Decision Advantage

Decision Advantage

Intelligence in International Politics from the Spanish Armada to Cyberwar

JENNIFER E. SIMS

To Marshall Collins, Jr.
Thank you for your contribution
to our country and our beloved town
of Salem, CT.

[signature]

12/28/23

OXFORD
UNIVERSITY PRESS

OXFORD
UNIVERSITY PRESS

Oxford University Press is a department of the University of Oxford. It furthers the University's objective of excellence in research, scholarship, and education by publishing worldwide. Oxford is a registered trade mark of Oxford University Press in the UK and certain other countries.

Published in the United States of America by Oxford University Press
198 Madison Avenue, New York, NY 10016, United States of America.

Library of Congress Cataloging-in-Publication Data
Names: Sims, Jennifer E., author.
Title: Decision advantage : intelligence in international politics from the Spanish Armada to cyberwar / Jennifer E. Sims.
Description: New York, NY : Oxford University Press, 2022. |
Includes bibliographical references and index.
Identifiers: LCCN 2021031278 (print) | LCCN 2021031279 (ebook) |
ISBN 9780197508046 (hardback) | ISBN 9780197508060 (epub)
Subjects: LCSH: International relations—Decision making. |
Strategic planning. | Intelligence service. | Military intelligence.
Classification: LCC JZ1253 .S56 2022 (print) |
LCC JZ1253 (ebook) | DDC 327.12—dc23
LC record available at https://lccn.loc.gov/2021031278
LC ebook record available at https://lccn.loc.gov/2021031279

DOI: 10.1093/oso/9780197508046.001.0001

1 3 5 7 9 8 6 4 2

Printed by Integrated Books International, United States of America

For my husband, Bob Gallucci

Contents

Figures

Preface

The historian Michael Howard once wrote: "The past is a foreign country; there is very little we can say about it until we have learned its language and understood its assumptions; and in deriving conclusions about the processes which occurred in it and applying them to our own day we must be very careful indeed."[1] It is, then, with perhaps unwarranted courage that I, a political scientist, have mined history for knowledge about intelligence, the world's second oldest profession. Historians such as Howard tend to dislike this sort of thing—and rightly so—because mistakes can damage the historical record for years.

If I beg to differ with their wisdom in this case, it is because the language of intelligence is not well understood within academia. Of course, scholars have grappled with the impact of intelligence organizations and programs on international politics. But few have dedicated themselves to establishing that common language or theory which might unlock lessons about what intelligence *has always been*, let alone why it has succeeded, failed, and perpetuated itself over millennia. This volume represents an effort to provide that language and to suggest its significance for our understanding of politics and history. In so doing, I derive lessons that might help us deal with the modern information revolution, including cyberwar, artificial intelligence, and mass deception operations.

The challenge, though enormous, has seemed worthwhile and feasible. One reason is that historians have developed substantial records of significant historical events, such as the Spanish Armada, the US Civil War, and the diplomacy before World Wars I and II. Without the rigorous methods of historical research, we would be left to cherry-pick stories or anecdotes rather than see and understand competitive learning contextualized within the larger flow of politics, diplomacy, and war. Given good historical records, political scientists have an important role. Without the rudiments of theory, we would be swimming in a morass of detail, or we would be waylaid by the discovery of secret triumphs irrelevant to historical outcomes. It has only been in recent decades that political scientists and historians have become interested in intelligence as a jointly pursued aspect of their respective disciplines. To this exceptional generation of scholars, including David Dilks, Mark Lowenthal, Ernest May, Robert Jervis, Richard Betts, Christopher Andrew, Geoffrey Parker, and others, we owe an enormous debt of gratitude. They have pressed reluctant governments to declassify historical documents and, thereby, have helped us all to learn from history.

Methodological differences have, however, sometimes become obstacles to joint study and better learning about intelligence. Without good theory, which political scientists have only belatedly begun to supply, researchers suffer from biases and so come to erroneous conclusions about the impact of intelligence on outcomes. For their part, historians often seem averse to theory, fearing it prejudices their work.

All of us, including scholars, entertain theories. Theory is, at its simplest, just a set of rules for sifting material, organizing it, and presenting it for edification. For example, writing a history of WWI employs theory if only to say that this cataclysmic event can be separated from the wars of German reunification and from WWII as a discrete event with its own causes, beginnings, and endings. One might as easily say that the two world wars are better understood as part of one particularly violent period in a more general European adjustment to the industrial revolution. If how one carves up history involves theory of some kind, then most historians and political scientists engage in theorizing at least at some level. The difference really is that political scientists put their selection rules up front and make their conclusions about cause and effect explicit. The inevitable lack of nuance in such work makes historians understandably uncomfortable. Political scientists theorize, however, so that the reader can follow their logic. They prefer to make their selection criteria rigorous and test those rules and theoretical propositions against historical evidence, even if doing so risks overgeneralization and a certain tone-deafness to the periods involved. Such approaches can have tragic outcomes if the work skips too lightly over the history, sowing distrust in the results, or makes too much of otherwise inconsequential historical data just because they can be counted. Historians know that, rich as the human past is, one can find evidence for almost any idea, weaving narratives, including outlandish ones, in support of it. What distinguishes storytellers and conspiracy theorists from political scientists is rigor: the latter invite challenges to their work from peers armed with facts and counterevidence.

It is with all these notions in mind that I have written a book theorizing about the phenomenon we call "intelligence" and how it has shaped the course of winning and losing in international affairs. To do this work, I have defined intelligence not as what modern intelligence institutions do, but as competitive, purposeful learning—an endeavor in which humankind has engaged since prehistoric times. The implicit claim is that intelligence springs from curiosity, is therefore integral to human affairs, and is an underappreciated form of power that helps some humans to avoid predation and others to accomplish it. Intelligence is therefore best understood as a tool shaped to competitive purposes. And, since the best judge of its success is the decision-maker who wields it, intelligence serves less some elusive truth or prediction than that decision-maker's advantage as he seeks to protect himself or his group from an observant and reactive foe.

Given that humans are born curious and committed to survival, we can assume history is full of intelligence successes and failures. We should, therefore, know more about not just what our species has done to survive, but how we knew how to do it. To accomplish this goal, I specify a rule or law: the architecture of competitive learning always involves five distinct pieces: decision-makers, platforms (access providers), sensors (sniffers, tasters, readers, feelers), processors (sense-makers), and communicators (transmitters). Whether the competition is a horse race, a baseball game, a political campaign, or international politics, these five pieces of the intelligence enterprise will always be involved.[2] To find intelligence activities, including in historical eras before the CIA, MI6, or Russia's GRU ever existed, it is necessary to look for these pieces and their connections. This study accomplishes this goal and derives from the research a strong hypothesis: the better these five pieces are, including in their integration with the decision-maker, the better the intelligence for competition; and the better that intelligence is relative to an opponent, the more likely the win. This approach also recognizes that the term "intelligence" should imply "engineered"—not delivered through luck or happenstance. Of course, states can achieve superior intelligence by engineering what seems lucky through strategic positioning, thus rendering intelligence better and cheaper than an opponent's. The conclusion to this volume suggests how to accomplish such seemingly effortless wins even as it establishes what the historical record suggests "better" means for each piece of the intelligence architecture, including when direct comparison with an opponent is not possible.

Because this book addresses these claims about intelligence in the context of international politics, I have adopted a case-study approach that takes deep dives into history—dives that will submerge the reader in historical detail. Readers familiar with the eras may find little new. This inductive approach is, however, informed by historians' concerns about rush to judgment and is purposeful. Rather than import prejudices from the present into the past, I have used the analytical tools just described to find intelligence activities as they may have existed before professional intelligence institutions were conceived, and to learn, if possible, what made particular arrangements of its architectural pieces better for one side than another. The idea is that, if intelligence is a form of power, centuries of practice may be able to tell us how to measure it, build it, and use it in a vastly different international system than the one we have today. What makes intelligence better ought not to be a mystery, or an artifact of the Cold War, but rather a lesson derived from centuries of experience that can be made relevant to a world of cyberwar, cyborgs, and artificial intelligence. In the last two chapters of this volume, I address some of these current and future challenges directly.

Acknowledgments

The ambitious task described in the preface to this volume could not have been accomplished alone. Although equipped with analytical tools to find intelligence in a complicated past, I am not a historian by training, and this fact presented problems. I anticipated hunting through a recovered past full of fine archival work, but a secondary literature possibly littered with the fancies, mistakes, or biases of well-meaning interlopers like me. The idea was horrifying. I remembered the opening of Walter M. Miller Jr.'s science fiction novel *A Canticle for Leibowitz*, in which a monk, foraging in a postapocalyptic landscape of the future, discovers a rare and cryptic document hidden in a subterranean bunker: "Pound pastrami, can kraut, six bagels—bring home for Emma," signed, Leibowitz.[1] Awed by his find and curious about its meaning, the monk scurries to his abbot, who, equally awed and mystified, wonders if the hand of the abby's namesake, the Blessed Leibowitz, was behind it all, working another miracle. As amusing as Miller's opening seemed to be, I was struck by the horror of his topic (nuclear apocalypse) and by his foraging monk, who unwittingly uncovered and propagated irrelevancies.

Still, it is in human nature to dig, find, and make sense of things. Learning from the past, the best we can do is to seek historians to help, which poses additional challenges. As a historian has written: "If contemporary analysis appeals to the authority of history, it should rely on more rather than less reliable historical scholarship."[2] So I sought out respected historians of the eras in which I would forage, conducting roundtables to get their input on draft chapters. I could not have been more fortunate in the help I received. I was honored and pleased, in particular, to have the help of Professor Geoffrey Parker, the eminent historian of Philip II, his lineage, his empire, and his age. Dr. Parker not only patiently helped me to navigate the overflowing literature on the subject, but also introduced me to other respected historians for the Civil War and WWI, many of whom agreed to join political scientists and intelligence professionals in roundtables on the book held at the Chicago Council on Global Affairs and the Wilson Center in Washington, DC. I owe these two institutions and their leaders, the Hon. Jane Harman and Ambassador Ivo Daalder, a great debt of gratitude. Besides Geoffrey Parker, core roundtable participants included Nicholas A. Lambert, Mark Grimsley, Mark Lowenthal, Christian Ostermann, Burton Gerber, Robert Gallucci, Rodney Faraon, Brian Hanson, Rachel Bronson, and Greg Treverton. The debates and criticisms flew; I benefited from all of them.

In addition to these roundtables on the manuscript, I sought guidance from contemporary experts in diplomacy, military combat, and intelligence. Together with my colleague and former CIA operations officer Burton Gerber, I hosted intelligence salons while I taught first at Johns Hopkins School of Advanced International Studies and then at Georgetown University. A number of the Georgetown University salons were funded through a special grant administered by the Security Studies Program at Georgetown University's School of Foreign Service. To the scholars and practitioners who participated in these salons, manuscript reviews, and recent online meetings, I owe particular thanks. While there are too many to mention, a few merit special mention (in no special order) for years of intellectual engagement and outstanding contributions: Robert Jervis, Keith Jeffery, Alexander Wendt, Richard Betts, Hank Crumpton, Michael Hayden, Jim Clapper, George Tenet, John McLaughlin, John McGaffin, Michael McConnell, Michael Brown, Loch Johnson, Austin Yamada, David Charney, Ernest R. May, John Fox, Michael Warner, Ronald Marks, John Moseman, Jim Bruce, Carmen Medina, Amy Zegart, Robert Wallace, Kathleen Kiernan, James R. Gosler, Roy Godson, Harvey Rishikof, Toby Gati, Tom Fingar, Daniel Kurtzer, Daniel Byman, Ellen Laipson, William M. Nolte, Albert C. Pierce, Elizabeth Stanley, Suzanne Kelly, Suzanne Spaulding, Nicholas Gallucci, Roger George, Randall M. Fort, Charley Allen, Christopher Mellon, and Eliot Cohen. And for her expertise as a prepublication copyeditor, tireless substantive critic, Spanish translator, cultural expert, and friend, I owe a particular debt of gratitude to Rosa DeBerry King. She has lived with this manuscript for over a year, improving it in many ways, including contributing the translation of a sixteenth-century manuscript in Appendix 2, and always encouraging me onward. These experts, scholars, and practitioners, while generously helping me over the years, bear no blame for any mistakes this volume may still contain despite their best efforts.

I extend great thanks to my students over many years who, although too many to name, know who they are and how much they have contributed. Vincent H. Bridgeman, Matthew Walker, Anand Prakash, and Megan Jackson deserve special mention for their enormous contributions, which included active and substantive engagement in many of the salons and critical contributions to delimiting the meaning of intelligence itself.

I also thank the prepublication staff of the Office of the Director of National Intelligence for their careful and efficient review of this manuscript. As is always the case, such review was solely for issues of classification and indicates no endorsement of the contents.

As sources of both financial and logistical support there have been no greater contributors than the Wilson Center, the Chicago Council on Global Affairs, and, especially, the Smith Richardson Foundation (SRF), without whose grant this book could not have started and certainly could not have been completed.

SRF officers Martin Strmecki and Nadia Schadlow have been great motivators. Their patient commitment to my completion of the task has kept me going even when the task felt overwhelming. Chris Juby, Ana Teasdale, and Jennifer Jun of the Chicago Council on Global Affairs helped with the production of the manuscript, including the organization of roundtables. In fact, many on the staff of the Chicago Council and of the Wilson Center in Washington, DC, were essential to the success of the roundtables.

And in bringing this book from manuscript to publication, my special appreciation goes to all at Oxford University Press for their smooth production of this volume and especially to David McBride for his patience and wise counsel throughout.

Finally, I owe most to the tireless patience of my husband, friend, editor, and substantive critic, Robert L. Gallucci. A diplomat, scholar, and professor, he has been a fount of wisdom, as well as a persistent realist, reminding me often of what his thesis adviser told him many years ago: "Do not try to write *Man, the State, and War*, just do a serious piece of work."[3] And so, I hope, I have.

1

Intelligence and Decision Advantage in International Politics

"Intelligence" is information for competition. The idea is simple: if you are in a horse race, playing football, at bat, or facing strategic nuclear war, intelligence helps you know better than other competitors how to get the outcome you want, decision by decision.[1] These decisions are particularly weighty in international politics. States compete to secure their interests in a world of few rules and the constant potential for war. During some centuries, such as the years from AD 1500 to 1700 in Europe, or 770 to 221 BC in China, states suffered near constant deadly conflicts.[2] More recently, the nuclear age has expanded the scope of interstate violence to put civilization itself at risk. Throughout all these epochs, intelligence has served choice, whether reckless or lucid.

The value of intelligence—often called the world's second oldest profession—seems indisputable. Yet experts have challenged that idea. In a 2006 article for *Foreign Affairs*, the well-regarded intelligence historian David Kahn claimed that "during most of Western history . . . warriors paid intelligence little heed, because it rarely helped them."[3] This same argument resonates throughout John Keegan's work *Intelligence in War*. "Victory is an elusive prize," Keegan writes, "bought with blood rather than brains."[4] Many theorists of international politics would seem to agree, dismissing the role of intelligence in their conjectures on the causes of war.[5] It is not that they overlook the importance of uncertainty; rather these academic Realists assume uncertainty is an unvarying attribute of the international system and look for causes for war, peace, and victory elsewhere, such as the size of armies, the nature of weapons, or strategies for their use. At the same time, however, they assume that the distribution of power shapes the movements of states and so must be knowable by all the Great Powers. Together these assumptions constitute an impossible proposition: that intelligence is both worthless *and* necessary for understanding the behavior of states.[6]

If such logic were not enough to drive intelligence professionals to despair, intelligence scholars seem just as pessimistic. Professors Richard Betts, Mark Lowenthal, and Abram Shulsky have noted that, even if intelligence is crucial for avoiding surprise, it can rarely unveil enemy intentions with any precision.[7] In reaction to expectations that a well-funded intelligence system should prevent surprise, Betts and others have urged humility. Just as the greats in baseball never

Decision Advantage. Jennifer E. Sims, Oxford University Press. © Oxford University Press 2022.
DOI: 10.1093/oso/9780197508046.003.0001

bat .500, let alone 1.000, they say intelligence cannot be perfected either. Thus, discussions of reform involve, even among the most knowledgeable, a depressing but necessary lowering of expectations.

Such guarded assessments raise interesting questions: Why, if intelligence cannot reliably warn, has it persisted for so long as an instrument of statecraft? Why, if intelligence is so useless, do states continue to invest great sums in it? One answer may be that hope simply springs eternal; but another may be that success rates are greater than scholars appreciate. Failures are newsworthy, but successes remain hidden until declassified long after the fact. We now know, for example, that US intelligence sources forewarned President John F. Kennedy in 1962 of the emplacement of Soviet ballistic missiles in Cuba, allowing him to act before the nuclear-tipped missiles were ready to launch. He shared imagery with allies to gain their support, ordered a military blockade to prevent additional missiles from reaching Cuba, and demanded that the weapons already there be disabled and removed. Soviet Premier Nikita Khrushchev used his ambassador, Anatoly Dobrynin, to explore trading the removal of American missiles from Turkey for the ones deployed in Cuba, and a deal was struck. Most scholars now understand that the outcome turned less on perfect knowledge than on *sufficient* knowledge for the right choices on both sides. In this instance, intelligence arguably saved both Superpowers from catastrophe.

Consider this: for every intelligence failure on one side, there was probably success on the other. The attacks on December 7, 1941 (Pearl Harbor) and on 9/11 were intelligence defeats for the United States, but wins for the attackers—at least in the opening battles of what turned out to be global wars. Is the best question not *whether* intelligence works but *how* it does so?

Why a Theory?

I will show in this volume that intelligence shapes outcomes in international politics. It helps leaders know the distribution of power among states, act more quickly and decisively in countries' interests, and so protect them from predation. I will make the case that intelligence can do so regularly and predictably because the factors that lead to success (knowing more than your adversary through purposeful learning) are identifiable, measurable, and buildable. In this sense intelligence is a form of power not unlike the military kind.

Pessimism or cynicism about this last point persists because we have lacked an overall theory of how intelligence works in competitions in general and politics in particular. Getting the practice of intelligence *reliably* right, regardless of the foe, requires such a theory. And while some theorists have tackled the problem, efforts so far have been disappointingly descriptive rather than explanatory. For example, intelligence is often described as a cycle: decision-makers secretly request information; collectors go get it; analysts discern its meaning and then send it on to the decision-makers. Failure is defined simply as a breakdown in the cycle. Missing, however, is any explanation of how the cycle breaks, how intelligence prevents surprise, or how it helps create it in other parties. The "cycle" might make a good model, but it is no guide to troubleshooting after failure occurs. In other words, it offers no general theory of how intelligence helps decision-making, how failures arise, or how best to make trade-offs among competing requirements.[8]

Intelligence has also been described as keeping secrets or stealing them from others, as the United States did during the Cuban Missile Crisis.[9] According to this test, which some believe suffices as theory, the more secrets an intelligence service collects the better it is; indeed, the more classified the product the better that product must be. Yet this test identifies and measures what modern intelligence agencies do rather than explains how intelligence succeeds and fails. Certainly, it would be unwise for any competitor to focus on learning only what others choose to hide, because that would tempt them to hide what is worthless in order to deceive, tease, or otherwise influence.

It follows that it would be just as unwise to guard most diligently only knowledge that is most secretly obtained rather than knowledge that is most advantageous to have, regardless of how it was obtained. Moreover, defining intelligence as secrets can blind collectors as well as decision-makers. When al-Qaeda terrorists surprised the United States on September 11, 2001, they gathered intelligence on their targets but used none of the secrets closeted away by the US government. They also acted openly, using their true names.[10] The intelligence they needed to succeed with their plan—airline schedules, piloting know-how, and target location—was freely available. Their tradecraft looked nothing like that used by the United States during the Cuban Missile Crisis, but it worked. So, clearly, intelligence cannot be just about gathering or keeping secrets.[11]

Finally, intelligence is sometimes described as the search for objective truth. At one level, this idea seems correct. Good intelligence represents what is, not what one wishes were true or what is true, relevant but unnecessary for competitive decision-making. A man surprised by a bear will not be saved by knowing the precise length of the animal's incisors. And it is in this sense that an intelligence provider's objective but undisciplined search for truth can be inappropriate and sometimes dangerous. Neglect of utility—the decision-maker's dilemma and what she needs to know to win—can lead practitioners to believe their work is a kind of science, and its defense almost a religious endeavor. Indeed, one senses the rather modern idea of "speaking truth to power" reflects a search for morality in what has long been deemed a shady profession. Although the biblical declaration "And ye shall know the truth, and the truth shall make you free" (John

8:32) is inscribed in the wall of the foyer of the US Central Intelligence Agency,[12] it does not take a theorist of international politics to know that political leaders rarely have the luxury or divine connections to build policies on ultimate truths. In the heat of conflict, decisions often have to be made before all the facts can be gathered. Policymakers simply want reduced uncertainty and, ideally, better assessments than those available to adversaries. Truth-finding, therefore, cannot be an unfailing guide to intelligence success.

Lacking a sound theory of intelligence, a practical problem arises: intelligence reform tends to focus not on time-tested principles, but on the last failure, which can be a poor guide to long-term success.[13] Yet the US government continues to study failures for the purpose of intelligence reform, risking sensitive inter-connected operations.[14] For example, following the treachery of Aldrich Ames, the CIA mole who in 1985 betrayed agents to Moscow, critics complained Ames had access to too many secrets. *Too much sharing* of sensitive material had cost valuable agents' lives. After 9/11, however, critics complained of too much se-crecy and *too little sharing* of sensitive material. They demanded that intelli-gence agencies loosen requirements for "the need to know" and institutionalize the "need to share." Those operatives who remembered the earlier lessons and resisted, having lost sources to Ames's treachery years before, were branded as "old school." Then, following massive data leaks by Chelsea (Bradley) Manning and Edward Snowden, both of whom had access to secrets well beyond their "need to know," sources were (predictably) jeopardized or lost. Reformers called, once again, for *better secrecy*. Intelligence experts worried that sharing had gone too far, empowering adversaries from Vladimir Putin to the Islamic State and al-Qaeda.

Regardless of one's position on secrecy, the seemingly varied lessons from past failures present a conundrum. If collection and retention of secrets are not al-ways essential to good intelligence, and the intelligence cycle is no guide to suc-cess, what is? Do enduring principles of sound intelligence practice exist—ones that apply to military battles, diplomatic standoffs, and attacks by terrorist cells regardless of country or historical era? How do we measure intelligence capabil-ities *before* intelligence failure and optimize our chances for success? How does intelligence relate to power and political theory writ large? Although intelligence theorists have worked diligently for years, convincing answers to these questions remain elusive. This volume aims to provide at least some of them.

Before doing so, however, I will mention five premises underlying the theory of intelligence developed in this book.

- First, the mission of intelligence is to help competitors act by illuminating opportunities for wins through competitive, purposeful learning. Failure and success in intelligence is therefore always relative to the competitive performance of others.[15]

- Second, this study presumes that national intelligence has to be understood in the context of international politics, which is characterized by conflict, anarchy, and the currency of power.[16] States compete using diplomacy and force—carrots and sticks—the effective application of which depends on what they know about each other.

- Third, cooperation for common purpose can only happen when states know the potential gains. In the absence of such knowledge, states will tend to augment their power unilaterally, even at the risk of triggering an arms race. Such spiraling insecurity is known among political scientists as the "security dilemma." Intelligence theory may offer an escape from it.

- Fourth, the attributes of repeatedly successful intelligence practices, discerned from historical examples, can help build a sound theory of intelligence and guide us to best practices, regardless of any particular distribution of power or technological context.

- Fifth, competitive learning happens naturally because humans are naturally curious. Formal intelligence services exist to accelerate matters. And while natural conditions (e.g., proximity to the English Channel) can make learning easier for some competitors than others (e.g., British ships versus Spanish ones navigating in a storm), in this volume, we are principally concerned with *engineered* informational advantages, even as we must recognize that they are helped or hurt by underlying conditions or the varying curiosity of presidents and kings.

To understand this last point, consider the evolution of the offense-defense military balance in Renaissance Europe after the invention of fortress-busting artillery. In 1440, an Italian author, Leon Battista Alberti, wrote a prescient treatise in proposing defensive fortifications built in uneven lines, "like the teeth of a saw."[17] His idea languished for some years until, in 1485, it was finally published. When Charles VIII of France invaded Italy with eighteen thousand men and a siege train of forty or more guns, he besieged cities, massacred thousands, and inspired the Italian states to augment fortifications in this way.[18] Eventually, Italian engineers propagated these new defensive ideas throughout the continent of Europe, redressing the former imbalance between fortress defenders and besiegers. Thus, the ingredients of power and the character of warfare in Europe changed through the *propagation of innovation* among engineers (natural information flows), *as well as purposeful learning* by princes (intelligence collection). Slow or impoverished learners put their fortifications at risk by doing nothing; others learned that new ideas were affecting outcomes, so they did something about it.[19]

The point is that, if innovations in the technology of war matter, then it matters who learns about such innovations first. This is an intelligence problem arising from the natural spread of ideas. Technologies and techniques become known, meaningful for war, and propagated widely and more quickly through competitive learning—a process that sometimes requires stealing secrets, sometimes voracious reading of military and scientific literature, and sometimes just having a country full of smart innovators and businessmen connected to national security decision-makers.

This opening chapter sets the stage for these kinds of insights by discussing what intelligence is, how it is best used, and how history can help illustrate the essential principles on which sound intelligence practice must rest.

The Essence of Intelligence

To avoid the mental trope of defining national intelligence as what modern intelligence agencies do—that is, covert action, signals intelligence, espionage, and the like—it is useful to think of it as a learning game. The purpose of this chapter is to share some opening thoughts about how one might identify this game as it has been practiced over centuries of war and peace. We need a method for finding the intelligence function in a world of pre-industrial, agrarian societies or in armies with no designated intelligence officers at all. A sense of essential attributes aids the hunt for examples by steering us away from biases about secrecy or categories such as "signals intelligence" or "imagery intelligence." Thinking of intelligence in such categories may help us understand its modern age, during which large intelligence bureaucracies focused on radar, infrared, and optical sensors, but it will likely be inappropriate or distracting when hunting for Renaissance-era intelligence.

Freeing ourselves from prejudices favoring modern intelligence practices also allows us to consider whether current intelligence pathologies may have once been smart practice. For example, whereas modern democracies eschew "politicized" intelligence or the twisting of facts to fit political preference, older societies would have regarded such objectivity as a cause for distrust. Sixteenth-century kings, recognizing politicization as the norm, made use of it when honing their intelligence capabilities. Political or religious affiliation indicated loyalty when state allegiances were weak. Monarchs sometimes neutralized such biases more by diversifying their intelligence advisors than by attempting to castrate them politically or religiously, which would not have lasted long, anyway.

The Concept of Decision-Advantage

To get to the essence of intelligence without triggering Cold War or 9/11 mindsets, it may help to consider a simple vignette unrelated to national security:

Imagine you live on a farm and have just rescued a very large dog, one stronger and heavier than you, with serious issues related to dog-on-dog aggression. She has surprised you more than once, barreling people over or spooking cows, horses, and their owners when launching at other canines on your leashed walks. This makes the two of you competitors: she has somehow learned that attacking other dogs is in her interest; you have an interest in changing her mind, while in the meantime avoiding dog fights and personal injury.

Unfortunately, your powerful new dog has a better sense of smell, sight, and hearing than you have—built-in sensors that help her track her prey and other dogs better than you can. She has a natural *intelligence advantage* over you in this regard. Moreover, if she senses a loose dog on your daily walk in the country, she can easily act faster than you, ripping the leash right out of your hand—what we might call *decision advantage*, or the capacity for rapid action based on senses tightly wired to nerves, muscle, and instinctual choice. She has *less uncertainty* than you do about where other animals are because she benefits from an acute sense of smell that distinguishes moles, rabbits, and cats from other dogs. Along the country road, *the terrain of uncertainty* is tilted in her favor, not yours, in contests involving dog-on-dog encounters.[20]

With all these natural advantages, will your dog necessarily win? No. This is because the practice of "intelligence" allows competitors to alter any competitive "terrain of uncertainty" for the purpose of overcoming opening disadvantages of this kind.

For example, as your dog's trainer, you have some intelligence assets that, with careful thought and planning, you can leverage. Although your senses are less sharp, you are taller. This "platform" advantage means you may, despite inferior eyesight, see farther down the road than she can. You also have a mobility advantage. You can scope out the battlefield while keeping her penned up. If you think ahead and map the terrain before taking her on her walk, you can choose your route so that your platform advantage can be used to best effect.

Second, although your decision-making may be less swift than hers, you can be more focused on the training than she will be. As she explores the roadside smells and hunts field mice, you can concentrate on reading signals and remembering the locations of gates and fences that can help you restrain your dog if another one comes along. In other words, you can compensate for her faster instinctual reaction times by using analytical indicators you know and trust. You might watch herds of horses grazing near the road, for example, because you know if they suddenly prick their ears at something approaching, your dog might not notice but you would. Thus, you could anticipate your dog's behavior better than she could.

In sum, by taking deliberate measures, you are *engineering tactical and strategic intelligence advantages* designed to overcome your dog's natural strengths to gain *decision-advantages* when training her. She is thinking tactically about multiple adversaries; you are thinking strategically about just one—her.

> Then it happens: the horses are craning their necks. You can see a distant movement, which is enough to know that, whatever it is, you are at risk of being dragged down the road in a few short minutes. You remember the gate you just passed and turn back before your dog notices that a horse and rider are about half a mile away, with a loose dog running behind. You have about fifteen yards to sprint to get behind the fence and control your dog. You get there in time. As the strangers pass, your dog is surprised, tries to lunge at them, but cannot. You have won this battle despite your opening competitive disadvantages.

Victory came in this instance from an *engineered* decision-advantage against a competitor with better eyes, ears, nose, and instinctual reaction times than yours. You adopted a targeted collection strategy based on your sole collection advantage—platform height and mobility—integrated with planning and analysis, to leverage what you could do better than your dog. Knowing your dog and how she made decisions, you planned how to get and use competitively acquired information to execute a sound strategy to control her.

Now consider this:

> The next time you walk your dog, a cougar stalks you and your dog from behind. Suddenly, the horses stampede in all directions, confusing you. Your dog growls, turns, and lunges, ripping the leash from your hand. Surprised, you at first have no idea what to do. You realize your focus on your dog made you prey to an unexpected competitor. Luckily, your dog, with her distracted sniffing, scanning, and instinctual decision-making, proved better than you at detecting and reacting to this new threat. Suddenly less an adversary than an ally, she is driving the cat back. You come to your senses, run toward the gate, and both of you escape.

This second vignette illustrates our opening conundrum. Whereas in the first example, good intelligence depended on focus, strategy and a plan, these capabilities were the opposite of what was needed in the second: sensors untethered to your strategy and quite independent of your control.

We surmise, then, that a reliably superior intelligence service must be responsive to decision-makers' requirements and yet, at *the same time*, capable of acting outside of those requirements to rescue those decision-makers from strategic surprise.[21] Intelligence policy seems to be about designing and maintaining a system that can do both without becoming unaccountable or unaffordable. This book argues that that is exactly what sound intelligence policy should be.

Gaining Advantage by Disadvantaging Others: Counterintelligence

The dog-walking metaphor has so far helped to simplify the concept of competitive intelligence and its components.[22] Yet a crucial element seems missing. The trainer did not consider how to keep the dog from watching and anticipating. The trainer did not consider distraction, blinders, or ear-plugs, altering her ability to sniff and see. What about information denial and manipulation, which are the tools of counterintelligence?

The purpose of *counterintelligence* (CI) is to gain decision advantages by controlling or degrading what others can know in ways that serve a competitor's interests. Generally, counterintelligence operations can be categorized as defense (blocking an opposing intelligence service) or offense (manipulating an opponent with intent to deceive or influence).[23] In either event, successful CI operations alter opponents' appreciation of facts in useful ways. Their primary purpose is to limit or change what competitors know, not to bring about specific political, military, or economic outcomes, which would be policymaking and, if secretly sponsored, covert action. In fact, the US government makes a legal distinction between counterintelligence and covert action based on political intent. In practice, the two activities may be indistinguishable.

Whether offensive or defensive, CI is an intelligence function that can only serve decision advantage if it is managed as part of the larger competition and the intelligence enterprise that serves it. Strong, positive intelligence is needed to know whom to block, or whether an opponent is being deceived. CI, while not intrinsically political, nonetheless requires an intimate understanding of strategy lest the opponent be lured in counterproductive ways or distracted at the moment he is meant to surrender. This volume will show that understanding CI's differences from and connectedness to both security and positive collection is therefore crucial to its success.

Counterintelligence and Security

The missions of counterintelligence and security are often confused, but they are not the same. Security connotes keeping sensitive information protected; its purpose is to protect against loss. Counterintelligence has a related but different driving idea. Its purpose is not necessarily to protect a given set of information, but rather to help one side win by limiting and manipulating what an opponent can know. The value of information for a counterintelligence officer will change, and security requirements will alter as strategy and tactics change.

For example, obsolete but still secret military plans might be usefully leaked to an enemy if they might be more disorienting than helpful to him. Such an attempt to twist an opponent's mind for one's own gain is an example of offensive counterintelligence; a security officer would never contemplate such a move. For security to be effective for counterintelligence, it must be a subordinate goal and selectively applied. Indeed, a master of offensive CI may purposefully weaken his own side's operational security in one area if the idea is to use that vulnerability or loss to distract an adversary from a more important effort in another area.

Given the differences between security and counterintelligence, officials often differ over priorities as policymakers seek to secure intelligence advantages.[24] Security is easier to understand and use than counterintelligence, so it often dominates. Especially in democracies, security seems honest, while counterintelligence can seem devious and even unethical.

Measurement also matters: security seems to be working so long as there are no losses; counterintelligence seems to produce little unless spies are caught or deceptions usefully deflect the enemy, which is an outcome often difficult to know and rarely publicized.[25] Whereas security officials protecting classified information have little reason to care about public information, counterintelligence officers might advise public officials to protect unclassified or "open source" intelligence if it could empower a dangerous enemy. After the 9/11 attacks, for example, blueprints of major bridges, dams, and other infrastructure across the United States were taken off the internet because they had competitive value for terrorists. Critics, focused on the problems of overclassification, often cannot recognize the problems of underclassification, missing the central issue: that protection of competitive information (intelligence) is essential and only useful if applied and removed at will. Obviously, such selective secrecy is (and should be) more difficult in a democracy than in an autocracy, but the cost of not having it is ignored at a society's peril.

In fact, when competitions increase in intensity and perceptions of threats rise, incentives for governments to withhold information will tend to be high.[26] Yet it is precisely during these more intense contests that good counterintelligence experts will watch for ways that *security* policies may jeopardize the overarching strategic mission that counterintelligence is meant to serve. Democracies are inherently less good at this kind of attentiveness. During WWII, for example, the US government decided to classify the formerly open scientific work of physicists recruited to the task of developing the atomic bomb. The disappearance of a whole category of formerly open research suggested to Soviet scientists that Washington was sponsoring secret research on nuclear weapons, leading at least one to report his suspicions to Joseph Stalin. What seemed a "no-brainer" for American security professionals was, from a counterintelligence standpoint, an obvious misstep.[27]

Despite the theoretical logic of seamless intelligence and counterintelligence operations, the practice of these arts is difficult to coordinate. Those who practice intelligence, counterintelligence, and security are often required to operate separately to some degree, especially in democracies. There is, in fact, always a threat to democracy in any optimized intelligence system that joins intelligence, military force, and the powers of arrest. Perfected abilities to gain information dominance, if not balanced by equally strong powers of oversight and budgetary control, can be used by those in power to keep that power, to hide the mechanisms by which they do so, and to deceive those to whom they are accountable.

It follows that democratic states that join the power to spy with powers of coercion, state security, and arrest put the balance between the governed and the governors in jeopardy. Dictatorships, autocracies, and oligarchies, not so constrained, institutionalize decision-advantage in favor of their supreme leaders.

Toward a Theory of Intelligence in International Politics

Although issues such as public trust, counterintelligence, and intrusive collection make the problem of designing a reliable intelligence system seem impossible, especially for democracies, this book is founded on the premise that the study of successful intelligence practices can help make it possible. Indeed, a number of the observations that will be derived from historical examples in this book deserve mention here because, while illustrating and refining the points made earlier, they run counter to conventional wisdom:

- Intelligence is a bespoke method for superior learning so competitors can execute winning strategies.
- Intelligence adds or subtracts from competitors' respective *natural advantages* in competitive information; so designing a winning strategy involves scouting these relative advantages and building on them.

- Intelligence for avoiding strategic surprise can never be just an extension of support to current policymaking; looking further down the road cannot help discover what is behind your back.
- Since successful intelligence varies by competition, failure in one instance can be no certain guide to best practices in the next.
- Competitors can sometimes share interests, become unexpected allies against a common foe, or seek jointly to deceive others, so the capacity to release intelligence may be as important to decision-advantage as the capacity to gain secrets in the first place.
- Every action one competitor takes has the potential to produce intelligence for the other side. Behaving predictably thus makes other competitors' intelligence easier, but also makes their own behavior potentially more predictable as well. Decision-makers can use this dynamic either to deceive or to build confidence for the purpose of lowering tensions among competitors.
- Counterintelligence cannot work and may do damage without coordination with policy-makers.
- Information security improves competitive prospects only if it takes a back seat to counterintelligence requirements.
- Decision-makers are critical to successful intelligence practice and, in fact, are an integral part of it. Although decision-makers in modern international politics often delegate intelligence gathering to others, their involvement in intelligence and counterintelligence is essential or they risk lost advantages and eventual defeat.
- It follows that any rules separating intelligence from policy are likely to lead to trouble.

In essence, then, this study confirms what seems simple common sense: smarter competitors tend to win. The devil lies in the details, which abound in the complex business of international politics. How do you get smarter faster than others when enemies are trying to stop you and the stakes are life and death? And how do you know when winning might mean sacrificing a current advantage for a longer-term truce? How can we study intelligence practices in a way that helps us anticipate winners and losers so that we can be among the former, not the latter?

Studying Intelligence in International Politics

If intelligence is to explain outcomes in international affairs, including how militarily weak competitors sometimes win, we need a more precise way to define intelligence than just competitive learning and to distinguish it from other similar activities, such as journalism. We also need to weigh the claims for it in competitions without rules and with the highest stakes imaginable, such as global war.

The challenges of this task are manageable for six reasons:

- First, this study will use a precise and consistent definition of intelligence applicable across historical eras: *the collection, analysis, and dissemination of information for decision-makers engaged in a competitive enterprise.* This activity can be done for decision-makers on one's side to help them gain advantage or "for" adversaries whom one wishes to disadvantage with false, untimely, or irrelevant information.

- Second, this study *distinguishes intelligence from informational context—* what we have termed the *terrain of uncertainty*—on which all competitors play. This distinction helps to ensure that decision-makers who benefit from luck or happenstance are not credited with *purposeful learning* when they should not be.

- Third, the research has included case studies selected for the quality of their historical records and their potential to stress-test the propositions outlined above. This rule precludes the use of recent events, such as the 2003 Iraq war or 9/11, but includes military and diplomatic conflicts as well as national security related manhunts, such as the search and capture of President Abraham Lincoln's assassin, John Wilkes Booth, which happened over a century ago, at the very end of the US Civil War.

- Fourth, *each case study will identify key decision points* that, given historical perspective, proved crucial to the outcome. Identifying such decisions will allow us *to trace the intelligence* on which those decisions were made to the roots of either success or failure. For example, we will trace what Queen Elizabeth I knew when she decided on an act of war against the much more powerful King Philip II of Spain, or when she kept her fleet in the English Channel instead of permitting attempts to interdict Spain's galleons farther away.

- Fifth, the evaluation of success and failure will turn on the extent to which reduction of relative uncertainty was based on any kind of engineered advantage, including deliberate exploitation of the terrain of uncertainty. Lessons will stem from how that successful engineering was achieved. Intelligence advantage will explicitly not be credited to lucky happenstance, revelation of objective but useless fact, or successful espionage without helpful result. Indeed, intelligence may be credited with success even if we now know that it was technically wrong, so long as it was right enough to help competitive decision-making achieve a winning result.

- Finally, we will treat existing intelligence services as part of the terrain of uncertainty at the opening of any new competition, leaving the deliberate use of such institutions and their contribution to competitive learning a matter for research, not assumption. The existence of a relatively expensive intelligence collection apparatus may imply an opening informational advantage—a lucky gift for an incoming official—but it only implies the capacity for, not the fact of, competitive learning. Moreover, that such an intelligence system might have "got it right" will constitute no indicator of success if it cannot "deliver it right" or if a new decision-maker cannot "receive it right" so that effective learning—measured by winning decisions—may be accomplished.

Three of these methods for mining the historical record require more careful explanation in order to avoid confusion: the distinction between intelligence-advantage and decision-advantage; the concept of the terrain of uncertainty as it applies to international politics; and the method by which key decisions can be traced to their roots in an informational sense.

Decision Advantage, Intelligence Advantage, and the Terrain of Uncertainty in International Politics

I have said that, in general, *decision-advantage* involves having more options than an opponent has, as well as the capacity to choose among them with greater certainty, timeliness, and impact than he can. Intelligence improves this capacity by delivering timely information that reduces uncertainty relative to an opponent's. Such an *intelligence-advantage* is achieved most efficiently by building on the *terrain of uncertainty*, that is, the competitors' relative knowledge, informational resources, and familiarity with applicable rules at the opening of conflict.

In the peculiar, high-stakes domain of international politics, however, no central authority enforces rules, constrains options or shapes the *terrain of uncertainty*, which involves a slew of factors beyond decision-makers' control. Warriors must scout the terrain before battle to find high ground and learn the strengths and weaknesses of their geographical positions; political leaders scout the competitive infosphere—the economic, political, and technological lay of the land—to learn the strengths and weaknesses of their informational positions relative to others. Understood this way, intelligence augments carrots and sticks but also creates a peculiar form of power that causes competitors to do what they otherwise would not, left to their own devices. Managing this weapon, like any weapon, requires discipline, care, and the avoidance of fratricidal effects. Just as one does not bring a knife to a gunfight or an aircraft carrier to a guerrilla war, so intelligence built for one kind of competition will not necessarily help with another.

Smart competitors can thus create opportunities for themselves. After all, states are bound by no rules in international politics that they have the wit, power, and interest to overcome. They can gain advantages by shifting the locus of the fight or by speeding up their decision-making in order to degrade their opponents' options relative to their own.[28] They can also gain advantages by constructing new cooperative architectures or belief systems for inter-state relations. Recall that *intelligence-advantage* implies superior competitive knowledge, while *decision-advantage* encompasses the larger idea of having richer and clearer options than the adversary has. Such richness includes, of course, knowing more about the adversary's decision-making than he knows about yours. It also involves knowing more about how to change how they think than they can change how you do, accelerating progress toward cooperation and transparency or downward spirals to dystopia.[29] Throughout history, intelligence has sharpened the weapons for interstate conflict, reinforcing antagonisms as well as the terms of peace. Yet it alone of all weapons in man's toolkit has the potential to reconstruct international politics in fundamental ways for the future.

Distinguishing Decision-Advantage and Intelligence-Advantage

A deer-hunting analogy helps highlight both the distinction between intelligence-advantage and decision-advantage and the reasons why both are so important in international politics. On open terrain, a hunted deer has lots of options, such as bursts of speed, changing course, freezing in place, or running from meadow to woods where he is naturally camouflaged. These options give the deer some decision advantages over the hunter. If the deer changes direction faster than the hunter can position himself and fire his gun or loose an arrow, then the prey gains decision advantage by *speed*. The hunter may track the deer better than the deer is tracking the hunter (*intelligence-advantage*), but still be at a *decision-disadvantage* if he is unable to aim successfully before firing. Note that the deer does not *engineer* this advantage; he wins simply by staying on the move.[30] Unwittingly, the deer is acting faster than the hunter can see, decide, and shoot. When purposeful, such a tactic may be referred to as getting inside the opponent's decision loop. The deer, who knows little about decision-loops or the elements of archery, is just naturally good at it. He cannot get better over time by learning about bows and arrows, only by getting faster through natural evolution.

In international politics, however, all sides are likely thinking about the competition, and capable of engineering how and when to shift strategies (get a gun) or speed up decision-making. Such engineering on both sides can be credited to intelligence, so the ideas of decision advantage and intelligence advantage in international politics are often closely linked. Furthermore, neither intelligence-advantage nor decision-advantage is a guarantee of victory, in part because competitions in international politics tend to endure. If every intelligence advantage is immediately used, the sources of that advantage are likely to be noticed and eliminated by the other side, making future defeats more likely. We can hypothesize, therefore, that during interstate conflicts, counterintelligence will be particularly important to decision-advantage. What an individual decision-maker *actually does* in diplomacy or battle—whether she uses the intelligence advantages gained—still depends on an individual capacity to learn and to make decisions, and a host of other intangibles, such as mental stability, phobias, and connections to the levers of state power. So we can further hypothesize the following:

- States that pursue intelligence-driven decision advantages will fare better in international competitions than those that do not.
- States will, over time, find their intelligence methods converging as they learn more about how winning decisions are made.

Finally, the concept of a terrain of uncertainty seems particularly important for international politics because it suggests that some qualities of leadership turn more on luck than merit. Leaders can look good by being in the right place at the right time or by engaging a relatively inept foe. There will always be something lucky for someone about the distribution of scientific knowledge, technological information, shared languages and loyalties, knowledge of authorities, and the like. We can hypothesize that some leaders will recognize that they can exploit this relative luck in the short term by designing strategies that capitalize on natural strengths or, alternatively, make up for relative deficiencies by speeding up their decision-making or luring an opponent onto more favorable ground.[31] Such recognition itself can be boosted by intelligence, which thus informs strategy. After 9/11, for example, some experts advised that al-Qaeda intended to lure US forces into the Middle East in order to better fight and defeat them. But it is equally true that states equipped with superior intelligence will have the capacity to lure others onto cooperative ground, thereby lowering the costs of outcomes in their collective interests.

This volume will show that, over centuries of international conflict, the terrain of uncertainty has involved a constant, transnational flow of talent, ideas, and innovation that has unevenly delivered "luck" and shaped governments' relative capacities to learn. Yet savvy leaders have learned to manipulate the terrain of uncertainty in their favor before crises and over the long term through the advancement of science, industry, education, language, freedom of religion, and freedom of the press.[32] Those states that invest in innovation and other forms of global "knowing" enhance their baseline capabilities to understand, anticipate, and mitigate threats when they arise. In this way, they minimize the additional resources they must invest in professional intelligence services while recruiting from a richer pool at lower costs when such investment is necessary.

Tracing Decision-Advantage to Its Intelligence Roots

The crucial distinction between intelligence-advantage and decision-advantage in international politics allows us to sort serendipitous knowledge from intelligence by employing the idea of purposefulness. If medieval kings learned from knights and monks, and civil war generals used horse cavalry and telescopes, their methods may have differed but their *purpose* was competitive learning. So the intelligence historian looking for unknown or alien intelligence practices must trace the connections between decisions and tools. She will need to use generic elements of purposeful learning, regardless of whether such tools were classified as intelligence assets. These tools can be sorted into four types:

- Platforms (such as ships, planes, embassies, people, prisons)
- Sensors (such as eyes, ears, antennae, cameras)
- Processors (such as computers or brains)
- Communications (such as flags, letters, telegraphs, telephones)

The idea that competitive learning requires tools derives from the notion that a decision-maker is, in the first instance, her own intelligence *platform* because she is the host for *sensors*, such as eyes and ears. These sensors, in turn, *communicate* through nerve signals to the brain so the decision-maker can act. She is, in other words, an integrated collection and sense-making entity. As such, humans are near-perfect systems for gathering their own intelligence.

Delegating or expanding the intelligence function to others involves employing more of each of these essential tools in some way. Competitors choose to do so because they want to gain better information on adversaries than their own faculties can provide, or than adversaries have on them. Most decision-makers feel smart enough; they just abhor relative uncertainty. They want help getting access to a competitor, perceiving what he is doing, understanding his purpose, and knowing how best to respond, given that competitor's knowledge and expectations.

The intelligence historian's task, then, is to identify whether relative knowledge was crucial to a winning decision, determine how that knowledge came to be (lucky or deliberate; through better learning or denial), who provided it, and what platforms, sources, processors, and communications systems were used. At what point was the information determined to be relevant to the competition? Was it protected? If it was not protected, was this due to an oversight, ignorance, distrust, the intent to deceive, or knowledge that the adversary was blind? If the latter, was this blinding engineered or simply exploited? It is important to remember that even when a formal intelligence process exists, it may not be effective or connected in any way to decision-making, in which case it is irrelevant. One then needs to determine what informal system is connected and how it works.

In actual practice, finding the intelligence function in human affairs can be tricky. Sometimes one can to do so by finding likely platforms and *tracing forward* to decisions or *backward* to spies. Professionals know to do this kind of thinking when designing collection systems, countering spies, or recruiting agents, and the results are often surprising. For example, after 9/11 the US Federal Bureau of Investigation (FBI) recognized that libraries were potential intelligence platforms for terrorists, triggering interest in gathering information on their use. The public reaction was immediately hostile, because most people do not think of libraries in this context. Libraries are held sacrosanct by a culture deeply rooted in the democratization of knowledge. Librarians collect books, store them for public use, and safeguard equal access to everyone. Most people do not think of libraries as part of an intelligence system, and rightly so. But, from an intelligence perspective, libraries can be intelligence platforms for learning how to build a bomb, finding maps, or meeting coconspirators without generating suspicion. From a counterintelligence standpoint, libraries can be sensor-rich collection platforms, having reference librarians and security cameras that can help identify odd behavior and trace networks of coconspirators. During an insurrection pitting students against a tyrannical government, the distribution and qualities of libraries, universities, and internet cafés are part of the terrain of uncertainty. A government may suspect that revolutionaries are using cell phones to organize, and so demand that telecommunications companies help find the leaders or lose lucrative contracts.

Although libraries and internet-capable cell phones constitute a readily understandable example of civilian "platforms" usable for intelligence, the historian of intelligence must remain open to finding less obvious platforms and sensors over centuries of practice and technological change. Prisons can be platforms hosting an array of sensors in the form of prisoners or guards. Ships can be platforms for viewing the vulnerabilities of enemy ports. Horses can be platforms for helping human eyes and ears cover wider battlefields. And insects can be platforms for getting nano-sensors inside buildings. What makes for superior platforms, sensors, and communications capabilities in any era or competition will vary, depending on technology, the nature of the competition, and the creativity of the competitor. What theorists and practitioners need to discover are the winning attributes common to them all. If we do, we will have the beginnings of sound intelligence theory.

Case Studies and the Use of History

Of course, one must be mindful of the dangers of using history for any purpose. It is often said that history is written by winners, incompletely recorded, and never fully repeated. It cannot be, therefore, a true science. Political scientists, nonetheless, use history to make generalizations about cause and effect—to generate theory—while remaining humble about the process. Leslie H. Gelb, working on documents related to the Vietnam War, noted that "writing history, especially where it blends in to current events, ... is a treacherous exercise." He went on to add: "We often could not tell whether something happened because someone decided it, decided against it, or, most likely, because it unfolded from the situation."[33] Nonetheless, he admitted to ascribing causality or linkages in order to help officials get things more right the next time. It is in this same vein that I have engaged in deep dives into history.

The historian Marc Trachtenberg has said that "the aim of historical analysis is to understand the past by reducing it to a story,"[34] and in the end, all stories must be simplified representations of the past and cannot, therefore, be definitive. The case histories in this volume are presented in this spirit and with these caveats. Although I have shared my conclusions in a series of roundtables with historians specializing in the periods covered by my case studies, there is no way to be completely sure of the findings. They constitute my best effort to distill the workings of intelligence from a complicated, irretrievable past.

The Ethical Dimension

Unfortunately, as intelligence sheds prediction or truth as its ultimate objective, it would appear to lose a foothold in democratic societies where ethics and accountability matter. I argue that the ethical foundation for intelligence rests on other, more compelling grounds. In fact, democracies are built on the notion that the world is full of competing truths. The value of national intelligence lies in its ability to keep states, including democracies, safe while enabling leaders to construct commonly advantageous ground for interstate relations. With good intelligence, states should be able to use the power they have to secure their interests most efficiently, and wars of misperception or folly should decrease. If, in the interests of misplaced morality, all competitors were to have equally abysmal intelligence services, wars of misperception would be more likely, and the winners more arbitrary.[35] Since good intelligence mediates between power and its effective use, the proliferation of its sound practice should make global politics less random, chaotic, and savage. Moreover, good intelligence has a leveling influence: so long as intelligence is deliberately fine-tuned, even states that are not great powers and are disadvantaged by poor circumstantial knowledge, can create decision-advantages and win.

Theories of good intelligence aside, it is important always to keep in mind that optimizing the capacity of a government to gain intelligence advantages over other states can undermine democracy and its legitimacy at home. This is because intelligence systems good for winning against terrorists, fascists, or invaders can be used domestically to suppress legal opposition. In other words, good intelligence can be quickly made bad for a democracy if it is turned against citizens who need to know whether to replace their governors. Many supporters of Edward Snowden, though conceding he revealed no illegal programs, lauded his revelations about the extent of the US government's new surveillance powers, which they found threatening. Political leaders or generals have used intelligence institutions to try to stay in power, compromising civil liberties in the process. President Nixon's resignation followed his exposed attempt to do just this in the 1970s scandal known as Watergate.

Intelligence power is dangerous precisely because it is designed to disadvantage adversaries, potentially empowering intelligence chiefs, enabling tyrants, and causing democracies to fail. Since fair competition is essential to representative government, intelligence policy entails a conundrum for all democracies. Harnessed to law and open to review, intelligence advantages are difficult to gain against foreign adversaries; yet, unharnessed from the rule of law, intelligence can undermine constitutional rights, including the power of the people to hold politicians accountable. An intelligence capacity capable of defeating foreign threats is worse than no good for "national security" if used to get a jump on the electorate, twist elections, and undermine the democratic way of life; yet an intelligence capacity completely open to public review is nearly useless against adversaries.

Dangerous as intelligence may be, this book reveals that balancing civil liberties and sound intelligence need not be a zero-sum game. Improving intelligence helped save democratic Britain from being overrun by Adolf Hitler's authoritarian, Nazi state; free societies generate technological advances useful for gaining intelligence advantages over autocracies; and even the turbulence entailed by empowering citizens with unfiltered internet access is the precursor to reaching the informational high ground as a nation, not just as a state. In fact, as both Britain and the United States learned during WWII, democracies with free markets and thriving private sectors have gained repeated informational advantages over authoritarian regimes, including in the intelligence domain. Freedom to innovate and experiment builds wealth, motivates learning, and puts democratic, capitalist countries at the cutting edge of technology. Such distributed learning lessens the challenges for intelligence, which can exploit the favorable terrain of uncertainty in a relatively free and prosperous state. Citizens, nongovernmental organizations, utilities, and corporations in sound democracies are more likely to collaborate to provide timely information against threats to their communities and to keep intelligence subservient to the rule of law.

Instruments of oversight and accountability, as we shall see, are the crucial enablers of consistent intelligence advantage for democracies. They foster trust between decision-makers and intelligence providers and, in democracies, among citizens, intelligence providers, and governors. Intelligence agencies that eschew rather than strengthen oversight institutions, including channels for protected dissent or whistleblowing, put intelligence advantage at risk. Electorates that celebrate dissenters who eschew institutionalized channels for protest or complaint also damage their own democracy. When unelected intelligence professionals or dissenters undermine decisions by the courts or evade accountability to their legally elected political leaders, intelligence oversight has failed and democracies have entered a world of hurt. Self-proclaimed champions of democracy who eschew oversight institutions to leak intelligence are not only disadvantaging their own elected officials relative to tyrants, imperialists, and fanatics, but damaging one of democracy's greatest reforms of the state: *institutionalized* public accountability for secrecy in decision-making of all kinds—accountability that is studied and careful rather than tabloid-ready or haphazard. At the same time, leakers who enable sound oversight potentially enable intelligence advantages in the future. A superior intelligence service in a democracy plans for leaks and penetrations and turns them to advantage.

The truth is, intelligence can never be disinvented, only improved. So the question for democracies has always been both simple and challenging: how can accountable intelligence systems be built that bolster the security of just social and economic systems and, thus, contribute to reducing instabilities from arms races, terrorism, and war?

Conclusion: Overcoming Prophecy, Prediction, and Other Shibboleths of Intelligence

The significance of this volume lies in both theory and method. It overturns conventional wisdom about intelligence practice by using the past to discover how intelligence used to work in order to offer insights into what intelligence services may be doing wrong today. As researchers build upon its findings with further case studies, current thinking about intelligence and its role in international politics should change.

For example, we will need to stop thinking of intelligence as stealing secrets or as the embodiment of highly accurate predictions or of truth. We will need to talk about underclassification as much as overclassification and find ways to make secrecy a policy choice, not an albatross. Of course, decisions sometimes require secret, factually accurate information, as when a bombing run requires stealth and knowledge of the exact geo-coordinates of the target; yet at other times they do not, as when Union generals, filled with uncertainty before Gettysburg, traveled on horseback, in the open, to learn *enough* about where General Lee might be headed to preposition themselves to advantage.[36] Combatants may even achieve advantages by eschewing facts in favor of prophecy if they believe the latter enables surprise because their opponents, *assuming that facts and reason matter more*, could fail to take account of it. If, however, such combatants actually believe they owe their win to divination and not to the adversaries' mistakes, they will likely lose the next time. The point is, intelligence is dynamic and comparative; the success and failure of an intelligence system cannot be analyzed apart from the opponent's system.

It follows that, even when employing rigorous analytical tools, we will need to stop thinking of strategic intelligence as high-confidence forecasting. The case will be made in this volume that strategic intelligence should map the terrain of uncertainty so strategists can make plans that leverage informational advantages. Rather than exhaust itself trying to analyze itself out of a state of uncertainty, strategic intelligence finds useful knowledge in existing circumstances. When strategic intelligence becomes equated with perfecting estimation, everyone begins arguing over guesswork and its best methodology. Gaming enemy behavior in this way can thus become a complicated art that depreciates the value of "just enough" intelligence. Lengthy pursuit of truth through estimation makes little sense when helpful hints about what currently *is* would do. Besides, intelligence and policymaking wars are stimulated by told-you-so debates among policymakers and analysts who believe themselves equally justified (or vindicated) in their guesswork. Such troubles partly reflect the tendency for estimates to become predictions—both living beyond the moment of decision. Absent the context decision-makers faced when forced to act before all data were available, estimative intelligence can look more obvious (or foolish) in retrospect than it did at the time it was offered, straining relations among all involved.

Finally, lionizing prediction tends to reinforce comfortable assumptions about a noninteractive foe—that is, one who does not know what you know about him or sticks to his plan regardless of your moves. Predictions can thus encumber rather than aid competitive decision-making. Worse, competitors known to have a firm prediction (or a widely accepted and highly confident estimative judgment) in hand are themselves more predictable than they otherwise would have been. Most successful deceptions turn on convincing an adversary of what he is already inclined to believe is true—a prediction—and then doing something else. Although "estimation" is a term preferred over "prediction" by intelligence experts because it implies contingencies and probabilities, it is often driven by the desire for predictive truth, with all the dangers for strategy, timely decision-making, and overanalysis that can entail. The case studies in this volume suggest that perhaps the most important role for estimation is in driving collection. Intelligence estimates reveal, after all, the gaps in what is known and so can support collection initiatives that reduce guessing to a minimum.

* * *

Although the stories that follow are complex, most of them boil down to lessons no more complicated than those in the vignettes used in this chapter. This study will show that, from the Spanish Armada to the twentieth century, relative knowledge has mattered in decisive ways and that it has more often been engineered than serendipitously gained. What it cannot sufficiently explain is that some leaders find solutions to conflict that transcend the win-lose dynamic. Intelligence, a fact-gathering enterprise, is not a good tool for enabling such vision, but it is good at identifying who has it and who does not. To the extent intelligence comes close to enabling vision, it is in its ability to rise above the present game to look for advantages elsewhere—what we will call true strategic intelligence.

That said, the following analysis suggests something more surprising than the importance of transcendent knowing: that states can build consistently successful intelligence systems and, in so doing, reduce the risk and consequences of silly wars. We might, indeed, go further to say that the spread of sound intelligence practices may provide the basis for responsible transparency among states and thus offers hope for a managed, as opposed to utopian, global peace. It would be remarkable indeed to learn that intelligence practice might be an ethical route to the avoidance of war, but such is the conclusion of this book.

2

The Spanish Armada

> In comparison with the king of Spain, we were like a mouse against
> an elephant.
>
> —Cornelis Pieterszoon Hooft,
> Amsterdam magistrate, writing in 1617[1]

The Spanish Armada's attempt to defeat England in 1588 represented an early, if
unusual, form of asymmetric warfare.[2] King Philip II of Spain, ruling the largest
and richest empire the world had ever known, planned to invade England, overthrow the Protestant Queen Elizabeth I, and re-establish Catholic rule. Philip's
Armada, a fleet of 130 ships laden with thirty thousand men, was to sail to the
Spanish Netherlands, where it would meet an army assembled by the Duke of
Parma. The combined army would then cross the Channel, invade England, and
topple the queen. Spain's expectations were high, so plans were already afoot for
the regime that would replace the Tudors in a country as poor as Spain was rich—
an impoverished place scraping by largely on the proceeds of trade in wool, privateering, and piracy.

Unfortunately for Philip II, events did not go his way. Queen Elizabeth's navy
harassed the Spanish fleet and drove it past the point of rendezvous with Parma's
forces. Philip's commanders, failing to join up as planned, were incapable of innovating on the fly. With Parma bottled up in the Netherlands by the free Dutch,
the Armada's deep-drawing warships were forced to wait at anchor off the coast,
then scattered as the English sent fireships into their midst. During the decisive
battle of Gravelines, English guns bombarded the Spanish ships at close range.
The degraded Armada fled north, unable to close and grapple with the English
ships and thus use superiority in soldiers to overwhelm the English crews. On
the journey home through storms and roiling waters off the Irish coast, many of
the Spanish galleons were wrecked; crew members drowned or were slaughtered
at the hands of looters and ransom hunters.

Historians have argued with varying degrees of confidence that intelligence
was either unimportant or irrelevant to the Spanish defeat. Some have argued
that intelligence mattered only insofar as Philip II seemed lacking in it: he repeatedly failed to foresee events.[3] And, although Elizabeth's spymaster, Sir Francis
Walsingham, had used double agents and decrypted messages to unveil the

Decision Advantage. Jennifer E. Sims, Oxford University Press. © Oxford University Press 2022.
DOI: 10.1093/oso/9780197508046.003.0002

Spanish king's prior plots to unseat his queen,[4] his network did not contribute much to English preparedness for the Armada itself.[5] Tactical knowledge related to England's last-minute defense, including the precise landing point for Spanish troops, escaped Elizabeth's notorious spies.

In fact, most scholars blame Philip's poor administrative style, his timing, and his strategy for Spain's loss—not intelligence.[6] After all, Philip II's "Enterprise of England" was hardly secret; it was a topic of discussion throughout Europe. And as for the English victory, unusually bad weather made England's defense seem more artful than it really was.[7] Philip himself credited his loss less to English wit than to a "Protestant wind"—an act of God that made the defeat seem, especially to the pious king, all the worse.

Past scholarship on this battle has, however, generally defined intelligence in narrow terms: as espionage or theft of secrets.[8] Such an approach depreciates the other ways competitive learning is accomplished.[9] If the question is whether informational advantages mattered to wartime decision-making and how they were achieved, neither an act of God on the one hand, nor evidence of vigorous espionage on the other, clinches the argument. Instead, the questions are *whether the battle for information decreased uncertainty for one side relative to the other and, if so, how England acquired its informational advantage and used it to win.* Answers to these questions require a review of the informational context in which this historic contest took place—that is, the "terrain of uncertainty."

To appreciate just one aspect of the terrain in this sixteenth-century case, consider that in Elizabethan times it was assumed that no one at sea could see beyond the visual range of a man in a crow's nest. Ship captains were not only ignorant of what lay beyond, but also *assumed it to be unknowable.* The terrain of uncertainty at sea was seemingly level for admirals on Spanish galleons and English fishermen alike, so long as they swayed from comparable heights above deck. This assumption, however, made disruption of the status quo profitable. Innovators sought to overturn conventional wisdom and sell advantage at a profit. In this case, entrepreneurial scientists, such as Leonard Diggs and a handful of other Englishmen, began to experiment. They developed a perspective glass in the 1570s that worked as a kind of early telescope.[10] The innovators seem to have shared the invention with English privateers, including Sir Francis Drake, whose apparently miraculous talents at predation became widely known. By the time of the Armada, Elizabeth had recruited Drake and other English privateers into her navy.

Of course, a single innovation in intelligence rarely wins a battle. The larger question is whether or not England developed an intelligence advantage by using the terrain of uncertainty in a larger way, and, if so, how.[11] English scrappiness may have counterbalanced Spain's better knowledge of far-flung seas, but did the English *knowingly* tip that balance or just get lucky? In other words, did they leverage opening advantages to design savvy strategies, achieve surprise, and win? To know that, we must first briefly consider the nature of the larger Anglo-Spanish war of which this one battle was a part, mapping the terrain of uncertainty that affected both sides. As royal houses girded for war, they either built on their respective opening advantages, or they did not.[12]

The Anglo-Spanish Conflict

Although the story of the Spanish Armada seems a simple story of a battle at sea, neither the battle nor the intelligence that supported each side can be understood apart from the broader Anglo-Spanish war. The Armada was part of a many-layered contest among the evolving great powers of the sixteenth century. In its broadest scope, the issue was whether or not the Habsburg dynasty's Catholic and imperial interests would prevail in Europe.[13] King Philip II, a member of this inbred but powerful family, was largely driven by family obligation and faith. The first required that he retain the lands won from France by his ancestors and acquire the resources for defending them; the second required driving Muslims out of the western Mediterranean and Christian Europe and stamping out Protestantism, which he regarded as heretical.[14]

Queen Elizabeth was driven less by faith, family, or prize than by fear: Catholic Europe opposed her rule and seemed intent on dethroning her. She held fast to the long-standing belief that all monarchs defended a collective interest in the preservation of monarchical power, sovereignty, and legitimacy as attributes of their lineage. This mindset explains, in part, her hesitancy to execute members of the nobility who plotted against her, particularly her chief rival, the Catholic Mary, Queen of Scots. It also explains her stiff embrace of the realm's rising merchant class, which both filled her coffers and chafed against Spanish dominion over the seas. She and other English nobility invested in merchantmen, privateers, and the technology they required to trade, raid, or steal. Such activities brought resources to her throne even as they emboldened others with claims to it, and set her on a collision course with the Spanish king.

Eventually, however, Elizabeth recognized that clinging to the transnational idea of monarchical rights would be folly. In the first place, her enemies regarded her rule and thus her "rights" as illegitimate. Second, she needed her merchants more than she did her distant royal relatives, whose notions of divine right were as split as Christianity was by the Reformation. Beginning in 1585, she not only landed an English army in the Netherlands to support Protestants rebelling against their Spanish king, but also sponsored her privateers' ever more violent raids against Spanish holdings. Finally, in 1587, she spilled royal blood herself by executing her Catholic cousin, Mary, Queen of Scots, and unleashed her most fearsome pirate, Francis Drake, against Spanish interests. With these actions, the undeclared Anglo-Spanish war became an open one, and the stage was set for the sailing of Spain's great Armada against her.

The Terrain of Uncertainty

Despite the retrospective clarity of this sixteenth-century, great power conflict, it was deeply confusing at the time, as living history almost always is.[15] Respected historian Fernand Braudel once wrote:

> The historian who takes a seat in Philip II's chair and reads his papers finds himself transported into a strange one-dimensional world, a world of strong passions certainly, blind like any other living world, our own included, and un-conscious of the deeper realities of history, of the running waters on which our frail barks are tossed like cockleshells.[16]

The mid-sixteenth century was a time of deep uncertainty about the future of Catholicism, the relationship of monarchs to each other, and the impact of the New World on the fortunes of rulers, the emerging merchant class, and the financial solvency of proto-states. Chance engagements could spark massive bloodshed, becoming acts of war. At other times, battles at sea or beheadings—even of nobility—led to nothing. Such structural characteristics of "knowing" in the sixteenth century created dangers of miscalculation and folly. But they also created opportunities for wily intelligence operators to exploit the assumptions and ignorance of opponents.

The contextual circumstances for the Armada suggest four types of strategic uncertainty that would affect relative knowing and, thus, the potential for competitive success:

- The stability of ruling regimes
- The nature of military power, especially at sea
- The effects of time and distance on assessing and exercising power
- Divine preference or "acts of God"

From the modern vantage point, it is easy to underestimate the last factor: the deep fears and false certainties surrounding the workings of a divine hand. But this "knowing" of the faithful contributed in important ways to what competitors believed they needed to know to win—that is, their intelligence requirements. By 1580, science, commerce, and religiously driven social change had distributed faith and uncertainty unevenly, creating dangers of miscalculation.

Opportunities were plentiful for exploiting the assumptions and ignorance of opponents. In these respects, Spain and England were both blessed and cursed in differing ways.

Stability and the Uncertainty of Rule: Disloyalty, Disunity, and Distrust

The most significant opening uncertainty for the queen had to do with the security of her throne; for King Philip II, it was imperial integrity, including the effects of piratical attacks on his financial flows.[17] Whereas the queen needed to identify her domestic enemies and track them, the king needed to track pirates and quell insurgencies. Spain, like other European proto-states in the sixteenth century, had a fractious population. As one historian reminds us,

> The typical polity of early modern Europe was not the homogenous and unitary nation state; rather it comprised a loose aggregation of territories formed over the course of centuries by marriage treaties, negotiated take-overs, and formal mergers. In almost every case an act of association laid down in detail the separate identity and particular privileges of the various constituent parts. In addition, each major component state retained its own economic, social and (above all) defensive interests long after incorporation, and they did not always coincide with those of the central government.[18]

Such incoherence plagued both England and Spain in the mid-sixteenth century, but while Philip II wrestled with regional interests, Elizabeth's adversaries challenged her legitimacy, making her more uncertain of her hold on power than Philip ever was.[19] She needed a relatively strong domestic counterintelligence capability just to secure her crown.

The reasons for Elizabeth's vulnerability were several. First, the Reformation had shaken authority structures. Protestants no longer accepted the pope as the universal arbiter of God's will, including monarchical legitimacy.[20] When King Henry VIII rejected papal authority over the Church of England, English Catholics fled or went underground. After Henry's death and the brief reign of his son Edward, the next Tudor heir, Queen Mary, wed Elizabeth I's future adversary, Spain's Philip II, and re-established Catholicism in England. Mary soon died too. Philip quit England and Mary's half-sister, Elizabeth, became queen. She embraced Protestantism, causing another Catholic diaspora and continued rebellion at home. Through all these royal changes, English Protestants and Catholics developed an ever more textured hatred for one another. Religious affiliation was often mercurial, hidden, and mutable.

For a monarch with limited resources, uncertainty does not get much worse than this. Queen Elizabeth had the pope as an implacable enemy with a long reach into Catholic Ireland and Scotland, as well as segments of her English population. She was in constant danger of losing her throne to those who opposed her rule, either on religious grounds or out of blatant self-interest. Many of the most dangerous of these enemies were duplicitous, such as the dissident Catholic nobility in the north who had supported the rule of Mary Tudor and yet stayed in England when Elizabeth took the throne. As long as her dissenting nobles had the loyalty of the people in their regions, the English state was weak from within and its politics as changeable as these nobles' vanities and whims. A group of them organized to depose Elizabeth and install Mary, Queen of Scots in 1569 in what became known as the "Northern Rising."[21] The queen's situation worsened when, in 1580, the pope blessed the idea of regicide, an act formerly considered "the zenith of iniquity."[22] To survive, the queen had to keep track of domestic threats and pretenders to the throne. Not surprisingly, this objective quickly became the focus of her intelligence effort.

Philip II, in contrast, benefited from broad religious unity among elites on the Iberian Peninsula and great popularity with most of his Spanish subjects.[23] To the extent the king felt his rule in jeopardy, it was from imperial overstretch.[24] He governed a heavy quilt of countries that his Habsburg family had stitched through marriage and might. As more lands were attached to the Habsburg realm, insurrection and uncertainty pulled at this stitching faster than Philip could effectively manage from Madrid. Dissent clustered on the peripheries, where taxes exceeded expected returns. Native populations were exploited, and English, Dutch, or French traders fanned the fires of discontent for their own gain.

The king's trusted councils, some of which overlapped in their purview, struggled to gather timely knowledge of routine threats as they arose.[25] Thus, despite a large imperial bureaucracy feeding him information, the king rarely felt he knew enough about his realm in its entirety to act decisively in any one part of it. Could the Netherlands be held while Turkey threatened Spain in the Mediterranean? Could English apostasy be addressed while treasure routes in Central America remained vulnerable?

Imperial instability in any single part of the empire made it difficult to muster the resources necessary for monitoring the rest; any part might incubate seeds of dissolution. Officials in Madrid could not keep up with developments on the boundaries of empire as fast as local adversaries could, particularly after sea lines of communication were threatened by piracy and rebellion after 1572. This new imperial problem led the Spanish in the 1580s first to wonder if the collapse of one peripheral holding would cause a domino effect in others, and then to consider if fighting in a peripheral region such as the Netherlands might forestall the need to fight rebellion or invasion at home. Gradually, the idea spread that "the day that Spain removes its armies from those provinces, we would inevitably see theirs in Spain."[26]

Indeed, the king's biggest uncertainty was probably Spain's hold on the Protestant Low Countries, across the Channel from Protestant England and next to Spain's traditional adversary, France.[27] The Netherlands in the mid-sixteenth century was a collection of provinces in which over half the population lived in two hundred towns and cities, at least 10 percent of which were fortified. Their populations had strong identities and cultures, and their politics were feisty.[28] The king's uncertainties in the Netherlands had only been somewhat alleviated by the presence of the Duke of Alba's army, which had marched there from Italy at the king's direction. The duke found the Netherlands inhospitable, especially to the west and north. The countryside was a swamp full of canals and dikes that, as one oft-quoted observer wrote, made it "an universall quagmire . . . the buttock of the world, full on feinees and bloud, but no bones."[29] In gifting this quagmire to Philip, Charles V had bequeathed a recurrent nightmare.[30]

The rebellious population in the Netherlands enflamed Anglo-Spanish conflict because it raised each side's worst fears: cross-Channel invasion for England and imperial rot for Spain. After 1567, both monarchs pricked and wounded each other there, spreading the infection. Dutch rebels fought Philip's rule and, while Philip's generals eventually subdued the southern provinces (Spanish Netherlands), the rebels to the north continued the fight from their fortified cities, founding the independent country of the "United Provinces" in 1581.[31] To English eyes, Spanish efforts to subdue the Dutch rebels seemed a possible threat to the queen's realm, only forty miles away by sea. Some on the queen's Privy Council saw a threat in *every* Spanish move. Men such as Francis Walsingham and the Earl of Leicester, the queen's favorite courtier, believed England needed to use force to ensure that Spain did not secure a Catholic base from which to plot against the throne, pressure England, and roll back Protestantism. Yet even these influential supporters of the Dutch cause had difficulty allying with a land so divided geographically and politically. Leicester was sent to lead the rebellion, was heralded as a savior, and then lambasted by the States General, which refused to work with him. From Spain's perspective, England was deliberately enflaming matters that related directly to the integrity and viability of the Spanish throne.

Thus, underpinning the growing conflict between England and Spain was a complex weave of political uncertainty: whereas the English queen needed to know if the Spanish army parked across the Channel would enable a Catholic insurgency against her, the king needed to know if a Protestant insurgency in the Netherlands would undermine governance there and suck him into a costly land war. Learning the answer to the queen's question, while no minor challenge, was inherently easier than learning the answer to the king's. England's proximity meant that her merchants could regularly monitor Spanish capabilities and hear news from the Dutch, while Spain's relatively long lines of communication back to Madrid caused delays and extended security issues.[32] Along either side of the English Channel, the terrain of uncertainty was not level.

Distrust

While strategic uncertainties did not always overlap, one respect in which they did was pirates. Neither monarch trusted them, while both recognized their potential for political disruption. Their unregulated adventurism put the queen's diplomacy constantly at risk, while at the same time threatening the king's finances. The king's fear of pirates and privateers—mostly English and Dutch—reflected his judgment that the homeland was at risk if the imperial periphery would not hold; the queen's fear of them reflected her recognition that she would be blamed for their predations against the mighty Spanish Crown. By the 1570s, Dutch and English privateers were breaking rules of maritime trade. The Spanish, taking offense, attacked English ships, thereby escalating matters.

Then came Sir Francis Drake. This privateer-pirate circumnavigated the world, eroding the king's reputation, defenses, and finances by recruiting native populations in Central America to attack Spanish treasure routes and enriching the queen's coffers at Spain's expense. By 1580, this English and Protestant sea captain had become an international celebrity, seemingly bent on undermining Spain's empire in unpredictable ways. When, in 1585, Drake recruited a group of privateers and advanced on Philip's holdings in the Caribbean with over twenty ships, Philip, not surprisingly, took this as a declaration of war. He assumed, probably incorrectly, that he was more vulnerable to men such as Drake than they were to him. He worried that pilots of Spanish galleons or ex-slaves from Spanish mines in America were learning the value of what they knew—the vulnerabilities of Spanish treasure routes on land and sea—and where to sell this knowledge. He was right to do so.[33]

Queen Elizabeth I had her own uncertainties about her privateers, pirates, and merchantmen. She, too, had reason to distrust them, although the nexus of piracy and royal insecurity had different implications in England than in Spain. The entrepreneurial spirit stirred up by the Age of Discovery and Protestant individualism created new sources of wealth for England, provided those sources could be harnessed to the queen's purposes. Therein lay her trouble: Elizabeth expected her privateers to help with her finances, but understood she had limited capacity to predict their success or control their provocative tactics, especially when they were at sea. As profit motives were injecting new questions of loyalty into the English class structure, the queen nonetheless had to rely on her nobles and merchants for the financing of her navy.[34]

The queen understood that the privateers she funded one day could engage in piracy the next, risking her money and aims for their personal objectives. Merchantmen such as Drake and his cohort John Hawkins, could break Spain's laws of overseas commerce, do business with Madrid, or attack Spanish ships according to their whim. English privateers became indistinguishable from pirates operating in the Mediterranean and Huguenot rebels operating in the northern seas. Sailing on floating fortresses of their own, they were almost as ungovernable by the queen as the Dutch city-states were for Philip II. Investing in privateers one day and arresting them as pirates the next, Elizabeth struggled with the challenge of lashing her sea captains to her foreign policy. Her uncertainties were, however, far less than those of King Philip II, who saw pirates as much more than sea-based thieves. He saw them as terrorists enabling insurgencies worldwide.

In sum, it would seem that the queen's uncertainties about the longevity of her rule should have been greater than the king's about maintenance of his empire. In fact, unrelieved uncertainties *on both sides* drove them to what was likely an unnecessary war, as we shall see in the following chapter.[35] Once war became inevitable, a crucial inequity would tip the scales to the queen's advantage: Philip II chose to invade. The queen had superior intelligence on her own turf. Communications were such that she could also learn faster than he could about Spain's imperial periphery in Northern Europe. The king, therefore, needed a relatively intense intelligence effort to match or surpass English knowledge of the Channel, of Catholic insurgencies in England, and of the latest outrages by the Dutch or English sea captains.

In short, Philip II's decision to invade ceded England the intelligence high ground: the queen could learn how to hone her counterintelligence network and work with her pirates faster than Philip could learn how to prevent her from doing so. Over time, her decisions would tend to decrease Philip's relative knowledge in these areas, while his decisions would sharpen hers. Initially careful to avoid getting drawn into the Protestants' war in the Netherlands or a pirates' war at sea, which would have made her domestic instabilities worse, Elizabeth found a way to lure them all into her own royal war against Spain.

Uncertainty and the Sea

In general, mid-sixteenth-century Spain had better knowledge of shipbuilding and piloting, better navigational technologies, and better maps of the major commercial shipping routes than any other great power. In fact, Spain had mastered war-fighting at sea as well as on land, which makes Queen Elizabeth's choice of war appear all the more astonishing. Yet Spain's dominance was more fragile than it appeared. The Age of Discovery had invigorated competition for mastery of the oceans, with all that meant for bringing science, particularly cosmology and engineering, into the competitive arts of navigation, shipbuilding, and warfare.[36] As a result, the techniques of warfare were more uncertain on the sea than on land.[37] And, of course, the two were linked: when shipping routes were at risk, travel on land became more hazardous for large armies in need of victualing; when land blocked a safe march, armies were transported by sea.[38]

Three characteristics of sixteenth-century seafaring carried particular uncertainty: the difficulty of distinguishing friends from enemies; imbalances in the distribution of navigational knowledge among Mediterranean and Northern European powers; and the effects of advances in mathematics on shipbuilding and naval strategy. Strategic intelligence could exploit these uncertainties and innovations to get the jump on adversaries.

Friend or Foe?

European seafaring was a kindling mix of collaboration, competition, and piracy during the mid-sixteenth century, with few indicators for who, at any moment, might strike a fire. This danger had been long developing. When Portugal was at the vanguard of exploration in the fourteenth century, her sea captains enlisted the Genoese to help navigate the coast of Africa. Henry the Navigator created a base in the impressive castle at Sagres where "navigators, chart-makers, ship designers, sailors, adventurers and explorers from all over Europe came together to pool their knowledge and expertise in a common goal: the exploration and conquest of new worlds."[39] Gradually, however, the spirit of common cause gave way to aggressive jockeying for advantage. Eventually, Pope Alexander VI had to divide the world between his feuding Catholic powers, Spain and Portugal, in a papal bull of 1493. This bull was later codified in the 1494 Treaty of Tordesillas (Figure 2.1), which placed a Line of Demarcation 370 degrees west of Cape Verde off the coast of Africa. This longitudinal division left Spain "owning" all trade to the west, Portugal all trade to the east, and England out completely. Friendly monarchs observed the rule; adversaries broke it.

Though perhaps settling matters for Catholic Europe—at least until Spain absorbed Portugal in 1580, effectively eliminating the Line of Demarcation—this treaty did not do so for Protestant England, or the French, English, and Dutch privateers who had begun preying on shipping routes and exploring on their own. In fact, the treaty, which was intended to clarify relationships of power, in some ways obscured them because it anchored signatories to the belief that matters were clearer than they really were. Portugal kept its knowledge of its sea routes secret; Spain, while more open to foreign commerce, insisted on licensing all Spanish pilots plying the trade. Both countries, but especially

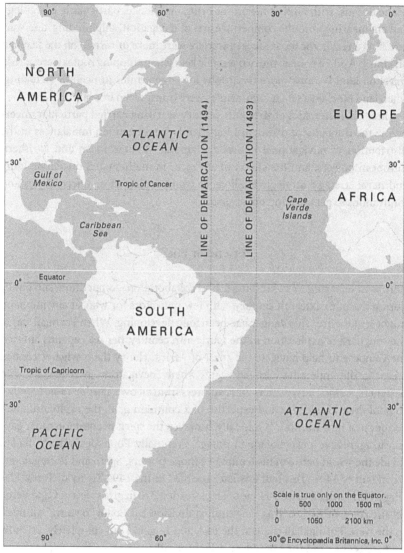

Figure 2.1 Map showing the line of demarcation between Spanish and Portuguese territory, as first defined by Pope Alexander VI (1493) and later revised by the *Treaty of Tordesillas* (1494). Spain won control of lands discovered west of the line, while Portugal gained rights to new lands to the east.

Source: "Treaty of Tordesillas," Encyclopaedia Britannica, https://www.britannica.com/event/Treaty-of-Tordesillas#/media/1/599856/140076. Accessed February 5, 2021. Courtesy Encyclopædia Britannica, Inc.

Portugal, punished any pilots abrogating the law, leading some of them to flee and, as we shall see, increasing uncertainty about what was known and unknown to foreigners about Iberian trading routes.

In contrast, English monarchs had long understood that merchantmen could be allies, co-opted by lax rule enforcement or bought outright and made privateers. Successful English sea captains of the day were also profit-oriented risk-takers. England's Henry VII, otherwise careful not to anger Spain, looked the other way when English traders, such as the elder William Hawkins, snapped up Portuguese pilots venturing to Brazil.[40] By the time Elizabeth I ruled, some of the best English sea captains seemed simultaneously privateers and pirates, acquiring Spanish seafaring licenses from Madrid while routinely breaking Spain's seafaring rules, such as the Line of Demarcation, for private gain and only selectively sharing what they knew with others, including other English merchants.[41] It was not much of a stretch for them to begin capturing foreign trade, crews, and vessels.

The Spanish came to regard certain merchantmen as criminals or pirates for whom the rules and courtesies of seafaring did not apply. English merchantmen, in turn, came to see themselves as powers unto themselves, ready to broker profitable deals with major powers. With such fluid concepts of the seafaring "game," discerning friend from foe at any point was difficult for both monarchs and sea captains. When one English privateer, John Hawkins, accepted assurances of safe harbor at San Juan de Ulúa while repairing his ships, the Spanish viceroy of Mexico ambushed him, killed or captured most of his crews, and sent the remainder limping home. Hawkins and his compatriot, Francis Drake, never forgot their mistake or forgave the Spanish for the deception, which cost the lives of many Englishmen and a ship of the queen's navy.[42]

Navigation

The dual-use aspects of seafaring, where honorable assurances and bloodletting coexisted, contributed to another uncertainty: how some were navigating open ocean and coastal zones to the detriment of others.[43] The Spanish seemed to have overwhelming superiority in all such matters by the mid-sixteenth century. In fact, they did not.

Improved techniques for travel in open ocean and along a nation's littoral had encouraged trade but had also increased the danger of attack from the sea. This led weak but savvy powers to hoard knowledge of their coasts. King Henry VIII, for example, who built England's first fleet of modern warships for his kingdom's defense, also built England's first lighthouse at Newcastle upon Tyne to lessen the dangers of navigating to port.[44] But the English king soon recognized his conundrum: lighthouses, like landmarks, were necessary for safe trade, but enemies could also use them to plan invasions. During the next century, the English generally eschewed lighthouses as a troublesome dual-use technology. The English did not build them in any quantity until the seventeenth century.[45] Of course, what was true of lighthouses at night was also true of buoy markers, church steeples, tall trees, and breaking water during the day. Good maps of them could be used to guide both merchant ships and invaders safely ashore.

Since the English Channel was key to England's defense and also treacherous, English and Dutch merchantmen familiar with its waters had precious knowledge that the Crown had reason to protect in ways Mediterranean powers poorly understood. As the naval historian E. G. R. Taylor has written,

> Whereas the Mediterranean Sea consists of a series of deep basins, the seas of north-west Europe are shallow seas. And because they are shallow—forming an enormous extension of the continental shelf—they are subjected to tides of exceptional range, and to tidal streams sweeping now this way, now that. As a result of the mutual interference of river and tidal streams there are deposits of river silt and long shore sand and shingle which are always shifting their shape and position. Depths are obviously of first importance, and the changes of depths twice daily with the tides.[46]

As the arts of mapping and navigating grew in importance for global traders, English seamen found advantages in staying inscrutable. They used the compass for orientation but, unlike Mediterranean captains, chose their courses by old-fashioned soundings and calendars of tides. Their specialized knowledge of how to navigate the shallow seas without "cartes and plates" was, in part, a cultural legacy; Northern European sea captains mocked those who relied on "sheepes skinnes" instead of wit and experience in seafaring.[47] As a result, few good maps on the Channel were available in the mid-sixteenth century; its secrets were embedded in the private notebooks or coded "rutters" of the English and Dutch merchantmen. These English sea captains thus knew their coasts and the Channel waters more from experience (either their own or their pilots') than from maps. This fact proved crucial during the sailing of the Armada because the English navy, built in good part on its merchant marine, could use the challenging northern seas as a weapon the Spanish could not parry. Although the latter had some competitive advantages in global or oceanic navigation, these advantages ebbed when ships sailed into ports unfamiliar to Spanish licensed pilots, and especially in the shallow waters of northern coastal zones. A strategy to fight there threw great informational advantages England's way.

Second, otherwise superior Spanish navigators lost advantages when they left their routine East-West treasure routes. Like those from other wealthy equatorial countries, the Spanish had long plotted courses beyond sight of land but at familiar latitudes, with some later forays into southern seas. Although they knew that the earth's rotation made geolocation a function of time as well as distance, they had not dedicated themselves to learning how to calculate it in oceans closer to the poles or with unfamiliar constellations of stars. While the developing conventions of longitude and latitude helped, ships' captains still had to translate two dimensions to three in order to accurately anticipate landings in northern seas.

Third, new technologies and geometry for plotting routes gave navigators and pilots growing advantages over less experienced noblemen serving as admirals. Crews on Spanish ships were forced to take orders from men who had little knowledge of weather or navigational calculations, while noblemen serving as admirals were forced to trust professionals for the very basics of situational awareness. Trust was strained in times of war, especially for officers for whom the results of open ocean navigation were about as good as "painting a house for a blind man."[48] Generally, the faster learners were admirals or captains who could overcome social barriers and earn the trust of experienced sailors.[49] The English proved better at this than the Spanish. Wily captains like Drake excelled at recruiting and bridging the gap between often lowly and sometimes foreign pilots and his regular crews. By the time he circumnavigated the globe, Drake was an expert pilot and navigator himself, even in unfamiliar waters, but he still valued and rewarded his skilled seamen.

In fact, Drake's relatively superior abilities in this latter regard proved essential to defeating the Armada. The dominant form of seafaring in the sixteenth century was still coastal "tramping," or the art of port-to-port navigation.[50] The special difficulties of coastal piloting in northern waters meant that the Spanish needed to recruit and retain English or Dutch pilots who could find their way out of navigational difficulties by the look of the coastline or the smell and taste of the sea and its sandy floor. The alternative was to steal. As already mentioned, some northern pilots recorded seafaring "codes" in logbooks known as rutters, which they jealously guarded for their clues concerning the safest routes into poorly mapped ports. Given the absence of good maps, acquiring these rutters or knowledgeable pilots could unlock the secrets of coasts and tides for invaders.

And here is where the English developed a wartime advantage: whereas the Spanish maintained a system for training pilots using traditional methods, the poorer English did not. English merchants, pirates, and privateers, such as Sir Francis Drake, trained their own pilots and recruited captured Spanish ones to help them raid targets in return for a percentage of the treasure gained. The English thus rose rapidly from dependency to supremacy in worldwide coastal navigation.

Just how rapid that rise was can be gauged by the fact that in 1558 probably not one, as late as 1568 probably only one, English seaman was capable of navigating to the West Indies without the aid of Portuguese, French or Spanish pilots. Yet, by the time of the Armada, a mere score of years later, Englishmen had gained "the reputation of being, above all Western nations, expert and active in all naval operations, and great sea dogs."[51]

At least some historians have credited Queen Elizabeth's counselor William Cecil (later Lord Burghley) with creating and preserving this strategic advantage. He protected English captains' specialized knowledge of the Channel while sponsoring raids and theft to secure the secrets of access to foreign ports. Unlike more traditional courts, the English one understood that lowly fishermen and merchants, many coming from hardscrabble backgrounds, could be valuable intelligence assets for the highest bidder and that maritime commanders plying enemy waters had to be excellent managers and manipulators of men.[52] This is one reason the Naval Board had privateers in the Royal Navy in 1588. The Spanish court was not ignorant of such matters; it just found the implications distasteful. Knowing that the absence or malevolence of a few experienced, roughneck pilots could blind a fleet and pry open an empire and all its treasure, the Spanish became expert at administrative control of pilots, while the English became expert at recruiting and paying them off with stolen Spanish booty.[53]

Uncertainty in Shipbuilding

A fourth seagoing uncertainty concerned the relationship of ship design to naval power. At the start of conflict with Elizabethan England, the Spanish dominated in this domain. Philip II had a massive fleet of ships purpose-built to imperial need. Every change in ship design entailed a trade-off among attributes of speed, weaponry, and storage capacity for feeding and hydrating soldiers aboard.[54] The Spanish, with a far-flung empire, deep pockets, and advantages in combined land-sea operations, dominated the market for the best shipwrights, most of whom worked along the Mediterranean littoral.

Spanish warships were widely regarded as the gold standard, incorporating advances in speed, agility, and firepower derived from long-haul treasure, escort, and amphibious operations. Spain excelled at designing and using galleons for the transport of soldiers who grappled, boarded, and overpowered the adversary at sea. Shipwrights designed their products to these requirements, albeit within the constraints of accommodating warriors with a sense of privilege: space for their own servants, armor, and even personal chefs. Thus, the largest paymasters—Spain and Portugal—set the standards for ocean travel, coastal trade, and battles at sea. Shipwrights knew not only how to build purpose-built galleons, but also how to modify merchant ships for warfare while retaining or improving their seaworthiness.[55] They altered galleons for oceangoing travel, joined squared sails to lateen sails for increased maneuverability, and plugged the sides of galleys and galleasses in order to make them ocean worthy.

Iberian and Italian shipwrights, at the top of their game in the sixteenth century, developed a mindset, however, about what could and could not be done with a boat. Design followed function, and the function of galleons, when purpose-built for war, followed the needs of the Spanish Empire. The largest Iberian galleons and carracks, topped by intimidating superstructures for guns and the housing of troops, became the models for all others. Even the English navy had the markings of Spanish design; Philip II, briefly England's king, had taken Henry VIII's upstart navy and modernized it using Spanish designs. So it was assumed—and not just in Spain—that the measure of naval power was the Spanish standard.

Yet this assumption was becoming dangerous for one driving reason: ship design was, by mid-century, escaping the mastery of the professional Iberian shipwright. In essence, there had long been just four ways to learn how to build a better boat: become an apprentice to an expert shipwright; buy that shipwright; discover his proprietary formulas; or steal the best ships, study their workings, and reverse-engineer them to create an improved model. The first option took decades. The second required a lot of money. The third required getting inside the shipwright's head, or decoding his scale models, the key parameters of which were a mystery to anyone outside the trade.[56] The fourth—stealing ships—became the métier of pirates and privateers. And they were learning from what they stole.

Over years of experience, pirates and privateers had come to understand that the high-capacity, castle-laden Spanish galleons were too heavy for the speed and maneuverability predators needed. The more the English raided Spanish ports and the more Spanish ships were defeated or captured, the more knowledgeable the raiders became about the nexus between ship design and performance in battle. Unable to afford new ships, they began to tinker, revise, and retrofit—experimenting with incremental change. Thus, by 1588, the terrain of knowledge about ship design was shifting from the old masters to pirates and privateers outside of Spanish imperial control, with all the implications that would have for changing naval doctrine and fleet tactics.[57] Aided by advances in math, these naval reformers were soon able to explain on paper the rationale for their redesigns to anyone with the resources to finance them. As we shall see, Queen Elizabeth I exploited this opportunity first, thanks to her opening advantages in access to privateers.

Time and Distance: The Uncertainty of Communications

The changing art of seafaring included an uncertainty of more general scope: unpredictable relationships between time and distance due to unreliable communications. In general, sixteenth-century monarchs could communicate better than rebels, merchants, and lesser nobles, yet even their decision-making often reflected delayed understanding of events. For example, after the Saint Bartholomew's Day massacre of Protestants in Paris in August 1572, information traveled to London faster by panicked refugees than by royal courier. Elizabeth's instructions to her ambassador—her later intelligence chief, Sir Francis Walsingham—arrived several days too late to be useful. Forced to appear before the king of France without guidance, the ambassador had to rely on his own wit.[58] Royal misperceptions and miscommunications were almost inevitable in such circumstances.

Decision-makers of all ranks had to map the most reliable routes for their messages. A letter that took a week to travel from Rome to Lisbon could take three months to get from Rome to Amsterdam because of the relatively bad roads and brigandage.[59] Roads linking great ports, capitals, and cities of trade, such as Brussels, Venice, Rome, Paris, Madrid, and Lisbon were generally best. These cities experienced wide ranges in delivery times even after the Duke of Alva made the Spanish Road famous by marching Spain's huge army along it in 1567.[60] This route was, in fact, less a road in places than a barely passable collection of traveling options connecting the Low Countries with points south. On any given day, the road could be direct and relatively fast or, with brigandage, washed-out bridges, and other blockages, circuitous and slow. As Philip II contemplated succession later in life, he explicitly warned his son about such uncertainties.[61] By then he knew that intelligence about safe lines of communication could be a source of significant advantage in war.

Matters were different at sea, but not necessarily better. News could sail relatively quickly along important coasts such as the Spanish Main or the Mediterranean littoral, but the difficulties of messaging from ship to shore made delivery unreliable. Most naval commanders used light, rapid ships to reconnoiter and communicate with the shore. These pinnaces were always at the mercy of the weather, and, once they made port, their messages to inland recipients depended on the availability of horses and couriers. If the pinnaces were those of an enemy coordinating an attack, coastal bonfires could alert inland villages, although these fires could also signal the invader that the moment of surprise was lost.[62] Sending messages the other way—from land to sea—was perhaps the most difficult because ships under sail were moving targets for pinnaces. Uncertainties varied by locale: whoever owned the shore tended to have advantages in local ship-to-shore communications. Philip II and his admirals would encounter this problem as they sought to share intelligence and coordinate land-sea operations for the Armada. Intrafleet communications were a different matter. Large royal fleets needed good communications, particularly Spain's treasure *flotas*, which, with much transoceanic experience, excelled at ship-to-ship messaging.

It is hard to appreciate from a contemporary vantage point the difficulties sixteenth-century monarchs had with communications and the uncertainties this weakness created for military operations.[63] By the time of the Armada, Spain and the Netherlands had been connected for over eighty years by a courier system through France. It included 106 relay stations and, by 1518, ostensible diplomatic immunity for communications among France, Italy, Germany, the Netherlands, and Spain. This arrangement meant, however, that France, a thoroughfare for traffic among royal courts and Rome, had the capacity to monitor, secretly delay, or intercept the communications of others.[64] And distance created vulnerabilities. Even the most powerful monarchs could have messages interdicted by criminals, spies, or irresolute allies.

Problems of this kind made intelligence—that is, *engineered advantages in learning*—a royal preoccupation. The Queen Elizabeth had to work at it. She shut her ports to deny cross-Channel communications when necessary and traveled the English countryside to hear gossip and petitions. Privy councilors with ties to merchants and mariners kept abreast of information of importance to the security of the queen.[65] And the queen herself interrogated her privateers after their voyages. After his circumnavigation, for example, Sir Francis Drake reportedly spent hours with her describing what he had learned about geography and Spain's worldwide holdings during his voyages.

In contrast, King Philip II's formal intelligence system and administrative councils flooded him with information. The king understood that communication meant power, so he spent resources on it. The Duke of Alba may have temporarily improved courier services from Milan to Brussels in 1567, but as noted earlier, this route was still filled with obstacles and threats that made communications unreliable. The king had to buy security for his couriers, fast horses for express service, and allies, including the pope, to guard his communications in central Europe. When these efforts were successful, which they often were, he enjoyed astonishing visiting dignitaries with news about developments in their own countries that even they had not yet received.[66] But he nonetheless remained uncertain about the timely delivery of particular messages at particular times—an intelligence requirement that haunted his decision-making during the sailing of the Armada in 1588.

The link between intelligence and decision advantage was, however, poorly understood. Because Philip believed that communications held the empire together, he wanted most of it to flow through him. Yet Drake's lightning tactics rendered the king's centrality to information flows a deficit for Spain.

He was repeatedly surprised and enraged by piratical attacks on his outposts. Descending like terrorists, the brigands struck and then disappeared before the king or his governors could react.[67] The king's advantages in communications had led him to reserve most decision-making to himself, but this policy only exacerbated his disadvantages in timely response to particular offenses by pirates on the periphery of empire.

This situation may have been discernible to a sophisticated intelligence service, but it was hardly clear to Philip II. Despite all his capability to communicate, the king did not appreciate those contingencies that could make ill-informed decision-making Spain's greatest vulnerability in war. He seemed to assume his commanders on the ground in the Netherlands, for example, would have sufficient information on fleet operations in the English Channel to coordinate with them. Yet none of his commanders at sea could know the information flowing to Madrid; they could not receive, let alone analyze, the massive flow of intelligence that emptied into the king's chambers each day; and while they sometimes knew more than the king about operations and tactics, they were limited in what they could decide without royal permission.

Indeed, the king's belief that only he could run his intelligence apparatus made him unable to do just that. Obsessed with secret writing and simple codes, he failed to study his admirals' and generals' requirements for "knowing" in battle. Codes and physical security would not matter if England had a superior capacity for more agile, informed decision-making in war. Whereas the English queen, with her relatively poor communications, delegated tactical information-gathering and naval decision-making to her sea captains, the king abhorred delegation of such authority. As a result, the communications terrain, including the capacity to get competitive information to decision-makers, would be tipped against the Spanish in 1588. By designing a complicated, coordinated, amphibious attack off hostile shores with key executive decisions left in his own hands, Philip unwittingly *chose* disadvantage. The question is why.

The Workings of God's Hand

The fourth major cause of uncertainty in the sixteenth century had to do with divine preference and the rise of the superstitious or incurious mind. If decision-makers believe events are directed by unseen and unknowable powers, then facts signify nothing and decision advantage becomes meaningless. If the decision-makers are monarchs who believe they, by divine will, not only know but represent such powers, then competitive faiths matter and God takes sides. Intelligence is reduced to the simple job of knowing God's will.

The problem for sixteenth-century polities was that Protestantism, which proposed that individuals could have direct relationships with God, threatened the institution of divine rule and the larger authorities of the Catholic Church. The ensuing storm darkened everything, creating fears of divine retribution.

> Elizabethan politics oscillated between realpolitik and religion, though this was a wider European development. For, whereas dynastic, chivalric, commercial, and personal ambitions had hitherto chiefly dominated the Renaissance stage, the polarization of rival religious creeds at the closing session of the Council of Trent meant that politicians increasingly saw themselves as combatants engaged in a cosmic confrontation between right and wrong. The concept of the "true church" that Catholics and Protestant promulgated in their diametrically opposed ways was pervasive; it ensured that pragmatism was overtaken by dogmatism, haggling by perpetual struggle, and compromise by persecution.[68]

Threats to the Catholic order grew with every "godless" Tudor success and growth in England's power. As the sixteenth century progressed, "Protestant" pirates, some of whom knelt to no God at all, were successfully feeding off Catholic empires supposedly protected by divine preference. Adventurers such as Francis Drake, a commoner with a mythical reputation as an antihero or an avenging angel, rose to knighthood and took tea with the queen. Devoutly Catholic Philip II, attempting to undercut Drake's growing power, called him satanic, which seemed only to increase his power. Drake played this devilish reputation for all it was worth, watching ships and ports surrender at the mere sight of him. The rise of such a powerful, transnational actor who repudiated the pope in Rome was part of a larger paradigm-shifting process underway throughout Catholic Europe.

The Tudor role in this shake-up of political authorities did not necessarily mean the English gained advantages from the consequences. Queen Elizabeth understood that pirates such as Drake valued profit and self-glorification more than God-fearing loyalty to the throne, which made her perennially suspicious. She attempted to embed loyal nobles on Drake's ships, only to have them killed, caponized, or sent home in disgrace. Drake tolerated no disloyalty or second-guessing at sea, even as he understood how his rule at sea jeopardized the queen's on land, putting his status with her in constant question. He was not alone. Protestant privateers sailing for the queen often preferred rich targets over Protestant England's best interests—although the combination of the two almost always prevailed.

Philip II and the forces of transnational Catholicism, nominally led by the pope, also had the problem of uncontrollable surrogates of questionable loyalty, but the king seemed inattentive to the threats they posed. All too ready to act on the pope's behalf, English Catholics agitated against the queen, conspired, and then betrayed Rome when the English caught or turned them. Sir Francis Walsingham, the queen's chief minister for espionage, pegged the mercurial agents well:

> The parade of "hired Papists," as Walsingham once termed them, and of disreputable Scotsmen, and of prison conmen who had served Mr. Secretary in his search for privy information were all liars of a lesser or greater sort. They lied to inflate their own importance, or to fill in a slack period when they hadn't found anything genuine to sell; they lied in hopes of playing both sides of the street, sometimes they lied for no reason at all.[69]

The confusion that zealots created for monarchs was compounded by monarchs' claims to divine insight and preoccupation with the worldly. The king veered from messianic certainty to paralyzing fears of error and micromanagement. The Protestant queen flirted with Catholic suitors, waivered in her support for the Protestant Dutch against their oppressors, and for years tolerated the murderous intentions of her Catholic half-sister, Mary. The Protestant ministers who caught Mary's treason and helped convict her of it got tongue-lashings and, in some cases, imprisonment in the Tower of London. Even Drake expected surprises from the queen, used spies to gauge his favor in court, and generally sought to stay well beyond her reach.

As secularism grew in the interstices between Catholicism and Protestantism, so did new loci of power largely anchored in business and banking. Drake and his piratical colleagues represented one facet of this new power, derived less through nobility of blood or religious affiliation than through intelligence-driven action. Drake learned to use information and thievery more than religious affiliation as currency in this pursuit. Yet, without an anchor in either political or religious elites, Drake found this balancing act difficult and monarchical loyalty tenuous. For all the tactical intelligence men like Drake might collect at sea, they suffered from lack of strategic information about the risks and gains of using it in any particular instance—even for decision-making on their own side. With no religious or political network to back him, Drake evolved into a transnational power in his own right, becoming more an ally with whom the queen liaised than a part of her governing religious and political elite.

Acts of God, Divine Will, and Superstition

Although Drake and his kind represented a form of transnational, secular power that threatened old authority structures, sixteenth-century Europeans still saw

God as a real player who would take sides in war. For the Spanish, God spoke through the pope and the king, who was therefore expected to topple the heretic queen. The queen's Protestant counselors were equally certain that the Roman church and its allies were corrupt, so war with Spain was justified, no doubt in God's eyes, as well. Drake believed "true religion could not survive in England unless the greatness of Spain were abased" and Rome put back in its place. "How can it be endured that kings and princes must kiss the Pope's foot?" Drake opined. "What a swindle!"[70]

Divine will was thus one of the most impenetrable sources of uncertainty in the age of sailing ships precisely because almost everyone seemed so certain of it. Most monarchs believed they could influence acts of God, such as storms, extreme tides, or the availability of victuals from the sea, through prayer. As a result, they were at certain times remarkably incurious, and at others in the thrall of prophecy, which could stir them and their people to act irrationally. Espionage is difficult when intentions are guided more by tea leaves than facts.

Indeed, superstition and speculation were running high in 1588, creating social turbulence unsettling for all monarchs. This year was, according to the prophecy of Cyprianus Leovitius, *supposed to be* one of divine intervention involving the overthrow of the Antichrist and the onset of the Last Judgment. According to one historian who has written on such prophecies,

> There would be "either a universal consummation and final dissolution of the world, or at least a general subversion and alteration of principalities, kingdoms, monarchies and empires." These prognostications were "rife in every man's mouth," and to the superstitious, signs were not lacking that Nature was in turmoil, confirming that some great cataclysm was imminent.[71]

Alarming sightings, such as "a vast number of fleas collected together on the window of the Queen's Presence Chamber" or "30 great fish commonly called porpoises" swimming up the Thames to the Watergate of the Queen's palace, put all of Europe abuzz. The possibilities for 1588 included "tempests, floods and earthquakes, snow and hailstorms in summer, monstrous births, even skies running blood."[72]

Regardless of whether Catholics or Protestants expected vindication, the effect of all this prognostication was to taint intelligence with omens, delay decision-making, and add tension and urgency to the widely anticipated Anglo-Spanish confrontation. Venetian spies reported that the astrological insights of emperor Rudolf II were so impossible to acquire that even Philip II's ambassador could not do so, which meant, of course, that he spent serious time trying. The emperor Rudolf was, in fact, seemingly paralyzed by his fears of the coming end of days, and that paralysis rippled out as a storm of anxiety through Christian Europe.

The terror affected military power in subtle ways. Mercenaries and other recruits began to dither over taking sides, fearful that their choice would land them in hellfire when God's judgment was meted out. It may have also increased the theatrical effects of surprise, suppressed courage in adversity, and amplified swings in morale among troops.

The next chapter reveals how such matters of faith and superstition sowed hubris, confusion, and a peculiar incuriosity in parts of Europe as the Armada sailed north. Despite damaging storms, the king urged it forward because he could not sort fearful prognostications, matters of faith, and facts. He was imprudent in his decisions not because he was uninformed, but rather because he believed himself so divinely informed that facts had become irrelevant.[73] This was a self-induced disadvantage that his intelligence operations could not overcome. Most of his courtiers were so certain God was on Philip II's side and Spain could not fail that they stifled bad news and dissent of any kind. The king was regarded by some as a saint, if not divine himself, until the end of his reign. Geoffrey Parker, the leading historian of sixteenth-century Spain and Philip II, has emphasized this point in particular:

> At the beginning of the reign, when he promoted a man of humble birth to be primate of all Spain, the wife of a courtier irreverently commented: "These are the miracles that the king now wishes to perform, and they seem very like those of Christ, who made men out of clay"; by its end, however, many of his servants and subjects genuinely saw him as the incarnation of God on earth, believed he had been a saint, and attributed miracles to him. Philip himself made no such claims—on one occasion he wrote "I don't know if [people] think I'm made of iron or stone. The truth is, they need to see that I am mortal, like everyone else"—but he seldom had qualms about exercising his absolute power over life and death.[74]

Helpful as such a widespread perception might have been for the security of his rule, the king's belief in an alliance with the all-powerful undermined his interest in intelligence.

Time and again the king pressed his policies upon unwilling subordinates, or upon taxpayers, on the grounds that his work was God's work. Philip once loftily urged a dispirited subordinate to take better care of his health "because you are engaged in God's service and in mine—which is the same thing." And throughout his reign, the king believed profoundly that God would provide whatever lay beyond human powers of prediction or execution. He repeatedly counted upon miracles to bridge the gap between intention and achievement and thus to fill the interstices in his strategic plan.[75]

As a result of the king's piousness, incuriosity had such a foothold in Spain that the court had a positive disinterest in intelligence contradicting royal assertion. The commander of the Armada, Medina Sidonia, tried to warn the king in 1588 about the obstacles to a successful naval attack that year, but the king's principal minister for foreign affairs intercepted the letter and refused to send it forward. "Do not depress us with fears for the fate of the Armada, because in such a [just] cause God will make sure it succeeds."[76]

Blind faith in the king's divine mission did not eliminate all rationality. The king's highest military commanders sometimes resisted his divinely inspired optimism. The Duke of Alba, for example, learning in 1571 of the king's belief that invading England was God's will, replied that "[God] normally works through the resources He gives to humans" and that Alba judged the resources insufficient.[77] While Philip II sometimes listened to such advice, he remained overconfident and often rejected it. Certainty bred hubris, predictability, and sloppiness.

The overall effect of this religious turmoil and uncertainty seems to have favored England in 1588. Philip II was so certain of God's backing at times that he seemed open to taking shortcuts in preparing for battle—a fact that the pope, less pious in this regard, may have considered when withholding financing for the king until he landed on English soil. Protestants, however, who tended to see God favoring those who worked hardest for him, believed the weather was something more to plan for than to pray about. They built ships suitable for varying winds—more maneuverable, speedy, and flexible—and so gave God some options.

Circumstance to Advantage: Intelligence at Work

In general, the context for decision-making in the mid-sixteenth century included uncertainties that distorted perceptions of power and encouraged risk-taking. We can summarize the "terrain of uncertainty" thus:

- Both sides knew that Spain was dominant in land warfare, but that Philip II's finances were stretched by conflict in the Netherlands and were vulnerable to any interruption in flows of treasure across the Atlantic.
- Both knew that their extended involvement in the Low Countries would likely drain their royal coffers with little prospect of a lasting, positive outcome. Likewise, each believed that withdrawal would jeopardize its rule at home.
- Both knew that the English queen's rule was in greater jeopardy than Philip II's, and that her strongest domestic adversaries were Catholic allies of Spain.

- The English Privy Council knew that the queen's vulnerability depended on developments in England, which they could know better than the king could.
- The Spanish king had the best archive of maps and naval data for most of the world,[78] but not for the north and its littoral regions, where Spanish pilots and admirals were relatively ignorant.[79]
- Spain knew best how to navigate most open ocean routes, manage large-scale intrafleet communication, and build classic warships.[80]
- English and Dutch merchantmen and privateers knew better than the Spanish how to navigate the English Channel and associated northern seas, recruit and retain foreign pilots, raid foreign ports, interdict ships, and achieve surprise in naval operations.
- Piratical English and Dutch "sea dogs" knew more about their own ships and crews, as well as the strengths and weaknesses of Spanish ships, than the Spanish knew about their own or those of the English. In fact, equipped with new tools developed through mathematics, English sea captains knew how to adapt ship construction to operational requirements and possessed a language for representing these changes to potential financiers.
- Catholics, defenders of a faith seemingly threatened by satanic pirates and a godless Tudor regime, were relatively certain that God was on their side, so they were relatively incurious competitors.

In sum, the terrain of uncertainty for Spanish and English combatants in the mid-sixteenth century was perilously lopsided for one side or the other depending on the kind and location of the fight: better for England the closer to her shores; better for the king in the Mediterranean or on the open ocean; bad for both but worse for England in the Netherlands. To capitalize on her opening informational advantages, Elizabeth needed to deter invasion and achieve operational and tactical surprise in the Channel—not fight a land war or a general engagement on the open seas triggered by piratical excess.

To deter constructively as opposed to provocatively, the queen needed intelligence, particularly from her mariners. She understood from years of experience, however, that England's natural advantages were not coincident with those enjoyed by her privateers. Outside the Channel, pirates might win tactical victories using strategies of surprise, but in large-scale engagements, Spain's larger fleet, better maps of the continent and oceans, better intrafleet communications, and skilled ship-borne soldiers would likely be decisive. Any English intelligence service worth its salt would have advised the queen, if she had to fight, to choose the very kind of battle Philip II chose: a naval battle in the Channel. A superior Spanish service might have anticipated the queen's intention to bring pirates into her navy, convinced the king to avoid engaging in the Channel, and shown him the advantages to be gained by killing Drake and his collaborators in Spanish ports. At the strategic level, Spain's informational advantages favored three options for war: an open ocean fight with the English navy; luring English forces into war on the continent; or, perhaps, surprise invasion of England via Ireland or from the sea. All the king's *worst* informational gaps would be triggered by an attempt to coordinate maneuvers in the Channel between an armada of ships and Spain's swamped army in the Netherlands.

Staring at her options, the queen had fewer choices, but more curiosity. She wondered whether to taunt Philip in the Netherlands, whether it might be possible to avoid war by reducing his treasure and finances, and how best to fight if she had to—specifically, how to win a naval battle, which seemed her only hope. As we will see in the next chapter, her Privy Council's intelligence operations mattered to these decisions. Her government learned that her privateers had a way of winning against the Spanish fleet that was scalable and, therefore, might overturn old measures of power at sea. Elizabeth cleverly liaised with her fractious sea captains, allied with them on the brink of war, and then controlled them with sharp tugs on the only tether she had—their food and ammunition. This policy may have been contingent, artful, and not entirely planned, but it was fully intentional in its cumulative effects. Her government deliberately sought piratical knowledge for revolutionizing English ship design. Then, through ruthless policies of official oversight, the queen deliberately tied piratical intelligence-gathering to the fight against the Spanish in the Channel. All the while, her precarious position on the throne was increasingly secured by her ministers' purposeful infiltration of enemy plots against her—a process that resulted in England's deep penetration of Catholic networks in Europe.

In contrast, Spain's superior knowledge of the oceans and capacity for intrafleet communications favored a fight almost anywhere *but* the English Channel. A well-informed king might have picked off the pirates threatening his fleet and lured the English navy away from the Channel where her ships could not long endure and her navy's relative inability to communicate would enfeeble English fleet operations. Such a ploy could have worked: just before the battle, the queen's had to refuse her admirals' pleas to be allowed to dash out of the Channel to engage the Spanish fleet en route. But the king did not entertain such ideas once his ships sailed. Instead he continued to believe, erroneously, that he knew enough of the Channel to win there. The Duke of Parma believed otherwise, but his uncertainties were overruled by the king's certain knowledge of God's favor. The terrible storms of 1588 created surprising conditions, but Philip's vulnerability to them was of his own making. In considering his opponent, Philip was mistaken in the same way leaders of powerful armies fighting in traditional ways with well-worn doctrine misjudge the advantages of guerrilla forces operating in their own homeland. So it was that the queen gathered intelligence about Philip's critical naval weaknesses and, playing David to Spain's Goliath, hit the giant be-tween the eyes.[81] Not only did she co-opt her privateers, but they designed her slingshot and became her stone.

Conclusion

Strategic intelligence fills the gap between what a government knows and what it needs to know to advance its interests in a competitive world. Because strategic choices can make filling this gap easier for one side than the other, mapping the opening terrain of uncertainty is a crucial first step for gaining decision advan-tage in military contests. Choices informed by strategic intelligence, in turn, fa-cilitate intelligence support to operations and tactics. This lesson will become clear in the next chapter on the specifics of Spanish and English decision-making.

The structural characteristics of "knowing" in the sixteenth century created dangers of miscalculation and folly for all; the effects were, however, very specific for Spanish and English prospects in war, depending on the strategy each side chose. The foregoing survey of what was generally known and unknown at the time reveals where advantages in this general knowledge lay, but has only hinted about how they were used, overcome, or lost. What remains is to understand how the *purposeful* acquisition and manipulation of competitive information rolled back or exploited uncertainty, and thus affected the Anglo-Spanish naval en-gagement in 1588. Intelligence systems, working in concert with policymakers, needed to fill in the blind spots for their own sides while enlarging them for opponents. Making bad strategic decisions may rest on poor mapping of the ter-rain of uncertainty, but a good intelligence service can still overcome that deficit.

The next chapter details how ill-conceived Spanish covert policies had exactly the opposite effect, damaging the king's own espionage network while stimu-lating the growth of the queen's. Philip made his situation worse by consolidating the loyalty of the English to their queen and improving the flow of domestic in-telligence to London. Instead of leveraging Elizabeth's uncertainties, he created the threat that filled them in, losing his embassy and other spies and agents in the process.

3

Gaining Decision Advantage in the Anglo-Spanish War

The last chapter described how the terrain of uncertainty would either stress or ease intelligence during the Anglo-Spanish war, depending on the strategies each side chose. What we need to know now is whether and how the queen and king each exploited, overcame, or ignored this terrain in their pursuit of competitive advantages.

To find answers, we need to identify crucial decisions on both sides and the reasoning behind them.[1] For example, in 1587 Queen Elizabeth decided to risk war against Spain.[2] This was a choice for *asymmetric* war chosen by the militarily *weaker* party in circumstances other than sneak attack.[3] It is tempting to assume miscalculation, but was it? Most historians agree that the queen was no fool, so it is possible she had intelligence that led her to think she could win. In this chapter, we will explore this decision, as well as others crucial to the outcome of Anglo-Spanish conflict in 1588: Spain's and England's choices regarding their respective interests and the marshaling of power to support them; operational choices about how and where to fight; and tactical decisions during the naval battle itself.[4] The task is to examine the extent to which intelligence clarified, lubricated, or muddied these choices for England and Spain.

Although the following analysis breaks the conflict down on three levels from strategic to tactical and analyzes decisions separately, it is important to remember that this discussion is somewhat artificial. Decisions related to grand strategy (addressing the largest interests of the Crown), operations (about how and where to engage to secure selected interests), and tactics (about how to fight in the moment) were all interlaced.

Informing the Pursuit of Strategic Power and Interest

The Anglo-Spanish conflict may have turned hot in 1586, but Spain and England had been engaged in a form of cold war since at least 1570. During the years in between, both monarchs alternately taunted and accommodated each other. Calculated in terms of relative power, classically measured, Spain should have been able to win a war against England relatively easily. Spain was militarily

Decision Advantage. Jennifer E. Sims, Oxford University Press. © Oxford University Press 2022.
DOI: 10.1093/oso/9780197508046.003.0003

dominant, France was weak, Catholics were belligerent, and the pope had authorized regicide. The king nonetheless hesitated. He had to counter the Turkish threat in the Mediterranean, maintain solvency through predictable flows of treasure into his coffers, and, in general, run a huge empire. To him, fighting battles in the north seemed like picking scabs: likely to worsen bleeding sores, especially in the Netherlands.

The king's hesitation offers a clue to the complexity he faced. At least until matters came to a head in 1585, Spanish and English interests were potentially reconcilable. Philip needed to subdue Northern Europe at reasonable cost; Elizabeth needed a secure throne and so could have helped quell the Protestant revolt in return for certain guarantees from Philip II. That the king not only missed an opportunity to heal his wound in Northern Europe but also did pick his scabs, making matters worse, suggests that he either had poor strategic intelligence from 1570 to 1586 or felt divinely inspired and therefore infallible. The queen's intelligence hardly seemed better; she chose to ally with the Dutch in 1584, provoking a war with Spain, just as the king's power in Northern Europe was consolidating.

Were no advisors painting a strategic picture for these monarchs, and, if not, why not? To answer this question, we examine each side's intelligence for two consequential decisions during these years: Spain's choice to use covert action to unseat the English queen; and the queen's decision to become involved in the Protestant rebellion in the Netherlands and thus to declare war on Spain.

Strategic Intelligence and Spain's First "Enterprise of England"

Given the king's opening advantages in strategic information, the story of how he lost them is worth detailed review. The lessons gained are timeless ones about treating covert action as a substitute for, rather than a tool of, normal policy and planning. Philip II knew his strategic interests required reducing the costs of empire and keeping his army solvent. Although Queen Elizabeth could have helped him in both these objectives, he persisted in believing she was more of a threat and more insecure on her throne than she actually was. This latter view was initially based on reports of the "Northern Rising" of 1569. The Rising followed Spain's invasion and occupation of the Netherlands in 1567, which led Dutch Protestants to come to England's shores. The sudden flood of refugees triggered English fears of invasion and emboldened Catholic dissidents. Among the latter were English nobles who plotted to replace their Protestant queen with a Catholic one, Mary, Queen of Scots. Although the king initially rejected Catholic proposals to invade England as he pursued war against Turkey (1559–71), he left belligerent diplomats to handle English affairs and report to him on their progress.

These Spanish diplomats claimed enough knowledge and connections in 1571 to propose a series of covert plots to overthrow the English queen. The king knowingly accepted risks by authorizing this activity. He knew that Spain's English collaborators had failed in the Northern Rising and that their future loyalty to Spain would be uncertain. Mary, Queen of Scots, while Catholic, was a Francophile who might eventually turn against Spain. Worse, he must have guessed English counterintelligence was on alert: not only was memory of the Northern Rising still strong in Elizabeth's court, but Mary, imprisoned on English soil since fleeing a rebellion of her own nobles against her rule in 1568, remained a magnet for dissidents.[5] Elizabeth's Privy Council saw her as a threat. The king nevertheless accepted his diplomats' advice that England's Catholic insurgents offered the easiest and cheapest way to end his troubles in the north.[6] The king's decision was based on a multifaceted intelligence failure in which he was complicit: the failure to appreciate the Elizabeth's superior grasp of her domestic situation; the failure to identify compromised sources purposefully meant to mislead; and the failure to link covert policy, including intelligence tactics and operations, to a coherent grand strategy. The story is one of shaky sources, double agents, politicized analysis, poor counterintelligence, and simple hubris.

The Ridolfi Plot

One of those who had been tangentially involved in the Northern Rising was a Florentine banker in London named Roberto Ridolfi. He was a trusted facilitator and courier for Pope Pius V and dissident English Catholics.[7] In January 1571, Ridolfi told the beleaguered Mary, Queen of Scots that he could enlist the pope and King Philip in a plot on her behalf. Mary agreed. Ridolfi then enlisted three men: a reluctant Duke of Norfolk, whose participation in the Northern Rising had already made him a suspect in the eyes of the Privy Council; an eager Don Guerau de Espés del Valle, the Spanish ambassador in England; and the pope. De Espés, who "strove to exaggerate and exploit any English slight or action that seemed to prejudice Spanish interests," was particularly enthusiastic. The plan evolved from simply exfiltrating Mary to regicidal warfare: assassinating Elizabeth as she toured the countryside, and then invading with Spain's forces from the Netherlands, led by the unwilling Duke of Alba. De Espés wrote up the plan as "The Enterprise of England" and sent it to the king, who sought the Duke of Alba's advice. Alba thought the whole plot implausible and told the king as much.

Astonishingly, Ridolfi pressed forward with the plan, went to Madrid, and gained the king's endorsement over Alba's protests. Philip informed Alba that

> no one can deny that this venture involves many and great difficulties. . . . In spite of all this I desire to achieve this enterprise so much, and I have such complete confidence that God our Lord, to whose service it is dedicated (because I have no personal ambition here), will guide and direct it, and I hold my charge from God to do this to be so explicit that I am extremely determined and resolved to proceed and participate, doing on my side everything possible in this world to promote and assist it.[8]

In addition to religious certitude, Philip's decision was based on reporting from de Espés, Ridolfi, and others who, over the preceding two years, had sought to whip up support for their plot by overinflating the disloyalty of English Catholics and, perhaps, Norfolk himself.

Almost from the beginning, however, Ridolfi's operation was penetrated, corrupted, and exploited by members of the queen's Privy Council. The ministers had seen much of the Spanish reporting because, having been stung by the Northern Rising, they had been watching all those implicated in it, including the Spanish embassy. They had been controlling the post and ports and intercepting couriers. In fact, Elizabeth I's decision to spare some of the traitors allowed her ministers to track them, discover new plots taking shape, and gather evidence against them.[9] Such activities were the particular responsibility of the queen's secretaries, sequentially William Cecil (later Lord Burghley and hereafter referred to as such), and Francis Walsingham. Burghley, who had adopted Catholicism under Mary Tudor before returning to Protestantism under Elizabeth, used his clerical bona fides to identify and penetrate Catholic networks. Traitors were caught, interrogated, and either turned or killed. The Spanish ambassador, de Espés, was an unwitting tool in this process—more valuable in luring co-conspirators into the English net when at liberty than when under arrest.

Ridolfi, in contrast, probably turned from the Catholic cause to Elizabeth's early on. Indeed, historians think it likely Ridolfi was a double agent who, in meeting with Philip in 1571, was executing a complicated sting at Burghley's behest.[10] If so, this was a sophisticated counterintelligence strategy employing both defensive measures (monitoring and tracking adversaries) and offensive measures (manipulating and influencing) to offer the Spanish a regicidal cause and then prevent it from happening.[11] Such manipulation meant, of course, that England's espionage apparatus might harvest some tainted intelligence. After all, its counterintelligence agents would be seeding the king's most malicious intentions before these intentions had fully ripened.

The queen's spymasters seem to have had a plan to guard against this problem. Elizabeth sent the king a diplomatic offer of reconciliation at about the same time Ridolfi was presenting his plot to him. With the king's decision in favor of the plot, Elizabeth's ministers grew more certain of his malign intentions. They apparently brought the privateer sea captain John Hawkins into the plot by having him offer to ferry Alba's troops across the Channel in return for release of Englishmen still imprisoned after Spain's attack at San Juan de Ulúa. The Spanish accepted. That they understood their intelligence deficit in the Channel probably made them easy prey for this deepening deception. Hawkins learned the size of the invading force and its landing point: Harwich in Essex.

Not surprisingly, the Ridolfi plot, which had grown into the first "Enterprise of England," failed. De Espés was kicked out of England, and his collaborators, except for Ridolfi and Hawkins, were imprisoned or killed—confirming that these latter two were complicit in Burghley's game and ruining Spanish intelligence on the queen's domestic affairs.[12] The king likely never understood the provenance and danger entailed in the plot because he had few reliable sources beyond those advocating it and inadequate operational counterintelligence. Whereas the queen had access to Catholics and Protestant networks through her ministers' espionage networks, the king's spies were either Catholics intent on convincing him of what he should do or double agents. Philip had expelled the last English ambassador to Spain, the Protestant priest Dr. John Man, for calling the pope "a canting little monk." Given so few ways to learn, the king could not appreciate how weak England's dissident Catholics were at any particular moment or how effective the English might be at tracking his agents' and ambassador's every move.[13]

There is evidence that one source may have been a counterweight to the distorted views coming to Madrid through de Espés's channel: in 1569, the Duke of Alba sent an agent, Christophe d'Assonleville, to England at the king's behest. Although his reports are not now available, this minister from the Netherlands knew England well and had good contacts there. From this and other sources, Alba and his successor likely knew enough to tell the king that plots to topple Elizabeth were highly risky and that Spain was poorly positioned to support any English insurgency. Their arguments suffered, however, from poor lines of communication back to Madrid. For example, although the king sent orders for Alba to open negotiations with the queen, this authorization took about three months to get to him. This delay, and the king's distraction over the Ottoman Turks, provided the opening for de Espés to propose and receive authorization for his "Enterprise of England." The king's intelligence apparatus never solved or even took account of his communications problems, which contributed to his seemingly erratic delegation of decision-making—first to de Espés, then to Alba, then back to de Espés—all of which added to the kind of confusion that plagued the Armada almost two decades later.[14]

Thus, poor Spanish intelligence policy and operational decision-making left England the beneficiary of Spain's (and the pope's) covert policies from 1569 to 1571. Philip's decision to support the opportunistic and largely tactical plan concocted by de Espés, Ridolfi, and his cohorts backfired: it drew the watchful eye of the queen's Privy Council, clarified the threat posed by Spanish forces in the Netherlands, and tempted England's greater involvement there. Although the queen's strategic intelligence was also poor, she became more strategically decisive because Spain's plots eventually convinced her that Philip was determined to overthrow her. She joined the French (Charles IX, backed by his mother, Catherine de Medici) in signing the Treaty of Blois on April 19, 1572. This startling agreement provided that any attack on one party would be viewed as an attack on the other. By putting the Spanish Netherlands in a vise between England and France and walling out Spain, it would have constituted a revolutionary development in the structure of international politics—had French Catholics not slaughtered three thousand Huguenots in Paris and ten thousand more in the provinces just a few months later, probably at Catherine's instigation. As word of the massacre spread, English Protestants assumed the Catholic conspiracy involved not just the French royal family, but also Philip II and the pope. Fury and fear thus eclipsed the effects of the April treaty.[15]

So it was that the Spanish king's mistakes, induced by covert action, had already, by 1572, begun forcing Elizabeth's hand in ways that compromised her long-term strategic interests. And, by uncovering a conspiracy they had helped to provoke, the queen's ministers set England on the path to war with Spain—a path they all knew was dangerous.

The Throckmorton and Babington Plots

The intelligence advantages flowing to the English endured long after the Ridolfi case was closed, in part because the queen's Protestant ministers now expected Spanish intervention, and so prepared to stay ahead of it. Francis Walsingham, who had replaced Burghley as principal secretary in December 1573, expanded the latter's espionage network and increased the vigilance of the state.[16] He gained personal control of significant customs operations in port cities, strengthened border patrols and connections to businessmen, funded piratical enterprises to find and exploit Spain's vulnerable flows of specie, and developed new ways to monitor all of Queen Mary's communications as she remained captive on English soil.[17] Burghley, known for his Catholic sympathies dating back to the years before Elizabeth's reign, retained sources among the Catholic diaspora;

Walsingham continued to track English Catholics in France and monitored their communications to English noblemen and merchants. Thus, both Burghley and Walsingham fed intelligence to the queen, albeit biased by their respective political inclinations and the offensive counterintelligence tools used to collect it.[18]

In comparison, Spain's intelligence on England worsened after the failed Ridolfi plot. By 1573, King Philip II was operating with little knowledge of how deeply Catholic networks had been compromised and how tightly the queen's Privy Council had wrapped her kingdom in a net of counterintelligence. It is unsurprising, therefore, that Spain became mixed up in more failed plots. In 1583, alert English border security agents working for the warden of the Middle Marches stopped a Jesuit dentist attempting to cross the border to Scotland. His equipment concealed secret letters to the Duke of Lennox, a French Catholic confidant of Mary's son, the young King James of Scotland. The doctor's capture soon unraveled what became known as the Throckmorton plot. This plan, supported by four hundred thousand ducats from Pope Gregory XIII, envisioned a joint invasion of England by Lennox out of Scotland and Henry I, Duke of Guise, out of France for the purpose of overthrowing Elizabeth and installing Mary as queen. Lennox had made his involvement conditional on Philip II's military and financial support, which he had been duly promised by Philip's new ambassador to England (1578–84), Don Bernadino de Mendoza. As usual, Philip had been hesitant. He had asked Alba's successor, the Duke of Parma (arriving 1578), and Santa Cruz, a top admiral, to study the invasion plan. Parma was as unenthusiastic about this plan as his predecessor had been about the earlier Ridolfi plot. After dithering, Philip decided against invasion, claiming the season was too late to attempt it, but probably also finding collaboration with the French too risky.

Although the initial plan was discarded when Protestant nobles captured the young Scottish king and exiled Lennox, it was revived shortly thereafter by Mendoza, whose intelligence failed yet again for reasons of poor operational security.[19] Walsingham had been monitoring the French embassy and opening Mary's letters because he suspected French collusion with a network of Catholic expatriates. His source, embedded in the embassy, reported that two Englishmen, Francis Throckmorton and Lord Henry Howard, were secretly adding to Mary's bundle of authorized letters. Walsingham blackmailed the French ambassador into exposing the plot, managing to do so without revealing his source. After Throckmorton's arrest, a search of his home revealed treasonous letters to Mary and a list of ports and havens for invading forces. Subjected to torture, Throckmorton revealed the Duke of Guise's complicity and the role that Mendoza had played in orchestrating much of the plot.[20] When Mendoza was told he would be banished from England, he seemed more boastful than concerned about the consequences for the king's intelligence: "Don Bernadino de Mendoza was born not to disturb kingdoms but to conquer them."[21]

The king also seemed to learn little from these developments. To both surrogates and enemies, his delegated decision-making had amounted to political endorsement of the plotting.[22] But, despite the repeated failures, the king named Mendoza his ambassador to Paris, where he went on to organize an extensive European espionage network—a counterintelligence catastrophe for the Spanish given the easy mark Mendoza had become for the English. Indeed, there is strong evidence to suppose that Walsingham and Burghley conspired to penetrate Mendoza's network again—this time in France—by setting up a Catholic nobleman, Sir Edward Stafford, as English ambassador and inducing Mendoza to use him as a double agent.[23]

Walsingham, convinced that the Spanish plotting would continue, tightened security around Mary and increased surveillance of her. Early in 1585, the queen placed Mary under the watchful eye of Sir Amias Paulet, a trusted Protestant, who effectively isolated her. Walsingham then used two double agents to gain her trust and penetrate her communications. The more important of these was Gilbert Gifford who, having connections with Catholic ringleaders in Paris, easily became the secret courier between Catholic exiles, the Spanish ambassador in Paris, the French embassy in London, and Mary. Pretending to devise an ingenious solution for secreting messages to the imprisoned queen using a beer keg, Gifford actually was providing all messages to Walsingham, who deciphered them, copied them, and then let them proceed on their way.[24] Walsingham thus uncovered the treasonous plans of a young and wealthy Englishman named Anthony Babington. He and Mendoza were again advancing the old template: a northern rising of Catholic nobles on behalf of Mary, an invasion force from Spain, and regicide. Their covert action, revived with a few new decision-makers, suffered the old, familiar results: Walsingham arrested Babington, hanged him, and then had him drawn and quartered, along with his English co-conspirators.

The notable point here is that not only was the king weakened by his intelligence, but every Spanish intelligence failure made English counterintelligence more powerful. Although these events cost both sides strategic inspiration and vision, England ended up the net beneficiary. That Elizabeth appreciated the defensive advantages she was reaping is evident from her expenditures: in 1582, England's espionage endeavors had received only £750 from the queen's coffers; by 1586 Walsingham had £2,000 to spend and reportedly had agents "in above forty several places" in Europe.[25]

The wrong lesson should not be learned here: Walsingham's successes obscure the fact that his stings and preoccupations with current events had created intelligence biases that the queen needed to overcome. He did gain repeated intelligence advantages over plotters at the tactical level; yet, by focusing almost exclusively on threats, he continued the narrowing of the queen's options that

Burghley had begun in the name of her personal security. Walsingham, as a Protestant advocate of war against Spain, may have pursued this tack intentionally. His focus on defense minimized the gathering of intelligence on options other than war, including how to find common ground on the Netherlands or how to exploit the divisions among a reluctant king, the unruly Ambassador Mendoza, Parma in the Netherlands, and Spain's French collaborators. His was a defensive mindset that proved excellent for catching criminals and traitors but poor at leveraging intelligence for larger political decision-making. The queen had to look elsewhere for this, and she did.

England's Strategic Intelligence and the Queen's Decision for War

Historians make a mistake when they consider intelligence to be largely secret spying and counterspying. The queen's strategic assessments of Spain's power and interests were not based on her espionage networks and counterintelligence alone. She developed her own sources. For example, in 1580 she chose to embrace Sir Francis Drake as an intelligence asset after he returned from circumnavigating the globe. The queen's decision was not an obvious one. Drake had gone well beyond any authorization given to him by the queen and had "crossed the line" of maritime demarcation set by the pope.[26] Although the hold of Drake's ship was filled with treasure, the queen could have impounded it while still imprisoning Drake in the Tower, thus mollifying Spain.

Francis Drake: Sea Captain, Privateer, and Intelligence Collector

Elizabeth had, in fact, good reason for her decision. Drake had returned with a new kind of treasure: good intelligence on Spain, ideas on how to get more, and knowledge of Philip II's strategic and operational vulnerabilities at sea.[27] He shared some of this intelligence in an hours-long audience with the queen, providing information on Philip's empire, including the resources and attitudes of native populations, navigational techniques, and maps. The maritime intelligence Drake brought back was generally kept secret in a liaison arrangement between Queen Elizabeth I and her privateer. Historians have recognized its importance:

> Drake did, of course, submit a journal and map of his voyage to the queen. . . . These documents must have been crammed with sensitive

information and valuable geographical data. Much of it would have been highly offensive to the king of Spain. It seems likely, then, that a policy of official secrecy prohibited public access to them. The queen may well have forbidden the publication of any accounts of the voyage at all. If so, the ban was relaxed after the Armada.[28]

This context is important for a full understanding of the queen's decision in 1585 to give him a commission of retribution against Spain and, later, to include him as an admiral in her fleet. Drake was a dual-use asset: an intelligence collector able to map Spain's geographical vulnerabilities and assess her naval power as well as a weapon useful for degrading it.

But the queen also realized, more deeply over time, that Drake did as he saw fit. "As Protestant hero and the ultimate authority on naval and maritime matters, he became a force in his own right as well as folk myth."[29] As discussed in the previous chapter, this element of uncertainty amounted to an intelligence problem for the queen, who knew she could not always trust Drake to have her interests foremost. Drake's independence was good if he brought her answers to vital questions, such as whether England could profit from Spain's imperial vulnerabilities, but bad if he threatened Spain at moments of his own choosing rather than hers, or if his weaknesses, interests, and actions made for potential vulnerabilities for England. The queen decided, therefore, to infiltrate Drake's crews, place loyalists on his ships, and after 1580, tether Drake to her cause with the promise of ships and funds. The queen knew that Drake had to be bought and watched. The relationship between ship and throne was less one of trust than of uneasy alliance—an intelligence liaison between competitors rather than a relationship of authority extending only one way.

The paradox was this: the more the queen relied on men such as Drake and John Hawkins for strategic intelligence and planning, which she clearly did, the more these sea captains should have been targeted by Spanish intelligence; yet there is little evidence Spain tried. This inattentiveness is surprising. After all, the queen's privateers were often grounded or uncertain of their pay when they returned home. Even if the king could not have recruited Drake himself, he should have been able to recruit members of his crew. There is little evidence the Spanish did so. They used Hawkins as part of the Ridolfi plot, so it is possible that they tried to recruit others, but failed. Drake was known as a master at recruiting and retaining crews; widely credited with extraordinary interpersonal skills, he demanded and received loyalty from pilots and seamen of all nationalities. In return, he sailed his ships with them, fought with them, and gave them stolen treasure. Infiltrating such tightly run ships for intelligence or sabotage would have been difficult indeed.

In any event, Philip II certainly judged Drake a threat. In August 1579, as Drake finished circling the world in his *Golden Hind*, the king started what would become a thick file on the English sea captain. Spanish estimates of Drake's plunder were as high as £600,000, much of which he had gotten at Philip's expense.[30] The king's ambassador in England reported a close and productive relationship between Drake and the queen that, the ambassador believed, portended a rapid increase in English maritime power. After describing the jewel-encrusted crown, diamond cross, and gold bars Drake had bestowed on her and members of her court, he wrote:

> The Queen shows extraordinary favour to Drake and never fails to speak to him when she goes out in public, conversing with him for a long time. She says that she will knight him on the day she goes to see his ship. She has ordered the ship itself to be brought ashore and placed in her arsenal near Greenwich as a curiosity.[31]

What the ambassador missed, however, was that the queen suspected that she could not own the captain, though she would try, and that promises of faith, loyalty, and treasure would not be enough for either party. As interested in retribution for San Juan de Ulúa as Hawkins ever was, Drake launched provocations against Spain at times when the queen wanted peace—a tendency that sometimes surprised and often angered her, limiting his usefulness as a strategic asset. That the king nonetheless saw the queen's relationship with Drake as a combined military threat is certain. He *assumed* Drake's predations were at the queen's behest and that she was forcing Spain to defend its treasure *flotas* and ports around the empire at great expense. That the king never was able to gather enough good intelligence on Drake to understand the sea captain's own vulnerabilities meant that he did not understand Drake's liabilities for the queen. As tensions between Spain and England grew, Philip wrote to his ambassador in London, Mendoza, pleading for intelligence on Drake's situation: "Tell me what has become of Drake and what you hear of the arming of ships. . . . It is most important that I should know all this."[32]

If Philip's diplomats and spies had had more aptitude than they did, they would have learned the reasons why, from 1580 to 1585, the queen was forcing Drake and his cohorts and crews to lie low. One reason was that she did not trust him to respect the diplomatic tightrope she was walking. She was also revamping her navy and needed new ships and new doctrine before provoking Spain at sea. Elizabeth had showered Drake with gifts and lands to compensate for his frustrated ambitions as a pirate and privateer, leaving him to absorb his new wealth and title as a knight and member of Parliament. Fine as this was for Drake, it could not help him sustain his crews, who relied on maritime predation for their

income. Philip II evidently missed a rich opportunity to recruit the most desperate among them.

Although Drake did not deliver grand strategic advantage as these monarchs
lurched toward war over the Netherlands, he and his piratical colleagues did provide the queen naval intelligence that emboldened her to rebuild her ships and
even risk war with Spain, as will be discussed in the next section.[33] In any event,
between the Dutch revolt against Spanish rule in 1572 and 1581, English policy
veered between presenting Spain with a threat or a crutch: Drake unleashed or
common cause against the French and even the Dutch, with conditions attached.
The Spanish did not understand the offers or the threats, partly because Elizabeth
had no ambassador in Madrid, so there was no trusted representative explaining
them to the king.[34] Thus, Philip's lack of sound representation and strategic intelligence in London was complemented by Elizabeth's lack of access to the Spanish
court. Diplomatic intelligence failed both ways. The result was poor strategic assessment and thus poor English diplomacy during more than a decade of proxy
combat and rising uncertainty in Northern Europe.[35]

The Treaties of Joinville and Nonsuch: Decision Advantage Spain?

Then, matters got even more complicated. In 1584, the Duke of Alençon (now
Anjou) died and William of Orange, the cornerstone of the Dutch revolt, was
assassinated, making a Spanish victory seem near but leaving a Protestant,
Henry Navarre, in line for the French throne. On December 31, Philip signed
the Treaty of Joinville, which allied him with Catholic Henry de Guise in his fight
against Navarre.[36] He also allied with a French Catholic paramilitary organization and married off a daughter to another royal claimant to the throne of France.
The sitting French king, Henry III, reacted by reducing support to rebellious
Protestants in the Spanish Netherlands. Surprisingly, Elizabeth decided shortly
thereafter (August 20, 1585) to sign the Treaty of Nonsuch, which provided significant monetary and military support to the collapsing Protestant cause.

Elizabeth's decision seemed a bad one, given England's relative weakness and
the Spanish king's consolidating power in Northern Europe. Key members of her
Privy Council had long argued that strengthening the Protestant Low Countries
was a form of insurance against Catholic predation whichever threat—French
or Spanish—might crystallize first. But now the Protestants were clearly losing
and Spain would see her move to back the Dutch in the worst possible light. Her
decision, in the context of a number of other aggressive measures, went beyond
the pursuit of leverage to a course of brinkmanship and probable war with Spain.

So why did she decide as she did? The queen leaned toward war because the Throckmorton plot and a growing body of intelligence, most of it wrong, suggested that the Spanish king had decided for war himself. The queen saw Philip's tightening grip on the Netherlands in the context of regicidal plots against her and a religious absolutism with which there could be no compromise. When, earlier in 1585, Philip had sought to tamp down the Dutch uprising by secretly deciding to terminate all Dutch trade with the Iberian Peninsula, including English ships, Elizabeth was ready to interpret the move as blatant aggression. She scoffed at his excuse that his need to refit his navy required that "all" foreign ships be included in the embargo. An escaped English captain brought to the queen the official Spanish document that suggested only Protestant countries were targeted. Elizabeth interpreted this intelligence as a clear indicator that the king wanted not only to starve Dutch traders, but to debilitate England. She might have been willing up to that point to sell the Dutch out for a bigger deal, had Philip proposed one. Now she believed the Dutch cause had to be hers as well, so she agreed to send scarce military resources to the Dutch and released Drake from his confinement on land to conduct more predations at sea.

The queen's decisions did not preclude feints toward compromise, just in case things went awry. Not long after news of Orange's death reached her in 1584, she had sent a long list of questions to her Privy Council asking, in effect, should Holland and Zealand fall to Spain, whether the king of Spain would attack her or economically strangle her realm.[37] The queen knew what everyone knew about the Netherlands: it was a quagmire for Spain and, thus, a drain on energy, morale, finances, and forces. There was a chance that, despite Philip's hostility toward her rule, he might want a way out, and that exploring one could at least buy her time.

One of the queen's channels to the king, kept alive since 1583 in a perfunctory sense by Walsingham, involved contact with the former Portuguese ambassador to England, António de Castillo, who had been recalled by Philip in 1582, two years after Spain's absorption of Portugal.[38] Walsingham had explored grounds for compromise before Castillo's departure and did so again in 1585 and 1587.[39] During this time, at least one of Philip's letters to Parma had suggested he had an open mind regarding strategic reconciliation. Neither the king nor the queen knew enough, however, to broker a deal, though they seemed to try. Sir John Crofts and Lord Burghley persisted in their efforts to sell out both French and Protestant aims in the Netherlands for a Spanish supervised calm guaranteed by the queen.[40] Although it is likely that by the end of 1585 Elizabeth had decided against any deal, the negotiations nevertheless continued as late as 1588, buying her time to prepare for war. If engaged in a deliberate misdirection, she was negotiating at the expense of Dutch trust—a poorly appreciated cost.[41]

Decisions for War

The queen's interpretation of Philip's embargo of trade in 1584 may seem now to have been a misreading of facts—a decision of strategic importance informed by tactical intelligence of uncertain importance. That view misses, however, her growing appreciation of the religious or absolutist dimension that was very much part of the Spanish worldview and that the document ordering the embargo seemed to confirm. Spain's actions were meant only to starve the Dutch into submission; the king released English ships on August 17, three days before the queen signed the Treaty of Nonsuch. Although the king was by this time obsessed by the idea of invasion, and the English court had made up its mind that Spain's intentions were implacably hostile, caution had so far prevailed. Evidence of the selective embargo, however, at last unified Elizabeth's ministers, energized English defenses, and prompted the alliance with the rebellious Protestants across the Channel. The queen released Drake and Philip began serious preparations for the Armada.

This dynamic—tactics undermining strategic interests, reinforcing the need for tactical maneuvers to gain advantage—was driven on both sides by perceived threat and the speed of current intelligence relative to strategic learning and influence. Religion did not cause such blinders. After all, the Catholic Duke of Parma counseled his king to consider options. It was the lack of intelligence for grand strategy on both sides that distorted perceptions of relative power and destroyed opportunities for peace.

So it was that, despite the king's release of English ships, the queen unleashed Drake in 1585 to conduct operations she knew favored surprise attack against Spanish ports and ships. The queen's decision was based on her assessment of Spanish intent and naval preparedness, despite almost certain recognition of her incapacity to control the consequences of Drake's actions. His fleet of twenty-five ships, eight pinnaces, and nineteen hundred men sailed to Galicia on September 24, where they raided, killed, took hostages, desecrated churches, and stole loot.[42] It is unclear to this day whether the Galicia adventure was part of the queen's plan or the peculiar design of Drake, who wanted to intimidate the Spanish king and provoke open war. Without doubt, however, the queen knew Drake had the capacity and will to take such actions and that he would, indeed, "singe the beard" of the Spanish king. His attacks infuriated the king, who received full assessments of the damage, which was both severe and embarrassing.

Thus, Philip II's tactical decision to overpower the Dutch rebels had become the trigger for better-informed, but still tactical moves on the English side.[43] Absent good strategic diplomacy, the queen was gaining advantage by reinforcing her opponent's belief that to beat England and restore Spanish prerogatives, he would have to beat Drake. This was not grand strategy but strategy of a more operational kind—perhaps enough to beat a relatively uninformed invader. If the queen could keep Drake close to her shores and under some kind of discipline, the Spanish navy would have to sail north and fight him in the English Channel. And here alone was the place where Elizabeth had some hope of winning. Although her own ministers found her approach indecisive, confusing, and even maddening, the queen was by the mid-1580s manipulating Spanish perceptions to her own advantage while buying time for building resources and a fleet to defend her realm.

Not surprisingly, the king finally decided for war against England in 1585 after receiving the news of Sir Francis Drake's landing in Galicia.[44] Once again, his strategy would be invasion; he would not take Drake's bait by trying to defeat him first. He agreed with Archbishop Rodrigo de Castro of Seville about the futility of a manhunt at sea: "What was the point . . . of chasing Drake, a fine sailor with a powerful fleet?"[45] Philip demanded, belatedly, a strategic analysis from his chief foreign policy advisor, Don Juan de Zúñiga y Requeséns, who concluded that invading England was the king's best and, indeed, only choice. The king accepted Zúñiga's framework and prepared to attack England. He reasoned that he could certainly do what he knew others had done in the past—invade from the sea. In the process, he would defeat Drake and put a stop to the endless and embarrassing drain on Spanish resources. As it turned out, his instincts played right into Elizabeth's hands.[46] The king had a mindset that precluded the gathering of intelligence on how the queen might defeat him.

Although neither side engineered an overall strategic advantage during the 1580s, it seems fair to conclude that the queen benefited from Spanish mistakes more than Spain benefited from England's. The queen's counterintelligence improved as Philip's foreign intelligence suffered with every failed plot against her, and Spain's failure to see strategic opportunities allowed Drake and the queen to sustain a tense embrace. Thus, Drake's exploits in 1579–80 and from 1585 to 1587 increased Elizabeth's power to threaten and deter, while her liaison with her "sea dogs" brought her intelligence. The queen did not make the king's mistake of confusing strategic intelligence with operations. She took Drake's *intelligence* but did not adopt his *strategy* because she understood his interests were not necessarily her own. Extraterritorial defense through offense was Drake's guiding precept—he often spoke of England's borders as coincident with adversaries' coastlines—but this reflected *his* preference for surprise attack, and the queen knew it. She understood that defense of her throne required secure communications in the Channel and a firm royal hand on Drake. In contrast, Philip II's overall advantages at sea and messianic drive made an amphibious assault on England seem less risky and intelligence seem less important than they truly were. Overseer of an empire and winner of multiple naval engagements, most notably against the Turks in the Battle of Lepanto, the Spanish king had a wealth of global knowledge. He lacked, however, the strategic grasp necessary to craft a winning plan for dealing with England and her pirates.

In a sense, both monarchs fell into war more than they decided for it. Poor strategic intelligence on both sides was in large part to blame. They had taken actions that deprived them of diplomatic intelligence, made their standoff worse, and increased the risks of war. Unfortunately for King Philip, his situation would prove far worse than the queen's. He received biased points of view from his commanders and showed hesitancy and confusion in his choices even though he had the luxury of the offensive.[47]

The absence of good strategic intelligence is often reflected in incoherent military strategy, and this was true in the Spanish case. There was discussion of "a landing in Scotland, of a blitzkrieg seaborne attack on the Isle of Wight, of a sudden solo assault by Parma's army on the coast of Kent, as well as . . . of amphibious assaults from Lisbon on Algiers and Larache."[48] The difference from Queen Elizabeth's situation was that Philip II had more options, fewer natural advantages in northern seas such as the Channel, and less and less intelligence of any kind to guide him. Philip received analytical estimates about the likely success of an invasion, but these all either lacked an assessment of English intentions and capabilities or got them wrong. When, late in 1585, Philip began to gather intelligence in a systematic fashion, his informants on England were "optimistic as to Catholic support for an invasion." He learned from agents' reports that "only twelve English counties were Protestant; that the old nobility and gentry would rally to the cause . . . and that the supporters of Mary, Queen of Scots would be friendly to Spain or neutral." Almost none of this intelligence was accurate.[49]

Intelligence for Weapons and Employment Doctrines

Although English and Spanish decision-makers misjudged their strategic options largely because of faulty intelligence, their operational and tactical choices were better informed. Yet even here the English gained an intelligence advantage, in part because the king chose to fight in Anglo-Dutch waters rather than luring the English fleet into his own. Spain went on the attack without knowing important facts about the Channel and the queen's ships, weapons, doctrine, and defenses designed for operations there. These gaps in naval intelligence were particularly striking, because England was spearheading a revolution in naval warfare that was an open secret.

The English Decision to Develop the Race-Built Galleon

The problem of English defense from foreign invasion had always been, apart from the Scottish back door, essentially a naval problem. Elizabeth's father,

Henry VIII, understood this and created an impressive naval force almost from scratch.[50] This fleet required maintenance and improvement to retain its effectiveness. Ironically, Spain's Philip II, briefly husband of Henry VIII's daughter, Mary Tudor, did so by patterning changes to the English fleet on the design of Spanish galleons.

Philip II deemed this change a major upgrade. Shipwrights in the early sixteenth century were secretive about their craft and those working at docks in Northern Europe had little access to Spanish designs before the ascension of Mary Tudor.[51] Most English ships up to this time had been built on the broader lines of the traditional carrack.[52] As Spanish ships began sailing into English ports during the reign of Queen Mary and King Philip II, English shipwrights naturally studied and adopted many of their most admirable characteristics.[53] By the time Elizabeth came to power, Philip was back in Spain and England had a fleet of ships that, though in need of general refurbishing, fit the template of the Spanish galleon.

Yet, beginning in 1577, the queen authorized a radical reconstruction of her fleet along "race-built" lines—a change that, had it not been taken, would likely have led to defeat in 1588.[54] Instead, by the time the Armada sailed, she had warships with advanced capabilities that optimized both artillery and maneuverability.[55] As one Spaniard observed aboard the Armada's fastest ship, the *San Juan Bautista*, the English could out-sail her "as if we were standing still."[56] And when it came to gunnery, the English had a decisive but hardly secret weapon in 1588: improved four-wheeled gun carriages that rendered England's larger artillery pieces at least one hundred times more efficient than were the Armada's largest guns.[57] Joined with more maneuverable ships, these "trucks" allowed the English to fire and reload more quickly than opponents could, battering them in time with the swells as they heeled over and providing an operational flexibility that the Spanish should have anticipated, but could not emulate once the Armada sailed.[58] English gunnery had been superior since the reign of King Henry VIII; however, it was the decision to combine the guns, Hawkins's race-built ships, and a new naval doctrine that gave England her edge in 1588.

What did the notoriously tightfisted Elizabeth and the members of her Naval Board know that led them to authorize such an expensive and apparently risky overhaul of England's ships and naval doctrine, and how did they come to know it? Philip II must have realized that his galleons were sailing against warships with these advantages; if so, how did he plan to deal with them?

The Role of John Hawkins: Collector, Analyst, Paramilitary Operative

The intelligence for the revolution in English ship design rested on a good source, the now familiar seaman and double agent John Hawkins, and on a revolutionary method for processing, exploiting, and propagating his insights provided by master shipwrights Matthew Baker, and Peter Pett.

First, the source: recall that John Hawkins, who had insinuated himself into the Ridolfi plot discussed earlier, had seen and fought Spanish galleons. He also had a theory of how to beat them.[59] To influence the queen, however, he needed her trust and to establish his bona fides by delivering useful intelligence. Hawkins's motives, like Drake's, went back to that Spanish deceit in the Mexican port of San Juan de Ulúa.[60] Both Hawkins and Drake had barely escaped the battle with their lives and, limping home, swore revenge.[61] The incident also gave both men firsthand experience engaging Spanish warships at close range. For example, the venerable English carrack *Jesus of Lubeck*, had been purchased in Hamburg during the reign of Henry VIII and rebuilt for cargo by Hawkins. When the Spanish attacked, her poor maneuverability prevented escape. The Spanish ships closed in to board and engage in hand-to-hand combat. Hawkins's crews, pulling away, dropped launches alongside to keep their distance from the Spanish. As the battle unfolded, the English used their better guns to full effect, sinking and torching the Spaniards' two warships.

Hawkins retained several lessons from this encounter. First was the importance of maneuverability under sail. Second was the Spanish preference for boarding over bombardment. Third was the potential decisiveness of guns. What the three lessons together signified was the advantage to be gained by innovating in ship design *and* naval doctrine; success would require moving from grappling and boarding to maneuverability and long-distance gunnery. We know that Hawkins had learned these lessons because, by 1570, he had begun to work with the private shipwright Richard Chapman, to rebuild ships designed to fight the Spanish. They worked at the Navy Royal at Deptford shipyard.[62] His father-in-law, Benjamin Godson, was then treasurer of the navy. Through this special connection, Hawkins had access to decision-making on the Naval Board.[63]

It was only two years after the battle of San Juan de Ulúa and one year after his return home that Hawkins, in partnership with Chapman, designed a new type of warship: the race-built galleon. This sleeker, lighter ship employed "a length to beam ratio of 3:1, . . . a deeper hull and draught than before, and a stepped but continuous deck for emplacement of . . . powerful guns."[64] The superstructure was kept low, which also lowered the ship's center of gravity and, added to other refinements, improved its handling and stability in rough seas or when firing guns. Chapman and Hawkins collaborated in building the first of this new type of warship, the three-hundred-ton *Foresight*.[65] Its success led to the refitting of the galleasses *Bull* and *Tiger* along race-built lines that same year. The galleons *Dreadnought* and *Swiftsure* (Figure 3.1), commissioned in 1573, were built with the aid of shipwrights Matthew Baker and Peter Pett respectively.[66] The performance of these ships was the nearest thing to perfection that the Tudor world could produce. Compared to other warships, Hawkins' race-built galleons could sail faster and closer to the wind . . . and they had less leeway—the sideways drift experienced by sailing ships when the wind was on the beam. In short, they . . . could out-sail the majority of other warships—particularly the carracks that made up the bulk of the Spanish fleet in 1588.[67]

Although Hawkins had designed and built a new platform, his motives were still largely business, private gain, and revenge. The information he used was his own expertise honed and applied to gain personal advantage. What turned Hawkins's private pursuits into intelligence for the Crown was the Naval Board's purposeful capture of his knowledge for the benefit of the queen. Members of the Privy Council were paying attention to new ideas about ship design and open to having private interests partner with the Crown. Innovative designs in hand, Hawkins won contracts to rebuild the queen's fleet. Chapman, the queen's royal shipwright, became his partner. Hawkins was treasurer of the navy by 1577 and, in 1578, his new ships, employing new tactics, won against the Spanish in the battle of Smerwick off the Irish coast—an engagement discussed more fully below.[68]

Galleon of the Royal Navy of Her Majesty Queen Elizabeth I of England

SWIFTSURE

Race-built Galleon, 1573

Tons burthen: 350 tons
Length: 74 ft (keel)
Beam: 30 ft
Depth of hold: 15 ft

Figure 3.1 English ship *Swiftsure* race-built galleon
Source: Original image courtesy of Alex Brown.

And now for the matter of analytical method: how did the famously tightfisted queen come to spend such astonishing resources on an overhaul of her navy? Convincing the Crown required convincing decision-makers of the advantages of the race-built design. Shipwright Matthew Baker provided the "means by which the Hawkins' race-built galleon design was explained for all to see."[69] This crucial point has been lost in controversies over who might claim the most credit for innovations in the Elizabethan fleet. Matthew Baker was the "innovative ship designer" who wrote an influential treatise on shipbuilding, *Fragments of Ancient Shipwrightry*, in 1582.[70] Military historian Angus Konstam has persuasively argued that Baker, along with his colleague Peter Pett were disciples of Hawkins's approach to ship design. According to Konstam, Baker's *Fragments* should best be seen as a vehicle for promoting that design:

> In his *Fragments of Ancient English Shipwrightry* (1582), Matthew Baker published a treatise that laid out the geometric proportions he used in ship construction. This formula revealed just how scientific the art of shipbuilding had become. While many shipbuilders continued to work on their own secret formulas of proportion and hull shape, or followed their own rule-of-thumb ideas about stability, the leading shipwrights were trying to codify the general ideas proposed by Hawkins. . . . It was up to the shipbuilders—men such as Richard Chapman, Matthew Baker, and Peter Pett—to interpret Hawkins's wishes and to build the ships. Baker's *Fragments* therefore represents an attempt to explain the Hawkins design so there was no room for mistakes—a move from art toward science.[71]

Here was a true innovation in naval intelligence. Even before his volume was published, Baker had a new way of designing ships on paper using advanced mathematics and geometry. His analytical approach was both scientific and portable, making negotiations over refinements in design intelligible for seamen, the Navy Board, and even the Privy Council. Thus, Hawkins's maritime knowledge was convincingly illustrated for the Navy Board and, presumably, the queen.

That Hawkins had unique information that was purposefully sought by national security decision-makers and presented in easily digestible form before the Armada sailed made him the source of intelligence advantage; for decision advantage, his information had to offer the queen not just cheaper or more elegant ships, but an edge against the Spanish at a competitively important moment. That this was so is suggested by Hawkins's official advancement as conflict with Spain became more intense. He was named treasurer of the navy in 1577 and was funded for the building of three new race-built galleons, the *Revenge*, the *Rainbow*, and the *Vanguard*, while conflict with Spain was still coming to a boil. All three of these new ships were finished in time to take part in the fight against the Armada in 1588. In fact, they were the standard-bearers for the queen's new navy. An annotated inventory of the fleet taken by William Borough, comptroller of the navy, described the best English warships as those meeting Hawkins's specifications exactly, emphasizing maneuverability and firepower rather than boarding to win battles. Indeed, by the time the Armada sailed, the last of the pre-Hawkins navy-built galleons, the *White Bear*, was considered slow relative to the newer ships.

That the Privy Council understood Hawkins's value to the queen is clear: when Hawkins's tenure on the Navy Board became contentious—as it was bound to be when he undermined the nobility's opportunities for graft and shipwrights' pride in their more conventional designs—important members of the Privy Council backed him, particularly the queen's espionage chief, Sir Francis Walsingham. Other backers included Burghley, with whom Hawkins corresponded directly, and Sir William Wynter, who had used the redesigned ships against the Spanish.

Protecting Knowledge of English Race-Built Galleons

Hawkins provided intelligence to the queen's navy, but he also seemed strangely careless with it, as he is known to have shared his inside information with a Spanish agent.[72] Perhaps Hawkins did so because much information was already available about England's new navy or he sought to "dangle" his services as a (double) agent for the Spanish. In any event, prior to the battle with the Armada, both sides knew what the redesigned English ships could do because they had witnessed their capabilities in action. Recall that in 1578, Pope Gregory XIII, who had dedicated himself to toppling the heretical queen, selected Smerwick, Ireland, for landing an invasion force that would serve, with Spain's backing, as a bridgehead for an attack on England. As in the cases of Spain's land-based plots, the Navy Royal was tipped off beforehand. England had a spy, Thomas Cely, in a position to warn of the Spanish preparations. Elizabeth sent a small squadron of her ships to confront the Spanish reinforcements, which included eight hundred to one thousand Italian and Spanish troops sailing under the flag of the experienced commander Juan Martínez de Recalde. Several of Hawkins's newly redesigned ships, including the *Swiftsure* and *Revenge*, demonstrated in the ensuing battle some of the qualities he had advertised. The English admiral employed operations and tactics that took advantage of the English ships' firepower and relative maneuverability.[73] He returned home victorious and became an even stronger supporter of England's new navy.[74]

By 1588—ten years after the battle with Recalde—the English needed to know if they had lost their advantage. The battle off Smerwick and widespread knowledge of the changing character of English ships made it possible the

Spanish had learned enough in time to change their ships and doctrine. Would Spanish admirals act on the probability that they would be outgunned and outmaneuvered once the Armada reached the Channel? Hawkins seems to have believed his innovations were widely known: "The common report that strangers make of our ships amongst themselves is daily confirmed to be true, which is that for strength, assurance, nimbleness and swiftness of sailing, there are no vessels in the world to be compared with ours."[75]

The question for the English was whether or not the Spanish were taking any countermeasures and, if so, what those might be. Although the English navy did not learn it beforehand, the answer was that the Spanish knew they needed to strengthen the sides of their ships to withstand increased firepower from English guns, so they did. Philip II feared that the English would "fire low" and "so inflict damage on the narrow vulnerable belt between the wind and the water."[76] The English navy, we will discover, only learned the extent of this Spanish retrofitting during the battle itself.

Yet the Spanish, showing little interest in changing their ships and doctrine in any fundamental way, remained unprepared for the kind of tactics the English fleet intended to use in 1588, and were unable to adapt on the fly.[77] Although they knew that the English would employ their guns more relentlessly than ever, they failed to grasp that the English innovation was not just in weaponry, ships, and doctrine, but in tactical intelligence in support of operations at sea. England's possession of maneuverable ships and larger guns gave English admirals the ability to learn and expand on new tactics, such as those they probably knew had been used by the Swedes, the Danes, and Danish allies in their war (1563–70) for control of Baltic trade, conducted largely at sea. In 1564, the numerically inferior Swedes beat the allied forces, primarily through maneuver and standoff gunnery rather than grappling and boarding.[78] During these battles, a significant number of ships were also lost to fire, unexpected explosions, and weather: in one instance, fourteen anchored Danish and Lubeckian ships were smashed against rocks when a strong wind transformed into a storm, killing fifteen hundred men. Maneuverability then and in 1588 meant opportunity to learn and to exploit opportunities in the midst of competition—in other words, to gain decision advantage at sea.

The Spanish Decision to Maintain Traditional Ships and Doctrine

Given such knowable history and evolution in ship design, what accounts for Spain's poor appreciation of English operational strategy in 1588? Why did Madrid lag in operational and tactical use of naval intelligence? One answer may be that Spanish captains, knowing that the English would employ their guns more relentlessly than ever, did not have a means to make this information relevant to decisions made at higher levels. The intelligence problem for Spain was less access to English naval innovations, which were hardly secret, than a mindset that divided the knowledge gained by ship crews during operations from those responsible for decisions regarding shipbuilding and naval strategy—namely, the king, his shipwrights, and his high-born admirals. Unlike the English Navy Board, the Spanish navy was set in its ways and had poor means for binding technological intelligence to weapons development, strategy, and operations. Institutionalized privilege was a common source of intelligence failure in an age of nobility and monarchy.

This Spanish deficiency was, however, more one of process than capability. The English did not know, therefore, the extent of their advantages at the time the Armada sailed. Archaeologists and historians have since examined the Armada's wrecks and records, reporting what was hardly evident at the time: "In gun mounting, the Spanish were a half century behind the English."[79] Spain's response to the English guns was *only* to reinforce the sides of their galleons; they did not re-examine larger matters of ship design and doctrine. Drake, Hawkins, and the rest of the queen's navy had to learn all this during the battle. They knew much of the Spanish fleet had been retrofitted from 1586 to 1588; they did not know the extent of the improvements, including whether guns and reinforced beams had been given high priority. The Spanish probably felt no need for more than the latter, given their operational plan. Spanish doctrine continued along the traditional lines of sailing in a crescent formation, guns defending fore and aft and broadsides used only close-in, as a precursor to grappling and boarding. As soon as the Armada sailed, that fact was obvious. One can only surmise that the Spanish considered the English advantage in maneuverability inconsequential.

Still, deficiencies of process and privilege cannot explain all. There is evidence that the king was worried about a naval confrontation with England, so why the Spanish navy did not do more still remains a mystery. Clearly, some of the king's naval officers were concerned about the development of English guns and what it meant for tactics because they advocated the thickening of hulls. Yet, beyond minor improvement in defenses, the Spanish navy drew few implications for their own ships, doctrine, and maritime operations. It should have been possible for Spanish admirals to imagine how the combination of English guns and maneuverable ships could make Spain's naval operations highly risky if not foolhardy. Philip II felt compelled to write to his commander the year the Armada sailed, reminding him that the English were likely to try to outgun him.

Philip's comment suggests, in fact, a further explanation for Spain's lag: not just mindset but *active preference* for traditional ways. Despite intelligence on English plans, there is evidence that Spanish nobility—and even admirals—stuck with past methods and weapons as a positive choice over the newer forms of warfare. They continued to believe they had an advantage in the kind of amphibious warfare they planned, which turned on the number of troops a ship could carry and their ability to get to shore. After all, their plan was to invade, not to defeat England in a battle at sea. Their objectives would be exclusively two: getting troops to shore and, if necessary, using those troops to overwhelm any ship that got too close. Spanish doctrine involved assigning its troops, experienced more on land than sea, to the initial loading of the guns, then having them rejoin their company for the ensuing hand-to-hand combat.[80] If challenged, they knew they could rely on their superior skills at grappling and boarding.

Thus, the ignorance that seems so surprising in retrospect hardly seemed ignorance at the time. Most salient for a Spanish admiral in 1588 was not the experiences of Danes and Swedes in Baltic battles decades earlier, but rather the victory in 1582 of their own celebrated admiral the Marquis of Santa Cruz against Portuguese resistance in the Battle of Villa Franca off the Azores. In 1580, Santa Cruz had conducted a successful amphibious assault on Lisbon, probably the best-defended port in Europe, causing the Portuguese claimant to the throne, Dom António, Prior of Crato, to seek refuge in England. When Spain threatened war if Elizabeth aided Dom António, the queen quit plans to help him. Dom António then left England for France and, eventually, Terceira in the Azores, where he held out against Spanish attempts to eliminate him. Santa Cruz finally fought Dom António's fleet in 1582, which included forty French ships and a host of English privateers. The French, led by Filippo di Piero Strozzi, a renowned French admiral, bombarded the Spanish with heavy gunfire and standoff tactics. In their eagerness to tighten the noose, however, Strozzi's warships finally closed in on the Spanish, who promptly boarded and overwhelmed them. The English privateers, seeing the shift of events, turned sail and sped back to the Channel.

To King Philip II, this Spanish success probably seemed both decisive and definitive. Santa Cruz, who had captured the French flagship and killed Strozzi, trumpeted his victory. Spanish morale and confidence, which had been undermined by the global exploits of Sir Francis Drake, skyrocketed. As one historian of the Armada has written: "Seeing his vaunted enemies cutting and running, Santa Cruz was moved to assure Philip that he would take on the whole might of the English navy at the King's command, and the flight of the English ships also had a strong influence on Philip's advisors."[81]

The Battle of Villa Franca suggested that to be victorious, the captains of well-gunned English ships would still need to grapple and board—that is, close in on the enemy. But this, of course, was wrong. The English could win if they just outgunned them, kept the Armada and Parma from joining up or the two from landing anywhere along the treacherous English coastline. Spanish intelligence failed to imagine such an outcome, so failed to imagine the Spanish admirals' disadvantages. The king believed that even if the English attacked, Santa Cruz could refuse to engage and sail on with reinforced hulls. And if Santa Cruz did decide to engage, the outcome would be the same as the one Strozzi received off the island of Terceira. Once faced with a tough fight, the English would flee.

With these thoughts in mind and trusting Santa Cruz, Philip gave him the latitude to choose operations and tactics. Before Santa Cruz suddenly died in early 1588, Philip wrote:

> Since the outcome of wars, and especially of wars at sea, are so subject to fluctuations in the weather and to the uncertainty of the information available to those who command armies and navies, I have absolutely nothing certain to tell you or precise orders to give concerning what should be done with the fleet. Since you are so competent and expert in both, it seemed best to delegate all this to you so that, according to the opportunities that occur, both for the navy to fight and for the pursuit of the pirates (i.e. the English), and in all the other things that may occur during your voyage, you will do whatever seems to you most appropriate.[82]

The king wrote no such thing to Santa Cruz's replacement, Don Alonso Pérez de Guzmán, Seventh Duke of Medina Sidonia. The inexperienced Medina Sidonia, who pleaded against the assignment, did not want all the responsibilities that his predecessor had been given, writing to the king, "I do not understand (naval combat), know nothing about it, have no health for the sea, and have no money to spend on it."[83] The king nonetheless insisted that he take on the task. The king's advisors, moreover, refused to countenance any hesitation: "Do not depress us with fears for the fate of the Armada, because . . . God will make sure it succeeds."[84] This mindset among Spanish admirals and their king meant the Armada sailed into the Channel with no plan B and no amiral empowered to make one up if necessary. The king thought he, or God, knew enough to win without one.

Informing Current Naval Strategy, Operations, and Tactics

Of course, Philip had long realized he needed a plan A. In addition to asking Santa Cruz, he had sought input from his advisor Don Juan de Zúñiga y Requeséns and the Duke of Parma, both of whom would advocate a cross-Channel invasion.[85] From his study of history, Philip knew that, since the Norman Conquest of 1066, seven amphibious landings on English shores had been successful. Successful strategies had been of three types: cross-Channel assaults with naval defense; surprise amphibious landings; and naval diversions to allow concentration of land forces and then cross-Channel attack.[86] Philip decided to draw from these past examples to prepare for war. This strategic analysis was smart and intelligence-driven—at least up to a point. What happened when the king drew operational conclusions suggests intelligence may achieve worse than nothing with one good analysis left dangling. As the historian Parker has put it: "That all three possible strategies received consideration in 1586–8 reflects credit on the vision and competence of Philip and his 'national security advisers'; that the king eventually tried to undertake all three at once does not."[87]

Before detailing how intelligence contributed to Spain's plan, it is worth emphasizing one point here: As Spain's offensive buildup gained momentum over several years, the king clung to a critical assumption: that England could be surprised. Surprise would be critical for any plan of invasion for three reasons: first, it would allow Parma to load his troops onto vulnerable barges and float them out to Spanish ships before the Dutch or English could prevent it; second, it would increase the chances that Drake might be elsewhere or otherwise unawares; third, it would allow Spain to land where English defenses would be minimal and unprepared.

Retaining a capacity for surprise in these particular regards, however, was in some respects unrealistic and in others ill-informed. In the first place, Parma had made clear that his ability to join up with the Armada depended on keeping the English fleet away—perhaps with a diversion of some kind. Yet the plan had the Armada assembling for all to see, and then sailing directly to Parma, which would bring the English there too. Second, although Elizabeth had trouble controlling pirates once they had sailed, she had repeatedly demonstrated her ability, when threatened, *to prevent* Drake and others from sailing. Current intelligence could have revealed that Elizabeth's privateers were ready to defend the Channel and have effective control over royal fleet operations there. Third, the English strategy, knowable in advance, was to keep the Spanish from landing anywhere along the coast, because once Spanish troops did, the English almost certainly would lose. Secret landing plans therefore gained the Spanish fleet almost no advantage of surprise, especially if it had to connect with Parma first.

Given the importance of surprise to Spain's plan, Philip's neglect of it has seemed inexplicable to most historians. The historians' error lies in confusing reporting about the Armada's launch and even its route, which had become common knowledge, with intelligence advantage, which can result from delivering an expected blow at an unexpected time. Philip may have believed success only required secrecy about the rendezvous with Parma and its timing, thus surprising the Dutch sea dogs monitoring the coast and perhaps leading them to believe Parma's forces would not be involved. Parma had reported that he thought he could manage to evade the Dutch if he knew just the moment when the Armada would arrive and delay boarding barges until then. Parma's larger point about surprise—that the whole operation would fail if the Armada could not keep the English relatively ignorant about that arrival and so away from the rendezvous—was lost in the exchange. So too was the point that Medina Sidonia would need to know in a timely way when Parma was ready for his arrival, lest both he and Parma be more surprised by each other than the English would be. As the preeminent biographer of Philip II, Geoffrey Parker, has remarked: "Medina's expectation that his messengers to Flanders would arrive—let alone return with an answer—in less than a week was patently absurd."

Similarly, the king received many *reports* of Drake's mastery of men and the seas, but ended up surprised by him even into the final days of the Armada's battle. This outcome was predictable. Few of the king's reports on Drake analyzed his employment by the queen, his vulnerabilities, including how he coordinated with his fleet (or not), chose victims (so could thus be baited), or antagonized others (so could be neutralized) in the coming naval war. The king probably received no advantageous intelligence on Drake because he had decided against fighting him. Drake's marauding had created superstitions, inflated his image, and expedited news of his exploits. Philip had decided that the only solution to Drake was to decapitate his sponsor. Drake's operation and the terms of his relationship to the queen certainly constituted a menace, but it was one that few Spanish agents understood and none could demystify for the king.[88] As Philip saw himself the sword of God, so he saw in Drake the Antichrist, whom God would have to handle.[89]

Spain's Operational Plan and Strategy

All this miscalculation raises the question of how such a cumbersome operational plan had evolved and on the basis of what intelligence. As mentioned previously, Philip had turned to several of his closest advisors for potential operational strategies for attacking England. Santa Cruz and Parma recommended different approaches that reflected each advisor's particular perspective.[90] In March 1586, the Marquis of Santa Cruz had drafted his naval plan, which entailed sending a large invasion fleet directly from the Iberian Peninsula to enemy shores. This plan was heavily influenced by his defeat of Dom António's troops and fleet in the Azores. Santa Cruz felt confident that he could lead Spain to victory again with an audacious naval attack and surprise amphibious landing at a secret location.

Although Philip liked the marquis's ideas, which were carefully laid out in a lengthy document, he had also asked Parma to produce his own strategy. As the king waited almost six months for a response, he began assembling troops, embargoing and refitting ships and exploring financial contributions from the pope, with whom he discussed a joint land-sea invasion employing troops from the Army of Flanders. Parma's proposal finally arrived on June 20, for an attack from the Spanish Netherlands using thirty thousand of the foot and five hundred of the horse already concentrated there. Whereas Santa Cruz believed he only needed to surprise the British concerning where and when his ships would land on English shores, Parma believed he only needed to surprise the British with the fact of his cross-Channel invasion; the English would be militarily inferior wherever the landing took place. Decision advantage for Parma therefore required a different kind of intelligence-advantage than that sought by the fleet: secrecy about if and when he would embark. If the English knew his role and timing, they could, in concert with the Dutch, easily sink his vulnerable barges. If they did not know in advance, the reporting of spies would be ineffectual: since the English coast was only eight to twelve hours away for his troops, Parma calculated that any Dutch or English spies learning of the embarkation would be unable to warn the queen in time for her to take action.

As mentioned earlier, the king could not decide between Parma's and Santa Cruz's plans. Note that these two plans were mutually exclusive: Santa Cruz's plan required massive preparations, operational flexibility, and good knowledge of the English Channel and its ports to execute a surprise *landing*; Parma's plan required massive land preparations, naval distractions to keep the English away, operational inflexibility, and good knowledge of the timing of the Armada's diversion in order to execute a surprise *embarkation* from a fixed point. The king, nonetheless, *decided to combine the plans* into a single, nearly impossible operation. With no adviser equipped to guide him through the uncertainties this decision would generate, he simply assumed the two plans would be better joined than either one would be on its own.

This choice seemed to result from a cascade of blunders that were not the king's alone. Parma's plan was unworkable even before it reached the king's desk, and Parma sensed it. He had endorsed the idea of involving the Spanish fleet if it could be used to distract the English navy with a feint to the west, perhaps near Ireland, so his troops could suddenly and swiftly cross the Channel, unnoticed until the last moment. Absent that engineered opportunity, fleet operations could endanger him by drawing the English navy up the Channel, putting all ports on alert. Philip took Parma's endorsement but misinterpreted his warning as a call for more security, not a new plan. The king knew his efforts to assemble his Armada had been obvious throughout Europe for months. The queen almost certainly expected him to attack. So the king decided on a "solution" to Parma's security problem that increased it even more: ordering the joining-up of his forces on sea with Parma's on land to secure the crossing. The timing of the meetup and cross-sea invasion would need to be perfect—an unlikely prospect given the uncertain communications in northern seas.[91] And if Spanish warships could not control the Narrow Seas between Dunkirk and Dover to protect

Parma's forces, even perfect timing would not be enough.[92] With the king's decision, a battle in the Channel would be almost certain, and Parma's troops likely
caught in the crossfire. Despite the high and varying intelligence requirements
for these Spanish plans, especially once they were combined, there is little evidence that Philip explored them. His advisors' disagreements became the salient
problem; he resolved it by combining their preferences, despite their incompatible intelligence aspects. He decided on a joint, amphibious landing launched
from a fixed point of rendezvous he could not keep secret, further sabotaging
Parma's security by telling the pope and his cardinals about his plan when he
knew that the Vatican leaked like a sieve. He probably believed he needed the
church's financial support and backing for his role as "kingmaker" once the operation was done. As Philip himself must have anticipated, however, knowledge
of his new "Enterprise of England" spread throughout Italy's diplomatic corps.
Walsingham's network of spies relayed developments, though the precise point
of landing on English shores remained unknown. With strategic surprise impossible, Philip needed either tactical surprise or Spanish command of the seas,
especially if Parma's troops were to be involved. The terrain of uncertainty, however, was tilted against Spain on both counts.

Given his chosen strategy, Philip needed to rectify the natural imbalance of
open-source information in England's favor: better knowledge of the Channel,
"eyes-on" monitoring of shipping traffic across the Narrow Seas, and the capacity
to watch Spain assemble its fleet in Lisbon. At least at one point, the king did appreciate his intelligence challenge and the importance of doing something about
it. Registering Parma's concern about security, Philip wrote to him in 1586 that
he knew he had

> the need to make the Channel safe, because of the risk of sending a fleet like
> ours to sail between France and England at the appointed time . . . without
> having a safe port in either, nor in Flanders (except for Dunkirk, which apart
> from being the only one available is not suitable for ships of large draft), forcing
> it to face the weather; leaving aside the general advantages, *and the more de-
> tailed knowledge of those coasts that the enemy fleet will have.*[93]

Philip thus understood in plenty of time before the Armada sailed that his
relative intelligence capabilities might matter greatly, but then he apparently
forgot about them, taking comfort, perhaps, in the voluminous stream of information flowing to him on all matters. These flows did not, however, help him
analyze Santa Cruz's view of the relevance of an old sea-victory at Villa Franca
to amphibious operations in the Channel; did not help him examine his and
Parma's assumptions about communications from ship to shore in the North
Atlantic or cross-Channel; and did not help him assess the reliability of sources

on English support for his "Enterprise." By 1588, in fact, Philip believed he did not need to probe any of these matters. He had decided the strategy was set. And if decisions had to be made in the course of battle, he would make them himself. With Santa Cruz gone, he believed he alone had the intelligence to effectively command, so he demanded "minute-by-minute" updates from his subordinates, constant sharing and consultation among them, but also complete faith in the "Enterprise."

Thus, the king's plans from 1586 to 1587 seemed alternately amendable or rigid and therefore unpredictable. A conceptual lock on his military strategy also locked in misconceptions about what he needed to know, given English counterstrategy and operations. "Believe me," he said even to his renowned admiral Santa Cruz, "as one who has complete information on the present state of affairs in all areas." Following Santa Cruz's passing, nothing was to be altered without Philip's express permission.

As Philip struggled with logistical challenges, his intelligence became increasingly inadequate. His bureaucracy had been filtering out intelligence incompatible with his perceived preferences and so was serving to make his decisions worse. Philip generally delegated administrative questions to his system of councils. For especially sensitive matters, he relied on his closest advisors, of whom the most important was Don Juan de Zúñiga y Avellaneda, a member of the king's Council of State, the Council of War, and the Junta de Noche, the "Council of the Night" on which Philip relied for special advice regarding the Armada.[94] The king and the members of this select board believed the king alone understood the will of God and the pulse of his empire. So it was that the Duke of Medina Sidonia, engaged in preparing the Armada to sail after the death of Santa Cruz, tried to get word to the king about his fleet's serious shortcomings. Secretary of State Juan de Idiáquez Zúñiga intercepted the analysis, chastised Medina Sidonia for poor faith in God, and blackmailed him into silence.[95]

The Queen's Operational Plan and Strategy

The queen's decisions were at least as difficult as the king's. She did not need to choose a defensive strategy and indeed allowed Drake to sail to Spain, where he damaged the Armada before it sailed. But, given Drake's unruliness and Parma's army, she knew piratical pricks against the Spanish Empire would not be enough. Needing a cheap plan for defense of her long coastline, the queen and her Privy Council settled, albeit fitfully, on a surprising counterstrategy: to fight a pirate's war with a royal sense of measure and purpose. So Elizabeth made Sir Francis Drake vice admiral of her fleet. She also put Hawkins and Martin Frobisher, her next best privateers, in her principal warships and made the genial, but relatively inexperienced Howard of Effingham her Lord Admiral. This structure meant, in effect, opportunistic warfare—a protean design for defense of her realm.[96] That Drake, formally subordinate and deferential to Howard, would nonetheless run the show soon became apparent. An early indicator was the role allotted to the high-born and experienced captain William Borough, whom Drake had commanded at sea the year before and had come to regard as a scoundrel and a mutineer. In 1588, as the queen awaited the Armada, Borough was accorded a minor role floating on a ship in the Thames.

The story of William Borough and Drake's attack on Cadiz in 1587 reveals how the queen's operational strategy against the Armada evolved and gelled. Thanks to the extensive reporting from Walsingham's network of spies, England expected that the Armada would soon be ready to sail out of Lisbon that year. The queen realized, however, that without precise knowledge of the Spanish fleet's timing, the costs of maintaining readiness might become prohibitive. To learn more or possibly even deter or delay an attack, Elizabeth authorized Drake to set sail for reconnaissance and opportunistic sabotage. Timing would be crucial. Spanish embargoing of ships and their assembly in Lisbon meant that coastal areas would be busy with traffic and inadequately defended for a window of time. Walsingham closed all ports to prevent news of Drake's voyage from leaking in order to achieve surprise. Perhaps to convince Philip of Drake's official backing, Walsingham revealed Drake's plan to Stafford, the queen's ambassador and likely double agent in Paris, who would pass news of Drake's voyage to the king and so strengthen his bona fides.[97] If this was the plan, Walsingham understood the problems of land-based communications and timed the leak almost perfectly for his purposes.

Ever protective of his own interests, Drake made sure his small fleet, which included Borough as vice admiral, got away before the queen changed her mind about the opportunistic part of his mission, which she did. She tried to order Drake at the last minute to steer clear of attacks on Spanish soil or against ships at anchor in Spanish ports. She may have been hoping to strike a last-minute deal with Philip; her backchannels to the king meant she continued to listen to evidence that negotiations with Philip might yet amount to something. But it is just as likely that she sought a measure of plausible deniability should Drake's operations go awry or the king stand down. In any case, Drake outmaneuvered her fast pinnace, thus preventing the delivery of any revised command.

Drake sailed to Cadiz, where he knew from captured Spanish sailors that several ships were being fitted out for the Armada.[98] Unexpected and unidentified, Drake's vanguard sailed into the harbor and, exploiting surprise, demolished between twenty-five and thirty-five enemy ships. He heard from captured mariners that Santa Cruz's galleon, the designated flagship for the Armada, was in the rock-strewn and perilous inner harbor, so he transferred to a light pinnace and led a small fleet to capture her. He won the ship, towed her out of the inner harbor, then looted and destroyed her. Drake then sailed from Cadiz to Cape St. Vincent, where he took command of several Spanish castles and proceeded to interdict supply ships, destroy fishing fleets, and intimidate troops seeking passage by sea to Lisbon.

As he was accomplishing all this, Drake was first astonished, then angry to find Borough, his vice admiral, objecting to his commands throughout. Then, having replaced Borough's command and having confined him aboard his own ship, Drake learned that the ship, with Borough aboard, had mutinied and sailed for home. Reduced in number, Drake's fleet, nonetheless, proceeded toward the Azores, where he captured a fabulous prize: the king's own treasure ship from the East Indies full of gold, spices, and silks valued at more than £114,000—more than the cost of building fifty royal galleons.[99] Furious over the news of Drake's attacks, Philip sent the Marquis of Santa Cruz off on another ineffective manhunt, which depleted his ships and supplies to such an extent that the Armada was delayed until the following year and many debilitated and demoralized seamen, including the marquis himself, died of typhus. Others simply quit. Meanwhile, Drake, loaded up with treasure, returned to England, where Elizabeth, acting displeased about his insubordination, nonetheless made him vice admiral of her fleet and humiliated Borough.

If Drake had failed in this preemptive strike and theft of riches, the fortunes of Drake and Borough might have been reversed and the queen's strategy would probably not have gelled. The essence of this strategy was to build on England's three advantages relative to Spain: first, better knowledge of the Channel and control of its littoral, with help from the Dutch navy; second, building the nimbler Navy Royal; and third, a better capacity for tactical intelligence—especially piratical talent for collecting it and using it for surprise. The latter was Drake's unique talent, the queen knew it, and the Cadiz mission proved it.

Tactics from Coruña to Gravelines: England Exploits the Terrain of Uncertainty

Queen Elizabeth's choice to leave operational strategy and tactics largely to her pirate-seamen in 1588 was a risky one, but she had few options. Her opponent's strategy was as yet unclear, and she had to prevent those three distinct possibilities Zúñiga had presented to Philip: the joining of the Armada with Parma's land forces for a joint invasion; a surprise assault by Philip's fleet somewhere along the coast; and a major fleet engagement in the west that would neutralize her navy and allow Parma unimpeded access to the Thames with his barges. She knew she could count on the Dutch for only so much. Suspicious of Spain's ultimate intentions, the Dutch would likely watch Parma, help defend the Narrow Seas, and bottle up Spanish forces in Flanders, but only if this could be done without endangering the interests of the free Dutch Republic.

The brilliance of her decision-making was in realizing that, though the Navy Royal was hers to direct, she could not know enough about the Armada or Philip's tactics to run things from London. The queen's vaunted yet ground-based, civilian intelligence apparatus could do little to support naval tactics and operations at sea. For the same reason that ship-to-shore communications were challenging, intercepting them was as well. Courier runs from ships were unpredictable and therefore difficult to interdict once the pinnaces reached shore. The queen understood that, to achieve superior situational awareness once the navies engaged, she needed to delegate both intelligence and decision-making to those conducting operations. She thus gave up tactical control to empower her greatest seamen. They had a proven capacity for gathering and assessing tactical intelligence to outwit, outmaneuver, and outgun the Spanish in battle—witness Drake's victory using tactical intelligence at Cadiz and to capture the Spanish treasure ship in 1587. The queen's decision thus capitalized on her natural advantages, while building on an intelligence one: her liaison with Drake.

To understand the size of this advantage, recall that before the Armada's sails were sited off the Lizard in 1588, no Englishman knew exactly how England's lengthy coast would need to be defended. Drake did know, however, how to create and exploit uncertainty in the Channel better than his enemies did. He was, of course, used to being on the offensive, and the English fleet now had to be in a defensive posture. Maneuverability and gunnery had been optimized at the expense of carrying capacity for troops, food, or ammunition. Traditional fleet warfare, risky and probably suicidal for England's race-built galleons, was not part of the plan. What was to emerge was a new form of naval warfare: piratical defense at sea, which entailed aggressive and deliberate intelligence-gathering through observation, stealth, and theft, then a foiling of adversarial operations through maneuver and surprise.

Such tactics would be challenging. Drake and Hawkins were used to taking the initiative and using the advantages of surprise more for quick offensive strikes than for defense or disruption. There was also the issue of loyalty among shipmates: although pirates and privateers were accustomed to raiding ships and ports for supplies as needed, and could certainly do likewise at war, their crews were unlikely to tolerate deprivations when political outcomes, not gold and jewels, were the prize. The English navy was therefore brittle and, to some extent, ungovernable. The queen's decision to delegate the defense of her realm to Drake was brilliant, but she also did not have much choice. And if Philip had understood her plan, he could have exploited the weaknesses in it. He did not.

Elizabeth's delegation of tactical decision-making did not include an abdication of overall authority. Elizabeth needed to balance Drake's fight against Medina Sidonia's fleet with defense against the possibility of a second, backup fleet sailing from Spain, a sudden move by Parma, or a sympathetic Catholic insurrection. To guard against these possibilities, she needed discipline in the chain of command, which Drake's celebrity status might disrupt. She needed a hold on Drake and his colleagues to be sure that they resisted their urge to go on the offensive, engage in, or be lured into, extraterritorial defense outside the Channel, or to pursue aggrandizing opportunities at the expense of fleet operations. For all these reasons, she controlled operations and tactics in two heavy-handed ways that almost proved her undoing: first, and as already mentioned, she left a relatively inexperienced but loyal nobleman, Charles Howard, as Lord Admiral in charge of naval operations. Second, she severely limited the ammunition and victuals allocated to her ships, which ensured the fleet would stay close to home rather than dart after easy, lucrative prey further out to sea. She also took a near-mortal decision to treat her sailors in the most miserly way, leaving many to die of illness and starvation when they finally came home. Yet, from her position as head of state, she had no sense in 1588 that defeat of the Armada would bring war with Philip to an end. She needed money and decided to get it through partial demobilization and the withholding of pay rather than with taxes on the wealthy, whose ships were the essential pillar of her navy.[100]

In any event, with Drake spearheading decision-making during battle, the fleet's tactical intelligence capabilities would be maximized, provided he was given the freedom to use all of his skills for reconnaissance. Even the English fleet's relative weakness in intership communications under sail might be overcome: by interdicting just one boat, Drake could learn evolving Spanish intentions—as he would eventually do with *Nuestra Señora del Rosario*. Flexible and tolerant, Lord Admiral Howard provided Drake great latitude for this kind of independent action, squashing complaints from others suspicious that Drake's opportunism would cost them. Howard also probably served as a damper on the egos and competitive mindsets of his privateers, who, though valuable for their knowledge of the seas, opportunistic tactics, and tight command and control of crews, were unpracticed in self-sacrifice for the interests of the throne. In essence, the fleet would conduct an early form of network warfare at sea. It was a first. As Arthur Nelson has written,

> The fleet would be able to attack or retreat at will, keeping the battle at long range and preventing a landing on the vulnerable southern coast. It must be remembered that in this war, for the first time, a major battle at sea would be fought under sail alone. The advantages of the weather gauge, the upwind side

of the battle, were just being realized and theoretical tactics had to be applied and proved.[101]

Thus, the naval operations that unfolded from La Coruña, Spain, to the small port of Gravelines in the Spanish Netherlands owed their outlines to the queen's well-informed decisions regarding the provisioning and manning of the fleet in late 1587.

Note that the queen's relationship with Drake in 1588 was an odd mix: both a competition between rival powers and a form of barter in which the queen gave Drake ships and rank in her navy in exchange for his capacity for tactical intelligence-based operations at sea. Her management of this sensitive liaison relationship was put to the test during the first months of 1588, when Drake's natural impatience and inclination for predation arose. The queen had authorized general mobilization in November 1587, and, by December 21, the Navy Royal and the merchant fleet had achieved an acceptable state of readiness. Drake, meantime, had put together a squadron of merchantmen at Plymouth consisting of six Navy Royal ships and a merchant pinnace. Rumors that the Armada planned to sail in January were creating a war-scare, so Drake sent two of his pinnaces, the *Spy* and the *Makeshift*, to do reconnaissance of the Spanish coast. He found little to suggest an attack was imminent, so he recommended going on the offensive with an attack on the Spanish coast similar to the one he had conducted the previous year. "With 40 sails of shipping we shall do more good on their own coast than a great many more will do at home," he wrote the queen and Council. The queen refused. Drake would have needed two months' worth of supplies for such an offensive plan, which would have provided too long a tether for a man both key to the realm's defenses and known for his opportunistic impulses. The queen made sure he did not have them.

The queen's decisions with respect to operations and tactics were not dependent on Drake's intelligence alone, of course. Her other advisers brought knowledge and expertise. The Privy Council had intelligence on Parma's forces in the Netherlands. Some of it came from the Dutch, who were liaison partners wary of English treachery that might leave them to counter the brunt of a Spanish blow. Despite Dutch concerns and the threat from Parma, the English fleet could not hover around the Narrows where the Channel meets the North Sea. Such a position would have left the southwest coast vulnerable. It would also have given to the Spanish fleet both depth of seas and the weather gauge (closer proximity to the westerly winds). The English would thus have forfeited their intelligence advantage in the Channel and the advantages of superior maneuverability. For these reasons, Lord Howard sailed his galleons and pinnaces to Plymouth in mid-April to join Drake's fleet, leaving a smaller contingent under Lord Seymour at the Narrows. Only Sir Henry Palmer patrolled near the Dutch coast to protect against any sudden moves by the Duke of Parma.

Although by some accounts the queen's best seamen disputed the need for splitting the navy in this way, the queen and her Council had intelligence that led them to distrust the Dutch allegiance to the English cause when it risked their own.[102] Dutch liaison and Burghley's network revealed that Parma was preparing to attack the Dutch on land in a ploy designed to mislead both the English and the Dutch about the Armada's target (defeat of the Dutch, not the English) and thus drive a wedge between them. He had dispersed his troops to create uncertainty, effectively pinning the Dutch down so they could do little to help the English fleet should the opportunity later arise. Parma's stratagem had, however, the unintended consequence of reinforcing the English decision to split its navy, as described above, to guard against Parma's next move.[103] This English decision did little, of course, to alleviate Dutch concerns about English intentions, but it did prevent what Parma really wanted: the English navy unified elsewhere and unable to interfere with his meeting with the Armada for the cross-Channel invasion.

Intelligence, Tactics, and the Decisions of Drake versus Medina Sidonia

The Armada left Lisbon for England on May 18, 1588 (Figure 3.2). Delayed by the weather and the lumbering pace of its slowest ship, the Armada was no further than Finisterre by June 9, when spoiling food and lack of water forced Medina Sidonia to seek haven for his fleet in La Coruña. A gale struck, dispersing and seriously damaging the galleons that had not yet made it into the harbor. Despairing over the extent of the damage to his ships and fearing the gale was divinely inspired, Medina Sidonia wrote to Philip suggesting the enterprise be disbanded and peace negotiations pursued.

Philip, in a fury, demanded that his admirals get on with it. He proclaimed it to be God's will that the mission continue. Medina Sidonia dutifully recalled his scattered ships, repaired them, and again set sail on July 12. Navigation errors and bad weather split and degraded the fleet, which was not reunited until July 20 with five fewer ships: four galleys unable to manage the rough seas and the flagship of the Biscayan squadron. Finally, in battle formation, the Armada hove to west of Fowey. There, Medina Sidonia, assuming the main part of the English fleet was to his front in the Channel, called a war council. Although his admirals wanted to surprise Drake's ships at Plymouth, Medina Sidonia refused, citing the king's instructions to join up with Parma. Intent on sailing for Dover, he did nothing to scout his opportunities.

In the meantime, Thomas Fleming saw the Armada's first squadron sailing off the Lizard on July 19 and quickly sailed his pinnace, the *Golden Hind*, back to

Figure 3.2 The Spanish Armada's course, 1588. Pine's engraving of 1739, of a tapestry then in the House of Lords.

Source: A Short History of the English People, by John Richard Green, illustrated ed., II, (London and New York: Macmillan and Company, 1893).

Plymouth to warn Drake. The latter, legend says, insisted he had time to finish his game of bowls before dealing with the Armada.[104] Drake knew, in fact, the rhythm of the wind and seas in his homeport and, using the cover of night and a slack tide, warped the fleet out of the harbor to achieve the weather gauge and surprise the Spanish. Lord Howard, following medieval practice, invited engagement by firing a single shot from his pinnace, the *Disdain*, into the nearest great ship. And so began the first, inconclusive fight between the great Spanish fleet and the Navy Royal. The skirmish revealed the agility of the English ships, their innovative capacities for in-line, broadside attack first one way, then the other, allowing guns to be reloaded on each side in between. The Spanish noted the uncertain range of the English guns, but also the English captains' refusal to close with the Spanish lest this maneuver enable enemy troops to board. The Spanish demonstrated their countertactics, which included baiting the English by letting laggards trail the fleet in order to tempt the English to close so they could grapple and board. Neither side caused much damage to the other, however, and Howard reported that the Navy Royal was simply "plucking the feathers" off the great Armada.

Yet the differences in fleet intelligence and innate flexibility soon became apparent. With Drake's ships out of Plymouth, the Armada assumed its tight crescent formation for the voyage east and its rendezvous with Parma. As Medina Sidonia headed for the Isle of Wight, he repeatedly tried to contact Parma to tell him he was on his way. These communications—so crucial to the king's strategy—proved poor. As the Armada nonetheless proceeded in a steady eastward pace, one of his galleons, the *San Salvador*, suffered a suspicious on-board explosion that led to several collisions among ships coming to its aid. Among these, the most damaged was the *Rosario*. Drake saw his opportunity to gather intelligence and, without authorization, took it. Although he was meant to lead the English fleet that night with a lighted lantern astern, Drake extinguished the light and, under cover of darkness, made his way to the *Rosario*, whose captain quickly surrendered. Drake and his crew not only looted the ship, but gained critical intelligence about its construction, guns, gun carriages, and crew. Drake wined and dined the captain, learning the poor state of the galleon's guns, the surprising thickness of her hull, and the fleet's order of battle and plan of operations. Drake was criticized when he returned to the English fleet for "going dark" and endangering the rest, but his intelligence proved valuable in subsequent battles: the English began to risk closer approaches when firing on Spanish ships and practiced repeated bombardment.

The first opportunity for the English to experiment with what they had learned happened off Portland Bill when the two fleets became becalmed within long-range fire of each other. Howard had attempted to maneuver between the Armada's flank and the English coast, but he lost the weather gauge (the position upwind of the enemy) and failed in the effort, leaving Martin Frobisher's huge galleon *Triumph* anchored along with five middle-sized ships near Portland Bill. At this point along the coast, unbeknownst to the Spanish but well known to the English seamen, roiled the treacherous Portland Race—a rapid tidal current caused by underwater obstruction. Medina Sidonia sent galleasses to board the *Triumph*, but, unable to cross the turbulent Race, they were forced to stand off, well within shooting range of the *Triumph*'s guns. Sidonia tried to support the galleasses with part of his fleet and also send part of his line to help Vice Admiral Juan Martínez de Recalde, who was cut off by Drake to the west. Howard used this opportunity to interdict and isolate Medina Sidonia's flagship, the *San Martín*, and bombarded her using close-in, broadside attacks by his entire line. When the Armada finally reformed, both Recalde's *San Juan* and Medina Sidonia's *San Martín* were badly damaged.

The English, out of ammunition and still chasing a relatively intact Armada, had learned two more lessons from these engagements: despite repeated efforts to pierce the Spanish hulls from midrange, the targets would not sink. They needed to get still closer, while continuing to prevent either boarding by the enemy or the latter's dash to land. Second, they likely realized that the Spanish probably had no experienced Channel pilots aboard, given how they had floundered in the waters of the Race. Admiral Howard reformed his fleet into four squadrons commanded by himself, Frobisher, Hawkins, and Drake. The objective now was to keep the Spanish from safe havens or bridgeheads at Portsmouth or on the Isle of Wight. Drake and Hawkins, using their wealth of knowledge from navigating the Channel, struck hard from the rear of Medina Sidonia's fleet, pushing the Armada closer and closer to Owers bank, a line of treacherous rocks that marked the far eastern entry into Spithead and Portsmouth. Just in time, Medina Sidonia's pilot saw the turbulent water and alerted him to the danger that the entire Armada might be grounded. Medina Sidonia took the Armada beyond the threat, but also beyond its last hope for safe haven before reaching Parma's point of embarkation.

The Armada was thus forced to anchor in the open off Calais Roads, upwind of Dunkirk's shoals but subject to strong tides and erratic winds there. Dunkirk's shoals extended for thirteen miles from the coast of the Netherlands into the sea and from Gravelines to Ostend. More shoals were at the estuary of the River Scheldt, covering Flushing. To pass, ships could draw no more than five feet of water at low tide and ten feet at half-tide—too low for large galleons to cross safely. Parma did not get to Dunkirk until July 27, but when he did, he could not move. The weather had made the sea turbulent, and without ships to protect them from the English, Parma's unarmed flat-bed barges loaded with troops and horse could not leave the coast. The Dutch, with 140 shallow-draft flyboats prepared to ambush, were hoping Parma would make an attempt; they became angry that the English blocked Parma's route and, thus, their opportunity to strike. Meanwhile, the English, seeing that the Dutch were not patrolling, distrusted their aims. Nevertheless, Parma remained bottled up and unable to join hands with the Armada.

Howard and his admirals, now confident that the south coast of England was relatively safe and wanting to further damage the Spanish fleet, anchored upwind of the Spanish fleet and made a new plan. The Eastern Squadron, under Seymour, had joined them with thirty-six fresh ships and some additional, but still inadequate, supplies of ammunition and shot. Knowing a fierce spring tide was due off Dunkirk, the English prepared eight fireships to send as unmanned incendiaries into the Armada for the purpose of dispersing it. They used big ships from their own ranks, instead of those prepositioned for this purpose near the Thames, in order to gain surprise. At midnight on July 28, Howard set the sails of the fireships. The Spanish tried to interdict and tow them off, but panic struck when one of the unusually large "hellburners" began exploding with gunfire, reminiscent of the famous fireship attack against Antwerp that had left eight hundred Spanish troops dead in 1585. Many of the Armada's ships cut their cables, collided with each other and drifted in the wind and tide. By morning, only five of the Armada's galleons, including Sidonia's flagship, were back at anchor. Howard's flagship and two smaller galleons pursued one of the large galleasses seen limping to shore, ran her aground, then looted her.

Meanwhile, Medina Sidonia reorganized the Armada. It resumed sailing in its tight-winged, crescent formation with Sidonia's own ship in the lead. First, Drake bombarded the *San Martín*, then Hawkins did, attacking as Drake sailed to the rear. When Howard rejoined the fleet, four hours after Drake had started the attack, a close-fought battle ensued. The Spanish stuck to their tactics, trying to grapple and board; the English continued theirs by tacking back and forth, but firing much closer in with repeated broadsides. English cannons were firing three shots to the Spaniards' one. The *Mario Juan* was sunk and the *San Mateo* and *San Felipe* were forced to beach on the Dutch coast, where locals slaughtered the crews. A sudden squall with winds from the northwest forced the rest of the Armada leeward toward the shoals, but the fleet managed to pull away, just in time, with a sudden shift in winds. Discipline was lost, however, as the terrible weather seemed God's wrath visited on the Catholic cause. Several of Medina Sidonia's officers disobeyed direction; he executed them to set an example. As the Armada sped northwest on a fresh wind, the English fleet gave chase, leaving the Eastern Squadron behind to guard against a sudden move by Parma or a sudden change of wind that might bring the Armada back.

Parma, however, had given up. As Medina Sidonia sailed north, hoping for a weather change but without a backup plan, Parma was disembarking his troops and returning to Brussels. With the gale pressing the Armada relentlessly north with no good maps, local pilots, or plans at hand, Medina Sidonia tried to get back to Spanish shores by sailing around the northern coast of Scotland, west of Ireland, then south to La Coruña. In gale-force winds, with hulls prone to leeward drift and lacking good navigators, many of the ships wrecked on Irish shores, where locals, some believing tales of a second Armada on the way, murdered the survivors.

Conclusion

Intelligence played a significant role in the story of the Armada, and perhaps a crucial one. The most important lessons will be discussed in the next chapter.

Here it is enough to note that intelligence took the form of open information-gathering by trusted agents, espionage, encryption, support to covert action, and theft at sea. It also rested, however, on natural advantages in "knowing" that the English were able to exploit, thanks to poor choices made by Spain. What probably blinded both protagonists most at the strategic level was the lost diplomatic intelligence caused by the decision-makers themselves.

The question remains, however: did Elizabeth *achieve* decision advantage, or did Philip II, in losing his, hand the queen hers? The foregoing analysis begs this question, but the answer is difficult and complex. England's weakness incentivized the queen to learn, while rendering her adversary overconfident. Indeed, the queen's engineered gains were at least matched by the king's incuriosity and overconfidence. The king and most of his Spanish experts overestimated Queen Elizabeth's vulnerability on her throne and underestimated her sources of strength. Although the queen could claim only twelve hundred paid officials in her entire realm, she nonetheless had an extensive—indeed global—intelligence network. Her favors, which seemed endlessly changeable, ensured that she would hear from all quarters in exchange for them.[105] Indeed, by the 1570s, court machinations, gossip, and internal political warfare were giving Elizabeth more insight into where she stood and where to keep watch inside her own country than the king realized. When Philip's plots threatened her, she built on this good fortune by cajoling, bribing, and seducing her nobility into an ever more robust intelligence network. In fact, the impressive number of Catholic plots against Elizabeth—twenty or more—and the tiny size of her government made it easy for foreign leaders to overestimate the queen's problems in securing her position and exercising power. Rather than seeking to learn how England was changing, Philip tended to rely on knowledge from his reign with Mary to estimate Elizabeth's Catholic opposition, failing to grasp that many English were shifting allegiances from religion to spoils.[106] A loose system was evolving in which governance recognized knightly honor, but also business acumen.[107] So Philip II developed a strategy predicated on an English weakness the queen had turned into a strength: knowledge of domestic plotting.

Thus, the paradox: so long as Philip II engaged in an effort to arouse domestic opposition to her as part of his grand strategy, the queen could win; she simply needed to develop stronger counterintelligence capabilities than Spain's far harder task of sustaining espionage capabilities inside England. This condition was eventually met thanks to Spain's relentless bungling of plots and intelligence gathering. By choosing to use political instability against her without a superior intelligence network in place, Philip made England's internal divisions a greater source of strategic uncertainty for himself than he fully appreciated. As the next chapter discusses, his ambassadors and spies arguably did more to increase his false sense of certainty and help Elizabeth manage hers than they did to speed her downfall.

As we consider the lessons from the Armada, it will be important to remember that intelligence performance in the sixteenth century cannot be measured against modern tradecraft. For example, few monarchs in that age expected unbiased reporting. Partisanship among spymasters and their agents afforded access to important information held by those with likeminded views. Monarchs tended to leave foreign espionage to their favorite and loyal commanders, nobles, and diplomats, most of whom held strong partisan views. Though seemingly flawed by today's standards, such Renaissance methods did not render intelligence irrelevant to outcomes or impoverish its results. When judging the impact of intelligence on those outcomes, it is relative advantage that matters, not tradecraft per se. The Elizabethans just had a different way of doing the business; when judging its quality, that business must be compared to that of the Spanish, not modern times.

4

Intelligence Lessons from the Spanish Armada

If the story of the Armada has one Aesop-like moral—simple and easily understood—it might be that certainty invites surprise. Spain was, by any measure, *certainly* more powerful than England in 1588. Yet the queen demonstrated a steely, intelligence-driven approach and, surprisingly, won. Indeed, in historical perspective, it is less the queen's indecision than the king's hubris that seems foolish. As the historian Geoffrey Parker has put it,

> After 32 years on the throne, Philip II regarded himself as both omniscient and divinely inspired—especially where English affairs were concerned. Having resided in and ruled the Kingdom himself in the 1550s, he believed forever afterwards that "I can give better information and advice on that Kingdom and on its affairs and people than any one else." Therefore . . . he attempted to micromanage every aspect of the Armada campaign.[1]

King Philip was *certain* of the superiority of his navy, although he knew little about how the English intended to fight with theirs in the Channel. Moreover, when he decided for war against the heretic queen and her piratical allies, he was *certain* God would have his back. The Armada's defeat, in the midst of unseasonably violent storms, astonished and crushed him.

Although there are many lessons to be learned from the case of the Armada, this lesson about the dangers of certainty—and mindsets in general—is probably most important. Two other important lessons will also be addressed: the opportunities and dangers of intelligence liaison; and, the requirements, pitfalls, and opportunities of covert action and counterintelligence.

Certainty and Its Relationship to Warning and Surprise

The overarching problem of hyperconfidence in human affairs, whether derived from faith, science, or prejudice, is that it dulls curiosity and incentives to learn. So, apart from notions of divine provenance, how and why did overconfidence arise in this case?

Decision Advantage. Jennifer E. Sims, Oxford University Press. © Oxford University Press 2022.
DOI: 10.1093/oso/9780197508046.003.0004

One reason had to do with mindsets, which are sometimes useful and sometimes not. Behavioral rules for thinking and acting tend to stick because they have helped others or seem affirmed by experiment. Such rules may be passed on as "lessons learned" to help train decision-makers to orient toward what they see, recognize any historical parallels, and then take appropriate action. Rules may be captured in doctrine or theory to convey lessons from one generation and transmit them to the next.[2]

Such was the case with Spain's doctrine for fighting at sea that featured the techniques of closing, grappling, boarding, and fighting. Spain had galleons, admirals, and soldiers that were all perfected to these techniques because King Philip II had repeatedly won with them. Most Spanish leaders had mindsets cemented by 1588, following wins against the Turks at Lepanto, Dom Antonio's mixed fleet at Villa Franca in 1582, and again at Terceira in 1583, when the Spanish succeeded in an amphibious attack. What the Spanish failed to consider was the strong possibility that their decades of wins meant the English might learn to fight in a new way—using ships as platforms for spying, maneuver, and gunnery—and that they might win that way. The Venetian ambassador to Madrid in 1588 understood at least part of what the king was blind to: "The Englishmen are of a different quality from the Spaniards, bearing a name above all the West for being expert and enterprising in maritime affairs, and the finest fighters upon the sea."[3]

A second reason hyperconfidence develops is that insecure leaders, valuing decisiveness, cover their insecurities with bravado. As that bravado spreads, subordinates copy the posture, deny threats, or just make stuff up. Just before the Armada set sail, the pope's emissary reported a conversation he had with a high-ranking Spanish officer:

"If you meet the English Armada in the Channel do you expect to win the battle?"

"Of course!"

"How can you be sure?"

"It's very simple. It is well known that we fight in God's cause, so when we meet the English, God will surely arrange matters so that we can grapple and board them. . . . But unless God helps us by a miracle, the English, who have faster and handier ships than ours and many more long-range guns, and who know their advantage just as we do, will never close with us at all but stand aloof and knock us to pieces with their culverins without our being able to do them any serious hurt. *So, we are sailing against England in the confident hope of a miracle.*"[4]

Confidence and decisiveness are important to leadership, but projected certainty, especially when accompanied by close-mindedness, is something dangerous. It can stifle collection of new intelligence, cause subordinates to with-hold intelligence that contradicts the leader's view or lead them to discount what they know because the commander has said it cannot be. Tortured by indecision on even the most minor of issues, King Philip II refused to acknowledge befud-dlement about a big one: his patchwork strategy against England. He projected absolute confidence when his Armada finally sailed, and would hear no evidence that would undermine it, even from his admirals.

In contrast, Queen Elizabeth I's indecisiveness, for all its appearance of weak-ness, had the salutary effects of causing enemies to underestimate her and subordinates to supply her more intelligence in the hope she would finally make up her mind. The test of her true mettle came during the battle in the Channel when, despite almost universal pleading from her advisors, she stuck to her ruth-less decision to withhold pay, victuals, and ammunition to her seamen so they could not drift off or quit. She needed to keep her vessels close and hold resources tightly because she was uncertain whether King Philip, having more resources than she, had a backup plan. That he did not was her luck and his intelligence failure.

This last point brings up a third reason for overconfidence: military superi-ority. Dominant competitors tend to be conservative with their innovations. They invest in their weapons and troops incrementally because anything more revolutionary might put their supremacy at risk. Such conservatism tends to make commanders incurious about how adversaries might overturn their ad-vantage at lower cost. For example, Medina Sidonia, not a seaman himself, listened mostly to admirals confident in the superiority of their old ways.[5] So even though Spanish ships began to be built on sleeker lines, those sailing off in 1588 still had the giant forecastles and sterncastles for carrying noblemen and their retinues, relatively few accomplished seamen aboard, and a pon-derous and unwieldy way of going. Nonetheless, the fleet was soon called "La Armada Invencible" (The *Invincible* Armada), its order of battle known throughout Europe, and its size expected to produce shock, awe, and an English surrender.[6]

Of course, even if the Duke of Medina Sidonia had had better ideas in 1588, he had few choices by that time. His predecessor, Santa Cruz, would have had to learn enough about his weaker opponent to have envisioned a future defeat, convinced the king of it, and sustained that conviction long enough to overhaul Spanish naval assets and doctrine. Such a challenge is rarely met probably be-cause the larger and more successful a naval or military force, the more difficult it is to see the need for change and to respond to innovations, especially if changes in doctrine are required. Gaining decision advantage requires discovery of a threat, reverse engineering, counterinnovation, retooling, and retraining. That is a lot of investment just to hedge against innovation by a seemingly weaker power.

Whatever its cause, hypercertainty has pernicious effects on learning and adapting in competition. Its remedy, cultivated skepticism, may have been the queen's secret weapon. Whether her uncertainty was a deliberate and managed design or not, it seems to have served her:

- Uncertainty increased her incentive to collect information and explore new things (Drake's circumnavigation), kept her open-minded to new, unexpected intelligence, and so led to innovation (her race-built galleons and accompanying doctrine of fire and maneuver).
- Uncertainty also rendered the queen relatively unpredictable to the Dutch and the Spanish, and made her close associates seem more open to betrayal than they probably were.

Note that the queen's indecision was advantageous because she was on the defensive and benefited from the king's striking deficits, rendering the downsides less dangerous. In contrast, Philip II's found "truth" (military supremacy and God's will) shaped his behavior in ways the queen's Privy Council could discover and use to anticipate his next moves. Such conviction also made him more incurious than he should have been about an enemy he thought he knew, but did not. The queen's actual or affected uncertainty about Spain's intentions and English interests in the Netherlands kept her advisors collecting intelligence to persuade her one way or the other. Her uncertainty led her advisors to levy new requirements for information on Mary's intentions and Catholic connections. The king's certainty did the opposite, at least at the strategic level by opening the door for what Nassim Nicholas Taleb has termed "black swans," or the arrival of the totally unexpected.[7]

Although we cannot be sure the queen's behavior was purposeful and intelligence-driven, her decision-making illustrates how theatrics and indecisiveness, combined with feigned ignorance, can incentivize collection and generate intelligence power. "Managed uncertainty" or indecision sounds bad, but it might also be called humility—a better understood, if often uncelebrated, characteristic of leadership. Managed indecision has as its driving idea the notion that skepticism may be good if calibrated to optimize intelligence advantage. Unless intelligence providers respect this idea too, they will view uncertainty and indecision as problems in need of fixing instead of engines of intelligence advantage. Falling into the certainty trap of "speaking truth to power," they can too easily let their "high-confidence" estimates of the enemy take pride of place over the unknown, inhibiting the continuous learning and calibration so necessary for winning against an innovating foe.

Queen Elizabeth I distrusted fervent anti-Catholic advisers who seemed certain of King Philip II's belligerent intentions before they had hard evidence that he had decided on war, making her more skeptical than she should have been about their evidence of plotting against her. Yet that skepticism also made them more industrious to prove their point. To the English government's credit, the fickle queen's few certainties, such as the common interests of monarchs in preserving divine rule, did not lead her to shut down her collectors who believed Philip II was conspiring to remove her. Walsingham kept collecting and uncovering regicidal plots that saved the queen's crown and probably her life.

Such lessons regarding uncertainty should not be interpreted as endorsing a waffling style of leadership when the requirements of competition are known. They simply underscore the importance of continuous learning and the problems attending hyperconfidence in such circumstances. Queen Elizabeth I and her Privy Council deserve credit for managing a factionalized and politicized intelligence service. By disowning partisans while keeping them employed, she squeezed operational intelligence advantages out of a system unable to deliver strategic ones.

Biases and Paradoxes

To identify remedies for hypercertainty, two of its most pernicious consequences merit more detailed treatment: its impact on competitive collection, and its effects on analytical support to decision-making.

First, consider the "certainty paradox" embedded in the Armada case study: *the more you think you know, the less you are likely to know relative to the adversary over time.* This observation suggests a theoretical proposition: the more uncertain a competitor is, the more that competitor will want to develop collection systems to reduce that uncertainty (i.e., increase its intelligence power); the less uncertain, the more likely resources will be shifted away from intelligence to augment other forms of power, risking an increase in uncertainty (and a loss of intelligence power) over time. This proposition does not mean, of course, that uncertainty is good or that having multiple, energized collectors ensures decision advantage. It means only that both are necessary if not sufficient for sustained intelligence advantage. If curiosity is as much a given of international politics as conflict, then stability requires constant learning because competitors will seek advantages in unwatched space. In fact, the lack of known enemies means intelligence managers should increase collection, not cut it, for purposes of warning. Put another way, there is no "peace dividend" for intelligence in international politics, where conflict is endemic. Cutting intelligence in peacetime invites predation.

Managing the certainty paradox is not easy because uncertainty, with its requirement for continuous learning, can frustrate budget managers and collectors unwilling to risk resources on what they regard as a largely settled case. This dynamic can lead to rifts between decision-makers and collectors. Walsingham, Queen Elizabeth's secretary, believed she had the evidence to go to war against Spain long before she did, and their relationship suffered. Yet managing the paradox may be even more difficult when decision-makers have made up their minds. For all his certainty about large matters, Philip II had insecurities that made him a micromanager. His certainty masked private doubts, which made him both predictable and uneducable at critical moments, much to the Duke of Parma's dismay. The irony is that, although some lauded him as "the hand of God," and therefore omniscient, he knew he was not. Philip confessed to his top admiral that he did not know how to find and beat Drake. Certain he could win a naval battle so long as he was not hunting Drake, the king did not drive his intelligence system forward to confirm he was right. Thus, he fell headlong into the certainty paradox.

To appreciate this last point, consider a counterfactual: the king could have sought to learn more about piratical vulnerabilities from English crews, or infiltrated them for purposes of mutiny, sabotage, deception, or espionage. English privateers had knowable and exploitable problems, such as how to defend themselves when forced to careen their ships, especially in tropical waters. They careened them in 1588, just before the Armada sailed, because their strategy relied on speed and maneuverability.[8] Furthermore, their ships could not stay afloat if their crews did not receive their expected compensation. Being opportunists at heart, piratical English seamen were prone to rebellion and tolerated deprivation only in the expectation of treasure. Particularly when pressed into service, as they were for the queen in 1588, they made for a volatile kind of crew, potentially bribable for the right kind of pay.[9] Their already low wages had not been paid for sixteen weeks at the time the Armada sailed. Drake knew these vulnerabilities because he not only knew his men, he was one of them. He resented the queen's tight fist and wore her defensive mission like a hair shirt. Spain did not, however, exploit these weaknesses.

Beyond arrogance, prejudice and weak counterintelligence were also to blame for the king's overconfidence. His admirals assumed the Armada's proper display of Spanish naval muscle would leave lowly English seamen cowering, even as these admirals knew the English had skills and knowledge they themselves did not possess.[10] The failed Ridolfi plot should have removed Spain's blinders, but did not. John Hawkins, a key author of England's naval revolution, had offered his services to the Spanish, who, taking the bait, revealed the limits of what they knew but gained little in return. They should have asked themselves why Hawkins, who had seemed so useful to Spanish aims, had nonetheless been set free by his queen after the plot failed. Was it possible that, in hiring Hawkins, the king had revealed what he did not know about amphibious operations in the Channel? By letting Hawkins go, was the queen rewarding him for helping her learn more about the king than he had learned about her—the essence of intelligence-advantage? Did she have a greater use for him that stayed her hand? Lacking a counterintelligence mentality, and thus a capacity to learn from their opponent's success, the Spanish did not pursue this line of thinking.

Certainty and Confirmation Bias

Whether history would have been different if the Spanish navy had learned more is impossible to know for sure. What we do know is that the king's premonition of certain victory made him *more* aware of evidence confirming his point of view than incentivized to learn what might be wrong about it. His stubborn mindset of superiority at sea, adopted after 1582, was based on a kind of battle the English had no intention of fighting. They had learned from the Spanish success that they must not be tempted, as the French admiral had been, to close the noose on the Spanish ships. They were determined in 1588 not to be boarded and beaten again, but to outgun and outmaneuver their adversary. When the Armada sailed into the Channel, the Spanish insistence on secrecy about where Parma's troops would land simply confirmed their incuriosity about the English plan, which was to keep them from landing *anywhere* through maneuver at sea.

In contrast, Drake continued to embrace his own and the queen's uncertainties about both his crews and Spanish capabilities. On the cusp of war, he wrote to the queen:

> Your Majesty would willingly be satisfied from me how the forces now in Lisbon might best be distressed, truly this point is hardly to be answered as yet for two special causes: the first that our intelligences are as yet uncertain; the second is the resolution of our own people, which I shall better understand when I have them at sea.[11]

He went on to warn the queen against employing her counterintelligence assets against him, as she had done the year before by forcing him to bring one of her noblemen, William Boroughs, with him on his sensitive mission against Spain. Drake told her now was not the time for such oversight. Instead, he argued for attacking the Armada before it sailed. He and Lord Admiral Howard were uncertain whether the Spanish planned to delay the Armada and so force the English fleet into such a prolonged readiness that the costs of victualing and wages would become unbearable. Moreover, Drake knew that if the Spanish knew the English plan and were acting on that knowledge, they might have improved gunnery, recruited better sailors, and reinforced hulls. In the face of such uncertainties and risks, Drake and, eventually, Howard favored going on the offensive, which would throw advantages to Drake. He knew better how to attack ships in foreign ports than at sea.

When the queen prevented her navy from conducting a preemptive strike against the Armada and both navies engaged in the Channel, Drake understood what the Spanish king did not: that the only critical facts for either side to know would be the peculiarities of navigating in those waters and the sailing capacities of Spanish ships relative to English ones. Everything, including Parma's crossing, would depend on mastery of the Channel; knowledge of wind, water, and relative maneuverability would be the pivot on which decision advantage would turn. With Drake's interception of the *Rosario*, he swung that door wide for the queen. He learned that Spain had simply reinforced their ships with little else up their sleeves. In the meantime, Spain had focused on keeping its destination secret, which was largely irrelevant to the English plan.

The certainty paradox can trip up any competitor fighting on his home turf, a failure Drake avoided by keeping his intelligence in play, and by recognizing that his adversary would likely seek intelligence to compensate. That Spain did not do this—say by preparing better maps or recruiting more English and Dutch pilots—makes England's intelligence collection look better than it was.[12] It is true that the queen's and Drake's actions together largely saved the English side. If Drake had not intervened to prevent it, the queen's fleet might have been divided in two, reducing its ability to prevent landfall. Without the queen, Drake and the other English admirals might have sailed away, trying to beat the Spanish as Drake was accustomed to, but risking an open-ocean fight. Yet the king's decision to invade the way he did, without the intelligence he needed, gifted the queen and her navy with limited choices: either fighting off the Spanish coast, whose littoral Drake's pilots already knew well, or in the Channel, where Philip's navy would be sailing relatively blind.[13] The king, believing he knew England and the Channel well enough, never truly understood his deficit and its implications.

Of course, there was more to the queen's advantage than luck and Philip's obstinance. She had made informed decisions years earlier because her collectors had learned how to design a purpose-built weapon against them, and showed her the advantages to be gained by investing in a new navy. Based on this intelligence, the queen had taken a risk years earlier that she probably would not have taken otherwise: to fund a navy suited to defending the Channel or short-term predatory stings, betting that the king would bring his navy to her, just as he had brought his regicidal operatives. Unlike the king and his advisors, who assumed they knew the essentials of fighting England when they did not, the queen, her Privy Council, and her Naval Board did not assume they could win against the Spanish, despite their known advantages in the Channel. This is how asymmetric wars are won by lesser powers: by gaining intelligence advantage.

Collection Gaps and the Lure of Intelligence Liaison

A second set of lessons from the Armada concerns intelligence liaison, which is not a friendship or even partnership but rather a form of bartering among competitive intelligence providers. Intelligence liaison may involve trading maps for agent reporting, providing territorial access for "sensors" in exchange for the information they gain, and the like.[14] Liaison arrangements may involve controlled transfers of selected pieces of the collection, processing, or the communications system itself, such as good sources, fluent speakers, a prison for interrogation, or a particular ship for carrying a sensor. Done well, liaison with another intelligence provider can extend the range of an intelligence system, allowing it to collect quickly on otherwise unfamiliar or unmapped terrain. Done poorly, it gives more leverage to the partner than intended, imports his vulnerabilities, or offers opportunities for deception.

So, what can the Armada case reveal about how to do intelligence liaison well? In general, the liaison between England's queen and the master seaman, Drake, is the best example. They both knew the limits of their partnership, calculated its value continuously, and ran counterintelligence operations to weigh the vulnerabilities each posed to the other. Yet the Armada case study may offer more lessons in how to avoid doing liaison badly. Spain had wanted a win on the cheap in the decades prior to 1588. The king trusted his ambassadors to work with preexisting Catholic networks, which the English were busy penetrating. Later, he had turned to the Vatican and partnered with the pope. Riddled with spies, however, the Vatican had leaked his plans.

It would seem that, even with "friends," the costs and benefits of liaison must be calculated to guard against dependency, deceit, manipulation, or penetration. Unfortunately, it is when intelligence is weakest that incentives for liaison are most powerful, the means for counterintelligence are most impoverished, and clues to the danger are most likely ignored. Without a strong capability to detect foul play, intelligence liaison is dangerous; but with few alternatives for filling gaps in collection, incentives are strong to look the other way.

The case of the Armada serves to highlight three sources of danger in liaison relationships:

- *Compromises in collection management*: Intelligence liaison involves partnering with another intelligence organization that will have its own process of vetting, placing, and communicating with its sources. Bartering for access to that organization's intelligence does not usually involve access to or involvement in all aspects of its business, even if poor management of collection may increase risks for all.

In the sixteenth century, intelligence bartering was especially risky because it usually involved factionalized proto-states and the transnational powers of the day: piratical and religious networks run by sea captains, cardinals and the pope. This political setting blurred distinctions between sources (individual "sensors" hired and vetted by an intelligence service) and liaison partners (intelligence organizations managing and exchanging their services for mutual gain). Mistaking the second for the first meant miscalculating the partner's power, interests and vulnerabilities. Some individuals, such as low-born sea captains, were more powerful than they seemed. And those that seemed powerful were difficult to monitor and manage. For example, the queen got intelligence from Drake in return for financing his voyages, but she could not manage his ships at sea or vet his crews. This meant that his collection priorities might not always align with hers and his actions could bring unwanted war. Drake recruited spies, ran counterintelligence and collection operations, and had his own agenda for increasing his power as a sea captain and entrepreneur. The queen had difficulty staying informed on how he might be complicating her plans, so she dealt with him by keeping him uncertain of her support, including the resources she would provide for his voyages.

- *New vulnerabilities*: An intelligence service may use its access to a partnering service to learn about or compromise its sources and methods. Even if the partner has no intent to betray the arrangement, a third party may use that service to gain access or exercise influence. Strong counterintelligence is essential, therefore, to effective liaison, even if political agendas are in alignment.[15]

Just as the queen realized that Drake could be a vulnerability for her, so the king understood the dangers of liaising with the pope, whose intelligence he knew would be skewed toward getting him to spend his resources on hopeless Catholic causes that would drain his coffers and weaken his empire. He also came to understand the extent to which the Vatican leaked and how that might undermine attempts to keep the Armada's mission secret.

Unfortunately, the king did not seem to realize that Hawkins, whom he hired as an operative, could damage him just as much, if not more, than the pope. This prejudice may have reflected an imperial mindset that divided the world into the powerful high-born and the lowly. Philip II generally treated privateers more as rogues than as competitors with whom he could productively liaise over time. Thinking of John Hawkins as an individual, not a competitor with a power base of his own, he hired Hawkins for an intelligence and ferrying operation for the exfiltration of Mary, Queen of Scots. In return, Philip II agreed to release crews that had been imprisoned in Spanish jails since San Juan de Ulúa. Not only did he and his advisors buy the unlikely line that Hawkins favored a Catholic England, but by making his reward a one-time prisoner release, they advertised their interest in his one-time use and their ignorance of his network's larger worth. Unlike the queen, the king failed to see the problems and opportunities of securing Hawkins's services on a large scale.

Again, a counterfactual may help to clarify matters: we do not know what would have happened had Spain offered perpetual trading licenses and ships to Hawkins or someone else like him. The historical record seems clear, however, that almost all privateers chafed under the queen's restrictions during the 1570s and 1580s and hungered after lucrative trading privileges. The king seems to have offered no deal befitting a knowledgeable, transnational entrepreneur such as Hawkins. Treating him as a hired source instead of a potential liaison partner, he miscalculated the danger Hawkins represented not only to Spain, but also to the queen.

- *Deceptive riches*: Liaison, which involves borrowing intelligence systems (platforms, sensors, processing, and exploitation), can dazzle the parties with cheap riches that mask their separate agendas and the benefits each party gains from the risks it is incurring.

On this point much can be learned from England's success in managing intelligence sharing. The queen clearly understood the risks of liaison with the Dutch, who shared intelligence to strengthen English support for their insurgency against Spain, and of liaison with privateers, who thought and acted like pirates. Using these relationships, the queen and her Privy Council were able to supplement regular intelligence with knowledge from well beyond England's own shores. The queen suffered from occasional duplicity, but her evident preparation for treachery in these relationships reflected her understanding of her liaison partners' incentives, which were closely watched by her Privy Council and, particularly, by Burghley and Walsingham. The Dutch, dependent on the larger alliance within which their intelligence exchange was embedded, suffered constant uncertainty about whether they would be sold out in a deal between London and Madrid.

From a historical perspective, the queen's liaison relationships look safer than they actually were at the time. While the Privy Council's oversight of the machinations of the Dutch was not unusual, its involvement in liaising with the queen's privateers was much more so. Walsingham and Leicester, in particular, understood that England's defense would rest with the queen's navy, so the Naval Board and Privy Council bartered for information from seamen—even those operating on the boundary of what was legal and certainly beyond the Privy Council's direct control. One reason John Hawkins seemed to the Spanish to be a convincing traitor was that he was an entrepreneur whose activities bordered on the criminal; he also had a convincing list of grievances against the queen and information to sell. But the Spanish did not do their counterintelligence homework. If they had, they would have learned that Hawkins had a better deal with his own government: new ships, commissions, and the prospect of more contracts to come.

Liaison differs from agent recruitment in at least two ways: the bartering quality of the exchange, and the long-term aspect of the arrangement. The queen understood that she would, in particular, need Sir Francis Drake's collection apparatus not just once but repeatedly, and that her requirements for intelligence were not necessarily his. He was her hound on a leash—constantly hunting for prey and alert to threats. She knew she needed to keep him both dependent and leashed, and that his loyalty would need to be bought. To his delight, she showered him with money, offered him ships, and made him a knight; to his frustration, she limited his voyages, underpaid his crews, and put spies on his ships. Her behavior was appropriate for a monarch who understood with whom she was dealing, for what purpose, and at what risk. For years Burghley had counseled the queen, wisely, that she should beware of Drake's purposes. He believed that Drake's voyages were "only profitable to himself and his companions, but an injury to the queen as they only irritated foreign princes."[16] The queen, needing her cheap riches, nevertheless remained on her guard against deceit and abandonment even into the battle in 1588, when Drake was her vice admiral. The origin of the king's relative blindness in 1588 lay in his lesser appreciation of his collaborators' mixed motives, his failure to offer them lasting returns, and his poor counterintelligence. When organizing the Ridolfi plot, the king's ambassadors leaned on Hawkins and others who promised to join their own intelligence networks to Spain's in return for favors. Neither the pope nor Philip II imagined that the English had assets in Spain that allowed them to monitor the plotters and run Hawkins as a double agent.[17]

This lesson is not that intelligence liaison can never work, only that the relationship is not or should not be about trust. As Drake and his queen could testify, liaison as an intelligence function has little to do with friendship and everything to do with counterintelligence. The theoretical proposition would seem to be threefold: that intelligence liaison is most dangerous when it is used to fill gaps in collection rather than supplementing it; the more dependent a competitor is on intelligence liaison, the more vulnerable that competitor will be to deception, manipulation, and engineered disadvantage; and, therefore, the weaker a competitor's counterintelligence capabilities (which necessarily include collection against the partnering service), the more dangerous intelligence liaison will be.

Counterintelligence

The English queen's spymasters understood that counterintelligence operations can improve intelligence collection. In other words, it is not just a way to defend against someone stealing secrets, but a way to know what your opponent wants or needs as well. Most important, *defensive* counterintelligence, such as locks, surveillance, and spy-catching, was often blended with *offensive* counterintelligence, which is the art of influencing the adversary's intelligence to affect what that service sees, hears, understands, and reports. Special dangers thus arose: by creating stings and embedding agents in Spain's covert actions, the queen's spymasters learned about hostile networks, but also reported the developments they had helped create as evidence of King Philip II's hostile intentions.

So it seems that offensive counterintelligence distorts enemy thinking at some peril to both sides. Consider the Ridolfi plot, in which the queen's Privy Council baited the Spanish king by assuring him that Catholics were a serious threat to Queen Elizabeth I and would rise up against her once the king invaded. While perhaps it was more true at the time than it would be later, the king held on to that idea for over a decade. If the king's counterintelligence had been better, he would have realized that those who lured him with notions of Catholic uprising were the ones who went free after the plot was foiled. This knowable fact should have made him discount everything those sources had told him in the past. That he did not question that past reporting became both England's and Spain's problem: the former because the idea of a Catholic rising made Philip less inclined toward peace than he otherwise might have been; the latter because it made Philip more fervent and less cautious than he should have been about his Enterprise of England.

The lesson here is that, if counterintelligence managers do not know the tool's full potential or its dangers while adversaries do, spies or bad sources can be harder to catch, positive intelligence collection can be hobbled, deception can be more difficult to recognize, and decision-makers can be blindsided. England became masterful in this sort of activity, while Spain suffered an almost pitiful collapse that contributed to the king's muddled thinking in 1588. To understand how this happened, and the opportunities lost to history thanks to mishandled intelligence policy, the story of the Armada must be considered from its underside—the back of the tapestry as it were.

To examine this hidden side of history, one needs to recall the basics of counterintelligence from the opening chapter of this volume. Strong positive intelligence treats counterintelligence as its partner, not its opposite. Neither can work well without the other, so they often share collection assets and jointly exploit the results in the service of joint strategy. This approach makes sense because positive intelligence can be empowered or sabotaged by counterintelligence, which seeks to block or influence how an opposing competitor learns through selective secrecy, surveillance, camouflage, and deception. If the purposeful blocking and shaping redirects an opponent in unhelpful ways or leads to misinterpretations about a competitor's natural inclinations, opportunities for dealmaking may not be understood as such by those collecting positive intelligence. If, on the other hand, knowledge about an opponent is kept from those trying to block him, the latter effort may fail and competitive advantage lost. Therefore, positive intelligence (learning) and counterintelligence (tracking, blocking, and shaping an opponent's learning) are best at delivering advantage when operating together—in fact, treated as operationally joined. Keeping and releasing secrets cannot work to advantage without knowledge of the enemy and what he or she needs to know to win. Expert practitioners recognize this fact, the sensitive boundaries between defensive and offensive counterintelligence, and the minefields of both.[18]

Counterintelligence operates at three levels, of which England practiced two and Spain just one. These levels correspond to the three levels at which competitors' respective intelligence services operate: the level of *grand competition*, including collection against the terrain of uncertainty and what competitors' private sectors and publics are doing; the level of decision-making, including what the polity's *government* will do; and the level of competitive learning, including what the targeted government's *intelligence services* are doing.[19] Countering a competitor's efforts to learn at these levels may be thought of as grand, big, and little counterintelligence (CI), corresponding to the level on which the adversary is conducting its intelligence operations.[20] An opponent's covert action or industrial espionage will seek to penetrate or manipulate its target's civil society, including businesses and media outlets. Efforts to counter such activity (grand CI) often require cooperation among a polity's law enforcement, religious, and private entities, such as prisons, churches, political parties, or even schools, in addition to military and government institutions. Given these requirements, Walsingham's portfolio on the Privy Council gave him advantageous authorities, including a deep reach into England's civil society, as well as responsibility for the queen's intelligence and espionage affairs. He was empowered in a way most modern democratic societies would not tolerate for reasons of privacy, civil rights, and due process. He empowered the queen with intelligence in a manner authoritarian leaders might want but democracies eschew.

In contrast, Philip II had no one, except perhaps the incompetent Mendoza, to oversee his intelligence and counterintelligence operations. He often tried to run them himself using the filter of his subordinate and often too agreeable governing councils and intermittent inputs from the Duke of Parma. He and Mendoza specifically targeted and vetted certain individuals for collection or influence, such as Hawkins, Ridolfi, and the like, but operating on this level was all Philip II seemed able to do. To run complex efforts to learn how the English were learning about his navy and use that to penetrate, sabotage, or delay what the English navy could know and do (as Drake did to him 1587) seems to have been well beyond his capability. Using speed, initiative, and learning-on-the-fly, Drake could know more about the vulnerabilities of Philip II's ports and shipping operations as he sailed along the Spanish coast than the king or his admirals could know in those moments. This superiority in tactical knowledge was one reason why Drake argued to take the battle to Spanish ports in 1588; his intelligence activities had tipped that terrain in England's favor. With the number of intelligence operatives targeting Spanish interests and limitations on his resources and ground-based communications, Philip was constantly off-balance in these regards. Grand CI requires a capacity for grand intelligence collection and, unlike the queen, who had privateers for this mission, Philip II had none, except perhaps the Vatican, against which he needed better counterintelligence, too.

This last point raises the question of why Queen Elizabeth tolerated the counterintelligence challenge Drake and his colleagues represented. Running operations against these privateers was not a simple matter. Although they were valuable to the queen's defense, these seamen objected to the queen's interference in their endeavors, if only because the success of their own operations depended on maintaining personal control, including over the risks of engaging with the Spanish. This dilemma exists wherever public-private interests overlap from a national security standpoint. If an entity's private operation or a firm's proprietary information is at risk, the decision about whether counterintelligence interests (the protection of that proprietary information from political adversaries) should outweigh business interests (continuing to do business with that foreign government or its firms) is far from straightforward. In some cases, the private entity may insist the decision be its alone, particularly when non-defense-related industrial espionage is concerned. Men like Drake in the sixteenth century certainly so insisted. Drake and the queen did not always agree about what to do regarding the information he collected; its collection risked the queen's interests, and her use of it sometimes risked damaging Drake's interests. Both sides could, based on these conflicts, refuse to collaborate in the future.[21] Recall that Drake reminded the queen as the Armada prepared to sail that if she tried to put another (counterintelligence) operative on his ship, all might be lost. He could not tolerate her second-guessing his operations—a point he was able to make because he was running his own counterintelligence operations against her, and he knew she needed him at that moment more than he needed her. In response, she shorted his supplies.

Of course, big CI—or the protection of government operations—cannot just be about catching spies; in sixteenth-century England it also involved allowing them to circulate around the throne to hear what the monarch wanted them to hear or know. If a foreign intelligence service is learning what the targeted country wants it to learn by stealing certain documents, for example, it may be desirable to allow the theft. Sometimes it is more important, for the sake of decision advantage, to find foreign agents and, instead of arresting them, selectively release intelligence and even "secrets" to them. The case of William Stafford, Elizabeth's seemingly traitorous ambassador in Paris, is a case in point. Walsingham well knew that Stafford was in cahoots with the Spanish in the run-up to war, but he either found it more to England's benefit to allow Stafford to convey certain information than to stop him, or he was actually employing him as a double agent.[22] It follows that the decision about how to fit counterintelligence operations—be they offensive or defensive—with policymaking is a matter that cannot be decided without the involvement of the policymakers themselves. It is thus incumbent on counterintelligence decision-makers to work with other government officials when shaping and executing counterintelligence policy. Obviously, this policy cannot be a purely law enforcement question, although law enforcement must be part of the mix or it risks arresting the wrong people at the wrong time for collecting intelligence they were meant to have.

Finally, little CI, or the protection of an intelligence service from penetration or manipulation, involves similar trade-offs requiring input from those responsible for intelligence policy. Neither side excelled in this domain because tradecraft was generally poor. In particular, codemaking lagged behind codebreaking, and cryptology was weak. The effects of poor tradecraft had implications for intelligence liaison, where the cost-benefit trade-offs of collaborative spying and counterspying are often subtle, complicated, and riddled with sensitive calculations concerning sources and methods. The cost/benefit calculation must be made by those closest to strategy and operations in the field and, in the case of agents of foreign powers operating in the homeland, in close consultation with responsible intelligence officials there.

Covert Action and Intelligence Support to Military Operations

The Armada story turned on the outcome of Spain's attempted covert actions, which kindled belief in Philip II's regicidal intentions, led to the ouster of Spain's diplomatic representatives, strengthened English counterintelligence, increased the number of potential double agents working for England, and reduced the availability of human sources for Spain. Such consequences of the Ridolfi, Babington, and Throckmorton plots demonstrate the dangers that attend covert action, which aims to change political, military, or economic events without revealing the perpetrator's hand. Covert action is secret policy that uses intelligence, not intelligence that dips into policy as counterintelligence often does. The perpetrator must make policy not just at the launch, but also at each step of policy execution.

Although covert action seeks to exploit vulnerabilities through clandestine sponsorship of open activities, it can hand intelligence advantages to an enemy, prompt the target to repair its vulnerabilities, and destroy sources in the targeted country, blinding the perpetrator. These dangers arise because covert action often requires energizing couriers, communicators, forgers, and storefronts in a common project, putting them at risk. It biases sources to the sponsor's preferred ends, and it forces assets to work together against deadlines at the risk of their own cover. The Spanish ambassadors' collection activities in support of operations to spring Mary out of her prison revealed the shape an attack might take and what Philip II felt uncertain about: how to join Parma's army to larger fleet operations.

None of this is to suggest that covert action is never wise, only that it must be well calculated. As we saw in the preceding chapter, the Spanish failed to take account of the effects of covert action on competitive learning. The essential problem was that the king's intelligence providers in London and France were also policymakers and plotters against the queen. Left to their own devices, his emissaries recruited sources eager to overthrow Elizabeth, not ones best suited to unbiased collection and risk assessment.[23] Mostly Catholics, these sources or agents sold their services to the Spanish more to influence the king than to convey good intelligence for careful decision-making. They wanted the powerful Spanish Empire to restore Catholicism in England. This kind of influence peddling was a lucrative game in the murky world of Renaissance politics, in which many tried their hand. But the king's intelligence managers had already decided on plans for invasion, insurrection, and even regicide.

Even in such circumstances, decision-makers need intelligence support to sustain operational advantages, as well as to know when to change policies. So long as regicide was the only game in play, few would look for intelligence related to Philip's larger interests. Thus, neither Philip's ambassadors in Paris and London, nor the agents they recruited, could help Philip frame the costs and benefits of regicide or rate the probabilities of its success. It was not so much that they missed opportunities to inform the king, as that they had no interest in gathering this kind of intelligence. Agents lost their lives with each failed operation, depleting the potential for human intelligence collection, while England's intelligence against them improved.

In any event, the resulting intelligence gap cost Philip strategic decision-advantage. His policies of covert action required superb tactical intelligence for successful execution, but destroyed his sources and intelligence infrastructure.[24] As mentioned before, the king could have leveraged the queen's fidelity to the monarchical concept and her impoverished situation to roll back her support to Dutch rebels resisting their king. Instead, his actions actually worked to liberate the queen, who had long felt constrained by the idea of divine rule, a principle she expected a fellow monarch and former suitor, such as Philip II, to defend. The idea that he would sponsor her murder had seemed impossible to entertain, until his agents' covert actions proved her mindset wrong and the queen's Protestants used the king's mistakes to their political advantage.

Thus, Philip's three failed covert actions created four more problems for him: a ramping-up of England's security; a rollback in access for his intelligence network there, most notably with the termination of his embassy in 1583; the development of a competing and independently controlled network of spies working for the commander of his forces in the Spanish Netherlands, which led to discordant decision-making in Brussels and Madrid; and greater certainty for the queen regarding Philip's intentions, even when these were in flux. The Privy Council tightened English security, created a bond of association that pledged all signatories to the defense of Queen Elizabeth's life, and promised death for would-be plotters and their beneficiaries. Philip's attempt to capitalize on what he thought were the queen's vulnerabilities thus caused a strengthening of the hawkish wing of the queen's Privy Council, and a closing of gaps in England's security arrangements. It deprived the king of intelligence for appropriately assessing his risks and capabilities in 1588.

The case of the Armada suggests that calculating the risks and gains of covert action depends on four assessments:

- *The likely risk to intelligence advantage*: If agents, moles (sources embedded in the enemy's intelligence or decision-making structure), or double agents are involved, a covert action increases the risk of their loss as the plotters' operations risk exposure of supporting communications and intelligence providers, eliminating their availability for intelligence collection on other matters.
- *The risk to decision advantage*: Covert action orients both sources and operatives to a cause, introducing a structural bias into intelligence reporting that may lead to miscalculation or policy manipulation for the perpetrator and intelligence advantages for the target. Indeed, the intelligence groundwork for a covert action is almost always laid prior to the policymaker's decision to execute it, making that decision potentially biased by intelligence skewed toward the views of those agents volunteering or recruited for the cause. By the time Philip II had a chance to weigh in on the Ridolfi plot, the reporting he was receiving was heavily biased, and many of the agents he trusted had been turned. Even if assets remain unbiased,

covert actions increase their risks, the dangers if they are captured, and their potential value as double agents.

- *The consequences of stress-testing the adversary's counterintelligence service*: Covert action will likely strengthen the counterintelligence apparatus of the opponent, especially if operatives are caught and turned.
- *Loss of policy control over operations with significant competitive consequences*: Supported by a small group of biased sources, secret policy-operations tend to become self-affirming and, for reasons of tempo, efficiency and plausible deniability tend to take on a life of their own. This factor makes decision-makers more comfortable with covert action than they should be, because they can delegate policymaking while washing their hands of the results.

These dangers do not mean that covert action is always a bad idea. The case of the Anglo-Spanish conflict suggests that covert actions are most likely to succeed under these conditions:

- *They are small in scale so that the execution can be envisioned to completion.* The Ridolfi plot, like nearly all versions of Philip II's "Enterprise of England," was too big in scope, had too many contingencies, and had too many moving parts for the Spanish to manage or even envision the outcome.[25] To be successful, policymakers have to know how, when, and where they will stick the landing, even if some changes are necessary in the air.
- *They are designed more to influence policy than to execute it.* Covert actions inclined toward *offensive counterintelligence* (manipulating how other competitors think), including those involving double agent operations, will tend to be more successful than the secret sponsorship of higher-profile lethal attacks.
- *They are executed by a liaison partner whose collection apparatus will absorb the risks if the operation fails.* Recalling the earlier lesson on liaison, however, the partner should care more about his own collection infrastructure than the sponsor does. Otherwise, betrayal of the sponsor and the dedicated assets will not be expensive enough for him. It is important to understand that Drake was often acting as a covert operative for the queen. She claimed plausible deniability for her sponsorship of his efforts to interrupt the king's treasure flows. In other words, she was in a position to deny the connection, and he was willing to pay the price should his missions fail. The queen's liaison with Drake may be considered one of the most successful covert action alliances in history.
- *They are supporting events on the verge of happening anyway, lessening the demands on secret intelligence sources.* The news of the Northern Rising in

1569 against Elizabeth's Protestant rule made Philip II think covert action might be easy. But covert action *after* an event does not have the same effect as enabling that event in the first place.

Confusing the enemy about whom he is fighting through secret sponsorship often creates a large initial advantage. But this deceit, which can lead to anger and blowback if revealed, may lead to lost advantage later. England's successful covert actions in the sixteenth century had attributes of offensive counterintelligence. The Hawkins deception sought to discern, and then influence, Spanish plans for an attack. It partly succeeded because it sought to twist a foreign plan that was ripening in the wake of the Northern Rising. This offensive operation was still dangerous, of course. Hawkins had to hand over intelligence that proved his worth in order to have influence. But it worked because Burghley and Walsingham had ongoing contact with Hawkins and ran independent agents who reported on Hawkins's moves. It worked because English *counterintelligence* seems to have been much better than Spain's. It would have been strategically successful, as well, if England had a good strategic collection capability separately establishing the king's intentions. In the absence of the latter, the former nonetheless produced decision-advantage.

The lesson here is fairly straightforward: secretly sponsored, open operations—what is today called covert action—whether designed for influence or some other political, military, or economic end, is unlikely to succeed without a ripe target, strong counterintelligence support, positive intelligence collection to corroborate results, and a deep bench of sources that can recover collection against the target if the covert action fails. Risks escalate if collection assets are few, the size of the enterprise is great, the action is lethal, and the secret sponsor's role is difficult to hide.

Finally, the issue of covert action reminds us how easy it is for intelligence to become politicized when it is asked to support secret policy. All competitors' frequent use of covert action in the sixteenth century reflected, in part, the politically charged nature of the times. The intelligence costs of such activities were underestimated because intelligence *was always politicized*. Recalling the terrain of uncertainty in sixteenth-century Europe, it is hard to imagine how either monarch could have overcome the politicization of their intelligence networks. Objectivity was hard to find in a world where place of birth, nationality, or race was less cause for trust than religious affiliation. And in this latter regard, the queen sprinkled her court with advisers of varying allegiances.

Burghley was perhaps the most unusual of these advisers in that he, a counselor to the Protestant Queen Elizabeth I, had once sworn allegiance to Queen Mary I, a devout Catholic and the former wife of King Philip II. Always suspect himself, Burghley's penetration agents ran terrible risks. For example, Burghley's protégé and ambassador to France, Sir Edward Stafford, provided evidence suggesting Spain's king was more indecisive than implacably hostile, which in fact he apparently was until December 1586 and perhaps even early 1587.[26] Stafford was judged by many at the time (and by most historians since) to have been a traitor; but, as already mentioned, there is evidence he was a successful double agent and in any case, he received Burghley's protection.[27] Similarly, Sir John Crofts's longevity on the Privy Council, despite his Spanish sympathies, may have reflected the queen's interest in countering Walsingham's anti-Catholic fervor. Some historians have suggested that Croft was a paid Spanish agent of influence. If so, he was never exposed as such.[28] It seems at least as plausible that the queen wanted Croft's Spanish connections and that she knew Stafford, as English ambassador to France, was running covert influence operations using the Spanish ambassador there.[29]

All this political ferment in sixteenth-century intelligence networks suggests a lesson contrary to modern intelligence thought: politicization, which distorts intelligence, need not ruin it. Indeed, when trust between decision-makers and intelligence providers is lacking, politicizing intelligence may be a means to regain trust and improved intelligence flows so long as managers make sure multiple channels for competing political "takes" exist. This is the brilliance of democratic politics: it eschews the conceit that facts have only one set of implications, and incentivizes people to gather them for the purpose of influencing and informing each other. The intelligence process can be a microcosm of the democratic process insofar as it seeks less to suppress dissent in favor of one point of view, than to organize dominant views according to their compatibility with a flow of facts competitively obtained.

Previewing the US Civil War Case: A Study of Battlefield Intelligence

The case of the Spanish Armada has been instructive for thinking about how intelligence worked across a range of decision-making—from grand strategies such as the Enterprise of England to tactics in the battle of Gravelines. It has helped to show how a weaker competitor could overcome a stronger one by wit rather than arms alone. Its lessons about the interconnectedness of learning from tactical to strategic decision-making will be instructive as we go on to examine in greater detail how intelligence can empower mass armies on battlefields. We will see that superior platforms, sensors, resources, and communications systems are not enough to ensure intelligence advantage. Connectedness to decision-making, including disciplined use of intelligence by decision-makers themselves, is also essential. We will explore how, obvious as this requirement may seem in theory, it is far less obvious in practice. Lacking attention to the challenge of how to support decision-making on the one hand and decision-makers' involvement in intelligence strategy on the other, an intelligence system can perform like water torture, trickling so slowly it drives a leader crazy or, like a misdirected fire hose, saturating troops but not helping them put out the fire.

As we move on to examine two battles during the American Civil War, it may seem problematic to analyze them separately from strategic decision-making for the larger war, especially because the Armada case demonstrated how strategic intelligence can set up operational decisions for success or failure. Confederate General Robert E. Lee's decision to move north toward Gettysburg, for example, was influenced by grand strategy, especially Richmond's decisions regarding the western theater of Confederate operations.[30] Recognizing that out-of-area factors can be lessened but never eliminated, we will consider the battlefields in which decision-making was relatively contained and only as commanders knew them through the intelligence systems they had at hand, not as historians with access to documentary records may understand them now. These battles will include First Manassas, Chancellorsville, and, briefly, the run-up to Gettysburg. Nevertheless, the reader should keep in mind that strategic choices made off the battlefield sometimes facilitated competitive advantages for one side or another, as they did in the case of the Armada, which was, in fact, a single engagement in a much wider and lengthier war.

5

Battlefield Intelligence: The Battles of First Manassas and Chancellorsville during the US Civil War

The protagonists involved in the case of the Spanish Armada had differing cultures, religious convictions, experiences at sea, and traditions of command in an empire on the one hand, and an island proto-state on the other. Although neither perfected intelligence in war, Queen Elizabeth won the battle of 1588 by exploiting Philip II's seafaring vulnerabilities, using her natural intelligence advantages, and managing her privateers, whose ships were the most capable intelligence-gathering platforms of the day. Her use of intelligence power was not the sole cause of her victory, but it improved decision-making relative to Spain's, and lowered England's vulnerability to unlucky twists of fate.

The American Civil War offers quite a different case of intelligence in war—one in which rival commanders shared military traditions, doctrine, and experiences. Both sides knew their opponents' interests, language, and purposes. In fact, many of the opposing officers had attended West Point together, and more than a few were friends at the war's start. The heroes of the Mexican-American War—Andrew Jackson and Winfield Scott—had established the military traditions that had shaped the first Civil War soldiers on both sides, including their common knowledge of weapons, communications, and military tactics.[1] And both sides had benefited from study of the Crimean War, including its rifled weapons, telegraph, use of railroads, and the like. Shared mindsets also meant shared misjudgments, such as the expectation that the war would be short and the first battle a decisive one.

Yet common perceptions gave way to uneven learning as the war progressed. Advantages in knowledge became less a matter of luck and more of artful strategy.[2] Commanders' evolving experiences led to refined judgments about what they needed to know to win, such as whether or not a road could be corded with existing fencing, where horse-drawn artillery could ford a river, how much time a marching column would need to outflank an opposing line, and whether or not to pursue an army in retreat. At least a few commanders realized something more: that mass armies required delegating complex collection missions and problem-solving to full-time intelligence officers. Whereas in 1861, neither the US army nor the Confederate army had a concept of intelligence policy, Union

Decision Advantage. Jennifer E. Sims, Oxford University Press. © Oxford University Press 2022.
DOI: 10.1093/oso/9780197508046.003.0005

Army General Joseph Hooker had one by 1863. He created a unit, the Bureau of Military Information (BMI), to manage collection against the enemy's order of battle and organize support for decision-making. Chancellorsville archived the result: stunning intelligence support for strategic surprise. Unfortunately, once Hooker's army mobilized, the BMI could not sustain this advantage on the battlefield because of mismanaged communications and secrecy. Nevertheless, Hooker retained the BMI so that it could learn from its mistakes. This decision proved a gift to his successor. As both armies raced toward Gettysburg, the BMI outdid Lee's capacity to process and deliver intelligence on the hoof. Federal forces were able to piece together the Confederate order of battle, while General Robert E. Lee was left missing his cavalry, which were his "eyes and ears." As historian Edwin C. Fishel wrote in his landmark study of the subject:

> The standard depiction of the battle of Gettysburg as the accidental collision of two armies marching half blindly is found to be true only for the Confederates. Their 150-mile march . . . was penetrated by soldier-spies whose findings enabled the pursuing Federals to cross the Potomac simultaneously with the main body of the invaders and unbeknown to them. The Confederates assumed dangerously dispersed positions across south-central Pennsylvania, their movements reported by fourteen locally organized groups of citizen-spies and scouts. Thus General Meade was able to foresee that the enemy would concentrate at or near Gettysburg. His forces seized commanding heights there and surprised the arriving Confederates, who never overcame the Federals' initial advantage of position.[3]

It is the trajectory from common knowledge to these sorts of competitive advantages that makes the US Civil War a particularly good case for studying the derivation of intelligence advantage on the battlefield. Shared history and leadership skills among officers ensured neither a level nor a transparent battlefield. Technological change was increasing uncertainty for both sides because it was affecting the potential killing radius of soldiers, the command radius of generals, and the influence of civilian leaders on military strategy.[4] Thanks to the telegraph, generals could better understand and shape larger battlefields, but presidents in Washington and Richmond could also second-guess battlefield operations, and newspapers could learn and leak tactics before their execution. Although President Lincoln considered knowledge of enemy movements to be at the heart of winning tactics and strategy throughout the war, he also believed it was "the most constantly present, and most difficult" of the challenges to be overcome if victory was to be achieved.[5]

This chapter explains why, despite their common martial history, the two sides at the start of the war were not equally positioned to learn of battlefield developments at Manassas and Chancellorsville and how, therefore, the challenges of overcoming these learning disabilities differed for both sides. The discussion in this chapter sets the stage for the next, which examines the intelligence behind specific decisions in well-documented battles. The first will be the First Battle of Bull Run (or "First Manassas," July 16–21, 1861), when General Irvin McDowell's army failed in its attempt at a surprise flanking movement only to be surprised in turn by the sudden appearance of Confederate reinforcements. The second will be the Battle of Chancellorsville (April–May 1863), when Union general "Fighting Joe" Hooker surprised Confederate general Robert E. Lee only to suffer a bigger surprise and defeat himself. Although the analysis of these battles largely relies on the work of well-known historians, it focuses on the role of intelligence in decision-making and so may change perceptions of what happened.

Before we examine particular decisions, however, it is necessary to review in greater detail the "terrain of uncertainty," factors that obscured the battlefields of First Manassas and Chancellorsville in 1861 and 1863, respectively.[6] As we do, we should recall what Ambrose Bierce, a Civil War staff officer, wrote about the fog of war:

> The civilian reader must not suppose when he reads accounts of military operations in which relative position of the forces are defined . . . that these were matters of general knowledge to those engaged. Such statements are commonly made, even by those in high command, in the light of later disclosures, such as the enemy's official reports. It is seldom, indeed, that a subordinate officer knows anything about the disposition of the enemy's forces—except that it is unamiable—or precisely whom he is fighting. As to the rank and file, they can know nothing more of the matter than the arms they carry. They hardly know what troops are upon their own right or left the length of a regiment away. If it is a cloudy day they are ignorant even of the points of a compass. . . . [W]hat is going on in front of him he does not know at all until he learns it afterward.[7]

In this chapter it will be these kinds of uncertainties surrounding the battles themselves that will be of greatest interest—not the grand strategic unknowns that affected higher-level decisions, such as if, or when, Britain might enter the war.[8]

Apart from the general fog of war, three broad areas of uncertainty plagued Civil War commanders of the eastern theater in ways they struggled to understand: the dimensions and topography of the ground on which they would fight; the effects of new technologies, such as rifled guns, aeronautics, and telegraphy on war-fighting; and, the skills and loyalties of Americans straddling sides and forced to choose.

Maps

Maps constituted a form of pictorial intelligence for both sides in the US Civil War. As one historian has written, "It is almost a truism that good marching equated with good mapping, particularly under the conditions that prevailed for Civil War armies maneuvering in mid-nineteenth century rural America."[9] Other historians have noted that during this conflict, "maps were tools of war as assuredly as were muskets, cannon and ironclad warships, allowing generals who would otherwise be limited to the narrow parameters of their own vision and the subjective reports of scouts, guides and local citizens to survey and command an entire theater of operations."[10]

While few historians have examined the intelligence implications of such observations, the implicit suggestion that maps were objective and scouting subjective is misleading. Maps used by generals at the start of the Civil War were analytical products produced by government bureaucrats, farmers, engineers, scouts, railroad men, real estate brokers, or other collectors, often for purposes other than war-fighting. Their accuracy and suitability for battle varied according to the interests of the sponsor and the skills of the producer. For battle, officers needed bespoke maps to gain advantages. So the question is: did preexisting maps or the skills of mapmakers relieve uncertainty more on one side than the other from 1861 to 1865?

Competitive reconnaissance of terrain would prove as important in the eastern theater as in any other during the Civil War—and maybe more so. Only one hundred miles separated the two capitals. The intervening ground belonged to a state belted with navigable rivers, exposed along a coastline, and split by the spines of Virginia's Blue Ridge and Allegheny Mountains, which ran from the outskirts of Washington north toward Gettysburg, and south toward the Confederate capital of Richmond and beyond.[11] The folds in terrain, including the lower Bull Run Mountains, could hide the movements of armies or be used to funnel troops through gaps to achieve surprise. Although commanders understood how important these natural features would be to the war, they were uncertain in the spring of 1861 which side would benefit most from them.

One might presume the Union started with a built-in intelligence advantage in mapping because of organizations such as the Corps of Topographical Engineers, which had been established in the early 1800s. Most of the Corps's engineers stayed loyal to the Union. Railroads were also concentrated in the North, which meant their baseline maps and infrastructure for surveying were accessible to the Union. Printers and publishers of maps, also concentrated in the North, had evolved rapidly through the 1850s. Following the laborious and expensive use of copper plates, the relatively cheap use of lithography turned map publishing into a profitable industry. Washington could also reproduce and disseminate maps more quickly and in greater volume than could the Confederacy, which had no engineering department at the start of the war.[12]

Yet Union advantages in mapmaking were limited. The government's existing maps, for example, were mostly inadequate for military use. The areas where the heaviest fighting would occur during the Civil War, including the Shenandoah Valley, were largely unmapped in 1861.[13] Although topographical maps made for commercial or railroad purposes provided some coverage, few were accurate, detailed, or on a scale useful for the movement of large armies. The reasons for the lack in Virginia were probably varied, but D. H. Strother, a topographical engineer with the Federal army, believed that the state's governors had deliberately rebuffed Federal efforts to map it. Virginia had "jealously maintained her constitutional impenetrability. No National scow was ever permitted to rake the mud out of her rivers, and no Federal engineer to set up his tripod on her sacred soil. The consequence was that reliable maps of the country could not be procured."[14]

Virginia's variable place-names also seemed designed to deceive anyone but a native. Cold Harbor was also Coal Harbor, which was not to be confused with New Cold Harbor or "burned" Cold Harbor, which was also known locally as Old Cold Harbor. The Union's maps for the military were, therefore, often old and confusing. Certainly, their bad intelligence complicated decision-making and infuriated commanders such as General Philip Sheridan. According to Earl B. McElfresh, Sheridan once asked a cavalryman a specific question while pointing to a map:

"Captain, how far is it to Green's Corners from this point?"

The Captain looked at him a moment and then answered: "What Green's Corners do you mean, sir?"

"Why in the valley between Harpers Ferry and Martinsburg."

The captain looked at the questioner a moment and said: "I have been in the valley since the battle of Antietam, but I never heard of Green's Corners before, and I don't believe there is any such place."

The little man (Sheridan) jumped up with the map in his hand, nervously tapping it with his finger and said sharply: "Well, sir, I will show it to you on the map; here it is; Tolbert send this officer back to the regiment."

He then turned to me and said: "Scout, do you know where Green's Corners are?"

"No sir, I never heard of it."

His eyes snapped and he looked as though he was about to kick me out of the room, when General Tolbert, who had been looking at the map, said: "Why Sheridan, you are all wrong; you have got a department map thirty years old. The new map has it down as Smithfield. The name has changed."[15]

Even when states had gone to some length to produce detailed maps for public purposes, as Maryland and Virginia did in 1852 and 1859 respectively, the surveying (i.e., collection) on which they were based was generally old, making the maps out of date when published.[16] Union generals could, therefore, be misled in believing a relatively recently printed map to be accurate. Moreover, not all maps were designed for military use, and so confused commanders in battle. Some commercial maps showed, for example, notional road and rail networks that, designed to lure investors, had never come to be.

Indeed, the Union's better access to prewar maps, such as the US Coastal Survey, sometimes bred overconfidence among military planners. Knowing the location of bridges and fords did not mean knowing their wartime utility for armies of men with six-horse teams and heavy artillery. Supply wagons for marching armies could weigh as much as four thousand pounds fully loaded, but much less when supplies were low. Whether a bridge would sustain the weight of any given wagon on any given march required an engineer's analysis in the context of his commander's requirements—in other words, maps supplemented by current intelligence. Without good intelligence, a seemingly fine civilian map could shape military decision-making much as light from a street lamp shapes a search for lost keys at night. Federal engineer Thomas Jefferson Cram famously prepared a map of a Virginia peninsula for General George B. McClellan's campaign against Richmond using the best existing ones he could find, some of which dated back to the Revolutionary War.[17] Unfortunately, his product failed to cover one critical feature that was beyond the margins of the coastal survey he had used as a reference: an abrupt change in the direction of the Warwick River. The river blocked McClellan's march more effectively than enemy troops could ever have done.[18]

Maps had to be relevant to particular military decisions to deliver advantages in battle, which meant most needed to be supplemented by scouting or engineers' reports. Commanders needed maps for some maneuvers that showed not only roads, but also fences needed for corduroying them so wagon wheels could get traction. Ones that failed to indicate marshes, and even minor changes in topography, were less useful to a marching mass of men and animals than ones that did. Engineers responsible for the surveying and construction of temporary roads, fortifications, and bridges became critical intelligence collectors who had to know exactly what their commanders needed, when they needed it, and according to their order of battle. Targeted aggressively by the enemy for what they knew, not just what they drew, these mapmakers and engineers on both sides guarded their personnel, plans, and annotated maps as if they were treasure.

The North's institutional advantages in mapping were important, but initially less important than its operational disadvantages in real-time scouting. Scouting and mapping were connected. A moving army needed to know roads and their quality, but also the distribution of forage for animals that, for just one moderately sized command, reportedly used twenty-four tons daily.[19] Generals courted failure if they ordered movements without reference to scouting reports on forage, elevations, fords, or the current attitudes of local farmers. Alternatively, commanders could achieve advantages by trapping otherwise stronger opponents on land believed to be barren or hostile to them. A Union general's failure to pursue a retreating enemy was sometimes less cowardice than uncertainty about agronomics: whether hungry soldiers and horses could be fed if he did.

Such disadvantages particularly affected battles in Virginia at the start of the war, when Union leaders such as General-in-Chief Winfield Scott held out hope that Virginians had sympathy for the Northern cause. Mapping land use for the purpose of using crops, water, or stored harvests for military purposes threatened to alienate citizens, undermining any hope of winning their loyalties. Well-founded or not, this view resulted in impoverished decision-making. As one Union commissary said on the crucial question of General Patterson's effectiveness in a council of war before the Battle of First Manassas: "The question of subsistence is here a question of transportation. Thus far, no reliance has been placed on the adjacent country. A day's march would compel a resort to it. *As far as known*, those supplies would be quite inadequate."[20] Patterson's failure to move at the crucial moment before the Battle of First Manassas, as we shall see in the next chapter, was, in part, a failure to know enough to gauge the risks of venturing deeper into Virginia. In any case, Patterson's stall enabled his opponent to slip away to reinforce Confederate troops in Manassas.

Yet, to be successful, scouts often had to augment maps with good intelligence from locals. And for the battles of both First Manassas and Chancellorsville, the locals were Southerners. This gave an advantage to the Confederates until Lee moved north. Locals could describe and sketch farms, fords, fences and even property ownership that, once verified, could be useful in battle. Rudimentary maps might be found mounted on the walls of homeowners or carried in the pockets of tradesmen. Their utility depended on whether anyone was able to verify or falsify them as an enemy approached. This was the job of amateur "topogs," or mapmakers familiar with the countryside or at home with its people; they often had an underappreciated advantage over professional engineers.

Although the Confederacy had certain built-in advantages in topographical collection and analysis on Southern soil, its civilian mapmakers still had to learn how to support the military, and commanders had to learn how to direct them. General "Stonewall" Jackson's foot cavalry achieved surprising speeds, in part because of good, purpose-made maps. Jedediah Hotchkiss, a former Virginia schoolteacher and amateur geologist, was one such "collector" brought into service for the Confederacy early in the war. His sketches, initially done on horseback with colored pencils, were often rudimentary, but effective.[21] Jackson ordered Hotchkiss on 26 March 1862, to make a map of the Shenandoah Valley, "from Harpers Ferry to Lexington, showing all the points of offense and defense in those places." As Hotchkiss put it: "This was the beginning of my career as a Topographical Engineer."[22] Thereafter, he employed two horses, a wagon, a driver, a compass, and the occasional local guide. Jackson used Hotchkiss's products to win his campaign against Generals Banks and Frémont in the Shenandoah Valley during the spring and early summer of 1862.[23]

Hotchkiss's role was not a singular one, but perhaps the best documented case. His techniques of economy and design highlight how truth-seeking can be overvalued, and purpose-driven simplicity undervalued in performing the intelligence function. In fact, his first mission as a mapmaker taught him that too much attention to detail could be costly: his position was overrun and he lost his tent, much equipment, "and his new, highly accurate, now virtually useless, map of Camp Garnett and Rich Mountain."[24] Learning from the experience, Hotchkiss became quick and efficient. General Stonewall Jackson felt indebted to his cartographer during the Valley campaign despite the fact that the Union's maps might be considered more detailed and, at least in that sense, more "true" than Hotchkiss's were.[25] Hotchkiss's simpler designs were timely and useful despite occasional gaps that were inconsequential for Jackson's purposes. His sketchbooks and maps showed *only what the cartographer knew Jackson needed to know* to move his troops: the *usable* gaps, elevations, and fords.[26] As the war progressed, real-time mapmaking became an indispensable adjunct to archived maps, engineering, and mounted reconnaissance. In fact, nineteenth-century mapmakers who could also scout and prepare relevant and timely products for their commanders were much like the coastal pilots of sixteenth century: the expert providers of last-mile navigation for men at war.

It is important not to exaggerate the oft-romanticized contributions of men such as Hotchkiss, or to infer that only the South had such skilled and trusted mapmakers. Jedediah Hotchkiss proved such a man for the South; John C. Babcock was probably his closest complement in the North. Robert Knox Sneden, served with the Army of the Potomac until he was captured in 1863 and imprisoned. His memoir provides good insights into wartime decision-making from a Northern mapmaker's perspective.[27] Yet it is the Hotchkiss example, in particular, that illustrates the important point best; that for intelligence purposes it was the *relative utility* of maps to battlefield decision-making that mattered, not necessarily their generic accuracy or detail. By using color, layout, and *the absence* of unnecessary facts, mapmakers could make their clients' decisions easier—saving them from becoming hopping mad, as Sheridan became when confused by details. Reaping the benefits of operating on home turf and the urgency that comes when intelligence is missing, the Confederacy enjoyed an initial edge in battle-specific topographical awareness that, over time, the North had to reduce in order to win.[28]

Technological Uncertainties: Guns, Wires, Balloons, and Equitation

If the technology of industrial-scale mapmaking proved a double-edged sword for intelligence—creating both opportunities and new vulnerabilities—this double edge was emblematic of technological change more generally.[29] The industrial revolution in the mid-nineteenth century had introduced improvements in firepower, communications, and transportation that brought uncertainties for commanders on both sides. Civil War historian Mark Grimsley has written that this was indeed a revolution in military affairs of the most profound kind—one that neither the Union nor the Confederacy understood at the war's start:

> The American Civil War exemplifies a military revolution. . . . (It) combined the mass politics and passions of the Wars of the French Revolution with the technology, productive capacity and managerial style of an emergent industrial Revolution. The result, foreseen by Lincoln in December 1861, was a "remorseless revolutionary struggle" that beggared the capacity to imagine its sweep, duration and effects.[30]

Military leaders, initially inexperienced with telegraphy's effects on battlefields, soon understood that rapid, long-distance communication could expand the traditional battlefield. If managed well, it enabled the swift maneuvering and synchronization of large armies. Extended horizons created, at the same time, the need to know more about the enemy over larger distances. Military campaigns and marching armies might cover sixty miles or more. Thanks to improved long-distance communications, commanders, who were used to focusing on the fight at their front, could be surprised by the sudden appearance of enemy reinforcements from afar or interventions from superiors hundreds of miles in their rear. Certainly, President Lincoln and Jefferson Davis, distant from battle, nonetheless monitored, second-guessed, and reallocated resources in ways generals in the field could not have anticipated in early 1861.[31]

Ironically, more battlefield intelligence for presidents sometimes meant greater uncertainty for their generals. Whether presidents' new access to battlefield intelligence crippled a field commander or not depended on his leadership skills, the number of those engaged in the battle, and his relative capacity to stay informed. The technologies that most influenced a commander's sense of knowing were those that addressed his deepest uncertainties: the power of the enemy, his ability to maneuver, and his ability to operate in the fog of war. In the case of the land battles, such as those examined in the next chapter, the relevant technologies included rifled, repeating, and breech-loading weaponry; communications, including signaling and the telegraph; and transportation, including rails, aeronautics, and equitation.[32]

Uncertain Firepower: Weapons and Warriors

Although military officers on both sides of the US Civil War had similar experiences and training at the start, they had to cope with two new uncertainties: fluctuating supplies of untrained volunteers and the arms with which those men would be equipped. Regarding the first, both sides had difficulties estimating the size of armies because recruitment, attrition, and reinforcements swelled and depleted their ranks precipitously, and sometimes unpredictably, especially as the war progressed. Generals were, therefore, almost always uncertain about the number of effective troops in their own ranks, let alone in the ranks of the enemy. The Confederacy probably had the greatest problems retaining numbers. As the Civil War historian Edwin B. Coddington has written,

> The South understandably had greater difficulty in keeping the ranks filled because of its much smaller white population and the fact that many men had to stay home to work in the factories, run the railroads, and maintain the food producing farms. In the name of states' rights and constitutional freedom many Southern governors vigorously opposed the Confederate Conscription Act of 1862 and impaired its effectiveness.[33]

It has become legend that General Lee coped with his disadvantage by estimating the worth of one Confederate soldier to be much greater than a Union one. Whether or not Lee deemed the Confederate soldier to be superior or cared about imbalances in forces, it is nonetheless doubtful that he "ever learned the exact number of brigades in the Army of the Potomac or their identities. At least in his correspondence and reports he never gave any indications that he had such knowledge."[34] He often sought intelligence on the matter and sometimes leaned, for lack of an alternative, on noncontextualized newspaper reporting or leaks. For example, after the Battle of Chancellorsville, Lee got hold of a War Department report showing Union general Hooker's forces, the Army of the Potomac, at 159,000 troops. He estimated the Union to have, therefore, a two-to-one advantage over him as he moved north toward Gettysburg. But this intelligence was already wrong. The numbers for the Federals had been falling radically; thousands of men had left the service after Chancellorsville as the terms of their enlistments had expired.

Those commanders estimating relative numbers had to cope not only with uncertain enlistments and attrition, but also with the common problems of counting troops in motion.

> During these periods of marching, countermarching, halting and fighting, the old routine of camp disappeared, many extra new duties came into being, and the "curse of straggling" set in. . . . Under these circumstances the regimental morning reports were apt to be slurred over or suspended; even if they were made according to regulations they were liable to be untrustworthy as to the number of men who could be placed in line of battle. What falsified the records even more was the practice of leaving large numbers of stragglers on the rolls as present for duty because their officers expected them to catch up with the marching columns.[35]

Such problems, according to General Henry J. Hunt, a Union officer, left everyone in the Army of the Potomac "at sea" and prone to "absurd exaggeration." Counts were "pretty much guesswork" because they were padded, or based on muster rolls instead of those "present for duty." Even the latter could not be interpreted as describing numbers available for the front line, because essential services behind the lines still needed to be done.[36] Such problems of assessment of one's own side were bad enough, but they were worse when each side attempted to estimate the other, especially when both sides had been on the move. The balance of forces at Gettysburg, for example, would be more difficult to assess than those at Chancellorsville, where the armies had been facing each other for some time.

Second, estimates of troop effectiveness depended, in part, on the weapons they carried, and this too, seemed impossible to know and then to appreciate in terms of tactics and battlefield planning. Even before the outbreak of war, rifle-muskets, rifled muskets, and rifled artillery pieces seemed likely to require changes in battlefield tactics and strategy.[37] The technologies of rifling promised more accuracy, longer range, and marginally faster fire when employing the easy-loading Minié ball. The advent of the breechloader and repeater meant potential increases in the speed and safety of loading weapons. Indeed, some theorists at the time foresaw the end of Napoleonic-style frontal assaults because of the power that rifles and rifled artillery pieces could give to defenders on the battlefield. Some modern historians have taken up this argument to criticize generals who attempted to execute such assaults during the war.[38]

It was not that rifling was new; the technology of rifling barrels had been available for a long time. What was new was the quality of rifles and the potential, at least in the industrial North, to widen the distribution of rifled weapons to the infantry—not just selected sharpshooters. Breech-loading rifles and carbines allowed for faster and easier firing, especially from horseback. Over the course of the war from 1861 to 1865, rifles or rifled muskets would become standard issue for the average soldier; breechloaders and repeaters would not. Military historians have since called the American Civil War the world's first "rifle war." If so, it was also the last musket one.

So it should have been the case that officers on both sides of the conflict would demand intelligence on the distribution of rifled weapons on the battlefield so they could adjust tactics to firepower. There is little evidence, however, that they did. Indeed, the rifle seems to have had only minor effects on decision-making and tactics. One reason had to do with both sides' preoccupation with supply, not relative distribution. Rifle-muskets only gradually displaced standard smoothbore muskets as the war progressed, while old, second-, and third-class weapons persisted in inventories. The Smithfield 1855 rifle became standard issue in the North in 1863, but breechloaders remained rare, and repeaters were never adopted as standard issue. If enlisting soldiers in 1861 were issued weapons at all, they were often of low quality. Until 1863, and in some instances throughout the war, soldiers might be equipped with any of the following weapons, ranging in caliber from .52 to .71:

- American Springfield Rifle Musket (.58 caliber)
- English Enfield Rifle Musket (.58 and .57 caliber)
- French rifled muskets (.577 and .58 caliber)
- Smoothbore muskets; flintlock, converted to percussion, including old Harpers Ferry smoothbores that were known for their buck-and-ball cartridges. Some said these weapons killed at both ends.
- The Austrian rifle Model 1854; most had such a wicked kick that men refused to fire them.
- Belgian rifled muskets, converted from smoothbore; according to one veteran, some of these were so antique "They might have been used in the Napoleon wars."[39]
- Dresden and Suhl rifle-muskets (.58 caliber); "Language fails when attempting to describe the grotesque worthlessness of these so-called arms."[40]
- Old shotguns and flintlock muskets marked 1776, etc.[41] These ranged in caliber from .54 to .71.[42] Most were considered second- or third-class weapons.
- Breechloaders; .52 caliber Sharps and Merrill rifles

Such a mix of weapons meant unpredictable effectiveness and tactical uncertainties on both sides, at least from 1861 to 1863. The result was a scramble for the best weapons possible under the assumption that advantage would flow to whichever side was best at it. Lieutenant Colonel Edward Porter Alexander, chief of ordnance for General Lee in 1862, thought the battlefield situation with respect to armaments was definitely skewed in the Union's favor.

[Before Second Manassas] I was occupied in re-accumulating supplies of ammunition, & in improving our armament of small arms, & of artillery, by our captures in recent battles, as well as by all the arms we could make or get in through the blockade. The great point desired was to equip all our infantry with the rifle musket, calibre 58/100ths, instead of the old fashioned smooth bore round ball musket, calibre 69/100ths, which nine out of ten of our men had to start out with. The former has a range of 1000 yards, the latter of only about 200. The enemy were armed entirely with the former, & we were at a great disadvantage until we did the same.[43]

Given such incentives, intelligence about how rifles would be used by the enemy mattered less than correcting the imbalance in their distribution. According to E. P. Alexander, the Northern advantage in both rifle-muskets and artillery continued until Gettysburg. Meanwhile, scavenging off battlefields, and shortages in ammunition had, presumptively, the greatest impact on effectiveness.

A second reason that innovations in weaponry had little impact on battlefield tactics had to do with prewar military intelligence. Before 1861, a great debate had been underway in the United States and Europe over what industrial-scale rifling meant for tactics. Some Europeans argued that linear formations would be made obsolete; rifles and rifled artillery would render frontal Napoleonic-style assaults too risky to execute. Rifling, they argued, meant that correctly aimed and fired weapons would be accurate at longer ranges. The theoretical range of the 1855 Springfield rifle could be four hundred to six hundred yards.[44] The old smoothbore muskets had an effective range of two hundred yards or less. Rifled muskets with the Minié system, which used smaller, easy-to-load bullets that expanded into the rifling grooves when fired, also offered a higher rate of fire. British theorists disagreed with their European counterparts. They tended to be conservative in estimating the battlefield effects of rifling, and expected that the effectiveness of old linear tactics and formations would hold on modern battlefields.

Influential American theorists, listening to both sides, tended to agree with the British. Most apparently believed that change would be incremental based on observations made during the Crimean War. Small units of sharpshooters had roamed the battlefield, picking off the enemy. Defending sharpshooters had countered them from trenches in advance of the line. Registering the lessons, the American army field manual was slightly altered in 1855 to incorporate French notions of how light infantry training might absorb the enhanced capabilities of the rifle-musket. Jefferson Davis, who would later become president of the Confederacy, reported to Congress that "the rifle musket would change tactics by forcing an increased reliance on skirmishers."[45] But that, basically, was all.

The issue was not fully decided as the Union and Confederacy went to war in 1861. Most observers had foreseen the need for intensive training if the rifle was to be effectively employed at longer distances. Lieutenant Cadmus M. Wilcox of the Seventh US Infantry, made common cause with Horace William Shaler Cleveland, "a zealous advocate of rifles," who called for the formation of rifle clubs so all men of military age could learn how to shoot with them.[46] These men believed rifles would change tactics forever; it was only a matter of when officers would wake to the fact and claim the advantage for their own side.

Given this background, Civil War commanders on both sides probably *expected* changes in battlefield capabilities related to rifle-muskets and artillery, while *remaining uncertain* about how these changes would play out in practice for a "national army of ordinary citizens."[47] At least in the earliest months of the war, they soon got their answer:

> The bursting of shells, the shrieking of cannon balls, the crashing as they splintered the trees . . . would have filled the soul of a warrior with ecstasy. Not being a warrior but a plain citizen, I saw nothing especially entertaining in such a hubbub. . . . We lay as flat as flounders.[48]

Even if, as modern scholars have determined, the rifle-musket would not significantly change the overall effectiveness of troops, the soldiers marching to war in 1861 and the officers commanding them could not have known this fact. Officers, therefore, used formations, drills, and the linear tactics prescribed by their common field manuals. These manuals were based on the 1835 version penned by the aged General Winfield Scott that had been updated in 1855 by Lieutenant Colonel William J. Hardee. Hardee later joined the Confederacy, which employed the same approach.[49] Given that army manuals confirmed long-standing linear tactics, adding only an increased rate for the double-quick and quick-step march, it is not surprising that, in the absence of more intensive and general training with rifles, killing zones generally remained the same as in the era of the smoothbore, as modern scholars have established.[50] And since smokeless powder was yet to be invented, smoke on the battlefield kept visibility low and killing ranges short, even as the rate of fire and potential accuracy improved.

Thus, although a rifle-related revolution was generally expected, Napoleonic tactics persisted, and frontal assaults were not necessarily eschewed. Both sides, despite scanty intelligence on the capability of defenders, tried Napoleonic frontal assaults at Maryes Heights (December 13, 1862; Battle of Fredericksburg, VA; c. 6,300 Federal troops killed); Pickett's Charge (July 3, 1863, Gettysburg, PA; 1,123 Confederates killed, 4,019 wounded); and Cold Harbor, VA (June 1864; more than 7,000 Federal soldiers killed or wounded).[51] In fact, even if intelligence had overcome uncertainties to reveal that defenders had advantages in rifles in these cases, it would likely have changed little. The flaws in these attacks had much to do with failures in the line, failure of support, and other tactical errors. Most of the soldiers killed in these assaults died within the range of the older smoothbores.[52] It was not that Wilcox and others were wrong about the potential of rifles, but rifles hit battlefields before the citizen-soldier had the necessary training and officers had the necessary tactical guidance for exploiting their new capabilities in battle. Rifles, therefore, probably changed morale more than they changed unit effectiveness from 1861 to 1863.

The point is that, although both Federals and Confederates had uncertainties about how weapons and training might affect battlefields, their decisions reflected the conservatism of their shared training and intelligence from the Crimean War.[53] With both sides so conservatively inclined, neither exploited the opportunities offered by the new technologies or collected intelligence on whether the other would do so. Of course, that rifling made no difference to most battles does not mean it might not have done so with better intelligence and so better decision-making. In theory, uncertainties about troop effectiveness *should have* implicated tactics and driven intelligence requirements. As already mentioned, Wilcox and others had strongly advocated just such an approach. That generals during the Civil War mostly did not see the need was probably due to their common mindsets. It was not that they believed effectiveness did not matter; it was that effectiveness turned on many unquantifiable factors, such as smoke, weather, disease, and bravery. Specifics on weapons distribution, and training probably seemed just a part of this amorphous unknown and thus relatively inconsequential targets for intelligence collection. That both sides arrived at this conclusion nonetheless made both sides "right" only because they were equally disadvantaged.

That said, some exceptions proved the rule. A Federal scout thought it worth reporting to Hooker that he overheard a Confederate surgeon say that "not 10 percent of the rebels are hit below the shoulders," revealing a problem that better training might fix.[54] And General Hays, during the battle of Gettysburg, deliberately arranged his riflemen in such a way that their greater range and rate of fire could overcome Confederates assaulting Cemetery Ridge. But such reporting and tactics did not seem to affect decision-making, much less intelligence collection, at the level of the brigade or army.

In summary, innovations in weaponry raised three intelligence-related issues: whether and under what conditions the quality of weapons on both sides might make for advantages or vulnerabilities on the battlefield; whether or not opposing commanders were aware of these conditions; and how the enemy's ordnance policies might change relative capabilities over time. The first question seemed answered for both sides by the army field manuals issued in 1855, which agreed on the basics of linear tactics, formations, and drills. Without much ability to change such basics once the war began, most commanders considered the second issue—what the new weapons could *theoretically* do—at best a secondary matter for intelligence. And, regarding whether one side or the other would produce superior weapons over time, the Confederacy did not have the resources to compete, while the Union did, but did not take advantage of it. The Federal chief of ordnance, Brigadier General James W. Ripley, eschewed the potential advantages of innovation in favor of standardized technologies, rapid resupply, and steady approaches to training and doctrine—decisions that caused tensions between commanders and headquarters.

Unfortunately, such ordnance-related questions were often poorly framed, the answers hard to come by, and advantages lost. Officers, as well as infantrymen, marched to the early battles in a state of profound ignorance:

We went into the great conflict necessarily unprepared, like an amateur chessplayer who might attempt a championship match without a knowledge of the strategic openings of the game. Our soldiers as a rule did not even know how to shoot, as we understand marksmanship now. It took us at least a year from the opening of the war to learn how to fight. The Confederates were somewhat better prepared at the start, and so had the better of the game in the early period of the war. This lesson should never be forgotten.

In considering the lessons of the war, any one, whether strategist or not, who is thoroughly familiar with its history, must be impressed with the ignorance of the enemy's numbers, position and movements, to say nothing of his intentions, displayed by our officers in the first year of the war. . . . War, like chess, may be played blindfold, but in neither case is the game likely to be won *unless the player knows the enemy's position and moves.*[55]

So both armies muddled through the first year, forgoing potential advantages.[56] By 1863, the Confederacy was "tolerably well armed" and the Federals mostly had rifled weapons.[57] But the choices made in Washington, Richmond, or even the upper levels of command remained generally uninformed by weapons' effectiveness, hospital statistics, or the effects of training and readiness on morale. When, despite constant pressure from President Lincoln, the head of ordnance for the Federals refused to order mass production of repeaters, the impact was felt most by the infantryman. They pleaded for the more effective weapons they knew existed.[58] Soldiers lost confidence in their weapons and, acquiring their own arms from home, local theft, scavenging, or unauthorized purchases, made do with what they had. Commanders, levying few requirements for intelligence on how deployed infantry were equipped and the implications of it, instead focused on counting the number of warm bodies and artillery pieces.[59]

Wires and Rails

One of the greatest military uncertainties on both sides at the start of the war concerned communications. The Crimean War (1853–56), in particular, had alerted most militaries to the likely impact of the electric telegraph, a relatively new invention, on strategic chains of command.[60] The British got busy developing undersea and underground wires that would soon spread throughout the empire. Most generals, including St Arnaud, Napoleon III's commander in the Crimea, were wary of linking battlefields to civilian decision-makers in government. Yet few official observers, including Americans such as the future Union general George B. McClellan, envisioned how critical the telegraph would become for the outcome of battles themselves. Between 1861 and 1865, the Federals' US Military Telegraph laid "15,389 miles of lines . . . with a total expenditure of $3,219,400."[61] War correspondents, reporting back using the telegraph, would make battlefields visible to generals, but also to their enemies and spies.

The communications revolution that would shock mid-century warfare was foreseeable, but the US military did not learn fast enough to prepare for it. One reason had to do with weak links between civilian innovation and the military profession. The communications revolution had begun in the 1820s and 1830s when an American scientist, Joseph Henry, working with electrical conductors, noticed relationships between changes in current, voltage, and the magnetic field generated around them.[62] Samuel Morse took these discoveries further, eventually patenting the electromagnetic telegraph. By the end of 1844, the practical implications of such research had become difficult to miss. That year, Morse had installed a complete electric telegraph line running from Pratt Street Station in Baltimore to the Supreme Court Chamber in Washington, DC. Morse sent his first message along it on 11 May, using a code of long and short bursts representing each letter of the alphabet.[63]

Although the military proved slow to appreciate the implications of Morse's work, the private sector was not. Entrepreneurs saw the telegraph as a way to direct traffic on railways and to facilitate broader, faster communications for businesses across the expanding country. Civilian telegraphers worked at varying speeds depending on their level of expertise, but railroad telegraphers soon became the best among them because the safety of trains depended on their skill. The United States had twelve thousand miles of telegraph lines by 1850 and perhaps sixty thousand by 1861.[64] Three great telegraph corporations existed at the outbreak of the war and connected most cities: American Telegraph, Western Union, and Southwestern Telegraph. (The exception was the Far West, where connection to San Francisco would take until the winter of 1861–62.) American Telegraph lines, which ran from east of the Hudson River and along the coast, met the Southwestern Telegraph lines at Chattanooga, Tennessee, Mobile, Alabama, and New Orleans. Southwestern Telegraph, headquartered in Louisville, Kentucky, was otherwise dominant in the South.[65] This telegraphic network, cooperatively run until 1861 by these few mammoth companies (and a few less consequential ones), soon became militarized, broken-up, enlarged, and sabotaged as both the Union and Confederacy awoke—albeit unevenly—to the need for control of intelligence and communications.

In fact, the situation was extraordinary. A huge, nationwide, segmented, privately owned infrastructure was positioned to affect the survival of Washington, the command and organization of mass armies, the role of cavalry and journalists, and civil-military relations. What remained to resolve was the question of control of the system's individual parts. Although less rich than the North in telegraph lines, the South's wires were also less exposed than Washington's were. At the time of First Manassas, the Confederates had working lines from Manassas to Richmond along the Orange and Alexandria lines, and working rails west from Manassas to Front Royal through Delaplane, at the foot of the Blue Ridge and just a few miles south of Ashby's Gap. Where wires could not reach, mounted couriers informed generals needing intelligence for coordinating actions in the Piedmont and the Shenandoah Valley. Shortly after his inauguration, Confederate president Jefferson Davis took advantage of the opportunities arising from the South's access to Northern communications. As early as February 21, he began to use American Telegraph lines to recruit Federal officials, such as signalmen, congressmen, and clerks, to the Southern cause—an activity that continued until late April. The wires from Richmond north to Washington and beyond remained open "regardless of how inimical to Northern interests was the content of what passed over them."[66] The Federals were not monitoring these lines for any intelligence windfall; they were simply not quick enough to realize their communications' vulnerabilities or the opportunities offered by their access to Confederate communications.[67]

The Federals' first wake-up call came within three days of the attack on Fort Sumter (April 12, 1861) when Washington telegraphed Lincoln's call for the mustering of seventy-five thousand troops in defense of the city over the same American Telegraph lines Richmond was using and apparently monitoring. Secessionists immediately began disrupting and damaging the railways running through Maryland to the North. Then, on 19 April, the South captured Harpers Ferry, Virginia, costing the Federals all communications through that point on the Baltimore and Ohio Railroad. This move forced all that traffic to transit through Maryland. Rebel mobs in Baltimore rioted, burned railroad bridges, kidnapped telegraphers, and busted up telegraphic lines. After 21 April, when telegraphic lines north of Baltimore were cut, Washington had to resort to couriers for communications beyond that city. Effectively isolated between two rebellious, slave-owning states, the Union was now blinded, vulnerable to decapitation, and at last fully awake to the situation. Federal troops took over the Washington telegraph office on 19 April and began official oversight of the company's operations—seven days after the Fort Sumter attack. The War Department still kept the lines to Richmond open, but prohibited American Telegraph operators from communicating with their colleagues south of the city and instituted censorship of all message traffic.[68]

Secretary of War Simon Cameron urgently appealed to railroad executives in Pennsylvania to come to Washington to restore communications to the north of the city. Thomas A. Scott and his junior colleague, Andrew Carnegie, agreed and by April 27 had accomplished the task.[69] Their handpicked men reconstituted the northern rail and telegraph lines, erected loops connecting the White House, War Department, and Congress, and extended them to military encampments surrounding the city for up to twelve miles in every direction. Scott also called in four telegraph operators from the Pennsylvania Railroad and stationed them at the War Department, Navy Yard, and Baltimore and Ohio Railroad depot, which served as US Army headquarters at the time.

So began the civilian core of what would become the US Military Telegraph Corps—a civilian component within the War Department. Despite this public-private partnership, however, telegraphic communications remained disorganized and confused. One reason had to do with money. According to the report of a telegrapher at the time, one entrepreneur financed all the changes in telegraphy around Washington, DC, that April and beyond: E. S. Sanford, President of American Telegraph. Sanford, "more than any other person," was owed "a debt of gratitude for furnishing nearly all the funds and supplies used by the corps in that department *for a period of seven months*."[70] Beyond that, resources were uncertain.

A second reason for confusion related to operational planning. Although railroad, telegraph, and government officials had saved Federal communications that April, their operations were not part of an agreed strategy. Several eminent civilian telegraphers had been brought to Washington, and some redeployed to critical commands, but these men were not part of the military chain of command and knew little about the needs of generals in the field. They formed an internal, exclusive network for decision-making on telegraphic priorities. Officers with the army's Signal Corps, for example, were instructed not to interfere with the network—a directive that would lead to major complications. On 20 May, Federal officials, realizing the potential importance of the telegraphic dispatches they had seized, belatedly began to read the Richmond traffic. Whatever advantage they might have foreseen, however, quickly disappeared. On 21 or 22 May a clutch of the highest officials of the American Telegraph Company decided to cut the lines from Washington to Richmond, leaving the Confederate line from Richmond to Alexandria, unaffected. The American Telegraph executives had acted independently, meeting and conferring by themselves on Long Bridge between Washington and Virginia.[71] The Federals did not cut the Alexandria line until they captured that city on 24 May.

The confused state of communications, intelligence, and decision-making would profoundly affect strategy and tactics during the first months of the war. In particular, the lack of prewar scientific and technological intelligence had practical and operational consequences for the terrain of uncertainty in 1861. Neither the military nor the civilians in the War Department were sufficiently in control to process the problem, let alone fix it. The Baltimore riots and loss of Harpers Ferry had driven home the Union's need for secure communications and private-sector expertise. Yet one month later, no one seemed sure who was, or should be, in charge for the purposes of strategic and operational planning. Decision-makers taking part in Federal war councils could not, and did not, take full account of the logistical challenges attending their options, such as the time required to deploy wires or the effects of redistributing cavalry on the relative speed of communications among commanders. Thus, as Irvin McDowell marched his Federal army toward Bull Run in the spring of 1861, telegraph lines failed to follow him to the battlefield, which was a mere thirty-five miles south from the capital. They bridged the Potomac but ended at least ten miles short, requiring scarce mounted couriers to complete the connection.[72] Perhaps more important: no reliable telegraph line or courier system linked Federal troops in the Shenandoah Valley with those at Bull Run. This gap in coverage south of the capital prevented the timely synchronization of Federal forces that would directly affect the outcome of that battle.

Although communications for the Federals were greatly improved by the establishment of the public-private partnership in telecommunications, it was born strained and remained so as the war progressed. The government's creation of the United States Military Telegraph (USMT), a quasi-civilian enterprise run by the War Department, meant that communications would seem an arcane aspect of war-fighting for some time to come. The USMT used the railroad's Morse coding system and transposition ciphers, which officers in the field could not interpret.[73] Generals and their staff became frustrated with communicators outside the chain of command and with War Department decisions that, uncoordinated with commanders in the field, threatened to affect the outcome of battles. Civilian telegraphers became frustrated with their noncombat status, their overlooked vulnerabilities, lack of rights as noncombatants when captured, and their lack of access to the councils of war despite their importance to battlefield outcomes.

This tension between officers and telegraphers became increasingly important over time. The Federals' first and limited expansion of telegraph lines evolved into a major effort extending to all theaters of war. "Mules and spools" linked chains of command, providing connectivity also between battlefields and the White House. Military communications and intercepts eventually took priority over all other civilian uses of telegraphic lines, not just those associated with railroads. "It developed from sheer necessity, a necessity so urgent that legal requirements were disregarded, to the manifest service of the Union. Its importance was so self-evident that no man, it is believed, ever ventured to impugn its legitimacy."[74]

Federal rails and telegraph, strung across the North, provided a relatively secure communications backbone for far-flung Union armies, tethered to it by thousands of miles of temporary wires. The investment in wire and connectivity was huge, and the South struggled to compete with it. The North's broad, interconnected, and flexible infrastructure provided a strategic advantage that would play an important role as the Union closed in on the Confederacy from both sides, squeezing its defenders in coordinated actions across a broad front.

Such strategic advantages for the North, important though they were, did not necessarily dictate the outcome of individual battles, especially during the early years of the war when the USMT and the US Army Signal Corps engaged in a debilitating rivalry. The Signal Corps was the brainchild of Albert Myer, who had developed a secret system for encoding communications by flag in the 1850s. His prewar pursuit of funding for his Army Signals Service had led him to reveal his secret techniques for signals intelligence to his deputy, Edward Porter Alexander. Unfortunately for Myer, Alexander joined the Confederacy in early 1861 and quickly established its signals service using Myer's techniques. Meanwhile Myer, a military man who appreciated the importance of connecting the battlefield to command centers, recognized the disarray in Washington and launched an ambitious effort to reorganize all military signaling, including by telegraph and from balloons. Myer's earliest efforts to innovate and integrate army communications foundered. As troops marched toward Bull Run in 1861, he was promoting the utility of balloons and struggling to untangle one as he transported it to the front. In contrast, his Confederate protégé's simple use of telegraphic signaling became part of Richmond's military command structure and gave Confederate general P. G. T. Beauregard a distinct advantage in the Battle of First Manassas.[75]

In the aftermath of that rout, bureaucratic rivalry between the fast-developing USMT and Myer's Army Signal Corps heated up. Myer's early failures reflected not just ill-timed ambition, but also the disarray in civil-military decision-making. Union general George B. McClellan, who had used telegraphy during his operations in West Virginia and Ohio, took Myer under his wing when appointed to replace McDowell in Washington. The USMT, in the meantime, had no clear chief for the first seven months of the war. This gap, perhaps reflecting expectations of a short war, contributed to the inconsistent development of battlefield telegraphy and, therefore, intelligence dissemination.[76] For example, Myer got enough traction in the army to deploy his relatively simple and accessible alternative to the Morse and Stager system, threatening to derail the nascent USMT.

The Signal Corps eventually attempted takeover of the USMT, causing rival, incompatible technologies to be employed on the same battlefield. Bureaucratic disputes led to fights over technology, with railroad operators advocating their difficult but trusted Morse codes, and Myer's Federal Signal Corps advocating an underpowered system that was more usable by the common soldier. This friction caused serious problems for telegraphers trying to support troops at Chancellorsville.[77] It would cause General Hooker to lose touch with his key commander, General John Sedgwick, as Hooker sought to squeeze Lee between their two positions. His competing telegraphic lines used two different security protocols and types of equipment that made traffic unpredictable, disorderly, and difficult to repair. Hooker, accustomed to instantaneous telegraphic intelligence at his headquarters, could not find out what was happening on his flanks in the midst of battle.

The next chapter examines more closely whether or not Myer's organizational ambitions cost decision advantage in early battles. It already seems apparent, however, that despite the Union's opening advantages in communications infrastructure and resources, early failures in intelligence policy undermined those advantages. Partly as a result of the communications snafus at Chancellorsville, the Union backed the Morse partisans, its Signal Corps handled only flag, rocket, and similar communications, and balloons were abandoned for the rest of the war.

In sharp contrast with the North, the South's advantage lay in its relative poverty and its scrappiness. Richmond managed rudimentary telegraphy and signals under one military organization throughout the war. There were no resources or deep pockets to fund rival start-ups. Whereas the better-equipped and better-funded Union forces suffered divisions among Federal telegraphers at least until the end of the Battle of Chancellorsville, the less endowed Confederacy improvised with less. Its Signal and Secret Service Bureau, run by Major William Norris, developed an extensive network of communications among agents, scouts, and saboteurs using both the telegraph, where feasible, and an underground system of safe houses and couriers reaching as far as Canada. This line of communication was used for everything from secret orders for assassination to transporting newspapers. Federal counterintelligence officers were hard-pressed to keep up. Defending or locating wires in civilian territory was one thing, but manhunts for couriers were another.

The Federals faced other issues as well. Although their better access to raw materials such as copper wire, batteries, and the like made the extension of telegraph lines over long distances far more feasible than it was for the Confederacy, the effort to do so was costly in more than dollars. Federals were often forced to use cavalry to extend and then protect these wires. Since copper wires were draped over fence posts, bushes, and tree branches for more miles, the Federals had a relative vulnerability in both secure communications and cavalry readiness for other duties. When commanders decided to pull scarce cavalry off telegraphic security or courier duties for scouting or screening, they sometimes failed to understand the risks they were taking regarding their own communications.

Without cavalry support, telegraphers' long lines were vulnerable, and so was the intelligence those lines carried. Often, telegraph lines fell short of where a message had to go. In such cases, cavalrymen were needed for delivery. Telegraphers sometimes had to become couriers themselves when cavalry were assigned other duties, leaving their stations undermanned and making themselves vulnerable to capture. The situation created strains on the Union side because civilian telegraphers were critical providers of military intelligence but disconnected from the chain of command and, therefore, from critical decision-making concerning logistics. When telegraphers complained about deficient security, gaps in pickets, or inefficient cavalry operations, they created tensions with the very commanders they sought to support.[78] Then too, when Federal forces were in retreat, civilian telegraphers and their equipment were sometimes overlooked or left behind. If captured, these civilians were usually not paroled because they were not in uniform. With many telegraphers dying in Confederate prisons, shortages in communicators became a particular battlefield problem for the North, which had come to rely on their skills but had no control over their recruitment, training, or deployment. Confederate telegraphers, on the other hand, were regular army and treated as such if captured.

Confederate commanders initially found the trade-off between communications, raids, and scouting difficult but not crippling. Certainly, General Edward Porter Alexander's memoirs recount the attentiveness with which Jefferson Davis set up the Signal Corps and supported telegraphy more generally. Yet when the Confederate cavalry operated on Northern soil—with the terrain of uncertainty tipped against them—commanders had to assess more carefully the trade-offs among couriering intelligence, raiding, screening, and patrolling. Confederate officers did not initially appreciate the importance of centralized management in these regards, and the learning was costly. In one famous example during the prelude to Gettysburg, Lee authorized General Stuart's cavalry to sweep north, a ride they used to sabotage railcars, capture telegraphers, and burn storage depots. The cost was grave, however. Lee lost situational awareness during his march north on enemy soil. Stuart, long criticized for this extended ride, was not solely at fault; the cavalry he left to screen Lee's march performed poorly as collectors of intelligence on the Federals—a mission that they reportedly did not understand they had. Stuart did at least send one dispatch alerting Lee that the Federals were on his heels, but the message, sent by courier, apparently never arrived.[79] Lee's cavalry orders, at least in this case, though operationally successful as narrowly construed, may have hurt Meade less than they hurt Lee.

The early failure to appreciate how the telegraph and the use of cavalry would affect civil-military communications, intelligence, and theater-wide military strategy did not last. In particular, the Federals learned to overcome Confederate advantages in communications on their home soil as Union cavalry and telegraphers became more adept at laying wires, hiding them, and threatening, recruiting, and bribing locals to keep them intact.[80] Gathering intelligence on where the enemy's assets were and how vulnerable they might be became a war within the larger war. Leaving enemy communications intact for intelligence exploitation was only one of several trade-offs commanders learned to consider when conducting intelligence operations. The "intelligence war" required a strategy too—one that fit with a commander's larger ends. Counterintelligence operations would backfire, for example, if cavalry raids to destroy enemy telegraph lines undermined the ability to learn enemy intentions or to hijack those communications systems for one's own purposes. Absent such a strategy, cavalrymen found themselves torn between fighting, blinding, and learning.

Finally, one of the most consequential effects of telegraphy for both sides had to do with the impact of the national press on war. The combination of the printing press, the telegraph, and rails made it possible for locals to get timely national news of the war, especially in the North. Although such connectivity between governors and the battlefield had been observed during the Crimean War, the implications became more apparent during the four years of fighting in America. Reporters traveled with the troops and penned stories on strategy, battlefield preparations, and encampments. Even reporters sympathetic to the Federal cause were eager to get scoops and to report them in newspapers that readily found their way south. The result was a sudden rush of public information on the war, including particulars on the morale, plans, and locations of the troops that made for good intelligence for the enemy. With the news industry particularly strong in Northern states, such open-source intelligence was particularly advantageous for the South.

Confederate generals were happy to acquire this windfall; Federal officers railed against it. Although civilian officials also despaired over the leakage of sensitive information, they could not fathom how to staunch the flow since they relied on newspapers to whip up public support for the Union's cause. Some generals, such as General William Tecumseh Sherman, prohibited journalists from marching with the troops. General Joseph Hooker tried threatening incarceration. Newsmen responded by encoding their telegrams so their editors could be kept apprised of Hooker's next move. Perhaps the most often cited words on the subject come from General Sherman, who, suffering from leaks of precious information to the South, admitted he wished he could get rid of every newsman in the world, although this would mean he'd have to "suffer reports from Hell before breakfast."[81] Of course, both sides eventually learned to use the press by planting stories intended to deceive the other side.

Equitation

Westward expansion in wires and rails had contributed to another significant development in military affairs: the revival of cavalry operations. As the US population shifted westward in the decades before the war, settlements pressed against or overlapped with Native American territory, generating friction and open conflict. So, with miserly contributions from Congress, a small cavalry, dominated by Southerners, began to operate largely in the west. No one at West Point had developed, however, a useful modern concept of cavalry operations. Romanticism clung to the strength of "spurs and sabre"—the Napoleonic idea of a cavalry charge. This antiquated notion, unsuited to most Civil War operations in the heavily wooded eastern theater of war, prevented most Union commanders from seeing their deficiencies in cavalry at the time of First Manassas.[82]

The problem was not just a lack of theory for cavalry operations with weapons more modern than the sabre; commanders had no concept of joint operations at all. They did not fully appreciate that the mid-century revival of scouting, screening, reconnaissance, and special operations so applicable to prewar conflicts in the west meant horses would become increasingly important "platforms" for mobile intelligence collection, security, and communications as well as combat alongside infantry operations in the east.

Although both sides suffered from their lack of vision, the Confederate cavalry began with some advantages. For example, the best horses and most experienced mounted shooters were in the South, although few commanders on either side fully understood the implications.[83] The South had sustained a relatively rural, agrarian economy in the decades before the war, whereas the North had urbanized. From 1800 to 1860, agriculture had claimed a steady 80 percent of the South's workforce, while the North's had dropped from 70 to 40 percent.[84] In the South, gentlemen bred horses, rode and raced their finest stock, and often hunted on horseback. Indeed, hunting was a widespread feature of Southern life that involved stealth, reconnaissance, speed, agility, and teamwork; it required well-trained mounts with endurance and jumping skills. Southerners' relatively superior knowledge of horses and horsemanship thus came naturally. They often came to war with their own mounts and initially had handier use of them.

Over time, however, both sides learned from experience, and built cavalries of commensurate skills. The North achieved rough equivalence with the Confederacy by the time of Virginia's great cavalry battle at Brandy Station in 1863.[85] By the end of that year, both sides were able to scout large land armies and to employ mounted partisan rangers, such as John Mosby's Virginia battalion or Union colonel Ulric Dahlgren's operatives, for purposes of intelligence-enabled raiding and surprise. They investigated and perfected equipment to help with the comfort and endurance of both horse and rider. One example was the McClellan saddle, designed by the aforementioned George B. McClellan, who led Union troops during the war. Known for his attention to readiness and logistics, he participated in a prewar military commission sent to Europe to gather intelligence on developments, including engineering, cavalry, and field equipment. As a result of this work, he designed a new saddle for the US Army that entered its stockpile in 1859 and was soon copied by the Confederate cavalry.

The Confederacy's overall advantages in horses and equitation skills nonetheless caused serious problems for the Union in the opening years of the Civil War—problems that modern historians sometimes treat as marginal if not romantic. Yet military officers fighting at Chancellorsville or Gettysburg would have regarded such condescension as naive. By then, they knew horses to be more than the heart of the fighting cavalry; they were essential to the emplacement and transportation of artillery, critical to the timely distribution of telegraphic wire, and crucial vehicles for the collection and communication of intelligence. Just as modern militaries require armored cavalry, including vehicles enrobed in sensors and communication and navigational equipment, the cavalrymen of the nineteenth century needed advantages in their mounts: durability, thriftiness, speed, intelligence, and training.[86] Cavalry horses provided the platforms for "all terrain" reconnaissance, screening, security, communications, and operational mobility. Speed enabled clandestine operations from raiding behind battle lines to extending, securing, and striking against lines of communication. The training, equipping, husbandry, and supply of horses were critical, therefore, to intelligence, command, and the outcome of battles.[87]

Given the importance of the warhorse, it is not surprising that both sides invested in getting the best stock they could; what is surprising is how many horses were lost, often through negligence and wasteful practices. Of a nation of five million horses in 1861, two million or more had died by its end. Supply and quality of stock were constant uncertainty, especially in the North during the first years of war and later for both sides.[88] Initially, the Federals did not have enough saddle horses for cavalry operations.[89] The Union's homegrown equines tended to be relatively "cold-blooded" or draft-like in appearance, which made them suitable for hitching to wagons or artillery but less so for speed or reconnaissance work.[90] In contrast, Southerners valued their Thoroughbred racing stock most highly and had long bred them for export. Although their purebreds were often too high-strung for the battlefield, the average grade (mixed breed) horse in the South tended to have some Thoroughbred blood, making them particularly suited to cavalry operations such as reconnaissance, raiding, screening, and mounted warfare.[91]

Thus, while both sides had problems requisitioning horses at the start of the war, the Union felt the problem more acutely. Northerners, who had generally imported their saddle horses from Southern states, experienced in 1861 the shock of interrupted supply. The Federals could not simply breed suitable cavalry horses to improve supply. Horses take several years to mature and even then are generally "green"—that is, unaccustomed to the requirements of harness or rider—until at least three years old. This meant that Union forces had to go to war with what stock they had, could requisition, or managed to buy or steal from locals. The quality was not always high—at least for the steady, thrifty, and fast qualities so prized by the military.

> When the Civil War erupted, Union Army military animal purchases were divided into two areas. The Quartermaster General's office procured draft horses and mules while the Cavalry Bureau purchased cavalry mounts. Both branches utilized the contractor system. Many difficulties were encountered in purchasing and the care of military animals. There was a lack of knowledge of the use and maintenance of animals by the troops, and it was reflected in the loss of horses due to malnutrition, disease, neglect or overuse. The situation became so bad that special inspectors were appointed and given wide latitude to correct problems. Orders were even issued authorizing transfer of cavalry officers and whole cavalry commands, to the infantry if the men were found neglecting their animals.[92]

The Union's disadvantages went still further: Many early Federal recruits were relatively inexperienced in the saddle, and so, unfamiliar with cross-country riding, jumping, river-crossing, and field reconnaissance.[93] Few had learned how to maintain a horse, let alone recognize and resolve health and training issues. Especially for the city-born shopkeeper, lawyer, or teacher, horse husbandry had been the purview of stable boys, not gentlemen:

> Once they climbed into the saddle, and it became obvious how powerful these alien creatures really were, the soldiers' attitudes went from one of disdain to one of fear ... men as frightened of the horses and riding as they were of the enemy. "The wild fumbling after mane or saddle strap, the terror depicted on some faces when the commands 'trot' or 'gallop' were given, are a lasting source of amusement," one observer noted.[94]

The general inexperience of the Northern recruit meant that, during early battles, officers had to deal with poor control or loss of artillery, terrorized mounts unable to courier messages, and hobbled reconnaissance capabilities. Although the Union developed a system for acquiring and distributing horses by lots, the best-bred ones went to commanding generals, while enlisted men received the more unsuitable or "green" mounts. One cavalryman training recruits described the resulting "circus" as more due to man than beast: "Many of the [men] have never bridled a horse nor touched a saddle."[95]

The Union's early problems with its most crucial "platforms" for war-fighting, communications, and reconnaissance manifested almost immediately. The Federal decision to march toward Manassas on 1 July 1861, was not executed until the sixteenth because the Union general-in-chief, Winfield Scott, and the commanding general, Irvin McDowell, were "waiting for horses."[96] Worse, prior to the battle, Scott forced General Patterson to give his regular cavalry to McDowell, despite giving Patterson the crucial mission of tracking Confederate general Joe Johnston's whereabouts in the Shenandoah Valley. Stripped of his "eyes and ears," much as General Lee would be before Gettysburg, Patterson had to rely for reconnaissance on a small number of inexperienced Pennsylvania cavalrymen. Scott, who seems to have had no concept of cavalry operations, failed to anticipate the degree to which his decision would blind Patterson as the Confederates moved to concentrate their forces. In contrast, Confederate general Johnston's cavalry reconnoitered, sent and received messages to Manassas and Richmond, and screened his movements.

The Southern soldier's connection to horses and mules was so deeply cultural and connected to known military needs that soldiers often sacrificed their own well-being for that of their mounts. In February 1863, before the Battle of Chancellorsville, Lee wrote to his daughter Mary that his army was "up to our knees in mud and what is worse short on rations for men & beasts. This keeps me miserable. I am willing to starve myself, but cannot bear my men or horses to be pinched. I fear many of the latter will die."[97] Lee's seemingly sentimental musing masked hardheaded calculation: He counted on his cavalry for reconnaissance and surprise attack and would take risks to preserve these capabilities. In a bold move before the Battle of Chancellorsville, Lee dispersed his horses to gain forage. By this time in the war, however, the North fully realized the worth of good horseflesh too. President Lincoln had a few choice words to say after Confederate John Mosby went through Union lines to capture a sleeping General Edwin Henry Stoughton, several of his staff, and, perhaps most importantly, their mounts. Lincoln complained that while he could "make a much better Brigadier in five minutes . . . the horses cost a hundred and twenty-five dollars a piece."[98] The joke had a point everyone at that point understood. Horses were the indispensable platforms of the war. The Union eventually instituted a remount program for breeding superior cavalry stock that lasted through WWII.

Over time, the opening disparities between Union and Confederate horses and horsemanship declined. Federals soon realized they were compromising their horses through ignorant practices, so worked to change them. Confederates suffered losses of forage on land ravaged by war, so struggled to maintain the quality and readiness of their mounts.[99] And, if Southern troops came to the war as, in general, better horsemen than their Northern counterparts, the Union probably overcame this advantage by 1863, when they held their own at the battle of Brandy Station and then attempted to cut Confederate lines of communication with Richmond.[100]

Balloons

If the South initially excelled at communications, reconnaissance, and raiding on horseback, the North had an early edge in a different form of mobile reconnaissance platform: balloons. Although some historians have discounted the importance of aerial reconnaissance to the outcome of Civil War battles, soldiers at the time debated the issue.[101] What seems certain is that balloons generated uncertainty; whether or not that uncertainty mattered, especially during the Battles of First Manassas and Chancellorsville, is a topic for the next chapter.

In fact, neither army could be sure at the time that balloons *would not* be decisive. Former Confederate signals officer Edward Porter Alexander said in his recollections on the war that he believed the Federals underappreciated aerial reconnaissance.[102]

> The very knowledge by the enemy of one's use of balloons is demoralizing, & leads them, in all their movements, to roundabout roads and night marches which are often very hampering. But the observers in the balloons should

be trained staff officers, not the ignorant class of ordinary balloonists, which
I think were generally in charge of the Federal balloons.[103]

Alexander had served briefly as a Confederate balloonist and thought the
platform's capabilities were unmatched, provided its user was properly trained.
In his view, even if the positive intelligence they provided seemed minimal, the
disruption Federal balloons caused the Confederacy should have made them
worth the expense. The Federals, however, came to a different conclusion. The
Signal Corps's wigwag, or flag-signaling, system using towers and high ground
took over the balloons' reconnaissance mission after Chancellorsville. Land-
based signal stations operated at substantially less cost and logistical trouble.[104]

Ballooning was hardly a settled art in 1861, and its military potential was unknown. It was only by the middle of the nineteenth century that "aeronautics" had
come into its own as a professional occupation.[105] Prior to this, American ballooning had been a curiosity largely confined to circuses and backyard hobbyists.
Yet, with the scientific experiments of men such as John Wise, Thaddeus Lowe,
and John La Mountain, ballooning with hydrogen gas and the exploitation of
high-altitude wind currents became feasible. By mid-century, ballooning had
become a fad. Financiers had even begun to back the planning and execution of
transatlantic voyages.

Thaddeus Lowe, one of the most ambitious of these early aeronauts, set the
prewar record for the largest craft designed for transatlantic travel. Built in July
1859, Lowe's giant balloon was christened *The City of New York* and reached over
200 feet tall. Its envelope had a diameter of 160 feet, a capacity of about 726,000
cubic feet of hydrogen gas, and a capability to lift over twenty-two tons. Lowe
attached his monstrosity to a thirty-foot-long lifeboat in case an emergency
landing might be required while flying above the Atlantic Ocean. The lifeboat
was equipped with a paddle wheel driven by a steam engine designed by John
Ericsson, the same man who designed the navy's first ironclad, *Monitor*, which
was to see use during the Civil War.[106]

Before the war, the hunger for aerial flight was mostly felt and satiated in the
northern industrial states. Lowe built his transcontinental airship in Hoboken,
New Jersey, where he could employ teams of seamstresses and thousands of
yards of imported Chinese silk. Lowe, La Mountain, Wise, and Lowe's other
competitors found financiers for their projects in the industrial cities of the
Northeast, though their travels sometimes took them over southern states,
alerting the South to the new technology and prompting interest there. Wise
and La Mountain's record-breaking, long-distance balloon flight was launched
in St. Louis, Missouri, on 1 July 1859, and finished on the eastern shores of Lake
Ontario the next day—an almost 804-mile journey lasting less than twenty-
four hours.

As the storm clouds of war gathered, Lowe took visiting Japanese officials aloft and publicized his balloons widely in the press. He demonstrated the eastern flow of the high-altitude jet stream and the westward flow of currents at lower altitudes with a voyage of his monster ship, renamed *The Great Western*, that started in Pennsylvania and came back to nearly the same point.[107] In April 1861, Lowe's longest untethered ascent floated him eastward from Cincinnati, Ohio, to rural South Carolina, where he landed among suspicious locals who almost took his life. Shots had already been fired at Fort Sumter, and South Carolina had just seceded from the Union.[108]

The potential for balloon aviation was thus widely recognized in 1861 and offered, it seemed, the new "high ground" in war (Figure 5.1). Despite these

Figure 5.1 Mathew Brady, *Professor Lowe's Military Balloon Near Gaines Mill, Virginia*, photographed 1 June 1862, showing inflation of the balloon *Intrepid* to reconnoiter the Battle of Fair Oaks; Lowe is standing to the right of the balloon and not visible in this image.

Source: Photo courtesy of the Library of Congress.

inklings of the advantage that might be gained, however, there was also plenty of uncertainty and even opposition in high places. General-in-Chief Winfield Scott was more than skeptical; he was hostile. During the Mexican-American War, one aeronaut had pestered him to use airships for aerial bombardment—something he had regarded then as preposterous.[109] Scott's initial judgment about the emerging technology became a mindset that persisted into the early years of the Civil War.

Scott's view was not without justification, even as late as 1861. Operators hawked their technologies around Washington, but they failed in one military-related launch after another. Part of the problem was adapting balloons to military intelligence. Operators often were good at flying, but did not know what to look for on a battlefield. Although launching a balloon might offer high ground for observation, tethered balloons alerted the enemy to one's position. Operators figured out ways to use the telegraph to report their findings; they also tried secrecy by doing ascents at dusk, although late summer thunderstorms put such flights at risk.

Other problems related to timely inflation and the cumbersome equipment needed to accomplish it. It took patience and a lot of equipment to inflate a balloon, lift an observer into the sky, and then determine the results. City gas could be used, but then the balloon had to be inflated in one place and transported to a point within range of the battlefield. The apparatus for inflating balloons away from cities was unwieldy and the requisite iron shavings expensive. Material to keep one balloon inflated day and night for two months required about one hundred containers of sulfuric acid, weighing about sixteen thousand pounds, and twenty barrels of iron turnings, weighing about ten thousand pounds. These materials were combined in heavy equipment to generate the gas required for inflating the balloons, which had to be towed along as the army marched.[110] In sum, the collection system's benefits had to be weighed against its costs, and the latter seemed relatively high, while the former remained unproved.

Military men were losing faith, but the Northern aeronauts, backed by the head of the Smithsonian Institution, urged persistence in resolving the problems of balloon flight in war.[111] Lowe made the case that balloon reconnaissance would be worth the expense and swore, if the army were to agree to it, that the South could not follow suit because there were no knowledgeable balloonists south of the Mason-Dixon line. Lowe even demonstrated how balloons could direct artillery fire by assessing and signaling damage from the air.

Eventually, the Federal army bought the proponents' arguments. A new balloon corps was established, initially under the Corps of Topographical Engineers. This aeronautical corps was linked, in turn, to the military telegraph to speed communications. Later, its management was transferred to the Signal Corps.[112]

The Union Navy purchased a coal barge and modified her by flattening her deck and adding one of Lowe's hydrogen generators. On 11 November 1861, it served as a launch platform for that service's first observational balloons—perhaps the beginning of naval aviation.[113]

Lowe may have been correct in describing the advantages—albeit limited—that aeronautics could deliver during the early days of the war; but he was wrong about the Confederacy's ineptitude. Richmond created a balloon corps as well—reportedly using donated silk dresses for the envelopes. At least one Confederate officer believed that balloons gave the side using them an advantage, because the surveillance demoralized opposing troops and forced them to march at night or undercover if they hoped to achieve surprise. As mentioned earlier, he saw the Federals' problems as related to whom they sent up: trained officers or that "ignorant class of ordinary balloonists, which I think were generally in charge of the Federal balloons."[114] The problems of balloon management were similar in this way to the problems of the telegraph; some private operators were ignorant of the users they supported and vice versa. In any event, the Confederate balloon was captured early in the war, ending the South's efforts with them.

Uncertain Loyalties

The third crucial area of uncertainty concerned public loyalty to governments. Especially at the start of the war, generals sought to avoid strategies and tactics likely to offend citizens, particularly in borderline states. Assuming the war would be short, Union generals initially tried to win battles as bloodlessly as possible to avoid economic distress and public blowback.[115] Winfield Scott, a Virginian, had such an opening mindset. Thus, early in the war, Union general George McClellan wrote to a Virginian who served as an aide to Scott: "Assure the General that no prospect of a brilliant victory shall induce me to depart from my intention of gaining success by maneuvering rather than by fighting."[116] Similarly, Confederate general Lee remained hopeful that his conduct of the war would inspire a sympathetic revolution in the North, bringing victory not just through battle, but by popular will.

Whether or not Scott's or Lee's estimations were realistic was an intelligence question rarely asked and even less often answered in the context of battlefield decision-making. Yet, uncertain civilian loyalties often affected strategy and tactics, complicating net assessment. Confederate general Edward Porter Alexander intimated after the war that had Federals recognized and appreciated the areas with Union sympathizers during the Peninsula Campaign of 1862, they might have designed a war-winning plan for victory and so saved the country several more years of war.[117] In any event, indeterminate loyalties increased insider threats on both sides and led to new roles for civilian secret services, including the use of private detectives and police in war. Their success, however, often turned on citizen-spies.

Citizen-Spies

In civil wars, citizens often have to choose sides, and their loyalties are suspect after they do. The result can be widespread uncertainty and vulnerability for combatants and noncombatants alike. At the outset of the US Civil War, for example, Washington was home to just over sixty-one thousand white residents, of whom two-thirds were loyal, according to Charles Stone, the city's inspector general at the time. This left an estimated twenty thousand potential covert operatives or spies.[118] Some bureaucrats chose the Confederacy without leaving their positions in the Federal government, making secret war-planning difficult in the capital, and leading to fears of insider threats throughout the war.[119] Although uncertain loyalties within the US capital proved an opening advantage for the Confederacy, the South's exploitation of it fostered a robust Federal counterintelligence capability that surpassed the South's over time.[120]

Historical studies of Civil War intelligence have sometimes confused the romantic exploits of amateur spies with effective intelligence for war-fighting. At other times, citizen-spies have not been credited enough for their deliveries of battlefield advantage. Without sufficient inquiry and criteria for judging, historians have tended to either overlook or overplay the roles of agents such as the Federals' Elizabeth Van Lew or the Confederates' Rose O'Neale Greenhow.[121] Stories of espionage during the Civil War abound because credible "cover"—the means that enables a spy to work without raising suspicion—permitted socialites, slaves, and farmers to pose as one persona but secretly be another.

What is needed to assess a spy's true value is less focus on tradecraft or heroism than on delivered advantage. Effective informers or spies require more than pretense; they require access to useful information and the capacity to deliver it to those who can use it to win. At the outset of the war, both sides were uncertain how to set up this "capacity to deliver" and capacity to understand what was needed for military decision-making. Opportunities for local informers increased when enemy troops were marching through their homeland, but most civilians did not know what or to whom to report, leading some generals to discount their worth.

Given the gap between commanding generals and civilian partisans, many of the best Civil War citizen-spies early in the war were those in positions both to learn what would hurt the enemy and to inflict that hurt themselves—fusing spying and decision-making together.[122] This threat caused persistent uncertainty among commanding generals on both sides. During the Battle of Fredericksburg, General Robert E. Lee complained about the Confederacy's lack of "zeal and energy" in moving supplies along the Richmond, Fredericksburg, and Potomac Railroad. He did not know that the superintendent of that railroad was Samuel Ruth, a member of Richmond's Unionist underground, who used his position to learn about Lee's requirements and then delay requisitions through increased paperwork.[123] Ruth was successful as a saboteur because he ran trains; he was successful as a spy only to the extent that he could act on the intelligence himself or connect his collection platform to the Union underground and from there to the BMI.

Ruth's situation was not unusual. Private companies that owned and operated "dual use" technologies such as advanced communications and transportation infrastructure empowered citizen-spies in both North and South, rendering their voluntary work useful. The civilian telegraphers who controlled the lines and codes—some just boys when the war began—and the engineers who ran trains transporting troops to battle were capable of garbling orders. They could slow engines to a crawl, making them among the most important and least heralded of civilian operatives. Similarly, the beginnings of industrial, mass warfare brought new opportunities for covert, as opposed to clandestine, spying in support of partisan action. Besides railroad employees and telegraphers, weapons manufacturers and journalists had opportunities to spy. Sometimes these covert operatives were helpful, and sometimes hurtful, to their respective militaries' operations, depending on how well connected and discreet they were.[124]

Although citizen-spies were sometimes incapable of delivering timely or useful information to commanders, opposing ones had to assume the threat from them was real, complicating strategy and tactics. Stonewall Jackson had a simple solution: he kept his tactics and strategies secret, even when fighting on his own turf. Similarly, Union general Winfield Scott kept his early war planning hidden from civilian and military advisers in case they sympathized with the South. His practice proved wise: his quartermaster, Joseph Johnston, opted for the Confederacy in 1861. Of course, secrecy had its risks as well and sometimes led to disabling mistakes when key decision-makers were kept out of the loop. Insider threats and the secrecy they engendered also created uncertainties within state and local governments, leading politicians to roll back civil liberties. When the city of Baltimore, Maryland, exploded in riots led by its secessionist mayor in defiance of the state's Unionist governor, Lincoln put the city under martial law and suspended habeas corpus.

The confusion over loyalties was almost unfathomable at the start of the war. Consider that both the police chief and mayor of Washington, DC, were Southern partisans and that President Lincoln attempted to recruit Robert E. Lee to command Union forces before Lee opted to take the side of the Confederacy.

While Lee took his time deciding, Federal planners had to decide how much they could tell him. The situation was not unusual. Many civilians in the Federal government, torn between their country and their home states, took their time before deciding, too. According to Edwin Fishel, "Some who went South helped themselves to military documents before leaving. And some obtained clerkships in Richmond. Although the situation offered the Federals an opening to plant their own men as spies in the Confederate bureaucracy, the opportunity was apparently not seized."[125]

In fact, few army officers in 1861 could anticipate how citizens would affect the fight on either side—except to know that they would be crucial both as combatants and as spies.[126] Understanding and mapping this human terrain was nowhere more difficult than in the Upper South, such as Virginia and Maryland, where pockets of secessionists or unionists could exist in close proximity, and loyalties might seem to shift with whichever army was marching through. Union general George McClellan, having beaten Confederate troops in western Virginia in early 1861, reveled in the adoration of the locals at roughly the same time that General Patterson, a two-day march away in Winchester, found them inhospitable at best.[127]

As the war progressed, human intelligence remained available but often unreliable on both sides. Overall, however, it was the Union that developed by 1863 the better system in the eastern theater for vetting sources—whether citizens, deserters, or prisoners—and integrating their intelligence into useful reports. What distinguished Lee's struggle that year to get good intelligence on his way to Gettysburg was less his missing cavalry than his relatively poor capacity to learn without it. The Federals' BMI had created covert reporting channels for citizen-spies capable of tracking Lee much of the way. By regularizing channels for reporting and collating the results, the BMI enabled agents with good intelligence to inform General Hooker's and General Meade's decisions.

The BMI may have been the principal source of the North's engineered advantage in 1863, but its success was not instantaneous. It had been proceeded by years of uncertainty. Perhaps its greatest analyst, John C. Babcock, had been corroborating sources and developing data on the Confederate order of battle for years. Between the Battles of First Manassas and Chancellorsville, Babcock and others had developed systems for vetting sources, interrogating deserters and prisoners, and delivering assessments of the enemy. Babcock, and men like him, made it possible for the BMI to form quickly and to prove its worth to the highest level of command. By the time Hooker faced Lee at Chancellorsville, the BMI was able to estimate Lee's forces within two percent of their official strength. If his successful surprise attack was based, among other things, on reporting from civilians, his confidence in that reporting rested primarily in the experienced managers of the military's newest secret service.[128] The provenance of the BMI's analysts and managers is therefore worth further review.

Secret Services in the Eastern Theater

Antebellum, semisecret, civilian associations were part of the "terrain of uncertainty" in 1861. Some of these associations were political networks that varied in their coherence and dedication to a competitive cause, such as winning an election, abolishing slavery, or seceding from the Union. Others were professional associations of detectives selling services to states and private corporations, which could employ them with few restrictions. Governors could legally hire spies; police forces were beginning to employ private "detectives" to hunt and capture criminals on the run; and, industrialists running railroads hired security personnel to deter and capture bandits attempting to rob their shipments. Many of these state-run and private forms of security bordered on vigilantism; their methods tended to be defensive, and keyed to worst-case analysis; and their objectives included sufficient productivity—real or fabricated—to ensure continuing financial support. Few of them appreciated distinctions between competitive learning (intelligence) and simple, threat-based warning for security purposes.[129] When war broke out, some of these informal or quasi-professional civilian "services" were adopted by or imported into the military with varying degrees of friction. Balloonists offered networked observational platforms but, as mentioned earlier, lacked solid understanding of the military requirements they proposed to support. Others had connections to decision-makers, but lacked platforms suitable for battlefield support. Railroad detectives, whose exploits had achieved celebratory status before the war, are perhaps the best-known example of the latter.

The advent of long-distance rails and communications had increased the need for wide-ranging manhunts as criminals exploited the concentrations of wealth and the nation's growing infrastructure for their own purposes. As the competition between thieves and mail, banking, and railroad businesses ramped up, it taught both sides much about the art of interdiction, running, hunting, and evasion—lessons that crystallized, at least for one side, in the hunt for Lincoln's assassin, John Wilkes Booth, in 1865. Private entrepreneurs were willing to pay a great deal to win these competitions, which turned on meeting force with overwhelming force at the moment bandits might strike. Demand was high enough for protective services that private detective businesses began to sprout, particularly in the North. These services profited when they overestimated their targets, causing businessmen to sink capital into protection of vulnerable operations and thus the deterrence of crime. Generally, it worked.

One successful security expert became nationally known thanks to such defensive techniques. In 1850, an Irish immigrant named Allan Pinkerton left the Chicago police force, where he had worked as a detective, to establish the Pinkerton National Detective Agency using a huge eye as a logo and We Never Sleep as its motto. Working to protect railroads over the next ten years, Pinkerton established a reputation for strict codes of conduct, securing communications lines, and saving railroads considerable sums. Among those he aided were the president of the Rock Island and Illinois Central Railroad, George B. McClellan, and his attorney, Abraham Lincoln. When war threatened and then erupted in 1861, McClellan became, at President Lincoln's behest, a Union general. Pinkerton worked first to secure the newly elected president in office, then got himself hired as McClellan's principal purveyor of military intelligence.

When Pinkerton took over security services in Washington, he replaced William C. Parsons, a quiet lawyer who had run early espionage operations for the War Department. Parsons had employed a topographer and was working with a handful of agents, who had begun gathering information on secessionist arms trafficking, disloyal Washingtonians, and the plans of the nascent Confederate army. Parsons was buffeted by the bureaucratic rivalries that infused the War Department in early 1861, as generals jockeyed for positions in the newly expanding US army. He was firmly attached to Colonel Joseph K. F. Mansfield, who soon became a brigadier general. Then in August, Parsons became ill and quit his job. When General George McClellan took over command of the Army of the Potomac, he wanted Pinkerton, a civilian detective, running Parson's spies.

The choice of Pinkerton was an intelligence policy decision of considerable consequence. The detective's security-minded orientation and organizational skills brought benefits and liabilities that would shape the North's early intelligence efforts, beginning in the capital city itself. The Confederates had long had a spy ring in Washington composed of female socialites, whose easy access to political and military elites had extended from Washington's peacetime politics into war. One of these women, Rose Greenhow, was notorious for her Southern and anti-Republican sympathies before the war, but equally for her politically mixed dinner parties. Her recruiter had been Captain Thomas Jordan, a West Point graduate and former US quartermaster who had joined Confederate general P. T. Beauregard's staff. Once employed as a spy, Greenhow sustained her Washington connections using the cover of her earlier purpose: provocative conversation. Except for adopting a simple code for communications, Greenhow did nothing new; she simply continued to entertain Washington's senior officials and military officers as she had done for some time.

Detective Pinkerton was, however, new to town and so found Greenhow's activities abnormal and suspicious. He staked out her house and caught her at espionage, but only arrested and imprisoned her *after the North's defeat* at First Manassas, by which time her contribution to the battle was complete. Pinkerton no doubt wanted additional evidence of Greenhow's treachery before arresting her, but this prioritized law enforcement over military intelligence. Experienced in protecting inflexible railroad tracks, scheduled trains, and fixed telegraph wires, he was better at security than he was at delivering operational advantage, including insight into enemy plans and deceptions.[130] His reputation as an intelligence professional nonetheless got a boost from the Greenhow case, as he was soon assigned a major role in support to military operations. Whereas preoccupation with security was workable in the defense of Washington, Pinkerton's culture of security was bound to skew his performance during military campaigns. Even the difference between "security" and "counterintelligence" escaped him.[131]

The notion that intelligence in war could be thought of as detective work in peacetime was Pinkerton's bias and, therefore, the Union's opening mindset, which it only slowly overcame. While later serving as chief of intelligence for General George McClellan, Pinkerton regularly overestimated the strength of the adversary, reinforcing McClellan's own tendency to exaggerate it. In the context of war, however, such overestimation can lead to paralysis and a neglect of the search for the vulnerabilities of the other side. During McClellan's ambitious march on Richmond, known as the Peninsula Campaign, Pinkerton's overreliance on human sources of questionable allegiance, combined with his desire to provide intelligence that comported with his commanding general's conservative nature, led to overestimates of enemy capabilities. Pinkerton remained a security officer, not an enabler of offensive strategy. It was not until the creation of the BMI that operational requirements, as opposed to head counts and manhunts, became intelligence priorities. Pinkerton's failures as an intelligence chief probably tainted, in turn, his reputation as a detective. When the hunt for John Wilkes Booth began in 1865, it was not Pinkerton who was called, but his chief rival, fellow detective Lafayette Baker.

Whereas the Union initially focused on security, the Confederacy focused on civilian espionage from the start, taking advantage of chaotic political conditions in Washington and the rapidly forming networks of insurgents animated by common cause. Yet, over the course of the war, its civilian networks did not achieve the organizational strength of Northern ones, for reasons that are not entirely clear. One problem may have been double agents. Among the first Southern recruiters of espionage agents was Virginia's governor, John Letcher, who had also been a member of Congress from 1853 to 1859.[132] Letcher enlisted US Army captain Thomas Jordan, Greenhow's handler, who recruited a network of agents in Washington. Jordan delegated the management of this civilian network to Greenhow when he left to join the Confederate army. Soon, however, a Union soldier from Wisconsin reported, after escaping from prison in the aftermath of First Manassas, that he had connected with Union sympathizers in Richmond who regarded Letcher as "claimed by the Unionists and trusted by them."[133] If Letcher was a double agent—a bold supposition, to be sure—this might help explain how Confederate civilian networks were rolled up so quickly after First Manassas and remained relatively weak.

In contrast, Union networks in the South seemed to have staying power, even though their overall impact on wartime decisions has been difficult to establish. One of the most prolific of them was based on an estate in Richmond owned by a southern aristocrat, Elizabeth Van Lew. Her Union sympathies were discounted by Richmond society because she came from a credentialed southern family.[134] But Van Lew began operating early in the war, apparently before the Battle of First Manassas. At some point after that battle, she began visiting Richmond's prisons, carrying messages to and from Federal troops and helping escapees. Rarely stopped or inspected, she used no particular cover other than her reputation, appearance as a harmless spinster, and her southern accent.

The point here is that too little attention has been paid to her role as the manager of an intelligence system, the "Union Underground," that established a reliable channel of communications from Richmond to the headquarters of Union general Ulysses S. Grant and back. Her agents were embedded in groups of refugees fleeing impossible living conditions or farmers with good reason to be on the roads distributing their scarce supplies. They were seldom stopped or questioned.[135] Van Lew's contribution to decision-making seems to have varied, however, depending on her access to those knowledgeable about Confederate tactics and strategy. She claimed to have placed an African American servant, Elizabeth Bower, in the Confederate White House, but the claim has not been definitively proven.[136]

Thus, the two sides in the Civil War came to the fight differently equipped for civilian assistance in managing and countering espionage for military operations. On the one hand, the North had more experience with securing its sprawling infrastructure and chasing down evildoers using civilian detective agencies; on the other hand, the South, which owned the territory between the warring capitals and the loyalties of one-third of the population of Washington, was better positioned to use citizens as couriers, covert collectors, and individual spies, but had little superstructure for organizing them. If Greenhow had the advantage of twenty thousand potential recruits with good natural cover, Washington had the advantage of having the resources for intensive counterintelligence campaigns. Unlike Richmond, which was surrounded by Virginia countryside, Washington officials knew they were surrounded by Confederate sympathizers, and took strong steps from the start to round up spies and their couriers.

The Confederacy did have within the War Department a unit known as the Confederate Signal and Secret Service Bureau, run by Major William Norris.

Norris gathered newspapers, ran spies and saboteurs, and maintained a clandestine communications network between Richmond and agents in Canada, Washington, and other locations in the North. Called the "Secret Line," the network would play a role in establishing connections among agents involved in President Lincoln's assassination. Its role in providing advantages to generals on the battlefield was slight, however. Unlike the Union's BMI, the Signal and Secret Service Bureau focused on communications, secret operatives, and (poor) encryption for the War Department.[137]

The Loyalty of Troops

Another uncertainty in the eastern theater had to do with order and fidelity within the military. Generals on both sides during the early months had to prepare to fight while sifting out spies, saboteurs, and resistors from among their recruits. Commanders sizing up men could not tell loyalties from appearances or family connections; determining them in the confusion of battle required distinguishing stragglers from deserters and the peculiar uniforms of a wide array of state militias. As a result, early skirmishing in northern Virginia led to incidents of friendly fire and casualties. Indeed, among the first actions of the opposing quartermasters were to issue standard uniforms to their respective armies to clarify matters.

Confusion persisted, however, because of shortages of materials and the rise of irregulars. The use of casually defined uniforms made adequate cover relatively easy for spies; standardized uniforms forced spies to steal the garb of the enemy or to replicate it more exactly. Soldiers therefore tended to rely on rules of thumb to distinguish between friend and foe. Accent, appearance, habit, or even geographical location became an indicator of loyalty. Military officers who understood the shortcuts became especially successful spies. For example, the North created, under the leadership of General John Charles Frémont, a cavalry unit known as the Jesse Scouts that specialized in infiltrating Confederate lines by simply dressing in gray uniforms and riding across. They used simple pass codes to recognize each other.

Uncertainties related to overall numbers, including desertions and re-enlistment plagued commanders very early in the war. Raw recruits and part-time militias were considered unreliable in battle until properly trained. In the early months of war, commanders were often as uncertain of the changing strength of their own numbers as they were of the other side's. Coming into office as commander in chief, President Lincoln thoroughly disliked this murkiness, so sent a sharp message to Winfield Scott: "Would it impose too much labor on General Scott . . . to make short, comprehensive, daily reports to me of what occurs in his department, including the receipt of intelligence?"[138] The president could not have liked his first briefings on the status of forces. The US Army east of the Mississippi was small—no more than four thousand enlisted men out of a total of seventeen thousand, many of whom would defect to the Confederacy. In February, the Provisional Confederate Congress had established a volunteer army under President Jefferson Davis; it would not institute conscription until 1862.[139]

Although both armies would balloon in 1861 as the sides prepared for battle, commanders continued to worry about marginal advantages in numbers and the fighting capabilities of their raw recruits. The men were mostly a ragtag group with little appreciation of how to fight in units, coordinate action, and take orders. Some in the North, such as the pro-Republican Wide Awakes, were self-organized political agitators who had simply taken up arms. Early Union recruits signed up for limited terms of ninety days, and some, exposed to the hardships of military life, resolved not to stay any longer than promised, even in the midst of battle. The resulting uncertainties plagued General Patterson and General McDowell before and during the Battle of First Manassas. If, as the next chapter will show, Patterson's estimates turned pessimistic when faced with the loss of his "three-month men," inducing caution, General Winfield Scott became strangely hopeful and therefore bold in the expectations he passed on to McDowell.

For its part, the Confederacy went from a largely volunteer army to passing a conscription law in 1862 that filled the ranks. The law also led to a spike in desertions. The law exempted from service all men with more than twenty slaves, causing resentment among non-slave-owners and the poor. And as starvation and destruction took hold, the poor realized defending their homes might require working their fields as much as fighting the Union. Many soldiers took unauthorized leave even at the risk of execution. In January 1863, before the Battle of Chancellorsville, Lee's army lost 1,878 men, most of them deserters. Out of the 708 who entered the army at that time, 287 were conscripts who had deserted, been caught, and returned.[140] This latter group could hardly be expected to fight well. They were there only because of a well-organized patrol system: a network of Southern housewives who had become adept at identifying and reporting deserters.[141]

Conclusion: Uncertainty, Requirements, and Intelligence Infrastructure during the American Civil War

Mapping the terrain of uncertainty before and during the early years of the US Civil War provides context for judging intelligence successes and failures on its early battlefields. As in the case of the Spanish Armada, this context matters because it would be wrong to attribute to either side superior intelligence capabilities when advantages flowed more from happenstance or luck than deliberate, competitive learning. For example, the North was lucky that it had detective agencies experienced in investigating trouble and informing decisions for private-sector businessmen; it only achieved intelligence advantages, however, when it was possible to reform those organizations to serve battlefield commanders' requirements. Recognizing good fortune and exploiting it for new competitive purposes is part of the intelligence business and deserves credit; but good fortune and smart exploitation of it ought not be confused.

In the next chapter we examine whether or not Civil War generals in the eastern theater recognized and exploited their built-in advantages or overcame their disadvantages at the Battles of First Manassas (1861) and Chancellorsville (1863). Although alike in their opening levels of confusion, each side in these battles differed in what they knew best by luck or happenstance. The Union, in general, had opening advantages in ballooning and communications, given that the expertise for telegraphy and the resources for extending wires were far greater in the North than in the South. The North was also better positioned to develop partnerships with industrialists—an important advantage given the Union's opening dependency on vulnerable communications and inability to control wires south of Washington. The Confederacy in the eastern theater had clear opening advantages in civilian spies, real-time mapmaking, and intelligence from Northern newspapers. The South also began the war with advantages in cavalry reconnaissance and encoded signaling with flags.

In considering the implications of these advantages, it is important to recall that informational advantages, whether engineered or not, do not always imply decision-advantage. In the first place, natural informational advantages are often obvious and quick to be eliminated. The North's opening advantages in rails and telegraphy prompted Confederate sympathizers to cripple Federal lines by cutting wires, destroying railroad tracks, and capturing telegraphers. Doing so triggered, of course, the rapid development of Federal security systems and public-private partnerships. Such intelligence "wars" are the natural process by which competitive intelligence improves, much as competition in weapons and tactics tends to improve fighting on both sides. For example, Southern advantages in horses and horsemanship had largely disappeared by the time of the cavalry engagement at Brandy Station in 1863, at which point these "mobile platforms" went from being a Confederate advantage to a Union one, thanks to the Union's infrastructure for requisitioning and moving heavy stock. This shift meant that the choices between employing cavalry in raids, courier, or reconnaissance duties became tougher and more consequential for the South than for the North as the war progressed.

A second reason informational advantages do not always lead to decision advantage has to do with the linked factors of organization and trust. Providing information deemed advantageous for one purpose does not mean it will be helpful for another or understood by a new competitor. Thanks to Pinkerton's expertise and connections, the Federals were initially better positioned to develop a trusted, organized intelligence service, but the detective's tendency to inflate enemy numbers—advantageous for railroad security but not for a marching army—meant that commanders could not rely on it for making decisions. The Union's Bureau of Military Information was created by 1863, but General Hooker still lost the Battle of Chancellorsville and his command of the Army of the Potomac, in part because the BMI's intelligence practices were not as good as General Lee's in lifting the fog of war during battle. Indeed, the BMI's operations were still contributing to that fog. The next chapter addresses the reasons why.

It is important to keep in mind as this analysis unfolds, however, that the opening balance sheet formulated here was not fully understood by either side at the outbreak of war—not just because it has been clarified by historical perspective, but also because neither side had a service providing strategic intelligence at the time. Although the case of the Armada has shown that a balance sheet derived from mapping the terrain of uncertainty is an essential part of good intelligence and strategic planning, the US Civil War resulted from secession, not premeditated attack. Both sides were thrust into war while standing cheek to jowl; they had little chance to deliberate about where and how they would fight.[142] Northern and Southern commanders struggled, therefore, with strategic and operational uncertainties as they contemplated their first land battle in 1861. At issue were command chains, political bosses, logistical matters, dual-use technologies, terrain, and the numbers and loyalties of those in the fight. Neither side would fully grasp at the start that this mix of factors, combined with innovations in weaponry, portended a revolution in warfare and years of armed combat. In such circumstances, whichever side could better exploit its informational advantages, or better organize its intelligence practices, would likely gain decision advantages. By 1863, at least a few commanders knew this truth and had improved the integration of intelligence operations into battlefield planning and execution.

* * *

We now move from the uncertainties and capabilities that circumstances dealt both sides, to an examination of how these hands were actually played in battle. Relative uncertainties in war that stem from long-term trends in technology and sociocultural developments may deliver starting advantages, but those advantages cannot be realized unless someone seizes them, builds upon them, and then uses them to fight. A wily opponent faced with a more powerful adversary can recognize the challenge and, using well-informed strategies, play to his own advantages. Yet the art of using intelligence for decision advantage also involves employing information at speed timed to the pace of battle.

We must remind ourselves, as we analyze intelligence in battle, that intelligence on "intentions" does not necessarily imply fuzzy estimation of what resides in an opponent's mind. One can steal an enemy's rather precise intentions by stealing his military orders without his knowledge or by intercepting his communications. A mole embedded within the opponent's command structure can sometimes keep such theft nearly continuous, so every change in plan is conveyed in a timely way.[143] Good intelligence accomplishes these gains while at the same time controlling the opponent's ability to get such gains himself.

Paradoxically, the better the command, control, and intelligence system of an opposing army (or one's own), the more reliable and productive its penetration will be for intelligence on intentions. Thus, as military headquarters during the nineteenth century grew, staff multiplied, and orders were issued in duplicate and archived, the gains in command were accompanied by gains in the dangers of lax security, misdirection, and leaks. It must never be forgotten that an intelligence system can be disrupted by the enemy *or by one's own inept apparatus*, causing indecision, confusion, and uncertainty. It is for this reason that we cannot judge intelligence power by counting the number of agents, the size of the organization, or the number of intelligence products produced. Intelligence power can only be measured by decision-advantage, which in turn rests on intelligence advantage. Good intelligence increases power on the battlefield but, poorly done, risks ruining it. The Civil War reveals, among other things, how and why this is so.

6

Gaining Advantage: First Manassas and Chancellorsville

Major General Philip H. Sheridan, a Union general in the US Civil War, once called intelligence the "great essential of success" in war.[1] To determine if he was right, it makes sense to compare cases similar in most ways but differing in the combatants' management of information. Engagements between the Confederates' Army of Northern Virginia and the Union's Army of the Potomac during 1861 and 1863 demonstrate how variations in intelligence practice affected decisions within the same theater of operations at the beginning of the war and then two years into it. Our interest in each side's ability to gain intelligence advantages means that we are as curious about how this was done in 1861, when the terrain of uncertainty held sway, as in 1863, when the competition had matured and relative advantage was, presumably, more deliberately achieved. Over time, the Federal and Confederate armies improved their knowledge of each other and the terrain on which they would fight, making advantages costlier to achieve, and potentially more decisive.

The Battle of First Manassas in July 1861 was the first major meeting of Confederate and Union armies in the field (Figure 6.1). Brigadier General Irvin McDowell, a middling graduate of West Point, commanded about thirty-five thousand hastily assembled Federal troops, many of whom had three-month enlistments soon to expire. Feeling the urgency of a shrinking force, he marched toward Manassas before he felt ready and without complete knowledge of enemy dispositions and intentions or the lay of the land. General Beauregard, also a West Point graduate, commanded about seventeen thousand Confederates. They took up defensive lines at the steep-banked Bull Run, just above the convergence of strategic rail lines at Manassas Junction, about thirty-five miles from Washington, DC. Farther west, in the Shenandoah Valley, Confederate general Joseph Johnston commanded roughly twelve thousand troops near the city of Winchester, Virginia. About twenty miles away, near Martinsburg, Union General Robert Patterson, had roughly fourteen thousand troops with which to prevent Johnston from reinforcing Beauregard. While McDowell hesitated as he groped for the knowledge he needed to cross Bull Run, surprise the enemy, and capture the junction, Beauregard called for reinforcements. To the Federals'

Decision Advantage. Jennifer E. Sims, Oxford University Press. © Oxford University Press 2022.
DOI: 10.1093/oso/9780197508046.003.0006

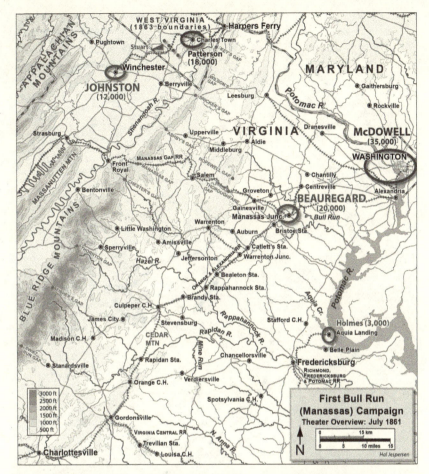

Figure 6.1 Map of the First Bull Run (Manassas) campaign, theater overview, July 1861

Source: Map by Hal Jespersen, www.cwmaps.com.

surprise Beauregard not only got timely reinforcements, but he and Joe Johnston won the battle.

At Chancellorsville, two years later, a far better prepared Union general than McDowell, "Fighting Joe" Hooker, led a surprise attack only to be surprised, in turn, by Confederate general Robert E. Lee's fast-footed tactics. Despite an impressive plan of attack and superior numbers (Figure 6.2), Hooker had paused, bewildered in the midst of battle. Lee split his army, surprised Hooker's flank, and forced him back across the Rappahannock River.

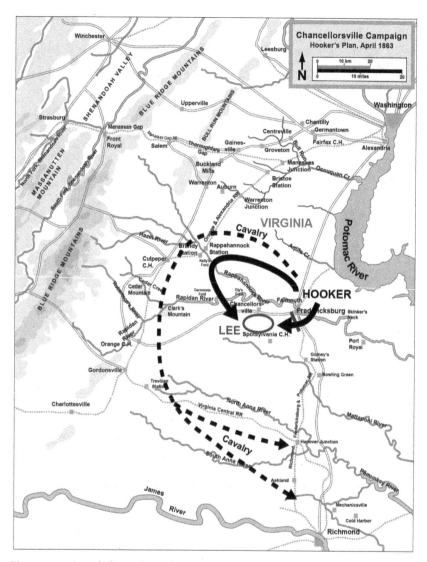

Figure 6.2 Map of Chancellorsville campaign: Hooker's plan, April 1863
Source: Map by Hal Jespersen, www.cwmaps.com.

History has judged both McDowell and Hooker harshly. They were indecisive at critical junctures, misused their cavalry, and failed to guard against the redistribution of forces that ultimately defeated them. Some historians have blamed the amorphous "fog of war" for their indecision. Others have blamed the Federal generals' leadership, though acknowledging that McDowell led green, undisciplined troops and Hooker suffered the effects of an exploding shell at a crucial moment. Few scholars, however, have suggested intelligence factors were important to outcomes.[2] After all, despite copious intelligence provided by his new Bureau of Military Information (BMI), Hooker still lost at Chancellorsville.

In this chapter the case will be made that intelligence played a crucial role in both of these Union defeats. The issue is not whether Federal troops had better all-source analysis after the creation of the BMI; they did. The issue is also not whether the Confederates had more spies in Virginia than the Federals had; they did. The question is whether in each case, Confederate commanders were better or lesser informed than were their Federal counterparts when crucial decisions had to be made and, if so, whether it was luck or engineering that made them so. We learned in the prior chapter that Confederate and Union decision-makers came into the Civil War with a shared history, but different opening advantages in knowledge and the capacity to learn. How did they use or overcome these opening positions? What accounted for intelligence advantages in each battle, and how did they affect outcomes? Was General Lee, as Civil War historian Stephen W. Sears suggests, unaware of how much he owed to "Dame Fortune," or was he, in fact, luck's godfather, and knowingly so?[3]

We begin this investigation with a discussion of the Battle of First Manassas,[4] which was a battle in the dark—that is, one shaped more by the underlying uncertainties on both sides than by illuminating intelligence strategies. The story is of battlefield advantage lost in Washington, as well as on the front lines. Despite superior numbers of troops, better equipment, and sufficient initiative to have outpaced Confederate communications and decision-making, Federal forces were beaten. The Confederates built on their natural gifts to develop an intelligence system that, while flawed, was sufficient in its overall capabilities to gain superior situational awareness from Winchester to Manassas. In general darkness, even a dim light can help one side win.

First Manassas: Confederates Gain Intelligence Advantage

With the Federal government's abandonment of Fort Sumter in April 1861, the Confederate occupation of Harpers Ferry, Virginia's vote to secede from the Union, and riots and vandalism in Baltimore, President Lincoln and most of his cabinet understood civil war was inevitable.[5] By the end of June, Union papers were crying, "On to Richmond"—a sign of the growing public impatience with Washington's efforts to gather troops, train them, and develop a coherent strategy. President Lincoln was just as impatient. He had already rejected General-in-Chief Winfield Scott's Anaconda Strategy, which envisioned a slow strangling of the South.[6] Instead, Lincoln wanted a decisive attack using the existing force of "three-month men" assembled to protect the city—ideally resolving matters before the Confederate legislature could meet on July 20.[7] In a show of resolve, he intended to use his speech to Congress on July 4 to ask for $400 million and a minimum of four hundred thousand more troops.[8] What he and his generals needed to decide was not whether to strike the Confederacy, but how best to make it a fatal blow.

Southern decision-makers, emboldened by Sumter and by Virginia's secession, also wanted a quick war. Confederate president Jefferson Davis had transferred his government to Richmond and had moved quickly down the Shenandoah Valley to secure Virginia's northern boundary at Harpers Ferry, his back door to Washington should Maryland secede. Union general Benjamin Franklin Butler, Andrew Carnegie, and President Lincoln had shut that idea down by, respectively, occupying Baltimore with Federal troops, securing rails and wires running through the state, and suspending habeas corpus to discourage rampant vigilantism.

Forced to adopt a defensive strategy, Davis had powerful incentives to learn when and where the enemy would move next. Northern newspapers were furnishing good information on the growing size of the US Army, the adequacy of its supplies, victuals, weapons, and the like, but they offered only speculation on the true strategy the North would pursue. News reports covered the activities of General George McClellan, who was winning battles in western Virginia; General Joseph Patterson, who was maneuvering near the mouth of the Shenandoah Valley; and Federal probes from Washington into northern Virginia. But no one seemed to know if these forces would be combined and, if so, under whom and with what initial objective.

The Union's Strategic Decision

Union commanders met with Lincoln and his cabinet on June 29, 1861, to discuss strategic options and to make a decision.[9] This meeting included the president; McDowell, recently put in command of the Department of Northeastern Virginia; General-in-Chief Winfield Scott; Captain Montgomery Meigs, an engineer responsible for constructing the Capitol dome; General Charles Sandford; Brevet Brigadier General (Col.) Joseph K. F. Mansfield, who commanded the newly established Department of Washington, including its espionage network; Brigadier General Daniel Tyler; Major General John Charles Frémont; and Lincoln's cabinet.[10] The issue to be resolved was which way to strike, against whom, and when. "On to Richmond" was one thing, but how to get there quite another.

As they considered their options, the Federal officers meeting at the White House had many of the same facts, provided in a similar meeting held on

June 25—a meeting McDowell had been unable to attend. Winfield Scott had outlined them:

> On both sides of the Potomac River at Washington, the federal forces, including the command of General Stone at Poolesville, numbered fifty thousand. In addition, Patterson had about ten to sixteen thousand more, making in all sixty-six thousand. Overall, the Union troops were better armed, equipped, and paid than their adversaries; but they were raw, had less artillery, and had almost no cavalry. Beauregard had at Manassas Junction, Fairfax and Centerville [*sic*] nearly twenty-four thousand infantry and two-thousand cavalry, all of whom had no pay, little food, poor clothing, and hostility to discipline. Nevertheless, his men had greater experience in the use of arms and longer drill than the Union troops.[11]

The men gathering on the twenty-ninth considered these facts with similar mindsets.[12] They held four perceptions in common. First, all were convinced, including the former appeasers in Lincoln's inner circle, that the Union would have to fight and beat the Confederacy. Second, all shared a deep respect for the general officer missing from the meeting: Major General Robert Patterson, a former regular army officer who was leading an army composed of Pennsylvania militia toward a Potomac crossing in western Virginia.[13] They knew Patterson wanted reinforcements, especially regular army officers, for a combined effort against what he believed should be the main target for any Federal advance: General Joe Johnston's forces in the Shenandoah Valley. Everyone in the room considered Johnston to be the most experienced general on the Confederate side and hovering far too close to Washington for comfort. Patterson had been pressing his plan to have McDowell join forces with him to defeat Johnston. Scott, who had initially supported Patterson's plan, had then "crippled" him on the seventeenth by recalling some of his best troops to Washington to counter Beauregard's growing strength at Manassas. Everyone knew Patterson was incensed about it.

Third, all the officers present had railroads on their minds. The Baltimore riots, which had disrupted the arrival of army volunteers, communications, and supplies to Washington, had underscored the importance of securing lines of communication for the defense of the capital. General George McClellan was making swift moves to secure the Baltimore and Ohio rails in western Virginia, capturing crucial rolling stock, telegraph lines, and intersections of road, rail, and water transport. General Butler had secured the eastern end of the line by occupying Baltimore to Washington's rear. The problem lay in the middle. Harpers Ferry, an important arsenal and the confluence of river, railroad, and communications lines, had been lost to the Confederates on 19 April. Though strategically important, the town was difficult to defend, so Johnston had left it on 15 June, having destroyed the rails, lines, and equipment located there. Johnston seemed to be falling back toward Winchester, on the line to Manassas. While doing so, he had detached Thomas J. Jackson's brigade to the railroad town of Martinsburg, where, on 19 June, Jackson had destroyed railroad tracks, trains, and equipment. The Confederates had thus acted quickly to sabotage rails—first on the Alexandria to Leesburg line below Washington, and then on the Baltimore-Orange line above it.

Lincoln announced he wanted to "bag" Jackson in the Shenandoah Valley—a desire felt widely among those taking their seats for the war council that day.[14] The implications of Jackson's latest move seemed grave: any move on Richmond would now have to go through Johnston's Confederates in the Valley or Beauregard's at Manassas; but, whichever way was chosen, the rebels could consolidate their forces faster than the Federals could join theirs. A secure, working railroad lay between Beauregard and Johnston, but not between Patterson and McDowell. Colonel Stone, not in attendance on 29 June, had been reporting the waxing and waning of Confederate strength as he tried to secure lines along the upper Potomac on the Maryland side. The rails connecting Martinsburg, Harpers Ferry, and Relay House (below Baltimore) were not only too far to the rear, but were either seriously damaged or threatened by vigilantes. The only potentially working line, from Washington to Leesburg, which lay just east of the Blue Ridge Mountains and below Harpers Ferry, was vulnerable to the forces gathering in Manassas, who could attack and pin the Federals against the Potomac. It seemed with each passing day that what should have been the North's natural advantage in rails had become an alarming Confederate one.

Finally, all the military officers in the room on 29 June were West Point men commanding an army of militiamen and volunteers. They were confident in their knowledge of military theory, if not necessarily field operations. For example, they all knew the contents of the army training manual and the tactics they would need to employ on the battlefield. Having studied Napoleon's victories, they feared a combination of Confederate forces as much as they were inclined toward joining their own. Along with the politicians in the room, they assumed that, in general, Confederate and Union troops were roughly equivalent in readiness. As Lincoln put it, "We must make up our minds that man for man the soldier from the South will be a match for the soldier from the North and vice versa."[15]

There were also, however, deep divides among those assembled. Tensions and disagreements simmered just below the surface. Some had to do with civil-military relations and authorities.[16] The military chain of command was clear: General-in-Chief Winfield Scott, despite his advancing age and infirmities, would make decisions—at least in theory. But the president and his cabinet were also part of the assembling war council. Lincoln and his secretary of state, William Seward, had already demonstrated that they would not nec-essarily defer to Scott, the "Hero of Veracruz," the "commander-in-chief," who was accustomed to dispensing rank and honors.[17] It was one thing for Lincoln to have rejected Scott's Anaconda plan for squeezing the South into submis-sion through blockade and siege. But in April, Lincoln, Seward, and Treasury Secretary Salmon P. Chase had involved themselves in what Scott regarded as logistical decisions, such as the resupply of Fort Sumter and Fort Perkins—even to the point of gathering their own intelligence and issuing conflicting orders for the deployment of the warship, Powhatan, without the knowledge of the navy secretary.[18] Beyond that, Lincoln had pressed Scott on the importance of tech-nologies Scott believed would be disruptive to Union forces, such as balloon re-connaissance, and had made decisions about the army's senior officers without due regard for Scott's advice—commissioning officers "with the same eye to-ward coalition building that he displayed in building his cabinet"—that is, with politics in mind.[19] As Scott considered his deep reservations about the coming war and current options for prosecuting it, he suspected that Lincoln would not shrink from running the war himself should his commanders seem indecisive or fail to advance on Richmond soon.

Second, while most men in the room assumed the war would be short and decisive, Scott did not. He had long worried that foraging and marauding by the Union's undisciplined troops, destruction of property, or mass bloodshed on Virginia's soil would consolidate Virginia against the Union and the South for the Confederacy more generally, especially in the critical border states. Even now, as he took his chair on 29 June, Scott had trouble shaking this idea. He sensed the continuing importance of winning or keeping the people's loyalties, even though Virginia had voted to join the Confederacy. A wise policy, in his view, would nurture Southern resistance to Richmond. A rush to battle with untrained, un-disciplined men would increase chances of panic, more bloodshed, and deeper national divisions. Eyeing the men entering the room, he expected McDowell, who owed his command partially to Scott, to agree with him—at least about the army's lack of readiness, if not the other merits of delay.[20]

Irvin McDowell, a freshly minted general with his first command, did worry about the greenness of his army. So far, however, he had been reticent to say so, except perhaps to Scott. McDowell had been a recent confidant of Secretary Chase, who had been among the most aggressive of the cabinet members, had long hungered for battle, and had supported him for the higher rank of major general. Although McDowell had humbly declined such rapid advancement, he still regarded Chase as a powerful benefactor, an ardent supporter of a swift march toward Manassas, and a critic of the more hesitant Scott. As early as 3 May, Chase and McDowell, who by then expected to get the command he would later receive, had conferred on how to secure Manassas by launching first onto the Virginia shore of the Potomac—a military operation the first part of which had then been successfully executed by Sandford on 23–24 May. Federals now occupied several camps ranging from Alexandria in the east to Falls Church in the west. McDowell thus saw Chase as more than a patron, secretary of the treasury, and the president's link to banks loaning money for the war. He saw him as a powerful interventionist.[21] McDowell knew, as he took his place in the war council, that he needed to deliver a plan agreeable to Scott, but also one that the president and Chase would endorse. Unless he was careful, he would be on a collision course with one or more of his seniors.

McDowell, relying on Meigs and Scott, likely felt ready. He had stayed abreast of what had happened at the earlier meeting on the twenty-fifth and so knew that the council had discussed the Union's superior strength and had failed again to support Scott's desire for a delay until the autumn. Montgomery Meigs had also assured everyone that adequate supplies would be ready as soon as the army would march. What McDowell may not have known was that Meigs knew that the army was short on wagons, horses, and other supplies, and would be so for at least several more weeks. Meigs's reassurances likely stemmed from either bravado or a desire to protect his relations with Secretary of War Simon Cameron, who was supporting the offensive, but failing at his job. Heading a department of fewer than two hundred people, Cameron had been long despairing that he had "no guns, no ammunition, no anything,"[22] He had turned to Seward and Chase for help, believing his task to be almost unbearable. Meigs, an engineer with a good mind for logistics, had taken private opportunities to urge him forward on logistical matters, and to shore up his deficiencies, such as managing contracts with materiel and service providers of unknown loyalties.

Among Cameron's deficiencies Meigs did not comprehend or could not address, however, were the War Department's shortfalls in managing the infighting in the new telegraphic and signaling services, nominally under Cameron's purview. The bureaucratic infighting had recently begun erupting in ways that affected operations. In fact, the first field battle among Federal communications officers was unfolding at Fort Monroe, even as the war council gathered on 29 June.[23] General Butler, the aggressive occupier of Baltimore, had been assigned to Fort Monroe near Newport News since 22 May, and had worked quickly to set up communications. He had asked Albert Myer, the chief of the army's Signal Corps, to help, and by 27 June, Myer had established a signaling service between the fort and an outpost at Newport News, soon supplemented by a US Military Telegraph line. When Myer tried to inspect the USMT officers, however, they rebelled, alerting their seniors at the War Department. Myer was then instructed to leave the USMT alone, convincing him he could not work with the USMT and reinvigorating his efforts to develop his own system using different machines.[24]

This internal intelligence fight was the first battle in what would become a tel-egraph/signals war between the hybrid private/public USMT under Carnegie's control in the War Department, and the army's Signal Corps, championed by the awkward, but persistent, Albert Myer. Cameron, if he was aware of that problem and similar tensions among balloonists, said nothing about them at the meeting of 29 June. Indeed, matters related to the logistics of aeronautics and telegraphy were lightly addressed, if at all, perhaps because Carnegie's team seemed the best organized of all at work at the War Department and Thaddeus Howe's successful balloon ascents at Falls Church had produced seemingly reliable maps for fifty miles in all directions.[25]

In fact, the excitement around aerial platforms hid serious problems with their potential use in battle. As Lowe would later state, the military officers riding with him had "sketched a fine map of the surrounding country and observed the movements of the enemy."

> When the map was shown to some Union volunteers "who were familiar with the vicinity of the Fairfax Court House, [they] at once recognized it, and the roads, lanes, stream and dwellings." Just as important was the discovery of Rebels encamped at the Fairfax Court House.[26]

These ascents were proving so productive that they had even changed the minds of skeptics such as Brigadier General Daniel Tyler. Unfortunately, they also fed the notion that the ground between the Potomac and Bull Run would be sufficiently known for any march across it using mostly existing maps and aerial reconnaissance.[27] Subsequently, but before the meeting of the war council on 29 July, Howe's balloons had been brought under the Bureau of Topographical Engineers. There, the idea that balloons could help provide intelligence during battle was not yet understood, so the logistical requirements for employing them were not widely considered.

The biggest *known* unknown, at least for McDowell, had to do with Patterson's influence and General Mansfield's intentions. Mansfield, in charge of the Department of Washington and the army's only espionage and reconnaissance unit, was no friend of McDowell's. He was known to have wanted McDowell's command, but had experienced some past friction with Scott that may have cost him.[28] In any event, Mansfield had been slow in releasing regiments arriving in Washington to McDowell's army, so McDowell probably found it unsurprising that topographical intelligence, maps, scouting reports, and the like had been slow to reach him and largely inadequate—a fact that became more apparent in retrospect than at the time. Topographical engineers and scouts reported to Mansfield through his subordinate, William Parsons, who seemed unable or un-willing to meet McDowell's needs in planning his attack.[29] McDowell had access to other spies, however, at least one of whom he had already deployed without Mansfield's say-so.[30] In any event, McDowell probably worried less than he should have about his lack of adequate scouting reports and other intelligence.

The bigger worry for McDowell was General Patterson and his operations in the Shenandoah Valley. Patterson still wanted the war council to endorse his advance as the primary movement, but he was short on wagons, short on supplies, saddled with three-month men, and dealing with hostile locals. Believing a foraging army would further enrage the citizenry and degrade the security of his position, Patterson had a sympathetic ear in Scott, the old Virginian. McDowell knew that if Scott sought a solution by depleting McDowell's army to appease Patterson, the offensive he was planning would be in trouble.[31] As McDowell prepared to make his presentation on the twenty-ninth, it was this problem of scarce resources and Patterson's competing claims to them that occupied his thoughts, not the threat posed to his own plan if Patterson could not play his designated role. In fact, McDowell's plan, which he was about to try to sell, had implicitly linked the fates of both generals, making the only truly vital resources the ones for mutual collaboration. McDowell proved himself blind to this implicit linkage, which was more dependent on communications than the division of troops between them. McDowell's presentation would nevertheless focus on numbers and the instruments of force, not intelligence.

The War Council's Decision

In fact, after some opening preliminaries, McDowell presented a plan to the council of war that made substantiating Patterson's reports, responding to his requests, and engaging with massive forces in the Shenandoah Valley seemingly unnecessary. Spreading out the generic maps he had, McDowell pointed out how he could defeat Beauregard with thirty-five thousand troops, but no less.[32] These troops would march on Manassas in three columns, with ten thousand held in reserve. Although Union forces would have to coordinate across columns, *so long as Patterson held Johnston* in the Valley, the war could be won *with McDowell's forces alone.* McDowell pointed out that the alternative—a move by him to support Patterson—would leave Washington exposed to rebel forces building under Beauregard, the aggressively-minded hero of Fort Sumter, while gaining no ground in the effort to hold Richmond at risk. With McDowell's plan, Patterson would know better than Johnston the precise moment of McDowell's advance, but at that moment, offering battle would not be enough; Patterson would have to engage in such a way, and for long enough, to prevent a combination of Confederate forces at Manassas.

Scott commended McDowell for his analysis and authoritative presentation. He said nothing about McDowell's assumptions regarding the necessity of good communications, an astonishing lapse given that Scott knew—and the telegraphers of the day knew—that Scott had been unable to find Patterson for several days between 7 and 17 June due to glitches in the wires and courier services. Patterson's massive army on the march had simply disappeared, albeit temporarily.[33] Stone had also reported that couriers were getting lost on unfamiliar roads north of the Potomac. If McDowell was going to depend on precisely coordinated movements with Patterson, there was reason to worry. But Stone was in the field, not in the room, so this point was not made.

Instead, Scott assured McDowell that, should Johnston make a move toward Manassas, he would have Patterson "nipping at his heels." The comment likely made General Sandford uneasy. He thought McDowell's plan unworkable and said so. But he stood alone. Chase, the president, and the rest of those assembled favored it. Scott determined that Sandford should go with his New York troops to reinforce Patterson, along with Stone's forces at Harpers Ferry, Wallace's regiment at Chambersburg, and a couple more from Wisconsin—all of which would be communicated to Patterson around 8 July. Scott would not get the delay he still desired; McDowell's advance was set to begin as soon as logistically possible.

In one sense, these decisions were good ones. Had these men taken Patterson's preferred course of sending McDowell's troops to him for an attack on Johnston and a march up the Shenandoah Valley, which had been plausible enough to engage Scott's strong interest and initial support, it is likely that Washington would have been overrun, losing the war in its earliest days. In another sense, however, the decisions were poorly informed for successful execution. McDowell's strategy had three unmet intelligence requirements: first, that Patterson have the capacity to sustain timely intelligence on Johnston and his movements; second, that McDowell know his route sufficiently well to predict and execute a set time for attack so that Patterson could be sure to have Johnston's attention at the critical moment; third, that Patterson and McDowell have good enough intelligence sharing that, if plans were disrupted, Patterson could improvise effectively. These intelligence demands were more significant than were those facing the Confederates. To frustrate the Federal plan, Johnston just needed to move toward Beauregard's forces at Manassas faster than Patterson could learn about it and react.[34]

The requirements for Federal intelligence seem so clear and the failure to address them so obvious, they beg the question of why an experienced general did not address them. Did Scott have intelligence that lessened these gaps or made them seem irrelevant?

Scott's Intelligence, June to July 1861

Scott's strategic decision relegating Patterson to a secondary role was based on reasonably sound intelligence. Federal troops had conducted incursions into northern Virginia that made clear that any movement by McDowell in support of Patterson would leave Washington dangerously exposed. Troops had accomplished "reconnaissance in force" through Fairfax Courthouse in late May; to Big Bethel on 10 June, when about three thousand Federals had advanced out of Fortress Monroe, fired on one another, and were driven back; and, toward Vienna, Virginia on 17 June, when Schenck's brigade had reconnoitered the Loudoun and Hampshire Railroad, finding it damaged. Although Confederates had put an end to these adventures rather quickly, ascents by balloons had revealed that Confederate outposts continued to dot the northern Virginia landscape.[35] Reports as of 26 June suggested Beauregard had about twenty thousand men compared with McDowell's fourteen thousand.[36] Although Scott knew that McDowell's troops would double in number over the coming weeks, the earlier forays had given him reason to believe that McDowell could not defeat Beauregard unless he had superiority in numbers.

Intelligence had also been mounting since mid-June that Johnston's threat to Patterson was less than Patterson had been suggesting as he moved to the Potomac. Colonel Charles Stone, attempting to secure the canal from Harpers Ferry to Washington, had reported the likely Confederate withdrawal from the former, but continuing threats at the ferries on the Virginia side.[37] Supplementing this intelligence, Mansfield had asked his spy chief, Parson, to send an agent, Kirk R. Mason, on three missions to Harpers Ferry to discern Confederate forces and their intentions. Mason reported on his last venture that, despite Patterson's protestations to the contrary, the Confederates were falling back toward Winchester.[38] This news was significant during the 29 June meeting because it suggested that the Confederates might be planning to consolidate in Manassas instead of joining near Harpers Ferry or Martinsburg for an attack on Patterson. Scott was, therefore, already inclined to have Patterson play a secondary role to McDowell in the first battle of the war. This assessment was partly why he believed he could draw down Patterson's strength on the seventeenth to reinforce Washington.

The second part of the decision—whether to endorse McDowell's plan without alteration—was, however, relatively more difficult and certainly less well informed. Topographical maps made clear that, while Patterson *might* be able to track Johnston's movements if he had enough cavalry, McDowell *certainly could not* because of the screen afforded by the Blue Ridge Mountains.[39] In addition, McDowell's old maps, spotty balloon coverage, and indifferent scouting offered little on how the terrain between the Potomac and the Rappahannock might affect the extension of telegraphic wires and the movements of thousands of men, horses, wagons, and artillery once the battle began.

Planning decisions for battlefield operations required data processed and exploited by informed engineers. None of the aeronauts had this skill or understood this purpose; even military observers carried aloft could not assess such factors as the sogginess of ground, the height of a river's banks, or the depth of its waters—all variables that changed with the seasons and especially in the spring. Even McDowell, fixated on the location and numbers of the enemies he faced, seems not to have understood his own intelligence requirements. And apparently no one at the War Department, or among his aeronauts, made him aware of them. After the successful ascents of Howe's balloons at Falls Church and the creation of the balloon corps, competing aeronauts engaged in the same kind of bureaucratic warfare that was embroiling telegraphers and the Signal Corps—internecine warfare sparked, in both cases, by a War Department strapped for funds and staff and looking for cheap solutions.[40] Within McDowell's command itself, occupation of the southern boundary of the Potomac had raised commanders' confidence in their knowledge of the terrain. Unfortunately, they knew the ground only about ten miles into Virginia.

The implication of this operational blindness was that McDowell's advance would not be smooth, and communication with Patterson could not be timely. Wires could be stretched and protected only so far, and telegraph messaging would necessarily go through Washington, specifically through Scott. In fact, the uncertainties of terrain meant that timing would be the greatest challenge the commanding generals would face. Scott probably knew this to be true because of erratic connections to Patterson. And Stone had reported his own communication problems in that direction when, at Poolesville, he reported that Mansfield's messengers did not seem to "understand the roads," forcing workarounds.[41] Telegraphic communications from Washington to Leesburg would likely remain vulnerable because of Confederate presence in the vicinity and the inherent vulnerability of wires that had to be guarded against vandalism.

Stone certainly appreciated the importance of his mission, if not the ambitious nature of completing it. He had sent his plan to Scott on 16 June:

> If I become satisfied that Harpers Ferry has been evacuated, and that a general retreat has been made, via Winchester, I shall cross the river by the upper ferry and ford, capture the force . . . occupy Leesburg, and open means of communication as rapidly as possible, with General Patterson on the one hand and General McDowell on the other, taking especial care to restore as rapidly as practicable, the transportation routes on both sides of the river down.[42]

Although Stone heard on 6 July that he would soon receive telegraphers for Harpers Ferry and Point of Rocks (along the Potomac near Leesburg), no evidence exists that stations were operating at either point when the battle commenced, or that the necessary couriers were in place at either end of the line. The correspondence around this time has been lost, so the telegraphers' recollections, recounted in their memoirs, that these stations were not sufficient are all the historical record offers on this point.[43]

Making matters worse, the idea of mobile reconnaissance escaped everyone except, perhaps, Mansfield and his engineers, whom McDowell had only lightly used. McDowell, in fact, later admitted that he had "no idea how to use cavalry."[44] Somewhere in the War Department, telegraphers knew that telegraphic lines would need to keep pace with McDowell's movements, but their requirements were slow to be met and poorly integrated into McDowell's plan. Although McDowell may not have worried about Patterson's end of matters, his plan should have contemplated his requirements for signaling across his columns and hearing from Patterson. Instead, the head of the Signal Corps, Albert Myer, was not ordered to report to McDowell (from Fort Monroe) until 17 July, and telegraphers' equipment dragged behind McDowell's marching troops. The telegraph office at Fairfax Courthouse, McDowell's headquarters, was not set up until 20 July, well after Johnston had already left the Valley to support Beauregard. It closed on 22 July after the Federal army had swept past in full retreat.

The lack of an intelligence infrastructure necessary for the complex operations was a *knowable* strategic gap that Scott should have understood and could have addressed with better planning, but did not.[45] That gap was not just in McDowell's planning, but in Patterson's and Scott's as well. Although Scott was probably the most knowledgeable about the communications problems along the Potomac during the war council on 29 June, he did not raise them. This oversight was egregious because attempts to connect to Patterson's moving army had already raised the communications intelligence problems that McDowell would soon be facing. As one telegrapher put it after the war, "It is somewhat remarkable that on the eve of this first great battle of the war . . . no adequate means of communication was kept open between Patterson and the War Department. As it would turn out, at the vital point in the movements, 17 to 21 July, Patterson received no communication whatever from the General in Chief."[46] He goes on to say:

As Patterson claims to have telegraphed information and for orders during these days, the trouble may have been at Washington City; but it is certain that there was no office nearer Patterson than Harpers Ferry. It would seem that the neglect was in Washington, if it be true as stated by him, that his movements "could at any moment be countermanded by telegraph," and that his first information of McDowell's defeat was three days thereafter, from a Philadelphia paper.[47]

Knowing what he did prior to McDowell's march, Scott should have either rapidly innovated using balloons and wires before the army marched, or he should have increased Patterson's cavalry regulars, but he dismissed the first and, by the time of the war council, had already recalled the latter—the principal existing means by which Patterson could monitor Johnston and make the necessary links to McDowell.

In fact, almost immediately after the war council was over on 29 June, Scott began to have doubts about McDowell's plan, but the steps he took made matters worse.[48] Apparently, he sent a former San Francisco vigilante and new government employee, Lafayette Baker, to spy on Confederate intentions. This was just one week before McDowell's army was due to march.[49] Scott wanted to know which general had more sway with the Confederate president, Beauregard or Johnston; the best place to learn the answer was Richmond itself.[50] Indeed Patterson, still convinced that he faced the greatest threat, wrote on July 5 that he had good intelligence that Johnston had been heavily reinforced and that those reinforcements had come from Manassas. This intelligence supported Patterson's view that he, not McDowell, would face the bulk of Confederate forces.[51] Patterson's report probably reinforced Scott's interest in news from Baker.

As luck would have it, Beauregard's troops had promptly arrested Baker in Manassas and had sent him on to Richmond by rail. There, he reported he had interactions with Jefferson Davis himself, which he subsequently claimed he relayed to Scott. Scott did send an intelligence report to Patterson on 11 July that, whether sourced to Baker or not, seemed to confirm the latter's view that chasing Johnston up the Valley (south) for purposes of engaging or interdicting him, would be unwise:

> The plan of operations of the secession army in Virginia . . . meditates a
> stand and an engagement by Johnston when he shall have drawn Patterson
> sufficiently far back from the river to render impossible his retreat across
> it on being vanquished, and an advance then by Johnston and Wise con-
> jointly upon McClellan, and after the conquest of him, a march in this di-
> rection, to unite in one attack upon the Federal forces across the Potomac
> with the army under Beauregard at Manassas Junction and the wing of that
> army . . . now nine miles from Alexandria. Success in each of these three sev-
> eral movements is anticipated, and thereby not only the possession of the
> capital is thought to be assured, but an advance of the Federal troops upon
> Richmond prevented.[52]

If this report were true, the worst thing Patterson could do would be to allow himself to be lured away from the Potomac, cut off from his supplies, and unable to retreat. But so long as Johnston stayed at Winchester, chasing him and thus extending Patterson's supply lines and communications was exactly what the Federal plan of "holding" Joe Johnston's forces in the Valley would require.

This intelligence, if believed, effectively placed a "hold" on Patterson, preventing him from putting his "hold" on Johnston at Winchester. To do the latter, Patterson would have had to risk falling into the Confederates' trap. Scott, nonetheless, sent the intelligence to Patterson only a few days before McDowell was to march, further muddying Patterson's orders. Dated July 9, which would correspond to the reported date of Baker's mission, the intelligence may have reflected a Confederate stratagem sent through Baker or some other spy.[53] If the intelligence did come from Baker, it should have been suspect, since the man had little understanding of the telltale signs of contingent military planning or deception. That Baker was able to return safely from Richmond, and at the same time report enough to be paid handsomely, seems to suggest that this report was indeed a Southern stratagem.[54]

Whatever the source, this late "intelligence" meant Patterson could not "nip at Johnston's heels" without entrapping himself. Given that Scott believed this intelligence was plausible enough to send on to Patterson, Scott should have alerted McDowell to Patterson's dilemma and revisited operations contingent on Patterson's ability to pin Johnston in the Valley. He did not. Instead, Scott's news ramped up Patterson's fears that he might have to fight Johnston with inferior numbers, giving him all the more reason to conserve his strength and avoid getting lured up the Valley. Scott seemed to understand this fix—at least at some level. When Patterson then asked Scott to endorse his plan to fall back to Leesburg, if necessary, he received Scott's approval. Patterson understood, therefore, that he had two operational requirements: First, that his demonstration on Johnston's front should be on the sixteenth, the date planned for McDowell's march; second, that he should beware of Confederate moves to lure him south for the purpose of entrapment. Patterson did not know whether McDowell had Scott's intelligence or understood his difficulties in light of it. It is not known, but seems likely, that Scott did not share the 9 July intelligence with McDowell, who apparently assumed throughout the battle that Patterson would hold Johnston according to the original plan. Scott apparently decided, for whatever reason, that changes were either unnecessary or impossible by 9 July.

In summary, the Federal strategy was deeply flawed because it ignored relative capacities to learn during battle. The Federals knew that the Confederates had communications covered because any move by McDowell toward Patterson would be in the open, that the rail junctions and wires from Richmond to Manassas and from there to the Valley were working better than the Federals'

lines through Leesburg to Harpers Ferry, and that the Southern cavalry was superior.[55] None of these Southern advantages were fully addressed when assessing
McDowell's plan. Although the war council had the requisite technology for
improving communications and observing wide expanses from balloons, the
members did not consider such matters on 29 June. Scott had based his decision
to endorse McDowell's operational strategy on either a misunderstanding of its
intelligence requirements, or concession to a majority's mindset once his own
preferences for conducting the war were shelved. Patterson, out of the loop, was
forced to rely on Scott's good judgment, which failed him.

Thus, McDowell went to battle believing Patterson could and would detain
Johnston in the Valley to prevent a consolidation of Confederates at Manassas,
and that he would do so whenever he engaged Beauregard.[56] According to
Brigadier General Tyler, Scott himself reiterated this promise to McDowell as
late as 13 July.[57] Thus reassured, McDowell focused almost exclusively on his
own operations and left the rest to the commander in chief.

The Confederacy's Strategic and Operational Decisions

Like the decision-makers in Washington, those in Richmond faced two threats
on two potential fronts without sufficient forces to win both simultaneously:

- One possibility was a two-pronged attack through the Shenandoah Valley
  (Patterson) and through Manassas toward the Rappahannock (McDowell).
  One of these fronts would likely be dominant, in which case Confederate
  commanders needed good intelligence on the timing and direction of the
  main Federal thrust in order to defeat it and then rapidly to reinforce the
  second front.
- A second possibility was a feint, with McDowell marching west, then whee-
  ling northwest to reinforce Patterson for a single concentrated strike against
  Johnston, who would need reinforcements from Beauregard—a plan that
  Federal commanders were, in fact, considering through most of June.

The Confederacy needed to develop counterplans for each of these scenarios.
Either scenario might begin with a march by McDowell toward Beauregard, who
would then want reinforcement from Johnston. But if the advance were a feint
and became a turning movement, Johnston would need to resist an early move
to reinforce McDowell in order to hold off a combined attack by McDowell,
Patterson, and perhaps McClellan while he waited for reinforcements from
Beauregard. The combination of the Federals' raids in Northern Virginia,
McClellan's perch just west of Patterson, Patterson's reinforcement and advance

in early July, McDowell's false starts around the same time, followed by Patterson's odd movements at the mouth of the Shenandoah Valley, kept Confederate decision-makers off balance. Beauregard and Johnston were at odds, vying for resources much as McDowell and Patterson were doing in Washington.

To combine their forces for defensive purposes, the Confederates, like the Federals, needed a plan for common situational awareness in battle. This required

- Knowledge of the comparative size, distribution, training, and readiness of troops, weapons, and mobile platforms, such as trains and cavalry on both sides;
- Advance knowledge of the planned direction, objective, and terrain of march;
- Alerts to enemy troops' actual movements; and
- A capacity for *joint appreciation* of what these movements meant in the context of both sides' strategies and operations (i.e., reliable and fast communications) in order to gain decision-advantage.

As their commanders tried to learn Federal plans, Beauregard's engineers rode over most of the terrain between Bull Run and Centreville, mapping roads, fords, bridges, and locations for signaling stations on high ground in the area around Bull Run. General Beauregard and his signalman, Alexander, spent considerable time surveying the land between Manassas and Centreville before McDowell marched. Beauregard arrayed his forces opposite the most useful fords between the stone bridge on the Warrenton Pike and Manassas Junction. Certainly aware of Federal balloon surveillance, he hid his men in trees and thickets while designing a counterplan for gaining the high ground. Alexander selected five elevated sites for signaling: hills stretching from Centreville to his own position on "signal hill," roughly six miles from the Run. It was from this vantage point that Alexander was able to observe Federal movements and alert those on the Confederate left flank that they were turned, ruining the full impact of the Federals' intended surprise. Johnston sent skirmishers forward to scope out Patterson's movements, destroy rails and equipment, and then fall back.

The most pressing requirements for intelligence could only be met, however, with good insider information about enemy forces, strategy, timing, tactics, and combined operations. Although Confederates had sensors in the form of pickets and signalmen arrayed across northern Virginia to detect any Federal advance—a form of tactical warning—they knew they needed reliable, timely intelligence related to the Federals' strategy if they were to have any hope of effective joint operations. In sum, they knew they needed *theater-wide*, operational warning for joint operations.

Herein lies the key to understanding the importance of the Confederate spy Rose O'Neale Greenhow, whose role has been debated almost from the moment the war concluded.[58] Greenhow sent two messages to Beauregard: one on the ninth, which he received on the tenth, and the other the night of 16 July. The first informed him that McDowell would march with his entire army toward Manassas sometime within the next few days. This report made clear that the next movement would be no feint and that the strategy the Federals had settled upon was McDowell's—not Patterson's or any other. Beauregard reacted by ordering his forward deployed forces to fall back to Bull Run once the advance began, likely to lure the Federal army toward his fortified points at Bull Run and Manassas Junction. Greenhow's second message provided the exact date, composition, and direction of McDowell's intended advance, triggering Beauregard's plea to Richmond for reinforcements. This message caused Davis to order Johnston to move in support of Beauregard *on the morning of the eighteenth*, which was three days before the battle actually would begin, and two days before McDowell would have a telegraph set up at his headquarters at Fairfax Courthouse.

Although Greenhow's detractors have argued that her information on the timing and direction of McDowell's attack was redundant because newspapers and retreating Confederate outposts provided plenty of warning without her, her supporters, including Beauregard himself, have testified that her role in alerting him to McDowell's moves and intentions was crucial. Indeed, because of Greenhow, Beauregard and Johnston knew more about McDowell's movements and intentions than Patterson did between 16 July and 19 July, gaining decision-advantage for the Confederacy. Greenhow supplied Beauregard with intelligence on how many reserves McDowell would leave behind, where he was headed, and what Patterson would do to support him. She delivered his objective, not just his date of march. This intelligence erased the Confederates' greatest uncertainty, which was the role Patterson would play. If, as discussed earlier, the intelligence flowing to Scott and separately to Patterson on 9 July was part of a deceptive stratagem designed to hold Patterson in the Valley, as it might well have been, it would now work to Confederate advantage.

In weighing Greenhow's contribution, it is important to recall that the Federals were themselves uncertain of their intentions until late June and, in response to Patterson's appeals, had been reinforcing him with troops, including the forces that had secured the Potomac under Colonel Stone. Until Jefferson Davis understood the moves Patterson would make, he had to wait to decide which of his generals should lead the Confederate defense. Greenhow's intelligence on 10 July, which made clear that McDowell's intended move on Manassas Junction would be no feint but the main attack, convinced Beauregard and Davis that the battle would be at Manassas, in Beauregard's front, causing Davis to prepare new orders for Johnston. After so much Federal indecision and repeated false starts, however, McDowell's intentions were presumably changeable, so Greenhow's second report on the sixteenth confirmed the need to trigger Johnston's move, and the precise moment it needed to be executed. Given that the Northern press was neither informed nor trusted on this point and Confederate pickets would get the information too late, Greenhow's intelligence was probably essential to Johnston's timely decision. The Confederates had a prearranged courier system that ensured that, given the lack of a working telegraph from Washington, Greenhow's role there would be supported by as speedy communications as possible. In the event, Greenhow's couriers took great risks to deliver her messages, suggesting their commanding officers valued them greatly. The question for modern historians judging Greenhow's performance was not whether her tradecraft was professional, but rather whether she was good enough in the moment to deliver a critical advantage. The record suggests she was.

Competitive Operational Decisions

Once McDowell marched, intelligence support to strategic planning gave way to support to military operations, for which the Federals were singularly unprepared. McDowell had planned to achieve surprise by coming around the enemy's right flank. Unfortunately, as we have seen, the maps McDowell had were missing important information about the strength of bridges or the fords over Bull Run. McDowell, who had been told this stream was "fordable at almost any place," soon found out this assessment was wrong for thousands of marching men with horses and artillery.[59] Parson's stable of spies and scouts, which could have provided McDowell with good intelligence on the usability of the fords, were neither deployed nor consulted before the march. So, in the midst of his advance, McDowell lost time as he resorted to scouting himself. His staff, small and ill-equipped for field reconnaissance, struggled to help fill the gap.[60] Across the Blue Ridge, Patterson held to his conviction that Johnston had thirty-five thousand men. Expecting McDowell to march on the sixteenth, he waited in Martinsburg and then made a demonstration toward Winchester on that day. That accomplished, he sidled back to Charlestown, secure in the knowledge that such a movement had been endorsed in advance by Scott, but confused about what he should do next.[61]

Unfortunately, unbeknownst to Patterson, General McDowell had stopped his march *for two days* just short of the Run, unwittingly rendering Patterson's demonstration, now bound to be seen as a feint thanks to Greenhow's intelligence, both premature and too brief. Expecting opposition, McDowell had started slowly and cautiously, sending skirmishers but no cavalry reconnaissance in front. Soon, however, muddy roads, slippery creek beds, and steep banks slowed his march, and engineers and telegraphers had to solve these challenges of logistics and wiring on the fly. By the time McDowell found a suitable crossing of the Run, achieving a poorly wrought surprise, Johnston had already learned via telegram and courier that he needed to reinforce Manassas and had moved that way. McDowell still did not know his lost advantage. Pushing Confederate forces back toward Henry Hill, he paused again, failing to exploit his hard-won advantage. These delays provided sufficient time for Johnston to get most of his forces to Beauregard, and successfully repulse the Federals with no interference from Patterson.

The Sources of Decision-Advantage

So, who or what was to blame for McDowell's defeat? That McDowell lost decision-advantages over the Confederates is clear. Scholars have long blamed his leadership, which was wanting. After all, he did not demand intelligence about Johnston's or Patterson's movements, so he did not get it. But was he the only one at fault? Historical works tend to blame Patterson more, agreeing with Scott's critique of him at the time. Arguably, McDowell felt little need for speed because he felt he had been relieved of considering enemy movements beyond Manassas and its environs. He was trusting Patterson to take care of them.

Whereas McDowell felt no need to acquire information dominance on the battlefield, in part because he was assured he had it, Patterson felt acutely both the need and the gap—so much so that he was paralyzed. Scott was the only commander in a position to see the entire picture. And while the commander in chief had a nagging hunch that things could go wrong, he did almost nothing to investigate and fix them. Scott deserved more blame than he ultimately got for his decisions, but he deserved blame as well for poor leadership of a chaotically run war machine. Balloon policy, mentioned earlier, was one known and poorly used tool, handicapped by a mismanaged War Department, competition among contractors, and poor adaptation to operational requirements. Other gaps had to do with human intelligence and counterespionage. The scouts and guides who had studied the terrain and could have aided McDowell were not effectively deployed or used. Some historians have suggested this neglect was McDowell's fault, while others claim that Mansfield, who controlled the War Department's scouting and espionage effort, was miserly because he wanted McDowell's command. These slips and gaps should have been corrected by Scott, who was commander in chief, and the only one in a position to coordinate the full array of intelligence assets on behalf of joint operations. Scott was, however, at the end of his very long and illustrious career; the challenges of modern warfare simply escaped him.

In the absence of strong central leadership, generals had to problem-solve on the fly. For example, McDowell's poor planning for fording Bull Run stemmed directly from the lack of relevant intelligence on terrain interpreted through the eyes of military engineers. McDowell relied on intelligence from locals that the stone bridge afforded the best crossing of the Run, and that it was mined. It was not. As the frustrated general reconnoitered along the Confederate right, he learned that the "road" leading to the ford he had planned to use was a mere cart path and impractical for his army. As McDowell's engineers sought a route for a flanking maneuver on the Confederate *left*, finally executing it, the Confederate signalman Edward Porter Alexander, perched on his hill, saw the sun glint off the Federals' bayonets and cannon and provided warning of the turn.

The Confederates' initial decision-advantages stemmed less from great competence on their side than from intelligence-induced delay on the part of the Federals. Greenhow's espionage was unprofessional, but it was better than what the Federals had and so proved good enough to help anticipate Patterson's subordinate role. Alexander's warning signal, while inspiring a vigorous and swift Confederate defense, was probably less important to the Confederate win than were the Federal gaps in communications and Scott's poor handling of intelligence. And while McDowell's delay in crossing the Run set him back, he might have pulled out a victory if he had followed up his initial wins with a vigorous pursuit of the demoralized Confederate forces.

Of course, intelligence was not all that mattered to the outcome of this battle. McDowell's delay for two hours after his initial tactical victories on Matthew's Hill, and before re-engaging the enemy, stemmed from the same tunnel vision that had prevented him from understanding the urgency of his movements east of the Run. In those crucial hours, one of Johnston's newly arrived commanders, Thomas Jackson, had time to assemble his troops on the field and earn his reputation for the impenetrable "stone wall" he presented to the enemy. Behind this "wall," the Confederates were able to reorganize their demoralized troops and integrate Johnston's additional reinforcements from Piedmont. Within hours of McDowell's tactical victories, his men were fleeing back across the Run—not just a defeated army, but a panicked mob.

From First Manassas to Chancellorsville

Good historians stick to facts; but there is much that can be learned about past events from what did not happen, but almost did. First Manassas, for example, might have turned out differently had the Federals used balloons to keep an eye on Johnston and to keep McDowell apprised of events in the Shenandoah Valley. Balloons, which had provided sweeping views of the enemy at rest outside of Washington, were ideal for long-dwell missions, and could have been deployed with telegraphic connectivity if preparations had begun back in May or June.[62]

Yet, even if balloons had been deployed out of Harpers Ferry too, someone would have had to think creatively about how to connect balloon reconnaissance to McDowell's battlefield with cavalry or extended telegraph lines. Winfield Scott's skepticism regarding balloons and his old-school approach to military communications may have prevented him from calling in the American telegraph executives and aeronauts for ideas about how to accomplish the connectivity McDowell's strategy required. Similarly, McDowell never thought of any innovative solutions because he had been told it was not his problem, when operationally, he must have known it most certainly was. After all, his adversaries went into battle with relatively secure communications to Richmond by rail from Manassas and Winchester. Jefferson Davis also set up two legs of a pony express for communications in the Valley from Staunton to Winchester. Unlike Federal couriers servicing the War Department, Colonel Stone and General Patterson in June and July 1861, these Confederate riders knew the roads.

The Federals' tactical and logistical problems at First Manassas were not of the same order as those experienced two years later at Chancellorsville. During the first battle, the problems turned on the difference between information and intelligence—a distinction the Confederates seemed to better appreciate at that time. McDowell's preliminary *information* on the Run—that it was fordable at any point—was true, but only for a local farmer or lone scout on horseback, not for a large army equipped with heavy guns trying to surprise a foe. Good *intelligence* would have identified the difference and set to work filling in the gaps. This crucial distinction between good information, which is true, and good intelligence, which is true *and competitively useful*, rests neither on secrecy nor on theft, but on understanding the meaning of facts in a competitive context. Stealing more prewar maps or deploying more balloons would not have solved the problem of finding fordable points. What McDowell needed was what the Confederates accomplished: advance work in the form of savvy scouts able to discern the opportunities and obstacles afforded by the terrain and how these would affect his decision-making.

The point is not that McDowell might have exploited such knowledge to achieve any surprise. After all, his surprise worked to some degree. Rather, he needed such knowledge to execute his operations *more quickly* than Johnston could move his troops to reinforce Beauregard, which was the key to winning in this case. Beauregard, whose tasks were primarily to know McDowell's plan and to delay its execution, was well positioned to do so with his communications links to Johnston, including through Richmond; his five signal hills; his weeks of scouting and occupying the terrain; and his network of spies in Washington.

* * *

Almost two years later, on 27 April, 1863, Union general "Fighting Joe" Hooker faced a set of strategic circumstances similar to those McDowell had faced at Bull Run. Having studied McDowell's mistakes, he believed he had a good plan to catch his opponent with a timely surprise—a strategy that rested on intelligence-advantage. He knew he had to have a better sense of where his enemy was and how he would attack him than his enemy had of him. Before attacking across the Rappahannock in 1863, near the town of Chancellorsville, Hooker *did* deploy balloons, and his Bureau of Military Information *did* think creatively about how to connect them to his headquarters. He still lost. As we shall see, Hooker, like McDowell, underestimated what he, his subordinate officers, and his intelligence providers needed to stay connected *during the battle*. In neither First Manassas nor Chancellorsville, were telegraph operators, aeronauts, or cavalry—all critical assets for battlefield communications and intelligence dissemination—integrated into military planning with this purpose in mind. They were neither briefed nor equipped to provide reliable connectivity across the entire area of operations. That Hooker blamed his intelligence, but kept his newly minted BMI largely intact after his defeat, offers a clue to what he knew had gone badly wrong, which we will now examine in greater detail.

Decision-Advantage at Chancellorsville

Hooker's effective surprise in outflanking the Confederates across the Rappahannock has been lauded as one of the best-executed surprise attacks in history. This success was not lucky; the attack was built on meticulous intelligence. As historian Edwin Fishel has put it: "Hooker's maneuver may fairly be regarded as an intelligence coup, conceivably the greatest one of the entire Civil War."[63] Looked at closely, however, that intelligence succeeded in part because the enemy's intelligence failed.

Hooker's Strategic Intelligence Advantage

In preparation for the coming battle, Hooker was determined to avoid the mistakes made prior to First Manassas. He had his chief engineer, First Lieutenant Cyrus B. Comstock, examine all the river crossings on either side of Fredericksburg for twenty-four miles. Comstock ruled out all but three: US Ford, twelve miles above town, and two sites lower down, where General Ambrose Burnside had crossed in his disastrous engagement at Fredericksburg the previous year. Choices thus arrayed, Hooker organized a unit under his chief of staff, Daniel Butterfield, for managing and scrubbing all available intelligence on what General Lee was doing and his order of battle. Hooker was particularly concerned about his own left flank, which was exposed to Virginia's infamous secessionist territory known as the Northern Neck, and the whereabouts of Lee's subordinate, General James Longstreet. Longstreet was elsewhere, but might reinforce Lee at a critical moment in battle, as Johnston had done for Beauregard at Manassas.

Hooker ordered his chief of security, General Marsena R. Patrick, "to organize and perfect a system for collecting information as speedily as possible." Patrick disliked his mission: "I do not fancy the class of men and think they do not fancy me." This led him, perhaps, to quickly find a colonel to manage secret service operations with whom he felt comfortable and who "appears well." He found such a person in Colonel George H. Sharpe, a lawyer with the 120th New York, who soon organized Hooker's secret service as deputy provost marshal general.[64] Thus unburdened, Patrick focused much of his attention on security, putting all postal services under his strict control and placing officers as detectives at supply depots.[65] Patrick preferred the company of lawmen to spies, so he left management of espionage to others.[66] Assisted by his chief interrogator, John Babcock, Sharpe managed all collectors, including those performing espionage, interrogation, and scouting, and coordinated collection from cavalry reconnaissance, balloon surveillance, signal intercepts, and telecommunications.[67] Nominally subordinate to Patrick, Butterfield, and Hooker, Sharpe still reported directly to Hooker in his role as intelligence chief.

Patrick and Sharpe limited General Lee's positional awareness with the tightest security and counterintelligence program the Federal army had yet experienced. This program included the rounding up of deserters through liaison with state and local officials; coordination of telegraph operations to preclude their use by deserters or spies; and, ultimately, at least two ruses to mask the trajectory of Hooker's intended advance. Patrick and Sharpe worked across the widest possible definition of the battlefield, and well ahead of the army's first move. As early as February, Patrick had begun recruiting the first Union sympathizers in the area. Two months later, Sharpe had increased the total number of agents to twenty-one.[68] By mid-April, coordination had begun with the navy's Potomac flotilla to prevent espionage and desertion on that waterway. Cavalry runs into the Neck began soon thereafter to disrupt Confederates' foraging and their lines of communications.

In all this activity, Hooker and Sharpe demonstrated what McDowell had so conspicuously lacked at First Manassas: a sense of the scope of the potential battlefield, and what needed to be known in its farthest reaches. He soon developed a cadre of soldiers willing and able to insinuate themselves within Confederate ranks, and officers dedicated to managing them.[69] Thus, Hooker's staff created the BMI that, as explained in the previous chapter, was the first instance in which all-source collection and analysis was delegated by a commanding military officer to a freestanding organization.[70] This organization, in turn, could and did enforce secrecy when needed, and authorized disclosures when advantageous.

In comparison, General Lee was strategically blind as he watched and waited. His situation contrasted sharply with Beauregard's and Johnston's before First Manassas. They, too, had been in defensive positions, but had more actively reconnoitered and prepared thanks to having narrowed likely scenarios to roughly three. Lee had a far less crisp estimation of what was coming than had Beauregard.[71] He did have an open telegraph line to Richmond, so he knew that his fellow Confederate general, Braxton Bragg, was in danger in Tennessee and that his own inactivity in the east made the situation worse for Bragg. He also knew Burnside, Hooker's predecessor, had headed south with his corps in February. But Lee joined President Davis in worrying that this might presage an attack on the Confederate capital the shape of which was hard to foresee.

Lee did not like his situation, so he started taking risky decisions in the relative dark. He sent divisions under Pickett and Hood south to counter Burnside, further diminishing his forces, and then sent Longstreet to command. When Burnside went west instead, Lee ordered Longstreet to remain in the Richmond area to collect provisions and forage for the starving troops back on the Rappahannock River. This decision meant that 25 percent of his veterans might be absent for the coming confrontation with Hooker, whom Lee found inscrutable.

> General Hooker is obliged to do something . . . I do not know what it will be. He is playing the Chinese game. Trying what frightening will do. He runs out his guns, starts his wagons and troops up & down the river, & creates an excitement generally. Our men look on in wonder, give a cheer, & all again subsides "in status quo ante bellum."[72]

Lee's long wait seems, in historical perspective, to have approached somnolence. For example, despite being encamped in Fredericksburg for months with Jedediah Hotchkiss at hand, Lee did not order good maps of the local terrain.[73] The lack of terrain mapping was likely no oversight. Lee knew his own side of the river better than Hooker did, and may have believed he could use this advantage to get an edge. Accurate maps, especially distributed to subordinates, could end up in an opponent's hands. Lee knew Hotchkiss excelled at fast, useful, tactical intelligence, even if his speed sometimes caused minor inaccuracies. Besides, he had learned that enlistments of many in the Federal army were coming to an end.[74] This information, which was incorrect, may explain why his strategy did not include a plan for Longstreet to reinforce him if conditions warranted. In any event, lying ill and quiet on the south bank of the Rappahannock, Lee was taking an enormous bet—a bet that he could beat Hooker's more powerful army with better local and tactical intelligence on the move.

The bet was riskier than he knew. Hooker had a spy, Isaac Silver, on Lee's side of the river who produced detailed intelligence on the strength, readiness, and disposition of Lee's troops, revealing a large gap in the Confederate lines, the absence of Longstreet, and the weakness of horses expected to pull artillery. The intelligence from Silver, supplemented by reports from a deserter about Jackson's position on Lee's right, reinforced Hooker's idea that his best shot would be to attack on the Confederate left.[75] General Hooker had determined by April 11, 1863, how he would use this and other intelligence to surprise Lee. Unlike McDowell, however, he held no war council about it. He entrusted his chief of staff, Butterfield, with a message to President Lincoln informing him of the plan that, secret from Hooker's own commanding officers, involved sending most of his cavalry around Lee's left. Meanwhile the cavalry, commanded by Major General George Stoneman, would move through Gordonsville, sever the Richmond-Fredericksburg railway to cut off Lee's supplies, and then engage Lee's retreating troops, whom Hooker expected to force back with the sweep around Lee's left flank. That turning movement would cross at US Ford, twelve miles above town. Thanks to the work of the informant Isaac Silver, however, Hooker contemplated enlarging the gap in Lee's defenses to make the western crossing at Kelly's Ford.[76] The question for Hooker was how to ensure the gap would not close before he needed to use it.

In a series of careful deceptions, Hooker reinforced the gap on Lee's left with the help of his intelligence apparatus. Signal officers had learned that Confederates could read the Federals' messaging; knowing this, they created "chatter" indicating that Hooker's cavalry would be ordered to the Shenandoah Valley in pursuit of Confederate cavalry commanded by Fitzhugh Lee. The Federals soon learned from monitoring Confederate communications that this fake message had been intercepted and repeated by Confederate signalmen. Indeed, the planted information seemed trustworthy intelligence to Lee, who directed Stuart to stay upriver to prevent Stoneman's forces from penetrating the Valley—a move that a Federal spy confirmed with reports back to the Union's BMI. Meantime, Hooker sent raiding parties to his left, into Northern Neck, where they faked a pontoon crossing and erected Quaker guns to deceive Confederate pickets and hostile locals.[77] Hooker sought to turn Lee's natural advantages in local intelligence against him by stimulating untrained observers to report such feints to

Lee. He succeeded. The commander of the Federal forces there reported a rapid buildup of Confederate forces in response, confirming a concentration far away from where Hooker actually intended to strike. By 15 April, Hooker was able accurately to write: "Up to late last night the enemy appeared to have no suspicions of our designs."[78]

General Lee was vulnerable to such deceits because he was short on scouts and spies and relied perhaps too heavily on local intelligence.[79] Although his cavalry was renowned for screening and reconnaissance, his army at rest had no integrated intelligence apparatus throughout the month of April. He did have some civilian spies inside Federal lines, much as Beauregard had had, but Lee's secessionists were ensconced in the "Lacey house" in Falmouth, where they had limited access to sources and could only communicate through window lights and hand signals. Within the bounds of Hooker's southernmost lines, these women were simply picking up the casual conversations of Federal pickets. They could send few details given the rudimentary messaging system.[80] Confederate counterintelligence was also poor. The Federals soon learned of their leaky pickets at Falmouth, and corrected the problem with even tighter security, including "house guards."

In any event, Lee's failure to keep pace with Hooker's development of an army-wide intelligence system had immediate consequences, including the likelihood Lee's advantage in agile intelligence for military engagement would not be matched by an advantage over Hooker in positional intelligence—that is, intelligence on the static relationship of forces prior to battle. Lee's cavalry and scouts, who should have been his most trusted collectors and purveyors of intelligence, were instead busy conducting raids behind Federal lines, threatening the forces at Hooker's rear, and protecting the Valley too far west. These activities brought little useful information to Lee regarding Hooker's forces, their disposition, or their plans, presaging the problems Lee would experience during his later march toward Gettysburg. "For days or weeks the only significant reportage on Hooker's army came from a Stafford County citizen who had picked up some information while imprisoned at Aquia," Hooker's supply depot to his rear.[81] Such weaknesses in Lee's intelligence system, combined with the fact that Federal signal officers had successfully decoded the Confederate signals alphabet and were reading enemy messages, meant that the situational awareness was heavily tilted in Hooker's favor. Historian Edwin Fishel thus joins Douglas Southall Freeman in concluding that

comparison of these intelligence successes and failures in the two armies in this period reveals that for the first time in the two years of war in Virginia, the Federals knew more about their enemy than the Confederates knew about them. A reversal of the "intelligence advantage" had been achieved in the first two months of Hooker's regime.[82]

This advantage crystallized on April 27, 1863, when Hooker, after weeks of bad weather, launched his surprise maneuver and caught Lee off guard. Hooker swept much of his army through the gap his ruse had secured to outflank the Confederate left. He used Kelly's Ford, much further west than the better-defended US Ford, and well within the area vacated by J. E. B. Stuart's Confederate cavalry, which was still stalking Stoneman.

Intelligence for Operations: Hooker's Relative Blindness

Although Hooker had an operational plan, it assumed, rather than provided for, coordinated intelligence:

- Following the crossing at Kelly's Ford on April 29, Hooker envisioned a pincer movement, with corps under General George Meade (Fifth), General Henry Slocum (Twelfth) and Major General Oliver Howard (Eleventh) marching on roughly parallel courses southwest, then east to ford the Rapidan, uncover the lower fords on the Confederate left, and move on Chancellorsville.
- Hooker would remain with the rump section of his cavalry on the Federal right at Morrisville to coordinate the main body of his army, using cavalrymen as couriers to supplement telegraph wires.
- In the meantime, General John Sedgwick's (Sixth) corps, positioned below Fredericksburg, would make its move to cross the river. Sedgwick would be supported by the balloon corps, which would continuously assess the Confederates on his front.
- Hooker would then follow Meade, Slocum, and Howard (30 April) to set up headquarters at Chancellorsville, where Hooker would command the entire army and the timing of everyone's movements.
- At the appropriate time, Hooker would signal Sedgwick to execute, first, a vigorous demonstration to pin Lee into a defensive position near Fredericksburg; and, second, an advance west with General John F. Reynolds's First and General Daniel Sickles's Third in reserve.
- Taking advantage of Sedgwick's moves and joined by Couch crossing at Banks Ford, Hooker would move toward Lee from the west, putting the latter in a vice.

- Hooker's cavalry, led by Stoneman, would in the meantime cut off supplies, reinforcements, and communications by attacking the Confederate lines to Richmond.

Hooker's strategy was heavily dependent on intelligence-supported maneuvers. He required intelligence on developments across a long front of over thirteen miles, but assumed he would have it because of the BMI. After all, the BMI had been coordinating dispersed intelligence assets, a telegraph system to communicate intelligence and decisions, and ruses underway to undermine the enemy's situational awareness for months prior to the attack. Moreover, with the army underway, the BMI had authorized Thaddeus Howe to ascend in his balloon, and then telegraph developments regarding Sedgwick's operations back to headquarters.

Hooker's flanking movement at the start accomplished the kind of surprise McDowell had wanted to gain two years earlier. Hooker had studied his intelligence requirements and believed he had all he needed for the opening moves of his plan to work in a timely, coordinated way, being "the beneficiary of one of the most salutary performances by an intelligence service in the entire war."[83] Unfortunately, executing the plan during the days following his surprise maneuvers required tactical, as well as positional, intelligence—intelligence for an army in motion—and it was here that serious trouble lay.

From Information Dominance to Lost Decision-Advantage: What Went Wrong?

What eventually transpired was a defeat worse than McDowell's—one that entailed a series of unfortunate oversights and bad decisions by Hooker that confounded his subordinates and have perplexed military historians ever since. Having executed a near-flawless surprise with superior numbers, Hooker ordered a pause at Chancellorsville to allow concentration of Federal forces, including the three corps that were marching east, and Crouch's divisions crossing lower down in front of Falmouth. When Hooker finally ordered his columns forward, however, he did so uncertain of Lee's whereabouts and without ensuring communications among his columns. Meantime, Lee had arrayed roughly forty-eight thousand men back to back, facing Sedgwick, the river, and Hooker. He then moved the last, largest faction, thirty-six thousand men, aggressively toward Chancellorsville with a stable of scouts who knew the land well, such as Beverly Lacey, chaplain to Stonewall Jackson. Eventually realizing Lee was threatening his disjointed columns with ambush, Hooker ordered his forces (roughly ninety thousand men) *back to Chancellorsville*, where they arrayed themselves in eastward- and southward-facing lines, anticipating the addition of the First Corps (fifteen thousand) from the north, and relief from a *coordinated advance* by Sedgwick's Sixth Corps from the east, on Lee's rear.

To Hooker's surprise, however, he could not seem to learn how Sedgwick was doing on his left. Stoneman's cavalrymen were away, and his telegraph was not providing a timely link between Fredericksburg and Chancellorsville. On May 1, as Hooker waited for intelligence on Sedgwick's whereabouts, Lee's cavalry discovered that Hooker's right was exposed and told Lee, who then contemplated a startling maneuver: further division of his thirty-six thousand troops facing Hooker for a surprise attack on Hooker's right. Lee delegated the execution of the move to Stonewall Jackson, who relied on locals and Jedediah Hotchkiss, to substantiate word of a route through the Wilderness that might be sufficiently distant from Union lines. When Hotchkiss found the route, Stonewall Jackson marched his men to attack Hooker's right flank and forced its collapse.

This move achieved tactical surprise for two reasons: First, it was done slowly and quietly through the Wilderness, widely thought to be impenetrable. Second, it dashed Federal expectations by breaking all the rules of warfare. As the Confederate general Edward Porter Alexander later put it, "One of the axiomatic rules of warfare is to avoid dividing one's forces in the presence of one's enemy. For it gives him opportunities to oppose your factions with his whole units, & to crush them in detail."[84] Indeed, Hooker, hearing erroneous reports of a Confederate retreat and nothing from the commander guarding his right, assumed he had battlefield advantage when he did not. Astonishingly, Howard, who commanded Hooker's right, had received warnings from his own men about the Confederate flanking maneuver, but had refused to send the warnings up the chain because he assumed Hooker, supported by the BMI, knew more about the battlefield than he did. Both men's assumptions were wrong. Out of a nearly impenetrable thicket of woods and brush, Jackson launched a surprise attack that folded Hooker's right wing back past his center.

Stonewall Jackson's attack actually helped consolidate Federal forces, but the Union general froze with indecision. As the battle raged around Chancellorsville, Hooker worried that he did not know whether or not Lee would be reinforced by Longstreet and whether or not Sedgwick had the will and capacity to fight his way west. In fact, Sedgwick, unsupported by any eastward advance by Union forces and lacking good intelligence on why, had decided to head back across the Rappahannock. Confused, exhausted, and suffering the effects of a cannonball striking too close to his position, Hooker nonetheless remained in command, eventually giving up his ground near Chancellorsville, and then all ground south of the river. The battle was over. Hooker had lost despite having had the advantages of opening surprise, an all-source intelligence organization, and superior numbers.

Federal Mismanagement of Collection Systems, including Communications

This defeat was not just a sudden turn of events induced by a dazed or debilitated Federal commander, as some historians have suggested. The loss was, instead, largely intelligence-driven.[85] Hooker's chances of success were diminished weeks earlier when he failed to distinguish strategic intelligence, at which he bested Lee, from intelligence for tactical decision-making, at which General Lee excelled because of his local spies, knowledge of the terrain, and solid communications support from his cavalry. Consider the decisions Hooker expected to make and the unmet requirements for supporting intelligence:

- After crossing at Kelly's Ford on 29 April, Hooker envisioned a pincer movement that would uncover the lower fords on the Confederate left, and move on Chancellorsville in synchronized fashion.

Yet Hooker's chief signal (and telegraph) officer, Samuel T. Cushing, had no knowledge of Hooker's plan to move as far west as US Ford until 27 April, when Butterfield ordered him to extend his wires to Franklin Crossing and then to Banks Ford. When Cushing was told to extend further to US Ford, he said he had insufficient wire to do so. Forced to improvise, Cushing cannibalized wire connecting Hooker's original headquarters to Belle Plain (to the Federal rear on the Potomac). This wire had been in use for months and was damaged and unreliable. Cushing, nonetheless, installed it because it was the only wire available.

- Hooker planned to coordinate from the Federal right using the rump section of his cavalry and telegraph wires.

Yet between 30 April and 1 May, the wires went completely dark due to breakdowns in the Signal Corps's unreliable Beardslee machines and, even after these were fixed, breakdowns in the wires Cushing knew to be defective. Butterfield reacted by ordering the USMT to take over at US Ford using Morse equipment. Although this change helped, bottlenecks in communications persisted, nonetheless, because of the faulty wires. Hooker, alarmed and (erroneously) suspecting sabotage, ordered an entire regiment to guard the main line along the river from US Ford to Falmouth, and to shoot anyone attempting to interfere with it.[86]

- Sedgwick's (Sixth) corps, positioned below Fredericksburg, was supposed to cross the river to threaten Lee's forces and, on Hooker's signal, to begin a demonstration that would pin Lee into a defensive position near

Fredericksburg. Then Hooker would signal for Sedgwick to advance west to meet the rest of the army with Reynolds's First and Sickles's Third in reserve.

The plan's requirements for a joint view of the battle went unmet because of poorly shared intelligence and broken communications. Sedgwick crossed 1 May at 11:30 a.m., with Howe's balloons reporting on Lee's positions from Banks Ford and Franklin Ford, sending reports that were not, apparently, received by Hooker, possibly because of the downed telegraph lines. In the meantime, Hooker had telegraphed Sedgwick to begin a vigorous demonstration at precisely 1:00 p.m. Sedgwick did not receive this telegram until 4:45 p.m. and, seeing the time lapse, did not know what to do with it. Hooker's staff ordered him to advance on 2 May, relying on Lowe's aeronautical reports of weakness on Maryes Heights (Figure 6.3).

That day, having suffered Jackson's flank attack, Hooker remained in Chancellorsville, as clueless about Sedgwick's progress as the latter was of his. Sedgwick and Lowe, up in his balloon, could only see smoke from the direction of Chancellorsville. Two sources of Hooker's confusion were his faulty telegraph and his lack of cavalry. The structure housing the telegraph at US Ford had become a hospital, operators had become part-time nurses, and wires were

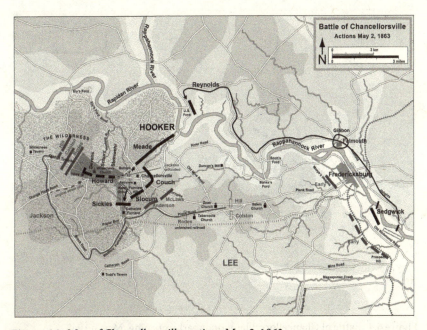

Figure 6.3 Map of Chancellorsville: actions May 2, 1863
Source: Map by Hal Jespersen, www.cwmaps.com.

broken in the chaos.[87] Hooker's order to Sedgwick (9:00 p.m.) to advance toward Chancellorsville was received by Sedgwick at 11:00 p.m., but, fourteen miles away, he could do little to relieve the pressure on Hooker, who had no idea where the rest of his army was located.

Accustomed to solid all-source intelligence, Hooker had already begun to suffer from its absence when, on 3 May at 9:00 a.m., the exploding shell knocked him out. Hooker was compromised by the injury, but his intelligence apparatus was already broken. By that night, Sedgwick had made only half the distance to Chancellorsville with his back to Banks Ford. A series of garbled communications followed: Hooker hoped Sedgwick could hold his position; Sedgwick asked if he should hold or cross the ford; Hooker ordered him to cross, soon after receiving a message that Sedgwick thought he could hold; Hooker told him to do so; but Sedgwick had already telegraphed that he had crossed at Banks Ford, so Hooker crossed the river himself (Figures 6.4 and 6.5). Throughout, Hooker's cavalry under Stoneman, which was supposed to have cut off Lee's supplies, reinforcements, and communications, had been doing a poor job; they would have been better employed for the kind of screening, reconnaissance, and communications that Jackson had been performing for Lee.[88] With his back to the

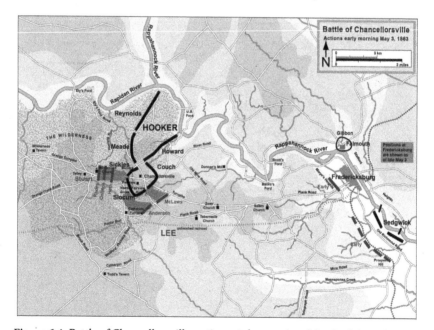

Figure 6.4 Battle of Chancellorsville: actions early morning, May 3, 1863
Source: Map by Hal Jespersen, www.cwmaps.com.

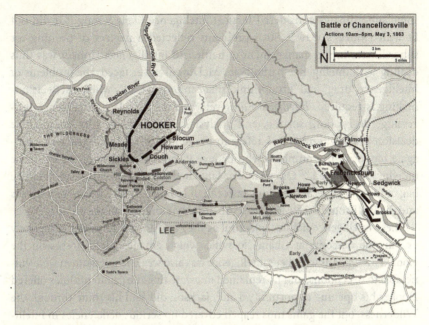

Figure 6.5 Battle of Chancellorsville: actions 10:00 a.m.–5:00 p.m., May 3, 1863
Source: Map by Hal Jespersen, www.cwmaps.com.

wall, Lee had options. Despite his advantage of position, Hooker believed he did not. The significant difference between them was their intelligence.

The Federals' loss of decision-advantage on 2–3 May rested on a disrupted telegraph and misuse of cavalry.[89] Although enabled with superior strategic intelligence at the launch, Hooker did not have sufficient intelligence to support tactical decision-making by either himself or his subordinates. Just as McDowell had lacked operational and tactical intelligence on Federal forces (Patterson) and the enemy (Joe Johnston) at First Manassas, so Hooker lacked this intelligence on his own forces (Sedgwick and Stoneman), and the enemy (Lee, Jackson, and Longstreet) at Chancellorsville.

The problems in 1863 were compounded, however, by elaborate intelligence capabilities that led Hooker to expect he could coordinate actions across a broad front when, in fact, neither he nor the BMI appreciated the intelligence wars underway on his own side or had envisioned how the requirements for intelligence would change once the battle had begun.[90] Making matters worse, Hooker's subordinates were so certain of Hooker's grasp of battlefield intelligence that they failed to report fresh intelligence up the chain of command in a timely way. Some believed that it had first to be coordinated with Butterfield, Hooker's chief of staff. In fact, given the perceived competence of the BMI, some subordinates considered tactical intelligence likely wrong if it did not fit with Hooker's view.[91] Such problems reflected a neglect of training for subordinates in the management of battlefield intelligence. Hooker was thus dealing with intelligence pathologies McDowell never faced: the problems of intelligence "drag" and "groupthink" that can prove deadly when fast decision-making is required. *Intelligence drag* refers to the time lags intelligence processing (decryption, sorting, and analysis) can introduce into competitive decision-making; *groupthink* refers to the tendency for intelligence to propagate based on the numbers who believe it, not the quality of the evidence on which it is based.[92] Once Hooker launched his offensive, Jackson and Lee began forcing Federal decisions faster than Hooker could disseminate orders and the BMI could create and disseminate a dynamic all-source picture.[93]

These intelligence failures, plentiful as they are, do not, however, completely explain the outcome at Chancellorsville, which entailed major losses on the Confederate side as well. Lee's intelligence was also weak; his signalmen were vulnerable to deceptions, and he remained unaware that the gap in his lines offered Hooker his opening opportunity. Later, Jackson did find his route through the Wilderness, but the gains thus reaped covered up serious deficiencies in intelligence gathering. Hotchkiss's crucial mapmaking in the midst of battle depended on the last-minute help he received from locals. Even as events began to go his way, Lee was perplexed by Hooker's flight back across the Rappahannock. To Lee, Hooker's defensive position at Chancellorsville appeared strong, but he did not know that Hooker felt weak because he had poor situational awareness and, in particular, believed Longstreet's divisions might be encircling him. Lee could not, therefore, "own" Hooker's intelligence disadvantage and claim the superiority he had.

Lee benefited from Union failures at Chancellorsville multiple times, but *created* advantages only three times: once when Stuart signaled Hooker's crossing at Kelly's Ford, giving Lee time to react; second, when he felt his way west from Maryes Heights with the help of locals; and third, when Stuart's intelligence and Hotchkiss's mapmaking enabled Jackson's bold move around Hooker's right— a move that also benefited from intelligence failures on Hooker's side. Thus, as Hooker fought for his reputation in Washington, Lee won one he only partly deserved. Even as Hooker's army shadowed Lee's movement north, and both sides positioned for the next engagement, the tables turned. Lee found himself at a surprising intelligence disadvantage, owing to his lack of situational awareness about the extended length of his army relative to the Army of the Potomac. As he moved north, the slim benefits he had had operating on his own turf disappeared. He found himself poorly equipped for strategic battlefield intelligence on enemy ground.

Conclusion: Intelligence Advantage before Gettysburg

Fighting Joe Hooker made a historic claim in 1861: "I was at Bull Run the other day, Mr. President . . . and it is no vanity in me to say that I am a damned sight better general than any you had on that field."[94] Hooker had a chance to make good on that claim in 1863. If outcomes are the measure, he did not. At Chancellorsville, Hooker's superiority in intelligence was fleeting because his innovative intelligence system lacked cavalry support and a robust, integrated telegraph that could transmit reliably among intelligence platforms and follow him into battle. Within hours of his surprise move across the Rappahannock, the same intelligence service that had made Hooker's master stroke possible had blinded him. This loss was no counterstroke by a superior intelligence service; it was the kind of self-inflicted blinding that happens when trusted headlights suddenly fail, leaving the driver worse off than if he had adjusted his eyes, his course, and his speed to the dark. On the road, blinded drivers pull over, which is exactly what Hooker did at Chancellorsville. In battle, however, such timeouts are dangerous. Opponents can use temporary blindness to win, which is exactly what Lee did. Accustomed to uncertainty, Lee groped his way forward and, eventually, to victory.

The Federals' loss led Hooker to resign before Washington's leaders could usher him out, but not before defending and protecting the BMI from attacks by those not privy to its operations. When Hooker handed the Federal army over to his successor, General Meade, the same intelligence service that had crippled him had regrouped for mobile service and was facilitating the army's swift move north. Thanks to extraordinary intelligence work, Hooker discovered Lee's trajectory, moved faster than Lee expected, and sent the Federal cavalry to Gettysburg, the spot where both armies were eventually to meet. This last decision was a lasting source of pride for him, just as Chancellorsville remained his shame. Hooker set up the victory at Gettysburg by solving what he knew had gone wrong in his last battle: mobile intelligence. Rather than reorganize the BMI, he demanded fixes to the cavalry and telegraph, and got them.

Indeed, the comparison of Chancellorsville and the run-up to Gettysburg highlights the importance of changing cavalry tactics to military intelligence in the mid-nineteenth century. As both armies raced north to Gettysburg, the Confederate cavalry screen established by Stuart initially hid Lee's advance down the Shenandoah Valley. But once Stuart broke toward Washington and stayed to the east of the northward-marching Federal troops, his utility to Lee *as an intelligence source* diminished rapidly, while it increased *as a potential counterintelligence operative*. He disrupted Union rails and broke telegraph lines. Thus, the intelligence dynamic that had held at Chancellorsville was reversed. With the benefit of integrated cavalry and the professional exploitation of sources by the BMI, General Hooker and General Meade stayed well apprised of Lee's advance, while it was Lee who seemed without headlights. The Federals learned of the likely meeting of armies at Gettysburg and so were able to choose the most advantageous ground on which to fight. As Lee was wondering whether he would face superior forces, the BMI was supplying Meade with a complete order of battle for the Confederates he would soon engage. With this superior intelligence, Meade knew he had no need to protect his rear, so could hold where he was. When Lee arrived on the battlefield, he accepted the gauntlet where it was thrown, regretting the absence of Stuart, his "eyes and ears."

* * *

This chapter has considered where intelligence advantage lay at critical decision-points during two Civil War battles. Before discussing their lessons in greater detail, an interim hypothesis seems worth mentioning: given that the Federals were on the offensive and lost decision advantages both battles, could it be that, at least from an intelligence standpoint, the offensive carries inherent intelligence disadvantages? Before the Battle of First Manassas, Scott's apparent trust in the advantages of the initiative seemed to have rendered him insensitive to the relative intelligence advantages the Confederates would have as soon as the Union forces marched. As Jeb Stuart once remarked: "The marching or transportation of divisions will often indicate the plan of a campaign."[95] The Confederates took advantage of those indications in both battles. McDowell's easily observed march and agent reporting on July 16, revealed Federal strategy in time for a fast, prearranged redistribution of forces on the Confederate side. Hooker's far more successful surprise built on his own insight into McDowell's defeat, allowing him to use secrecy to gain an opening advantage despite marching first.

Although one may be tempted to agree with Stuart about the intelligence-advantages of the defender, it seems more likely that the trouble lies less with the greater intelligence demands of an offensive, per se, than with the tendency of an attacker, especially one bent on surprise, to assume an intelligence-advantage and thus to overlook the necessity of securing and maintaining it. The Federals' offensive strategies in both battles were peculiarly prone to intelligence-related mistakes of this kind. The point is that Hooker, McDowell, and Scott lost decision-advantage; that they were on the offensive did not make that loss inevitable. If an offensive or defensive strategy is to work, it must have a built-in appreciation for the terrain of uncertainty, and a plan for using or compensating for it.

Recall that intelligence enabled Hooker's surprise offensive, but then collapsed. Despite the *knowable fact* that his telegraph wire was unreliable, Hooker first chose to send most of his cavalry, the primary source of mobile, battlefield intelligence collection and the crucial link between his short telegraph lines and his field commanders, on a mission to disrupt Lee's lines of communication with Richmond. Then, when the telegraph failed, Hooker wrongly assumed the enemy was the cause and chose to send more cavalry to guard the telegraph lines. Combined with Stoneman's occupation elsewhere, this poorly informed decision meant that the complex battlefield on May 2–3 would remain dark to him. Hooker's situation was not the result of bad luck; he *designed* his strategy around far-flung intelligence and communications assets incapable of delivering comparable images of the battle to the generals that would engage in it. If he had not kept his plans secret from his engineers and intelligence providers, perhaps Hooker would have been able to adapt intelligence to strategy. But he did. In contrast, Lee, commanding a numerically lesser force, sustained his cavalry's communications and kept his mapmaker, Jedediah Hotchkiss, and Stonewall Jackson's "foot cavalry" close at hand. This simple system gave him a view that the other side lacked, allowing him to plan and execute a surprising flank attack and the confidence he needed to engage at critical moments.

Considered this way, the Battle of Chancellorsville, in which Lee was outnumbered almost two to one, turned less on troop numbers than on leadership—a skill owing much to good intelligence, which lubricates choices more on one side than the other. Once Hooker's initial surprise was achieved, winning battlefield advantage flowed from the relative disposition of collection assets, their connectedness to chains of command, and commanders' analytical abilities to exploit it. The Union's new all-source intelligence bureau was neither mobile enough nor sufficiently connected to all commanders to sustain its opening advantages. Intelligence advantage at the operational level lay as much if not more in the adaptability of intelligence systems to battlefield tactics and decision-making than in any simple comparison of the number of spies, couriers, analysts, or codes on each side. And that adaptability depended as much on the sophistication and audacity of the user as the artfulness of the provider.

7

Intelligence Lessons from the Battlefield

The Battles of First Manassas and Chancellorsville offer timeless, over-arching lessons for intelligence. A familiar one is that strategic decisions have consequences for intelligence support to the battlefield, increasing the need for engineered advantage relative to the adversary. Spanish admirals learned this lesson in the sixteenth century when their Armada planned to deliver shock and awe along the English coast with inadequate maps and relatively poor knowledge of the currents. "Fighting Joe" Hooker learned something similar at Chancellorsville when he could not sustain opening intelligence advantages achieved in one position on enemy turf later. His strategy of surprise was brilliant, but its supporting intelligence architecture was not; it could not shift from high levels of secrecy, and a transparent order of battle for a few decision-makers, to coordinated action, distributed decision-making, and intelligence on the move. Common situational awareness among generals was needed both before and during the Battles of First Manassas and Chancellorsville; Scott and McDowell underestimated the requirement in 1861, and Hooker was too intoxicated with his superior numbers and opening intelligence advantages to prepare for it in 1863.

Getting confused on these matters has consequences for other areas of intelligence, including data collection and analysis. Union generals often seemed to care more about using intelligence to measure enemy forces than to find and exploit competitive advantages in those forces' relative distribution. Scott, for example, questioned Patterson's credibility as an intelligence provider before First Manassas because the latter repeatedly overestimated Johnston's strength from June through early July. Yet Scott failed to see what Patterson could: that while numbers were important to relative strength, they were not the source of Johnston's advantage, which was that Johnston appreciated the evolving distribution of forces and the constraints on Patterson better than McDowell, Patterson, or Scott did. Knowing one's own side better than adversaries do is fundamental to gaining intelligence advantage in most competitions. During First Manassas, Scott knew less than Beauregard and Johnston did about critical constraints on his own side—a wartime loss of "that essential of success" for which Scott was uniquely responsible.[1]

As we consider this and other lessons from these battlefields, we must proceed cautiously. The prescriptions resulting from the lessons discussed in this chapter

Decision Advantage. Jennifer E. Sims, Oxford University Press. © Oxford University Press 2022.
DOI: 10.1093/oso/9780197508046.003.0007

offer keys to winning on *these* battlefields. The general rule that one must engineer intelligence advantage leaves the specifics in any particular case contingent on circumstances. For example, whereas General McDowell might have benefited from just one clue about Confederate general Joe Johnston's movements in order to cross Bull Run in time, General Hooker had to have all-source analysis from multiple collectors to achieve his initial surprise at Chancellorsville. In Hooker's case, the requisite knowledge came from an archive of data built from scouting reports, engineering studies, balloon ascents, cavalry forays, and espionage networks. Similarly, tracking an opposing army in motion, as Hooker's army did on its way to Gettysburg, was the culmination of months of work, not just a single find or a lucky moment. As Lee moved his army north, the disparity in *engineered* intelligence power between Union and Confederate forces became apparent.

One general conclusion that can be derived from these cases is that superior intelligence requires creating opportunities for both the lucky find *and* successful puzzling. Union general Joseph Hooker's intelligence policy—to support the BMI rather than blame it for Chancellorsville—handed his successor an intelligence capability that proved important to his victory at Gettysburg: an archive of data, experienced analysts, a flexible, integrated telegraphic operation, and a solid network of sources and handlers. Hooker's careful remodeling of the BMI and related operations proved enough to achieve intelligence advantage for an army on the move, not just one at rest. Union generals Meade and Ulysses S. Grant would use and improve Hooker's system for the rest of the war.

Keeping these general points and cautionary ideas in mind, it is worth discussing a few lessons that concern the most intimate aspects of the intelligence process, including communication, aligning "truth-seeking" with problem-solving, public-private partnerships, and building trust between the providers and users of intelligence.

Communication: Pillar of Superior Intelligence

It may seem that the essence of intelligence is sourcing, analysis, or secrecy, but in truth it is not any one of these. Without the ability to connect knowledge to decision, none of what we consider to be intelligence tradecraft would matter. The battles covered in these case studies have illustrated this point, from the failure to connect Generals Patterson and McDowell during the Battle of First Manassas, to the failure of a factionalized telegraph system to keep Hooker informed of Sedgwick's whereabouts during the Battle of Chancellorsville. Connectivity of intelligence to decision is the crucial hidden enabler of intelligence power. If commanders are too confident or too ignorant to secure it, they risk operational disaster. Mcdowell was arguably ignorant; Hooker was overly confident; Scott was simply derelict.

Hooker's greatest disadvantage was his dependence on a divided and broken telegraph system for a battle plan that required superb communications across a broad front. The general compounded this problem by deciding not to tell his collection managers and telegraphers enough about what he intended to do. They had, therefore, insufficient wire for extending communications as far west as Hooker ultimately decided to go before crossing the Rappahannock. As one of the Morse men would later write of his experience at the crucial intersection of the two lines:

> All business from Falmouth, where part of the staff remained, and from Sedgwick [Sixth Corps], who crossed at Fredericksburg lower down, came to James Murray and myself. We handed it to the Signal people for re-transmission. For the two days, business was very heavy and A. Harper Caldwell and Jacques at Falmouth sent it to us so rapidly that we handed the Signal folks as much every five minutes as they could transmit in an hour. We were obliged to send most of the messages to Hooker by orderlies; half a company being detailed for that purpose. The consequence was, the Commanding General and his subordinate commanders became totally disgusted at the inadequacy of the Beardslee telegraph, and it was immediately after turned over to our people.[2]

Problems with the telegraph lines included the large volume of intelligence flowing through them and the apparently haphazard sequencing these flaws induced in the traffic flowing to Hooker and back to Sedgwick. As a consequence, Hooker's decisions about whether to order Sedgwick to advance east or cross back over the river became both confused and ill-informed. Hooker seemed indecisive; Sedgwick seemed changeable—at one moment insisting on retreat, the next ready to press the fight westward.

Hooker's system of signaling and communications was suited more to an army at rest than one on the move. Superior strategic intelligence cannot follow decision-makers into battle unless there is a workable plan for it to do so, and Hooker had none. Although he understood better than Scott, Patterson, or McDowell that successful strategic planning rests on superior knowledge, he seemed slow to grasp that its execution must do so, as well. This lag may have had to do with the unique status of the US Military Telegraph Corps (USMT) within Hooker's larger command. Although the Signal Corps with its Beardslee telegraph system was subordinate to him, the USMT technically was not. In any case, both Hooker and his telegraphers saw the latter's job as enabling army operations by carrying out a specific mission, not contributing to strategy.[3] The BMI and Hooker's staff, in turn, failed to fully understand the logistical constraints under which telegraphers were working and the consequences these would have. Without timely appreciation of Hooker's plan to cross about twenty-five miles north at Kelly's Ford, telegraphers in the Signal Corps and USMT had to jury-rig a flawed system on the fly, reducing the impact of all collectors feeding intelligence into that system. When problems arose, the competing Morse and Beardslee operators tended to point fingers—continuing shenanigans that had plagued the two telegraph operations since before First Manassas.

For intelligence to accompany troops into battle, its managers must have a flexible architecture for collection and communications and know where commanders are going and what they intend. *Such connectivity can only be provided if military decision-makers bring intelligence policymakers into strategic and operational planning.* Relying on the BMI and his immediate staff, Hooker overlooked his experts in telegraphy and aeronautics, who in turn were relying on orderlies and cavalry operations over which they had little say. Not fully expert on the systems they purportedly managed, officers within the BMI and headquarters' staff were poor advisers on the collection and communication challenges Hooker faced. Without access to Hooker's strategy, no telegrapher or platform manager—whether Thaddeus Lowe, Stoneman, or Babcock running spies, could appreciate the vulnerability of communications until they broke.

This gap was especially odd given improvements in the Federal cavalry. Unlike McDowell and Patterson, who had inadequate cavalry during First Manassas, Hooker had, in general, a capable, reorganized cavalry. He misused it. Hooker's decision to send Stoneman to cut off Lee's communications with Richmond might have been a judicious gamble, but it meant that he had no reliable system in place for backing up weaknesses in his wires—a knowable problem. He eventually did send some cavalry to guard the wires when they began to fail, but he assumed the problem was sabotage (enemy counterintelligence) when it was not. The consequences of these missteps included more misallocated cavalry and heightened sense of panic. Hooker's decision to retreat back across the Rappahannock reflected in part his uncertainty about Sedgwick's advance, but also whether Longstreet's forces would soon be reinforcing Lee—intelligence his intelligence service should have been able to provide.

In contrast, Lee profited from good communications with his cavalry throughout much of the battle. Much as Hooker's strategic assets had found the vulnerability in Lee's lines before battle, Jeb Stuart found Hooker's exposed right flank during it, and rapidly communicated this knowledge to Lee. This advantage was the predicate for Lee's decision to move Jackson into the gap on Hooker's right flank—a move he left to Jackson to design. And this attack drove a stake in the heart of Union forces, squashing morale and collapsing the confidence of mid-level officers.

It is worth noting that Hooker's best collection capabilities, such as balloons, signals stations, deserters, and farmer-spies were essentially fixed assets that depended on stationary communications systems for connectivity. Lee's collectors were predominantly mobile, with communications built-in. The latter included not just cavalry, but also mounted guides and mapmakers, such as Jedediah Hotchkiss.[4] During battle, Lee relied on Hotchkiss's skills at rapid map-making, asking him to draw specific routes, including enemy obstacles, within minutes to hours of a decision to move. Hotchkiss copied his maps and distributed them to all who needed them in real time to ensure common situational awareness. In this way, Lee kept proximate to his collectors—that is, not by tel-egraph but by physical proximity—as the battle unfolded. That was enough for him, because he never expected more.

There is, in fact, a curious lesson here. When good communications are lost, intelligence operations do not simply fail to inform; rather, they make any blinding worse by setting up the expectation of knowing and then not delivering. In such circumstances, gaps in intelligence may seem pregnant with meaning when they are not. Hearing nothing, commanders may assume all is well or im-agine the worst—both perhaps more debilitating for the dashed expectations that come from knowing what it is like to be well informed.

Recognition of the intelligence-communication nexus does not imply there was, or is, a simple prescription for using it to achieve superior intelligence in war, such as destroying the communications and intelligence operations of the other side. War is, at its heart, a form of communication: the convincing of one side by another that it will lose or has already lost. Decisions to end a war require the loser to learn it is defeated and to convey that knowledge and any terms of surrender across all lines of engagement. The transition from war to peace requires good risk calculation and informed interactions on both sides. So it follows that sound intel-ligence policy can involve protecting, and perhaps even upgrading, the learning capabilities of the opponent. Even at the tactical level, military strategies some-times involve, as Hooker's did, the intent to distract or mislead, which requires the enemy to see what you want him to and then react to it. Prior to Chancellorsville, both sides, but particularly Union forces, postured for the other as part of influence campaigns. So protagonists have at least some interest in preserving each other's ability to gather intelligence and to communicate down the chain of command. Decisions on which enemy communications to leave intact, to influence, or to de-stroy have to be part of intelligence and war-winning strategies.

Mapping: Lessons in the Relationship of Truth and Accuracy to Intelligence

General McDowell may have had plenty of *accurate* maps in June and July 1861, but he lacked *competitive knowledge* about the terrain those maps represented. In other words, he had good information, but poor intelligence. Strange as it seems, accurate maps can hurt a battlefield commander if they do not convey what he needs to know. For example, maps can mislead if commanders using them are tempted to guess what they mean for battle based on what they see drawn within them, as McDowell did when planning his march toward Bull Run. He learned during battle that the fords shown on maps might have been suitable for a farmer's wagon or a single man on horseback but were not for a six-horse team pulling a heavy gun. And a "road" might not be viable for an army if it forced it to march two men abreast. And if accurate maps vary enough in scope or detail, commanders engaged in the same or a related battle may have trouble coordinating their movements. These lessons from First Manassas were important. The Federal army proved slow to learn them. McClellan's officers erred during the subsequent Peninsula Campaign by extrapolating the course of rivers using highly accurate but nonetheless misleading maps.

For all these reasons, mapmakers and topographical engineers who served as both collectors and analysts were critical to decision-advantage during the Civil War. The good ones collected preexisting maps but then verified and extended them by riding routes and gauging distances. Jedediah Hotchkiss's support to Confederate generals Lee and Stonewall Jackson illustrated this kind of decision-advantage. By using color, layout, and the absence of unnecessary facts, Hotchkiss made his generals' battlefield decisions easier. Such maps were often less "true" than the more formal variety prepared as records of past battles, yet they succeeded if they addressed commanders' immediate questions. The further lesson here might be that perseverating on truth-finding, understood as perfecting detail and accuracy, can waste resources and cause intelligence to fail by encumbering decision-making with what might be called "intelligence drag." As a veteran of the Mexican war, Lee was aware of these kinds of intelligence problems. He found a way to keep his topographer glued to the requirements of competitive context rather than mapping "truths" prior to battle that might prove irrelevant to it.

Public-Private Partnerships and Their Oversight

The problems of logistics—procuring, storing, and distributing supplies in war—are well beyond the scope of this study, which has focused on decisions during two discreet battles. It is important to note, however, that intelligence was important to this larger wartime endeavor, which required either public-private partnerships or the nationalization of industry for the cause. With industrial growth rapid in the lead-up to war, "Napoleonic War tactics met modern weapons with devastating results."[5] The challenges for intelligence were commensurate. The Confederacy's ordnance general, Josiah Gorgas, attempted to meet this challenge by collaborating with railroads, weapons manufacturers, cotton mills, shoemakers, and miners. The Confederacy got progressively better at locating domestic stockpiles and bargaining with foreign suppliers, thus reducing the ordnance gap it faced at the start of the war. And, as already discussed, the Union partnered with telegraph companies and the railroads to turn civilian communication networks into a military telegraph system.

Such public-private partnerships differ from intelligence liaison insofar as they are contractual arrangements in which the interests of the contractor are subservient to those of hiring party. Knowing how, when, and with whom to partner is part of the job of intelligence support to logistics. At the start of the Civil War, neither side was very good at it, but the Confederacy seems to have been better—perhaps because its challenges were so grave. The Confederate who stood out for his mastery of logistics was Gorgas, who excelled at locating supplies, deploying agents for procuring them in Europe, and then balancing public and private blockade running to get them into Southern ports. The North was less desperate and so, perhaps, more slothful in meeting its intelligence challenges in logistical matters. The mid-nineteenth-century entrepreneurs who were innovating in communications, reconnaissance, and weaponry were mostly working in the North. Their products offered potential advances in effectiveness, but also threatened to undermine military doctrine and add to the challenges of commanding armies. As of 1861, the US Army field manual had changed little, leaving commanders on both sides complacent, if not ignorant, about how these innovations might affect battlefield performance. Among the few who kept an eye on opportunities in the private sector were those coming into the army with business backgrounds, such as General McClellan, an experienced railroad man who brought his private detective, Pinkerton, into his army with unfortunate results.[6]

In general, however, the US military was not an aggressive innovator or "first adopter" of technology during the early months of the Civil War, despite the rate of technological change in precision machining, communications, and aerial reconnaissance. Once the war began, both sides relied on traditional, proven tactics supplemented only at the margins with insights that had been gleaned from the Crimean War. Even the USMT, created by a team of private-sector entrepreneurs embedded in the Union's War Department, seemed created as an afterthought. Fully realized capabilities, such as rifled, breech-loading repeaters, the telegraph, and balloon reconnaissance were haphazardly introduced and their full potential left unrealized until late in the war. Although the counterfactual cannot be proven, poor intelligence from scientific and technological quarters before the war may have cost more men and beasts on the battlefield than required for the outcomes obtained.

Even when public-private partnerships were appreciated and implemented, they did not always work smoothly to satisfy intelligence requirements on the battlefield. Conflict among competing private-sector balloonists and competing telegraphers pitted private interests against each other, undermining operations. Confederate generals, reliant on railroads, came to understand that civilian engineers outside their command and control could be recruited as spies or covert operatives, slowing trains or reporting troop movements. For their part, entrepreneurs such as Thaddeus Lowe often found their collection platforms misused, misunderstood, and denigrated, even by military overseers attempting to bind them more thoroughly to wartime chains of command. For his part, Lowe was justifiably accused of mismanagement of his finances, which lowered the military's trust in his operations.

The necessary connection between competitive learning and technology drives both the requirement for private-public partnerships and intelligence oversight of them. And it was sound oversight that was lacking. Decision-makers cannot leave collection management to private entities, who will likely defend their methods, especially if these are connected to commercial interests. Such was the case with Lowe, who nonetheless brought an irreplaceable expertise to running his highly complex reconnaissance operation. The battles of Manassas and Chancellorsville also illustrate the dangers that can accompany the professionalization of an intelligence service in which collectors compete, and come to see accurate data production as one thing and decision-making another. If such ideas are allowed to take hold, intelligence becomes an end in itself, to the detriment of decision-advantage. Sharpe's BMI was lauded for collecting and analyzing the Confederate order of battle at Chancellorsville. Celebrating its success at that, its central managers seemed unaware that their semiprivate collection architecture, engineered for surprise, would be unable to support Hooker on Sedgwick's, let alone Longstreet's, *movements*, which constituted a different, although related, challenge. The users of intelligence are properly its first-tier managers and so responsible for extinguishing the commercial interests and fratricidal conflicts that can ruin it; but, in the context of the battlefield, decision-advantage requires almost always delegating collection management, oversight, and platform operations to someone unbeholden to any private-sector interests. And these subordinates must be sufficiently trusted to bring to decision-makers honest reports on the constraints within which collection systems are operating, along with potential solutions.

The Civil War battles of First Manassas and Chancellorsville provide plenty of evidence for this requirement for public-private partnership and intelligence oversight. Telegraphers, aeronauts, and signalmen, sometimes in alliance with industrial interests, competed for footholds in the infrastructure for war—occasionally at the expense of military missions. Intelligence innovators, such as balloonists John Wise, Thaddeus Lowe, and John La Mountain; the USMT and the Army Signal Corps; and heads of detective services, such as Pinkerton and Lafayette Baker, engaged in repetitive and destructive turf fights. Commanders and their intelligence managers needed to recognize these fights and put a stop to them before they endangered missions. They failed to do so before both battles. Sound oversight, which requires two-way flows of information between users and intelligence providers, *enables* intelligence as much or more than it constrains it. With centralized collection management and systemic oversight in place, intelligence providers can be relieved of destructive fratricidal conflicts, and given greater discretion to get their jobs done.

Managing All-Source Analysis and Collection

So, if central management of a collection system is necessary for gaining battle-field advantages, who should do it and how? Decision-makers tend to trust their closest intelligence advisors, lean on them for advice, and assume they will take care of fratricidal intelligence wars, even if those providers do not understand or know how to fix them. Colonel George Sharpe, who set up the BMI for Hooker, was an analyst and then Hooker's trusted advisor on all aspects of intelligence, in-cluding all-source intelligence and, by implication, the health of the intelligence system overall. During the Battle of Chancellorsville, Sharpe proved to be, how-ever, sometimes ill-informed and in any case dependent on collection platforms and communications over which he had only haphazard oversight. As a result, he could not explain to Hooker the risks and gains of the decisions he was taking on the intelligence he would need. One historian sympathetic to Sharpe's predica-ment put the blame on Hooker: "Hooker's refusal to properly prepare his staff for the operation due to excessive security had prevented the Signal Corps officers from ordering enough wire to support the attack."[7] And yet this judgment is only fair insofar as all intelligence—a delegated function of command—is the respon-sibility of the commander.

In fact, Hooker had delegated the *distribution* of all-source intelligence to his chief of staff, Major General Daniel Butterfield. As one historian has put it: "No matter where the reports originated—whether from the uncooperative cav-alry jealously guarding their ancient role, the eager to cooperate balloonists, or the team players in the Signal Corps, Butterfield made sure they circu-lated among all the players," and it was to him that individual collectors often appealed when they felt misused.[8] Still, while Butterfield circulated collection to the BMI analysts, he did not for the most part *manage it*. Collection man-agement was largely left to the Corps commanders and the private "owners" of the platforms and sensors involved. Thus, Hooker never understood the dangers of using degraded wires or poorly repaired balloons because he was never told. Instead, he depended on Butterfield and Sharpe, who in turn relied informally on telegraphers and civilian aeronauts, bullying them to make do with what they had once they finally learned Hooker's plan. For example, in the final days before Hooker's attack at Chancellorsville, an army captain with little understanding of balloon technology was put in charge of all aeronautics—a move that, supported by Butterfield, caused Lowe to lose heart before the battle and quit after it. Without its expert manager, the platform and, indeed, the entire collection system fell into disrepair. It was only when Hooker, in need of tracking Confederate movements after the battle, demanded urgent aerial reconnaissance that he learned his master of aerial reconnaissance was gone. And at this moment, the lack of a crucial source became the BMI's problem—that is, Sharpe's problem. The same proved true when Stoneman's cavalry operations went awry and the BMI could not locate Longstreet's forces; the only collection the BMI controlled were human agents and deserters, who were either agents of deception or otherwise poor at answering such questions.

The prescription for avoiding such intelligence failures is not self-evident. The danger in having all-source analysts or chiefs of staff serve as system managers is that they often have to prioritize the synthesis of large quantities of data needed for decision-making in the moment over understanding, coordinating, and managing the methods by which these data are obtained. The faster the decision-making, the more difficult and yet essential time management becomes. Fine-tuning all-source collection for any decision, and the next one after that, requires an appreciation of all potential sources, the differences in how they operate, their vulnerability to deception, and the constraints on timeliness and reliability of products. The more collectors there are, the more onerous this task.

Central management of collection is crucial when forces are on the move and collectors in conflict. Yet creating new central managers with powers to oversee and regulate creates tensions and can degrade performance by increasing bureaucracy and decreasing the morale of collectors. The BMI may have relied on the cavalry for critical intelligence and communications, but relations were tense because of the latter's preference for its autonomy and non-intelligence-related missions. Similar tensions arose in the BMI's relationships with telegraphers, whose performance depended on wires of varying quality and machines that were obtuse. Aeronauts, uncertain of their standing with military superiors, had financial and operational difficulties they were reluctant to share. BMI managers, not in direct line of command, were eager to provide answers to decision-makers under pressure and so were largely incurious about the problems in collection architectures supporting them. Such poor collection management can lead to defeat in contests with simpler arrangements such as those employed by General Lee.

Yet simplifying collection and tying it more directly to the commander is not always the best solution. On the battlefield, Lee sacrificed capabilities for more direct access to his collectors: mapmakers, cavalry, Signal Corps, newspapers, and secret agents. *It would seem that collection management requires a central platform manager who is trusted by collectors because he understands the components of each collection system, its relationship to all others, and the value of each to all-source analysts and the decision-makers they support.* The BMI lacked this understanding and connectivity because, as discussed above, the military had innovated by partnering with private interests but lacked the necessary flexibility and oversight within military chains of command. The cost was unstable organizational relationships that caused intelligence to fail before it could get better. In fact, failure in this case was probably necessary to perfect a revolution in military affairs: the integration of intelligence support to military operations within headquarters itself, and thus, the military chain of command.

Before leaving this point, it is important to note the subtle danger that arises when all-source analysts, trained to eschew collection bias and managerial interference, are promoted to managerial roles and asked to run intelligence systems they poorly understand. Because of their search for accurate information, all-source analysts can become more invested in arcane puzzles than smarter decision-making or a better-functioning intelligence system overall.[9] For this reason, rising intelligence professionals should spend time in all aspects of their business. Analysts, collection managers, and decision-makers should be trained to see their respective missions as connected to all others. At the same time, they should be expected to press their interests, disagree, and even compete for resources. The engine of intelligence thus generates power, but central coordinators do the shifting and transmission of that power. They must be as familiar as possible with all the puzzles being worked and all collection systems used, including their private-sector elements. They should be directly accountable to the commander, either by being his all-source analyst, too, or by acting in concert with him. It follows that decision-makers must know and confide all plans and decisions to whoever is responsible for the functions of collection management and all-source analysis, whether or not these functions are combined.

Intelligence Victories Hide in Operational Defeats

If intelligence problems must be fixed in the midst of war, surgery is required. After First Manassas, however, Congress had chopping blocks rather than surgery in mind. Politicians needed to find blame for the humiliating defeat, and so sent Patterson and Scott, two war heroes, into a wartime political battle to save their reputations. This politicized review led to finger-pointing and both generals' retirement, but contributed little rigorous thinking about underlying intelligence problems.

Intelligence policy continued to flounder as Washington launched another search for blame after Chancellorsville. This time however, Hooker, convinced of the value of the BMI, insisted on surgery. He laid heavy blame on Stoneman and on the Signal Service, whose telegraph functions were subsequently transferred to the USMT. Although Hooker lost his command, his protection of the BMI meant that it survived largely intact along with its network of human agents and archived data. Hooker and later General Ulysses S. Grant understood that the BMI represented something revolutionary that had to be preserved:

> Hooker [had] obtained a picture of the enemy's situation as coherent and complete as the supply of information permitted. This was an innovation: Hooker invented a process and a product now called all-source intelligence. Actually, it was a re-invention, for General Washington had engaged in all-source intelligence by virtue of being his own spymaster and also the one to whom the other sources, the cavalry and individual scouts, reported.[10]

Hooker understood that the BMI's methods were fragile for transforming seemingly worthless tidbits into useful knowledge, including collaboration among collectors, analysts, and accountants. He had watched his intelligence officers solve complex puzzles during the weeks of planning prior to his attack. He had appreciated how the accumulation of data had revealed Lee's order of battle, and he had participated in the methods for filling in gaps or influencing the enemy. The BMI had extended his eyes and ears, increasing his trust in what he knew before his attack.

The intimacy between intelligence and command that Hooker had created was no fluke; it was at the heart of the innovative approach he had instituted, however imperfectly. The idea was twofold: to bring together and store all battle-relevant information, and to relieve a commander of the job of analyzing and directing intelligence himself. By relieving commanders of some of that burden, the BMI fostered respect and, eventually trust. But the accretion of that trust took time, especially for commanders used to doing intelligence work themselves.[11] After the disaster at Chancellorsville, the BMI won only grudging support from Hooker's relatively inexperienced successor, General Meade, who never fully trusted it.[12] General Ulysses Grant did. He kept the service close to him through the campaign to capture Richmond and the battle of Appomattox Courthouse.[13]

Grant's intelligence in later battles owed a fair measure of its success to Hooker's light touch as a reformer in 1863. Hooker appreciated how the BMI worked, so he understood the hidden costs of disrupting an intelligence system in the midst of conflict. Such costs include the danger that reformers will not consider the requirements for the next battle or what went right (not just wrong) in the last one. Good intelligence performs like any complex system, such as a thoroughbred horse or a Formula One car: change the tires, the shoes, the octane, or the grain and the effects will be felt throughout. The better and more tightly tuned the system, the more consequential the effects for better or for worse. Had the BMI lost certain collectors, analysts, or managers, or even just shuffled their portfolios, agents recruited and developed over months of work might have been lost. The staff of the BMI did not just crunch numbers, they coordinated and collected human intelligence. Changes of staff could have meant the loss of critical skills in elicitation and interrogation and severed connections to civilian spies throughout Pennsylvania, Maryland, and Virginia. If intelligence "reform" had jeopardized the steady accumulation of data in accessible archives, which are often the least exciting products intelligence officers produce, years of work might have never been recovered.

Binding Decision to Knowledge

Although Union knowledge of the Confederate order of battle mattered greatly during the run-up to Gettysburg, how the BMI came to know it seemed, for most men commanding, fighting, and dying on the battlefield, very much "in the weeds." Binding decisions to someone else's learning—learning that is, in turn, largely based on persistent, archived collection—depends on trust. That fact may be one of the most important, but least understood and respected aspects of the intelligence business. Trust, in turn, depends on reliably positive outcomes for both decision-maker and intelligence provider over time. Decision-makers need to know how knowledge was gained, and providers need to know how and why it was valued in order to develop two-way confidence in the process.

Hooker, in this sense, was unusual. Most decision-makers favor collection for themselves or their shooters, not for jigsaw-puzzlers worrying a larger strategic problem whose significance is not yet clear. In modern intelligence services, even professionals forget this crucial point: Lacking a database with which to compare new information, one cannot fully judge its significance and, therefore, learn from it. Good analysts know, for example, the vital importance of sustaining seemingly nonproductive sources when the context merits it. These Civil War battles have demonstrated what may be unappreciated by inexperienced officers: that an absence of collection ought not necessarily impugn sources and may, in fact, validate them. Reports of nothing may be finding something, such as a gap in an enemy line or, in modern times, a missile that did not launch or a nuclear plant that is (still) not operating. Fortunately for the Union Army in 1863, General Hooker understood the relationship between persistent collection, pregnant gaps, and good estimative judgments of the enemy.[14] Decision-makers who take the time to understand why data collection and all-source analysis matters will gain significant advantages against those who do not. A trusted relationship among analyst, collector, and decision-maker is essential, therefore, if this kind of learning is to be achieved.

A related point is that one cannot judge the value of a source by the activity level of its target alone. Predators are, after all, often motionless before they pounce; silent canaries indicate a coal mine is safe, and quiet dogs can be Sherlock's clue to the familiarity of a murderer. Some sources tell their stories in silence or by registering nothing over time. Knowing the meaning of gaps requires knowing what could be there but is not—that is, having an uninterrupted history on the target. Gap analysis involves special expertise. Recall the importance of a police stakeout of a criminal lair; the whole point is the wait. If the watch is disrupted to chase one active, but insignificant, fugitive, knowledge on how to bring down the whole gang could be lost. But intelligence providers must also understand that, if the active agent is executing a decisive attack, to wait is to lose. So sometimes a data archive necessary for tomorrow's decision must be sacrificed for decision-advantage today. On a battlefield, waiting may either be wise or, alternatively deadly; to know which, and to accept the attendant risks, requires not just patience, but also knowing your enemy's habits as well as your own. Such knowledge in turn requires intimacy among collectors, analysts, and decision-makers.[15]

Secrecy and Intelligence-Sharing: The Good, the Bad, and The Ugly

Secrecy seems a simple thing: keeping secrets is good and losing them to the enemy is bad. Yet, as in many other matters related to intelligence, the truth is much more complex. Some of the most difficult intelligence policy decisions involve deciding what matters more: keeping a secret, giving it away, or some combination of the two. Hooker understood the conundrum to some extent because he engineered a deception to avoid revealing Federal capabilities to read Confederate communications, which he nonetheless was putting at risk. In other words, he knew that one sometimes had to risk losing secrets to the enemy to gain an advantage.

Hooker was not, however, a master of this game. He did not appreciate that the need for secrecy must be reconciled with the need for sharing on one's own side. Hooker kept so many secrets from his own team for fear of losing them that he handicapped his intelligence providers. His telegraph operators were surprised not just by the length of the Federal lines at Chancellorsville, but also by the volume of communications that the army's movements would demand at a single point (US Ford). As a result, Hooker's telegraph was soon overwhelmed by them.

Such difficulties were not Hooker's alone. Union officers had long had trouble balancing secrecy with sharing. Even an experienced officer like Scott did not tell McDowell about Patterson's constraints during the Battle of First Manassas or share with him the intelligence that seemed to reinforce Patterson's inclination not to extend his lines, leaving McDowell to assume that the timing of battle could be his to determine. Secrecy left subordinate generals and their communicators confused.

The solution to balancing the need for secrets with advantageous release of them would seem to have three parts: improved security; improved intelligence-sharing among subordinate decision-makers, including those responsible for intelligence support; and a policy for flexibly applying these capacities as strategy and tactics require. Hooker would have been taking great risks to share his secret plan with competing civilian and military telegraph operators whose infighting was a security risk even before the battle. That Hooker neither fixed the infighting, nor developed a plan for enlightening key subordinates, doomed the execution of his plan. Similarly, Scott neither understood the importance of civilian telegraphers before First Manassas, nor integrated their operations into an overall plan. He seems to have expected Patterson, isolated from the main battlefield, to figure things out on his own. In fact, Scott's secrecy about Patterson's inability to move or to communicate in a timely way seems a more pathological secrecy than Hooker's ever was—less a failed effort at achieving decision advantage than a deliberate hiding of a problem Scott discounted or believed he could not fix. Scott's pathology bordered on the privatization of intelligence: that is, the willful distortion of intelligence for personal ends—in this case to camouflage confusion and indecision before the battle, and incompetence afterward.

The third part of the solution, a capacity for selective secrecy, is perhaps the most challenging because of its demands on decision-makers themselves. If commanders are untrained in the arts of collection, secrecy, and proactive release, they may be more surprised than the adversary about the consequences of their decisions. Collectors working on their behalf may not know what information matters and so fail to deliver it. Commanders may misunderstand what they see, believing others know more than they do. In Hooker's case, lower-level commanders believed, correctly, that they could not see the whole picture but concluded, incorrectly, that they should therefore ignore what they were seeing and hearing on the battlefield. General Charles Devens, commanding a division on Hooker's right under General Howard, learned of Stonewall Jackson's flanking movements, but, in the context of headquarters' assertions that the rebels were retreating, discounted the importance of what he knew. He failed either to send the intelligence forward or to act on it by reorienting his own forces. Devens shared with Howard the belief that information of military importance generally flowed down the chain of command, not up it.[16] While neither Howard nor Devens was known for his initiative, both almost certainly believed their superiors knew best.

Unfortunately, such lessons suggest that classification systems are not enough to resolve the tensions between secrecy and advantageous release. Secrecy always seems the surer way to decision-advantage. As a result, releasing intelligence—especially planning to release it—can get short shrift in training and operations, even when winning may depend on it. And while rules for classification and declassification may be necessary, they tend to create rigidities. The wisdom and capacity to *change the rules* during battle or alter the flow of intelligence—whether sensor to shooter, sensor to analyst, or both—is both necessary and more difficult to teach. Commanders need subordinates who understand the significance of intelligence, who know who needs it too, and who have the courage and initiative to act on that wisdom.[17] When the requirements of secrecy lead intelligence organizations to weed out plucky individuals, to insist that rules for intelligence dissemination be backed up by uncompromising penalties for abrogating them, potential agility is lost.

The challenges and opportunities of advantageous release are underappreciated, even within militaries that otherwise understand the importance of flexible communications. Although they know unexpected tactical situations will likely arise, key commanders may be killed, or communications may break, they resist the idea of situational declassification (providing classified intelligence to uncleared decision-makers) when such breakdowns occur because it can easily lead to a breakdown in discipline or leaks. The only answer is training and preparation:

- Include collection managers and communicators in all classified operational planning.
- Have these managers prepare alternative routes for intelligence dissemination in crisis.
- Train all intelligence handlers and decision-makers in advantageous release, not just secrecy, and give them the tools to get it done.

The route-mapping for intelligence should work much as Google maps do for drivers on overcrowded roads: provide options for drivers so they arrive on time, regardless of roadblocks, traffic jams, or faulty equipment. Intelligence managers at all levels must know who the key decision-makers are, and then ensure communications are sustained regardless of where troops, pilots, commanders, or negotiators go.

It is worth emphasizing here that, whenever the "rules" of good intelligence conflict, sound policy resolves matters in favor of tactical, operational, or strategic decision-advantage, not rules of process, doctrine, or procedure. In this regard, militaries have advantages over diplomatic services because chains of command are usually obvious. Before the Civil War battle at Antietam, General McClellan benefited from an alert junior officer's decision to bring him one un-analyzed and uncoordinated piece of intelligence. General Lee's Special Order 191, which was found in a field wrapped around cigars, revealed the Confederate disposition of widely dispersed forces. The officer understood not only that valuable intelligence can be found in the enemy's trash but also where to take it. Similarly, good instincts were demonstrated over a century later when, during the first Persian Gulf War, mid-level US military officers noticed that intelligence dissemination among the combat services was broken, and fixed it outside of channels. Several developed workarounds, such as trusted "buddy networks" to move intelligence where it needed to go, rather than through preauthorized gateways.[18] Superior intelligence services train intelligence officers to appreciate the value of intelligence to decision-making as different from its source-related classification, which must be considered as well. They must be trained to treat flexibility as an asset potentially as valuable as classification, depending on the competitive context.

Gaining Advantage from Covert, "Gray," and Open-Source Intelligence

A fourth set of lessons from the Civil War concerns intelligence methods in which secrecy plays a purposely specialized or limited role: gray, overt, and covert collection. Overt intelligence collection is the gathering of public information (e.g., commercial maps, library books, newspapers) for competitive decision-making.

Covert collection (as opposed to "covert action") is the open observation of an enemy on behalf of a clandestine sponsor.[19] It is the latter that most interests us here, but it must be distinguished from more clandestine and open methods. During the US Civil War, civilians on both sides openly observed troops as they marched, camped, and even fought. Sometimes these reports were secretly volunteered; at other times they were secretly prearranged—a network of "open spies" with hidden reporting channels. The observations in such cases often appeared to be innocent, while the sponsorship and reporting were secret or clandestine.[20] Train watchers and port watchers were used in a similar way during WWI and WWII with much success.

"Gray" intelligence differs from overt and covert types, although some overlap may occur in practice. Gray intelligence is privately owned information that is deemed useful for a separate competitive purpose. Examples might include a foreign scientist's preliminary research results, or a corporate executive's PowerPoint presentation.

All three of these forms of intelligence—covert, gray, and open-source—share one common feature: the independence of the collection platforms involved. That is to say, the original collectors (surveyors, journalists, corporate executives) wholly own their own means of collection (platforms and sensors) and tend to be more available when one is fighting on familiar ground. These features make them difficult or impossible to manage, but also cheap and useful because they can hide in plain sight. During the Civil War, farmers, housewives, slaves, and merchants could conduct daily business while keeping alert to the enemy, and covertly reporting what they learned. Journalists did the same, but did all their reporting overtly.

Dependency on these methods involves hidden dangers, however. During the Civil War, both sides made use of such covert, gray, and open-source intelligence without always understanding the extent or implications of their dependency on it.

Lee's craftiness in using covert sources did not mean his intelligence assets were in any overall sense "better" than Hooker's; rather, his advantages were at least partly attributable to the terrain of uncertainty with its embedded open sources that were working against Hooker. This was Lee's luck, not sound intelligence planning. As Lee moved into Pennsylvania, natural advantages in overt, covert, and gray collection shifted to the Federals. As both armies left the Rappahannock and marched north to Gettysburg, Lee's extended lines were visible to an observant, compliant population secretly passing detailed intelligence to Federal headquarters. Thus, the situation that had held at Chancellorsville was reversed, and the terrain of uncertainty became biased in favor of the North. The run-up to Gettysburg demonstrated that the terrain of uncertainty shapes tactical and strategic advantages in decision-making that intelligence organizations ignore at their peril.

Yet the point here goes further: Because covert, gray, and open-source information is often independently collected, superiority must derive less from good management of collection than from superior capacity for handling and analyzing information flowing in unregulated volume. Being flooded with open-source information of varying credibility will not help, and may confuse decision-making. Compared with the Confederacy, the North's BMI had a better capacity to absorb, assess, and distill masses of information generated by partisans and deserters, and could check individual reports against an intelligence picture provided by all-source analysts.

Of course, operating on one's own soil or in a friendly environment increases the chances of getting relatively good covert, gray, and open-source intelligence, thus relieving the analytical burden. The danger is that complacency may take root, as it did with General Lee. Lee lost his self-awareness, as well as his sense of the enemy's location, as his strung-out forces marched north in 1863. As President Lincoln remarked in an apt barnyard analogy: with a chicken's head here and its feet stretched away over there, some place in the middle had to be skinny. What he did not say was that the chicken's sorry state should have been known to the chicken well before any fox got to it. It follows that a plan that tracks the fox without mapping the chicken is not a good plan at all. Put another way: intelligence focused on the enemy will have trouble recognizing the vulnerabilities motivating him. Intelligence services need knowledge of their own soil—terrain that a vigorous opponent with a strong intelligence service will prepare to exploit.[21]

Conclusion

Good military commanders, recognizing that intelligence is power, must engineer intelligence advantage just as they engineer advantages in weapons and troops. In choosing the ground on which to fight, commanders deal—wittingly or not—the opening cards for competing intelligence services. After the death of Stonewall Jackson at Chancellorsville, General Lee had to create tactical intelligence anew. Yet he sent his cavalry chief off on a mission that depleted his means for tracking the enemy at a time when his forces were vulnerable. Federal cavalry not only learned of Stuart's absence, but moved into the vacuum left behind. Federal cavalry conducted heavy scouting along the Potomac to General Lee's rear, where they learned Lee's position almost precisely. When Lee finally arrived on the battlefield, he accepted the gauntlet thrown, regretting the absence of Stuart, his "eyes and ears."[22]

Thus, while gaps in Confederate intelligence helped set the stage for Lee's defeat at Gettysburg, General Lee was, in a crucial sense, their author. Comparing battles at First Manassas and Chancellorsville reveals that the Federals' intelligence system showed marked improvement, while Lee's did not. Indeed, Beauregard's use of espionage behind Federal lines during First Manassas—amateurish but adequate relative to the Federals' effort at the time—stands in sharp relief to Lee's mishandling of his assets before and after Chancellorsville. Lee's intelligence failures prior to Gettysburg illuminated his earlier dependence on General Stonewall Jackson, who was a significant part of his more informal intelligence system. Although Jackson, who had outmaneuvered Federals during his famous Shenandoah Valley campaign, had done so on his own turf. He was a master in the use of secrecy, surprise, stratagems, scouts, and mapmaking before battle, not just afterward.

The role of commanders in choosing terrain is only one way, however, that decision-makers affect intelligence in war. Every decision has potential repercussions for the military's capacity to observe, learn, and act. General Lee did not know how Hooker planned to move before Chancellorsville. Unlike Beauregard and Johnston before First Manassas, he did little mapping and more waiting. This choice could have been disastrous for any other commander or in other circumstances. Consider the example of General Winfield Scott, who, seemingly disinterested in counterintelligence before battle, failed to discover that the Union's secrets had leaked and that the Confederates would, therefore, render McDowell's multipronged attack a wasteful use of time.[23]

Part of the Union's problem before the Battle of First Manassas flowed from the correct assumption that information superiority naturally inheres in the offensive. Confederates, holding the same assumption, were energized to overcome Northern superiority. Thus, Jefferson Davis authorized the creation of a spy network in Washington as early as April 1861, and had recruited a head of his army's signals intelligence effort well before the Federals had organized their own. Federal commanders discounted how engineered intelligence could alter outcomes, for better or worse.[24] Scott's dismissive attitude toward intelligence strategy led directly to failing courier and telegraph systems, poor links among his generals and civilian guides or spies, and failure to conduct even cheap reconnaissance.[25] A confounded president walked to the War Department to inquire why balloonists were not being equipped and used, but the War Department still dragged its feet.[26]

* * *

The lessons discussed here relate to communications, collection, industry, and secrecy during two Civil War battles and the run-up to the battle at Gettysburg. Together with lessons from the Armada, we have discovered additional evidence about what leads to success and failure for intelligence in war. Before moving on to learn lessons from diplomacy, it seems important to consider one particular aspect of military operations that bleeds into peacetime operations as well: the problem of intelligence during national-security-related manhunts, treasure hunts, and chases.

We have already considered several aspects of the problem: the challenge of providing "intelligence on wheels" when commanders move from waiting to chasing, from planning to engaging the enemy, or from battle to pursuit. Drake hunted for Spanish treasure galleons, the Spanish hunted for Drake, and the Federals hunted for Stonewall Jackson and Lee in the Shenandoah Valley. Some of the requirements for a chase seem obvious: a faster horse or ship, a better spyglass, and better knowledge of the terrain. The case studies have shown that pursuing an enemy behind his own lines or occupying enemy territory increases operational exposure to both clandestine and overt collection, especially if a hostile population is ready to swarm against the invader, trafficking in phony information and stealing. Such vulnerabilities can deliver intelligence advantage to an otherwise slower or weaker opponent. Yet there is still more to know on this topic, especially when a chase or a hunt is hyper-asymmetric—that is, when one side has a far better inherent ability to hide than the other does. It is one thing to find the proverbial needle in a haystack, but another to find one particular needle in a stack of needles. The following chapter, therefore, will extend our discussion to what we might now call a complex contingency: the Union's hunt for President Abraham Lincoln's assassin, John Wilkes Booth, as he fled across belligerent lines during the concluding months of the US Civil War.

8

Intelligence for the Chase:
The Hunt for President Abraham Lincoln's
Assassin, John Wilkes Booth

Before we examine the history of diplomatic intelligence during the twenty-first century, manhunts merit closer attention. After all, international politics has never been just about battlefields and diplomacy, but also evasion, interdiction, and predation: finding spies, terrorists, pirates, assassins, international drug dealers, illicit weapons, and other dangerous materials as they travel across war zones, through failed states, over international waters or across state borders. Philip II pursued Sir Francis Drake; Union forces pursued Stonewall Jackson through the Shenandoah Valley; and the US government pursued the instigator of the 9/11 attacks, Osama bin Laden, into Afghanistan and Pakistan at the turn of the twenty-first century.[1]

Whether or not hunts become matters of international politics turns less on the scale of the provocation than on their implications for state security. The Oklahoma City bombers of 1995 caused devastating loss of life, but were not agents of a foreign power. Americans were horrified, but did not view the attack as increasing the vulnerability of the state.[2] At the same time, the *perception* of vulnerability may not always be entirely rational. Philip II, a rich sixteenth-century king with a vast empire to finance, felt vulnerable to a sea captain with a flair for pinprick attacks on Spain's overseas treasure routes. Austria-Hungary, a twentieth-century empire allied to Germany in 1914, felt vulnerable to the Black Hand, a loose, transnational terrorist network of insurgent Serbs. After 9/11, the United States felt vulnerable to al-Qaeda, even after destroying its organization in Afghanistan and eliminating many of its leaders and operatives. The vulnerability in each case arose from felt terror, the fear that an adversary capable of surprise predation would attack on ever-larger scales. Such felt vulnerabilities may arise in response not just to terrorists, but also to weapons traffickers, drug runners, and violent, criminal gangs. Thus, how the triggering act is perceived would seem to condition the subsequent chase—an opening clue to the idea that counterintelligence, especially offensive counterintelligence or perception management, might be especially important to outcomes.

The analytical question that follows, then, is whether uncertainty and its remedy, intelligence, have different requirements for success in these kinds of

Decision Advantage. Jennifer E. Sims, Oxford University Press. © Oxford University Press 2022.
DOI: 10.1093/oso/9780197508046.003.0008

international contests than they do in military battles or diplomacy. The answer to this question lies in the special dynamics of transnational races, chases,
and interdictions, and how the choices made during these contests differ from
decision-making for war and diplomacy.

The search for President Lincoln's killer, John Wilkes Booth, is a revealing
case study in these regards. The simplicity of the chase—finding a famous actor
and assassin on the run—is set against a political backdrop of a fractured state
teetering between war and peace. The victorious Union general, Ulysses S. Grant,
put it well when he learned Lincoln had been shot: "I did not know what it meant.
Here was the rebellion put down in the field, and starting up in the gutters; we
had fought it as war, now we had to fight it as assassination."[3] Perceptions of
threat, its likely sponsors, the rules of the hunt, and the loyalty of citizens were all
at issue.

We are not interested here in the full story of the assassination. Historians have
thoroughly covered Booth's motives, preparations, and capture. We are only interested in knowing what intelligence requirements, met or unmet, contributed
to Booth's capture. Against Booth, a neophyte in almost everything except the
theater, the Federals started with a tremendous advantage. By 1865, the informational terrain (mapped in Chapter 5) had been amended by years of war during
which Union cavalry met or exceeded the skills of Confederate horsemen. The
methods of linking telegraph to cavalry operations had been improved, and generals better understood the limits of detectives as intelligence officers. Yet there
were also new uncertainties. Booth's capture would be a chase rather than a battle,
and the prey would choose the route. Whether or not he chose well, the context would hover between the laws of war and the constitutional requirements
of due process. Urgency, threats to security, and suspect loyalties were bound
to create a toxic mix for both sides. Such were the peculiar uncertainties in the
immediate aftermath of Appomattox, which marked the defeat and surrender
of General Robert E. Lee but not the war's final closure. Richmond had fallen,
but Jefferson Davis was on the run. In fact, General Sherman received news of
Lincoln's death while still negotiating surrender with his Confederate counterpart and, not sure of the impact, chose to keep it secret from him. Citizens living
in the Confederacy's borderlands knew the war was over, but many had not yet
given up. In fact, no one was certain about what would come next.

On this modified terrain of uncertainty, a tense contest would take place that
would grip the attention of both Confederacy and Union. Although the outlines
of the fascinating, often romanticized story of the hunt for Booth must be appreciated for the intelligence piece to make sense, the focus will remain on the key
decisions each side made and what they knew when they made them. The analysis begins with Booth's attack. Tactical intelligence-advantage tempted Booth
into acting before he was fully prepared to achieve the strategic advantage he was

seeking, which was a heroic revival of the Confederate cause. His decision to attack when he did was a spontaneous reaction to the news, shared by the owner
of Ford's Theater, that the president would attend that night's show, *My American
Cousin*. Booth knew the theater and the show so well that he felt certain he could
time his attack to the moment when only one actor would be on stage and the audience would be transfixed.[4] So he decided to act on his intelligence-advantage,
grab the moment, and let the rest take care of itself.

The Search for President Abraham Lincoln's Assassin

Shortly after 10:00 p.m. on 14 April 1865, Booth entered the presidential box at
Ford's Theater. Armed with a steel blade and a derringer pistol, Booth aimed at
the back of Lincoln's head and fired. The .44 caliber bullet coursed diagonally
through Lincoln's brain. Booth then stabbed Lincoln's companion, Major Henry
Rathbone, leaped from the presidential box, and crashed onto the stage, breaking
his leg. Shouting, "Thus to tyrants," and "The South is avenged!" Booth headed to
the theater's back exit with an army major, Joseph B. Stewart, in pursuit.

As Booth mounted his waiting horse, his part in the conspiracy to decapitate
the Union government was almost complete. His co-conspirators were targeting
Lincoln's secretary of state, William H. Seward, and Vice President Andrew
Johnson. What he did not know was how his fellow conspirators had played
their roles, and if his larger purpose, to reignite the passions of the Confederacy,
was any closer to being achieved. He did not stop to think, however, because he
believed he did not need to. There was no backup plan, no decisions to be made.
Spinning free from his sole pursuer, he galloped toward the prearranged rendezvous spot in Maryland, hoping the others would show up.

Booth would soon learn that his collaborators had not only failed, but would
soon be characterized in the press as monstrous, incompetent, or both. One con-
spirator, an out-of-town Confederate veteran named Lewis Powell, had slashed
at the incapacitated and house-bound Secretary Seward. Seward's unarmed
caretakers had defended him, saving his life. Powell's young sidekick and guide,
David Herold, had heard the violence and fled. In fact, at the very moment Booth
was riding away from Ford's Theater, Herold was galloping up Fourteenth Street
on a stolen horse with the owner in hot pursuit. Powell was running too, but
unfamiliar with the streets, spent that night in a tree. George Atzerodt, who had
been told to kill the vice president, had gotten drunk and lost his nerve. Both
Powell and Atzerodt would soon be caught, their plot revealed, and their thug-
gish behavior trumpeted by the press.[5]

As Booth rode toward the city limits, he needed one last actor and Confederate
sympathizer to do his job: John Matthews. Booth had left Matthews an important

letter to the *National Intelligencer*, asking him to mail it "unless I see you before ten o'clock tomorrow; in that case I will attend to it myself."[6] The letter named the perpetrators and their purpose: revenge against the Union for predation against the Confederacy. As Booth rode toward Maryland, the most important intelligence he lacked was that Matthews, a horrified witness to the assassination, had already destroyed Booth's letter. Booth also did not know that Seward, though attacked, had been heroically defended; and that Lincoln, though mortally wounded, was not yet dead.

Washington Reacts: Decision-Advantages Gained and Lost

Washington was soon in chaos. A mob had formed at Ford's Theater, threatening law and order with attacks against Confederate parolees, prisoners of war, and suspected sympathizers. During these first hours of chaos and confusion, news traveled quickly through the streets, including to the door of secretary of war, Edwin McMasters Stanton. Four decisions he took proved critical to gaining decision-advantages over Booth:[7]

- First, Stanton decided to verify what he had been told. First, he went to Seward's house, where he confirmed the attack on the secretary of state. Then, as mobs were gathering and against strong advice, he fought his way to the Peterson Boarding House to confirm the condition of the president.
- Second, he urged Vice President Johnson to stand aside and let him take charge. Johnson's agreement may have reflected his weakness or his judgment that, should the Confederacy be behind the attacks, the secretary of war would need to command Washington's new, complex battlefield. In either case, Stanton's decision to grab the reins and Johnson's relinquishing of them, ensured that the government would stay unified.
- Third, Stanton decided to act as if the assassination were an act of war, while working to defang the Confederacy. The Peterson House would be a temporary War Department headquarters that would serve as the clearinghouse for all relevant intelligence for the battle to come.[8]
- Fourth, (and perhaps simultaneously), Stanton arrogated to himself all civil and military decision-making power, and clarified the chain of command.

As Stanton considered these first moves, he took an inventory of what he knew, what he did not know, and what his intuition told him. In fact, he seems to have relied on his mindset, which altered only in the face of verifiable facts. Stanton knew, for example, that the attacks were a conspiracy of some kind; he did not initially know who had sponsored them, the identities and number of attackers, and whether or not the conspirators were planning more. Yet to Stanton, the whole business smelled of organized Confederate retribution.[9] He knew that in late 1863 and early 1864, the Union had authorized several secret cavalry raids on Richmond designed to free prisoners and damage communications. None of the raids had succeeded, but the last had led to political embarrassment: papers on a raider's body seemed to indicate that his mission had included the killing or capture of Confederate president Jefferson Davis and his cabinet.[10] Lincoln's assassination and the attack on Seward looked a lot like Richmond's payback. If it was payback, the first order of business would be to protect all the cabinet and to get the South to stand down.

With this frame of mind, Stanton thought Booth's act called for more than a response from police; the challenge was a complex contingency with profound implications for national security. He therefore began to put together a multilayered strategy. First, Stanton identified three potential adversaries—the perpetrators, the mob, and the Confederacy—and developed plans against each. The first required a manhunt; the second required the re-establishment of national law and order; the third required military defeat and political prostration of the South. Second, he decided to slip "a curious reference" into his first informational telegram on the attack (sent at 2:15 a.m.). Referring to the cabinet meeting of the previous afternoon, he mentioned that Lincoln "spoke very kindly of General Lee and others of the Confederacy."[11] The reference was "an apparent invitation to indignation at the ingratitude of a treacherous foe" and "implied that he had already concluded the assassination was a Confederate plot, *or that he wished it portrayed so to the public*."[12]

Much of this was familiar terrain. After all, from the outset of the war, the Lincoln administration had contained murderous mobs in Baltimore, hunted civilian spies within the city, and fought the Confederacy. What was new was the expected surrender of the Confederacy and the necessity of securing the peace, which was still being negotiated.

As Stanton contemplated additional steps, he knew the advantages of war powers, especially the power of propaganda or offensive counterintelligence. As secretary of war, he had had little issue with wartime arrests of journalists or manipulative use of propaganda. He had ordered the arrest of reporters and publishers of *New York World* and *Journal of Commerce* in 1864 over deceptive stories about the "failing" Union cause that threatened to undermine public confidence in the North. Indeed, when in a wartime frame, Stanton appreciated few constitutional boundaries. When George McClellan had been nominated to run for president against Lincoln, Stanton had assembled a file of rumors and innuendo to fuel conspiracy theories against McClellan. He also had begun investigations into secret societies and subversive organizations for the purpose of discrediting Lincoln's political opposition. He had even been accused of staging well-timed show-trials of "traitors" in order to affect election outcomes.[13] So good was he at offensive counterintelligence, that one of Stanton's biographers has called Lincoln's secretary of war also his "Minister of Propaganda."[14] So it is unsurprising that one of the first things he would do after the assassination would be to frame events in a way that would maximize public sympathy. With the public on the government's side, citizens might provide information for the manhunt while denying it to the perpetrators.

None of this is meant to suggest that Stanton was an aspiring tyrant, only that he had a well-established mindset that helped him act in decisive ways, even when current intelligence was scarce. He knew the costs and risks of the frame he would choose for the manhunt: if one of war, civil liberties might be curtailed, war might be rekindled, his methods later criticized, but the assassins likely eliminated quickly. If, on the other hand, he chose to observe the constitutional requirements for a manhunt, laws would be respected but his tools circumscribed and the actor-assassin might win his audience, escaping death.[15] He chose war.

Stanton's warrior mindset and personal knowledge gave him an intelligence advantage across all three competitions. Decisions quickly followed in each of the three fronts of the new civil-military battle:

- *The war:* Stanton sent a telegram summoning the commanding general, Ulysses S. Grant, back to Washington. Based on Stanton's authority, the quartermaster general, Montgomery Meigs, ordered the military to clear the streets, man the guns, and place extra guards at forts and prisons in anticipation of any next move by the perpetrators.

By 4:00 a.m., evidence from Booth's hotel room had suggested that Stanton's hunch about Confederate sponsorship was correct, and that decision-makers in Richmond were likely involved. This intelligence meant Booth might seek refuge there.[16] Stanton nonetheless telegraphed major cities on the east coast and in the message to Baltimore demanded that trains be searched and bridges guarded.[17] Thinking more like a warrior than a hunter, he was still trying to establish the enemy's order of battle. He issued a blizzard of instructions through his subordinates that diverted cavalry units to the mission of scouring the country for the assassins and any Confederate co-conspirators.

- *The manhunt:* Instead of immediately putting the Washington authorities and police in charge of the investigation, Stanton opted for joint operations, despite the risk that military involvement in handling evidence might compromise eventual prosecutions.

Stanton telegraphed the chief of police for New York City at 1:10 a.m., asking for his best detectives. By 2:00 a.m., orders were issued to arrest anyone attempting to leave the city by road or water—three hours after Booth had crossed the Fourteenth Street bridge into Maryland. Although by 3:00 a.m. Stanton was certain it was John Wilkes Booth who had shot Lincoln, he still saw Booth's act in a larger security context so, by 3:20 p.m., had hired the counterintelligence specialist Lafayette Baker to aid in the hunt.[18]

- *Managing the mob and shaping public opinion*: Stanton began influence operations by releasing selected intelligence to the public. His purpose was to pressure the South while channeling public anger into widespread efforts to track and catch Booth.

Lincoln died at 7:22 a.m. on 15 April. By 9:00 a.m., the news had reached the streets of New York City and Baltimore. Washington's morning newspapers included details about the safety and security of most cabinet members, the identity of the murderer, and Booth's physical appearance; by 12:00 p.m., word of Lincoln's death had spread to most major cities, and Johnson had been sworn in as president. Telegrams to Baltimore, New York, and other major Northern cities gave Booth's name, description, and likely trajectory—from Washington toward Saint Mary's and Calvert Counties. Lafayette Baker soon blanketed the country with wanted posters, descriptions, and pictures of the fugitives. The news was full of the reported cowardice, vanity, treachery, and bloodlust of the perpetrators. "Cincinnati: 'The universal feeling is one of terrible wrath.' New York: 'People appear perfectly horrified, and the utmost rage is felt toward all known secessionists and rebel sympathizers.'"[19]

Treating Lincoln's assassination as a complex contingency cost time. It also expanded the definition of "winning" from capturing criminals to securing the Union. The city had not blocked all exits until three hours after Booth had crossed the Fourteenth Street bridge into Maryland, which meant that he and one accomplice, David Herold, had been able to escape. Still, as Stanton saw it, organizing for a complex response to the assassination was fundamental. He needed law enforcement to help catch Booth and the military to secure the state from a potentially reinvigorated Confederacy.[20] The trick was to achieve an extra-legal victory for the Union without creating either more grievances for war-weary civilians or more martyrs for the South. Military and police operations, begun separately, became barely cooperative.[21] As news reports generated public outrage and motivated the hunters, cooperation increased. Military units provided horses to police, and high-ranking army officers pledged to help locate the perpetrators even as they worked to secure the city.[22] Joint military and police patrols raided Mary Surratt's boardinghouse and Booth's room at the National Hotel.[23] Having the cavalry involved in police operations did make it difficult for the latter to preserve evidence, but mobs were so violent at locations such as Ford's Theater, that security had to be left to military men for whom the requirements of legal procedure took second place to crowd control.

Once Stanton established the basic structure of decision-making, however, actions flowed relatively quickly. The Thirteenth New York Cavalry patrol left Washington at about 5:00 a.m. on 15 April, the morning after the attack. Led by Lieutenant Dana, the patrol headed for Piscataway, Maryland. Arriving there by 7:00 a.m., Dana began reporting back to Washington the rumors and tips he was hearing. Washington, in turn, issued bursts of intelligence for the hunters. Although civil resistance to this militarized form of law enforcement would build, it would not do so faster than the hunters would work or the Confederacy would collapse, making Booth's cause hopeless.

The Fugitives' Early Decision-Making: Exploiting Luck and the Terrain of Uncertainty

Unfortunately for Booth, he had no way of staying abreast of the news. He knew Richmond had taken no active part in his spontaneous attack on Lincoln, but he hoped a reinvigorated South and confusion about the assassinations would keep Washington from catching him before he found sanctuary in the Confederacy. Although he planned to ride ahead of the news, he almost certainly expected Confederates everywhere to applaud and perhaps even take credit as the news spread. It all depended on the letter—his manifesto—that he had left with Matthews. Strangely, Booth relied only on the publication of this document and his dramatic act to sway public opinion his way. As a celebrity rather than a street artist, he had always played to paying audiences; he did not know much about recruiting audiences and sustaining their support. He therefore took some bad decisions:

- Riding to the rendezvous point, Booth decided to tell Sergeant Cobb, who was guarding the bridge at Eleventh Street, his true name and where he was going (Beantown).

Although we do not know why Booth made this choice, it may be that he thought his name was famous enough to cause the sergeant to open the bridge, which was by rule closed at that hour. In any event, Cobb let him pass but remembered his name and his destination.

- When Booth reunited with Herold at Soper's Hill and heard his story, he decided to forge on according to plan.[24]

Booth probably assumed that Seward was dead and Powell caught. Booth could not know George Atzerodt had failed to attack the vice president, or that he would soon be arrested following a series of silly errors. With these two co-conspirators missing, however, Booth must have realized that the Federals would soon learn the outlines of his escape route. He had cultivated it for months—indeed from the time he and other Confederate agents had conspired to kidnap Lincoln rather than assassinate him. Sticking to his plan risked riding into a trap.

Booth's immediate difficulties were mounting, however, so his tactical decisions began to drive strategy. He needed to know what to do next, and his old plan, his co-conspirator Herold, and the Confederate network in Maryland seemed to be all he had. In this connection, the loss of Atzerodt was costly indeed. Atzerodt, was a blockade runner from Port Tobacco who was strong and knowledgeable enough to get them across the Potomac River.[25] The journey to Confederate Virginia also required crossing land that was so swampy that horses and riders unfamiliar with safe routes could be sucked down to their deaths. Booth needed more than Herold's minimal knowledge and skills. It was already obvious his horse would be no asset; she was an urban rental, demonstrably skittish, and ill-suited for negotiating the wilderness at night. Historical evidence suggests she fell during Booth's initial ride out of the city, scraping her shoulder, dumping Booth, and probably adding trauma to his injured leg. Booth probably regretted not having the locally bred horses he had sought to buy when kidnapping had been the plan. He had even bought a one-eyed horse for the purpose. His quick decision to kill Lincoln in the theater had rendered many such earlier arrangements irrelevant or obsolete.

- Following his original plan, Booth decided to head to his next destination, Surrattsville, Maryland, which was a known rebel hotspot thirteen miles outside of DC. Mary Surratt owned a tavern and safe house there, where the conspirators had prepositioned weapons. There Booth told the tavern manager, his old friend John Lloyd, that he had assassinated the president.[26]

In retrospect, both choices seem odd. The US government had known for years that the town was a nest of Confederate sympathizers and had revoked Surratt's license to operate her tavern as a US Post Office in 1864. Even if Booth were certain that his co-conspirators had not been caught, Surrattsville would be one of the first places the Federals would likely think to look for the assassins. Nonetheless, Booth and Herold stopped there to pick up weapons, perhaps because they believed their need for them was greater than the risk of being followed. This calculation proved wrong.

- Leaving Surratt's tavern, Booth decided to attend to his broken leg by heading for the home of Dr. Samuel Mudd, despite the detour this required.

Booth was now likely working from memory. He knew Mudd had been a Confederate sympathizer and previous co-conspirator. Six months earlier, Booth had traveled to Canada, where he had met a network of rebel couriers and operatives that specialized in blockade running, maintaining safe houses, exchanging intelligence, and shepherding spies from the North back to Richmond.[27] It was through this network that Booth had come to know Dr. Mudd, Mary Surratt, who owned the boardinghouse in Washington and the safe house in Surrattsville, and Mary's son John, who was a Confederate courier. His connections were old, however, so he and Herold may have decided not to reveal to Mudd what they had done. In any case, Mudd gave the two fugitives a room and set Booth's leg with what he had on hand.

- Around 5:00 a.m. the morning after the assassination (15 April), Booth decided to stay at the Mudd farm for the day and resume the journey the next night. His back and leg were sore, and he needed sleep.[28]

Since he probably had no plan to go to this farm as part of his escape, Booth may have reasoned that even if Atzerodt and Powell were caught, no one could know he was there. He probably also still believed he was ahead of the news, which traveled relatively slowly in this poor part of Maryland where telegraph, roads, and a rail network were lacking. He did not know that the War Department had already sent reports to all major newspapers and that telegraphers were setting up at Point Lookout on the Maryland peninsula, extending wire in what had become standard operating procedure in support of cavalry operations. Moreover, the provisional governor of Virginia, F. H. Pierpont, would soon do his part—probably at Stanton's request. Telegraphing the War Department in Washington, he condemned Booth's crimes, calling him a "dastardly agent of treason."[29] Despite Pierpont's prominence as a longtime Lincoln loyalist, this announcement, coming after Richmond's occupation, helped shift the hunt for Booth from a simple chase to a hunt for a villain whose capture might smooth Virginia's path back into the Union:

The recently loyalized *Richmond Whig* characterized the assassination as "an atrocity which will shock and appall every honorable man and woman in the land." "A hellish crime," declared Confederate general J. R. Jones. Robert Ould, the South's agent for the exchange of prisoners, thought that in its harm to the rebel states "it is the worst—Lee's surrender was nothing to it." A leading Copperhead journalist wrote, "It seems marvelous that there should live one human being so warped in judgment, so steeped in wickedness, so hardened in devilish fanaticism as to be capable of this deed."[30]

Detached from such news, Booth did not appreciate his vulnerability and the extent to which Washington's joint operations were closing in on him. His entire plan had turned on his personal celebrity and the support of the Confederacy's networks, whom he expected would protect him. He was wrong in this judgment. Stanton had made the matter one of war and peace. Given General Lee's surrender and Jefferson Davis's flight from Richmond, the political landscape had already shifted.

This turn of events had operational consequences for Booth's escape. Collaborators would now face increasing risks for helping the perpetrator of presidential assassination and for a cause running counter to the interests of a dissolving Confederacy. While Booth and Herold slept, new fears among diehard Confederates would make pursuit swifter than they knew. When Herold came down for lunch on 15 April, he and Booth had no idea Dana's cavalry patrol had reached Bryantown, which was less than ten miles from Mudd's farm. Booth remained in bed, refusing to eat. By 3:00 p.m., Herold had realized that Booth would need a carriage because he could no longer ride, so he and Dr. Mudd went to Bryantown to look for one.[31] When Herold saw Dana's patrol there, he sped back to the house, leaving Mudd to learn from the townspeople (if he did not know already) of Lincoln's assassination and the danger his family now faced.[32] Herold told Booth of the presence of cavalry in Bryantown, forcing a crucial decision: to attempt a daylight escape as soon as Booth could mount a horse, or to wait for Mudd, who might either provide critical intelligence or return with troops to arrest him.

- Based on his first good intelligence since leaving Washington, Booth now knew his hunters were gaining on him. He decided to trust Mudd.

Booth knew the territory was threaded with dangerous swamps that neither he nor Herold could navigate; his only option was to wait for the doctor. Mudd returned from town around 7:00 p.m., reportedly furious that he had been misled about Booth's actions and intentions. Whether or not Mudd had conspired in the past with Booth, he probably now wanted the men off his property. Mudd described potential escape routes and presumably trustworthy contacts: Confederate operatives William Burtles and Captain Samuel Cox.

Following Mudd's directions, Booth and Herold headed south, but were soon hopelessly lost (Figure 8.1).

Booth's decisions were, from this point forward, shaped largely by chance. Encountering a local man, Oswell Swan,[33] Booth offered him money to guide them through Zekiah Swamp to Captain Cox's farm, Rich Hill.[34] Booth took a risk in hiring Swan, but he was desperate. Swan was a part black, part Native American farmer with Union sympathies. Cox was a rich, known Confederate sympathizer. Of the two, only Cox knew about the assassination at this point (1:00 a.m. on the sixteenth). Swan agreed to take the strangers to Cox's place. So on Easter Sunday, the threesome arrived at Rich Hill. Relieved, the two fugitives threatened Swan with his life if he were to say anything, then went inside. Swan waited for his payment.

Cox gave the fugitives some food and sent them back outside to hide in a nearby pine thicket, telling them that their next guide would announce his arrival

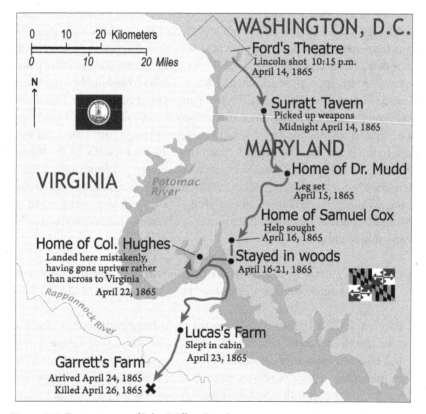

Figure 8.1 Escape route of John Wilkes Booth
Source: Courtesy of Wikimedia Commons.

with a coded whistle. Seeing Swan waiting for his money, Booth and Herold paid him more than they had originally agreed and watched him go.[35] Then they went to hide in the thicket as they had been told.

The fugitives had no choice but to trust Cox and the guide Cox would provide. It seemed their luck was holding when the guide turned out to be Thomas A. Jones, a veteran intelligence operative whom Booth had met months earlier when being introduced to the Confederate network operating from Richmond to Canada. Jones had experience as a signalman ferrying Confederate contraband across the Potomac. His track record as an intelligence operative was good, thanks to a reportedly inscrutable face and a code of honor that instilled trust among those with whom he worked. Booth and Herold soon developed that trust as well.[36]

Jones was also, however, Cox's foster brother and best friend. The Confederate agent had agreed to do his family a favor but, apparently, was not happy to do so.[37] The risks of this operation were high and the returns likely worthless. When Booth asked his new guide what the public thought about the assassination, adding that he looked forward to getting across and into the heart of the Confederacy, Jones stalled. He told Booth he would help ensure his safe passage across the river, but it could only be done by going to ground and waiting for an opportunity.

- Booth, now tired, frustrated, and depressed, decided to agree with Jones's plan.[38] He and Herold would hide in the thicket until Federal forces had scoured the area and moved on in their search.

Booth was now totally dependent on Jones to provide his intelligence. Although the dense, swampy land worked in the fugitives' favor, it did so only if they stayed hidden and relied completely on their guide. Jones started bringing the fugitives intelligence in the form of newspapers full of bad news, which reinforced their dependence on Jones. Over the next five days, Booth learned that the Confederacy had denounced him, that Abraham Lincoln was widely revered now as a martyr, that Seward still lived, and that Booth's letter to the *National Intelligencer* had apparently never been published. Worst of all, the city of Baltimore was reportedly "in mourning" and the *Intelligencer*'s publisher, John F. Coyle had proclaimed that "Booth was no cavalier. . . . On the contrary he was a cold, cautious, cowardly planning knave." His fellow actors and friends had even denounced him.[39] These were all hard blows for a man who had fancied himself a hero of the South.

Although the tide of public opinion should have made Booth suspicious of what Jones might do, he still felt safe in the agent's hands just as he still expected to be welcomed by a like-minded Virginia. Few historians have suggested he was wrong to trust Jones and his plan. As one chronicler of the assassins' flight has written: "A lone Confederate agent [Jones], without resources and nearly penniless . . . checkmated the frantic pursuit by thousands of men being orchestrated from Washington by Secretary of War Stanton."[40]

Yet "checkmate" is far too strong a word. Jones, in fact, may have already been planning to distance himself from the assassins, perhaps even at the risk of sabotaging Booth's long-term plan. Although Jones has long been seen as a wily but committed enabler of Booth's designs, this judgment may reflect Jones's retrospective self-glorification more than fact. Jones's actions were suspicious. His strategy of hiding Booth in place, for example, gave time and decision-making advantage to the Federals. They used that time to set their net: deploy the telegraph through southern Maryland; advertise Booth's dishonor; blanket the area with cavalry; interrogate Swan and Mudd; secure the river; and, in the meantime, secure General Joe Johnston's surrender. By the time Booth would get to Virginia, formerly friendly and open Confederate doors would be closed to him.

Jones's actions served his interests as much, if not more, than they served Booth's. Jones, like everyone else on the fugitives' escape route, wanted to be sure that Booth would not be caught while in his care. He still had a job to do for the South and intended on keeping it. As for what might happen to Booth later— that mattered more to Booth and Herold than it did to Jones. Even Cox, a longstanding Confederate loyalist, was wary of Booth; he had suspected the fugitives of plotting to steal his horses even after he had offered to help them. And with the reward for Booth so high, Jones was probably thinking that punishments for aiding Booth's escape would be even greater. Indeed, it is no surprise that Jones, who became aware of the $100,000 reward for Booth, did not turn the man over. Doing so would have revealed his and Cox's complicity and, perhaps worse, made life among Southern loyalists next to impossible thereafter. All Booth's enablers would almost certainly be executed; anyone ratting on Booth would be dishonored in the South. Given this calculation, Jones was not interested in taking any higher personal risks in the near term to avoid lower ones for Booth later on. So Jones, with his own neck and the larger Confederate network to worry about, kept Booth outdoors, on someone else's property, in a swamp.

In the meantime, having noticed Federal interest, albeit casual, in boats along the river, Jones secured his skiffs, leaving one visible while hiding the other as a backup. Jones also directed his former slave to use the first boat to fish daily and to disembark at a favorable launching site, thereby establishing a pattern that would raise no suspicions about the boat's purpose. Then, Jones waited for his opportunity. On 18 April he heard that Union troops were preparing to chase a false rumor some distance away from his location, Port Tobacco. By advertising their intentions in a town known to be a rebel stronghold, the Federals had gifted Jones with time, distance, and the knowledge that he had the advantage of both.

Jones waited for the troops to quit the area, then went back to the pine thicket, collected Booth and Herold, and, on the night of the twentieth, sent them across the river by compass direction. Indeed, Jones decided not to ferry them himself and, more surprisingly, did not tell them about the river's dangers that might cause them to veer wildly off-course. Although it is impossible to know whether Jones's neglect in providing warnings was purposeful, certainly he knew the river and its ways. As one chronicler of events has pointed out:

David Herold was a competent enough navigator of the Maryland and Virginia coastal marshes, creeks, and rivers, but he was not a professional seaman. And it was one thing to ply the waters during daylight hours while hunting for pleasure, another to run them at night when in danger as the object of the hunt. Herold had never made a trip across the Potomac under conditions like these: under pressure, pursued, and in near total darkness. Thomas Jones, seasoned agent, had done it hundreds of times.[41]

Long motivated by the Confederate cause that would outlast the war, Jones's habits of mind had, perhaps, become instinctual. In fact, the Confederate underground had long relied on him to manage risks, and he likely did so in this case. When Jones finally brought Booth and Herold to the river, he put them in a boat on a moonless night and pushed them into a river with strong, contrary currents and tides. According to some reports, one oar was broken and the boat leaked so badly Herold had to bail it out with his hat.[42]

Jones almost certainly knew what he was doing. Public sentiment was turning rapidly against the assassins; even goodwill in Virginia might not last long enough for Booth to find sanctuary anywhere. Furthermore, Jones had read the same papers Booth had read and knew the latter's deeds were judged by some Confederates as damaging to the Southern cause. Jones, still in touch with Confederate networks, probably understood the growing liabilities of his charges (and his own growing dangers) better than the fugitives did. Still working for the Confederacy that night, Jones's first order of business was to protect himself, Cox, and their long-standing network, lowering their risks, if necessary, at the fugitives' expense. As Jones guided his charges to the river, he refused them shelter in his house and hid them in the less seaworthy of his two boats despite knowing they would be fighting the worst of the river's currents and tides at that time of night. Although Jones later claimed a Confederate hero's cloak, he probably pushed his "packages" into the river expecting—perhaps even intending—for them to die.[43]

Jones's behavior was predictable given his interests and the larger game of which he was a part. Jones knew Booth's actions were not rekindling, but rather jeopardizing, the Southern cause, which was now to get prisoners back, retain state sovereignty, and achieve a favorable peace. If that cause went bad, Jones's network would still be needed.

Booth and Herold, still fixated on their single act of "glorious" retribution, appreciated none of the nuances to their situation. Thanking Jones profusely as he drifted away, Booth assumed he had made a friend while gaining an advantage over his Federal pursuers. He had accomplished neither. Shortly after losing sight of Jones that night (the twentieth), he and Herold went adrift, heading in the wrong direction on the Potomac River. The desperate men landed the morning of the twenty-first still on the Maryland shore after traveling more than five hours north while trying to row southwest. Refused help by the proprietors on the shore where they landed, the exhausted fugitives hid and made no further attempt to cross the river until the night of the twenty-second.

Capture or Death?

In the meantime, Stanton and his manhunters had achieved significant successes with multiple arrests, including Powell, Atzerodt, Mrs. Surratt, and John Lloyd. The search had also been narrowed from the entire eastern seaboard to southern Maryland.[44] In fact, Stanton's team had the opposite problem from Booth's: as public sentiment swung in their favor, they were swamped with scattershot information from too many eager sources, much of it insufficiently organized or aligned with decisions about where to go next. The Federal government's handsome rewards had generated many false leads, one of which on 18 April had taken Federal troops on the wild goose chase that allowed Jones to send Booth off. The hunters were becoming frustrated and exhausted. As one officer of the Eighth Illinois Cavalry put it following an inconsequential interview with Dr. Mudd: "In vain we scoured the country in all directions. I was out with my Company night and day. With us were some of the most expert detectives of the United States, but all our efforts to trace [Booth] further failed."[45] As the hunters accumulated tips, sources had to be evaluated on the fly, and intelligence distributed to cavalry on the move. Interrogations were sometimes rushed and held under less than ideal conditions.

Stanton nonetheless had two advantages over the assassins: cavalrymen and other interrogators, and a shifting political terrain. Stanton kept his teams working jointly by keeping rival detectives out of each other's lanes. When, on 19 April, the "all-seeing eye" Allan Pinkerton finally learned about the assassination and offered his services, Stanton turned him down. Instead, he spread word of rewards and kept his chains of command clear, embedding detectives like Lafayette Baker within the cavalry. This system eventually brought sources to experienced interrogators in the military. For example, Oswell Swan, the local freeman who had guided the fugitives to the Cox family home, "came in and reported."[46] Hazelton's cavalry unit went to Rich Hill with Swan, interviewed Cox, and arrested him. Then, on 21 April, Captain Lovett of Dana's cavalry unit considered where Booth had encountered Swan, and followed up on his old suspicions about Dr. Mudd. Lovett went back to Mudd's farm, interrogated him further, and became more suspicious. Searching the farm, he found Booth's riding boot and arrested Mudd. In short order, cavalry units started casing out nearby river crossings as ships patrolled the nearby shoreline. In the meantime, thanks to intelligence from interrogations of Mudd, Federal officers had updated news on Booth's and Herold's appearance. They zeroed in on the Potomac and its crossings, picketed the shoreline, and sent cavalry down the river by steamer in anticipation of seeing their prey somewhere near Jones's property.[47]

The Federals at last started putting together the larger picture. Cavalry reconnaissance had long identified Jones's boat as one of those that might be used to cross the river. They also knew Jones's history as a Confederate spy and courier; the proximity of the rebel stronghold of Port Tobacco, hometown of one of the now captured assassins, George Atzerodt; and the limited mobility of the man they were chasing. Believing Booth must have passed through Jones's location, the Federals descended on Jones's farm on the twenty-third. They were too late. They could find no evidence against Jones that could incriminate him in Booth's deed or in facilitating his escape. On the twenty-second, the very night the fugitives had ventured out onto the river again, the navy instigated a "rigid" blockade of the Potomac. All boats were to be searched and confiscated or destroyed.[48]

It is something of a miracle that Booth and Herold made it across the river, but they did. Once on Virginia soil, however, their lack of intelligence led to shock at the stiffness of their reception, and to more poor decisions. They received stingy aid or none at all from Southerners—even Confederate loyalists and safe house proprietors—who once might have been willing to aid any Confederate heading south. That Booth and Herold expected a sympathetic public is clear from their decisions: they no longer hid, but traveled openly. Although they adopted cover names and a story to go with them, such tactics were useless. The Federals had blanketed the area with photographs and descriptions. Ferrymen, such as William Rollins who took the fugitives across the Rappahannock River, were bound to notice a man on crutches and recognize his face. Moreover, Booth's and Herold's cover stories—that they were wounded Confederate soldiers and brothers named "Boyd"—did not hold up in the midst of Confederate country where knowledge of families, military units, and their commanders ran deep.

A lucky break for the Federals would soon bring the Sixteenth New York Cavalry to Virginia in hot pursuit of the assassins while most of the other manhunters were still spinning their wheels in Maryland. Major James

O'Beirne sent a telegram with a false lead about two men crossing the Potomac on the sixteenth. When the telegram arrived on 24 April in the War Department, Detective Lafayette Baker, who had been irritating everyone with his competitive snooping for leads, happened to be there. Baker put together a team that included his cousin, Luther Baker, along with another detective and a detachment of the Sixteenth New York Cavalry under the command of Lieutenant E. P. Dougherty. Equipped with maps and photographs from the US Army Medical Museum, the team headed toward the Rappahannock, traveling first by steamer. They disembarked at Belle Plain, Virginia, and then headed for Port Conway, where they would cross the Rappahannock. The team entered Port Conway on 25 April. Baker interrogated the ferryman, Rollins, who soon relayed all he knew, including the fact that Booth and Herold had been accompanied by Confederate soldiers, who mentioned going to Bowling Green. Worried that this was evidence of a larger and long-suspected Confederate plot, the hunters picked up their pace, crossed the river, and galloped off on their pursuit. Meanwhile, Major O'Beirne, who had sent them the false lead about the 16 April river crossing, had become convinced he had been wrong. Now searching the pine thicket where the fugitives had once rested, he reported his error and begged Washington for a compass and map. No one in Washington was coordinating the hunters, however, so the chase in Virginia proceeded nonetheless.[49] In this instance, lack of coordination among collectors served the Federal cause.

Although the Federals had made mistakes up to this point, Booth's mistakes were comparatively worse. Unaware of how fast the telegraph could trigger War Department decision-making and mobilize cavalry in 1865, Booth had replaced secrecy with indiscretions. When, on 24 April, the fugitives had met Confederate soldiers on leave from Mosby's Rangers, Booth had confided all in hopes of protection, thereby losing whatever advantages he had left. Although these soldiers had escorted Booth and Herold to Richard Garrett's farm, one of them eventually betrayed Booth to the Federals by taking them to the fugitives' hideout. The Garrett family had, in the meantime, become suspicious and had locked Booth and Herold in a tobacco barn. In the well-known denouement, the manhunters charged onto the Garrett farm in the middle of the night and demanded the fugitives' surrender.[50] Herold gave up, but Booth refused to do so. The manhunters burned the barn, and, as Booth hesitated to come out, a trigger-happy cavalryman shot him. Paralyzed from the neck down, Booth died just a few hours later.

Historians have wondered why the manhunters negotiated with Booth for so long on the Garrett farm and reportedly even comforted him with whiskey and blankets during his last hours. The answer seems to be that Stanton wanted Booth captured alive to avoid creating a martyr for the Confederacy. Booth alive was a Confederate liability; with the wrong kind of death, he threatened to become a Union one. Besides, Stanton still wondered if a larger Confederate conspiracy had enabled Booth's plot and might yet be revealed through forced confessions. He wanted swift, effective, military tribunals with as little opportunity for Confederate propaganda as possible.

Booth's decision not to surrender may have been cowardice or lust for fame—that is, wanting a last shot at being the author of his own play. He almost certainly wanted a hero's death, which was exactly what Stanton, and now the Sixteenth New York Cavalry, hoped to avoid. In the end, the Federals gained even this last advantage. Booth died with no audience other than those who had dispatched him, and in circumstances of passion (one soldier's rogue shot) rather than of cold calculation. Stanton won authorship of Booth's ending, characterizing everyone involved in the plot as traitors deserving military justice in a time of war. Eventually, the public denounced Stanton for rushing legal proceedings against civilians in military courts—an act subsequently deemed unconstitutional by many. In any event, the conspirators, including Mary Surratt and John Lloyd, were soon executed; Mudd, Cox, and Jones were not. In fact, Cox and Jones were only briefly imprisoned. Their network continued its operations for years afterward.

Lessons

The search for Booth remains a classic of its kind. It challenged intelligence operations in three particular ways: the search covered a complex, domestic "battlefield" of transnational importance; the hunt required mass surveillance; and its outcome involved open sources (media, collectors, and communicators) outside the direct control of either side.

These special features of the hunt for Lincoln's assassin generate too many enduring lessons to cover all here, but four in particular stand out.

1. All hunts require perception management; complex hunts turn on it.

Law enforcement officers engage in relatively straightforward hunts. The operations may be complex, but the public's support for finding lawbreakers is usually a given. Indeed "community-led policing" is about attentive nurturing of that public consensus to generate leads about crimes before they even happen. Savvy criminals can still play to the public using Robin Hood narratives or other celebrity gimmicks, but they almost always work from a disadvantage at the start.

Booth began to lose when the Federal government succeeded in framing his act as a war crime while simultaneously prosecuting the Confederacy's surrender. This decision carried some risk. In a state of war, civil laws of the belligerents may not pertain, and passions can make punishment for disloyalty to one's own side seem greater than monetary rewards from the enemy. Yet Stanton's chosen frame of war offered gains as well. It justified extralegal use of the cavalry, a stretching of evidence and procedure, and leverage against a Confederacy that was seeking favorable terms for surrender, including return of prisoners of war, which was a passionate cause for the population at large. Stanton's bet was that these factors were the currency of intelligence more than hoped-for monetary rewards that, if Confederate defeat had not been imminent, would not have compensated for the dishonor of turning in a fellow rebel.

Still, even with Stanton's contextual advantage, Booth did not have to lose. Complex hunts involving near-war conditions or transnational movements cannot take public support for granted. Instead, public loyalties and changing legal constraints must be mapped as part of the terrain of uncertainty—not just at the start, but as long as the hunt is underway. Intelligence delivers an advantage when it continually senses these public attitudes—seeing the enemy through the audience's eyes—and thus contributes to the managing of perceptions about it. In this way, intelligence for hunts tends to balance law enforcement with offensive counterintelligence (manipulated learning). The latter will involve not just the hunted, but also the public who, as potential hiders and finders, will always be deciding to help one side or the other out of shared passion or self-interest. This kind of influencing in complex hunts amounts, however, to policymaking, because explanations of why the hunt is underway, and how the target is behaving or will be treated, will have domestic political fallout and implications for future state security.

In fact, hunters and hunted in international politics almost always seek to shift the terrain of uncertainty in their favor. For example, an attacker's purpose may be to generate support for a cause or to terrorize a population, perhaps through martyrdom. Booth initially thought that escape would be a lesser priority than triggering panic or wounding so deeply that the scar would be left for generations to see. When he failed to achieve this goal, he began to fear for his life. The challenge for the hunter is to reframe the act of martyrdom as insanity, apostasy, or war in order to change public perceptions in his favor. Intelligence that does not appreciate this larger matter of framing the contest and limits itself only to an objective appraisal of the attacker's purpose will not help the hunter win. Indeed, it may make his losses worse.

Similarly, an attacker who fails to frame his actions with a compelling narrative, as Booth failed to do, increases his chances of losing. Booth did not want to be captured or killed, but he cared just as much about not being perceived as a common criminal. His aim was a "heroic" (ego-driven) reigniting of the Confederacy, which depended on the public's perception of him—a perception he believed he had managed for years on the stage with great success. Stanton needed to deny him that—even in death. Ironically, Booth, a celebrated actor but sorry soldier, succeeded in his attack but failed in this larger, more theatrical purpose. It never occurred to him to rehearse the scene in which he captured the sympathies of his audience. If he had done so, he might have recognized that Secretary of War Stanton, who had been doing propaganda and offensive counterintelligence for years, posed the greatest threat to his larger purposes.

That Booth did not realize this fact meant he did not know his enemy, and so was in trouble from the start.[51] Indeed, Booth did not think about the competition in any kind of sophisticated way. Stanton did, and quickly won a larger audience to a common cause. Later, however, even Stanton became trapped. Unable to shift his own wartime frame, he continued to assert the need for military justice past the moment when the public proved willing to tolerate it. His abrupt military prosecution of the plotters became the subject of civil division and dissent for years afterward.

It follows that the first intelligence questions after an assassination, or other attack of international significance, should be about perpetrator, purpose, and public loyalties or sympathies. The second question should be whether winning will be only about capture and if not, what the larger objective is and what is required to gain it. Stanton's most important advantages came from asking and answering these questions at the very start of this hunt. Although he was wrong in assuming that the larger author of the assassination was the Confederacy, he was right that Washington's best move was to threaten a resumption of a war unless the Confederacy would disown Booth's act. The move was risky. If the wrong narrative about Booth's act "went viral"—such as retribution for the Union's covert action to kill Jefferson Davis—the hearts and minds of the South could have hardened, and the war reignited. Stanton knew he needed to be careful. He wanted Virginians to disown Booth's act more than he wanted to prove Richmond's involvement. This attitude shaped the Federal hunt, with its accompanying narrative.

2. Successful hunts require that the hunter have collection dominance.

The hunt for Booth was a contest in which neither side had, in any absolute sense, what we might call "good" intelligence collection. It was a dimly lit game won by small advantages and a fair amount of luck. Still, the Federals had a surprising degree of collection capability because they could employ an already mustered and experienced cavalry, use it in extrajudicial ways, embed detectives within its ranks, and link all units back to Washington through a deployed telegraph. By comparison, Booth and Herold lost their navigator, Atzerodt, the first night, had poor access to newspapers, and were losing Confederate sympathies by the hour.

Booth's difficulties were partly his own fault. That the context or terrain for this manhunt was complex and, therefore, generally dark initially worked in his favor. This advantage derived from the extra burden the structure of a hunt places on the hunter because the prey has endless choices about where to go, but the hunter must make the right choice with every decision. That Booth stuck to his plan increased his risks as soon as he learned that his colleagues were lost and possibly captured. That meant that they might have been turned into collectors for the hunters, reporting on his plans. By continuing on his route, chances were growing that he would be riding into a trap.

When a hunt involves substantial advantages in collection for the hunter, including close access to the target, it can be transformed from chase to interdiction. An interdiction requires knowing where the target will be ahead of time so that prepositioned assets can intercept it. Avoiding an interdiction by erratic running will eventually exhaust even a well-informed target or prey, increasing advantages over time, and eventually forcing the target "to ground" or into hiding.[52] It logically follows that once a target stops moving, his advantage of choice will go away, while the opportunities for the hunter to preposition assets will go up. In the absence of collection dominance, however, the hiding target's trail will go cold and the target may win. This happened three times to Booth: once at the Mudd house, where he waited too long, allowing the cavalry to blanket the area; once in the pine thicket, where he waited for the cavalry to spread thin as they followed false leads; and once at the Garrett homestead, where he waited too long given the hot trail he had left after crossing the Potomac.

It would seem that Booth's best strategy in the pine thicket would have been to use Jones to plant false leads throughout the county in order to disperse the cavalry. The hunter's best counter would have been to offer rewards for correct leads and to generate sympathy for the cause among locals. Booth got lucky (a false lead did come up, with the expected effect), while the cavalry apparently tried not to overplay its hand. The danger for hunters is that intrusive monitoring may sour people over time or even alienate them completely, thus undermining the advantages time naturally provides. Stanton understood the problem, so he conveyed a sense of urgency to everyone involved.

In the absence of a cooperative population, interdiction will tend to rely more heavily on other forms of collection, including interrogation. But interrogation is a special art in international manhunts where complex cultural, legal, and evidentiary rules will come into play. This complication affected the hunt for Booth. The Federal cavalry, experienced perhaps with interrogating

Union sympathizers, deserters, and Confederate soldiers protected by the laws of war, were not initially as effective interrogating hostile citizens afraid of the consequences of either arrest or retribution. One reason the Sixteenth New York succeeded in tracking Booth was that its armed cavalry officers were able effectively to threaten Confederate veterans, while its embedded detective, Lafayette Baker, knew how to spot and interrogate civilians, such as the ferryman, Rollins.

Booth had, however, power to change these circumstances. Consider what might have happened had Booth tried to escape north to New York, where the population was actively mobilized against him. Although he would have had trouble avoiding an enraged public, safe houses used by the Confederate "line" existed in the north. And Stanton would have had more difficulty keeping the military in charge of joint operations than he did in Port Tobacco or Fredericksburg. Law enforcement, rather than the cavalry, would probably have had greater powers of detention, interrogation, and arrest. It seems likely that Booth might have been caught just as swiftly, but the collection would have come from citizens providing tipoffs to police, increasing the chances of trial and publicity for his cause. Instead, Booth's decision to stick to his plan meant Federal collection would necessarily depend more on the military, and decisions at the moment of capture would rest more with a cavalryman's mindset than a law enforcement one.

The point here is that Booth's decision about where to hide thus constrained or expanded the tools likely to be used to track him. And the degree of collection dominance is likely the greatest determinant of outcomes for hunters involved in complex manhunts. That successful hunts demand collection asymmetry in favor of the hunter makes them somewhat different than tactics on a battlefield. Eliciting intelligence from a hostile citizen is a specialized art in human "sensing" or human intelligence that is, in some ways, different not only from battlefield interrogations, but from recruiting and running agents as well. In complex contingencies, experienced detectives may be as good or better than intelligence professionals or military interrogators in gaining decision-advantage. In any event, interrogation requires special training and talent.[53]

When skills in interrogation are weak and populations hostile, chases or interdictions will require technical collection, which can perform as a complementary method for tracking. Technical collectors that can hover (stake out) and move (chase) can replace the need for a cooperative population. The Booth case suggests something nonintuitive: that, so long as there are enough collectors to follow all incoming tips and all collectors are accompanied by those empowered to arrest or kill, hunters may fare better if they *are not* well coordinated. The tip that led to Booth's capture proved erroneous—a fact that the captors did not know until after Booth was dead. Unwitting of the mistake, the Sixteenth New York expanded the search to terrain ignored by all other collectors.

Had the assassination happened earlier in the war, Booth might have been a needle in a very large haystack, tilting advantages his way. As it was, the terrain was tilted more against him every with each passing day. The crucial variable was the degree of Stanton's dominance in collection capacity, sensitized to the boundaries of public tolerance.

3. Manhunts raise special ethical and legal challenges, particularly for democracies.

The last point has another angle: the historical hunt for Booth masked risks that would have been more apparent if his act had been less catastrophic, or the story less abbreviated. Booth died on the Garrett farm, but Stanton, still operating in a wartime frame, insisted on conducting a military-led hunt and military tribunals rather than criminal prosecutions of the perpetrators. His choice raised ethical and constitutional issues for which he was widely criticized then, and even now. Still, in terms of the competition as he saw it, he surely won: the Confederacy succumbed, Booth and his most intimate conspirators were executed, and an orderly transition to the Johnson administration was secured. All Stanton suffered was a damaged reputation.

Yet if the hunt had continued much longer, the political situation might well have swung back in Booth's favor. Waning wartime conditions were leading to greater public compliance with Federal authority on Confederate soil, but also to a greater public interest in normalcy and constitutional due process. If the introduction of high politics or war into chases and interdictions leads governments to eschew or change the law and, in extreme cases, to use illegal, extraordinary means, the consolidation of peace leads to revived public interest in civil liberties. Rebels can see advantages in getting states to overreact, because overreach fires up popular resistance to the state and encourages a desire for a return to constitutional procedure, which may expose wartime overreach and dismissal of cases. Stanton had a relatively easy time of it because, with the public already used to wartime privations, his method of joint police, private detective, and military operations seemed just more of the same. Even as the public interest began to shift back to due process, Stanton benefited from recent memories of the wartime context, an enemy's defeat, and a nation mobilized by anger over the assassination.

It follows that a state engaged in complex manhunts on the edge of war must consider the boundaries of public tolerance for both the hunt and the envisioned endgame or risk capturing the target but losing the strategic goal. This lesson means that collection for interdiction may have to be scaled back in peacetime, and its methods kept in reserve should public cooperation surge again.

4. Successful manhunts require centralized management with delegation of collection and decision-making authorities.

Consider the freedom of maneuver the cavalry and Lafayette Baker's team had as they launched on their missions. Stanton took risks deploying military units throughout secessionist Maryland and Virginia while still attempting to secure the terms of the Confederacy's defeat. Yet that decision proved essential to his success. We now know Booth's group acted alone, but no one in Washington the night of the assassination knew that fact, so the first crucial hours had to be spent learning who, exactly, the enemy might be, where he was going, and who could best counter him. Pursuing Lincoln's killer was, therefore, a single thread in a complex contingency. It involved law enforcement, counterespionage, and cavalry officers hunting an indeterminate network of perpetrators with connections to insurgents in Canada. As matters of state intersected with an emerging transnational manhunt across Union and Confederate terrain, competitive decision-making had to take account of the interests of locals, state governors, and the military chain of command, which varied across the map. Stanton minimized the problem by operating within a wartime frame. Still, the competition was potentially boundless, lawless, and multilayered.

The more people involved in such a complex contingency, the more difficult it is for intelligence providers to understand who needs to know what for their particular job, whether they can legally know it or not, and even if they can, whether or not it is wise to share. Although choosing the frame of war, Stanton delegated decision-making to police, detectives, and the military, and then embedded intelligence collection in their midst.[54] The cavalry unit chasing Booth in Virginia threatened one Mosby Ranger's life to get him to lead the unit to the Garrett farm where Booth was hiding. The unit in Maryland proceeded far more cautiously with Mudd, probably because they were on Union ground, even if that particular ground had nurtured secessionist sympathies for most of the war.

Herein lies terrible trouble for intelligence services engaged in manhunts. Democracies require different procedures for intelligence-gathering against criminals, insurrectionists and enemy combatants; by embedding intelligence capabilities among friendly combatants, law enforcement can be perfected for the chase, but also influenced by political and military purposes of the hunters, which may vary over time and place. "Setting the net" on the edge of war, as Stanton did in the swamps of Maryland, is different from doing so against drug runners operating from Los Angeles to Mexico City. Even inside a single country, rules may vary for hunts. New York City police tracing illicit weapons-traffickers can run up against police in southern states with more liberal gun laws. A government fighting an insurgency may view curfew-breakers and petty criminals as national security risks, but risk public outrage if it acts on it on the insurgents' home ground. Yet once an attack happens and the state is in jeopardy, that same public may accuse government officials of being too cautious.

To complicate matters more, the decisions law enforcement officers make (arrest and prosecute, or kill), the tools they may use (investigation, surveillance, prosecution, and imprisonment), and the terrain on which they usually operate (the homeland, including its legal order) have limits and chains of command different from those to which most national security leaders or soldiers are accustomed. If circumstances put either police or national security officials in charge, these leaders may misunderstand their limits and authorities, leading agencies to question the lanes in which they should operate and, in some circumstances, even the directions in which each should be driving. If the target is an agent of a foreign power, as Stanton initially supposed Booth was, then that power can use all the devices of its intelligence apparatus to set factionalized hunters against each other.

Such tension and volatility in decision-making stresses standard intelligence practices. Intelligence officers may resist cooperating with police because the latter do not seem to "get" what intelligence is. Police counter that, in fact, they do seek intelligence advantages against criminals but in service to the law, not politics. Police can see intelligence officers supporting diplomacy and war as potential lawbreakers uninterested in the legal requirements of domestic operations, and too ready to jeopardize their long-term interests in safe streets and neighborhood watches with door-busting methods of pursuit. Military officers may see police as a drag on operations and become frustrated with intelligence officers unwilling to overstep their authorities on domestic soil when national security is at stake. And adversaries can exploit this split unless advance preparations for joint operations prevent it.

Although such infighting is bad for national security manhunts, the fact is that, in healthy democracies, collisions between policing, national security, and counterintelligence *should* occur. The solution is to set up protocols designing domestic intelligence architectures before a crisis, and training police, "the cavalry," and intelligence officers on their use before it is authorized. Stanton benefited from the extensive experience the cavalry already had in joint operations, but such experience cannot be taken for granted. There cannot be one type of architecture any more than there is one type of threat. In modern times, for example, hackers, bioterrorists, transnational criminals, and assassins will each demand different sorts of pursuers, enabled by different kinds of collection platforms and communications. In complex contingencies, when all lanes must drive in the same direction in service to the federal government, the requirements of legal choice should become intermixed with the requirements of political decision-making, statecraft, and judicial oversight; it therefore becomes essential to prepare for varying types of collection and the means for intelligence sharing.

The issue then becomes how to create and when to trigger such protocols and authorities. Stanton simply took over. But that cannot work in most circumstances. Protocols related to domestic intelligence collection and sharing among hospitals, police, port authorities, and national security agencies could be designed to be triggered by declarations of war or similar states of emergency. But states of emergency, war, and peace are not always clear in any one country, let alone across international borders. The more protocols there are, the more complicated decision-making will become. A sound intelligence system servicing transnational manhunts must be able to navigate in such chaos, informing decision-makers of the rules of the road under which they are operating at the moment, if necessary. And this requirement means that delegated operations with dedicated intelligence support should ideally be guided by a single, central authority that acts as a clearinghouse for intelligence on the changing rules that must be observed across the competitive space and over time.

Herein lies a central problem for intelligence support to international hunts or interdictions: some foreign countries will have clearer rules and more established protocols than others. Interrogations in one country may involve torture that is illegal in a partnering state. If states' vital interests seem to require that foreign laws be broken or "due process" for terrorist targets be curtailed, there can be no central clearinghouse for anything. Diplomacy enters the mix at this juncture, and the road map for operations becomes a subject for negotiation at all levels, from the unit commander demanding cooperation from a local official to an ambassador asking that intelligence officers not be jailed for breaking laws. In effect, political leaders, diplomats, military commanders, intelligence officers, and police engage in at least three very different "games" with different rules.

States depend on a legal framework for basic order but are tempted to eschew it during chases for the security of that very order. Thus, the paradox: intelligence-gathering finds advantages in flouting rules during missions to preserve them. This is a peculiar dilemma that first Lincoln, with his suspension of habeas corpus in the aftermath of the Baltimore riots, and Stanton, with his pursuit of Booth after the assassination, both experienced. The dilemma has persisted with the rise of mature democracies and their institutionalized intelligence services. Coming to decisions about legal boundaries has meant purposeful hobbling of the state in order to secure citizens against potentially rogue state power. Still, whenever national security seems in jeopardy through assassination or terrorism, the costs and gains of such hobbling are inevitably relitigated. Stopping terrorists with a nuclear bomb in an American city might seem worthy of extreme measures; but absent public disclosure of such threats, democracies prefer applied justice—lawfully rendering a criminal to the United States for prosecution. Between peace and war, manhunts can throw decision-makers for a loop.

So the opening question of this chapter—whether intelligence support for manhunts differs from support to more traditional diplomacy and military engagements—has answers. Based on this case, the differences are mostly matters of degree and emphasis. Manhunts would seem to require the hunter to emphasize the following capacities:

- Knowing the enemy *and one's own side* (police, military, diplomats, intelligence, and public) as well as possible but at least as well as the enemy does;
- Knowing how to win public support through superior narrative building;
- Achieving superior *knowledge of the terrain*, especially as it relates to public opinion, updated for all collectors and decision-makers;
- *Superior human collection capabilities* and situational awareness using evidence-based policing, nonhostile interviews, and intelligence-oriented interrogations;
- Centralized command but lenient control for coordination of diverse collectors operating under a variety of legal frameworks and rules, with special provision for independent action when necessary;
- Preparatory training and advanced protocols for joint operations;

Stanton benefited from conditions of war, teams experienced in joint operations, and the infamy of his opponent. He therefore met almost all of these requirements. He relied not just on instinct, but on intelligence facilitated by his reassertion of the frame of war through which all were made to see Booth's act. He established the martial order, strategic framework, and flexible chain of command that allowed the cavalry, supplemented by police and detectives under Lafayette Baker, to sort the law-abiding from rebels, collect the tactical intelligence necessary for a successful chase, and deliver it to the right place at the right time. There were mistakes, of course. But seasoned cavalry officers, well informed by an active telegraph and a supportive command structure, could take the initiative to track down leads as they saw fit. Thus, Colonel Lovett had a hunch about Dr. Mudd that he could pursue, while Captain Doherty flew south toward the Rappahannock because of a report of two men crossing the Potomac near there. The report later proved false, but the fast action put Federal troops near Booth's path, so Doherty was able to pick up on his trail.

It follows that, if the hunted target is to win, he needs to disrupt all of the hunter's capacities listed above: to shift the pursuit onto friendly terrain, create and sustain a compelling narrative, sow confusion and distrust among the pursuers, and build on trusted intelligence relationships with his supporters. Booth, a skilled actor, had no intelligence system supporting him and no method to win his audience for either his act or his larger purpose. His ploy to reignite the Confederate cause depended on a theatrical moment and a single letter left with an unwitting acquaintance who failed to deliver it. Booth did not know about the failure until days later. A narcissist, he may have believed his fame and theatrics would be enough to win hearts and minds to his cause but, if so, he was ignorant of his audience. The assassination had no trappings of Southern honor; the attack on Secretary Seward, who was bedridden at home, reportedly sickened even Booth when he heard of it.

Unlike Stanton, whose mindset served his intuition, Booth's mindset did not; he saw himself as a star on center stage in a vast theater. He assumed his play would be applauded and that positive reviews would follow, at least among Southerners. This actor, knowing his lines, was reduced to scribbling them in a personal diary.

In contrast, Stanton's mastery of telegraph and newspapers meant he controlled the curtain, the stage, and the lights. As the chase evolved, Booth's lack of preparation meant he had to rely on intelligence supplied by those in positions to aid, harm, or thwart him and with motives affected by every new announcement by the government of rewards for information and punishments for aiding the conspirators. Lacking any intelligence strategy, Booth had few options other than to believe what he was told by those along his escape route.

Conclusion

After the assassination of Lincoln, the hunt for Booth was a matter of state, not just because the conspiracy had targeted the president and his immediate constitutional successors, but also because an inability to capture the assassins would have projected weakness at a moment when a rekindling of the Civil War was still possible. This was no rare historical moment. Saboteurs, insurgents, terrorists, and fanatics have often sought to trigger fights involving greater powers. Great powers have recognized the challenges of manhunts and so, until modern times, have rarely attempted them and have usually failed when they have tried. The Anglo-Spanish conflict involved multiple hunts for Sir Francis Drake.[55] In fact, the interdiction of Drake and his small band of ships became a matter of empire for the Spanish—not just because he threatened the treasure *flotas* on which Philip II's army depended, but because, by exposing a vulnerability that others could exploit and forcing a chase, Drake had the power to increase Spain's vulnerabilities while damaging the credibility of its worldwide defenses.[56]

In fact, sending the cavalry and navy after Booth probably seemed to some as foolish as sending the Spanish navy after Drake; after all, Stanton himself believed the Union was still vulnerable to decapitation by the Confederacy. History shows, however, that such use of the cavalry was not foolish and not just because Stanton's intelligence operations were maximized that way. In the terms of one ancient Greek fable for success, Stanton became both hedgehog and fox: he kept his sights on the one big strategic objective, which was beating the South, while chasing Booth through swamps and pine thickets like a fox.[57] King Philip II never operated that way. Neither, of course, did Booth.

Yet the cases of Booth and Drake also contain a crucial, structural difference: in the case of Booth, the hunters knew his mission was over; in the case of Drake, he still had worse he could do. The former was a chase in which the adversary simply sought to hide, while the latter was an interdiction in which the adversary's worst attack might yet be coming. In both types of cases, however, spies, military officers, policymakers, and police have to work together outside of their comfort zones. Most successful national security-related manhunts involve this feature of joint operations, which can best be improved by building and testing potential architectures for them beforehand, and then exercising them internationally.

In fact, the multinational nuclear nonproliferation community, counterterrorism programs, and counterdrug operations have been dealing with these issues for years, sharing lessons regarding intelligence support across operational domains. In especially complex, nontraditional cases, democratic societies may still lose their bearings because the rules are uncertain in the specific circumstances of the case at the same time that the larger objectives of partners are suddenly both more consequential and less trusted. Terrorism and assassination, are, therefore, often successful as a form of asymmetric war against democracies. Booth just did not have a clue about how to prosecute one.

9

Intelligence Support to Diplomacy

In the previous case studies, we looked at how military intelligence affected strategy and tactics during a famous battle of the sixteenth century, on two battlefields of the American Civil War, and during the hunt for President Lincoln's assassin just five days after Appomattox. In these cases, intelligence did not necessarily lead to good decision-making; it sometimes got things wrong, distorted matters, or failed to persuade. But the combatants and hunters rarely doubted the value of gaining intelligence-advantages. The commander who knew more than his adversary had opportunities to win, whether or not he had superiority in weapons or warriors.

The following chapters deal with far less straightforward cases involving diplomatic and foreign-policy-related decision-making.[1] Like the military, diplomats seek "wins"; unlike the military, their wins sometimes require working with the enemy—a circumstance that introduces interesting ethical and risk-related issues.[2] One of the twentieth century's most prominent diplomats, Henry Kissinger, has written, for example, of the distaste Americans have sometimes had for the British tradition of dealing with enemies:

> In its entire history Great Britain had not often had the luxury of confining negotiations to friendly or ideologically compatible countries. Not having enjoyed anything like America's margin of safety even at the height of its power, Great Britain negotiated with ideological adversaries as a matter of course regarding practical arrangements relating to coexistence. Throughout, a clear working definition of the national interest had enabled the British public to judge the effectiveness of its statesmen. The British might experience occasional domestic disputes over the terms of a particular settlement, but almost never over the wisdom of negotiating.[3]

This British idea underpins classical diplomacy as it has been conducted for centuries. Even if individuals, tribes, lords, or states are so at odds they are willing to risk war, negotiations can work to secure interests at less cost. And even when peace is desired, diplomats may threaten sanctions in order to reconcile competing interests, then run the risk of spying to determine compliance with them.

To effectively sanction, threaten force, or negotiate treaties, diplomats need knowledge of political and military capabilities on all sides. Diplomatic

Decision Advantage. Jennifer E. Sims, Oxford University Press. © Oxford University Press 2022.
DOI: 10.1093/oso/9780197508046.003.0009

intelligence is therefore similar to military intelligence insofar as it requires appreciation of relative power, but differs from the military kind insofar as it entertains the possibility of both win-win solutions with adversaries and the use or sharing of intelligence to get them.

In fact, diplomatic operations include a combination of intelligence, communications, foreign policymaking and negotiation that vary according to the requirements of foreign policy. The influential US diplomat, George Kennan, once said that the central function of a diplomat is "to serve as a sensitive, accurate, and intelligent channel of communication between one's own government and another one."[4] Kennan may be best remembered, however, for policy advocacy. At the beginning of the Cold War, he authored a cable from Moscow that stiffened US resolve to "contain" the Soviet Union as a long-term strategy.[5]

Another foreign policy expert has emphasized the linked functions of intelligence and negotiation when conducting diplomacy: "The uncertainty about whether a deal is possible and if so what it would look like is what negotiators are paid to resolve."[6] To accomplish this goal, negotiators need to find out how much an ally or adversary will resist a diplomatic advance, and then their bottom line— that is, the worst deal for them that they would nonetheless accept if pressed. This makes diplomats professional intelligence collectors as well as negotiators, using carrots and sticks to elicit information for a deal. Clumsy efforts to collect intelligence on such issues can, however, break diplomatic trust and trigger the collapse of an alliance, the end of negotiations, or even escalation of a conflict, making diplomats more leery of risky intelligence operations than soldiers are. Recall how Queen Elizabeth's backchannel negotiations with Philip II threatened her alliance with the Dutch before the Armada sailed.

In fact, in diplomacy's influence-operations, intelligence is both valuable and full of risks. For centuries diplomats controlled these risks by developing a code of conduct, or rules of accepted diplomatic practice. The most powerful states tended to be the most constrained by those rules, because breaking them put at risk the very norms or institutions they had established to maintain order. Such, arguably, was one fatal flaw of British diplomacy in the era of total war from 1914 to 1945: British diplomats tended to gather information and signal their ideas and intentions through trusted diplomatic channels, and expected others to do likewise.[7] British diplomatic culture regarded information gathering as a gentlemanly affair. Comportment and discretion were good indicators of loyalty and the capacity "to masticate the mass of our Foreign Office papers," an indicator of intellectual perseverance.[8] Correlli Barnett has described British diplomacy during this period as having

> something of the air of a British family motorist of the era, proceeding with
> cautious deliberation and much hand signaling down the middle of the road

in one of the under-powered and upright saloons then produced by the British motor industry; and British diplomacy was, like the British driver, apt to be at once bewildered and indignant when cut up by faster operators.[9]

As we shall see, the irredentist Serbs and the vengeful Austrians proved to be "faster operators."

And yet to suppose that diplomacy has generally been a gentleman's game would be a serious mistake. Resolving conflicting interests short of war can be a nasty business indeed. Diplomats need to anticipate warlike behavior, outfox adversaries, lower the costs of conflict, and negotiate, compromise or even consort with former enemies. They rarely have the luxury of clear battle lines, firm objectives, or consistent allies. Toward the closing years of WWII, for example, diplomats scrambled to understand how conflicting interests among wartime allies might affect the coming world order. Intelligence services of the time both sorted matters and, arguably, exacerbated them. Moscow ran aggressive espionage operations against its allies, having recruited scientists involved in the Manhattan Project for developing nuclear weapons. In the notorious Gehlen affair, Nazis in Germany after WWII became protected Western intelligence assets targeted against rising Soviet power—an astonishing turn of events that both reflected and fueled the developing Cold War between the United States and the Soviet Union.[10]

Pragmatism in support of edgy diplomacy necessarily puts intelligence in a state of moral jeopardy even if secret learning through distasteful means prevents a cold war from going "hot." This is especially so in democracies that cultivate virtuous paradigms of political competition and friendships based on them. Hostile intelligence services, in turn, use such morality-based paradigms as avenues for penetrations—such as accessing a security-conscious target by penetrating a less secure liaison service regarded as "friendly" and "democratic" and, therefore, above suspicion. While it is challenging for negotiators to see collaborators and allies, with whom they are building and maintaining deals, as part of this larger, ruthless game, it is even more difficult to see and to tolerate one's own intelligence services playing that game, too—often at some risk to one's own diplomatic portfolio.

The contingent nature of diplomatic intelligence thus entails tasks, risks, and operating adjustments quite distinct from military intelligence in war. The two cases we will examine in the next few chapters consider diplomacy on the precipices of WWI and WWII—times we now regard as prewar, but at the time were regarded as peace. Fear of war was high, particularly before WWII, though few imagined how bad these wars would actually be. The source of the fear was new weaponry and the fragility of newly interdependent economies. Warmaking had expanded in the eighteenth and nineteenth centuries, claiming an increasing share of states' resources, including the blood and treasure of entire populations. War had become potentially grander, uglier, and more decisive than it had been in prior conflicts among the great powers.[11]

At the same time, *relative* power was changing in mysterious ways: industrial might mattered *if* access to raw materials was relatively assured; financial muscle mattered *unless* the blowback of using it hurt more than it helped; marginal superiority in air power was an asset *unless* one's factories were significantly more vulnerable from the air than the adversary's; larger populations mattered to battlefield superiority *except* when those populations proved disloyal, or too uneducated to handle the weaponry of modern war. Such ambiguities in the distribution of power, brought about by sociopolitical, economic, and industrial changes during the nineteenth century, allowed states such as Austria or Italy to punch above their true weight in the diplomatic marketplace. Others, presumed weak, pulled rabbits out of hats: Japan won the Russo-Japanese war of 1904–5, and Serbia shocked almost everyone by winning the Balkan wars of 1912–13.

Before turning to these cases, however, it makes sense to review additional ways in which diplomatic decision-making in peacetime is both different from, and similar to, military decision-making in war.

Similarities between Diplomatic and Military Intelligence

Although the haggling and the bazaar-like quality of diplomacy make its intelligence support more complex than for straightforward contests of blood and iron, there are important similarities between them. Diplomacy, like successful military command, requires measuring power so threats are credible and sanctions appropriate. Diplomats are interested in peacetime deployments of force and knowing foreign reactions to them because these can bolster (or undermine) calculations of foreign resolve. As in military strategy, diplomacy also requires knowledge of domestic support and readiness for war should diplomacy fail, which is a kind of net assessment.

Thus, to a significant extent both diplomacy and military decision-making depend on calculations of relative power. This common interest made for significant overlap in their requirements for intelligence collection when professional intelligence organizations first started to form. From 1876 to 1878, for example, British statesmen lauded "the assistance which has been so frequently and so ably rendered to the Foreign Office . . . by the Intelligence Department of the War Office."[12] Later, managing the boundaries of empire, the British statesmen learned how actions in India might trigger imperial Russian reaction elsewhere with the help of intelligence from military attachés. Their increasingly joint and systematic efforts, which extended to assessing Japanese capabilities against Russia in the early 1900s, brought the idea of "national" intelligence from throne room to modern bureaucratic practice: the collection of civilian and military strategic information for the coordinated exercise of state power in peace and war.[13]

WWI and WWII rapidly extended these joint diplomatic and military practices, so civilian institutions dedicated to national security expanded in number and size. By the time the Cold War began in the late 1940s, diplomats were coping with a host of military issues, such as a nuclear arms race, strategic deterrence, and the peacetime dangers of the nuclear fuel cycle for the proliferation of nuclear weapons. Foreign ministries, and particularly the US Department of State, became as fluent in the language of national force structure and deterrence as they had been in knowledge of foreign languages, borders and maps, royal houses, and religious affiliation in centuries past. When, in 1950, President Harry Truman wanted a review of "our objectives in peace and war . . . in the light of the probable fission bomb capability of the Soviet Union," it was a civilian banker, Paul Nitze, who led the joint diplomatic and military effort.[14] The Superpowers' national security staffs grew, with the most influential foreign and defense advisors focused on shoring up alliances and the avoidance of strategic nuclear war. This shift did not mean cultural and political matters were no longer important for great power diplomacy; rather, the principal business of diplomacy—furthering the national interest while avoiding strategic nuclear war—rested relatively more clearly on closely calibrated relationships of force.

Differences in the Diplomatic and Military Arts

Yet joint needs does not mean that diplomatic and military intelligence requirements have always been identical. Their requirements for decision-advantage have varied sharply. Although diplomacy sometimes enjoys the clarity of a battlefield, often it does not. Diplomats bargain with allies and enemies, which in either case can be a murky, dangerous business. This ambiguity is the first and probably most significant difference between diplomacy and military affairs. Diplomats may choose to negotiate to a stall on North Korea in the interest of working issues backchannel with China, for example. Similarly, a negotiator may shift from confronting to accommodating an adversary in order to "deal up"— that is, gain more value for power in a political exchange that becomes "win-win" instead of clear defeat for the other side. Allies can also put each other's interests at risk, while maneuvering for advantage on larger matters. US diplomats have, for example, chosen to overlook differences with Israel over espionage, re-exports of defense technologies, and settlement policies in order to advance the prospects for a negotiated peace in the Middle East.

Although haggling over agendas is not normal for opposing commanders, it is diplomats' métier. Negotiations have slowed the proliferation of nuclear weapons, eased the consequences of the Soviet Union's dissolution, and strengthened borders through alliances. Relative advantage in diplomacy, however, is harder to measure than on the battlefield. Although there are times when the classical idea of winning certainly applies, a state's peacetime interests are often subjective. Winning or losing may depend on one's point of view. Sometimes there is consensus about what would be the best outcome of negotiations with an adversary or what would constitute a loss. But diplomacy may take years to bring results, the gains may seem small, and the "wins" may be distributed among multiple players. A diplomatic win might flow from a mistake, such as unintentionally threatening another state that reacts by offering an unexpected concession. Successful diplomacy might de-escalate tensions by negotiating confidence-building measures or even releasing classified evidence of benign intent when the other state's intelligence is poor. Gaining decision advantage in diplomacy is, therefore, a murkier goal than in military affairs. One sometimes *deals with enemies* instead of, or in the process of, *defeating them.*

A second difference between diplomacy and war-fighting has to do with risk-taking—a topic mentioned earlier. Civilian policymakers often seem uncomfortable with espionage and what might be called the "dark arts." This is not because diplomats are more squeamish than their military counterparts; it is rather that their risk calculations are different. They win—that is, gain decision-advantage—by influencing a political marketplace. The exposure of clandestine activities on the soil of others can turn friends into enemies, lend persuasive power to opponents, and put delicate political strategies at risk. Spies caught behind enemy lines are one thing; those caught before the lines are drawn are quite another. For this reason, premodern diplomatic intelligence employed princely emissaries, ambassadors, and consuls, who were charged with delivering, as well as gathering, inside information. Protected by their royal connections on one end, and their utility to host governments on the other, they served for centuries as the intelligence gatherers and conveyers for kings, with their dual role tacitly acknowledged by the developing concept of diplomatic immunity. Diplomats, therefore, learned to take the risks of close access and intelligence collection and analysis themselves, and distrust the delegation of such maneuvering to others less invested in the outcomes. Since the institutionalization of intelligence services, however, professional officers have tended not to credit diplomats with intelligence expertise, despite often relying on diplomatic platforms overseas and diplomatic reporting for political insight. Diplomats, in turn, have become more self-reliant and less receptive to the intelligence analysis. Yet at the heart of gaining decision-advantage in this context is the development of trust between diplomatic decision-makers and the broader intelligence system in which they operate.

Third, unless diplomats are working for a great power with global military reach, the intelligence necessary for diplomacy will usually be broader in substance and geographic scope than that for military planning and operations. Diplomacy demands a special kind of readiness, including baseline information on all matters of potential interest to the state. Many states, such as Saudi Arabia, Israel, or Brazil, have global interests without commensurate military engagement. Even Superpowers cannot plan to back up all their political interests with military muscle. Without wide-ranging intelligence, diplomats cannot anticipate opportunities, avoid diplomatic surprise, frame priorities, or bring influence to bear on others by persuasion, threat, manipulation, or distraction, such as shifting a competitor's attention from one contested realm to another. If military decision-makers think in terms of theaters of operation or war, diplomats and other civilian national security decision-makers think in terms of a global bazaar in which everyone is selling something, and every deal is potentially connected to all others.

Fourth, unlike military decision-making, decisions regarding diplomatic logistics (embassy construction, visa processing, passport control, consular services, diplomatic security, communications, etc.) are not commonly integrated with diplomatic policymaking. Part of the reason for this difference is embedded in history. Diplomats before WWI were usually recruited from the upper classes and were often expected to pay for operations out of their own pockets. They learned to make do with little and to recruit locals to deal with buildings, communications, and other administrative functions. The prior culture persisted even as diplomatic operations became professionalized; most diplomats remained disinterested in decisions about where and how to build embassies, how to solicit resources, or how to establish and secure communications. The diplomats in the Foreign Office in late nineteenth-century Britain were so used to making do with antiquated record-keeping, archiving, and communications systems that they delayed reorganization for years.

Yet nowhere has the classic division between diplomacy and its supporting operations been more apparent than in the twentieth-century US Department of State. Policymakers and management staffs have generally divided themselves into two separate career hierarchies: the former attending minimally to technology or logistical planning; the latter acting as if policy mattered little to decisions regarding management, communications, and intelligence. Moreover, department managers, whose decisions on global resources affected Foreign Service reporting, communication, and security, have for decades distanced themselves from the government's intelligence apparatus, including the department's own Bureau of Intelligence and Research. Diplomats and negotiators have launched new diplomatic initiatives or evacuated a country in crisis only to be surprised by the suddenly inadequate communications, security, and high-level intelligence. As ambassadors locked facilities in times of crisis, intelligence agencies have knocked on those same doors, requesting an expansion of access. Thus, whereas military logistics are the meat and potatoes of readiness, diplomatic readiness has proven to be an elusive concept. The problem arose for the British after the industrial revolution; it is apparent in the United States as the Foreign Service struggles to play in complex interagency operations after the information revolution. With some notable exceptions, such as shuttle diplomacy in the Middle East or the hunt for hidden weapons in Iraq, US diplomacy has seemed confined within a nineteenth-century model of inflexible, geographically frozen overseas fortresses. The point here is not that this is the way diplomacy must be; it is that this is the way history has generally shaped diplomatic practice and culture, particularly in Western democracies. Few successful decision-makers in the military think in this bifurcated way about policy and operations.

Fifth, unlike military decision-making, diplomacy often eschews formal chain of command to focus instead on political access and leverage. Although the degree to which this informal process dominates will depend in part on the political characteristics of the government, influential decision-makers on any particular issue may have seemingly irrelevant portfolios. Diplomats may suddenly get new missions or choose to work around opposing decision-makers, ignoring rank and formalities. Lacking chain of command as a reliable guide, intelligence providers in the gray world of diplomacy must scramble to identify who decides, what they want, and how to influence a constantly shifting cast of adversaries. They must also track and enable influence across issue areas, working many fronts at once. Diplomats' readiness to work outside normal channels makes them intensely competitive, eager for specialized support, and resistant to the estimative judgments of others with less access to the corridors of power. Most diplomats believe themselves to be good "intelligence" officers themselves, and want their information from direct contact with foreign sources or trusted intermediaries.[15]

In the late nineteenth and early twentieth centuries, as we shall see, diplomats and political leaders employed citizen adventurers, royal princelings, financiers, industrialists, and, of course, military attachés to satisfy their changing needs for information. Sometimes the results were bad. The German kaiser's brother, for example, Prince Henry of Prussia, paid a royal visit to Britain's King George V before WWI, and heard the king muse that Britain would likely stay neutral should the continent become embroiled in war.[16] While the king did make that remark, he had no decision-making power, so the intelligence was irrelevant. The kaiser, nonetheless, liked what he heard and, pronouncing the word of a monarch good enough for him, threw his support more strongly behind Austria's advance against Serbia. Note that, bad as the kaiser's intelligence was, his opponents would have needed to track all his intelligence providers, including his peripatetic sibling, to fully understand German intentions.

Sixth, diplomacy involves influence—what some have termed "soft power." This effort can extend from the exchange of students and the holding of cultural events to disinformation campaigns and propaganda. Such practices increased in size and impact as a consequence of the industrial revolution, creating opportunities for the crafty to sway the terrain of uncertainty one way or another. For example, before WWI, the French and Russians were distributing funds to the press in foreign countries to influence public attitudes and so pressure policymakers. In 1905, the Russians hoped for support for a French loan, and the French wanted Germany to back down on Morocco. For the latter purpose, Théophile Delcassé gave the press intelligence on British military planning designed to threaten Germany. Such "inspired" articles in the press were often a reflection of political alliances among publishers and politicians—not just bribes—and could infuriate diplomats as much as help them. In this regard, at least, the diplomats of the early twentieth century shared with General Sherman and Secretary of War Stanton of the Civil War era decidedly mixed views of journalists. The difference was that a diplomat like Grey or a politician like Stanton could be a propagandist, while generals on the battlefield often could not spare the time.[17] The point is that diplomats regularly decide how to make open-source information work for them, even if those valuing a free and independent press are relatively constrained in their options.

For the foregoing reasons, perfecting the art of military intelligence does not necessarily suffice for gaining decision-advantage in diplomacy. To explore how to do so requires examining cases for which documentary records are rich, and successes and failures are clear. Both requirements are met for the period from 1900 to 1945. During this time, governments were superintending a great leap from organized military intelligence to integrated national intelligence geared toward managing state power. The leap was an inelegant one. In nineteenth-century democracies such as France's Third Republic or Britain, bureaucratic struggles developed between civil and military authorities. In fact, decision-making in most early twentieth-century European governments was so factionalized that it was confusing even to those governments themselves—a situation made worse by erratic communications.

WWI occurred on the edge of a great transition from informal or ad hoc national intelligence to organized professional intelligence systems for integrated state action. As the age of monarchs came to an end, European militaries, rocked by fluctuating civilian politics, drove stability into decision-making by creating inflexible plans. The militaries' means of coping with what we have been calling the competitive "terrain of uncertainty" increased the uncertainties for the civil authorities. Military management of intelligence for diplomacy led to disastrous decisions. Civilian management of military strategy through heavy-handed intelligence policy illuminated how battles can be lost when armchair strategists make mistakes. For these reasons decision-making on the precipice of WWI and WWII offers a good example of how decision-advantage may be gained or lost. The outcome of the Great War included the development of civilian intelligence systems serving both war and diplomacy. The use of them in the buildup to WWII propelled most modern states to organize the national intelligence services that would dominate the Cold War.

Complex as the analysis may be, a close examination of early twentieth-century diplomacy suggests that, to the many hypotheses on the causes of the Great War that already exist, we ought add another: immature, competitive intelligence organizations that were neither charged with comprehensive support to those determining "national" policies nor capable of providing it. As a result, confusion was rampant as governments pursued policies that were internally inconsistent, diplomats became targets for disinformation, factions within politicized intelligence agencies developed sources to bolster their own preferred positions, and militaries chose among constrained options rather than among emerging opportunities. Diplomats, unaccustomed to nastier, industrial-grade intelligence operations, either pulled a "Hooker," idling at a crucial moment, as the British foreign secretary was before WWI, or, more like Lee, lurching forward more on instinct rather than on good, comprehensive intelligence.

The decline of thrones and the rising power of labor, industry, and mass armies weakened the traditional architecture for intelligence for which royal emissaries and embassy platforms had long served as post and beam. Bewilderment followed. In just one example, Dayrell Crackanthorpe, the Serbophile British minister in Belgrade during the aftermath of the Balkan wars of 1912–13, relied more on a "Servian officer of his acquaintance" and "the official denials of the Belgrade government" than on field reporting to assess the extent of Serbian repression of minorities in its conquered territory. As one historian has observed of his skewed reporting: "Already, one might argue, the events unfolding in the Balkans were being viewed through the geopolitical lens of the alliance system."[18] That the British Foreign Office eventually came to recognize Serbian atrocities does not diminish the point that it did so ineptly and belatedly. In this way, the Great War evolved out of a slow-rolling diplomatic crisis of acute misperceptions. Later adjustments, including the development of open-source, scientific, and national intelligence systems during WWII, may explain why the later Cold War never went hot.

As we delve into cases of civil decision-advantage in the early twentieth century, it is important to keep a methodological point in mind: the conjoined development of formal institutions for military and diplomatic intelligence never monopolized the intelligence domain. New forms of intelligence-gathering, using information from private industry and journalism, also influenced decision-making. Private sources of civilian intelligence sometimes filled in where more formal forms of diplomatic and military intelligence could not. Although diplomatic history speaks to us in documents, which are generally the preserve of governments, its language ought not mislead us about methods and practices that, by their nature, resist organizational capture. Sometimes letters, memoirs, and biographies provide clues to diplomatic intelligence that documents do not.

Of course, the archaeology of intelligence practices cannot slip into fanciful storytelling, either. What is needed are both a plumbing of archives for evidence of intelligence support to diplomacy, regardless of its source, and careful use of theory, which unmasks intelligence activity masquerading as something else. In the last chapters of this volume, we will look at the revolution in intelligence that is unfolding in the twenty-first century—one in which the agent of change has been the information industry. This industry, offering unprecedented access to information for all those engaged in politics and war, has thrown decision-advantage back to the pre-Westphalian era, when gaining it was almost as hard for a monarch as for a peasant. Then, the source of narrowed advantages was intelligence scarcity, not wealth; whereas the peasant had limited vision because of his immobility, the monarch had limited vision because of the lies and deceptions of his informants. Though not equal in the volume of information flowing to them, both feared losing their lives to the unexpected. Today, in the sea of information available, securing information advantages and avoiding surprise and deception are again difficult for both governors and the governed; the root cause now, however, is information overload, not scarcity.

* * *

Before leaving this introduction to diplomatic intelligence, it is important to mention the special problem of intelligence on "intentions," which theorists of international politics sometimes cite when discounting the importance of intelligence in international affairs. Their error is in supposing a noninteractive terrain and, thus, a need to see into the future to know what an enemy will do. In fact, however, an adversary's "intention" during peacetime can often be discerned directly from decisions already taken. Before WWI, for example, ambassadors collected and provided intelligence on official planning, but also learned of foreign leaders' intentions from those people present when decisions were made. As we shall see, the British ambassador to Austria-Hungary learned that Vienna intended to deliver an ultimatum to Serbia from someone who had been in the room when that decision was made. Similarly, Hitler told his top generals of his concrete plans for Austria, Czechoslovakia, Poland, and France well before he pulled off his plans. Facts about "resolved intentions" or strategic plans were not the problem; getting decision-makers to believe them was, especially when sources had to be protected and so remained unknown, or were known but remained mistrusted.

Learning intentions may turn on the occasional indiscretion, but also on access to the records of decision-making. Governments capture their decisions in minutes or notes from cabinet meetings. The theft of such records can provide intelligence on intentions as real as counts of dreadnoughts and the tracking of ships at sea inform on naval intentions. Considering again the example of Britain's nineteenth-century conundrum in Asia, modern scholarship has revealed the relatively good British system for extended early warning. In fact, one military attaché's reporting from St. Petersburg judged Russian expansion unlikely. This reporting was not speculation based on mysterious analysis of the tsar's temperament or crystal ball-gazing, but was, instead, a reasoned conclusion based on facts: the disposition of Russia's forces, intercepted documents recording the tsar's decisions, and other meeting minutes. Colonel Frederick Wellesley, enjoying good access to the Russian War Office, could thus reliably collect and analyze intentions, observing, "I can obtain anything but I would like to know what is of special interest at home, so as to be guided in my future conduct."[19]

Finally, it is important to stress that in such circumstances, the test for intelligence is whether policymakers get the information they need for the most advantageous outcomes possible. Note that, because diplomacy involves clashes of interests, the issue is not whether the outcomes are the "best possible" for one side, but rather the most advantageous possible for that side given the power and influence of the other. Although gauging that sense of adequacy may be necessarily somewhat subjective, the relative knowledge behind the maneuvering to get there—the cost-benefit analysis—is discernible and, at least to some extent, measurable. Behind such maneuvering lie both the threat of force and the intimation that a state "knows" the consequences that it seeks, wants to avoid, and can inflict if it does not get its way. When a state knows these things better than an adversary does, then it may be said to have diplomatic "decision-advantage." On the other hand, threatening the use of force or other forms of sanctions without knowing whether or not they will be effective, can be imposed, or will incur excessive costs would be pure folly. These kinds of "knowing" are just a few of the objectives of intelligence support to diplomacy—a tough agenda, indeed.

10
Knowledge and Diplomacy in the Era
of Total War

On 28 June 1914, Serbian nationalists assassinated the Archduke of Austria, Franz Ferdinand, and his wife, Sophie, while they rode in an open car through the streets of Sarajevo. International reaction was initially muted and then, suddenly, it was not. Scrambling on the steep slope toward war, diplomats sought to secure advantages by mobilizing troops, influencing publics, and shoring up alliances. Nonetheless, in just a few weeks Europe was in flames. By the end of it, Russia had imploded, Austria-Hungary had disappeared, and about nine million soldiers and ten million civilians had lost their lives. Most diplomats had not foreseen either the consequences of the assassination or the devastation that war would bring.[1] Historian Raymond Aron has put it simply: "The explosion in 1914 was the result of diplomatic failure."[2]

Indeed, the trajectory of international politics from 1900 to 1940 seems littered with diplomatic failures. The peace treaty signed at the Palace of Versailles in 1919 was a failure.[3] Even US president Woodrow Wilson, who had promoted the League of Nations at the time, could not get the agreement passed by the US Senate. France, the United States, and Britain advocated self-determination, but then watched Italy annex territory and subjugate populations. Germany reoccupied the Rhineland, swallowed Austria, and exceeded its caps on military aviation, army, and general staff. Most famously, perhaps, British prime minister Neville Chamberlain declared in 1938 that he had achieved "peace in our time" by trading Czechoslovakia's Sudetenland to Adolf Hitler in return for promises that German aggression would cease. Chamberlain's hope was soon dashed as Germany devoured the French ally bit by bit. Nazi forces invaded Poland in 1939, and then, in the spring of 1940, swept through France so quickly that within seven weeks Hitler's army was marching down Paris's Champs-Elysees. In his book *Strange Victory*, historian Ernest May wrote of WWII: "If leaders in the Allied governments had anticipated the German offensive through the Ardennes, even as a worrisome contingency, it is almost inconceivable that France would have been defeated when and as it was."[4] Yet France fell so fast and unexpectedly that British forces barely scrambled home in time.

Setting aside the issue of blame for the mass slaughter in both these world wars, why did those Great Powers ostensibly interested in avoiding total war

Decision Advantage. Jennifer E. Sims, Oxford University Press. © Oxford University Press 2022.
DOI: 10.1093/oso/9780197508046.003.0010

nonetheless fail *twice*? Was intelligence to blame? Respected historians have long suggested that uninformed decision-making was part of the problem. In his multivolume analysis of WWI, historian Luigi Albertini wrote that "during this crisis ... any move which might have been effective in bringing about a peaceful solution either came too late or was not acted upon in good faith."[5] Officials were, according to a more recent historian, "sleepwalkers" disconnected from reality.[6] A close reading of the literature and supporting documents before WWI and, to a lesser extent, WWII suggest that even experienced statesmen were confused about the implications of their international commitments, ignorant of the decisions others were taking, and poorly informed about the nature of the modern war they were risking.

Statesmen in general, not just diplomats, seemed strangely ignorant throughout this era. As Austria moved against Serbia in 1914, the German kaiser reacted to King George V's intimations of conditional English neutrality by trying to stop his own army's westward march toward war. Not only was he confused about King George V's role and influence, he was infuriated to learn that he could not stop his own war machine.[7] Kaiser Wilhelm was not alone in his misdirected inquiry; even republican France appealed to the British king for intelligence on Britain's intentions, gaining nothing. Yet the kaiser's poor understanding of his army's operational constraints was particularly striking because he prized his command of his army. The Austrian emperor was hardly better informed. Having sent his troops south to fight a local war against Serbia, he was astonished that, once Russia mobilized, he could not turn them around in time to engage the Russians in Galicia.

For their part, Russian statesmen seemed confused about whether partial mobilization against Austria was possible, let alone desirable. The British Cabinet seemed so muddled, it could not decide what to do about the Austro-Hungarian ultimatum for over two weeks—despite rolling declarations of war in other capitals, and the German bombardment of Liège in neutral Belgium. Foreign Secretary Edward Grey shifted from studied neutrality in the developing crisis to a more unstudied type, barely hinting at Britain's intent to back her Entente partners, France and Russia, should Germany decide for war. When urged to send the British Expeditionary Force to support France as the Germans moved into Belgium, Grey knew at last what to do, but seemed uncertain about how to get it done.

Despite the attractiveness of the sleepwalking hypothesis, however, contemporaneous accounts and the autobiographies of participants in WWI suggest the problem was not somnolence. Statesmen of the era have generally described an almost hyper-awareness of the magnitude of the stakes, a reflective judgment that seems supported by the marginalia on the mountain of memos and telegrams, as well as the public speeches and national debates prior to WWII.[8] Participants later claimed, with some justification, that bureaucratic and party politics had obstructed communications among capitals and prevented information sharing within them. For example, Britain's Grey argued he had been constrained by a divided Cabinet, surprised by the extent to which Anglo-French military plans depended on an early British deployment should Germany attack, and shocked by others' prescient estimates of the duration and cost of the war. Observing that Britain's secretary of war, Lord Kitchener, had warned in early August 1914 that the coming conflict would likely last years and drain Britain's coffers, Grey later mused that "it was never disclosed how or by what powers of reasoning he made this forecast."[9]

This chapter will show that most of this uncertainty sprung primarily from changes in the tools available to states and the authorities they had to wield them. The industrial revolution had so altered decision-making within states and relationships of force among them that those seeking to manage international politics knew too little too late to do so competently. If generals and admirals were marginally better at it, this was because they had more seasoned methods for acquiring and using the clandestine forms of intelligence than diplomats did. That this diplomatic era was dark did not mean, of course, that intelligence advantage had disappeared; it just meant that the seeming "winners" at any moment could still be losers in the larger, more dimly lit game.

The Terrain of Uncertainty, 1900–45

To simplify matters, it is possible to identify four broad trends that generated uncertainties for European statesmen during this period: the new wave of industrialization; the related rebalancing of British and German power and its effects on alliance structures in Europe; the diffusion of decision-making authority within modernizing governments; and the rise of politically mobilized citizenry. To these structural changes, statesmen added another: national intelligence institutions. The growth in these institutions offered new, but poorly understood, tools for understanding friends and enemies while putting traditional diplomatic sources at risk.

The point of reviewing these trends and the uncertainties is to lay the groundwork for understanding the search for advantages in diplomatic knowledge and decision-making before the two world wars. Formal intelligence services were still not the exclusive means by which statesmen sought competitive knowledge, but professional services were beginning to displace traditional methods, in part because reliable knowledge was so important and yet so hard to find.

These were profoundly confusing times, whether leaders admitted it or not. Most did not. Diplomats, like military commanders, needed to understand relationships of force as well as other forms of influence, to share such knowledge selectively with those they sought to influence, and to exploit informational advantages against likely adversaries—the basic stuff intelligence services promise, but may fail to deliver when they are as new, weak, or untrusted as they were during this era. Uncertainties about economic conditions, how industrialization might be changing warfare, or even how other states were learning, were as important to diplomats' work as uncertainties about who had connections or authority in foreign capitals. The awakening to these basic truths was slow all around, causing serious miscalculations everywhere. This chapter explains why.

The Effects of Industrial Change

Political developments of the late nineteenth century were seen largely then, as now, as emanating from the industrial face of power. Pursuing applied science and expanding commerce could, regardless of intentions, manifest as threat and thus blur the line between war and peace. The aerial revolution, for example, begun in 1903, brought exciting commercial applications that, at the same time, inspired experimentation with aerial combat, bombing, and reconnaissance.[10] Rails were integrating large territories into single markets, but also unifying potential theaters of war. French loans to build a Russian railway threatened Germany's border; German moves to build a rail line from Berlin to Baghdad raised fears that the kaiser would soon exploit Ottoman weaknesses and threaten Russian or British interests in the Caucasus and Persia.

Diplomats understood that the laying of rails might seem a flexing of muscle, but also that economic interests could drive choices in ways that only made it seem that way, enflaming popular passions and making intentions uncertain all around. A redistribution of power, interest, and uncertainty was underway in the guise of good business. As military services integrated the new technologies into their plans and operations, calculations of advantage fluctuated according to the availability of raw materials, factories, and supply chains, many of which linked the economies of the Great Powers together. In such circumstances, answering diplomatic questions, such as whether a trading partner would risk conflict or whether a given level of factory production was an indicator of belligerent intent, involved a host of unknowns.

The challenge was not only in assessing power and threat. New technologies were also changing how states learned, influenced, lured, and bullied.[11] Industrial advances became subjects for diplomatic study, but, to read opportunities and threats correctly, diplomats needed experts who understood the implications of complex technologies and the requirements for their production. For the aging class of Europe's upper-crusted diplomats, the challenge was initially met with confusion and uncertainty. Part of the reason had to do with new opportunities for collaborative and accelerated decision-making.

Although scientists, industrialists, military officers, and diplomats had new incentives to share information among themselves, they had little experience in doing so. A lot had changed since the American Civil War, when generals had to accept the existence of a hodgepodge of weapons on battlefields, including some "antiques." By the late nineteenth century, industrialists had improved mass production and distribution, while innovators were introducing and sharing dual-use technologies across international borders. In such innovative times, even military leaders had trouble relating new technologies to power, interests, and intentions. General Ferdinand Foch, observing a 1910 air race in eastern France, offered the opinion that "flying . . . is merely a sport, like any other; from the military point of view it has no value whatever."[12] Foch was wrong, of course. By 1914, "aeroplanes" were proving useful in war; by 1938, they were the focus of diplomats' efforts to contain an arms race; by 1940 they were spearheading the battle for Britain upon which the fate of the British nation (and thus the fate of Foch's France) would depend. With military requirements lagging capabilities, industrialists had a weak grasp of wartime needs. Military assumptions about needed supplies at the start of WWI proved wildly off. Industrial capacities to meet the challenge initially fell short, but then surged to meet increased demand.[13]

Given such military and industrial uncertainties, it is hardly surprising that statesmen and diplomats had trouble calculating the relative distribution of power. In just a few decades, the age of air power, with its capacity for war-winning surprise attack, was raising fears of diplomatic paralysis for which foreign ministries were, for the most part, analytically unprepared.[14] Equipped with few theories of what to do about the peacetime threat and little knowledge of the technologies involved, diplomats joined with the military in fixating on relative numbers and playing for time.[15] Civilians criticized them, not for failure to think strategically, but for failure to count. Reports of numerical imbalances in rails, ships, or airplanes could trigger public outrage, causing political leaders to get jumpy and waste money on arms races that only heightened tensions with little gain. Perhaps the most famous example of this link between innovation, popular passions, and diplomatic uncertainty was triggered by Britain's development of dreadnoughts in the early twentieth century. These massively armored ships grabbed media attention, made other ships seemingly obsolete, and inspired naval ambitions among rising powers that had the industrial capability to imitate Britain's feat.[16] In short order, the kaiser demanded a German navy to rival Britain's but with no solid theory for how it would be used. He ended up with an expensive vanity project that, besides riling the British, drove a wedge between his admirals, his generals, and his chancellor. The resulting arms race exacerbated Anglo-German relations already troubled by the Anglo-French entente.[17]

To say that turn-of-the-century diplomats, awakening to the explosion of dual-use technologies, had to become fluent in military affairs still understates their problems, however. Diplomatic advantage turned on two additional drivers linked to the industrial revolution: communications, especially cable and wireless, and mechanized cryptology.[18] Some states were benefiting disproportionately from developments in these two areas. London, for example, could quickly take the lead in oceanic cable-laying because of her dominance at sea. The advent of steamships permitted navigating in straight lines regardless of wind and weather, which in turn, made feasible the laying of transoceanic wires. Britain set about designing redundant subsurface cable routes for herself while tapping or cutting enemy cables as needed—steps Britain took at the immediate onset of WWI. Germany apparently did not notice that the cutting, laying, and repairing of cables was a target-rich enterprise, so failed to attack it. Thus, Britain was able to use slow, poorly defended surface platforms to lay, lift, and snip at will, even into WWI.

Communications

The pre-WWI map of Britain's strengths and weaknesses in this area is worth closer study because it reveals the value, not just of terrain mapping, but of open-source intelligence. The development of Britain's communications advantages did not rest on steamships alone. It was both commercially driven and serendipitous.

The serendipitous part deserves special attention because of what it reveals about how imperial reach and profit-seeking can tip the terrain of uncertainty, making intelligence easier for one state than others. One example of the East India Company's unscripted role as a serendipitous collector for the British prior to WWI involved an inquisitive surgeon with the company in Southeast Asia. He discovered that the Palaquium gutta tree produced a strange product, samples of which he sent to London. In 1851, Michael Faraday, the discoverer of electromagnetic induction, investigated the product's unique characteristics as an insulator. He discovered that the material was the best available for protecting copper wire from seawater. At the time, oceanic communications were still carried by ship because no one had learned how to insulate the cables. Faraday's find was, therefore, both revolutionary and consequential for trade, travel, diplomacy, and war.

The discovery of gutta-percha, together with the advent of steamships, helped launch the British-led explosion in undersea cables.[19] The first transatlantic cable was laid in 1858, and within a decade, reliable transoceanic communications had been established. By 1892, the cable networks had reached about three hundred thousand miles of lines; by 1902, telegrams could be sent across the globe in less than an hour.[20] Ten submarine cables owned by five corporations lay beneath the North Atlantic; the shortest submarine distance stretched nearly nineteen hundred miles.[21] The Eastern Telegraph Company of London owned the longest network of cables, supplemented by its Eastern Extension Company. Thus, Britain had prepositioned itself to reroute, interdict, or simply read German cable traffic prior to WWI.

Although the British navy realized the strategic importance of its dominance of the worldwide cable system, the effects on competitive learning seemed unevenly understood by diplomats and statesmen. Well before WWI, London had subsidized the growth of the cable system and had encouraged foreign countries to land their cables on British soil or near her shores. When London used this access to identify and cut German cables carrying transatlantic communications before WWI, however, German and American traffic had to be rerouted. Forced onto fewer cables, the communications of both the neutral and the belligerent slowed considerably, while London's capacity secretly to intercept and read messages secretly improved. As the cable war progressed, the British advantage lay in knowing best which cables carried what traffic—an advantage that lay largely with the navy's Office of Naval Intelligence, run by Captain (later Admiral) William Reginald "Blinker" Hall. According to the historian of intelligence Christopher Andrew,

> Hall kept most diplomatic intercepts to himself. "He had" in the opinion of "Bubbles" James, "unbounded confidence in his ability to decide how much of the information in the messages should be passed on to other Government departments." Hall usually decided that other departments could be trusted with very little—and even the little was usually disguised.[22]

When a German telegram offered an alliance with Mexico in return for entering the war on the side of the Central Powers, London was, however, able to reveal the plot to the neutral US government. What London's intelligence services did not confess at the time was its method: spying on German and US communications. Instead, they claimed a source in the German embassy in Mexico. This British deception of an intended ally, now the well-known story of the Zimmermann Telegram, exploited an American innocence and dependence that did not last long. After WWI, the United States sought a cable-laying capacity to rival Britain's, at least in the Western Hemisphere.[23] The British effort to maintain a monopoly on communications routes to South America in the 1920s resulted in a peacetime, cable-laying "war" off the coast of Florida that included revelations about British cable-tapping in peacetime. Network protection became a new, costly, worldwide priority for Britain and all her rivals in the cable war, requiring a flexible navy and superior local threat assessments, especially where cables emerged from the sea. Even Germany, which lagged in submarine cable-laying, eventually became aware of the importance of owning, mapping, and cutting cables at sea; Berlin ran special operations to take down Britain's cable stations in the first months of WWI.

Perhaps the best example of this connectivity-vulnerability dynamic, however, was the invention of radio. Wireless communications permitted vehicles in all operational environments to be centrally coordinated and, by the interwar period, deployed for real-time deterrence, surveillance, and diplomacy.[24] Coordination of platforms on land, sea, and air allowed for new "joint" operational strategies. The speed with which radio penetrated the realms of diplomacy and war was astounding at the time. By 1896, Guglielmo Marconi had freed information from wires; by WWII, radios were enabling clandestine coordination of spies, covert communications from port watchers, and "wolf packs" of submarines capable of finding Allied surface ships, radioing locations, and clustering for attack. Radio communication enabled tank warfare to evolve into the fast-rolling German blitzkrieg, which overwhelmed France in 1940, catching British statesmen flat-footed. The Japanese navy used wireless radios to coordinate the surprise attack on Pearl Harbor.[25]

Statesmen and diplomats shared in the military's uncertainties as they sought to assess shifts in the balance of power caused by capacities for wireless communications in peacetime.[26] As one historian has succinctly put it: "The pace of change had quickly exceeded the ability of the government to keep up," so they stumbled forward, feeling their way.[27] The going was slow. In the United States, the 1912 Radio Act did not require that station owners be American citizens, so foreign governments were free to set up radio stations on US soil. In fact, in 1913 the German Telefunken company owned Atlantic Communications Company (ACC) in Sayville, Long Island. The ACC communicated regularly with the US Navy's Atlantic Fleet. According to historian Jonathan Weed Winkler, one young naval lieutenant, Stanford C. Hooper, saw what others did not:

> If there were German naval radio officers at Sayville, Hooper confided, it was entirely possible that they were learning the US Navy's radio procedures by listening in to the fleet's radio traffic. In the event of war, it might be possible for the station to transmit fake or disruptive messages to the navy as it moved along the coast. If this were the case, it would not be possible to change the navy's codes in time.[28]

Hooper's note flew to the desk of the secretary of the navy, who circulated it among his senior staff. The nation was at peace, but Hooper had determined that the Germans were spying on US soil. Could the navy monitor what they were doing, and if so, would it be legal? Wireless communication was speeding up decisions, but also rendering them more complex, swamping leaders with information, and introducing new vulnerabilities.

The resulting uncertainties handed advantage to the sharpest analysts and innovators. Engineers were learning to find wireless devices through direction-finding (locating clandestine emitters), to intercept them, and to map radio loads and links (traffic analysis).[29] Although the British began with a lead across most sectors of the communication revolution (albeit less so in radio than cable) the United States, France, and Germany were not far behind.[30]

In general, sailors and soldiers came to understand the intelligence-related implications of the revolution in communications—especially the need to balance security with timely use—faster than diplomats did.[31] The latter tended to presume privacy in communications when they had none, or authority to decide matters when others were gaining the ability to work around them. While this problem will be examined in greater detail below, the point here is that, with communications becoming cheap, mobile, and fast, officials and envoys seemed more impressed with their access to timely policy interventions than with the new vulnerabilities this networking entailed.

Over time, however, governments learned. Clandestine wireless communications led to a boom in intelligence and sudden busts in peacetime, as well as war. The result was the advent of "intelligence war"—battles among standing intelligence organizations to gain timely, competitive knowledge. The German services famously used analysis of wireless traffic during the interwar period to destroy Stalin's successful spy network known as the Red Orchestra. Thanks to wireless communications, Britain was able to create a phony spy network that successfully manipulated Hitler's chain of command during WWII, and Hitler in turn knew about almost every clandestine agent Britain sent to run sabotage and espionage operations behind enemy lines.[32] To deploy as an agent in the era of total war was to leap into an ocean of uncertainty, thanks to the revolution in wireless communications.

Brain Drains?

The importance of engineering know-how during these years suggests another source of intelligence advantage: the global distribution of intellectual firepower. Immigration, education, and economic opportunity were playing important roles in the redistribution of innovation among states. Scientists and technologists sought freedom to innovate and, as they moved in search of it, brought valuable knowledge about how to lure or recruit others doing state-of-the-art research. Long before the Manhattan Project assigned scientists to the production of atomic weapons, Britain, Germany, and the United States were attracting immigrants with scientific and technological expertise from poorer or more turbulent countries. For example, Britain welcomed Russian chemists during the upheavals before the Russian Revolution. When Britain suffered an unexpected shell shortage during WWI's Battle of Neuve Chappelle, London's new Ministry of Munitions recruited a number of them to devise substitutes for cordite, a key component of gunpowder that was in short supply.

Who would gain and who would lose in this great shuffle of the intellectual deck was difficult to know at any given point. It depended on what scientists believed about state policies, including whether research or funding might be restricted, immigration policies would permit relocation, and whether the lives of scientists and their families (as in the case of Jewish scientists in Germany) were in danger. Thus, the great sorting of talent became a source of both advantage and uncertainty in international politics. The United States was a particularly important beneficiary of these trends. From 1880 to 1920, US industry attracted a surge of immigrants into its rapidly developing automotive, steel, and communications industries. The US government also began investing in basic science as its large public research universities grew in size and stature. By the 1930s, the United States had become a leader in physics, attracting scientists such as Enrico Fermi and Albert Einstein, who, in turn, sought the colleagues, resources, and freedom necessary for the pursuit of their research interests. Einstein, a Swiss citizen, was visiting the United States when Hitler came to power in Germany in the 1930s, and chose to stay, becoming a US citizen in 1940. His colleague Leo Szilard, who left Germany at the same time, emigrated to the United States in 1938. Szilard wrote the famous 1939 letter to President Roosevelt, which Einstein signed, warning about the scientific feasibility of nuclear weapons. Szilard's initiative, along with the British MAUD report, led to the decision to launch the Manhattan Project—a secret effort to build an atomic bomb.

At the same time, enlisting the scientific community in national security presupposed that scientists would work as intelligence providers for the government, keeping secrets as necessary. Yet enlisting civilian scientists in this way raised problems. Governments had learned that scientists were not only important intelligence sources on weaponry, encryption, and surveillance, but also on the state of foreign research on such topics. The more connected scientists were to foreign colleagues, the better their work and their intelligence, but also the more suspicious their work seemed—at least to government officials concerned about security. Indeed, as hostilities waxed and waned, so did the willingness of scientists to report on each other for the benefit of the state. Reginald Victor (R. V.) Jones, a leading British innovator in the fields of radar and infrared technology between the world wars, wrote with fond recollection of his collaboration during the 1930s with the German scientist Carl Bosch, who, returning to Germany before WWII, became instrumental in designing the guidance systems for V-2 rockets.[33] Jones eventually became one of the scientists dedicated to destroying those rockets. Soviet nuclear physicists alerted Joseph Stalin to the possibility that the United States and Britain were building a nuclear weapon by reporting a drop-off in publications by their US colleagues. Their "open sources" confirmed the implications of Britain's MAUD report, which had been stolen by Stalin's agent in Britain, Donald Maclean: The Soviet Union's *allies* were developing an atomic bomb and keeping it secret from Moscow.[34] In response, Stalin ordered Lavrenti Beria, his espionage chief, to recruit US scientists and collect atomic secrets. By the end of the war, Soviet spies were working at Los Alamos and elsewhere.[35]

The point is that the industrial revolution had sharpened a complex and long-lasting dilemma for states: while freedom of information seemed the antithesis of gaining and retaining informational advantages, scientists also knew secrecy jeopardized their work.[36] The tension between scientific openness and national secrecy persisted—at least in democratic capitalist states—creating distrust and uncertainty. Applied science, nonetheless, brought big rewards to those scientists willing to work within the confines of classified programs. Big firms, such as Consolidated Aircraft Corporation (later Convair), Marconi, Krupp, and Kodak, took on the basic research necessary for advancing their respective industrial bases for national defense and intelligence, especially after WWII.[37] The "military-industrial complex" became a powerful engine for harnessing scientific innovation to dual-use technologies. By mid-century, the earlier naiveté in official circles about civil society's importance for warfare had diminished substantially, but suspicions about the political influence of the military-industrial complex grew, particularly after a military hero, President Dwight D. Eisenhower, issued a warning about it. WWII was the engine that drove this change and still stands as the prime example of the effects of scientific intelligence on war. Not surprisingly, the British physicist at the heart of it all, R. V. Jones, dubbed WWII "The Wizard War."

Automated Signal Enciphering and Interception

As the telegraph, telephone, cable system, and wireless radio improved the timeliness of information, governments began to network more. Only later did they recognize the importance of intercepting and protecting their communications, often adopting methods of competitive industries in the private sector.[38] As we will see in the next chapter, the learning curve was steep because the advance of electromechanical enciphering and decryption was more rapid than most users knew during the late nineteenth and early twentieth centuries. Defense required knowing how to evade, encipher, and deceive during conflicts characterized by constantly evolving modes of communication and ever-faster decision-making.[39] For many traditional diplomats, the burden seemed too much, and the methods often offensive. By 1945, however, civilian statesmen and diplomats were fully involved in offensive techniques, included tapping wires, deploying aerial antennas, and mechanical decryption.

The two capabilities—encryption to secure knowledge and description to exploit and disrupt it—had long been wedded to one another. For centuries secret communications had been a manual process involving codebooks and ciphers. Cryptology, or the art of encoding, enciphering, decoding, and decrypting data, had been around for centuries. But in 1883, Auguste Kerckhoffs authored the first book to grapple with cryptology in the mechanized age. His *La cryptographie militaire*, published in the French *Journal des Sciences Militaires*, addressed the demands on encoding brought by the telegraph, wireless, and other forms of communication involved in industrial warfare.[40] As WWI approached, the importance of secrecy in battlefield communications led to a focus on enhanced encryption for war. Although only two of the Great Powers, Russia and France, had a significant ability to intercept and decrypt electronic communications before WWI, all of them did by the end of the Great War.[41] The Germans used signal interception in early battles on the eastern front to gain significant advantages at Tannenberg and Lodz, but eventually found themselves repeatedly undermined by superior Allied codebreaking.[42] The victors gleaned the intentions, not just capabilities, of German commanders,[43] and all sides, including statesmen and diplomats, learned the lesson.

Machines aided in the formulation of ever more secure codes and ciphers from 1900 to 1940. With their dissemination across expanding communications networks, cryptology developed into a profession and, indeed, a national industry. This advent of automated encryption brought with it organizational change, partly because it required industrial production and vast resources, and partly because its benefits were considered so certain that it just made sense to adopt system-wide applications. Whereas commanders and diplomats once managed separate codes and cipher systems, states soon began to consolidate "signals intelligence" and machine-aided cryptologic systems. States' deepest secrets could be protected by state-of-the-art encryption across civil-military domains. It seemed to make sense to require all components to adopt the same state-of-the-art enciphering machines and methods. Yet if those methods could be penetrated, then all government communications would be vulnerable. Such opportunities and difficulties suggested the need for something new: the need for *national* intelligence policy.

One of the first issues of national policy had to do with automated encryption. It is not surprising given the heated industrial competition of the late nineteenth century that many of the first innovators of automated encryption systems focused on commercial applications. It is more surprising that the German government assumed after WWI that commercial methods and hardware could be retroactively classified and made secure enough for government-wide applications thereafter. The confidence to do so rested in the German leadership's belief that multi-rotor machine encryption could never be broken *even if* the enemy attempting to do so had the hardware and knew the method. Herein lay great opportunity for states seeking decisive advantage in WWII.

The story of how the Allies exploited machine encryption to gain intelligence and military advantages during WWII is now well known.[44] In essence, the Allies were able to read Nazi encrypted communications using machines that deconstructed German (and Japanese) encryption methods. The story of how they were able to do so has a long history and accounts often underplay the commercial origins, German mistakes, and Polish foresight that enabled Allied successes against Nazi submarine warfare in the Atlantic and in the D-Day landings in Europe. The Dutch inventor of the Enigma rotor system, Hugo Alexander Koch, was part of the early multinational race for commercial encryption. Koch sold his patent rights to a German, Arthur Scherbius, who marketed the device at the congress of the International Postal Union in 1923. The rotor-based innovation was publicized in *Radio News* and in flyers printed in English and German. A few years later, the German government bought it, adapted it for use by all its military and diplomatic services, and tightly controlled all related information.[45] In the meantime, the Poles had acquired the device too and were developing methods to break it. Their work eventually benefited the British and French, who extended and expanded the effort while testing their own methods of machine-based encryption.[46] The vulnerability of Enigma derived from both understanding its mechanics and exploiting how it was used; repetitive phrases and failures to change rotors opened opportunities. It is now widely known that the "Ultra" products from exploited German Enigma machines proved critical to the defeat of Nazi Germany. As Brigadier E. T. Williams reported in 1945, "It is contended that very few Armies ever went to battle better informed of their enemy."[47]

This background to the encryption revolution illustrates how the industrial revolution accelerated the seemingly mundane and unclassified provenance of some types of intelligence-advantage—that is, through commercial "tipping" of the terrain of uncertainty. New intelligence techniques are often derived from unfettered commercial profit-seeking industries. States without such capacities for innovation can stay abreast by simply buying or stealing commercial equipment in the expectation that it might become classified intelligence-related hardware. The latter may entail industrial espionage, but the former is simply savvy "open source" intelligence collection.

Systems Engineering

The industrial revolution brought an explosion in sensors and platforms, but also the connectedness of things through improved communications and engineering. The late nineteenth century saw achievements in audio detection of wireless transmissions, optics, sonar, and, by the 1930s, radar. Commercial leadership in these technologies offered diplomatic, military, and intelligence advantages to those states gifted with the resources and creativity to harness sensors to decision-making faster than their competitors could. The source of advantage was fourfold: sensor innovation, platform mobility, timely transmission, and the interoperability of all three.

It took little, of course, for spies to benefit from advances in cameras. Marrying cameras to moving platforms, especially airplanes, was another matter. The result was confusion and uncertainty about the relationship of technical progress to military power. For example, although Germany led the world in the precise milling of glass lenses suitable for clear photographic reconnaissance before WWI, the French were close behind and, as discussed earlier, surpassed the Germans in aerial systems engineering.[48] Engineering requirements were driven by performance and initially involved a great deal of experimentation. Engineers made cameras for homing pigeons, balloons, kites, dirigibles, and airplanes.[49] As "aeronauts" mastered their flying machines, they wanted automated, optically flexible cameras so they could pilot, navigate, evade, and reconnoiter all at the same time.[50] This meant cameras had to be stabilized and adjusted for appropriate resolution with minimal condensation.

Engineers did not have to be pilots to improve intelligence collection systems; indeed, they often worked across multiple platforms so efforts to adapt each could be more efficient given the capabilities of the others. "System integration" within and among platforms became a valuable and increasingly specialized objective. As aerial platforms progressed, pictures had to be taken from faster-moving, higher-flying aircraft, the film dropped off, and then prints made and analyzed. Reconnaissance systems employed radio communications, couriers, and ground-based photo-interpreters. System managers became critical to gaining advantages because they could keep useful intelligence flowing so pilots could focus more on flying the aircraft than seeing through clouds or remembering details. Photo-analysts, in turn, would not have to fly in order to develop pictorial mosaics from airborne platforms, map terrain, and interpret factory production rates. They gradually specialized in "signatures" related to particular weapons or factory operations, such as the flow of traffic, plumes from industrial stacks, and the like. Improvements in resolution meant aerial platforms could fly at higher altitudes at lower risk, or lower altitudes at higher gain, according to specific needs, such as avoiding antiaircraft fire or collecting close-ups of disturbed earth for indicators of vehicles, bunkers, troops, or refugees.

The ability to adjust the qualities of sensors to platforms and targets, fueled by the communications and encryption revolutions, brought certain advantages, but it also meant that intelligence managers, platform operators, and manufacturers had to work together. The job required an interdisciplinary skill: knowledge of the target, the performance parameters of platforms, sensors, sensor-processing, and communications devices. Competition in this new specialty grew fierce, with innovators in a race to adapt some breakthrough in, say, film processing or optics to faster planes or low-light conditions in clandestine settings. Platforms, cameras, and navigational skills had to be optimized together. Altitude, vibration, and camera placement affected resolution and clarity in the air, on ships, and in high-stress situations on the ground.[51]

Some platforms and sensor operations demanded more teamwork than others. If short on one capability, a state could ally with another to close the gap, creating new opportunities for joint ventures and secret trades managed through intelligence channels. And with such teamwork came the potential for betrayal, new vulnerabilities, and new openings for espionage by the other side. It is often said that it takes a network to fight a network, but it is also true that it can take just one spy to know that network. And those penetrations—of radio stations, airplane industries, lens manufacturers, or undersea cables—could usefully happen in peacetime, among friendly states whose industries were just trying to earn a profit.

Thus, uncertainty increased with improvements in the connectedness of national security infrastructures, including communications, reconnaissance, and espionage systems. The tighter the systems engineering, the more vulnerable the entire system was to any weak link, sudden security lapse, or deficiency in civilian production capacity. The testing of these systems, while at first public, soon became secret state-sponsored endeavors that military commanders rarely shared with their civilian counterparts, often for fear of leaks. Private-public partnerships became a pathway for gaining knowledge of an enemy's capabilities, boosting the importance and risks of industrial espionage in peacetime. While German industry initially excelled in optics, the French generally kept a lead in systems engineering in the aeronautical domain, demonstrating the utility of aerial reconnaissance in military exercises during 1911 and deploying the capability to Morocco the following year. Both German and French capabilities were insufficient on their own, however, and rode on a private sector whose secrets were difficult to keep.

In the ensuing competition, the United States and Britain benefited from French advances in reconnaissance. As the Allies shared their technical capabilities in airborne imaging and systems engineering, intelligence liaison and inter-allied trust also strengthened, creating mutual dependencies. The British pioneered on-board film development and photo analysis, while the French focused on hardware: aircraft and cameras. The Russians took a temporary lead in the development of "monster," multi-engine airplanes, but lacking sophisticated aeronautics and optics, they relied on visual collection that was harder to share.[52] After the 1917 revolution, however, Russia lost some of her best aircraft designers, including the engineering genius Igor Sikorsky, who emigrated to the United States. His Connecticut-based company, Sikorsky Aircraft, soon spearheaded the development of the helicopter.

Intelligence liaison had thus begun to extend beyond sharing secrets to the sharing of expertise in industrial and scientific problem-solving across the government-industry divide. Shortages of lenses, such as the British (1915) and the Americans (1917) experienced during WWI, reinforced the importance of industrial supply for modern, technical intelligence capabilities. Moreover, states began to recognize that *intelligence policy* was directly related to winning and that systems engineering, so necessary for gaining informational advantages, required *collection strategies*. The great powers thus focused on selective investment in new intelligence systems, such as platforms, sensors, communications, and their systematic co-engineering.

Given that the military did systems engineering for weapons systems and intelligence was integrated into war-fighting, most technical collection systems became the creatures of service-related platforms, sensors, and communications. The creators and designers of these technologies, nonetheless, became important for the new *national* intelligence mission, including diplomacy. But whereas the military understood how these systems performed, diplomats often did not— especially their operating capabilities, vulnerabilities, and communications constraints. As the military perfected their intelligence systems, diplomats and statesmen came to rely on them without knowing how they worked or could be tasked. In all matters of technological systems involving military platforms, the services tended to make the decisions about systems integration, but also about what to share with colleagues in peacetime. This situation would not change in the United States until the creation of the Central Intelligence Agency (CIA) and its civilian scientific and research components during the early years of the Cold War. In partnership with Lockheed, CIA developed the high-flying U-2 and SR-1 reconnaissance aircraft (projects AQUATONE and OXCART). The CIA joined with the Air Force in developing CORONA, the country's first imagery satellite.

Aerial systems were not the only technological advances or even the most important, but most advanced systems relied on military innovation. Platforms and sensors were mixed and matched in dizzying array. As states developed fast-moving planes, propeller-driven ships, and undersea platforms, they also sought to track the enemies' or hide their own. Developments in surveillance and reconnaissance included Sound Navigation and ranging (sonar), Radio Detection and Ranging (radar), and Infrared sensors. Radar used radio waves to determine the location, speed, direction, and altitude of objects. Infrared sensors enabled tracking of heat emitters, such as bombers, at night. Sonar used pulsed sound waves to track ships and submarines at sea. As technologies improved and sonar became more refined, sound waves generated by a particular kind of propeller became its "signature." These identifying signatures could then be matched against records of how particular ships had sounded in the past, allowing analysts to identify them. Managing threats in peacetime became ever more entwined with military operations, demanding more closely coordinated decision-making among diplomats and soldiers.

Yet even if military systems took the lead in national intelligence missions, civilian intelligence collectors and users were implicated. This new world of electronic intelligence connected everything. The concepts of electronic signatures and systems engineering were widely applicable. Telegraph and wireless operators—even undercover spies operating radios behind enemy lines—could be found by picking up their communications (signals) and identified by oddities in their keystrokes (signatures). The importance of a wireless operator to a network could be gauged by the electronic traffic he received and emitted (traffic analysis), his location determined by "direction-finding" (DF) antennas hosted by ships and trucks, and his movements verified using signature analysis. In this way, collection systems began to augment each other in a web of capabilities hard for targets to avoid.

Over time, intelligence services developed databases of recorded signal types, codes and ciphers, signatures, and the like. Every piece of electronic equipment left its telltale mark in some form. Vacuuming up noise from the environment, separating signals from other noise, and then "reading" this collection became a specialist's job.[53] The capability to process hums and whirs and translate them into the type or name of a ship required especially advanced "processing and exploitation" (P&E). Thus, the earliest forms of "measurement and signature intelligence" (MASINT) developed as an important intelligence discipline alongside signals intelligence (SIGINT, electronic intelligence (ELINT), and photographic intelligence (PHOTINT). Those militaries that had experimented earliest, and recorded soundings longest, became better than others at locating, identifying, and tracking the ships, planes, and spies of friends and foes.

The birth of the age of technical intelligence (TECHINT) meant that better-organized and industrialized states generally did better at gaining advantages through systems engineering—a fact that has led some intelligence historians to overemphasize organizational reform in remedying intelligence failures of all kinds. Advantages also flowed, however, to capitalist states where creativity trumped organization and innovators could profit from paradigm-busting discoveries rather than seeing them immediately classified. Strong entrepreneurial incentives, educational programs, healthy financial sectors, and incentivized venture capitalists enabled less centralized, capitalist polities to capitalize on creativity and thus gain important advantages over those less well-endowed or more socially and politically constrained.

The catch was that, while *civilians* could radically improve intelligence systems through commercially driven sensor development and systems engineering, the platform-specific requirements for national security operations could give away the sensing mechanism to enemies with whom commercial firms might conduct joint ventures. Government officials first ignored this development, then noticed it with alarm, and then sought to control it through expanding governmental reach into the private sector and retroactive classification of activities and commercial products, as happened in the case of the prototype of Germany's WWII encryption machine (Enigma). Protected by classification walls, however, professionalized system managers were in danger of becoming too conservative in orientation—that is, tempted to preserve or incrementally adjust existing capabilities at the expense of engineering new, disruptive technologies into any part of the collection system.

Conservative bias in engineering reflects the system-wide implications of changing any one piece of a larger whole. In some ways, there was nothing new here. Recall how the shipwrights responsible for Spanish galleons so protected and incrementally adjusted their designs that they began to meet the emperor's needs by producing ships that looked more like floating cities than naval weapons. Back in the sixteenth century, it took English innovation to reinvent naval warfare, creating much uncertainty in the process. The industrial revolution created a modern version of this dilemma. By the middle of the twentieth century, intelligence "readiness" had become ever more tied to collection infrastructures whose relative capacities were increasingly difficult to measure.[54]

Imperial Contraction, Balances of Power, and Alliance Politics

The burst of innovation in the late nineteenth century was part of an international shift in the distribution of economic power that proved easier to appreciate in retrospect than at the time. This shift was massive, global, and affected relative capabilities as much as absolute ones. From 1880 to 1938, Britain saw her share of world manufacturing drop by more than half (from 22.9 to 10.7 percent), while the newly unified land power, Germany, saw her share increase (8.5 to 12.7 percent) despite the devastation of WWI. Over the same period, the US share more than doubled (14.7 to 31.4 percent); the French share declined (7.8 to 4.4 percent). Austria-Hungary's share initially lagged at 4.4 percent and then disappeared after her defeat in WWI.[55] The United States overtook Britain in per capita levels of industrialization; Germany overtook France in the same measure by a wide margin.[56] Between 1913 and 1925 European manufacturing soared, crashed, then barely recovered, while manufacturing in the rest of the world, even leaving out the United States and Russia, steadily increased.

Not all industrializing states suffered the resulting uncertainty in equal measure. Large land empires, for a variety of reasons, escaped some of the worst dilemmas of rapid growth, such as volatile markets, weak legal systems, vulnerable transport and communications, or unreliable trading partners. The United States, for example, came out of its civil war with relatively stable political institutions and the prospect of a large, secure, and integrated market. The serendipitous development of rapid, long-distance communications and protection from European threats enhanced the capacity of the United States to expand westward across the American continent.[57] For most European powers, however, the explosion of industrial innovation generated existential angst, destabilizing the political foundations of the international system, which had long had Europe at its core.

In describing the sticky nature of the ensuing political adjustments, historian Paul Kennedy has identified Berlin's West Africa Conference of 1884–85 as the symbolic zenith of Old Europe's primacy. Here, the great powers, especially Germany, Britain, and France, contended over the boundaries of empire; Japan, still seemingly exotic and diminutive, was not invited; and Russia and the United States played marginal roles.[58] For the Great Powers intent on drawing imperial boundaries, "The fate of the planet still appeared to rest where it had seemed to rest for the preceding century or more: in the chancelleries of Europe."[59] Yet, as Kennedy went on to observe, in less than one lifetime, Europe would lie in ruins; nuclear weapons would be dropped on an expansionist, militarized Japan; Austria-Hungary would fracture into a collection of small states; and the world would square off between the formerly peripheral powers, Russia and the United States.

The stickiness of international politics during this time of rapid change rested on the gaping divide between changing power ratios and intelligence about them. Strategic shifts in power caused spikes in uncertainty long before the technological revolution brought, ironically, the intelligence systems necessary to reduce them. In the interim, prejudices and biases filled the gaps. Although statesmen exuded confidence, strategic uncertainty—that is, uncertainty about how best to align power and interests given the designs and capabilities of others—was nearly universal. So was the persistence of mindsets that filled in the unknown with analogy, anecdote, and prejudice. Declining empires had transitory diplomatic advantages in such an environment, because others presumed them to be more powerful than they increasingly were. Such was Britain's transitory advantage from 1900 to 1940. Her formidable history and her commercial and financial muscle in peacetime masked, both for her and her challengers, London's actual, relative decline in usable power.[60] In fact, when WWI broke out, Britain suffered disruption of the global commons as much, if not more, than any other state.[61]

This uncertainty at the turn of the century was not Britain's alone. As strengthening trade in strategic materials among the Great Powers contrasted ever more sharply with the threats they seemed to pose to each other, peacetime incentives, military capabilities, and security interests seemed in terrible misalignment. Germany and Britain, for example, remained industrial giants and trading partners with deeply entwined economies, and yet also political competitors with war plans against each other. By the interwar period, Germany and Russia were hostile, but their trading relationships had deepened. Britain, losing confidence in imperial defenses, ended up coordinating war plans with France and accommodating the power of Russia while politically estranged from both, leaving them uncertain of her allegiances. Before WWI, Germany was politically allied with the economically weakened and politically irresolute empire of Austria-Hungary, with which Berlin calculated fewer common economic interests than with London. With the interests of the Great Powers so intertwined and contingent, alliances seemed politically important but economically irrelevant, if not ill-advised.

Still, in the remaking of international politics, it was London that would witness the greatest restructuring of power. The mask was finally removed, and British heroism was on display in her plucky retreat across the English Channel at the start of WWII. The Battle of Britain has been memorialized largely because London's finest hours were also desperate ones.

Britain's Imperial Decline

In fact, of all the uncertainties shaping diplomacy from 1900 to 1945, the relative decline of the British Empire was probably the most confusing for all the other Great Powers. This confusion stemmed not just from London's capacity to mask its relative decline in traditional forms of power, but from her continuing ascendency in all forms of learning, fueled by her global reach. This was, indeed, the same core capability on which Elizabeth I had built her power, albeit now used for retaining it: relentless inquiry and exploration.

From the late eighteenth century through most of the nineteenth, London had spread wealth through an open financial and trading system supported by a generous, if often self-serving, stockpile of geographic and scientific knowledge. Imperialists had sponsored scholarship, exploration, and theft of artifacts with the help of the East India Trading Company, the army, and individual adventurers who banked or published the results.[62] One such British adventurer, Sir Richard Burton, was described in the 1911 *Encyclopedia Britannica* as a pioneering amateur archaeologist whose areas of interest "coincided with areas which have since become peculiarly interesting to the British Empire."[63] The poorly hidden implication was that Burton's contribution to imperial knowledge was purposeful and, in any event, highly useful. As one historian has written,

> From the early years of Victoria's reign there had been a flowering of all manner of academic disciplines with the intention of listing, filing and describing the nature of the diverse range of peoples within this Empire. It was amateur, random and passionate. Very little in its aims had any link whatsoever with military intelligence. But as the century wore on, the high command was very gradually to see the usefulness of this vast store of knowledge.[64]

In fact, armed with maps, languages, and contacts among diverse peoples, British diplomats and generals could leverage their smallish presence on the margins of empire better than almost any other competitor they might meet there. In this sense, Britain was, by the late nineteenth century, in a position similar to Philip II's Spanish Empire during the sixteenth century: secure so long as no rival had the knowledge and temerity to orchestrate a coordinated attack on her far-flung vulnerabilities.[65]

Britain's imperial pursuits had, however, enriched states that would by the end of the nineteenth century pose existential threats to that empire.[66] Britain's small army had been sufficient when potential rivals had been distracted by internal social upheavals on the Continent. After all, her global reach rested more on naval strength than on land forces. But this benign environment did not last. France had become an imperial rival in Africa and the Far East. Russia's growing power threatened British interests in Eastern Europe, the Mediterranean, India, Persia, and east through the Koreas and China. Although Germany, created mid-century out of Prussia and its lesser neighbors, seemed Britain's natural ally against an assertive France and a westward-reaching Russia, she had also become a worrisome continental powerhouse. After first defeating the Austrian Empire, she had beaten France in 1870, annexed Alsace and Lorraine, and tightened her Triple Alliance with Austria-Hungary and Italy. Kaiser Wilhelm II then chose to foment Anglo-French friction overseas to gain a still freer hand for Germany on the Continent.[67] By 1900, continental powers were looking outward, hungry for the resources needed for their expanding industries.

The British felt the pressure. Their country's financial infrastructure still dominated worldwide trade, but the empire included by this time about 12 million square miles and some 25 percent of the world's population. The costs of maintaining and defending such an expanse had become too burdensome to sustain.[68] Given that Britain's navy could not provide active defense everywhere at once, deterrence through coercive diplomacy had begun losing credibility. Any disturbance on the periphery, now transmitted by cable to European capitals within hours, seemed perilous. Such contradictions in British power from 1870 to 1940 made all other great powers uncertain about the nature, pace, and importance of Britain's imperial decline. Although that decline is still the subject of vigorous historical debate, the results are not. By the outbreak of WWII, British power was exposed for what it actually had become: her citizens sailing their boats across the Channel not to rescue entrepreneurs, insurers, or their financial houses, but to rescue the army so it could defend the British Isles. That everyone was surprised by the turn of events is testimony to how uncertain and obscure British decline had been before that moment.

Thus, by the end of the nineteenth century, disruptive forces had become strategic, incremental, and relentless. Britain's imperial dilemma was her impossible choice: countering a continental European threat *or* one in India; *or* one in the Pacific. The problem was not just theoretical. As Britain's foreign minister before WWI, Sir Edward Grey, mused in his memoir,

> British interests touched those of France and Russia in many parts of the world; and where interests touch, an atmosphere of ill-will is always dangerous. The blackest suspicion thrives in it, like a noxious growth under dark skies in murky air. The most simple and straightforward acts of one Government are attributed by the other to sinister motives; the agents of each Government on the spot prick and stir their Colonial Office at home with accounts of what the agents of the other Government are doing; the smallest incident may assume proportions that threaten the peace between great nations.[69]

Britain's response to this mix of financial and political pressures was to eschew long-term strategies and commitments. She helped strengthen Turkey against Russia during the Crimean War (1853–56), then courted Germany as a bulwark against Russian expansion. Rebuffed by Germany, she softened relations with France in 1904 while stiff-arming Russia, France's principal ally against German power. She backed France against Germany in the Moroccan Crises of 1905 and 1911 and defended her colonial position in Africa against insurgency and German interference in the Boer War. Britain's uncertainties thus became everyone else's. As her oceanic empire gained importance for industrial competitiveness but its borders became too expansive to defend all at once, her choices became more inscrutable and threatening to others. Germany and Austria-Hungary began to fear encirclement as British relations with France and Russia warmed but did not ripen into alliances. By the 1900s, Germany was flexing its muscle with new colonial aspirations, railway projects extending eastward toward Turkey and Persia, and a naval building program that, by focusing on dreadnoughts, seemed aimed at threatening Britain at sea.[70] Not surprisingly, London took offense, increasing uncertainties on all sides.

The problem, again, was stickiness. Britain still strode the world stage as if a guarantor of the global commons for international trade, when in fact, her capacity to defend sea lanes was not keeping up with the challenges. Her naval strategies at the turn of the century were designed less to bring troops to far-flung battlefields than to support her financial and commercial interests.[71] Prescient British industrialists, financiers, and statesmen had come to believe that interdependence meant vulnerability, so plans were developed before WWI to use London's financial and commercial muscle to shorten any Great Power war. Uncertain whether such economic muscle would work, Britain's leaders simply acted as if it would. The plan proved unsupportable.

Such flexible policies in defense of empire seemed purposefully deceptive to almost all the great powers. Indeed, if Britain had gained her empire in a fit of absent-mindedness, she was seemingly withdrawing from it in much the same way.[72] Britain's global presence, full of vulnerabilities and advantages, required a grand strategy; although others often presumed she had one, the truth was that she did not. As British foreign secretary Sir Edward Grey wrote in 1925:

> If all secrets were known it would probably be found that British Foreign Ministers have been guided by what seemed to them to be the immediate interest of this country without making elaborate calculations for the future. Their best qualities have been negative rather than positive . . . and they have generally shrunk from committing themselves for future contingencies, from creating expectations that they might not be able to fulfill, and from saying at any time more than they really meant. On the whole, the British Empire has been well served by these methods. It has, at any rate, been saved from capital and disastrous mistakes; such mistakes as are made by a great thinker, calculating far ahead, who thinks or calculates wrongly.[73]

Grey, no "great thinker" by his own lights, was in fact, reflective of a conservative culture suspicious of "grand ideas" in general.[74] Thus, British statesmen confused those seeking to assess British power and interests at the turn of the century, including each other.[75] Although British statesmen such as Sir Edward Grey may have eschewed any sort of coherent vision, they risked disadvantaging themselves, as they did when choosing to defend Siam (1893) against the French only to discover no interests there worth the risk.[76] Grey later confessed, "It seems incredible that two great European nations should have become nearly involved in war about anything so ephemeral."[77] For their part, French statesmen who before WWI were investing in an entente with Britain as a constraint on Germany and Austria-Hungary, rightly complained of a British foreign policy establishment that saw, in Grey's words, its "best qualities as negative rather than positive," that "shrunk from committing," and deliberately avoided "creating expectations."[78] Britain seemed the artful mongoose, constantly bobbing and weaving. By WWII, the weaving and bobbing would look less artful than pathetic to Hitler, and thoroughly deceptive to Stalin. Nevertheless, when and where Britain would stiffen or feint became the kaiser's, Hitler's, and Stalin's uncertainty and her own, peculiar, advantage.

Germany and Austria-Hungary suffered most, perhaps, from the uncertainties attending Britain's imperial and continental policies. The German kaiser's erratic decision-making during this period reflected partly his impulsive nature and partly frustration with British wobbliness advertised as strategic balancing. Unlike France and Russia, who negotiated tacit spheres of influence to glean Britain's imperial boundaries and reduce tensions, the Central Powers had no such methods or understandings, which meant unrelieved diplomatic, if not military, ambiguity. In this context, conspiracy theories thrived. Take, for example, Britain's deference to France and Russia in the Balkans. To decision-makers in Germany and Austria-Hungary, it was inconceivable that the British might not see this true source of instability in Europe and not have a plan to deal with it. After all, Russia's rising power entailed not just a mass, modernizing army, but one motivated by dangerous notions of protecting popular Slavic interests in Central Europe.[79] As one Austrian bureaucrat, Berthold Molden, opined just prior to the outbreak of WWI as he contemplated British potential intervention against Russia, London's ostensible entente partner:

> English politicians *would have to be blind* not to see that Russia is at the centre of a conspiracy directed against the integrity and autonomy of Austria-Hungary, a conspiracy which, in the final analysis, is as threatening to England's existence, because this conspiracy will be ever more violently pursued the longer and the more undisturbed one allows it to grow. Its success would mean the predominance of the Tsarist Empire in the entire region between the borders of Germany and India.[80]

From this pre-WWI Austrian perspective, *any* negotiations between Britain and Russia on *any* subject had the look of artful design. With diplomats in the thrall of their own strategic analysis, the basis for knowing differently would remain unexplored.

In fact, English politicians did not, in general, share the Austrian view of the Russian threat—at least not until after the Bolshevik revolution. The Austrian misconception, shared in part by the Germans, would play out in the crisis of 1914 in the form of ill-founded estimates of British policy and then virulent hostility. Reacting to a telegram from St. Petersburg on 30 July 1914, Kaiser Wilhelm II leaped to worst-case assumptions about British intent, deriving from her past jumpiness a hidden conspiratorial purpose:

> The net has suddenly been closed above our heads and with a scornful smile England has achieved the most brilliant success for her tenaciously pursued, purely anti-German Weltpolitik, against which we have proved helpless, while, as we are struggling isolated in the net, she weaves from our alliance loyalty to Austria the noose for our political and economic annihilation. A terrific achievement that deserves admiration, even from one who is ruined by it!![81]

The kaiser had long been prone to create out of his own imperial jealousies and Britain's variable policies such phantoms of strategic conspiracy.[82] But his eccentric imaginings masked a truth: British fickleness added to the uncertainties brought about by imperial disorder in the Russian, Turkish, and Austro-Hungarian empires.

Whither Germany and Austria-Hungary?

Britain's relative decline in power and related imperial overstretch were not the only sources of global uncertainty. The rise of Germany, tethered to a crumbling Austria-Hungary, triggered them, as well.

Ever since unification, Germany's leaders had realized they had a choice to make: whether to stay satisfied within Germany's continental bounds; to expand territory by exploiting opportunities in Eastern Europe; or to develop an overseas empire. What they would choose constituted the second major source of diplomatic uncertainty. As already mentioned, Count Otto von Bismarck had used war, political coercion, and diplomatic balancing to create the German state. When Germany took Alsace-Lorraine in 1870, France received a wound that would not heal.[83] Nothing Kaiser Wilhelm did helped stabilize the situation. By the turn of the century, Germany appeared to be planning either a blue-water navy to attack British power on the high seas and the Far East, or a continental land-grab by allying with Austria-Hungary and Turkey on the way to absorbing their crumbling empires. In all this, seemingly minor decisions became major diplomatic issues. Germany's ally Austria-Hungary managed a diplomatic coup against Slavic interests in 1908 by acquiring formal control over Bosnia-Herzegovina, threatening Russian interests. When, over the tsar's objections, the kaiser approved a Prussian general, Otto Liman von Sanders, to head a military mission in command of Turkish troops, the seemingly minor matter stole headlines.

In this toxic stew of British vulnerability, German growth, French vengeance, and Slavic nationalism, the European Great Powers arranged themselves into a series of opposing groups: the pre-WWI Triple Alliance of Germany, Austria-Hungary, and Italy against the Entente powers of Russia, France, and (fiddly) Britain; then, the post-WWI League of Nations versus revisionists; and then, during WWII, the Allies versus Axis powers, now including Japan. These ententes and alliances were problematic less because of their rigidity than because of their deceits. Allies were almost as hostile to each other as to their professed enemies. Alliances were roiled by internal sabotage: subterfuge, influence operations, and misdirection in military affairs. Before WWI, the British distrusted the tsar and his anti-liberal polity. The Russians distrusted the British, who were encroaching on neighboring Persia, sympathizing with anti-monarchists, and befriending Russia's archenemy, Japan. The French and British, although committed to a security-related entente, still resisted political cooperation with each other. Germany felt lashed to the fate of an albatross, Austria-Hungary, whose decay was threatening to infect all of Central Europe. Italy and Austria-Hungary, ostensibly friendly, in fact detested each other thanks to contending interests in the Balkans. Even within the Dual Monarchy, the Austrians distrusted the Hungarian Magyars and the latter resented their second-rank status.

WWI did little to resolve the uncertainties surrounding Germany's growing power, what she would do with it, and how others, including fickle allies, might respond. If anything, it made long-standing structural uncertainties worse. Russia, weakened by the struggle and internal rebellion, imploded, raising the risks of continental instability, including labor unrest stirred by communist ideology. Austria-Hungary, weak before WWI, fractured into small states whose borders would still be tempting for Germany but indefensible by anyone else. France and Russia, the best candidates for containing Germany, distrusted each other more than ever. WWI and the Treaty of Versailles confused statesmen into believing that the problem of German power could be solved, but neither the war nor its end had done much to resolve it. In fact, both the war and its settlement had brought the United States, a reluctant giant, into the mix.

The rise of the United States in the late nineteenth century, with its confusing mix of isolationist and expansionist impulses, complicated diplomatic assessments of relative power. After Washington's neutrality, and then intervention, against the Central Powers in WWI, the United States kept a chokehold on the British and French with demands for repayments of loans that were, in turn, linked to wartime reparations from Germany. Economic and financial uncertainties skyrocketed with tariffs, the collapse of the banking system, and the resulting depression. In the prelude to WWII, Hitler's rebuilding of Germany caused French and Russian uncertainties, not just over whether or not London's accumulating financial and military weaknesses would lead Britain to accommodate Germany at their expense, but what the United States would do about it—if anything.[84] The United States seemed, after all, the new arbitrator of global power balances. Germany's rise and Britain's decline made any US intervention on the European continent both consequential and uncertain, even for her allies. After all, the United States had long distrusted imperialist Britain, and, with the outbreak of WWI, had been slow to come to her defense. In the run-up to WWII, Britain was rightly uncertain of US backing, while Stalin assumed a British-American conspiracy designed to engage Hitler's war machine against Moscow. That all three ended up WWII allies is surprising; that they spied on each other is not.[85] Stalin, uncertain of how power and interest would shake out, ran spies against his military allies; President Roosevelt, aware of the espionage but uncertain of how the war would go, refused to let the FBI arrest them.

In sum, alliance systems throughout the era of total war were less rigid than poorly informed; they were intrinsically weak while appearing as militarily strong. Allies withheld intelligence from each other while jointly exercising their forces and professing their earnest commitments. The question of Germany's future, remaining structurally unresolved by her defeat in WWI, would become the flashpoint for the Cold War between the Soviet Union and the United States after WWII.[86] Throughout this period, the vital interests of Europe's great powers thus overlapped with Britain's greatest relative blind spot: the continental interior of Eastern Europe. Germany's choices were heavily dependent on British ones, but London had come to rely on France, which it barely trusted, for the knowledge she needed to frame her strategic choices there. In choosing to be indirectly involved in *knowing* Balkan affairs, Britain also became less attentive than her strategic interests actually dictated when it came time for *doing something*—a particularly dangerous mistake when rivals believed the opposite.

Unfortunately, by July 1914, "Cabinet governance" in Britain meant strategic indecision, not by institutional necessity, but by choice. British and German indecision, therefore, was intertwined in the run-up to both world wars. For any government to estimate Germany's next move required understanding what Berlin expected of London. But for any government to know the rank of British interests required seeing past her shaky commitments on the Continent and the tactical political and military choices she was making to sustain her empire. These were difficult calculations for London, the mongoose, to make; the snakes found them almost impossible.[87]

Who Decides for the State?

Before WWI, the concept of national intelligence was new. Intelligence flowed differently to the military and naval forces on the one hand and to civilian decision-makers on the other, so tended to reinforce competing mindsets within governments. When learning within governments is unevenly accomplished or compartmented within competing bureaucracies, not only does policymaking become difficult, but evidence of state intentions can be more difficult for other powers to see and to interpret. Before WWI, for example, the British foreign secretary's information on overseas matters came mostly from official represent-atives, such as his own and foreign ambassadors, and the press. Sir Edward Grey's mindset was that of a powerbroker intent on balancing between power blocks.[88] Among his most respected interlocutors was the German ambassador to London, who himself was an Anglophile. In contrast, the British military's focus was on its obligations to defend France. Anglo-French military assumptions and intelligence-gathering and sharing had a distinctly anti-German aspect that France came to trust. These two "frames" within the British government seemed compatible until the threat of war proved they were not: war planning required swift deployments of an expeditionary force; diplomatic planning required a pause so the cause of aggression and the rights of neutrals could be assessed. The concept of *national* decision-making based on *national* intelligence was missing.

This problem had two faces: knowing one's own national purpose and assessing the intentions of adversaries. Governments presented increasingly difficult intelligence targets for diplomats because, if one wanted to know what Britain would do, it no longer sufficed to steal a document off the desk of the king or his foreign secretary. Governmental decision-making, even in places that still had monarchs, had become factionalized. It had become more difficult for political elites to mirror-image—that is, to consider what they might do in an-other government's place—because that required knowing the pressures polit-ical elites were under from their militaries, their industrialists, their journalists, and their publics. Intelligence was more needed than ever, but governments, gathering peacetime information from industrialists, bankers, and old-school diplomats found it easier to know about the preferences of kings and the inter-connectedness of trade and finance than about the plans of Balkan terrorists, for whom global trade mattered little. This block helps to explain why, though the

Balkans may seem today to have been an obvious tinderbox for global war in 1914, London discounted the chance of it, and had only two obscure diplomats providing direct intelligence on the topic: one in Vienna who learned little about Balkan intrigues from the secretive Habsburg court; another in Belgrade who, being a quiet, low-level functionary, decided during the crisis of July 1914 to go on holiday.

Of course, for reasons already mentioned, if London's Foreign Office had instead had first-rank ambassadors in the Balkans, Italy, Romania, and Bulgaria prior to WWI, it is not at all clear they would have been able to learn much more than the lesser ones did. The communications revolution, the spread of democracy, and the rise of factionalism made decision-making authority uncertain in almost all European governments. The first brought revolutionary ways for statesmen to learn about foreign plans; the second brought the decline of monarchical authority; the third introduced contests for power within governments. All three trends increased opportunities for getting access to foreign government information, but decreased the ability to understand from such access what states would actually do. And so, compounding the confusion, ambassadors and governmental envoys began making government policy on the trot.[89] To begin to understand the complicated nature of diplomatic decision-making, the great uncertainties driving it, and the attendant failures of diplomatic intelligence, it is essential to understand the changing role of monarchs, which the next section does in greater depth.

The Decline of Kings

In 1914, monarchs, once the embodiment of states, still carried the title of "sovereigns." Yet by the end of the nineteenth century, the roles of European kings and emperors were variable and almost everywhere in decline. Christopher Walker has described the problem well:

> Whether or not they intervened aggressively in the political process, the continental monarchs nonetheless remained, by virtue of their very existence, an unsettling factor in international relations. The presence in only partially democratized systems of sovereigns who were the putative focal points of their respective executives with access to all state papers and personnel and with ultimate responsibility for every executive decision created ambiguity. A purely dynastic foreign policy, in which monarchies met each other to resolve great affairs of state, was obviously no longer apposite. . . . Yet the temptation to view the monarch as the helmsman and personification of the executive remained strong among diplomats, statesmen and especially the monarchs themselves.

Their presence created a persistent uncertainty about where exactly the pivot of the decision-making process rested. In this sense, kings and emperors could become a source of obfuscation in international relations. The resulting lack of clarity dogged efforts to establish secure and transparent relations between states.[90]

In general, European monarchies were giving way to parliamentary democracies, but their glidepaths were uncertain.[91] Politicians understood monarchical power was waning, but what this meant for decision-making seemed uncertain in particular instances. Even the weakest sovereigns occasionally intervened in affairs of state, sometimes with significant results. Britain's King Edward VII had very limited powers, but his dislike of the German kaiser, Wilhelm II, led him to sponsor a coterie of like-minded diplomatists into influential positions. These officials helped mend ties with France. In what turned out to be an influential trip to that country in 1903, the king pulled off a public relations triumph that helped pave the way for the entente between the two colonial rivals.[92] In contrast, King Edward VII's successor, George V, chose not to exercise what little power he had. The new king's diffidence did not prevent the Austrian foreign minister from expressing relief at the crowning of a sympathetically-minded sovereign. He anticipated, wrongly, that George V's decisions would matter as much as his predecessor's had. The German kaiser was to make the same mistake when, as recounted earlier, he mistook the king's reported musings about British neutrality for the commitment of a fellow monarch in a time of crisis: "I have the word of a King and that is enough for me!" he exclaimed.[93]

But therein lay the uncertainty of it all: kings *usually* did matter but sometimes did. Even as late as WWII, monarchs could change a nation's course or rally public will. King Leopold III of Belgium surrendered to the Nazis instead of following in the footsteps of his father, King Albert, who led Belgian troops in 1914. King George VI rallied the British after Nazi Germany defeated France in the opening months of WWII. Monarchs could not be discounted when assessing the unity, fighting capacities, and staying power of mass armies. Indeed, it was in recognition of their influence that Hitler sought to capture or kill King Haakon VII of Norway and Queen Wilhelmina of the Netherlands at the outbreak of WWII.[94] The heart of the matter from an intelligence standpoint, therefore, was as simple then as now: to know a state's intentions one had to know who would decide; gaining advantage required gaining access to him, her, or them. The problem was that no one really knew at any given moment who these "deciders" were.

If legally disempowered monarchs, such as Edward VII, could surprise in these years, so could legally powerful monarchs who did not use their authority, or did so in capricious ways. In Russia, Tsar Nicholas II assumed the throne in 1894 without a plan or much interest in international affairs. The tsar could, and did, demand briefings on most minor ministerial decisions, but this often meant that he was "engulfed in trivia while matters of real import fell by the wayside."[95] Even when he decided on a plan, such as extending Russian power and interest to the Far East during the 1890s, it tended to grow out of his private associations rather than the workings of his ministries. Historian Christopher Clark has noted that the tsar had "no personal secretariat and no personal secretary, so outsiders could use direct, personal connections to influence his decisions."[96] Russian business associates kept him informed about commercial opportunities in the Far East and encouraged him to defend Russian interests there.[97] So it was that after 1900, Russian attention veered away from Central Europe just as the Balkans were heating up, and despite the more conservative leanings and pronouncements of the Foreign Ministry.[98]

Whether or not the tsar's choices were wrong, they seemed capricious and confusing to those outside his inner circle. Russia "operated what were in effect two parallel official and non-official imperial policies, enabling Nicholas II to pick between options and play the factions off against each other."[99] After Russia's surprising defeat by Japan in 1905, Russia's senior executives created a Council of Ministers that gave government decision-making more coherence. But the tsar still had power and used it to work around his ministers in ways that made Russian decision-making difficult to fathom.[100] As one historian has put it: "The consequence of autocratic intervention was thus not the imposition of the Tsar's will as such, but rather a lasting uncertainty about who had the power to do what—a state of affairs that nourished factional strife and critically undermined the consistency of Russian decision-making."[101] Although Stalin's creation of a dictatorship in the 1920s clarified matters, the Soviet government's decision-making still had a volatile and secretive aspect that persisted long after his death in 1953.

Joining the general confusion was Austria-Hungary, whose sovereign decision-making seemed at once so complex, centralized, and sloth-like as to make the state both ungovernable and unfathomable. For decades, especially since Austria's defeat by Germany in the wars of German unification, the empire had been in decline. In this weakened state, Austria had joined with Hungary to shore up its imperial system. The Compromise of 1867, which the emperor had endorsed, resembled a Rube Goldberg contraption: a dual monarchy consisting of Austria and Hungary, both of which retained their capitals (Vienna and Budapest), separate constitutions, governments, parliaments, and, respectively, their German and Magyar aristocracies. The Austro-Hungarian state, as distinct from its separate parts, recognized the emperor, Franz Joseph, as its sovereign. Franz Joseph, who was also king of Hungary, presided over a Common Ministerial Council composed of the foreign minister, who was the highest official in the state, the Austrian and Hungarian premiers (minister-presidents), a joint finance minister, and the war minister. The council supposedly had authority over all the resources of the state, but was, in fact, a glorified discussion group that stood apart from the tight hierarchy of the military. In addition, the archduke retained his own military think-tank that helped to compensate for his exclusion from the emperor's decision-making circles. Despite Franz Ferdinand's high rank, he "was entrusted only with purely decorative tasks and all military measures were taken without his knowledge."[102]

The byzantine nature of Austria-Hungary's decision-making processes made negotiating with her difficult. If the Viennese ministry's executive authority came into question, that authority could not always be traced to the emperor. During the Bosnian crisis of 1908, Emperor Franz Joseph, had "behaved as if [he] were in virtual retirement." Most outsiders recognized the influence of the foreign minister, Count Alois Lexa von Aehrenthal, but at times the latter's power seemed to matter less than the vicissitudes of imperial decline.[103] Von Aehrenthal's successor, the relatively inexperienced Count Leopold von Berchtold, once called his ministry a simmering cauldron. He was probably referring to von Aehrenthal's diplomatic recruits, most of whom shared their mentor's hawkish predilections and conspired to control their new chief. At any rate, during the three and a half years before WWI, the Austro-Hungarian emperor attended none of his council's thirty-nine meetings, which meant that Berchtold, who once admitted to having no notion of the southern Slav question before taking office, was, at least in theory, setting policy.

When the archduke was assassinated in 1914, however, it was the Austrian army's chief of staff, Baron Franz Conrad von Hötzendorf, backed by von Aehrenthal's former recruits deep within the Foreign Ministry, who drove the choice for war against what Conrad called a "dangerous nest of vipers," by which he meant Serbia.[104] Few outsiders understood the power of Berchtold's lower-level colleagues at the time. Most foreign diplomats looked for the emperor's reaction out of habit and protocol, but guessed decisions were being made in Berlin, which was actually not the case in this instance. Unless steeped in court politics and the workings of ministries, ambassadors seeking authoritative views of Austria in those crucial days had a difficult chore knowing where to go. They also had a mindset that looked to political hierarchy rather than to soldiers or upstarts in the bowels of ministries.

Franz Joseph's chief ally, Germany's Kaiser Wilhelm II, also believed he was more master of German foreign policy than he often was, and in that variance lay destabilizing uncertainties for all those who sought intelligence on German policy.[105] In the wake of the Agadir Crisis of 1911, for example, the kaiser used reporting from a German naval attaché in London as rationale for a new naval law provocative to London, while his chancellor used contrary reporting from his ambassador to continue a policy of détente. To make matters worse, Wilhelm's leadership style—divisive and often disturbingly spontaneous—was matched by his awkward diplomacy, which included random comments to foreign governments on, for example, the prospect of settling a surfeit of Germans in underpopulated eastern France; German aspirations to "target" Latin America; the violability of neutral Belgium's borders (made to the Belgian king, no less); or the prospect of alliances with (or against) the United States, Russia, Japan, or Britain, depending on his mood. He was, in a sense, a one-man deception operation, constantly keeping others off-balance, but without any logical plan.[106] His direct relationship with the chief of the general staff meant that significant military decisions could be taken without the knowledge of civilian ministries or even the navy. The result was confusion, especially among those outside the Triple Alliance. For those experienced diplomats within that alliance, however, the German government's fragmentation made its decisions malleable. In this sense the volatility Hitler demonstrated in his meteoric career before WWII seemed not unlike Kaiser Wilhelm's. Foreign leaders could not be sure until on the brink of war whether Hitler was a serious governor or, like Wilhelm, more of an "inveterate geopolitical fantasist" from whom steadier minds could wrest power.[107]

Factionalism and Civil-Military Relations

The development of factions deeply rooted in government was another signature feature of this period, and contributed to the uncertainties of policymaking. Factions of all kinds had long existed in government, but the rapid bureaucratization of the state during the late nineteenth century allowed factions to take root and use regulations, or bureaucratic power, to undermine or work around established authorities. We have already seen that King Edward encouraged a Francophile faction within the British Foreign Office that remained in place after his death. Von Aehrenthal's young "rebels" constituted a more powerful faction—strong enough to pursue an aggressive solution to the Slavic nationalism after their mentor's death, and into years when the ministry had become weaker.

In Russia, the creation of the Council of Ministers after the tsar's catastrophes in the Far East lent an appearance of unity, but ministers' access to the tsar still existed under the "right of individual report." The Fundamental Laws of April 1907 reserved foreign and military policies to the tsar, making the Duma (state assembly) irrelevant, and obviating need for coordination among ministers. Indeed, the tsar's hostility to conciliar institutions locked in the tendency for factionalism in his government.[108] Factionalism in Russia was at least as strong, therefore, as the individual initiative of the ministers at any point, and the willingness of the chairman of the council to enforce discipline.[109] As historian William Fuller has observed, "Since all the ministries of state were competing for limited financial resources, the military's monopoly on information could serve to deny its rivals ammunition for argument."[110] The result was policymaking chaos and, from afar, something of a diplomatic black hole.

An excellent example of the result in policymaking terms was the Bosnian annexation crisis of 1908, mentioned earlier. This crisis, which established many of the mindsets governing the outbreak of WWI, is worth highlighting. Russia's foreign minister, Aleksandr Izvolsky, acquiesced to Austrian annexation of Bosnia-Herzegovina, apparently with the tsar's personal backing, in exchange for Russian interests regarding Turkey. Rival factions led by the council chairman, Pyotr Stolypin, and Russia's finance minister, Vladimir Kokovtsov, opposed the deal and the way it was made, despite Izvolsky's technically legal right of "individual report" to the tsar. That von Aehrenthal, Izvolsky's Viennese counterpart, ostensibly assumed the latter's authority was one thing; that the experienced Izvolsky misplayed his hand within his own government was quite another. The mistake cost him his job. He soon was replaced by Sergei Sazonov, a relatively junior diplomat, who had learned the lesson of his predecessor: not to get ahead of Stolypin, who intended to keep Russia out of foreign adventures until the country could regroup from its defeat by Japan. When Stolypin was assassinated in 1911, what Russian unity there was splintered, and a new group of Slavic nationalists took charge, leaving Sazonov's authority highly variable. Strong diplomats in the field, particularly men such as Nikolai Hartwig, the Slavophile ambassador in Belgrade, began to make up Russian policy on their own. With so much in disarray, foreign interlocutors had trouble learning what Russia was *actually doing*, let alone *intending to do*, as conflict in the Balkans flared again in 1914.

Autocracies were not alone in struggling to unify around a coherent foreign policy. Sir Edward Grey, who served as Britain's foreign secretary from December 1905 to December 1916, later claimed that the character of parliamentary systems and Cabinet government was, in fact, the problem for formulating policy in the lead-up to WWI. Accused of untimely decision-making and general opacity, Grey argued in response that he was required to follow Cabinet rules. Divided between liberal-imperialists and relative isolationists, Herbert Asquith's Liberal government had to achieve consensus before matters could be decided. In the British case, in other words, indecisiveness was built into the system so that all governing factions had their voice. In essence, Grey was arguing that democratic government worked as it should have worked in 1914; Britain meandered into world war on purpose.

The record of Grey's decision-making, which will be examined in the next chapter, makes his claim suspect. The fact remains that Grey's double-track policies—accepting military coordination with France as part of a deepening bilateral entente, while publicly claiming impartiality in continental affairs—fit with

the jury-rigged nature of late nineteenth century accountability in politics generally and foreign policy in particular. There seems little question that Grey was
well suited to these times. Projecting an aloof indifference to politics, he nonetheless made secret plans with colleagues for ousting certain party members or
plotting power grabs, and was known to compartmentalize information for bureaucratic ends.[111] Claiming inability to drive Cabinet decision-making in 1914,
he nonetheless clearly did so in 1911 when he authorized agreements with France
for Anglo-French military and naval coordination, but kept these decisions from
the Cabinet. At least one authoritative historian has noted that Grey's own "posture of gentlemanly diffidence belied an intuitive feel for the methods and tactics of adversarial politics," including "secretiveness and a preference for discreet,
behind the scenes dealing."[112] Another has called him "the most insular of foreign secretaries."[113] A political opponent, Arthur Ponsonby, identified in him "a
certain mystery that attracts."[114] Grey seemed to deliberately distance himself,
even at times of crisis, while maintaining a political toolkit that included the use
of special bureaucratic and extra-institutional power. All this reclusiveness, factionalism, and secrecy made policymaking in the British Foreign Ministry unex-
ceptional for the times, but also contributed to the ambiguity and indecisiveness
of these years. Given Britain's relative decline in power, and divisions within the
country at large over the course of empire, opacity in the Foreign Office risked
making British policy even more inscrutable and destabilizing.[115]

Although much of the uncertainty attached to Cabinet government had dis-
sipated by WWII, Neville Chamberlain's vacillation over the best means for
managing Germany between 1937 and 1938 seemed not all that different from
Foreign Minister Grey's before WWI. The similarity may be partly explained by
the uncertainty of decision-making in an era of barely disciplined party politics.
While we will explore both men's use of intelligence for decision-making in some
detail in the next chapter, the point here is that British governance in the interwar
period was fully part of the transitional era between the rule of sovereigns and
the sovereignty of the people.

The situation for republican France was different from Britain's but perhaps
even more opaque. France's internal divisions produced a constantly changing political leadership that accentuated the influence of bureaucratic politics
on state decision-making. From 1899 to 1940, France had a total of forty-nine
changes in prime minister, with only Raymond Poincaré's government of 1926
lasting as much as three years, and most failing to complete even a single year
in office.[116] This political merry-go-round fed the independence of influential
professionals, particularly the powerful Centrale in the Foreign Ministry, which
had access to intercepted communications through the *cabinet noir*. Deeply anti-
German, these bureaucrats of the Quai d'Orsay opposed a nuanced policy toward Berlin, sought to undermine conciliatory moves during the first Moroccan

Crisis in 1905, and subsequent Algeciras Conference, and positively provoked confrontation thereafter.[117] In the process, these bureaucrats ran up against influential and equally long-serving French diplomats, such as Paul Cambon (in London from 1898 to 1920), or his brother Jules Cambon in Berlin. By 1911, the Cambons favored some flexibility toward Germany and railed against the rigidity and *esprit de chicane* with which the Quai managed relations with Berlin.[118] Like-minded senior ambassadors, such as the Cambons, met privately whenever possible, sending personal letters to avoid the Quai's system for internal surveillance. Such factionalism, encrusted with parallel information channels, bureaucratic procedures, and exclusive networks of influence, led to rapid shifts in French policy. It also bred uncertainty for all those seeking authoritative representation of France's position on diplomatic matters. These interested parties included Russia, which feared French betrayal, and the English, who noted French anti-German machinations and suspected her intentions, even as the Anglo-French Entente Cordiale strengthened through coordinated military planning.

After the Great War, and certainly by 1939, French decision-making had somewhat clarified as a result of structural reforms, and the leadership of Édouard Daladier, the centrist prime minister after 1938. Daladier held multiple portfolios and had the ability to build coalitions that papered over differences.[119] Then, too, a more organized intelligence service had emerged, as it had in Britain, but here under the central direction of the army's Deuxième Bureau. This service had begun to feed intelligence to most senior officials, including those in the Foreign Ministry. Still, the French were surprised by the German invasion in 1940, and lost to a less well-equipped German force. This outcome seems more surprising than it should be. Although we are now concerned more with diplomacy than military operations, it is worth noting that, in his book *Strange Victory*, historian Ernest May documents confusion within the French services over where intelligence needed to go once it was collected. By his account, French intelligence only looked good from 1900 to 1940 if you ignored its accessibility to those who needed it for specific decisions. Taking May's argument further, such accessibility had to be compared to Germany's. As we saw at First Manassas and Chancellorsville, it is not just absolute capability, but also relative accessibility of intelligence to decision that matters—and it can matter as much as, or more than, relative strength in troops and iron.

In any event, for the first few decades of the twentieth century, the decline of monarchs brought statesmen increased authority for decision-making, but variable knowledge about tasking and analyzing military and naval intelligence for diplomatic purposes, or keeping and sharing such intelligence, when managing the risks of war. This meant, of course, that they struggled to understand whom to influence in foreign governments and how best to do so in a crisis. If France with its relatively long experience with professional intelligence could claim

some minor advantages in these regards, Russia may have been the most disadvantaged. As William Fuller has written of Russia before WWI: "From the most
insignificant consulate in Persia to the Council of State, civilian diplomats were
blindly ignorant of Russian military reality, while soldiers were confused about
the goals of foreign policy." This condition, however, existed throughout Europe
and, as Fuller noted, "the disassociation was of capital importance in precipi-
tating the First World War."[120]

Mysticism, Nationalism, and the Rise of Popular Sovereignty

If the locus of decision-making matters to intelligence, then the growing power
of the masses during the late nineteenth and early twentieth centuries complicated the search for decision-advantage. At the most critical moments, a ship
of state could be steered by their passions. That public opinion mattered to state
power is evident in simple numbers: on the precipice of WWI, France called up
for military service 250,000 men annually; Russia 335,000; Germany 280,000;
Italy 100,000; and Austria-Hungary 103,000. Military power was directly related
to conscription, which was, in turn, directly related to public will. Since the defeat of Napoleon, European statesmen had understood that war among the Great
Powers would involve the masses, but had remained uncertain about whether
they would show up in uniform, on the factory floor, or behind barricades.
Especially within Austria-Hungary, the military services depended on minority
nationalities to fight. As states employed ever-greater percentages of labor in
large arms-related industries, and extended the franchise, public support for
threatening or using force had become both critical and uncertain. The extraordinary consumption of men and materiel during WWI only accelerated these
trends.[121]

It follows that journalists could gain power as popular intelligence providers
and "influencers" of public opinion; demagogues could skip intermediary
decision-makers and appeal directly to "the people." In fact, as the static power
of monarchs declined relative to the enduring power of the masses to fight,
work, strike, and vote, even declining monarchies understood the need to load,
arm, and pull the trigger on the public's will. The uncertainty rested on how to
accomplish this feat, which seemed to require both good intelligence on public
support for policies, including polling and political campaigns, as well as capacities for influence, including newspapers and propaganda. Democracies
were better at the first than the second, although they were learning. Declining
autocracies tended to be better at the latter than the former, about which they
were *not* learning. The genius of the fascists in the run-up to WWII was their
mastery of both.

For most of the era, however, governments' influence on the governed was uncertain for three principal reasons: first, advances in communications enabled popular resistance to government policies; second, the rise in science triggered a counter-rationalist movement involving mystics, Ouija boards, and séances that engaged more passion than reason; third, new ideologies and race-consciousness were compromising allegiances to the state. The withering of trusted institutions, such as king, class, and church, and the rise of new, unfamiliar ones, such as parties and bureaucratic government, led to a sense of social dislocation and a hunger for belonging. Secret societies blossomed, transnational political movements sprang up, and governments lost control of social and political agendas. Popular resistance worked in both directions: people might resist war and refuse to fight, but they could also be persuaded to demand intervention, becoming more bellicose than their governments deemed wise, given the interests at stake and the likely consequences.

Popular Unrest

Such exacerbated tensions between governments and governed created new uncertainties for diplomats. Modern sources of strength for the nation-state were becoming embedded, as Correlli Barnett once wrote of Britain, "in the nation itself, the people; their skills, energy, ambition, discipline, initiative; their beliefs, myths and illusions," and in how all these elements interacted within the polity.[122] Instabilities were bubbling up from populations enthralled by their new political consciousness and capacities to know, act, and disrupt. Citizens had already learned they could man barricades, vote, or refuse to march to war; now they knew that they could strike or work double shifts and so had an ongoing impact on state power. National press organizations became public sources of intelligence and so grew in political power in almost all capitals. By the early twentieth century, citizens felt more informed, more engaged in politics and more certain of their opinions, even though fed, often, a highly politicized diet.

The impact of this evolution on state intelligence was broad and sustained. To learn what governments could or would do required learning what officials thought their populations would allow or demand, and such calculations proved complicated. Public attitudes were not just reported in the press but shaped by it; and reporters did not always fact-check their material. Some journalists were conspiracy-minded or politicized. Others were bought by foreign interests running propaganda campaigns. Regardless of the merits of the sources, transnational communications spread rumors or news, helping individuals "know" about national developments in a timely way and organize for common cause.

Pan-Slavism inspired a network of anarchists from Belgrade to Istanbul, accelerated the unraveling of the Habsburg dynasty and, combined with Turkish weakness, sparked the Balkan wars of 1912–13. The Black Hand, the terrorist organization that perpetrated the 1914 assassination of the archduke, got its tactical intelligence from organized news; the perpetrators learned about Franz Ferdinand's itinerary from the press. Austria-Hungary was not alone in its vulnerability to mass movements and terrorist organizations inspired by the communications revolution. The British feared insurgency in Ireland and Indian revolts sponsored by networks extending as far away as Canada and the United States.[123] By 1917, the Russian Revolution had brought democrats, then Bolsheviks, to power through the organization of anti-tsarist networks. And a diaspora of "White Russians," intent on restoring the monarchy, flooded Europe, establishing a wide-ranging network there. Fundamental to all this turmoil was the increased learning power of the public amid institutions not designed to cope with it.

The importance of worldwide communications to democratic adjustment cannot be overestimated when assessing the uncertainties of the times. As people felt more empowered, public opinion was becoming more unpredictable, swinging from deference to anger with little warning. And governments knew it. Queen Victoria's diamond jubilee celebration was an event of the masses, as well as the throne, and was only topped by the May 1910 funeral of her successor, King Edward VII—a stunning spectacle that included a host of European monarchs on chargers, but also a public transfixed, either in awe or opposition, by the British throne.

> So glorious was the spectacle . . . that the crowd, waiting in hushed and black-clad awe, could not keep back gasps of admiration. In scarlet and blue and green and purple, three by three the sovereigns rode through the palace gates, with plumed helmets, gold braid, crimson sashes, and jeweled orders, flashing in the sun. . . . Together they represented seventy nations in the greatest assemblage of royalty and rank ever gathered in one place and, of its kind, the last.[124]

As late as WWII, King George rallied the population by walking with his family, during the Battle of Britain, among bombed-out buildings in central London.

Yet the public response to such displays was best understood as engagement, not submission. Their awe and allegiance were not inconsistent with the realization that monarchical power was built on the sweat off their backs. Labor understood its power. Strikes could stop governors in their tracks; insurgency could overthrow tsars. The communist movement, spearheaded by Moscow and institutionalized in the Communist International, raised fears in democratic governments precisely because its narrative about worker empowerment resonated with a populace struggling to secure social equity. Such demands worried governors unsure how to meet them. The split was not just rich against poor or struggling entrepreneur against entitled nobility; it was also about the legitimacy of the state and the ideas and principles underpinning it. The Spanish Civil War, which broke out in April 1936, pitted republican leftists, supported by Moscow's communists, against nationalists supported by fascists in Italy and Germany.

That Britain brokered an international agreement (that no signatory observed) to stay out of the upheaval in Spain was hardly surprising.[125] In the face of such centrifugal and transnational political forces, governments feared losing the support of a media-conscious electorate and were, therefore, uncertain about their latitude for exercising force. Whereas prior generations of diplomats had mostly free hands in the conduct of foreign affairs, statesmen were increasingly bound to their democratizing polities whose shifting attitudes could confound the best-laid plans. Ignoring public pressure risked loss of public confidence, but acting on flighty public opinion risked diplomatic impulsiveness, irritation abroad, and costly conflict. Before WWI, Sir Edward Grey lamented Britain's awkward Balkan policies, which he believed reflected less Britain's national interests than the British public's dislike of Turkish oppression, especially in Macedonia. To some degree, Grey felt trapped. As he told the French in May 1914, "Whether [Britain] engaged in a Continental war or kept aloof would depend on public opinion in Great Britain when the time came."[126] Hitler had a different view; he later showed how to unshackle governors using the populist drugs of nationalism, corporatism, and xenophobia whipped up by propaganda and "influencers" in the press.[127]

The new, popular journalism elevated news executives to new heights of power and tempted all statesmen to use propaganda as a peacetime instrument of statecraft. Covert action—secret sponsorship of political, economic, or military activity—became a more regular governmental tool ranging from simple propaganda to insurgency and assassination. The learning curve was steep, and the blowback from failed operations was often costly. In the 1920s, for example, the British government discovered that the Bolshevik government, in an attempt to influence talks on an Anglo-Soviet trade agreement, had been selling tsarist diamonds to subsidize the left-leaning *Daily Herald*. British Cabinet members, appalled by the attempted subversion, struck back by leaking the intercepts that proved Moscow's role but, in doing so, compromised their intelligence sources, effectively shooting themselves in the foot. In response, the Soviets adopted the unbreakable "one-time pad" form of encryption, blinding British policymakers.[128]

Journalists became influential sources of information, particularly if they had access to high levels of government decision-making, and sometimes replaced diplomatic channels of uncertain trustworthiness. Newspaper editors readily accepted official "news" for publication, and expected, in return, to gain access to high-level policy and plans; as a result, "open source" information was collected and analyzed by embassies, military services, and foreign offices. At times, the lines between journalists, intelligence agents, and propagandists were faint to nonexistent; certainly, governments made extensive use of "inspired" articles to convey official thinking or preferred positions. In the United States, President Woodrow Wilson came into office distrusting his State Department and, so, collected intelligence on the Mexican Revolution using a trusted journalist.[129] In 1914 Germany, the journalist Viktor Naumann, a confidant of Wilhelm von Stumm, who was then head of the political department in Berlin's Foreign Office, acted as an intermediary with officials in Vienna. The overall effect was a loss of discipline and greater uncertainty in the conduct of foreign affairs.

Counter-rationalism . . .

In the explosion of information attending the nineteenth-century industrial revolution, there were few metrics for truth. Crown heads no longer decided, religion no longer mediated, but neither initially did scientific truths. Technological and scientific discoveries, in fields as diverse as genetics, anthropology, and wireless communications, energized "scientific" investigations into eugenics, Loch Ness monsters, and communicating with unseen beings of all kinds. It is no fluke that "wireless communication" through Ouija boards and paranormal seers surged during this time. Open-minded, credulous citizens measured their children's skulls to discern their optimum careers, went on cruises to hunt for modern-day dinosaurs, and tried paranormal communications through the use of séances, mediums, and tarot.[130] Some of the investigators gained fame, independence, and larger political profiles in the process.

These trends affected governance through the fueling of extreme, sometimes exclusive political agendas.[131] Networks of secret societies, such as the Masons, used quasi-religious rituals to enforce allegiances and became targets for the recruitment of intelligence operatives and, not surprisingly, counterintelligence infiltration.[132] Indirect effects included increased uncertainty about what one knew, even when confronted with facts, and greater certainties about the unknown, thanks to conspiracy theories. Anti-Semitism and unsubstantiated fears about Jewish plots were on the rise throughout Europe, contributing to increased violence against Jews and refugee flows to Palestine, which, in turn, enflamed Arab hostility toward Jews and an uprising against Britain that flared on and off from April 1936 to November 1938.[133] Statesmen, sure of facts, could not be sure in what irrational way others might read them. In the midst of the July Crisis of 1914, for example, the kaiser opined to the Austrian ambassador that the tsar's chief advisor was "probably the War Minister, but it seemed that the faith healer Rasputin was still exerting a decisive influence over him."[134] Conservative British member of Parliament and future foreign minister Sir Samuel Hoare had the same impression in 1916, but concluded that the "desolate monk" was actually the instigator of pro-German "Dark Forces" seeking to twist the purposes of the tsarist regime.[135] And fantastical rumors of German infiltration, spawned by British novelists before WWI, fueled British war scares that led directly to the rise of Britain's counterintelligence service.

... and the New Political Ideologies

Although the printing press and the telegraph gave each person, whether fanatic, fantasist, or foreign minister, a larger sounding board for his or her ideas, contending philosophies battled for adherents, raising the temperature of domestic politics and projecting weakness abroad.[136]

A widespread sense that old institutions were in jeopardy, in turn inspired popular and ideational resistance to monarchical and bourgeois power in the forms of Marxism, socialism, communism, and fascism. The rise of violent social movements, in general, and pan-Slavic terrorism in particular, were fully part of this upsurge in radicalism within Europe. Some used their competitive information to vote politicians out of office; others used their new empowerment for assassination, infiltration, revolution, or terrorism (the Bolsheviks, the Black Hand, and the Communist International).

The problem was not confined to weak European governments, but those with strong governing institutions and some capacity for domestic intelligence fared best. Informed governments could manage, co-opt, or exploit activism on the streets if they could get ahead of the agitators. For example, the rise of German sabotage operations in the United States during WWI triggered a popular backlash that included support for the anti-immigrant Palmer Raids—and even a form of domestic vigilantism. The FBI condoned, and then co-opted, the semi-private American Protective League. Empowered by the passage of the Espionage Act, the FBI rapidly took charge of domestic security and put private enforcers out of business.[137] In contrast, the Nazi Brownshirts and Mussolini's Blackshirts embodied violent radicalism that Hitler both inflamed and manipulated in service to the German state. Whereas the United States flexed its constitutional muscles to contain domestic passions, Hitler's Germany exploited its vigilantes and monopoly on force to spy, arrest, and kill domestic opponents. Although Hitler could not hide such actions from world opinion in an era of popular passions, he could sell them as necessary. Like Benito Mussolini, he was initially seen as more the master of monsters in a circus than as the monster himself.

Somewhere in between was the government of Serbia. Serbian nationalists had become, following their victories in the Balkan wars, both empowered and ungovernable. Here, organized unruliness was more evolutionary than surprisingly new. Serbian militants, who had murdered the king and queen some years before, had subsequently infiltrated the army and the government. By 1914, their networks had morphed into public-private secret societies. The Black Hand, probably the most militant of these terrorist organizations, was headed by Apis ("The Bull," aka Colonel Dragutin Dimitrijević), the head of military intelligence in Belgrade. Deeply embedded within the Serbian state, and often at odds with the Serbian prime minister, The Black Hand was, by 1914, willing to risk war with Austria-Hungary in the name of Serbian nationalism—regardless of what Serbia's public leaders might think or decide. Such threats to rule, especially emanating from regicidal assassins, were so destabilizing that even some Slavs in Russia, champions of Slavic nationalism, could not tolerate them.

That such extremism would lead to international instability might now seem obvious, but if and how it would do so was at the time not obvious at all. In 1914, when the Austrian archduke's assassination was still fresh, no one in a decision-making capacity in Germany, France, or Great Britain understood that the Black Hand had engineered it; to the extent they considered the matter, they believed instead that Narodna Odbrana (Serbian National Defense), was responsible—a critical distinction because the latter was a political secret society sanctioned by Serbia. Few governments other than Russia recognized the importance of this difference. Most had not learned to penetrate or influence secret societies successfully before WWI.

Austria-Hungary was right to fear for its longevity, but neither it nor any of the other Great Powers had an intelligence system suitable to the threat, with the possible exception of Russia. If the Great Powers had understood the true source of the assassination in 1914, it is possible war over Serbian complicity could have been avoided because the rationale for a punitive strike against the government in Belgrade would have disappeared. By WWII, governments were much more aware of the need to target transnational groups directly, but not appreciably better at it.

Counter-rationalism was not, however, just a fad for mystics or fuel for terrorists during the buildup to WWI; it would certainly be wrong to dismiss its effects as that transitory. Indeed, counter-rationalism probably found its most potent expression in the syndicalist movement of the French socialist theoretician, Georges Sorel. Emphasizing the importance of intuition, passion, and will, Sorel launched a nationalist movement fused to a form of socialism that fully embraced state capitalism, thereby seeding the national socialist movement of the interwar period. Although the precise sources of twentieth-century fascism may still be debated, the impact of the national socialist movements of this period, especially in its virulent form under Adolf Hitler, is not. Hitler's vision drove a criminal and hate-filled agenda linked not just to Mussolini's Italian form of fascism, but to a broad, multinational social movement with long roots back through the nineteenth century. Nazism seems to have grown out of anti-individualistic and antidemocratic notions of popular rule. It was of a piece with political movements that embraced racial exceptionalism as based (erroneously) on scientific "facts" and the benefits of conflict and competition Darwin had outlined, albeit twisted for irrational, conspiratorial purposes.[138]

Thus, state capitalism, race-based nationalism, counter-rationalism, and political extremism were thriving in many forms from 1900 to 1940. Nazism was, of course, a particularly virulent mix within this trend, but seeing Hitler's movement in its context helps to explain the delay in recognizing Nazism for what it really was. Uncertainty about what Nazism meant for international politics grew out of a generalized and misguided certainty that all peoples were not equal, that the superior should rule, and what mattered most at any given moment was the virility of the state, measured by the genetics of the nation and the will and passion of its leaders. Adolf Hitler was admired among many Europeans and Americans before he was feared or reviled, and in that admiration—uneven and volatile because largely ideational—lay practical political uncertainty for others.

Clear as these ideological revolutions and changes in public norms and attitudes may be in retrospect—we know now how important socialism, fascism, and communism would become to the evolution of international politics between WWI and WWII—they were not so clear from 1900 to 1938. The heuristics of the age shifted radically and unevenly in just a few short decades. Before the outbreak of WWI, empires and thrones were European symbols of national cohesion; by 1943, Uncle Sam was such a symbol for the United States, the swastika was for Germany, and the hammer and sickle for the Soviet Union. In Britain's case, the king's popularity and notions of noblesse oblige helped stave off antimonarchist impulses, but those impulses still seemed to threaten established order and national unity.

In sum, states had to take the temperature of volatile, impressionable, and sometimes irrational and ill-informed publics when assessing state power in the early twentieth century. The politics of the age of total war were revolutionary, innovative, and populist, but these dynamics overlaid a hunger for empire and strong, if not necessarily monarchical, sovereigns. The point is rather that in the age of total war, civilians—industrial magnates, workers, soldiers, journalists, insurgents, or informants—had heightened, if widely varying, powers to affect national security for better or worse. And while some governments got a grip, sometimes dangerously tight, on the passions of their populations through ramped-up intelligence and counterintelligence services, uncertainties about loyalties persisted.

The Growth of Institutionalized Intelligence

The combination of technological, ideological, and political effects of the industrial revolution made for a dark period in international politics. In such circumstances, statesmen have two options: lift the darkness or go on instinct. Between 1900 and 1940, most governments sought to lift the darkness. To do so, some tried to reform foreign ministries and created or expanded national, civilian intelligence services. Foreign ministries, intelligence institutions in all but name, began to adjust to the need for the well-educated, not just the blue-blooded. Military institutions began more regularly to share their intelligence products with civilian partners. National intelligence services began to track decision-making authorities for the purpose of delivering timely intelligence among diplomats, warriors, law enforcement, and statesmen. As professional intelligence services met statesmen's needs, the latter developed a measure of trust in these services. Winston Churchill, particularly effective as a wartime leader from 1940 to 1945, learned to wield the intelligence instrument because it was ever more closely fitted to his hand during the interwar period. One of the earliest to appreciate the utility of national intelligence, Churchill insisted on access to it, even during periods when he was out of office. Trusted by certain colleagues to keep secrets, he was one of the few private citizens allowed to have it.

Yet the professionalization of intelligence also created new uncertainties. National intelligence institutions, because they controlled classified information, threatened to create bureaucratic winners and losers. Official intelligence services could subordinate any single decision-maker's need to the needs of others, stamping out personal networks and private initiatives before official channels for intelligence-gathering were any good. Even if a government's intelligence advantages increased overall, any given official's access to it might suffer. Moreover, old biases threatened to become institutionalized, and new ones threatened to raise tensions. With regard to the former, foreign ministries became protective of their role, while military services had an interest in having nascent intelligence agencies back their services' threat assessments. Civilian intelligence services risked heightening threats out of a need to justify their existence.

In any event, the military (and civilians) paid a price for adopting institutionalized rules for intelligence-sharing and keeping what the state knew, and how it knew it, under new or elaborating systems of secrecy. Before the attack on Pearl Harbor and US entry into WWII, for example, Admiral Husband E. Kimmel, commander in chief of the US fleet and the US Pacific Fleet, was denied access to the routine flow of top-level intelligence as a matter of national security policy. Washington's warnings of Japanese attack were too vague and too late to protect the Pacific fleet from devastation.[139] In other cases, the intelligence was provided, but highly sensitive sourcing was obscured. During the WWII battle for Crete, the British reportedly lost battlefield advantage because the British managers refused to tell the commanding general that intelligence on German plans came from decryption of German Enigma messages. Told the intelligence came from a human spy to protect the source, the commanding general discounted its value and suffered the consequences.[140]

The point here is not that it was bad to create national intelligence services. Rather, it is that any remodeling of decision-making systems, including the flow of intelligence within them, comes at some cost. From the gain in knowledge these services offered had to be subtracted the new opportunities for institutionalized pathologies, such as the politicization (political corruption) and privatization (career-motivated corruption) of intelligence at the national level that could, in turn, offer foreign intelligence services openings for access to intelligence policy and high-level decision-making. So the question remains: did the sudden growth of national intelligence services mold the terrain of uncertainty favorably for some but not others?

Institutionalized Uncertainty

Although meant to lift the veil on international politics, new intelligence services initially increased confusion more than they illuminated matters. That governments became increasingly secretive, holding sensitive foreign intelligence from even insiders with a need to know about it, reflected new recognition of the importance of intelligence advantage, wariness of foreign states, and growing distrust of radicals within their own populations.

At the same time, as the collectors and validators of purportedly "authentic" information, national intelligence services became wielders of more bureaucratic power than their products often merited, and before most statesmen had developed trust in them. The result was confusion, leaks, retribution, and uncertainty. Stalin's solution to the growing bureaucratic power of his intelligence services was the repetitive purge; Hitler's was to manage his own open-source collection while playing intelligence services, such as his treacherous Abwehr and the SS, off one another.[141]

Yet by the end of WWII, intelligence institutions were poised to make an enormous contribution to the outcome of war. And the ones that did best in WWII were the ones that recognized and overcame their earlier poor performances.

Discerning good tradecraft and good intelligence policy was not in any statesman's manual. The challenges posed by the development of civilian intelligence bureaucracies went beyond trust to the unity, organization, and effectiveness of governmental operations. Intelligence institutions initially made organizational relationships more confusing and fraught with tension.[142] It is important to remember that early civilian intelligence services were underdeveloped compared to military ones in almost every European power. With the decline of royal and ecclesiastical power, and the rise of industrial warfare, emissaries from throne and church seemed to matter relatively less, while military power in terms of weapons manufacture seemingly mattered more. Early civilian intelligence institutions tended to follow the pattern. This fixation on military means made diplomacy contingent on military advantage to the exclusion of almost anything else. Hitler was among the few who understood that intelligence on the masses mattered, and that it could be used to gain decision advantages even when the military balance was against him. The emergence of civilian intelligence institutions eventually enabled other statesmen to learn how to tailor the instruments of power to their desired ends.

Progress was, however, slow. Diplomats and military and commercial attachés resented the rise of professional intelligence services whose operations put their own missions at risk. Democracies relied on diplomats for intelligence well into the interwar period, not just because spies were distrusted, but because statesmen believed diplomacy was responsible for maintaining the norms of international discourse. In 1929, US secretary of state Henry Stimson cited ethical reasons for terminating the jointly funded US Cipher Bureau ("Black Chamber"), a civil-military decryption unit, despite its stunning successes in decoding Japanese communications during the Washington Naval Conference.[143] In Britain, civil-military collaboration was better, but the learning curve was steep. Diplomats were horrified about what they learned foreign counterparts were saying about them in communications intercepts. They sought to shut down collection and reporting in ways that ultimately blinded them.

Espionage was another matter, however. British spy scares in the early 1900s led to the creation of espionage (MI6) and counterespionage (MI5) units that enabled the government to chase down leads, winning over a few British ministers in the process. After WWI, reforms of the Secret Intelligence Service (SIS) brought policymakers in closer touch with its intelligence-producers, including the code and cipher organization. In brief, this arrangement centralized the national intelligence function by placing representative sections of each intelligence service at SIS headquarters to refine targeting of collection as "consumers" required. At the same time, under the guidance of the SIS chief of service, Quex Sinclair, the service began tapping into the technological possibilities offered up by industry, and began thinking creatively about the counterintelligence dimension.[144] Sinclair set up clandestine radio communications with his over-seas posts and resumed the practice of opening the diplomatic bags of foreign governments. Still, unschooled in the careful use of intelligence advantages, ci-vilian leaders had "spasmodic" interactions with intelligence professionals and regularly mishandled products.[145] For example, angered by Communist infil-tration of the labor movement during the 1920s, one prominent minister made intelligence on Moscow's operations public. Moscow simply changed its codes, making intercepts unreadable and ruining intelligence production.[146]

The short-term effect of these recurring problems was to cause intelligence professionals to mistrust the statesmen they served, and vice versa. Where in-ternal trust was weakest, such as in postrevolutionary Russia, intelligence officials underwent loyalty tests, fled, or were killed. The Bolsheviks' most serious intelligence-related losses were the tsar's cryptologists, who left in great numbers and, by the end of WWI, were working against the Soviet state. In response to the termination of the US Black Chamber, the unit's head, Herbert Yardley, leaked his entire operation in a "tell-all" book the government tried, unsuccessfully, to suppress. Its revelations about the collection of Japanese diplomatic traffic led Tokyo to lodge a formal protest over the unfair negotiating processes the United States had used during the Washington Naval Conference of 1921. Although the military picked up the slack in US signals intelligence, the diplomatic blowback of Yardley's move was obvious. In France, mistrust was almost institutional-ized. The Quai d'Orsay, which had received intercepted communications since Cardinal Richelieu established his *cabinet noir* was, by the 1890s, successfully decrypting most of the communications of the Great Powers. Yet, accustomed to politicized intelligence, French statesmen used their relatively good access to secrets for personal political gains, including domestic electoral advantage, po-litical retribution, and bureaucratic rivalry.[147]

Bureaucratic rivalry was fueled by the naïveté of statesmen and diplomats new to intelligence, but also by incompetent tradecraft among newly minted professionals easily duped by forgeries and double agents.[148] In Britain, national intelligence capabilities grew largely outside of both the Foreign Office and the military chain of command. Although the War Office Special Section, first cre-ated for battlefield intelligence during the Boer War, began limited offensive operations against Germany in 1905, it was not until 1909 that the Admiralty and the War Office collaborated to create the civilian Secret Service Bureau (SSB). The SSB worked mostly for the army and navy before WWI, addressing primarily technical questions related to the German naval threat, not national requirements for peacetime decision-making or strategic warning. It did not produce much of value. A post-WWI British official report was highly critical of both the SSB's operations and its products.[149] For example, some influential human intelligence in these early years came from freelance Brussels espionage agents, who, taking advantage of permissive Belgian laws, openly advertised their services or offered secret intelligence exchanges.[150] Most of this intelligence, based on forged documents and compromised agents, was bad. Poor tradecraft persisted into the interwar period as SIS's sources on Bolshevik Russia, perceived during these years to be Britain's most dangerous threat, mostly came from the monarchist diaspora. These agents needed money, wanted to be recruited, but had lost access. They sold known forgeries. Their recruiters compromised themselves and their operations by persistent wishful thinking.[151] All this incompetence reflected inexperience and untested tradecraft. But it also reflected the inherent tensions and uncertainties attending the competition between intelligence gatherers, who develop sources, and counterintelligence officers, who are paid to suspect them. The quality of each depends on the other, even if the constant friction generates heat as well as light.

Incompetence, corruption, and bureaucratic rivalries set both decision-makers and intelligence officers on edge. French statesmen were vulnerable to their intelligence services and fearful of retaliation. Competing with France's *cabinet noir* before WWI was the Sûreté nationale, which, following its successful work on Japanese codes during the Russo-Japanese War, acquired a full-time cryptologic unit in 1907.[152] Both units were plagued by inaccuracies and politicization in the run-up to WWI, with the latter generating such serious leaks that France lost access to all German codes just before the outbreak of war, putting Paris at a serious disadvantage at the outset. Following the war, France had six independent intelligence organizations, including the Quai's *cabinet noir*, the Sûreté nationale, the intelligence units of the army, navy, and air force, the unit serving the ministry of colonies after 1937, and the intelligence arm of the Paris prefecture of police, which was dedicated to domestic intelligence and counterintelligence. The Foreign Office did not control or, indeed, have regular access to any of the last five of these intelligence organizations, their requirements, or their products. In fact, the most important of the above services for gaining a unified national view was the intelligence division (Deuxième Bureau) of the army general staff. Unlike in Germany, the army's intelligence organization "effectively controlled all spies and all interception and decryption of communications."[153] Its head received and reported all photographic intelligence and managed counterintelligence as well. The Deuxième Bureau encompassed the Service de Renseignements, which did signals and human intelligence and employed a staff for liaison with and reporting from all the other collectors of intelligence across the government. Without good relations with the Deuxième Bureau and, by extension, the army leadership, a prime minister operated in the dark.[154]

Another effect of institutionalized intelligence was heightened domestic surveillance and public distrust, with predictable effects on political leadership, which both needed to get domestic intelligence and feared blowback from it. Emblematic of the problem was the institutionalized art of covert intelligence triggered by newly important defense-related industries and wireless communications. Hostile powers could recruit "watchers" to keep tabs on factories, ports, or trains, and secretly report back to their foreign sponsors. As early as WWI, such covert collection—overtly sensing, but clandestinely sponsored—began to make significant differences in war.[155] Wireless radios also aided clandestine espionage. The Soviet Union ran a particularly innovative network of spies before and during WWII, the Red Orchestra ("Rote Kapelle"), that used business cover, open observation, and wireless communications to expose German plans.[156] Because of the ease of setting up such networks, countering them was difficult. Covert spying and sabotage, once exposed, prompted counterintelligence initiatives, domestic surveillance, and, in some cases, overreaction by governors.[157] Eventually, oversight institutions and legal frameworks for counterespionage and surveillance caught up, easing the problem, especially in democracies.[158]

After WWI, however, the institutionalized response was to protect intelligence institutions through added secrecy and the compartmenting of intelligence. Statesmen worried about subversion leaned ever more on counterintelligence organizations. They learned that without good, reliable sources, counterintelligence could be a wasteful, bottomless pit. Yet when sources were good, domestic surveillance paid off. The police, experienced in manhunts, were relatively quick to employ new technologies such as wireless intercepts and direction-finding (DFing) for peacetime counterespionage.[159] In several countries, police worked with intelligence institutions to hone the latter's tradecraft, despite the threat this collaboration posed to civil liberties. When labor demonstrations erupted in the 1920s, possibly sponsored by Moscow and linked to the Communist International, Western governments empowered domestic intelligence agencies to ferret out perpetrators using domestic penetration agents and signals intercepts on their own soil.[160] Prosecuting agents required proof of illegalities, but these were poorly defined short of criminal acts. In the United States, fear of foreign agency led to vigilantism, as well as the passing of espionage acts and the ramping up of federal policing. When public anxiety waned, or the reach of counterspies and police went too far for public tolerance, civilian dissidents, as well as political leaders, pushed back, sometimes blaming intelligence agencies for overreach, sometimes crediting them with preventing it by police. Especially in democracies, aggressive counterintelligence was sometimes more debilitating than empowering.

Mindsets

If the professionalization of intelligence was slow to lift the darkness infusing international politics before WWI, then statesmen should have been confused and slow to act. The next chapter reveals, however, that most of the decision-makers who brought on WWI were far from indecisive. In fact, despite profound uncertainties, statesmen *acted with confidence and alacrity* in bringing about a war that was in none of their interests. During the buildup to WWI, statesmen seemed, if anything, *more certain* about the future than ever. Even Winston Churchill, credited with clearer vision than most politicians of the time, believed, for example, that the international gold specie standard anchored the international system and ensured stability—a bulwark against war. "Everyone knows," he said in 1908, "every single businessman knows, it works delicately, automatically, universally and instantaneously." He then prophesized that it would endure at least until "the year 2000 had dawned upon the world."[161] In fact, the gold specie standard effectively ended with the outbreak of WWI.

The paradox of increasing certainty in an uncertain world underscores the importance of mindsets to decision-advantage. Mindsets, a combination of fixed and interlaced assumptions, help decision-makers act when information is scarce or ambiguous. Mindsets can supplement intelligence with the fruits of experience—that is, help guide and expedite decisions when everything seems dark. At other times, however, mindsets simply mislead or discourage learning, and so contribute to intelligence failure. Britain's leaders genuinely *believed* in 1914 that Europe's Great Powers would remain at peace for the foreseeable future. Because the costs of war seemed too high, if war came, it had to be short. In fact, when the Great War came, it persisted for years as governments simply printed money and took out loans. Germany's leaders *were certain* in 1914 that Russia would soon surpass her in power, collude with a revanchist France, and attack; in fact, Russia was riddled with domestic unrest that would lead to revolution in 1917.[162] Austria-Hungary's decision-makers were *sure* they could solve the Balkan problem if Germany had their back for a quick assault; she lost the war, and the "Balkan problem" persisted in its aftermath.

Mindsets can do worse than mislead; they can reduce demand for good intelligence. For example, the success of the British-organized "concert" of powers in the Balkan Crises of 1911–13 fed the notion that strategic warning was not crucial since crises could be managed. This mindset was comforting because it rested on traditional images: of Austria-Hungary as an empire; of Russia as a powerful guardian of the Slavs; of Britain as an attentive broker of power on the Continent; and of European Great Powers, in general, as investors in European stability. In fact, Britain's diplomats were inattentive to peasant unrest and the growth of terrorist networks throughout the region; Russia was more tail than teeth; Germany saw Austria more as albatross than empire; and Serbia, Vienna's nemesis, had beaten back the Turks and doubled its size. These trends, knowable by 1912, were surging *beneath* the crusty paradigms nurtured by many of Europe's most influential statesmen. Indeed, the peace agreement at Versailles that ended WWI testified to the persistence of this Great Power mindset. Its negotiators created a host of weak and indefensible states, again with the presumption that a concert of Great Powers—now the League of Nations—would suffice to maintain peace there without the collective will or intelligence to sanction, deter, or employ force in a timely way.

It was not just that, coming from privileged classes, governors retained a fear of barricades, confidence in gold, and an awe of the British Empire in their bones. The problem was also that, before WWI and the professionalization of national intelligence services, financiers and diplomats still sought their best intelligence by talking to themselves. Foreign ministries tended to be "clannish"; diplomats were often related to one another; and Britain's Foreign Office, despite its reforms, seemed dedicated to preserving its upper-class character. All of this amounted to a kind of international groupthink, which made appreciating modern trends difficult at best.[163] After all, the Habsburg Empire had stood for generations as a fixture at the heart of Europe. By 1913, though sickly and pocked with poverty, Austria still carried the imperial mystique. It boasted a population larger than that of France or Great Britain, territory stretching from Switzerland half way to the Black Sea, significant natural resources, and an age-old culture that captivated most Europeans.[164] That Austria-Hungary's internal divisions were hollowing out the empire faster than it could compensate in an age of industrialization and social upheaval was knowable, but few in the elite wanted to know, since the implications for European stability were so awful. Although the empire was "a heap of paradoxes and anachronisms," perhaps unsalvageable by its "pantomime parliament," betting against the Habsburgs just *seemed* wrong.[165]

Mindsets give way, however, in the press of threats to vital interests, the relentless accumulation of facts, or the rise of a new generation of decision-makers. German statesmen, tethered to Austria and Italy in a Triple Alliance, gradually came to understand Austria's weaknesses better than most of their colleagues in Paris and London because these weaknesses posed a direct threat to Germany. Their Viennese colleagues, understanding this too, feared Germany would cut the tether. The result was posturing and disinformation. Each ally sought to convince the other that the Triple Alliance had teeth in order to prevent it from falling completely apart. Both sets of decision-makers also had reason to hide what they knew from others who, should they be shaken from nineteenth-century complacency and images of a concert of Great Powers, might try to achieve European outcomes at Austria's and Germany's expense. And those "others" were already shedding old-world views. From 1900 to 1940, bureaucratic reforms in most of the Great Powers were bringing a new generation of diplomats, intelligence providers, and attachés into government.

This incremental process initially exchanged old uncertainties and diplomatic surprises for new ones. For example, shortly after the turn of the century a new wave of British diplomats perceived the kaiser's ambitious naval program as an existential threat that, in their relatively modern minds, republican France simply did not pose. When London deepened relations with France first, then her ally Russia, the kaiser was both furious and surprised. His expectations contrasted sharply with the open minds of a new generation of British diplomats for whom Waterloo was ancient history. One might conclude that, if the ability to exploit enemy mindsets to gain advantages is at the heart of offensive counterintelligence (deceptions and stratagems), the ability to change mindsets is an attribute of sound leadership; in its absence, matters take what may seem to be an inevitable course.

Nevertheless, old-school diplomatists only slowly relinquished power and, in the meantime, often resisted new methods for learning, such as the building of better sources through their national intelligence services. Even as new intelligence systems took hold, they often locked in old ways of thinking, becoming trusted before their tradecraft or products merited it. Formal intelligence services often gathered information faster than they could evaluate and secure their sources, making them more useful for reinforcing biases than busting them and, thus, serving as channels for opposing governments to convey their deceptive stratagems. The best example of the latter was, perhaps, the Trust, an antimonarchist deception conducted by the Russian Cheka after WWI. The Cheka used double agents posing as anti-Bolshevik monarchists. To communicate securely with each other, these posers exploited the trust of deceived intelligence services in the West to send messages through their respective governments' diplomatic bags. The Cheka operatives thus were able to earn the trust of monarchist networks and lure anti-Bolshevik émigrés to their deaths back in Moscow. Many western European governments fell for the ruses because intelligence services were inexperienced with them. Inexperience did not last. Using coordinated police and communications surveillance, the British disrupted Comintern networks during the interwar period. By WWII, the British were running sophisticated deception operations against Nazi Germany. And that expertise included knowledge that mindsets of all kinds—including belief in the epistemological supremacy of espionage—are fodder for deception.

Although the general problem of mindsets played a role in this dark period of international politics, it is important to recall that individual statesmen's mindsets varied. Personal attributes mattered in a way this analysis cannot address in any generalized manner. As Christopher Andrew has noted about the British statesman, Winston Churchill, "Not the least important aspect of [his] superiority over Hitler as a war leader was his much greater grasp of the role and importance of intelligence."[166] The difference was not just that he understood the value of collection, but that he understood the need for context and analyzed each piece in relation to the whole. Indeed, Churchill's competence in this regard may have reflected a forcing function: initially without a professional cadre of analysts to support him, he had learned how to read raw intelligence, make sense of it, and protect it, long before most others did. Churchill was a transitional figure—a leader accustomed to gathering and analyzing his own intelligence, but also cognizant of the growing role of professional expertise in the processing, if not the "all source" analysis or management, of it.

In contrast, Hitler, who understood Central Europe better than most of his competitors did, made serious mistakes because of his mindset about weak democracies and popular will. When his military attaché in Washington said, with little good evidence, that the United States would never side with London and Paris, Hitler believed him. It follows that, to know what Grey, the kaiser, or Hitler knew at key moments, and whether or not they had methods for attaining informational advantages, one must examine all their sources, not just the ones security services generated. It follows that blaming policymakers' decisions on the failures of their secret services begs important questions about what specific individuals thought they knew, thought they needed to know, and attempted to learn, whether through those services or not.

Conclusion

I have made four arguments in this chapter about the diplomatic terrain of uncertainty prior to WWI and WWII:

- First, that the darkness engulfing diplomatic decision-making from 1900 to 1940 flowed mostly from the effects of the industrial revolution and imperial decline. These factors contributed to perceptions of vulnerability, particularly for Austria-Hungary and the Ottoman Empire, but later for all the European Great Powers; obscured relationships of power; accelerated the race to achieve intelligence dominance; and disrupted authority patterns.
- Second, while irrationalism was rampant, advantages accrued to those states that recognized the importance of educating scientists and engineers, competing for them, and funding their research, eventually on industrial scales.
- Third, the transition of national intelligence functions from diplomatic and military establishments to professional national intelligence organizations confused decision-making between 1900 and 1940. Although the resulting uncertainties affected all states, it seems reasonable to hypothesize, given lessons from the prior case study, that those, such as Britain, that responded by reforming intelligence-related institutions gained advantages over those, such as Stalin's Soviet Union, that repeatedly purged them.

- Fourth, once established, professional intelligence services posed a threat to regimes, whether democracies or autocracies, because they challenged old mindsets with the relentless presentation of "facts," including those clandestinely acquired. Trust in those facts required, in turn, trust in the bureaucrats, agents, and clandestine processes with which statesmen were unfamiliar. Intelligence had shifted in the minds of leaders from the "eyes and ears" of the cavalry or royal siblings to the "cloak and dagger" of espionage institutions. Those states that had systems of governance that could adapt to the shift fared better than those that could not or would not.

Although no European state was likely to achieve a lasting advantage over others in such circumstances, the British at least came to understand, belatedly, that they needed an overall vision for avoiding the worst consequences of national unrest, surprise attack, and imperial decline. Out of this vision, Britain's Commonwealth and its special relationship with the United States would be born—a relationship that had, at its core, the most vigorous and lasting intelligence partnership the world had ever seen.

* * *

This chapter represents an effort to map the information environment during the era of total war. The next examines key decisions to determine how well statesmen learned, how they tried to improve their intelligence, and how, in specific circumstances, they gained information advantages over competitors. Did they use national intelligence institutions for peacetime espionage, cable tapping, or clandestine influence operations? It was not necessarily obvious to them that they should do so.

Before WWI, foreign ministers still sat atop the main engines of foreign information collection for national policymaking: their networks of ambassadors, envoys, and consular officers. The inherently political missions of diplomats did not yet seem separate from, let alone incompatible with, intelligence collection, transmission, and analysis for national security decision-making. Diplomatic information-gathering, conducted by a transnational elite, was widely accepted, if not always trusted.[167] But this reliance on diplomats also meant that intelligence advantages followed national or imperial footprints, while vital interests were expanding beyond them. The problem for British diplomats was, of course, that the decision for where and when war would come would not be theirs. That they knew more, in general, about politics from the Americas to the Far East did not mean that they had such advantages in a particular place, such as Serbia. It was there that Austria-Hungary could, and did, drag a blinkered Britain into world war.

Understanding Diplomatic Decision-Advantage:
Methodological Issues for the Period
from WWI to WWII

A few methodological issues arise as we move on to investigate how advantages in knowing affected diplomatic decisions before WWI and WWII. The first concerns how to bound relevant decision-making, given ambiguous chains of command and the overlap of domestic politics and foreign policy in the tracing of statesmen's decision-making. Learning styles differ among statesmen and diplomats more than they do among military commanders, who are trained now, as they were a century ago, in command, procedure, and doctrine. In comparison with military decision-making on the battlefield, national decision-making in the early twentieth century seems to have had an almost laissez-faire aspect. After all, Tsar Nicholas once said that he learned all he needed to know about British strategy from reading *The Times*.[168]

To solve this problem, the analysis will once again focus on key decisions, but will have to include the informational basis for all those influencing them—a daunting task that leaves open the possibility that someone not in the room or outside the evident chain of command played a larger role than the historical record suggests.

The second methodological issue concerns the definition of a "diplomatic win" in historical context. For example, that we now know that the era of total war involved horrific loss of life does not mean that we know that decisions to go to war in July 1914 were somehow wrong for the states that made them at the time. Diplomacy does not fail when war comes, any more than police patrols or cavalry fail if their operations reveal "hostiles," and battle ensues. Keeping order at lowest cost is the mission, which extends to re-establishing order once threats to it are addressed. The tremendous shifts in global power generated by the industrial revolution required adjustments to the international order of some kind; to believe that Austria-Hungary was wrong to gamble on war in 1914 is either to superimpose a preference for today's map of Europe on a nineteenth-century imperial regime, or to suggest that we know what the counterfactual outcome (a negotiated settlement) would have been when we do not. War, Vienna's chosen alternative to negotiation, had a chance of success in 1914, even though we now know it hastened the empire's demise at horrifically steep costs.

To simplify this methodological issue, we will focus the WWI discussion on Austro-Hungarian, German, and British decision-making before the ultimatum to Serbia was delivered, and on the Munich Crisis of 1938. In both 1914 and 1938, Britain had a clear interest in avoiding war, while first Austria-Hungary, and then Germany, were clearly intent on fighting one. These circumstances lend a crispness to the identification of decision-advantage that is missing when examining

Russia's options, for example. That we know Britain's foreign secretary in 1914, Sir Edward Grey, moved a reticent Cabinet to arms may look like a historical success, but it ought not prejudice our evaluation of whether he failed to demand intelligence on Austria-Hungary's plans before Britain's choices distilled into the single option of war. Vienna's plans and intentions were knowable; they were determined at a Council of Ministers meeting on 7 July, where full German backing was authoritatively (if erroneously) asserted. London proved, however, largely incurious for weeks. Although Grey eventually did move the British Cabinet to war, he did so only after Germany had violated Belgian neutrality and, thus, international law. In the meantime, Germany and Austria controlled what Britain knew about their most critical decisions. As a result, the German kaiser got war before Britain could stop it, but also, arguably, a wider war than he wanted. That he miscalculated concerning British and, then, American intervention was a serious mistake perpetrated by bureaucrats with single-minded focus. Similar errors plagued Hitler in 1938 and 1939. Failed strategic intelligence helps explain why Germany started and lost two world wars fought over the same ground and similar stakes.

Diplomacy always involves a contest over information even if intelligence-sharing is part of negotiating mutual wins. When, however, irreconcilable interests are involved, intelligence is the art of getting more wins than losses. Diplomatic decision-advantage is, in such circumstances, no different from the military kind, although more complex because of its impingement on domestic politics, its bartering dynamics, and its potentially global scale. With each new decision, informational advantages can be lost or gained, but the effects inevitably ripple forward, making decisions either progressively easier or more difficult.

Still, even in the run-up to war, determining whether intelligence advantages contributed to winning decisions can be difficult. Leaders may decide to forfeit tactical intelligence advantages to gain strategic advantages later, risking the chance that changes in leadership might cause the original rationale to be forgotten or lost. Such forfeiture of near-term informational advantage for long-term gain is, unfortunately, often difficult to uncover from the historical record, making leaders look more ignorant than they were, and agents look unproductive when they were anything but that. Intelligence may also not register clear wins until strategies play out and policies or forces clash. The following cases explore decisions and strategies that played out as global war, so unearthing their provenance is worth the effort.

11

Gaining Diplomatic Advantages
before World War I

Let me testify to this, my fellow citizens, I not only did not know it
until we got into this war, but I did not believe it when I was told that
it was true, that Germany was not the only country that maintained
a secret service. Every country in Europe maintained it, because
they had to be ready for Germany's spring upon them, and the only
difference between the German secret service and the other secret
services was that the German secret service found out more than the
others did! (Applause and laughter) And therefore Germany sprang
upon the other nations at unawares [sic], and they were not ready
for it.

—President Woodrow Wilson, speech, 5 September 1919[1]

Although we now know that professional intelligence services played minor roles
in the diplomatic decisions of the Great Powers before WWI, this chapter will
show that intelligence, understood as competitively acquired information, still
mattered. Statesmen gained intelligence advantages *despite* the general uncertainty of the times and the weaknesses of national intelligence services. In a climate of great uncertainty, however, even "winning" decisions of the moment can
be ill-informed and damaging in the long term. The results, in this case, plunged
great powers into a debilitating war. By the time Nazi aggression threatened to
plunge the world into WWII, intelligence services had improved, but not enough
to spare the great powers from catastrophic choices.

The complex history of the era of total war has led to a substantial literature
on war guilt, particularly regarding WWI. We need not revisit all the arguments
about causes and blame here. What we want to know is whether intelligence-
advantages led to diplomatic victories and, if so, when and how they did.

Regarding WWI, historical scholarship makes this much seem clear: Austria-
Hungary, backed by Germany, attempted a local war against Serbia that required
swift action before other Great Powers could learn of it and react. At most,
both powers planned a wider European war only if it proved necessary.[2] After
7 July 1914, Austria-Hungary's plan implied a joint intelligence strategy with

Decision Advantage. Jennifer E. Sims, Oxford University Press. © Oxford University Press 2022.
DOI: 10.1093/oso/9780197508046.003.0011

Germany: *withholding information* to achieve surprise; *releasing information* to shape perceptions; *sharing information* to coordinate diplomatic and military contingencies; and then *gathering and assessing foreign reactions* so that strategy and tactics might be adjusted in time. The questions are: First, did Berlin and Vienna actually have such an intelligence strategy, or were they making ad hoc, poorly informed decisions? Second, to what extent did other powers attempt to learn what they were up to, and how good were they at doing so?

To answer these questions, we will look at four critical decisions in the lead up to war: Austria-Hungary's July 7 decision to launch a war on Serbia; Germany's decision to provide her support; Britain's decision at that time to look the other way; and Russia's decision not to—a choice that spared Russia the surprise and paralysis that later afflicted Britain. These four decisions constituted the foundation for the July Crisis, which exploded with Austria's 23 July ultimatum to Serbia, progressed with Russia's general mobilization, and concluded with rolling declarations of war that, following the German invasion of Belgium, at last included Britain as well.

What is striking is how far removed from uncertainties described in the last chapter seem the discussions in which these decisions were made, and the poverty of intelligence involved in the making of them. While airplanes, cameras, wireless radios, automated encryption, and the tradecraft of human espionage were all revolutionizing capacities for assessing foreign powers, diplomatic powerbrokers were not using them, or even asking first-order questions about how they might affect national security strategy. While scientists, businessmen, laborers, financiers, and artist-philosophers were exploding out of the intellectual confines of the preindustrial world, the statesmen deciding events in July 1914 thought and acted comfortably within them—certain of what they knew, and incurious about what they did not.

In fact, a review of these decisions sheds light on a point often missed in the histories of this period: for three weeks or so, Austria sought to manipulate the decision-making of other Great Powers through policies that today we would call "information operations"; yet this effort, which initially had all the markings of an intelligence success, was not one. Austrian statesmen thought they knew what Germans were thinking when they did not, expected decision-makers in Britain to know more than they did, and wanted those in Russia to know less than they did. Any informational advantages gained were serendipitous, not engineered, and were therefore slowly recognized and quickly lost.

Vienna's Council of Ministers Decides for War on 7 July, 1914

Nine days after the assassination of the archduke, the Ministerial Council of Austria-Hungary met under the chairmanship of the emperor's foreign minister,

Count Leopold von Berchtold. Count Alexander von Hoyos served as secretary, and Conrad von Hötzendorf, chief of the general staff, attended as a guest.[3] In the course of four hours, the members of the council generally agreed to a strategy for regaining the Dual Monarchy's power and international standing through a preventive, local war triggered by an ultimatum Serbia could not possibly accept. They planned that the war would stay local by means of a surprise fait accompli, German deterrence of Great Power intervention, diplomatic initiatives to bind Romania to German purposes, and secrecy. This last tool would lower the risks of leaks and Italy's preemptive defection from the Triple Alliance. Details would be hammered out later.[4] These decisions constituted the strategy that guided Austria-Hungary's actions until the outbreak of WWI.[5]

The council members could rapidly take these decisions for two principal reasons: First, as discussed in the prior chapter, most members came to the meeting on 7 July with a common mindset, including intent on securing the Dual Monarchy at a moment of existential peril; second, their presumptive leader, Foreign Minister Berchtold, had a plan that seemed strongly supported by the intelligence available to the council.[6] The intelligence was, however, politicized, privatized, and incomplete, leading council members to believe, wrongly, that they had advantages that could be sustained.

Mindsets and Their Intelligence Consequences

The common mindset, in addition to elements described in the previous chapter, had a special Central European twist in this instance. As recently as December 1913, the tsar's minister in Belgrade, Nikolai Genrikhovich Hartwig, had thrown down a gauntlet: "After the question of Turkey it is now the turn of Austria. Serbia will be our best instrument. The day draws near when you, Bulgarians, will have Macedonia and when Serbia will take back *her* Bosnia and *her* Herzegovina."[7] Since Bosnia had recently been annexed by Austria-Hungary, most council members saw the assassination as part of a well-understood diplomatic battlefield pitting order against insurgency, and Austro-Hungary and Germany against Serbia and Russia. Almost no one on the council saw investigation into culpability for the archduke's assassination as necessary, or their rights of retribution as questionable. The perpetrator was presumptively the Belgrade government in collaboration with the pan-Slav cultural organization Narodna Odbrana, founded in 1908 in the midst of the annexation crisis, and linked to the government in Belgrade.[8] They viewed the newly victorious and enlarged Serbia as a threat not just to the emperor, but also to the tsar, kaiser, and king. Although a changing constellation of power on the Continent had complicated the old "concert" of conservative powers, council members nevertheless believed that the aftermath of regicide offered their best chance for settling accounts in the Balkans without triggering Great Power war.

The consequences of mindsets are often difficult to identify, but in this case, they are not. When Foreign Minister Berchtold decided to change the agenda for the 7 July meeting from the advertised topics of security and culpability for the murders to the question of retribution against Serbia, council members did not oppose the decision. By changing the agenda, however, Berchtold suppressed intelligence—whether wittingly or not. Potential sources of that intelligence were the finance minister, Leon Ritter von Biliński and, perhaps, his nemesis, General Oskar Potiorek. Biliński served as the Dual Monarchy's administrator for Bosnia and Herzegovina. In that capacity, he had met with Serbia's minister in Vienna, Jovan Jovanović, before the assassination and had received from him a specific warning about the danger to the archduke. At the time, Biliński did not report what he had learned to Berchtold, perhaps because he believed the report too vague or redundant. Vienna had received copious intelligence about the Black Hand's conspiratorial agenda and its bitter feud with the Belgrade government, including as recently as the first months of 1914. After the assassination, however, Biliński's intelligence was important both for reassessing Belgrade's culpability and for determining how Russia would perceive any Austro-Hungarian attack on Serbia, given what Russia likely knew Vienna had been told by Belgrade's emissary. Biliński knew that his source, the Serbian envoy, had strong associations with the Black Hand, and was in a position to know about the threat. Biliński also knew the envoy was taking great risks in informing him—almost certainly at the direction of the Serbian government.[9]

Yet Biliński had not wanted to hear about the threat at the time, and he certainly did not want the council to dwell on the warning after the assassination. A Slav himself, he had begun experimental policies of conciliation toward Slavic protestors in the provinces that had been strongly opposed by General Potiorek, who commanded security forces in Bosnia-Herzegovina. Their rivalry had peaked in the weeks before the assassination, during which Potiorek had barely escaped death himself. As the 7 July council meeting approached, Biliński probably also feared that he would be embarrassed by his former advocacy of a more lenient policy toward the Slavs.[10] Berchtold's switch in the agenda spared Biliński some embarrassment and allowed the latter to keep to himself his intelligence about Belgrade's effort at forewarning, which reduced Serbia's culpability.[11]

This silence, the indirect consequence of a collective mindset that discounted any need to investigate, would prove disastrous. Belgrade's attempt to forewarn Vienna had likely already come to the Russians' attention, making Vienna's accusations against Narodna Odbrana suspect, and retribution against Belgrade even less legitimate in Russian eyes.[12] By failing to explore the issue, Viennese decision-makers underestimated the likelihood that Russia would see Vienna's evidence against Belgrade as trumped-up, its retribution as unjustified, and its policies as deceptive.

Berchtold's Plan and Its Intelligence Underpinnings

Berchtold's power as Austrian foreign minister, including his command of diplomatic intelligence, constituted the second reason for the swift decision-making on 7 July. According to tradition, diplomacy was one thing and war quite another. Until decisions for war released the military to settle accounts, the foreign minister, reporting to the emperor, could control the diplomatic agenda with little input from the military.

Berchtold moved swiftly. As early as 1 July, the usually reticent foreign minister "commanded and managed" decision-making in Vienna.[13] He continued to do so during the council meeting of 7 July and through the rest of the crisis.[14] His purpose was to further a plan for swift attack and subjugation of Belgrade—an uncharacteristic position for the usually cautious foreign minister. The outlook for Austria-Hungary had long been grim, her situation needy, and her German ally seemingly unreliable. In prior crises, Berchtold had supported the emperor's inclination to avoid war. The foreign minister and the council had generally relied on the principles of Great Power "concert" to preserve a larger European peace.[15] Following the assassination, Berchtold's new plan abandoned these principles based on intelligence he thought was solid. It was not.

Before discussing this intelligence in detail, it is important to note that Berchtold relied on a disciplined, tightly driven policy process within his own ministry. In fact, by June 1914, the Foreign Ministry was in the grip of a cabal of hawks who were inspired by the conservative idea of old Austria restored to her prior Habsburg glory.[16] Berchtold's predecessor, Count Alois Lexa von Aehrenthal, had recruited these men, who were neither schooled diplomats nor objective intelligence providers. Regarding themselves as operatives, they had a preference for the kind of bold moves their mentor had made during the Bosnian Annexation Crisis of 1908.[17] They included Baron Alexander von Musulin, Count Alexander von Hoyos, Count János Forgách (former minister in Belgrade), Count Frigyes Szapáry (ambassador to St. Petersburg), Baron Leopold von Andrian-Werburg, Baron Georg von Franckenstein, Emanuel Urbas, and Ottokar Czernin.[18] Led by Forgách, these hawks believed they knew what Austria needed to do in response to the Sarajevo outrage: a decisive strike against Serbia. They had, indeed, already assembled most of the intelligence they needed to make their case.

Austria-Hungary's Intelligence Prior to the Decision for War, 7 July 1914.

Six crucial intelligence products supported Berchtold's plan for a swift strike against Serbia: evidence of Russian encirclement provided by the Austrian ambassador to Romania; evidence of Russian machinations in Serbia and Bosnia after the assassination; evidence from espionage of secret Anglo-Russian naval talks; a comprehensive analysis of Russian motives and Austro-Hungarian options; analysis of Britain's likely neutrality in any European conflict; and, perhaps most crucially, evidence of German backing for whatever Vienna chose to do in retaliation for the assassination.

The first critical pieces of intelligence concerned Russia. One important one came from Ottokar Czernin, the Austro-Hungarian ambassador in Romania and older brother to Otto Czernin, who was a member of Aehrenthal's diplomatic cabal mentioned earlier. Romania was the fourth, albeit secret, member of the Triple Alliance of Germany, Austria-Hungary, and Italy. According to Czernin's reports from mid-June, relations between Bucharest and the Entente powers, particularly Russia, had been improving—and dangerously so. Moreover, Romania's long-feared defection had, for all practical purposes, already occurred. Czernin had strong evidence for this view. Just a couple of weeks before the archduke's assassination, Tsar Nicholas had visited Romania, where the king had welcomed him warmly. The Romanian people had seemed unusually enthusiastic. What's more, Sergei Sazonov, the Russian foreign minister, had "conspicuously crossed into Transylvania to show support for the Romanians who lived under Magyar rule."[19] This development alarmed Budapest and Vienna's Foreign Office because Hungary had a significant Romanian population that posed an irredentist threat.

Romania's loss to the Alliance would, from a military perspective, double the size of the Russo-Austrian boundary along Austria's northern (Galician) frontier, increasing the potential threat from Russia if Austria were to send troops south to fight Serbia. Should Romania become neutral or slide into the Russian camp, which seemed to be the tsar's purpose, Austria would have a greater vulnerability to her rear, increasing the importance of a timely German intervention and reminding all of Austria's relative weakness and dependency. Czernin's analysis grimly described how others saw the Dual Monarchy in mid-June 1914:

> Since last year and the behavior of Austria Hungary during the [Balkan] war, the firm conviction has grown here, as in many other parts of Europe, that the Monarchy is an entity doomed to downfall and dissolution, that at the partition of Turkey we have inherited nothing from her but her fate—that, in other words in the near future the Hapsburg Monarchy will be put up to European auction.[20]

The ambassador went on to describe what he believed to be a deliberate Russian policy of encirclement designed to exploit the monarchy's weakness: "Before our eyes in broad daylight, plain for all to see, the encirclement of the Monarchy proceeds glaringly, with shameless effrontery, step by step. . . . And we stand by with folded arms interestedly observing the carrying out of this onslaught."[21] This analysis of Austria's dilemma was not new—the idea of encirclement had been repeatedly expressed in Berlin and Vienna—but it offered new evidence for it, while emphasizing the need to take corrective action soon.

Two additional pieces of intelligence had made Russia's malign intentions seem both more vivid and more credible. First, the Austrian military attaché in Belgrade had sent back numerous press clippings that called for pan-Slav "liberation" in the wake of the assassination. Potiorek had also informed the ministers in Vienna that agitation in Serbia made restoring order in Bosnia nearly hopeless. This intelligence reconfirmed the dangerous connection between Serbian unrest and fragility within the empire proper. To make matters worse, Russian fingerprints now seemed all over the disturbances: Nikolai Hartwig, the Russian ambassador in Belgrade and an influential advisor to the Serbian minister-president, Nikola Paschich (Pašić), had reportedly played a game of bridge after hearing of the assassination and had refused to lower the Russian flag. Having long fanned the flames of pan-Slavism, Hartwig now seemed to be implicating Russia in the atrocity, if only by his public indifference to it.

To Austrians, the newspaper reports of Serbian protests, especially in the context of Hartwig's rude reaction to the outrage, seemed the play of a Russian hand.[22] Such news from Belgrade was laced with rumor, but it complemented the word on the street in Vienna, where spontaneous demonstrations were taking place outside the Russian embassy as early as 2–3 July.[23] Despite lack of authoritative conclusions regarding the true sponsors of the assassination, Austrians seemed convinced that Russia's puppet government in Belgrade was to blame, and that the time was ripe for taking care of the Serbian problem.[24]

Another piece of intelligence on Russia concerned secret Anglo-Russian naval talks, which seemed to confirm the threat of encirclement. Berchtold likely knew of this intelligence through his contacts in Berlin, but it is unclear how many other members of the council knew of the sensitive sourcing behind it. Berlin's source was a German spy embedded in the Russian embassy, and the secrecy of his information made the naval talks seem particularly suspicious.[25] In fact, discussions of an Anglo-Russian naval understanding had been underway for some weeks. Russian Foreign Minister Sazonov had been referring to them in messages to his ambassador in London.[26] Now rumors of the talks were out in the street. Hearing of the leak but not knowing its source, the British foreign minister, Sir Edward Grey, felt compelled to deny before the House of Commons that Britain had any naval commitments to Russia, but he did not deny the discussions. He followed up by meeting with the German ambassador. In light of the spy's intelligence, however, Grey's clarifications seemed unconvincing, particularly to those sitting around the table in Vienna on 7 July.

Within the highest councils in Vienna, these new pieces of intelligence reinforced the perceived urgency of the monarchy's situation, but did not frame choices. Berchtold knew prior to the council meeting of 7 July that he needed to galvanize the council to action, which required German buy-in. He needed a comprehensive analysis pointing to practical next steps that council members and their German counterparts could endorse. Just such a study had been sitting, fortuitously, in the Foreign Ministry on the day of the assassination. Weeks before and at Berchtold's request, Franz von Matscheko, senior section chief for the Balkans in the Austrian Foreign Ministry, had prepared a paper on the challenge facing the Dual Monarchy in the wake of the Balkan wars and new Russian policies. He had finished it on 24 June, four days before the archduke's murder. Matscheko's paper was just what Berchtold needed.

Overall, Matscheko's analysis captured the council's preexisting worldview, but it added details and spelled out a course of action. On the upside, according to his analysis, Bulgaria seemed to have awakened from its earlier pro-Serbian trance. The new Albanian state also offered a bulwark against Serbian advance. On the downside, tensions with Italy were increasing, Romania's loyalties were uncertain and Serbia had doubled in size. The contraction of Turkey in Europe meant she could no longer serve as a counterweight to Russia there. And Franco-Russian policies had taken on a more aggressive character since Agadir and the election of French prime minister Raymond Poincaré, who had worked with Russia to tighten the noose around the Triple Alliance (among Germany, Austro-Hungary, and Italy).[27] In the author's view, none of these adjustments were the simple playing out of changing power relationships on the Continent. Rather, the tsar's aims were driving the power shift now underway—an aggressive, modern step in Russia's two-hundred-year "march to the sea." In this context, Russia's diplomatic initiatives and increasing military capabilities threatened an offensive war within a few years.[28] The upshot: Germany, no less than Austria-Hungary, had to fear for the future, which could be salvaged only with swift action. The memo prescribed a more assertive foreign policy to thwart Russia's encirclement and the building of new fortifications to compensate for the loss of Romania.[29]

Although the initial draft of 24 June emphasized diplomacy to shore up the Alliance, Berchtold took the opportunity in the aftermath of the assassination to add words suggestive of the need for immediate *military action* against Serbia:

The whole consequences of this heinous murder cannot yet be fathomed today. At least, however, it has delivered the indubitable evidence, if such was still required, for the unbridgeable difference between the Monarchy and Serbia as well as for the danger and intensity of the pan-Serbian movement which will stop at nothing. . . . All the more important is for the Monarchy the necessity to tear apart with a determined hand the threads which her opponents want to weave into a net above her head.[30]

This addition to the memo reflected the views of Berchtold's advisers in the Foreign Ministry, who planned to trap the Hungarian premier, Count István Tisza, into support for an attack on Serbia.

Berchtold had known well before the 7 July meeting that he had to neutralize Count Tisza, who had concerns about the kaiser's volatility on Balkan matters. On 30 June, Berchtold and Emperor Franz Joseph had agreed on the possible need for a military strike, provided Germany concurred. But the emperor had asked Berchtold to coordinate with Tisza, who, on 1 July, had conveyed to the emperor his concern that Berlin might leave Vienna in the lurch.[31]

Berchtold was not concerned. He had intelligence from the German ambassador and the influential reporter Viktor von Neumann that the kaiser would now back a preventive war.[32] Berchtold saw his problem more as one of neutralizing Tisza's opposition rather than exploring German views.[33] He decided to take the revised Matscheko memorandum, which Tisza had originally inspired (minus the veiled call for war), as the analytical basis for approaching Berlin.[34] Berchtold presented the memorandum to the emperor on 4 July and received the latter's authorization to send it to the German kaiser, covered by a personal letter from the emperor implicitly conveying the need to use force to sort out the Serbian problem.

Although these documents contained no *explicit* decision for war, Berchtold selected Count Hoyos, chief of the cabinet in the Foreign Ministry and one of the most hawkish of Berchtold's small group, to deliver them to Berlin *in advance* of the council meeting. In this way, Berchtold hoped to bring back intelligence on Germany's official position that would erase all possible doubts about German backing for war.

During meetings in Berlin with acting foreign minister Arthur Zimmermann, Hoyos went well beyond the emperor's official memorandum to elaborate on the energy and commitment with which Austrian action against Serbia would occur. He even referred to possible territorial adjustments that would come from Austria's expected victory over Belgrade. None of Hoyos's musings reflected an official Viennese, much less Hungarian view; Austria-Hungary's Council of Ministers had yet to meet. Indeed, Austria's ambassador, Ladislaus von Szögyény-Marich, held parallel conversations with the kaiser that did not cover the sensitive topic of territorial spoils. But Hoyos knew what he was doing. His aggressive talk was meant to convey Vienna's resolve, the necessity for which had been made clear by Hoyos's hawkish contacts in the German Foreign Ministry.

If Vienna wanted German backing for whatever the Council of Ministers might decide, including the question of war, there could be no wavering. Hoyos thus returned to Vienna with what he and the ambassador believed to be a "blank check" from Germany for Austrian action as she saw fit.[35]

The impression that would be left in Berlin was that Austria had not yet made up its mind, which was technically true. In fact, the intelligence Hoyos brought back to Vienna and which Ambassador Szögyény-Marich's report seemed to support—that Germany would have Austria-Hungary's back no matter what she decided to do on the Serbian question—poorly reflected the more complicated reactions of the interlocutors in Berlin.[36] In fact, implicit in the formal reply delivered by the German chancellor was a split opinion in Berlin and, in fact, in the mind of the kaiser himself. While formally approving next steps for Austria-Hungary's proposed diplomatic initiatives, the kaiser believed other (military) measures were for Austria to decide. Informally, the chancellor, on behalf of himself and the kaiser, advised attacking Serbia quickly. But, as Hoyos's report made clear, this more explicit support for the immediate use of force was conveyed by the chancellor as his unofficial view.[37] For his part, the kaiser seemed confused. He had told German chancellor Theobald von Bethmann-Hollweg on 5 July that he did not want Germany on record as supporting war; on 6 July, he nonetheless seems to have authorized the chancellor's informal message urging Vienna to conduct a quick strike; and on 7 July he told the head of Krupp industries that "this time" he would not "back down" if war should be necessary.[38] The kaiser seemed to want a local war without his fingerprints—an odd form of support, and certainly no "blank check."

Hoyos's mission to Berlin thus returned with diplomatic "intelligence" for the council's deliberations on July 7 that was full of unanalyzed contradictions. Not only did the German kaiser, Austria-Hungary's most important ally, approve of prompt action, he *insisted* on it, according to Germany's bilateral ambassador in Vienna. At the same time, the German government expected the Viennese government *to decide for itself* what Austria should do regarding Serbia. Although Berlin promised to "stand with" Austria, it would do so as a *good ally*. There were no specifics offered about what this meant in the context of a defensive alliance that included Italy, whose interests Vienna planned to ignore as it launched its offensive. Germany's diplomatic delivery of "full support" included no assurances that military coordination in support of Austrian war planning would be forthcoming.

Berchtold, nonetheless, heard what he wanted to hear about German intentions. He told the chief of the general staff, Baron Franz Conrad von Hötzendorf, that "Germany will stand by our side unequivocally, even if our operations against Serbia will bring about the great war. Germany advises us to strike at once."[39] Berchtold assumed Germany would provide military support for an immediate, limited war with Serbia, even if the Russian army were to become involved.

Conrad, who wanted war, knew better but said nothing. When Hoyos reported that Zimmermann had said that the German military was ready, Conrad laughed at him and said Zimmermann did not know what he was talking about.[40] Forgách, Berchtold's advisor in the ministry, nonetheless reported Berchtold's interpretation to Tisza: "We could rely on the full support of Germany in a potential action."[41]

Given what we know from the previous chapter about the disconnects between military and diplomatic decision-making at the time, Berchtold was taking an extraordinary analytical leap. Indeed, Forgách's message to Tisza seems good evidence, along with Hoyos's report, that the council meeting on 7 July was in fact *engineered* to take the decision for war. No pressure seems to have been put on Conrad to explain whether and how Germany's military support could be effected. And Conrad, for reasons of his own, did not offer any warning before the council meeting of 7 July or, as we shall see, during it.

Berchtold had, however, one other concern that he thought might affect the council's decision. If Russia were to mobilize and Germany's deterrence fail, Britain might become involved. In a Great Power war that included all the Entente powers, Germany and Austria could lose. It was with regard to this last point—Russian and British intentions—that a second analysis from Berchtold's ministry seems to have influenced him. On 6 July, an official in the ministry, Berthold Molden, wrote a memo that included, in addition to many of the points in Matscheko's analysis, an estimate of British capabilities and intentions with respect to the contingency of an Austrian attack on Serbia.[42] Noting that Austria's interests lay in a bolstering of the Triple Alliance without triggering a war with Russia, he argued that the chances of the latter would be reduced "probably also by England's attitude":

It cannot be assumed that England would consider a war involving the entire European continent as lying in her interest, quite apart from economic considerations which [sic] must confront her. For England, a German victory would be unwelcome, a victory of Russia would also be extremely uncomfortable; *she will therefore strive, as much as it lies in her power, to work for localization of an Austro-Hungarian war. Sensibly England would welcome a defeat of Serbia and the accompanying moral defeat of Russia.*[43]

Molden's analysis was a wild estimate, even if British behavior had long been erratic in these regards. Despite the certainty with which he wrote, Molden appears to have had no new evidence to back up his speculations. What he got correct was obvious: Britain did not want a European war. What was missing or incorrect was knowable: London's assessment of the likelihood that Austria would attempt to conduct a local war without Germany's backing, and of Russia's capacity to limit war in response. Britain thought the chances of either to be negligible.[44]

In fact, there is no record that Count Ottokar von Czernin, the chargé d'affaires in St. Petersburg, had conveyed to anyone in Vienna the Russian foreign minister's warning that cross-border retribution of the kind Austrian newspapers were advocating would be a "dangerous road" that Austria ought not take.[45] Moreover, Molden offered no sound military argument that Russia could partially mobilize without triggering a full German mobilization. German involvement, given her long-standing plan to attack France at the outset of any European war, meant larger European complications would necessarily follow that might force Britain's hand. Thus, the very signals Austria hoped for from Germany—particularly a willingness to defend the northern frontier—would be signals that Britain had to intervene on the side of the Entente. Whether a choice had to be made between surprising Britain with a fait accompli or recruiting her to Austria's punitive cause and limited aims remained unanalyzed. The critical issue, which remained implicit in the analysis—how Britain might best be prevented from intervening on the Franco-Russian side—was left unanswered by either the German or Austrian ambassadors in London. In fact, it was never asked of them.[46]

Intelligence for Decision-Making on 7 July

What remains to review is the impact all this deliberately acquired and circulated information—that is, "intelligence"—had on the deliberations of the council. Although, as mentioned earlier, we do not have a list of all those who read the intelligence recounted above, we do know that during the 7 July meeting, Berchtold elaborated on Matscheko's and Molden's boldest ideas.[47] These included the notion of encirclement, joint jeopardy for the dual alliance, and the need for an Austrian offensive before time whittled away all military advantage. He left the issue of British neutrality in the coming conflict—arguably the most uncertain point—presumptively aside. After first acknowledging that the assassination raised issues of internal security in Bosnia that had to be addressed, he pointed to the need, before all else, of using the situation afforded by the Sarajevo outrage to deal with Serbia "once and for all" with a "show of force."[48]

Presupposing the need for such a "decisive stroke," he reported that he had made Austria's case to Germany with "very satisfactory" results. Berchtold reported that the kaiser and his chancellor had "emphatically promised us the absolute support and aid of Germany in the eventuality of a warlike complication with Serbia." With respect to Italy's and Romania's interests, Berchtold mentioned little or nothing of Germany's suggested diplomatic initiatives to strengthen the Triple Alliance, emphasizing instead that Berlin agreed that "it would be better to act and await eventual claims to compensation." It was, therefore, Berchtold's plan, he told the council, that Rome and Bucharest would *not be apprised* of Austria-Hungary's plans. With respect to the Russian problem, things could only get worse and inaction would seem to be weakness to all other powers. The debilitating "process" working against Austria had to be stopped, and better now than later. Assuming an informational advantage implicit in acting quickly, Berchtold insisted that it would be best to use it to get "in advance of our foes" by a "timely reckoning with Serbia," because waiting would make such moves more dangerous.[49]

These words must have satisfied Conrad, the chief of the general staff, though they no doubt also made him squirm. The chief was only a guest at the council (he was to brief its members in a special session later that day), but Berchtold had already coordinated with him concerning the Hoyos mission to Germany and next steps. Conrad had long been a leading advocate for war against Serbia and had continued to advocate this line after the assassination, so his views fit neatly with the hard-line views of Berchtold's clique of hawkish advisors. Indeed, Conrad had urged the foreign minister as early as 30 June to recognize that the assassination was the moment for demonstrating strength through force. This implied implementing Austria's long-standing war plan against Serbia—a plan that entailed sending divisions south (Plan B for "Balkans") while holding other forces in reserve to augment troops on either the northern or southern frontiers, as necessary.

But Conrad also knew more intelligence than he likely shared, even in his later classified briefing. He knew that Austria's situation was far more dangerous than anyone around the table suspected, including Berchtold. In fact, Conrad's *withholding* of intelligence was almost as important as what he said in the days immediately following the assassination. Conrad knew five crucial facts better than anyone else:

- First, the treason of his former chief of military counterintelligence, Colonel Alfred Redl, meant that the Dual Monarchy's basic mobilization options were now known to the Russians. Redl's betrayal, discovered in May 1913, had forced expensive and complicated changes in Austria's military structure, but this remediation had not significantly changed mobilization plans, which were inflexible, slow to execute, and potentially contradictory to the requirements of the alliance with Germany—a fact that the Russians almost certainly now knew. That "conditions and prospects would never become better" was true, but conditions and prospects had also never been worse.[50]

Russia's military superiority, at least with respect to contingencies involving the Dual Monarchy, had already arrived.[51]

- Second, the chief of the German general staff, Helmuth von Moltke the Younger, had informed Conrad the month before that the German army *would not deploy in the east to support Austria at the outset of a European conflict.*[52] Conrad had been hoping for *more* German troops in the east, given Romania's changing status and the growth of Russian power. That hope had been dashed.[53] After hearing Moltke's revised plan for a European contingency in May, Conrad had complained in his diary that Austria was no longer a state, let alone an empire, because it was unable to operate independently.

- Third, Conrad knew that, given the defensive character of the Triple Alliance and Germany's military plan as described above, Vienna needed more than a promise to execute "alliance obligations" from Germany. To have any hope of pulling off a quick offensive against Serbia, *active diplomatic and military deterrence of Russia* would be required—neither of which were part of Germany's view of its obligations.[54] It was in this sense that Conrad realized the Hoyos mission had not received the assurance from Berlin that Austria needed for a local war.[55] Germany had, indeed, no plan for a limited war, or even a military deployment doctrine suitable for an active strategy of deterrence, and Conrad knew it.

- Fourth, Conrad knew that the civilian diplomats in Berlin, and even the kaiser (as opposed to the general staffs), didn't know what they didn't know, so promises of "full support" were empty of practical significance. The chancellor's affirmation of "alliance solidarity" did not reassure Conrad. Recall that he had laughed when Hoyos reported that Germany's acting foreign minister, Zimmermann, said he was "certain" that Germany "was strong enough to wage the war on both fronts alone," if necessary. Conrad had told Hoyos that Zimmermann did not know what he was talking about.[56] In truth, the German plan entailed a six-week war in the west against France before turning east against Russia; its inflexibility would be an open invitation for Russia to mobilize locally against Austria. Any Russian moves would, therefore, force Germany to provide allied "support," by launching a larger European war that would be, at best, a crapshoot.

- Conrad also knew that Austria was not ready for that European war. The reasons were personally embarrassing, which might explain how little he spoke of them during the early days of July 1914. The enormous expenses incurred since May 1913 in the cover-up and remediation of the Redl scandal, which had implicated Conrad's own son, had left its mark on the army and on him.[57] Redl had delivered a huge intelligence advantage to

Russia during his years of spying. Combined with budgetary restrictions and a certain hardheadedness in traditional military quarters, Redl's damage (intelligence on troop strength, communications lines, and war plans) had been considerable and long-lasting.[58]

Fearful of his own culpability in the Redl affair, Conrad was loath to report to civilian authorities the actual extent of Redl's damage. Furthermore, Conrad was confident that German military intelligence understood Austria was particularly weak along its northern frontier.[59] This frontier could, in theory, be reinforced with a mobile reserve but, despite Conrad's efforts, Austrian forces lacked the mobility, reconnaissance, and tactical warning to do this in a timely way. Aircraft for such missions were far fewer than Conrad had long wanted, while the Russians suffered no similar deficiency.[60] Germany could fill the gap in warning intelligence, of course, but such a critical dependency was itself unnerving. Once Germany's vital interests were jeopardized, Berlin could always use her superior intelligence to jerk Austria-Hungary's chain, forcing reinforcements from Vienna, and thus losses against Serbia, at a time of Berlin's choosing.

In sum, Conrad understood that no matter what assurances German *statesmen* had delivered, Austria-Hungary would not be master of her own military fate should she attack Serbia. Conrad almost certainly understood that a surprise attack in July 1914 could not produce a fait accompli. Such a feat required an endgame for which neither Germany nor Austria had a mutually acceptable plan, especially in the likely event that Russia considered mobilizing to compel Austrian retreat from Serbia. The Austrian army did not have the troops or railway system in place to allow a rapid deployment south to fight, win, and hold Serbia while forcing Russian troops to a halt on Austria's northern frontier. And if Germany came to Austria's defense by launching a wider war, Russian mobilization would trigger Austria's alliance obligation to counter Russian forces in Galicia while Germany finished fighting France—an obligation she would be unable to fulfill while securing gains in Serbia.[61]

There is evidence that Conrad lacked critical intelligence that may have skewed his judgment. He had wanted, for example, more aerial reconnaissance before the crisis of 1914, and he lacked critical intelligence on the condition of rails across Austria. In July 1914, Russia could run over 250 trains to the common frontier per day, whereas the Austrians could run only 153.[62] But with his mind made up, Conrad had no incentive to know more about the disaster he suspected was coming and was, in fact, unavoidable. It did not occur to him or to those statesmen making decisions in early July that what he did not know might make a difference to diplomatic decision-making.

That the bad odds for Austria were on Conrad's mind on 7 July is, however, beyond dispute. After the assassination, while speaking to the editor of the

Österreichische Rundschau, he alluded to his military angst over a war against Serbia: "In the years 1908–9 it would have been a game in which we could see all the cards, in 1912–13 it would have been a game with some chances of success, now it is a sheer gamble."[63] Actually, Conrad knew it was worse than that. He knew that the Germans were not preparing to deter Russia on Austria's behalf, only to defeat her, so an attack on Serbia effectively meant a European war. Yet, bad as the odds were, they were better than the odds would be a year or two later, given Russia's growing military capabilities. Conrad's view fit with Matscheko's: things could only get worse. But his grim conclusion about Austria's military position was kept even from his emperor. Franz Joseph had asked him on 5 July what Austria, having struck Serbia, would do if then "everyone will attack us." Conrad answered with a question: "But Germany will cover our rear?" Disturbed, the emperor reframed the question: "Are you *certain* of Germany?"[64] Conrad was noncommittal in replying, "Your Majesty, we must know how we are placed"—a disingenuous response, because he knew the answer, which was no.[65]

Although Berchtold had invited Conrad to brief the council on Austria's military capabilities on July 7, and he eventually did so in secret session, he likely did not share his deep pessimism. It appears that he did not even share his estimates of the time it would take to prepare an attack. To do so would have served to strengthen the arguments of Tisza, who still opposed military action lest it seem more like opportunism than retribution. In fact, Conrad saw hope for Vienna only in triggering world war; Count Tisza saw hope only in the patient diplomatic effort to build a stronger Triple Alliance. It seems likely that Conrad found it useful to support the Foreign Office's preference for a swift, local war *precisely because* a decisive victory over Serbia was effectively impossible without a European war. Indeed, there was no "local war" option that did not entail loss of the monarchy, *unless* Germany triggered a world war, since Austria did not have the troops to occupy Serbia for any length of time, let alone defend against an aroused Russia.

In any case, how could Conrad tell the council that his stewardship of the military had left Austria a mere satellite of Germany? Conrad knew that if the council decided to use force, it would be faced with an impossible subordinate decision: whether to save the Dual Monarchy from Russian invasion or from Serbia's pan-Slav insurgency and irredentism. The whole point of Vienna's lurch toward war was to save the Dual Monarchy, yet any of the options for use of force made that objective impossible. Irony of ironies, this had happened under his own watch—the watch of a military man who was one of the empire's most vocal hawks. Conrad briefed the council for the purposes of net assessment; he did not deliver one. Instead, he simply advocated attacking Serbia, knowing the consequences, but keeping them to himself.

The question is why. Some historians have suggested that Conrad chose to be desperately heroic for the sake of his lover; others have argued he did not have the intellectual ability to understand Austria's military dilemma.[66] But neither of these explanations seems as likely as the notion that he appreciated the dilemma, but saw Austria's situation as so desperate that only force of will in the context of general war could overcome her limitations. Indeed, given Austria's mobilization plans, it seems he planned to force Germany's hand by luring Russia into a deliberately created vacuum in Austria's north so Germany would have to implement its only planned option: attacking France through Belgium. Although we cannot prove this was true, certainly such brash planning was in his character and capacity. Unlike other military chiefs in Europe, Conrad had total oversight of Austria-Hungary's military establishment, from training to intelligence, reconnaissance, budget, planning, operations, liaison with Germany, and command.

Unfortunately for Berchtold, Conrad's withholding of intelligence on German military plans led to a later surprise for the Austrian foreign minister. Looking back, he confessed:

> I was completely ignorant of the fact that for Germany mobilization meant immediate entry into war. We did not know that the German plan of war implied from the first mobilization day offensive military operations and the violation of the neutrality of Belgium, and we hoped that if worst came to worst England would remain neutral.[67]

In any event, when Berchtold made a strong case on 7 July for striking Serbia, he expected Conrad's full backing—and he got it.[68] The council proved, however, to be no rubber stamp. In particular, Count Tisza smelled a rat. He knew the council meeting was a setup orchestrated by Conrad and the Foreign Office. These agitators for war were throwing the risks of Russian intervention in Hungary's lap. Romania's defection from the Triple Alliance threatened Hungary most of all because Bucharest had designs on Transylvania, Tisza's home turf. The Matscheko memorandum, which Tisza had supported, and perhaps even partially drafted in its original form, had emphasized the need to *strengthen* the Triple Alliance with new initiatives *to lure Romania and Bulgaria*, not to start a war. He therefore agreed with the memo but not the interpretation now being given to it. In fact, the framework for his advocacy of strengthened diplomacy had been stolen from him and used to argue for war, leaving him with no compelling counteranalysis.

Tisza hated "cleverness" and "parliamentary tactics."[69] He would not consent to "a surprise attack upon Serbia without a previous diplomatic action," and resented the fact that Hoyos, ostensibly sent on an intelligence mission, had ventured down this dangerous path in Berlin. Precipitous action without a diplomatic predicate would, in Tisza's view, reduce the Dual Monarchy's standing in all of Europe. Rash use of force against Serbia would trigger enmity among all except, perhaps, the Bulgarians, who were at the moment too weak to be of help. And even if force were the best option, Tisza pointed out, "It was not for Germany to decide whether we ought to strike against Serbia now or not"—a view Conrad knew, and could have told him, was in error.[70]

Personally, Tisza saw trends that were positive, such as the opportunity for a diplomatic opening to Bulgaria and Turkey, and the possibility of luring Romania back to the fold. These trends could strengthen the Triple Alliance over time, possibly even enlarging it. The declining birth rate in France might also free up more German troops for the fight against Russia at some future date. The first step, according to Tisza, should be "hard," but not impossible, demands conveyed to Belgrade. A diplomatic success would, Tisza argued, raise the monarchy's prestige and prevent the complications that would arise from resort to arms and a multi-front war, including with Romania. But if war should prove necessary, territorial demands must be eschewed because they would trigger a wider war. Russia would fight to the death to keep Serbia whole and, in any case, Hungary could not absorb more Serbs within the Dual Monarchy.

The rest of the council worked to change Tisza's mind. Berchtold began by making two points in response: First, Russia's increasing birth rate would more than compensate for France's declining one, so this point was irrelevant;[71] second, the Romanian problem would likely get worse, so concern about Bucharest's view could be no argument for inaction at the present time. Besides, Romania's King Carol had already said he could be of little help if war were to occur. Although Berchtold offered no evidence on these points, Tisza was not prepared to counter them. In truth, Russia's population actually had, like France's, been on decline since 1870.[72] And Germany had reasons for believing the Romanians might be lured back into the fold.

In any event, the imperial and royal premier, Count Karl von Stürgkh, supplemented Berchtold's arguments with domestic intelligence from the field, namely from General Potiorek, governor of Bosnia and Herzegovina. Potiorek had made clear in his reports that establishing internal security in Austria would be impossible without taking care of the external, Serbian threat with a "forcible stroke" first. Could Austria keep these two provinces of Bosnia and Herzegovina without stopping Serbian subversion at its source? Could she ever establish order there?

Minister Biliński, anxious now to back Potiorek and appear tough on Slavic unrest, supported Stürgkh's comments. Without swift action against Serbia, he opined, Bosnia would be more unmanageable than ever. Yet kTisza objected, pointing out that there was no evidence for this assertion, and that better administration of Bosnia could fix the problems there. Although Stürgkh disagreed with Tisza on this point, he agreed on another: that the question of force was for Austria to decide. And this was the larger matter. It was obvious from the intelligence Berchtold had collected over the past three days that the kaiser wanted swift and decisive action. If Austria failed to act now, Berlin might not be so willing to back Austria in her next time of need.[73] No one, including Tisza, questioned whether the kaiser knew the capabilities of his own military; it was just assumed that he did.

Then Stürgkh made a crucial point that was to infuse all subsequent decisions as an untested, but widely accepted assumption: if an immediate attack was eschewed so an ultimatum to Serbia could be issued and rejected first, and this was done primarily out of concern for hostile reactions abroad, as Tisza seemed to argue, then those diplomatic actions taken "for international reasons," *would have to be certain to result in war* and were, beyond this, just "a matter of detail." Stürgkh's comment seemed no more than a side-point, but it became a fundamental, and largely unexamined, assumption in the coming weeks. The logic was clear: if war was desirable, diplomacy to assuage its downside risks should not work against the desired plan. The diplomatic tool would be, in essence, for denial and deception only—a feint designed to gain time and international goodwill for Austria's war against Serbia, and nothing more.

Here was the point at which diplomacy and its positive intelligence function— the gathering of good information for decisions—parted ways. The council desired a war limited to either a swift, bilateral strike or a somewhat larger conflict among Germany, Austria-Hungary, and Russia. Diplomacy was viewed as an alternative to such a war, and therefore, just a sideshow. But diplomatic channels were also expected to manage matters and help discover solutions to prevent a global catastrophe. After the Hoyos mission and the council's decision to keep its intentions secret, however, diplomatic intelligence for subsequent decision-making in Vienna essentially ceased.

The Council's Decisions

With Berchtold's and Stürgkh's ideas in mind, the Council of Ministers thus came to three decisions that essentially locked down Austrian policy after 7 July:

- First, the ministers agreed that action against Serbia, whether warlike or peaceful, had to be swift.
- Second, military mobilization was "not to take place until after concrete demands have been addressed to Serbia and, after being refused, an ultimatum has been sent."

- Third, that "a purely diplomatic success, even if it ended with a glaring hu-miliation of Serbia, would be worthless."

These last two points logically rendered the first one a decision for war, whether it could be swift or not. In the coming days, the agreement on "con-crete demands," that is, tough requirements that Serbia could nonetheless meet (Tisza's preference), became an ultimatum designed to be unacceptable to any sovereign state. Anything short of that threatened to be that "purely diplomatic success" which would, in the minds of most of the Council members, mean de-feat. So the two-step process envisioned in the second decision—demands that, once rejected, would become an unacceptable ultimatum—became conflated into one. Diplomacy was to have only two tasks: to prepare in secret and then deliver such far-reaching demands that a Serbian refusal would be certain; and to open, by means of a cynical diplomatic deception, "the road to a radical solu-tion by means of a military action." Tisza's reservations, equally unsupported by convincing intelligence, had only persuaded the council to muddy its purpose and adopt a poorly framed strategy of diplomatic deception, not to reverse the decision for war.

The council took its decisions believing, erroneously, that Vienna's strategy of surprise gave her an enduring informational advantage that lowered risks. Members believed they had good information on the German government's views and the evolving security situation in the Austrian-Serbian border areas. Moreover, Vienna would continue to enjoy advantages of the initiative in de-ciding what to do about the assassination. The council, comforted by a uni-formity of view, failed to assess whether their presumed advantages in "knowing" could be sustained. Yet knowable facts, if analyzed, made it extremely unlikely intelligence-advantages could be sustained over the coming weeks:

- As a result of Redl's espionage, Russia had wiped out Austria's espionage net-work to such an extent that it had not recovered.[74] Moreover, Russia could intercept and decrypt all Austrian communications out of St. Petersburg, compromising any reporting on developments there, while the same was not true of Austria's ability to intercept Russian communications out of the Balkans and Austria.
- German decision-makers, seeking to distance themselves from Austrian actions, were scheduled to be out of country or on leave, and thus, relatively out of touch for liaison with Austrian diplomats and military attachés over the following weeks.
- Although Serbian and Russian penetration of Austria-Hungary was known, the extent of it was not fully understood. Suspicions were high that the Russian ambassador in Belgrade had extensive sources throughout Bosnia.

All this meant that Russia was bound to notice quickly any unusual military preparations that would need to be taken before Austria's ultimatum to Serbia.

- Diplomatic reporting was poor to non-existent. For example, Russia was no longer run by the advocates of peace, such as the former prime ministers Pyotr Stolypin or Vladimir Kokovtsov, but by these men's successor, the hostile Slavophile Ivan Goremykin and his "ambitious" cohort and minister of the interior, Nikolai Maklakov. The German ambassador in St. Petersburg, Count Friedrich von Pourtalès, knew this power shuffle had taken place, as his memoirs make clear, but "among the German documents there is not a single telegram or report from him in this sense, while there exist telegrams to the opposite effect."[75]

- Intelligence on British intentions was barely considered, despite London's history of brokering peaceful outcomes in the Balkans. Vienna planned to keep London in the dark in part to avoid such brokering initiatives, but without consideration of what London might do instead, or what signals from London might indicate that Vienna's plan would not work. Vienna assumed that the British would be distracted by imperial problems, such as the crisis in Ireland (and they were), but her ministers failed to plan for what would happen once she was not.

- Vienna had no assurances that Germany, which would likely have the best intelligence on developments in London, Paris, and St. Petersburg, would share that intelligence with Vienna.

- Reporting on Serbia and Russian activities there would decline precipitously as soon as the ultimatum was rejected and Austrian representation withdrawn.

- Intra-alliance intelligence-sharing with Italy would end as soon as Rome realized Austria-Hungary was acting against Italian interests and without forewarning.

In other words, having informational advantages over Belgrade on 7 July did not necessarily mean the Austrian Council of Ministers could sustain competitive advantages or situational awareness over the other Great Powers. No one, however, explored this problem and its implications for what Vienna might know right after the ultimatum was delivered, or one day into her offensive.

Summarizing the Austrian Case

One of the Council of Ministers' problems was a collegial style of decision-making that made intelligence questions seem contrary to a developing policy and made group-think more likely.[76] Despite the opening inclination toward war, group-think was, in this instance, less a passive than an engineered condition. A cabal of hawks, led by Berchtold, shaped the situational knowledge of those ministers sitting around the table on 7 July and the information flowing to the emperor. In the immediate aftermath of the assassination, these ministerial staffers sought evidence to support their position through private exchanges, such as those with influential German publicist Victor Naumann, who, in urging a swift strike, claimed official Germany would support it. They then launched a mission to Berlin that produced highly politicized reports on Germany's official point of view. These staffers used this intelligence to steer Austria-Hungary toward war.[77] Key members of the cabal would continue to meet throughout July, ensuring the necessary steps would be taken to achieve their goals. With the ministry running all intelligence operations in support of the council's deliberations, it was unlikely that intelligence would reach the council that ran against Berchtold's preferred outcomes.

Still, the outcome need not have been what it was. The council members bore responsibility for the outcome, as well. Tisza made good points but failed to press them or back them up with his own intelligence. Although the ministers' mindsets meant that standards for credible intelligence were low and their deference to the foreign ministry high, no one considered how they might know if their premises were wrong, or how they might change course if new intelligence suggested they should. It was not just that several senior decision-makers had reasons to hide what they knew; no one challenged the collective assumptions that allowed a rush to judgment. As a result, the "known unknowns" were not discussed or turned into requirements for diplomatic or military intelligence. For example, the council seemed to take for granted that other powers, *learning little* while Vienna secretly prepared, would nonetheless *learn enough* to comprehend the limited goals, legitimacy, and defensive thrust of Austria's attack and, thus, avoid a continental war. This was wishful thinking. Neglect of the intelligence implications of their strategy mirrored neglect of intelligence in its design.

The decision to use force against Serbia rested on the untested assumptions that the war could be kept short, thanks to military superiority over Serbia, and localized, thanks to secrecy, Russian intolerance of regicide, British indifference, and the German deterrent. No one checked whether the sources for these beliefs were biased or, if valid, whether the necessary conditions existed for them to endure. In fact, both the providers and withholders of intelligence were highly politicized; they shared only the intelligence that supported their views. Whereas an engaged and witting monarch, such as Queen Elizabeth I, might have used a rival set of intelligence operatives to ferret out cover-ups and expose danger, no strong central leader was available in 1914 to play that tough role in Vienna.[78]

The Foreign Ministry owned diplomatic intelligence in Vienna, and that ministry had an agenda.

Berlin Decides to Ride to War on Austria's Back 1–6 July 1914

Some experts have blamed the absence of strategic planning in Vienna on German pressure to strike Serbia before it was too late. Austria had, arguably, little time to think. According to this view, Vienna relied on Berlin's superior worldview and was bullied into the fight. Certainly, the kaiser was volcanic when learning of his ambassador's calming advice in Vienna immediately after the assassination. "The Serbs must be disposed of, and that right *soon!*" he wrote.[79] The ambassador got the message and quickly changed his tune.

To discern the causes of Vienna's intelligence failure requires addressing Berlin's culpability for Austria's hasty mistakes in intelligence and strategic planning. What were decision-makers in Berlin thinking when they urged swift action? Did the kaiser have intelligence on Austria-Hungary's plans and, seeing their intelligence gaps, recognize the perfect cover for a larger war? Or was the kaiser anticipating an outcome far different than the one Austria delivered into his lap when the crisis came to a head at the end of July?

Most historians agree that Austria-Hungary's decision-making on 7 July was influenced by the notorious "blank check" Berlin had seemingly provided the day before. Believing Germany had offered an unqualified promise of military cover necessary for a short local war, Austria's statesmen were more confident than they should have been. Indeed, some historians have suggested the German "gift" to Austria on 6 July was less a banker's check than a Trojan Horse, because the Germans knew what Conrad knew, and fully intended to use Austria's desire for a limited strike against Serbia as cover for their long-incubating plan for a wider European war.[80] Still, other historians have suggested that no blank check was intended; the kaiser's assurances of support did not mean that he expected to be out of the loop on subsequent decision-making or the intelligence that would support it. Indeed, as the July Crisis came to a head, German chancellor Bethmann-Hollweg sent a telegram to Vienna registering just this point: "We are, of course, prepared to fulfill our duty as allies, but must decline to let ourselves be dragged by Vienna wantonly and without regard to our advice, into a world conflagration."[81]

From an intelligence standpoint, this contrast between Berlin's swift, confident decision-making on 5–6 July and yawning gaps in specific knowledge is striking. The historically momentous German decision, which was conveyed to the Austrians on 6 July, seemingly flowed from estimative judgments based on very little: two Austrian documents and what two Austrian emissaries had to say.

How could this be? Were the Germans in fact confident and decisive in the run-up to global disaster?

The German Assessment: 5 July 1914

In truth, German decision-making from 5 July to 6 July was neither confident nor decisive, and certainly not based on any consensus view. Unlike in Austria, decision-making in Germany during these early days of July 1914 involved no single meeting or recorded moment of choice for which we have complete documentation. The meeting that comes closest to such a moment was one the kaiser held at the Neue Palais in Potsdam on 5 July. It was here that the key members of the Reich considered the Austrian documents suggesting war and the best German response to them. If the meeting looks, in retrospect, as if it fit well within Germany's long-standing plan for global war, in fact, it was not a serious, deliberative meeting of minds on this score. It was the Austrians that made it into one.

The members of the German group at the Neue Palais included, in addition to the kaiser, the chancellor, Bethmann-Hollweg; the chief of the Military Cabinet, Moriz Freiherr von Lyncker; Minister of War Erich von Falkenhayn; the kaiser's military aid, Hans Georg Hermann von Plessen; and the foreign minister, Gottlieb von Jagow. All these officials shared a common set of core beliefs that reflected historical, as well as circumstantial, knowledge.[82] They generally believed they needed no new intelligence to make these assessments:

- The military power of Russia was growing relative to Germany. Only military forces in being would have a decisive impact on war.[83]
- Russian military capabilities were insufficient, however, for winning a continental war in 1914. This "fact" was known in St. Petersburg, as well. Therefore, although the temporary superiority of Germany in Europe would end in a couple of years, deterring Russia from attacking would not be difficult in the meantime.[84]
- The tsar controlled Russian defense policy and did not want war.[85] The tsar had, however, a strong interest in defending the monarchical principle, especially given his own domestic problems. This stance would bias him *against* support for the regicidal Serbs, should Vienna punish them for the Sarajevo "outrage." (This view was, however, known to be wrong by the Austrian ambassador to Russia and probably also the German one.)
- Britain, plagued with domestic issues and imperial vulnerabilities, did not want to fight a continental war.[86] London was therefore likely to stay neutral should conflict in the Balkans come about.[87]

- Germany and Britain were natural allies because Russia was a threat to the latter's empire, and Germany was a bulwark against Russian power on the Continent.
- The Austrian emperor was old and weak-willed, but his authority over Austrian policymaking was certain, especially in the wake of the archduke's death.
- The weakening of the Triple Alliance (because of Serbo-Russian machinations in Austria and incompatible interests among Italy, Austria-Hungary, and Romania) had made continental stability uncertain, and worse with every passing year. If a European war had to be fought, which seemed likely, better now than later.
- German leadership was essential to allied strength. (It had failed in the past due, in part, to the kaiser's vacillation.)[88] Germany was no better or worse off than any other Great Power with respect to its intelligence capabilities.
- The rise of the Left in Germany presented a danger that could be alleviated through war.[89]

We know from the prior chapter that some, if not most, of this analysis was wrong, and that the Germans should have been, at the very least, uncertain—especially concerning comparative power relationships, the tsar's ability to exercise his authorities, and the strength of the Russian government's antiregicidal motivations. For example, no one at the Neue Palais on 5 July seemed to have appreciated the change that had come about in Russia as a result of the new membership of its Council of Ministers—a group far less likely to back down than Russia's decision-makers in 1908. There is evidence that the German ambassador in St. Petersburg, Count Friedrich von Pourtalès, understood the change, but there is no record that he discussed the implications with Berlin.[90] The shared paradigm among German statesmen, however, seemed too long-standing to be open to debate; indeed, the Austrians' analysis reflected in their documents fit well with the Germans' worldview.

On 5 July, with his advisors arrayed before him, the kaiser emphasized the emperor's claim that the time had come for Serbia to be "eliminated as a power factor in the Balkans." He added his impression of Austria's resolve, as conveyed by the ambassador. Wilhelm had already told the Austrian emissary earlier that day that Germany would fully support Vienna. But he had also indicated that he would need to consult his chancellor, whom he was sure would agree. The kaiser did not intend to vacillate now, as he would repeat several times over the next few days.[91] His confidence stemmed from a twofold certainty: that the Austrian spine needed stiffening and that the Russians would not intervene to stop a punitive, limited strike, especially given the recent circumstances of regicide. The kaiser did not want Austrian weakness on display. He wanted the emperor to launch a swift, punitive, local war that would restore respect for Austria-Hungary, and thus, the Triple Alliance, within Europe.

The kaiser expected his advisors to agree with him, and for the most part, they did, as Plessen's contemporaneous summary suggests:

> Our opinion is that the Austrians should act against Serbia the sooner the better and that the Russians—though friends of Serbia—nonetheless will not participate. There is the threat of Rumania abandoning the Triple Alliance, and an alliance between Turkey and Bulgaria is on the horizon.—H.M. departure for his North Sea cruise is to proceed undisturbed.[92]

Plessen's summary makes the discussion on 5 July seem almost perfunctory. In light of the formal reply to the Austrian inquiry (analyzed below), the senior officials in Potsdam may have believed the Austrian emperor's appeal was largely about his proposed diplomatic measures. While the emperor seemed to be contemplating some forceful action against Belgrade, he had not made up his mind to do so. The idea of urging him forward seemed appropriate, especially to the kaiser.

Yet, from an intelligence standpoint, it is striking that no one asked the military representatives what might result from such urging. For example, no one apparently asked whether the Serbian army could be defeated by the Austrians alone, how long it would take, and if not possible, what Germany could do short of launching a continental war.

The answer to this incuriosity may lie in the expectation that Austria would not act; but evidence suggests there was some concern she would. In fact, amidst the quiet in the room of the Neue Palais floated disquieting ideas, unspoken concerns, and some skepticism. First, Bethmann-Hollweg did not bring up the problem of likely British reactions to an offensive move against Serbia, although it was weighing on his mind. A German spy's secret reports of Anglo-Russian naval negotiations, including speculative talk about British support for a (simulated) Russian landing in Pomerania, had been "devastating" to him because they signaled the possibility that British neutrality or even disinterest could not be presumed.[93] If these Anglo-Russian negotiations moved forward and some kind of alliance ensued, it would be, in his view, "the last piece in the chain" encircling Germany and spelling her doom in any continental war. Worse, he no longer trusted intelligence coming through official channels from London. He had come to believe Berlin's ambassador, Prince Karl Max Lichnowsky, was "much too blue eyed" and was being duped by the British.[94] Neither he nor the kaiser could therefore be confident that they would have timely, unbiased analysis of British reactions to a limited strike. In fact, for Bethmann-Hollweg, the situation felt worse than 1912. This time, circumstances threatened to bring about a world war and "a revolution of everything that exists." As Bethmann-Hollweg was to confide to his aide on 8 July, he believed that "if the war came from the east and Germany marched to aid Austria instead of Austria marching north to aid Germany, there was a chance that the war could be kept to one front and that Britain would not intervene."[95] But he did not test this idea on the general staff, who had rejected such a scenario when Conrad had asked for it several months earlier. Deeply pessimistic already on 5 July, the chancellor, nonetheless, apparently kept his counsel.[96]

Second, most of the military officials in the room should have understood that the kaiser's idea of "support"—simply approving a strictly local war between Austria and Serbia while reducing the threat of a European war—was exactly the opposite of what the Austrians probably wanted. They probably wanted Germany to promise *to deter* Russia and, if necessary, *to march* to Austria's aid if other Great Powers intervened. After all, the German general staff knew what Conrad knew: that Austria was too weak to fight a local war alone. There was no scenario of Austrian punitive action with complementary German military "support" that could reliably deter Russia and not trigger a continental war. The German general staff also knew that, given Conrad's plans, a punitive strike would entail defeating the Serbian army at whatever price that required, creating a military weakness in Galicia that the Russian general staff would almost certainly press to exploit. The general staff also knew that the Russians knew the basic war plans of the Alliance, thanks to Redl's espionage. This knowledge was a wasting asset for them. So the kaiser's expectation that the tsar's antipathy to regicides would override military considerations likely reflected his ignorance of these latter factors.

Whether the military officials in the room truly understood the depth of the kaiser's ignorance of these matters is unknown. There is evidence to suggest they did not: when the kaiser was told at the peak of the crisis in late July that Germany had no contingency plan for a mobilization in the east that didn't also entail mobilization in the west, his fury dumbfounded his military aides. The kaiser knew that Germany's war plan required Austria to counter Russia while Germany fought France, but he did not realize the plan was impossible for him to change at will. The new logistics involved in mass warfare had made last-minute changes in that plan infeasible, cutting into his power (and the power of other statesmen and diplomats) to make credible trades, threats, and bargains.

For their part, the German military should also have known that, given the scale of modern war and its likely consequences, flexible force deployments would be critical to statesmen's national security strategies in peacetime—including last-minute efforts at deterrence to avoid a global catastrophe.[97] In any event, such consequential operational issues did not, apparently, come up on 5 July. There were no exchanges between military and diplomatic authorities regarding strategy, contingency plans, or net assessment that would have prompted answers to such intelligence questions.

One possible reason for this lack of debate at the highest level of German decision-making was skepticism about the need for it. At least one senior official, the minister of war, apparently assessed the documents from Vienna as constituting no explicit warning of imminent war or even a request for backing for one. In Falkenhayn's view, the Austrians had eschewed war many times before, so, while there might be need to bolster Germany's shocked ally, there seemed little need to raise military contingencies. Falkenhayn wrote about the meeting to Moltke, chief of the general staff, that same day:

> H.M. felt justified in drawing this inference [Austria's intention to attack Serbia] from the words of the Austrian Ambassador. . . . I was not present during this conversation, so am unable to permit myself to form any opinion in this matter. . . . [These] documents did not succeed in convincing me that the Vienna Government had taken any firm resolution. Both paint a very gloomy picture of the general situation of the Dual Monarchy as a result of Pan-Slav agitations. Both consider it necessary that something should be done about this with the greatest urgency. But neither speaks of the need for war, rather both expound "energetic" political action such as the conclusion of a treaty with Bulgaria, for which they would like to be certain of the support of the German Reich. This support should be granted with some indication that it would, in the first place, be a matter for Austria-Hungary to take the requisite steps which are in her own interest.[98]

Although Falkenhayn's understanding seems to have been quite different from Plessen's account of the same meeting quoted above, it more nearly reflected the state of play in official circles at that time in Vienna. It lacked, however, an appreciation of the plotting underway in Vienna's foreign ministry or the grip that cabal had on the decision-making process—plotting of which, as we shall see, the German ambassador to London was at the time well aware. As in Vienna, so in Germany: military and diplomatic intelligence was not always shared, so decision-makers often had incomplete understanding of developments.

In any event, the war minister claimed in his message to Moltke that he was not alone in his views. According to Falkenhayn, Bethmann-Hollweg believed the kaiser's annual naval excursion should proceed as planned. Astonishingly, the war minister thought the chancellor was not only unworried, but actually at ease:

> The Chancellor, who was also in Potsdam, appears to have as little faith as I do that the Austrian Government is really in earnest, even though its language is undeniably more resolute than in the past. At any rate, not only has he raised

no objections about the Scandinavian journey taking place, but he has even recommended it. *Certainly under no circumstances will the coming weeks bring any decisions.* It will be a long time before the treaty with Bulgaria is concluded. Your Excellency's stay at the Spa will therefore scarcely need to be curtailed.[99]

Falkenhayn evidently interpreted the discussion of "support" to Austria on 5 July as revolving around initiatives Vienna wished to take to expand the Triple Alliance, not of immediate military action, for which a decision would have been needed very soon. When he asked the kaiser if any military preparations should be made, Wilhelm II answered with a brusque no. Since Falkenhayn knew that military support for a quick Austrian military strike against Serbia would have required some preparation, Falkenhayn relayed his reassurances to Moltke that he need not rush home.

In fact, the kaiser's flawed thinking was not transparent to Falkenhayn or to anyone else. The kaiser believed German "support" for Austria entailed helping keep the war local, which in turn, required keeping Germany politically and militarily *disconnected* from the punitive strike. He did not know or ask whether such a hands-off policy would compromise German preparations should a wider war become necessary, because he believed that any Austrian move had to be seen, in both its timing and objectives, as unilateral retaliation for the regicide. The kaiser said to Bethmann-Hollweg on 5 July that "it was not our business to advise our ally what to do as a result of the Sarajevo murder. On this Austria-Hungary must make her own decisions." But he then added, "We must refrain from direct suggestions and advice all the more because we must use all means to prevent the Austro-Serbian conflict from widening into an international conflict." Thus, the kaiser believed it would not be so much military deterrence (covering Austria's rear), as Germany's demonstrable noninvolvement that would serve to manage Russian perceptions and thus constitute "support."

The chancellor therefore recommended no change in the schedules of senior leaders because any changes would have signaled German complicity in the consequential decisions Austria was about to make. Unfortunately, the chancellor was as uninformed as the kaiser about Germany's military constraints. Neither he nor the kaiser, discounting Russian involvement, asked for an assessment of how decision-makers in St. Petersburg might see Germany's "noninvolvement," or a net assessment of what the German military could do if Russia began a partial mobilization on Austria's borders.

The German Decision: 6 July 1914

Berlin's decision about how to respond to the Austrian documents, recorded on 6 July in the form of a briefing to Hoyos and the bilateral ambassador, thus seems to have been more of a political punt than a bold move to risk a European war. This conclusion is, however, somewhat misleading because it graces the decision with too much deliberation. The apparent ease of decision and lack of debate reflected poor intelligence-sharing and, at the same time, the ambiguity of the Austrian documents and their representation. Convinced Russia's malign purposes were behind her deepening entente with Britain, but also that the tsar would not risk war over an incident of regicide, the kaiser expected Austria to pull off a swift, successful fait accompli that his own military discounted because of its very improbability. He did not, evidently, think very deeply about the matter.

On 6 July, both Hoyos and Szögyény-Marich met with the chancellor and Undersecretary of State Arthur Zimmermann to receive the German government's formal reply. According to the ambassador's subsequent report, the chancellor emphasized in his formal communication Germany's full support for Vienna's proposed diplomatic moves.

- The German government specifically endorsed opening discussions with Bulgaria so long as these did not affect obligations toward Romania, and would authorize the German ambassador in Sofia to negotiate in this sense if the Austrian ambassador asked him to.
- The German envoy to Romania would keep the king of Romania apprised of these developments and remind him of his interest in suppressing Romanian agitation "against us."
- Regarding Serbia, "The German Government is of the opinion that [Austria] must judge what is to be done to clarify the relationship; in this [Austria] could—whatever form our decision might take—certainly count on Germany, *as ally and friend* of the Monarchy, to be right behind her."[100]

In short, Germany's precise and formal assurance of support was only for diplomatic actions that included reaffirmation of long-standing Alliance commitments. In the carefully crafted language of diplomacy, this formal reply was hardly a "blank check" for military cover in the case of an offensive Austrian attack on Serbia at any time and for any purpose. The Triple Alliance was, after all, a defensive one, and Germany's responsibility as "ally and friend" had to be understood in that limited context (i.e., no attack on Italy's interests and no forcible annexation of territory against the interests of Germany or other Alliance partners, etc.). But, at least in Szögyény-Marich's view, the chancellor hinted at such broader support later and more informally: "During the further course of conversation I ascertained," Szögyény-Marich wrote, "that the Imperial Chancellor like his Imperial Master considers immediate intervention on our part as the most radical and best solution for our difficulties in the Balkans."[101] But even this formulation was no blank check. The key was immediacy. The longer one waited, the less punitive and the more offensive it would appear. Germany had not, at this point, made any formal decision on military preferences. No *military* cover was made explicit, though it was certainly inferred by the Austrian council of ministers.

As we have seen, all subtle distinctions made by Bethmann-Hollweg and in turn by Szögyény-Marich soon became blurred in Vienna's foreign ministry, where objective analysis was in short supply, interest in parsing the meaning of words low, and the decision for war already made. Here we need to recall that on 6 July, Forgách, a member of the group of young imperialists, sent a telegram to Tisza: "Kaiser Wilhelm had it reported to His Majesty that *we could rely on the full support of Germany in a potential action*. According to Kaiser Wilhelm's opinion we should now not wait any longer with an action against Serbia. We should not let this present favorable moment remain unused. Russia was today not ready for war and Germany stood on our side as a faithful ally."[102] Phrased this way, the kaiser's views seemed part of the formal German response, not informal musings for Vienna to consider. And Forgách's implication that Germany's promise of "full support" extended to German military cover in the east for a limited Austrian war to the south was pure speculation at best or, at worse, deception.

Intelligence Support to Entente Decision-Making

From our current perspective, it seems extraordinary that Berlin and Vienna would overlook their requirements for information during this early stage of the crisis—indeed fail to consider all their sources. Yet both the context provided in the last chapter and the immediate circumstances explain why, for the most part, they did. In the first place, the Central Powers believed Britain and France were distracted, so maintaining an intelligence advantage over them would hardly be difficult. In particular, British statesmen were seen as overwhelmed by the rebellion in Protestant counties of Ulster due to the likely passage of the Irish Home Rule bill. As Churchill wrote of 1914:

> We cannot read the debates that continued at intervals through April, May and June without wondering that our Parliamentary institutions were strong enough to survive the passions by which they were convulsed. Was it astonishing that German agents reported and German statesmen believed, that England was paralyzed by faction and drifting into civil war and need not be taken into account as a factor in the European situation?[103]

For their part, French decision-makers were transfixed throughout the month of July by the convoluted trial of a murderess. The lady in question had shot a journalist for exposing her secret affair with a former prime minister, whom she had later married. Distracted, the Foreign Ministry overlooked warnings by the French ambassador in Belgrade that a crisis was brewing in Austro-Serbian relations. Worse, the murder-scandal led to politically motivated disclosures of French intercepts, a changing of codes, and thus, the loss of French access to foreign communications the very month that war planning in Austria had begun. What should have registered as a crisis in intelligence policy was hardly mentioned in official French communications.

The second reason for Germany's presumption of intelligence advantage had to do with improved relations between Germany and Britain that turned, in part, on strong, past bilateral communications. They had worked out resolutions to the Limon Sanders affair, which had involved the sensitive issue of German training of Turkish forces under the nose of the tsar; the Baghdad railway, which involved a German opening to Persia despite Russian fears of it; and on moderation of the naval competition.[104] As recently as 24 June, Foreign Minister Grey had reassured Berlin that he would keep direct bilateral channels open should a conflict arise again in the Balkans.[105] Indeed, Grey had come to rely on the German ambassador to help smooth relations and stay abreast of developments. In these conditions of distraction and dependency, Berlin had some reason to believe it could manage British reactions to a swift blow against Serbia.

Yet none of these explanations for German optimism explain the seeming indifference with which Grey followed the situation in southern Europe post-assassination—indeed, they beg the question. Given his prominent role in brokering the last Balkan crisis, mounting Russo-German tensions, and London's new vulnerabilities on the home front, why didn't he or his ministry recognize the catastrophe that was brewing or, at the very least, ramp up intelligence in anticipation of trouble?

By his own later confession, Grey believed at the time that "European peace had weathered worse storms than any that were visible above the horizon." How did he come to such a conclusion, given the provocation of regicide and the passions unleashed in the press on all sides? He had been, after all, at the Foreign Office "in the centre of all the troubles" for many years. How could he believe that "it was natural to hope, even to expect, that the same methods which had preserved peace hitherto . . . would preserve it still"?[106] Was this experienced minister's decision not to get immediately and directly involved based only on these hopes and happy expectations—in short, on an outdated mindset?

The British Decision to Stand Aside, 6 July 1914

The problem was, of course, that Grey was only interested, as he said himself, in what was visible above the horizon, not what was just beyond it. His policies were, as a result, largely reactive and his requirements for intelligence, as opposed to general information, largely contingent. He therefore failed to grasp decision-advantage when it fell into his lap.

On 6 July 1914, Grey met with the German ambassador, Prince Karl Max von Lichnowsky, in the Foreign Office. The men were comfortable with each other, having developed a relationship over Lichnowsky's tenure at his London post. This meeting, however, brought unwelcome intelligence from Germany. Lichnowsky had stopped by Berlin on his way to and from Silesia on 29 June and 5 July and met with Chancellor Bethmann-Hollweg and the acting foreign secretary, Zimmermann. During these discussions, he had learned about the strong faction within Austria's government that was intent on using the incident of 28 June for unleashing a war on Serbia. Lichnowsky, according to Grey's account, spoke to Grey in private terms. He advised that he believed Austria was in the grip of intense anti-Slav passions and that, while he did not know details, he knew "for a fact" that the Austrians "intended to do something." It was "not impossible" that the government would take "military action" against Serbia because some compensation in the form of humiliation for Serbia was required.

Lichnowsky explained that Germany's dilemma was simple: "If she told the Austrians that nothing must be done, she would be accused of always holding them back and not supporting them. On the other hand, if she let events take their course, there was the possibility of very serious trouble." Then the ambassador added that "there was some feeling in Germany . . . that trouble was bound to come and therefore it would be better to let trouble come now, rather than later."[107] Lichnowsky specifically identified Bethmann-Hollweg as among the pessimists.

It is hard to imagine a more straightforward warning of a coming crisis than the one delivered by Lichnowsky to Grey on the very day that the chancellor delivered his supposed blank check to the Austrians. The warning was underscored by Lichnowsky's repeated reference to its "private" and "delicate" nature, which suggests he might have gone beyond his formal instructions in sharing what he knew.[108] In fact, Lichnowsky's report to his own government on the meeting with Grey omits any reference to his warning about Austrian war plans and the chancellor's support for them.[109]

Grey responded by declaring himself ready to "mitigate difficulties" and, "if clouds arose," to prevent the storm from breaking. He later mentioned the exchange to the Russian ambassador, Alexander von Benckendorff, who promised to inform St. Petersburg. But Grey decided to do little beyond this. Rather than hearing this intelligence as a warning, it seems Grey took it as evidence of the intimacy of his personal relations with his German interlocutors, which probably seemed a good sign he could keep matters under control.

If Grey's inaction on 6 July forfeited a chance for gaining a jump on Austrian plans, later intelligence seemed to undermine any reason for it. Sir Maurice de Bunsen, ambassador to Vienna, initially had few insights to offer, but on 7 July reported that the usually perceptive Russian ambassador there, Nikolai Shebeko, was discounting the chance of Austrian aggression. On 6 July, Shebeko had told Bunsen he thought war unlikely. The Austrians knew that isolated combat with Serbia would be impossible, as it would trigger Russian intervention. Upon reading Bunsen's report, Sir Arthur Nicholson, Grey's permanent undersecretary (the number two position in the Foreign Office) advised Grey that he agreed with Shebeko; Nicholson judged him a "shrewd man" whose opinion should be given weight.[110]

Reassured that Austria planned no aggression, Grey sought to reassure Lichnowsky again that Britain appreciated improving relations with Germany and that Anglo-Russian naval discussions entailed no commitments—that English hands were still "free." Unbeknownst to Grey, the timing of this message was poor. Just forty-eight hours earlier, Austria had taken the decision for war, predicated on English independence from her Entente partners. For his part, Lichnowsky said he was "hopeful" that the German government "might have succeeded in smoothing the Austrian intentions with regard to Serbia." These comments, if sincere, show he had already lost the chancellor's confidence, was cut out of Berlin's secret decision-making, and perhaps was already being used as a tool for deception. In any event, Lichnowsky repeated Berlin's hope that England and Germany would stay in touch in order to "keep things right." Grey, while mentioning the importance of keeping Austrian demands within bounds, nonetheless promised to continue the same policy he had pursued during the Balkan Crisis and to do his "utmost to prevent the outbreak of war between the Great Powers." Lichnowsky reported to Berlin that Grey was "in a confident mood" and "cheerfully" of the view that there was "no reason to be pessimistic about the situation."[111]

Over the next few weeks Grey saw it as his job to keep Russian in check. This required, in his view, seeking Lichnowsky's counsel on German efforts to constrain Austria and applying delicate pressure in St. Petersburg. The latter aim was challenging given the tensions rising over British gains in Persian oil fields at Russian expense. In Grey's eyes, it seems the problem appeared as one of process, not objectives. He needed to work the levers of influence among touchy Great Powers jointly committed to European stability, not to gauge conflicting interests and plans in the context of structural shifts in European power—a shift whose potential for inducing instability hinged, in part, on Britain's own fickleness. In keeping with the times, Grey was thinking in incremental, rather than strategic, terms. As Luigi Albertini has written of this moment:

The truth was that it was on Berlin and Vienna, not on St. Petersburg, that he [Grey] should have brought pressure to bear. But the Foreign Office was still blind to this and remained so even after receiving other alarm signals contained in two dispatches from Bunsen in Vienna.[112]

The two dispatches to which Albertini refers are those of 16 and 17 July. In the first, Bunsen wrote: "My informant states that . . . Austro-Hungarian Government are in no mood to parley with Serbia, but will insist on immediate compliance, failing which force will be used. Germany is said to be in complete agreement with this procedure." In the second report, he added his source for the first: Count Heinrich von Lützow, ex-ambassador at Rome and confidant of Berchtold and Forgách. All sources reported the Ballplatz in "an uncompromising mood" and that Lützow in particular wondered "if I knew how grave the situation was."[113]

The answer, in fact, was that neither Grey nor the ambassador—indeed, no one anywhere in the British government—knew how grave the situation was at this moment. As late as 20 July, Grey was privately urging the Russians and Austrians to pursue bilateral discussions. This suggestion became policy on 22 July when Grey, astonishingly, suggested Russian cooperation with Austria in the framing of the demands to which Serbia would be required to comply. Grey's proposal reflected less intelligence on what was actually feasible, given the tremendous distrust then evident in Vienna, Germany, and St. Petersburg, than an incurious mindset fixed on the notion of Great Power "concert." The French president Poincaré, upon hearing Grey's suggestion, called it "very dangerous" and less preferable than direct French and English pressure on Vienna.[114]

Perhaps of greatest concern, however, should have been the "intelligence" Grey conveyed to Berlin and Vienna through the Austrian ambassador on 23 July, the very day of Austria's ultimatum to Serbia. In this conversation, Grey referred to the damage "a four-power war" (i.e., one in which England would stay neutral) would cause, thus implying that London would not come to the support of her Entente partners, just as Vienna and Berlin most desperately hoped. As Albertini has written: "It never entered his [Grey's] head that, in speaking to the Austrian Ambassador of a Four Power war, without so much as hinting that England might become involved, he was encouraging Berlin and Vienna to intransigence and war."[115] Albertini goes on to say:

Hence during this first phase of the July crisis at any rate the hesitancy and ineptitude of British policy is not to be sought in Cabinet dissensions, the Irish question, fear of offending Russia and the like. A perusal of the documents shows that up to 23 July there is one explanation pure and simple; namely

Grey's utter failure on the one hand to understand what was going on, what was told him and what was reported from the various embassies, and on the other to grasp that Austrian aggression against Serbia would bring in first Russia and then Germany and France.[116]

And such aggression would thus pose an existential question for Britain as well.

That Grey could conceive of British abstention in a four-power war reveals the significance of the intelligence he was missing: the degree to which his own military's war plans and French war plans were interlocked. Years of intelligence-sharing and war planning among the militaries had made the "entente" with France something of a military and naval alliance in which French and British ships divided up the seas between them and British troops filled critical gaps in defensive lines.[117] Relying on old mindsets, diplomats in Britain, as in Austria and Germany, had little appreciation for how the military intelligence, and net assessments to which they were not privy, would affect the playing out of their options on the edge of war.

Sazonov's Failure to Deliver a Sharp
Warning to Vienna on 17 July

That Grey's ignorance crippled him is certainly understandable; that the relatively well-informed Sazonov was similarly crippled seems less so. Russia did not want war over the Balkans, but her leaders were filled with hostility and suspicion regarding German intentions for Constantinople and the Straits. With mindsets primed to see German intrigue, decision-makers in St. Petersburg more quickly perceived the implications of the assassination, and the gravity of the situation, than Britain did. But, despite good intelligence, they missed a key opportunity to sharply warn Vienna. That they did not, however, was of less consequence than Britain's failure, if only because neither Austria nor Germany would likely have been deterred had they done so. What Russia did gain from its intelligence-advantage, however, was timely preparations for war.

Russia's collection architecture in the Balkans was based on an espionage network that was deeply embedded in the Slavic underground, the Black Hand and pan-Slavic cultural organizations, and in liaison relations with the Serbian government. Russian policymakers determined almost immediately that the assassination was linked to Bosnian insurgents, and that Austria had no right to countermeasures against the Serbian government. For Russia, therefore, collecting intelligence on Serbian culpability seemed less relevant than collecting on Austrian and German intentions. And on this, St. Petersburg had sources:

- Russia's ambassador in Vienna, Shebeko, was attentive and able. He reported that Berlin was fanning the flames for war shortly after the assassination—albeit somewhat before that proved technically true. He also kept track of key Viennese officials handling matters in the Austrian Foreign Ministry. Of particular note was the role played by Count Forgách, infamous in Russian official circles for having attempted an anti-Serbian deception campaign in the past; in fact, he was regarded more as an offensive counterintelligence agent who forged documents during a 1909 trial of Serbian conspirators than as a diplomat.[118]
- From the diplomatic circuit, Russian decision-makers had also learned of connections between the kaiser and the dead archduke, who was erroneously believed to be head of a "war party" and a stooge of Germany. In the aftermath of the assassination, Russian officials thought it likely that Germany would be pulling the strings on retaliation.
- Russia's ambassador in Serbia, Nikolai Hartwig, though an ardent Slavophile, knew Serbia was militarily weakened in 1914, and was counseling caution while sounding alarms. His intelligence indicated that the Serbian government had no official involvement in the outrage, although some of its members were implicated and President Nikola Paschich had some foreknowledge of it. It is likely that Hartwig even knew of Paschich's attempt to warn Biliński of the assassination plot.[119] In any event, Hartwig died suddenly of a heart attack shortly after the assassination, temporarily reducing intelligence flowing to Russia.

These sources on the Serbian government's noninvolvement in the assassination fueled early Russian suspicions regarding "Triplice" intentions. Then, just one week after the Austrian-Hungarian government had decided on war, supplemental intelligence arrived in St. Petersburg suggesting that war was the plan.[120]

- On 14 July, Russian cryptologists deciphered a telegram from Berchtold to the Austrian chargé d'affaires in St. Petersburg asking for the precise date when the French foreign minister would be leaving the Russian capital after long-planned inter-allied discussions there (23 July).[121] The request seemed ominous in the context of other diplomatic intelligence: Russia's head of chancery, Baron Moritz Fabianovich von Schilling, reported that the Italian ambassador, Marchese Andrea Carlotti di Riparbello, had asked how Russia would react if Austria were to take "serious measures" against Serbia. Schilling reported that Carlotti "thought it possible" that *Austria believed Russia, being of peaceful mind, would not adopt forcible measures for the protection of Serbia*"[122] and that the government there was planning on delivering an ultimatum. The ambassador in Vienna, Shebeko, reported similar news.[123]

- On 16 July, the same day Bunsen had informed Grey of the Austro-Hungarian plans for use of force, Shebeko echoed that warning. He wrote a letter reporting on Tisza's somewhat bellicose speech to the Hungarian parliament, in which he claimed that "every state, every nation must be in the position to wage war and must desire war as ultima ratio, if state and nation are to continue to exist."

- Shebeko separately stressed the point that Bunsen's Italian interlocutor had said Vienna *was assuming* Russian nonintervention in any punitive strike against Serbia and that this misperception could lead to war.

Shebeko recommended that Sazonov urgently convey to "the Austrian cabinet" how Russia would, in fact, react if Austria were to present demands unacceptable to the dignity of Serbia. He also suggested a (poor) means for doing so: the Austrian ambassador, Szapáry, due to arrive in St. Petersburg the next day.

Despite Shebeko's advice, the underlying intelligence, and his own growing sense of alarm, Sazonov decided not to deliver a strong warning to the Austrian government on 17 July. His reasons had to do with last-minute intelligence received through trusted but actually corrupt, diplomatic channels. In fact, neither German nor Austrian ambassadors were good channels for intergovernmental communications, having become by this point more agents of influence than sources of intelligence.[124] (At this time, neither Sazonov nor Shebeko knew that Austria's ambassadors had been instructed by Berchtold to keep plans "dark.") Szapáry, a member of the most hawkish Austrian cabal, took this instruction particularly seriously; when he arranged to see Sazonov on the seventeenth, he was intent on acting his part in the Austrian deception. When the two officials met, Szapáry "completely reassured Sazonov," who decided he need not issue threats given the ambassador's "guarantee of the pacific intentions of his Government." Sazonov told Schilling the ambassador had been "gentle as a lamb."

Szapáry's disposition, as opposed to the underlying facts, had a large impact on the Russian foreign minister. Once Szapáry's lamb-like presence was gone, however, the Russian foreign minister seems to have reconsidered the situation. For example, he commented to Britain's ambassador, Sir George Buchanan, that Austria's possible ultimatum to Belgrade was worrisome enough to make "precautionary military measures" worth considering. He also showed Shebeko's telegram to the tsar, who opined that demands from one state to another presaged war. With Sazonov's failure to deliver a sharp warning to Vienna on 17 July, the window arguably closed for using diplomacy to deter Austrian aggression. So began the unfolding of the July Crisis and European war.

* * *

Historians have analyzed the unfolding of events from 23 July to 1 August (the July Crisis) looking for war guilt. Yet, arguably, once the ultimatum was presented to Serbia on 23 July, options for maneuver were so tightly constrained, and intelligence channels so compromised, that none of the Great Powers could frame and then convey the collective interest in avoiding European war and steps that might bring that about. A Europe-wide war was not what German and Austrian civilian officials had planned on 7 July; but they had been under the misapprehension that neither Russia nor Britain would likely intervene, given the provocation of regicide and conditions of Austro-German military dominance, initiative, and surprise. They were wrong, not just because of poor intelligence, but because their own schemes of deception distorted calculations of interest all around, especially given the poverty of sound intelligence practices in most Great Powers. Indeed, it was not until 24 July that officials in London "began to be seriously worried by the situation."[125] So it can hardly be surprising that London was slower to rein in its Entente partners than both German and Austrian officials had hoped.

On 25 July, Grey proposed, too late, that the "disinterested" Great Powers act together for peace in St Petersburg and Vienna. By 26 July, the tsar was already initiating the "period preparatory to war." On 27 July, Germany rejected the British proposal for a conference. Austria declared war on Serbia on the twenty-eighth and began shelling Belgrade on the twenty-ninth. As the kaiser urged Berchtold to arrange a "halt in Belgrade," Moltke was urging Conrad to commence a general mobilization. The tsar ordered Russia's mobilization on 30 July; the emperor of Austria-Hungary ordered general mobilization on 31 July. The next day, Germany declared war on Russia and France declared war on Germany. Austria did not declare war on Russia until the sixth of August.

Decision Advantage, 7 July 1914

Our purpose up to this point has been a quite limited one: to examine how decision-makers informed themselves during the earliest stages of the crisis of July 1914. Did they gain or lose intelligence advantages in the process, and if so, how?

The diplomatic challenge implied by the Central Powers' strategy was threefold: first, *to prevent the Entente powers from knowing* about and, thus, preempting an Austrian strike against Serbia; second, once this local war was launched, *to convince these same powers of the Triple Alliance's intent* to contain the conflict; third, should containment prove impossible, *to shape British perceptions of who was at fault* for triggering a wider war so London, the least committed of the

Entente partners, would stay neutral or perhaps even defect to the side of the Central Powers. In sum, insofar as the initial strategy of the Central Powers was, in fact, to pull off a quick strike while, at the very least, managing the risks of a wider war, it required the allied Central Powers to

- *know in detail* the military constraints on their options and the options of their adversaries, and thus, the meaning any military moves would convey;
- *know best* what Austria planned against Serbia;
- *discover foreign perceptions and shape the narrative* of a just, local war;
- *learn* if Russia were to decide to counter Austrian moves in time to take deterrent actions, as well as *monitor* signals that Russia might be ready to trigger a wider war;
- *monitor* each other's actions and commitment to the joint strategy; and
- *suppress countermessaging* about the Central Powers' war aims despite an unruly press and government.

Their secondary strategy, in the event a wider war proved necessary, required

- *knowing* whether Britain was thinking of coming into the conflict at any point in order to deter her in a timely way from doing so;
- *influencing British intelligence* so that London would be convinced of the risks of entry and place blame for the wider war on France and Russia (offensive counterintelligence); and
- *monitoring* how Britain was responding to threats and incentives for neutrality.

In other words, even if the Central Powers' assumptions were correct that the Entente powers could be kept ignorant or unprepared until a local war was complete, decision-makers in Berlin and Vienna needed to retain intelligence-advantage and, thus, manage the contingency of wider war if this proved necessary.

Nothing suggests that decision-makers in Berlin or Vienna understood the intelligence requirements their strategy implied. They, therefore, failed to engineer a system for making sure those requirements were met. Following its endorsement of Austrian purposes, Berlin kept all its most senior decision-makers out of Berlin, away from the diplomatic circuit, and shut down its most influential asset in London, its own ambassador; Austria-Hungary kept its ambassador out of St. Petersburg until mid-July; and neither Berlin nor Vienna stayed in regular communication about the progress of Austrian war-planning or the wording of the ultimatum itself. Instead of an intelligence strategy, the allies had an uncoordinated, simple-minded policy of denial.

This analysis suggests that the early informational advantages enjoyed by civilian officials on Vienna and Berlin on 5–6 July were, for the most part, based
more on happenstance than craft, and almost all were forfeited by 7 July. In contrast, by 16 July, the Russian foreign minister probably knew more about Russia's
competitive position and interests than the Austrian foreign minister knew about
Austria-Hungary's. Unfortunately, Russia's range of options was limited by the
inability of others to gather intelligence. Britain's Sir Edward Grey arguably knew
least about how his country's interests were implicated, had no capacity to ferret
out the intelligence he needed and, therefore misunderstood the risks he was
taking with each decision. Contrasted with Berchtold, who successfully managed a Council of Ministers, Grey was more tool than shaper of a Cabinet view.

Viewed this way, the opening decisions that led to WWI arose from blind,
unimaginative, and incurious statesmen more than militarism, nationalism,
industrial capitalism, or even balance-of-power politics. Intelligence was the
Phantom of the Opera: seductive, potentially empowering, but elusive. Haunting
European statesmen for years afterward, gaps in intelligence in 1914 inspired
growth in national intelligence services during the decades leading up to WWII.

Conclusion

In fact, the "surprise" of 23 July reflected more the poverty of intelligence for
all than advantages engineered in Vienna. As we shall see, British decision-
makers relied on Berlin's Anglophile ambassador in London just when he was
losing access in Berlin. Russian statesmen seemed better informed than they actually were, given what they needed to know. The tsar did have a surveillance
apparatus for counterrevolutionary purposes and, at least initially, a Russian ambassador to Serbia who had infiltrated his host government and the pan-Slavic
underground. The advantages Russia gained, however, only prevented the kind
of paralysis that was to afflict Britain, and it was Britain that was key to the two-
front war Russia needed to win. Once Germany backed Austria's plan for a quick
coup de main, Russia could not make a deal with Germany to localize the conflict because Russia could not allow Austria-Hungary to defeat Serbia. Germany
and Austria failed to appreciate that Russia's new foreign policy decision-makers
would perceive a Serbian defeat as more threatening to the tsar's regime than
any regicidal band of ruffians. Russia's leadership quickly surmised, erroneously,
that the kaiser was using Vienna's moves purposely to launch a wider war. The
kaiser's failure to understand this fact constrained his options and constituted
Germany's crucial intelligence failure. Austria's failure lay in the assumption that
Germany "had her back" for deterring Russia.

Before briefly considering how the rise of professional intelligence systems affected European decision-making in 1938, three crucial lessons from the tragedy of WWI merit highlighting:

First, the superior knowledge Viennese statesmen had of their own situation at the start of a conflict blinded them as events gathered momentum. They enjoyed, in early July 1914, the sort of temporary clarity of vision General Hooker had before the battle of Chancellorsville. In both cases, certainty about the array of forces and how surprise could be achieved led to complacency about intelligence-gathering once plans started to unfold. The difference in these two cases was that Hooker had an integrated intelligence system whose officials could analyze and eventually fix the problem. The kaiser and the emperor had two disconnected intelligence systems—military and diplomatic—without the capacity or interest in doing so.

Second, advantages can flow from the timely *release* of intelligence, not just from withholding it. Gaining decision advantage is all about manipulating the balance of information among competitors, which can entail marketing, sharing, and purposeful "leaking," as well as, theft. Russia or Britain could have mitigated the effects of Austria's deceits had they had effective and secure means for uncovering them and *delivering trusted intelligence* to Vienna and Berlin. The diplomatic corps was weak, however, so they needed other liaison relationships, double agents, agents of influence, or "inspired" releases to the press.

Yet this deficiency among the Entente powers was less than that suffered by Austria-Hungary and Germany. Vienna's Council of Ministers had decided on a strategy that required an intelligence capability it did not have at hand. The ministers and their German backers planned a local war that was, in fact, more likely to trigger the world war they did not want, because of the very strategy of deception they considered essential for its execution.

Third, by compromising their most trusted intelligence channel, diplomacy, the council of ministers also compromised its ability to use it. On 7 July, at least one influential Austro-Hungarian council member judged diplomacy—the principal means by which states learned, as well as influenced each other—to be a "detail" rather than key to achieving their purposes. Decision-makers in 1938 would be less naïve, but still confused about how to manage intelligence during a global crisis.

12

Intelligence and Decision in 1938

> I asked the General straight out "What is Germany's aim in Europe today?" Goering replied "We want a free hand in Eastern Europe. We want to establish the unity of the German peoples. . . ." I said "Do you mean to get Austria?" Reply "Yes." I said "Do you mean to get Czechoslovakia?" Reply "Yes."
>
> —British intelligence agent Malcolm Christie, reporting on a conversation with Nazi Reichsmarschall Hermann Goering, 3 February, 1937

European decision-making in the run-up to WWII differed from early July 1914 in at least one striking way: national intelligence organizations had become heavily involved. The "Interwar Period," beginning with the Versailles settlement of 1919, involved the monitoring of German compliance with terms Berlin regarded as vindictive and illegitimate; and the Communist International was infiltrating labor organizations, threatening to turn labor activism into transnational agitation and social revolution. Intelligence and counterintelligence operations in France, Britain, Italy, Germany, and the Soviet Union all ramped up.[1]

Yet history has generally judged French, British, and American statesmen's decision-making on these matters, especially German resurgence, as poor. The British policy of diplomatic bargaining with the Nazi Reich, shorthanded as "appeasement," seemed at first rational, if weak-kneed; then simply irresponsible, if not irrational. Hitler steadily and relentlessly overturned the settlement of WWI by rearming, moving into the Rhineland in March 1936, absorbing Austria in the Anschluss, and dismembering Czechoslovakia in 1938. After handing the Sudetenland to Hitler in the infamous Munich Agreement, British prime minister Sir Neville Chamberlain wrote to the archbishop of Canterbury: "I sincerely believe that we have at last opened the way to that general appeasement which alone can save the world from chaos."[2] The next year, Hitler took the rest of Czechoslovakia and invaded Poland. France and Britain declared war. Thus, close on the heels of WWI, the "mad catastrophe" that was to have ended all wars for generations to come, began WWII.[3]

In fact, the Munich Crisis of 29 September, 1938, has come to symbolize both the dangers of negotiating with a ruthless adversary and the fecklessness

Decision Advantage. Jennifer E. Sims, Oxford University Press. © Oxford University Press 2022.
DOI: 10.1093/oso/9780197508046.003.0012

of national security intelligence. Appeasement has seemed a testament to wooden-headedness and intelligence gone badly wrong.[4] Chamberlain should have known that, by trading a piece of Czechoslovakia for Hitler's promise not to swallow the rest, he was giving away that country's principal defenses: forts, banks, and industry—arguably the last defensible line against Hitler's expansion eastward.[5] Hitler was neither as erratic as Kaiser Wilhelm II nor as obtuse; he had not just hinted at empire building, he had announced it to be his purpose—along with exterminating all non-Aryan peoples within that empire—in his 1925 book, *Mein Kampf* (*My Battle* or *My Struggle*).[6] By 1938, Hitler's Reich *clearly* threatened not just Germany's eastern neighbors but British forces as well. And it is not just in retrospect that "appeasement" in general, and the Munich Agreement in particular, seem ill-informed; Chamberlain's opponents at the time thought so too.[7] Churchill called the Munich Agreement "a defeat without war."[8]

Whether intelligence operations caused British miscalculation is not, however, the correct question because it presupposes Chamberlain miscalculated. It would be as biased as asking whether Britain's foresight in its rearmament and alliance-management were victories we might attribute to intelligence— that is, the foresight to know better than Hitler how to prepare for war in 1938. Presuming neither miscalculation nor prescience, we must ask instead whether and how intelligence informed strategy and tactics. If the goal of intelligence is to help states improve their relative positions at least cost, the test is not whether intelligence divined some future truth but whether it helped participants understand their relative power and thus achieve diplomatic wins, such as gaining time to prepare for war. In this case, it is intriguing that Hitler claimed at the time that the Munich Agreement was a terrible defeat. Perhaps he knew something that history, knowing his future, has since disregarded.

Before tackling the problem of pre-WWII decision-making, it makes sense to dispense with the issue of cowardice as an explanation for Chamberlain's decision-making in 1938. Although caricatures of Chamberlain suggest he was weak, dull-witted, and inept, such depictions are false. Recent scholarship has shown that the prime minister's problem was hardly spinelessness.[9] As early as 1933, when he was appointed Chancellor of the Exchequer, Chamberlain had identified Germany as Britain's greatest threat and had argued for increasing funds for armaments.[10] After becoming prime minister in 1937, his determined grip on foreign policy forced his foreign secretary, Anthony Eden, to resign. The uncertainties of the age—economic volatility, British decline, shifting ideologies, and public loyalties—were hardening agendas and stiffening leaders. Chamberlain was no exception.[11] He, like Hitler, disliked opposition and was infuriated by mockery and disrespect. Political opponents found his "cold intellect" alienating.[12] One key detractor called his "bark as bad as his bite."[13] Even Churchill respected Chamberlain as "a hard-bitten pioneer."[14] One well-respected historian has written that "except possibly for Margaret Thatcher, no peacetime British prime minister has been so strong-willed, almost tyrannical."[15] In fact, Chamberlain's sense of the German threat and pressure to increase spending on weapons of war, which contrasted sharply with the Labour Party's antimilitarism, led to a Conservative sweep in the elections of 1935.

If Chamberlain's apparent caving to Hitler was not a lack of toughness, then was it a matter of judgment? Chamberlain may have supported an arms buildup, but he repeatedly forfeited any advantages gained. Yet here again historians are amending once-familiar critiques of Chamberlain and the other appeasers. "Recent studies of General Gamelin, of France's prime minister Édouard Daladier, and of Britain's long-maligned prime minister Neville Chamberlain," writes one, "not only explain why they were thought to be heroes before the debacle of 1940 but why they *deserved* to be held in high regard."[16] Indeed, the policy of appeasement was so widely supported at the time, it seems unreasonable to blame one man's idiosyncrasies for it. More plausible than cowardice or incompetence is the notion that information flowing to decision-makers led to studied, collective choice. By the time of the Munich Agreement, Britain's leaders valued intelligence; Chamberlain is known to have given more weight to it than had his two predecessors.[17]

Returning then to the issue of wins and losses, both sides had reason to complain about outcomes, but did one side lose more, and was intelligence to blame? Hitler later believed he had lost twice to Chamberlain in 1938: once in the spring when London misconstrued German planning for an attack on Czechoslovakia as an imminent threat, warned Hitler, and made him appear to back down, losing face; a second time in September, when Hitler's plan to take Prague was trimmed to a messy absorption of Sudetenland. By most careful accounts, Hitler was miffed both times. Certainly, he regretted the outcome of Munich—a delay in German expansion east—more acutely than Chamberlain did. Chamberlain lamented the loss of the rest of Czechoslovakia in 1939, but Britain's avoidance of war until 1940 helped London's efforts at transatlantic diplomacy and military production from 1938 to 1940.

Although the counterfactual—what would have happened if appeasement had not been Britain's policy—cannot be determined, it is far from clear that a more belligerent policy could have been prevented war, shortened the Nazi regime, or elicited cooperation from Stalin. Even a delayed war constituted a diplomatic "win" for Britain if decision-makers at the time thought Czechoslovakia mattered less than buying time for achieving a more favorable military balance, if not a less bellicose adversary. Achieving any such favorable outcome required good knowledge of how to strike an advantageous deal, ideally without triggering war on unfavorable ground. Did Chamberlain have such insight and, if so, where did he get it?

Of course, to be in Chamberlain's shoes was to be uncertain of what would happen next. In diplomacy there is no fighting, tallying the dead, and recording the win. Every day the adversaries have you in their sights, jockeying for position, seeking to snatch victory from defeat. Playing the long game is, in fact, the only game in international politics, even if the home team might bench you for misplays or to make substitutions. Did Chamberlain know all this, and prove better at the long game because he understood better than Hitler did the devastation another great power war would bring to Europe, including Germany? Or did Hitler snooker him and just regret gaining only a partial prize?

Exploring these issues involves investigating the intelligence behind statesmen's decisions to negotiate Czechoslovakia's fate rather than fight for it, comparing British to German decision-making at comparable moments. Negotiations of this kind are influenced by three assessments: strategic intent, informed by maps of the terrain of uncertainty; the relative military power or "muscle" behind the negotiators; and by each side's intelligence on the stakeholders' objectives, constraints, and red lines. This chapter may not resolve all questions about appeasement, but it will show how intelligence oiled or soiled the machinery of maneuver as decision-makers searched for diplomatic advantage in these three areas.

Deals often look bad when made with enemies, especially after war ensues. But it is nonetheless true that, while allies are useful, peace can only be secured by dealing with enemies—through bartering, muscling, bluffing, or some combination of all three. Diplomatic wins must be judged in the context of the moment, as each side seeks to know the other's bottom line, when multiple futures are possible, and when relationships of force are uncertain. The side better at projecting power and fathoming an opponent's soft spots while concealing his own is more likely to achieve a favorable diplomatic outcome.

So, considered in these terms, how did Chamberlain's intelligence compare to Hitler's? To answer this question, it is necessary first to understand that Hitler's primary objectives from 1937 to 1938 were domestic because his European plans were so aggressive and his assessment of France and Britain so dismissive that his generals objected. He knew he needed to build his military while subjugating any leaders, who believed they, not Hitler, were the guarantors of the state. Not knowing Hitler's intelligence operations against his military, the allies did not know to be skeptical of sources within the German military who thought they knew Hitler's mind when they did not; in fact, they were being positively manipulated.

Hitler's Intelligence Operations against His Generals and His Decision to Take Czechoslovakia

In late 1937, Hitler planned to invade Czechoslovakia, but he was uncertain of his ability to get his generals to comply. In this regard, he knew more about the military than his German predecessors had known about it before WWI. In fact,

most of the uncertainties of the interwar period were an extension of those before the Great War, including the question of military submission to civilian rule
and who decided security questions for the state in times of peace.[18] By 1937,
Stalin was busy erasing these uncertainties by purging the Soviet army and intelligence services; France was still wrestling with the aftershocks of the Dreyfus
Affair; and Britain was expanding the Committee of Imperial Defense, creating
the military circulating branches of its Secret Intelligence Service (SIS or MI6),
and eventually constituting the Joint Intelligence Committee to coordinate a national intelligence point of view. In Germany, the army was the embodiment of
the state and its command structure—almost a state within the state. For Hitler,
uncertain authority over army decision-making was simply intolerable. So his
first battle was an internal one, and his first intelligence problem was learning
who his opponents were on the German general staff.

Most observers in 1937 believed the German army anchored the state in rationality and order, and, in a very real sense, it did. The German army was conservative and committed to the integrity of its chain of command. Hitler, however,
could not tolerate any center of German power not completely under his command.[19] He had conducted the blood purge of the competing Brownshirts (SA)
in 1934 and had declared the army to be a pillar of the German state—one whose
faithfulness he would never question. But then he did. By 1937 he had intelligence that there was insubordination at the army's highest levels.

Hitler's Intelligence for Command

Given Hitler's plan for continental hegemony through coercive diplomacy and
war, insubordination was among Hitler's greatest concerns. He knew that, to absorb Austria and Czechoslovakia, he needed the army's absolute loyalty. The army
was, however, stiff, conservative, and protective of its institutional prerogatives.
Taking on this institution would require a peculiar form of domestic intelligence,
skillfully employed. Hitler prided himself on his ability to discern loyalties,
ambitions, and capabilities, relying heavily on his own grasp of the facts.[20] So he
began testing his army generals and ministers to find out who might resist him.
He had Hermann Goering, head of the Luftwaffe (air force) and its communications intelligence unit, the Forschungsamt, and Heinrich Himmler, an occultist,
eugenicist, later architect of extermination camps, and leader of the Nazi Party's
fighting Blackshirts (SS), to help him.

One meeting seems to have played a particularly important role prior to
Hitler's moves to absorb Austria and Czechoslovakia. In November 1937, Hitler
ordered General Werner von Blomberg, his minister for war, to assemble a small
group of advisers to discuss pressing issues related to rearmament, such as the

priority among the services for the allocation of resources. Hitler also invited Baron Konstantin von Neurath, his foreign minister, and Hermann Goering. In fact, only Goering knew in advance what Hitler was planning to do. The Luftwaffe needed resources, so Goering supported wholeheartedly Hitler's plans to absorb Germany's resource-rich neighbors—plans that would soon need to be executed.[21] Other attendees included army commander in chief Colonel General Baron Werner von Fritsch, Admiral Erich Raeder, and Colonel Friedrich Hossbach, Hitler's liaison with the high command.

According to the memorandum of record, Hitler soon turned this meeting on logistics into one on grand strategy. Germany, he insisted, had to expand through the application of force no later than 1943–45 because "Our relative strength would decrease in relation to the rearmament . . . carried out by the rest of the world. . . . It was while the rest of the world was fencing itself off that we were obliged to take the offensive."[22] Hitler mentioned both Austria and Czechoslovakia, an ally of France, as targets for takeover in the interim. These moves had to be opportunistic, capitalizing on France's internal weakness, her fraught relationship with Italy, and Britain's imperial overstretch. He argued that London could not address conflicts in the Mediterranean and Far East while also preventing Germany from achieving its goals in Europe. In effect, Britain's imperial uncertainty and habit of tactical thinking could be used against her.[23] The strategy entailed operational risks, but risks of the kind Bismarck took in creating imperial Germany through blood and iron. Besides, Hitler asserted, neither Britain nor France was as powerful as simple military comparisons might suggest; action needed to be taken before these adversaries had time to arm.

Hitler's speech was a shocking confirmation of his most radical aims, but it also was something else: a means to ferret out resistance at the highest levels. According to Hossbach's later recollections, the meeting became volcanic. Despite the familiarity of Hitler's themes, his articulation of the operational implications led to "sharp exchanges" among the participants.[24] The generals, except for Goering, were appalled and they said so. They argued that his plan of expansion by force posed risks far greater than any Bismarck had assumed. France had military superiority; a war between Paris and Rome would occupy only an insufficient fraction of French forces. Fritsch declared that Germany could not defend her industrial centers from a French attack, particularly given her capacities for swift mobilization and Germany's relative inferiority in fortifications and motorized and mechanized divisions. Blomberg joined Fritsch in insisting that Britain and France not assume the role of enemies of the German state. Neurath agreed. Only Raeder seems to have kept his counsel.

Unfortunately for the attendees, Hitler was not asking for their intelligence assessments or advice. The issue for him was less strategy than authority. He believed he could use diplomacy and force to outmaneuver foreign opponents, but only if his decisions were unconditionally and immediately executed. His mindset was of a religious order, one that did not simply filter information but also prescribed action regardless of conventional calculations of risk.[25] This secular religion in turn shaped his need to know who under his command was outside the faith.[26] The November meeting gave him the answers he needed.

Hitler had reasons for suspecting the men in the room. Although in 1933 he had ordered his agency for communications intelligence, the Forschungsamt, not to wiretap members of the Nazi and military elite, he had allowed Goering secretly to do so.[27] It therefore seems likely that Goering and Himmler brought Hitler incriminating evidence about the generals' felt prerogatives and contrary views before this occasion. Hitler had meant it, however, when he said in 1935 that he alone would be the judge of their actual disloyalty. And so, as he listened to these men's reactions to his grand strategy, Hitler concluded that most were unsuitable for his high command. For example, although Fritsch had been cautiously supportive of remilitarization of the Rhineland and rearmament more generally, the commander of the army still spoke as if he believed that he was the supreme authority within the sphere of military operations. Hitler probably knew that during the Rhineland operation Fritsch had been wary of what France might do, believing he had options that Hitler had not expressly authorized.

Blomberg, Hitler's minister of war, seemed a different kind of problem. Although he had instituted loyalty oaths and the "Heil Hitler!" salute, he had also displayed an alarming case of the nerves in 1935 over Hitler's repudiation of the Treaty of Versailles and plans to rearm. Then, during the remilitarization of the Rhineland, he had delivered a telegram to Hitler from Germany's military attaché in London predicting Britain would intervene. Blomberg had behaved, in Hitler's view, like "a hysterical maiden."[28] Similarly, Foreign Minister Neurath, a servile diplomat apt to "wag his tail" around Hitler, nonetheless opposed Hitler's expansionist program and coercive diplomacy as likely to lead to war.[29]

The reactions of these men to his plans told Hitler all he needed to know. For the kind of European operation he planned, he needed a cohesive army he could grip and use like a scalpel, and civilian statesmen who, unflinching, could anesthetize the targets of aggression. Given that these men offered neither a good grip nor a steady hand, he needed to get rid of them, which in turn, required ruining them among their peers. Hitler could not afford to fire his generals outright and risk a general army revolt. So, Hitler had his Security Service unleash domestic covert actions to discredit those who had raised objections or failed to endorse his vision at this crucial meeting.[30] Within weeks of the November 1937 gathering, Blomberg and Fritsch had been implicated in manufactured scandals (the Blomberg-Fritsch affair) and were forced to resign. Neurath, promised renewal of his appointment, instead found his retirement "accepted." He became an advisor with little or no line authority over decision-making. These domestic maneuvers got rid of powerful internal opponents without offending the army and without raising foreign suspicions

Although Hitler thus gained intelligence advantages over his own army, he did so at the risk that his plans would leak or become known to the intelligence services of his enemies. Imagine if a French or British intelligence asset had been capable of infiltrating Hitler's November meeting, placing a microphone there or stealing the subsequently written memorandum of record. Hitler's strategy and clandestine, antimilitary maneuvers would have been revealed. His documented intent, combined with his subsequent actions, would have left little for estimative analysis to guess about his strategic intentions and control of his military. But no such agent or microphone was there. In fact, as will be discussed below, SIS collection inside Germany was weak and the ambassador, Neville Henderson, wary of its risks. He relied on diplomatic channels compromised by deceptive German contacts.

So it was that, while foreign governments were taking comfort from Hitler's apparent reliance on the institutionally independent German army, Hitler was moving to end that independence using secret means and covert operations. Similar ferreting-out of resistant generals followed similar meetings. In 1938 he ousted General Ludwig Beck, chief of the general staff. Beck was a particularly visible target because he wrote his objections in memoranda to Hitler himself. In early August 1938, Hitler called a meeting of senior commanders and other officers at Juterborg, south of Berlin. Before the meeting took place, Beck's superior, General Walther von Brauchitsch, elicited the views of the military leadership regarding the developing "Plan Green" to use force to occupy the Sudetenland and eventually all of Czechoslovakia. The latest draft had included language anticipating the possibility of having to fight France, sending shock waves through the military leadership. Beck, who was highly respected, objected. He was the most outspoken of those in the military who had long believed Hitler's plans would trigger a broader war and, thereby, the ruin of Germany. But Beck's intelligence was bad; he blamed Hitler's *advisors* for the plan. An attendee at the meeting, General Walter von Reichenau, commander of an army at Leipzig, told Hitler of Beck's beliefs and other murmurings of dissent. Beck was dismissed.

The secret intelligence war Hitler waged against his generals reaped a huge intelligence-advantage, because his adversaries continued estimating that the German army had more sway over Hitler than in fact it did. As we shall see, this assumption led policymakers in London to listen to voices that not only had no access to Hitler's plans, but were cut out or set up as foils. In his internal intelligence war, Hitler used Goering's surreptitious wiretaps, personal encounters, entrapment, and a group of military snitches seeking to elevate themselves at the expense of their peers. And he ran counterintelligence operations to learn the extent to which his maneuvers were known or likely to be compromised by his internal foes.

The more formal kind of intelligence came from Himmler's Gestapo (secret police) and Schutzstaffel (SS), which became the Nazi Party's private army, and sometimes the Abwehr, Germany's secret military intelligence service led since 1934 by Admiral Wilhelm Canaris. Canaris's organization also ran human agents overseas and secretly sponsored provocations.[31] It was, however, primarily Himmler's SS network of police and internal spies that kept tabs on threats to Hitler's regime.[32] By 1938, Hitler had situational awareness and information dominance over his military.

Hitler's Intelligence before Munich: The May 1938 Decision to Take Czechoslovakia in October

The second critical decision Hitler took in the run-up to Munich concerned the timing of his planned absorption of Czechoslovakia. For this decision, his intelligence proved inadequate, though he was slow to realize it. In his own mind, as he wrote in *Mein Kampf*, the issue of timing turned largely on public opinion, whose momentum once created could be seized and, he believed, controlled.[33] But Hitler underestimated the difficulties. People had been his primary source of political power, and he had consistently gained from his populist rhetoric. Although he knew popular complacency, ignorance, or resistance could cripple him, as he believed was happening to the governments in Britain and France, he did not believe this could happen to him. He was good at stirring popular passions, so it followed that intelligence advantage would flow from propaganda and influence operations—sources of power that mattered more than minor shifts in military balances. By late May 1938, after the Anschluss with Austria had met with popular enthusiasm beyond even his expectations, Hitler believed conditions were right for taking Czechoslovakia, preferably through coercive diplomacy, but if necessary, by judicious use of force prompted, of course, by some kind of provocation. Although the objective was not new, he now had a precise date in mind: October 1. He called in his generals and told them to prepare Plan Green.

Hitler's precision and confidence in giving this order sprang from his belief that he had mastered offensive counterintelligence: deception and propaganda. He knew that to threaten war without evidence of Sudeten grievance would alienate the masses and delay his plan. He needed the German Czechs to demonstrate distress in order to validate his threats of intervention and to gain legitimacy. The Sudeten German party was, however, represented in Prague, which had been trying to accommodate its demands. The party leader, Konrad

Henlein, seemed relatively "level-headed, patient and tractable" and had, in fact, long been a source for French intelligence. Unbeknownst to the French, however, Henlein had been playing a double game. Hitler had been providing secret subsidies to Henlein's organization, which was, in fact, a Nazi party, in order to gather intelligence and stir up unrest. In this way, Hitler would not have to wait on opportunities with all the problems of timing that would entail. Instead, he could create realities as he wanted them, when he wanted them.[34] This presumed, of course, that Henlein did not strike a separate deal with Prague, or that Prague did not suddenly decide to crack down on the insurgents, forcing Hitler's hand with respect to timing and putting public support at risk.

Hitler's diplomacy of force involved achieving objectives through the kind of "chemical solutions" proponents of appeasement also envisioned: adjusting national borders without triggering premature war among the great powers. But there was a difference. Whereas the appeasers saw such solutions as the objective of multilateral negotiations, Hitler saw the chemistry as his to mix, especially after the Anschluss. As Joseph Goebbels commented when Lithuania gave up Memel in 1938 without a fight: "If you apply a bit of pressure, things happen."[35] Believing that "the political understanding of the great masses . . . is not sufficiently developed for them to arrive at . . . general political opinions by themselves," Hitler could manipulate them and thus achieve a freedom of action democracies were constitutionally unable to replicate. "The majority of humankind . . . is inert and cowardly," he believed, so the role of a great leader was to arouse the masses with simple slogans that bind them to his cause.

> The great masses' receptive ability is only very limited, their understanding is small, but their forgetfulness is great. As a consequence . . . all effective propaganda has to limit itself only to a very few points and to use them like slogans. . . . The purpose of propaganda is not continually to produce interesting changes . . . but to convince; that means, to convince the masses.... A change must never alter the content. . . . In the end it always has to stay the same.[36]

In short, "Hitler held the masses to be as stupid as they were powerful."[37] In his mind, every failure on the part of foreign governments to oppose his actions, such as rearmament, the remilitarization of the Rhineland, or the Anschluss, was another indicator of his sway and their relative enfeeblement. He was incurious about foreign governments' capacities to understand or sway the people; he simply assumed they could not.

Hitler's confidence in his relatively good ability to know and control mass opinion was based on several factors. First, Goebbels, who was largely responsible for Hitler's influence campaigns, was good at his job. As minister of public enlightenment and propaganda, he controlled German press, radio, and film.

Hitler knew he could use the media to bring his version of reality to the people, and then track the results. Second, Hitler closely monitored the press himself and "insisted on extracts, not summaries."[38] He had Otto Meissner, his press chief, place a thick folder of press clippings by his bedroom door every morning. Goering, who had established Germany's large agency for intercepting communications, intercepted and reported the communications of foreign journalists so Hitler could compare those intercepts with what editors decided to publish.[39] Third, Hitler questioned foreign visitors on popular opinions back home, adding their responses to his personal analysis of political trends.

What Hitler did not know was what good diplomats could have told him: that a statesman such as Chamberlain was particularly well attuned to public opinion because his office depended on his being so; beyond this, Chamberlain was a skilled propagandist himself, well versed in influencing the press when the need arose. To Hitler, diversity of national views in foreign polities revealed weakness; the absence of dissent indicated a strong state. This belief that the power of public opinion had to be harnessed because publics were stupid helps explain why Hitler believed diplomatic reporting on complex decision-making in foreign democracies to be almost irrelevant.[40] Whereas popular authoritarians such as he and Benito Mussolini could get ahead of events, Hitler believed foreign government officials in liberal democracies were captives of public opinion, not shapers of it. Statesmen dealing with legal oppositions such as Roosevelt, Chamberlain, and Daladier were doomed, in Hitler's view, to manage only consequences. So he was incurious about the one dimension of power that he thought most crucial: how foreign electorates learned.

Influence Campaigns

This bias did not mean, however, that Hitler had no interest in shaping views in Paris and London. In fact, he seems to have used a sophisticated form of double-agent operations to do so. By keeping some relatively benign dissenters in his foreign ministry, he could not only put a reassuring face on his regime, but also provide soothing sources for a diplomatic circuit anxious for peace and looking for German officials to help keep it. One such person was Baron Ernst von Weizsäcker, a former naval officer, monarchist, and by 1938, a career diplomat serving as number two to Joachim von Ribbentrop in the Foreign Ministry.

To understand Weizsäcker's usefulness for Hitler's intelligence policy, one must appreciate the role played by his boss. Ribbentrop's servility to Nazism and Hitler, in particular, made him the cartoon for Nazism in the British press and a suspected éminence grise at home. While serving in his prior capacity as ambassador in London, Ribbentrop had realized that Hitler cared little for information on British policy, so he had reported about the lives and attitudes of British politicians, promoted Hitler's ideas in social circles, and hosted sympathetic members of the British aristocracy and Nazi sympathizers during their visits with Hitler. Ribbentrop had, in short, figured out Hitler's preference for officials who could influence the enemy through deception and persuasion rather than simply report, which newspapers could do. Pleased, Hitler chose Ribbentrop to replace the weak-kneed Neurath, and eventually called him "the greatest foreign minister since Bismarck."[41] Ribbentrop's access to Hitler was unrivaled, even by most of Hitler's generals.[42] Whereas the latter initially believed themselves more powerful than their Führer in matters involving war and state security, Ribbentrop knew where power lay and swiftly accommodated himself to it.

Such a man surely knew that his number two presented a problem. In the first place, Weizsäcker held Ribbentrop in low regard and viewed him as dangerously influential. Second, while Weizsäcker wanted a greater Germany too, he found Nazis embarrassing.[43] By 1938, his loyalty to Hitler stemmed not from Nazism, but from the Anschluss, which had begun to restore Germany's status as a European imperial power. Weizsäcker resisted, however, Hitler's grand strategy, including plans for the use of force in a larger European context. Instead, he favored negotiations, bartering, and sleights of hand to which Britain and France might acquiesce. When responding to Ribbentrop's complaints about military dissenters, he observed, "Whoever loves the German Reich and its Führer cannot counsel war." And while he believed that Czechoslovakia was destabilizing Europe, he also advised that Germany had "no military recipe for defeating France and Britain... war would therefore end with our exhaustion and defeat."[44]

Given Hitler's purge of his military and the dumping of Neurath, Hitler's and Ribbentrop's tolerance of constant dissent from such a high-level official seems strange. Weizsäcker conveyed all his views with some vigor not just to Ribbentrop, whom he considered naïve and dangerous, but to his contacts in the diplomatic circle—primarily the British ambassador, Neville Henderson. He was, in fact, probably Henderson's most important source within the German government. And herein lay Hitler's advantage: a senior diplomat was consistently delivering a two-part message as heartfelt as it was useful: Hitler was being poorly advised by warmongers and, if diplomats worked together, they could resolve outstanding issues without war. "If Paris and London would make it clear that their primary interest was peace and stability in the region," he intoned, "new territorial arrangements could be worked out, genuinely reflecting the principles of 'self-determination' and 'nationality.' "[45] Weizsäcker was thus an advocate of that very "chemical solution" for the Sudetenland that appeasers also sought; he made Hitler seem both rational and bounded regarding his aims.

In sum, Weizsäcker was a source providing diplomatic intelligence that advocates of appeasement in Britain and France could cite from the highest reaches of the Nazi Reich in affirmation of their preferred policy. Whether the policy of appeasement was seeded from Germany into Britain through Henderson or simply found receptive audience is unclear. What is clear, however, is that the success of Hitler's policy of coercive diplomacy required appeasement from the other side if it was not to provoke premature continental war. Weizsäcker, wittingly or not, provided the intelligence to Britain that made appeasement seem workable. If Britain's or France's military intelligence had been better, disconnects between Hitler's strong-arming of military dissenters and tolerance of diplomatic ones might have revealed his deceptions.

There seems little reason to believe that Hitler or Ribbentrop failed to appreciate Weizsäcker's opposition to the use of force against Czechoslovakia. He stated his views repeatedly and insistently during the summer of 1938—well past the time Hitler had approved Operation Green and sidelined anyone in the military who disagreed with him.[46] It is likely that Hitler deemed Weizsäcker useful for undermining the arguments of those in foreign governments advocating a resort to arms.

In fact, Weizsäcker spent considerable time trying to influence the British government; he hoped London would come to see Germany as less a competitor than a revitalized European bulwark, managing the industrial, financial, communist, and racial tides reordering the power relationships in Europe. Weizsäcker was, in this sense, the perfect foil because he truly believed what he was saying: "I have said to Henderson once again that this is not a game of chess but a rising sea. One cannot make the same kinds of assumptions as in normal times with normal reasons and normal people."[47]

Hitler's use of diplomatic channels for deception was mirrored in his discounting of diplomatic intelligence in most of his decision-making. Because he was using diplomacy to deceive, it is hardly surprising that he did not trust diplomatic reporting himself. By the end of the summer of 1938, the British were learning about his shocking disregard for intelligence coming through diplomatic channels.

When the German Ambassador in Paris, Johannes von Welczek, reported his strong impression that France would reluctantly be obliged to honour the obligation to the Czechs, Hitler simply pushed the report to one side, saying it did not interest him. Hearing of this, Lord Halifax pointed it out to the British Cabinet as evidence that "Herr Hitler was possibly or even probably mad."[48]

It was in this context—an appreciation of Hitler's probable dictatorial powers combined with his unwillingness to trust standard channels of communication, that Chamberlain decided to fly to Berlin in September to solve the crisis over the Sudetenland.

Chamberlain's Decision to Meet Hitler and Then Negotiate Partial Dismemberment, September 12, 1938

Chamberlain was ahead of Hitler in at least one regard: whereas Hitler had to craft an intelligence policy to alert him to those domestic officials who contested his views, Chamberlain had a Cabinet and opposition party to do that for him. In general, he felt well-equipped on foreign intelligence. After all, he had his foreign ministry and his ambassador in Germany for diplomatic intelligence; MI6, his foreign intelligence organization running agents overseas and liaising with the French; MI5, the domestic security service, to track treachery at home, and the press to help him know and influence public opinion. Like Hitler, he too believed the opinions of the masses could be decisive. And given public distaste for war and sympathy for German revisionism, Chamberlain's government saw the drawing of red lines in any particular place in Europe as prejudicial to a broader settlement.

This point requires emphasis: Chamberlain's idea by 1937 was that a peaceful restructuring of power could be stabilizing, especially if it squelched irredentism by reunifying nationalities and eliminating small, nonviable states. By 1938, therefore, most of the Cabinet believed that what was needed was an understanding of the grand bargain Hitler had in mind. The debate between appeasers and confrontationists was not so much about the restructuring of Europe in principle—most agreed that the Versailles Treaty ending WWI had been unfair to Germany. Rather, it was about whether Germany envisioned a settlement that might, taken as a whole, be tolerable. For the radical anti-appeasers, Hitler had no limits in mind and had a "package" he planned to acquire by force once diplomacy had delivered all it could. So, they argued, Britain should stop delivering.

To understand these differences in thinking and "knowing" among British officials before Munich, including how they used intelligence to support their decision-making, it is useful to review a high-level meeting held in London on 8 September 1938. The subject was intelligence coming from a secret German source, Herr X, who had recently risked coming to 10 Downing Street to alert the government about Hitler's intention to move on Czechoslovakia. Herr X was a credible source at the time. His real name was Theodor Kordt, chargé d'affaires at the German embassy; his brother worked for Ribbentrop. Kordt was pressing the British to deliver a public warning to deter Hitler from carrying out his plan for Czechoslovakia.

Neville Chamberlain's close advisers requested an urgent meeting to decide whether or not to act on Kordt's advice. In attendance were Chamberlain's foreign minister, Lord Halifax, his special advisor, Sir Horace Wilson, his Chancellor of the Exchequer, Sir John Simon, and the permanent undersecretary at the Foreign Office, Alexander Cadogan. As Chamberlain greeted them, his advisors were in a grim state of mind. Hitler had absorbed Austria in May. Now France was pressing Britain for support to deter Hitler from swallowing another weak state. On 30 August, the British Cabinet had decided to keep Berlin guessing about what it would do—an outcome that reinforced Chamberlain's inclination to maneuver. Kordt's intelligence was, however, arresting in both its precision and prediction: without a firm stand by Britain and France, Hitler would "march in" on the nineteenth or twentieth, which would be earlier than previous intelligence had indicated. According to the source, a stiff warning would lend weight to the inclination among some German generals to resist Hitler's orders. Time was of the essence if the British government wanted to stop him.

Chamberlain's Views and Policies

As Chamberlain considered this new intelligence, he did so in light of his own policy of appeasement, which was based on judgments and premises shared by most of his advisors and Cabinet:[49]

- *The need for time.* Traditional British diplomacy had long had something of the mongoose: agility, focus, and tactical response. But this approach had presumed adversaries would not and could not coordinate across her imperial expanse. The rise of Japan, its flirtations with Germany, and the communications revolution had rendered such assumptions untenable. At the same time, changes in the Commonwealth's constitution made wartime coherence uncertain and its defense almost impossible, particularly against an alliance of Germany, Japan, and Italy.[50] Britain could handle pop-up threats, but not a concert of enemies stretching from Central Europe to Asia. Chamberlain and his advisors therefore believed Britain needed time to separate these potential enemies and build arms to gain superiority over any combination of them.
- *An ordering of threats.* Of the global challenges Britain faced in the late 1930s, Germany's had become the most pressing.[51] The Bolshevik threat had loomed largest in the 1920s, but Stalin's purges and internal problems had weakened the Soviet state. In contrast, Germany's power had increased to the point that she could attack her neighbors more easily than Britain or France could defend them. In October 1936, the Air Ministry staff had submitted a paper to the Committee of Imperial Defense saying that Germany's aims were not just to build a force in phases to some reasonable cap, but to expand air power as fast as possible in order to have the capacity for a knockout blow against Britain.[52] In fact, Britain now—in September 1938—appeared vulnerable to a knockout blow from the air.[53] The ICC had

issued an influential report saying that Germany, a totalitarian state, could manage its finances and conserve raw materials in ways Britain could not.[54] By September 1938, intelligence reports estimated that the German air force included 927 long-range bombers, with London as a primary target.[55] Joining France in defense of the Low Countries was of increasing importance because, should they be overrun, their territories could be used to launch bombers across the Channel.

- *The expectation that the German threat was resolvable.* The Italians seemed open to steps that might secure a broader British settlement with Germany.[56] Besides, the War Office "still placed some residual faith in the role of the German high command as a rational brake on the wilder foreign policy impulses of Hitler and the party 'extremists.' "[57] Hitler's aims seemed to reflect the will of the German people, who had legitimate grievances stemming from the draconian settlement imposed by the victors at Versailles.[58] Since Germany's maladjustment to Europe's postwar structure was a man-made problem, reasonable men could fix it.[59] To get a fix, however, it was important not to embarrass Hitler or let him believe he was being encircled by hostile powers.[60] A peaceful settlement with Germany on the restructuring of Europe would allow Britain to focus on defending her interests in the Far East, block the encroachment of Soviet-sponsored communism, and use British naval power to deter Japan.[61]

- *Alliances, therefore, were difficult and dangerous.* Czechoslovakia was indefensible and could offer no help in the containment of German power. War Office intelligence reports since 1933, and especially since Germany's absorption of Austria, had made this clear.[62] Indeed, any European alliances could provoke German fears of encirclement. The Soviet Union, a natural counterweight to Germany's growing power, was a long-term threat to European order.[63] Even France, a necessary counterweight to Germany, had made irrational commitments to the defense of weak Central European states. A weak, defeatist France could endanger Britain through precipitous action or injudicious bluff. And, of course, US neutrality laws made US support unlikely, especially if British policy seemed unreasonably stiff.

- *Hitler was rational; war was not.* Chamberlain spoke for many British officials when he said that he "could not conceive of anyone's wanting war."[64] Although WWI had demonstrated the enormous costs and futility of great power war, it also left memories of carnage reawakened by the Luftwaffe's bombardment of Spain during the latter's recent civil war. Chamberlain knew Adolph Hitler was a brutal opportunist, but he also believed him to be rational—acting in Germany's interests to reverse a punitive peace. There was nothing insensible about building German power, including air power, so long as it was not for a war of aggression.[65] Even Hitler's July 1934 move against Ernst Röhm's pro-Nazi Brownshirts, since termed the Night of the Long Knives, seemed to demonstrate Hitler's sensible choice of his disciplined army over his thugs.

Most of Chamberlain's Cabinet and advisors shared the prime minister's premises regarding the primacy of the German threat and the likelihood that Hitler's aims could be limited. The specific issue was whether the dictators' aims might be incompatible, nonetheless, with British interests. Skeptical, Anthony Eden had resigned his position as foreign secretary earlier that year, prompting the British government to reassure the United States:

> There was above all no truth whatever in the press rumours to the effect that Great Britain now contemplated the negotiation of an agreement with the dictators at any cost. On the contrary, no agreement of any kind would be entered into with any dictator country unless it was entirely apparent that it was consonant with the principles which had hitherto guided British foreign policy and would result in general appeasement and hence in the preservation of peace.[66]

In sum, at the end of August 1938, most of London's decision-makers believed a firm stand against Germany could cost a world war for which Britain was as yet unprepared and indeed peculiarly vulnerable, while accommodation might perhaps satisfy the Führer's vision for a greater Germany. To explore that possibility in the case of Czechoslovakia, Lord Runciman had been sent to mediate the Czech crisis, searching for a way to accommodate Sudeten German grievances within a more loosely structured state. London remained unsure how much the viability of that state should really matter, beyond its importance to perceptions of the integrity of French commitments to her allies.

It should be noted here that the British policy of appeasement did not *assume* Germany's aims were tolerable; to the contrary, it was designed to tease out the answer to whether they were tolerable by accepting Germany's revisionist purposes while establishing principles for peace. Such a process required, however, knowing *who set* Germany's preferences and, if Hitler, then his authority to force them on his army during peacetime crises, given reports of dissent among some officers. Chamberlain was inclined to meet Hitler's demands, so long as they remained reasonable and limited, such as protecting the German Czechs in the Sudetenland. To ferret out Hitler's intentions, Chamberlain had a secret "Plan Z," which involved negotiating with Hitler face to face. As Chamberlain's advisors took their seats, the prime minister considered how much of it to share.

The Foreign Secretary's Dilemma

Chamberlain's senior advisors mostly shared his view on Britain's best strategy, appeasement, but remained uncertain how to implement it in the Czech case. The locus of the greatest angst was the Foreign Office. On one side of this disagreement was the permanent undersecretary, Alexander Cadogan, who believed Hitler's aims were uncertain and worth exploring; on the other side was Cadogan's predecessor, Robert Vansittart (also known as Van), who still advised the foreign secretary and took Hitler's book, *Mein Kampf*, at face value. He believed Hitler's aims were intolerable and that Britain should take "a firm stand" even at the risk of war. Cadogan was in the room that day; Vansittart, disliked by Chamberlain and almost everyone else, was not.

The foreign secretary, Lord Halifax, found himself constantly in the hot middle of this debate between his two subordinates. The antithesis of Anthony Eden, Halifax liked keeping a low profile and exercising quiet influence. His demeanor suited his responsibilities, which included not just foreign policy but also management of British diplomatic reporting and the secret intelligence services. Unfortunately, recent reporting from these sources had accentuated the deepening difference of views within his department. On the one hand, his ambassador in Berlin, Sir Neville Henderson, said that Hitler was a reasonable man. He was reporting that the German state secretary, Baron Ernst von Weizsäcker, thought a "friendly message" to Hitler about the Cabinet's "difficulties and apprehensions" would be the appropriate next step in limiting tensions.[67] Halifax knew that the French representative in Berlin, André François-Poncet, supported this view. François-Poncet, reportedly Hitler's favorite among Berlin's diplomats,[68] portrayed him "as determined to redress Germany's grievances, inclined to be impetuous, but realistic enough to be restrained by awareness both of Germany's comparative weakness and of the costs of war."[69] This reporting, together with that provided by the War Office, strengthened Halifax's view that Hitler listened to careerists in the Foreign Ministry and his military. German generals had repeatedly relayed to British diplomats their interest in preserving peace with the Western powers.[70] And Halifax had met Hitler himself and had found him rather unimpressive. In fact, Hitler was so unassuming that Halifax had almost handed him his coat, thinking he was a doorman.[71]

On the other hand, Halifax knew that Vansittart had reliable sources that saw Hitler as a monster. One of Vansittart's best sources, Group Captain Malcolm Christie, had seemed to demonstrate good access to Hitler's plans and the Luftwaffe's production rates by correctly estimating them over time. Now Christie was reporting that Hitler had not only set his sights on all of Czechoslovakia, *but on all of Europe*. This man had forewarned of the Anschluss and the earlier Czech crisis. He seemed able to relay intelligence soon after Hitler took decisions.[72] He had been a key source on German air power as well, contradicting the Air Ministry's own intelligence by revealing that no brakes were, in fact, being applied on production of German aircraft.[73] Although the Air Ministry had countered that reporting, it had eventually conceded it was correct.

Vansittart's support for his source had put Halifax on the spot and created bureaucratic enemies. Now, in September, Christie's reports were causing more bureaucratic trouble by mirroring French intelligence and undermining Chamberlain's policy. Vansittart had told Halifax of his conviction: German superiority over combined French and British forces made it rational for Hitler to press for supremacy. Halifax had seen reporting that the number of German soldiers that year (1938) had exceeded what the War Office *had expected for 1943*. But even if Vansittart seemed to have point, he also had a way of making trouble.[74] Chamberlain, for example, did not want him in the room. This made Halifax's problem more complex.

Vansittart was not happy to be cut out. His sources on Hitler's decision-making went well beyond Christie. He had set up a private spy network when he was permanent undersecretary (1930–38). Kept secret from most of the SIS, his "Z" network was run by a British businessman named Claude Dancey, who used officers under business cover. Vansittart also paid attention to reporting from MI5 agents he had helped put in play when he was permanent undersecretary. For example, he had encouraged the Security Service to penetrate the German embassy in London, where it had recruited the diplomat Wolfgang zu Putlitz. Motivated by hatred of the Nazis, Putlitz had provided detailed information on decision-making within the German foreign ministry and embassy.

Vansittart had also urged MI5 to spy on the London office of the Auslands Organization, an association of German Nazis living abroad. By May 1936, MI5 had determined that the Auslands Organization was "a ready-made instrument for [German] intelligence, espionage and ultimately for sabotage," with over 288 Nazi Party members and 870 Italian Fascists—a finding that had led Winston Churchill to dub the organization the "Nazitern."[75] Vansittart and MI5 had substantial evidence that the organization was an important source of intelligence for Hitler. Hitler's uncanny ability to anticipate British political moves after his march into the Rhineland in 1936 was based more on its reporting than the more alarmist warnings coming from his embassy in London.[76]

Vernon Kell, head of MI5, was one of the few who agreed with Vansittart that appeasement was useless because Hitler had long been implementing the road map he had laid out in *Mein Kampf*. "It is emphatically not a case of irresponsible utterances which have been discarded by a statesman obtaining power."[77] Like Vansittart, Kell was not reticent to share his opinion.

Halifax read the MI5 reports and could not dismiss them, but Vansittart's methods were irritating and his prescriptions impossible. In the first place, Vansittart believed that Hitler could be "stopped" only if France and Britain, with the support of the Soviet Union, presented a firm, united front against German aggression. Any process that suggested malleability to Hitler's next demands or involved the exclusion of Stalin would, in Vansittart's view, be taken as weakness, embolden Hitler, and lead to another world war. Halifax, however, abhorred Stalin and found Vansittart's argument tantamount to a bluff: both reckless and politically tone-deaf. A united front was hardly possible given that voters in both France and Britain wanted peace and saw at least some of German grievances as legitimate.

Second, Vansittart's recommendations tended toward impractical clandestine operations. He wanted to use secret maneuvers to iron out differences between the Sudeten Germans and Prague, thus presenting Hitler with a fait accompli. Intrigue was not, however, Halifax's style—diplomacy was—and the ambassador in Berlin, Henderson, believed *that* would work. Henderson knew senior officials in the Foreign Ministry who insisted Hitler would bend to a moderate approach. Besides, if the alternative to appeasement were done deals, Britain would have to create these realities on the ground through conspiracy and coups de main. Again, this was simply not in Halifax's comfort zone, even if there was a chance such intrigues might work, which he doubted.

Third, Halifax suspected that Vansittart had a rigid mindset biased against Germany and, worse, seemed to cherry-pick intelligence to fit his views. As early as May 1933, Vansittart had predicted that "the present regime in Germany will, on past and present form, loose off another European war just so soon as it feels strong enough.... We are considering very crude people who have few ideas in their noddles [sic] but brute force and militarism."[78] Halifax also knew Vansittart's sources shared his views, and some just wanted a greater Germany without Hitler. One had to guard against their advice, which was to have Britain risk war for the purpose of encouraging the army to revolt and thus force Hitler out.[79] Vansittart admitted that his German sources "thought that, if they fed me with sufficient evidence, I might have influence enough to arouse our Government and so stop it (the invasion of Czechoslovakia). Of course they were wrong, but we tried."[80] So, it was not unreasonable for Halifax to suspect that Vansittart's red line on Czechoslovakia reflected the preferences of his Czech sources who, though unnervingly right about Hitler's tactical moves, were also politicized insofar as their interest was to save their country no matter what. Britain had larger matters in mind. Vansittart's lack of discretion in such matters was a central reason he had been demoted from permanent undersecretary to "senior adviser" without line authority or portfolio.

Fourth, Halifax regarded Vansittart as a sneak. The man had gone behind the rest of the Foreign Office to meet privately with Alexis Leger, a French intelligence expert who had been named secretary general of the French Foreign Ministry in 1933.[81] Leger shared Vansittart's views and contacts with Henlein, leader of the Sudeten Germans. Halifax knew about these maneuvers, seeing the relationship with Leger as positively conspiratorial.[82] Halifax also knew that Vansittart had been colluding with Winston Churchill, Chamberlain's most prominent critic, to feed the latter Vansittart's latest "intelligence" on overseas developments. Although in this instance his actions were hardly sneaky—Churchill got the briefings right in Vansittart's office, and he got them, too, from Major Desmond Morton, head of the Industrial Intelligence Center—such briefings made Vansittart difficult to remove without causing political difficulties of all kinds, and Vansittart knew it.[83] Halifax could not dismiss the man without sending the wrong message to those in France and Germany who were, for differing reasons, watching for and worried about signs of weakness in London.

All this said, Halifax did not want to dismiss Vansittart. He wanted to get the man's intelligence for the same reasons Churchill did: it was riveting. Over the summer, Vansittart's sources in Germany had confirmed reporting coming to Leger through one of his female agents. She had reported that the Germans were negotiating with the Hungarian government to gain joint action against Czechoslovakia in the near future. The Deuxième Bureau was also running a source, Hans-Thilo Schmidt ("H.E."), whose brother was a German general. He had reported that Hitler was pressing the reluctant general staff for an attack sometime around 25 September.[84] Although most of this warning had been shared with SIS, Cadogan and the Committee of Imperial Defense, Schmidt's reports regarding Hitler's larger plans still seemed conjecture. Without proof one way or the other, the question remained: was Germany trying to right the (limited) wrongs of Versailles such that a comprehensive solution could be found, or was Hitler a madman seeking continental domination? It was because this question had not yet been answered that Halifax believed listening to Vansittart was prudent, if disagreeable.

As Halifax took his place in the meeting with Chamberlain, he thus felt pressed between two strong, irreconcilable positions. For reasons of temperament, he sided with Cadogan, but as a matter of prudence he had to listen to Vansittart. After all, if recent reporting from Berlin was correct, Hitler had ignored his own diplomatic intelligence that France would go to war over Czechoslovakia, which either meant the future of Sudeten Germans was vital, or Hitler did not fear war, or both.[85] Halifax had already told the Cabinet that, if the intelligence on this incident was true, Hitler was probably mad. As Halifax looked around the room, he probably wished Vansittart was there to make his case yet again, so others might be made uncomfortable too.

Cadogan

As Alexander Cadogan took a chair near Halifax, he was both perplexed by Halifax's continued tolerance of Vansittart and confident of his own view.[86] He did not know what Germany would do next, but he did know the right course for Chamberlain to take. Whereas Vansittart believed Hitler's intentions were clear, Cadogan accepted the SIS (MI6) view that they were uncertain, and that diplomacy could still uncover and change them. As he put it in his own diary at the time:

> If everyone in Germany is mad, and if all are bent on our destruction, disaster *must* come. Therefore, the best we can do is to put it off. Therefore we *must* try and talk with some of them and encourage some of them. It's no use shutting our eyes and hiding our heads in the sand and doing nothing.[87]

Cadogan believed diplomatic intelligence to be at least as important as the more secret kind, and better at enabling the tactical arts of influence provided it could determine who was pulling the strings. He knew that the Foreign Office had relatively good access to Hitler's government and that Chamberlain relied on diplomatic intelligence for his decision-making. Confidence in diplomatic channels did not mean that either he or Chamberlain distrusted secret sources, only that both thought them relatively thin and their product highly estimative, if nonetheless useful on occasion.

Cadogan was, within the Foreign Office, principal overseer of the Secret Intelligence Service (SIS or MI6) and Britain's Government Code and Cryptologic Service (GC&CS). He knew that GC&CS had failed to crack German high-grade codes and ciphers, and had little from other lower-level German sources.[88] He nonetheless got along well with the SIS chief, the widely respected Hugh ("Quex") Sinclair. The relationship was close, in part for bureaucratic reasons. The Foreign Office had come to play a major role in the operational targeting, planning, and reporting of the SIS ever since investigations after WWI found deficiencies in coordination.[89] "Circulating sections" had been set up in SIS headquarters to disseminate all incoming intelligence to those who needed it, including Vansittart in his new role.[90] But it was Cadogan, who now met regularly with Sinclair to discuss the latest intelligence and the reliability of sources.[91]

Sinclair judged the German government's objectives in Czechoslovakia to be uncertain, but he believed accommodation with Hitler might be possible. The intelligence in August that had, as Cadogan admitted, made his "hair stand on end" had not dissuaded Sinclair from this view.[92] Sinclair's assessment, estimate, and prescription (soon to be memorialized in an 18 September memo entitled "What is to be Done?") were all rolled into one: given German military dominance and

Berlin's expressed interest in national unity, the Czechs should be told to give up the Sudetenland or stand alone if they did not. If Vansittart's intelligence was politicized at its source, Sinclair's was politicized too, but with the official authority of MI6..

Although Sinclair was not at the 8 September meeting, Cadogan was there to relay his estimate and prescription. Most of the men listening to Cadogan appreciated that his and Sinclair's views were actually more estimate than fact-based assessment. They did not, perhaps, appreciate how weak the basis for SIS's estimate was, however. In fact, the weaknesses ran deep:

- SIS officers and agents (recruited spies) in Europe, were generally incompetent. Managers reported serious deficiencies in recruitment, training, tradecraft, and operational security.
- Few agents or their handlers were educated on scientific matters, despite their importance for understanding force balances and strategy. One group captain at SIS headquarters circulating reports to the Air Ministry found most agents more able "to tell what they saw rather than what they knew."[93] This lack of expertise was apparent to the service branches, which remained generally skeptical of reports coming in through SIS channels.
- Overseas SIS officers operated clandestinely under the cover of passport control officers (PCOs), which meant they were increasingly swamped with refugee processing, so less and less time was left for collecting intelligence.
- British ambassadors in general, but notably those in Italy, Germany, and the Soviet Union, did not like the PCOs' secret functions, so resisted allowing cover operations in their country or minimized the security necessary for their effective operation. At the same time, the British embassies in Germany, the Vatican, and Italy leaked like sieves. Officials in London found one Italian national employed by the embassy in Rome guilty of espionage, but the ambassador refused to believe it and had not dismissed the man. (The spy would not be kicked out until well into the war.) The legation to the Vatican was unsecured within a building owned by the Italian armed forces. And the embassy in Berlin was at the mercy of its German porter, who had keys to everything.[94]
- Funding for SIS operations was poor and the Foreign Office was largely to blame. Sinclair sometimes had to beg his own relatives for money. As PCOs had been steadily cut, recruitment of personnel was slow. Overseas agents generally lacked not only operating funds but also wireless communications, which meant that requirements for intelligence and responsive information were not received in a timely way.
- SIS reports were, for the most part, poorly coordinated with reporting from other departments. The Foreign Office resisted the idea of any interagency

committees, such as Industrial Intelligence Center (IIC) or the Joint Intelligence Sub-committee (JIC) of the Chiefs of Staff, being responsible for "political intelligence." FO resistance meant the JIC was ineffectual until at least the outbreak of war. The IIC, which initially shared office space with the SIS, was detached from it physically by 1934 and administratively by 1936, becoming subordinate to the Department of Overseas Trade. It too had insufficient resources for its job, which was to monitor overseas economic and industrial developments, including German rearmament.[95]

- Regarding Czechoslovakia in particular: SIS's chief asset could not be run directly but only through the Czechs. SIS had the same kinds of problems Halifax pinned on Vansittart. For example, Paul Thümmel (Agent A-4), was embedded in the Abwehr, and run by the Czech intelligence service. Although he seemed to supply excellent intelligence, he could not be tasked directly. Reports were summarized by the Czech service, and SIS lacked a method for ensuring that his reporting was not influenced by Czech interests.[96] Liaison with the Czech service should have been more suspected of compromise than it was.

In recent weeks, these matters had gotten worse: the station chief in Vienna had been effectively run out of town and the staff of the PCO removed; the Dutch Station was penetrated; and leaks were continuing from the Italian embassy, with no one sure who was responsible. PCO cover had become thin to the point of pretense.[97]

Cadogan knew most of these weaknesses and had concluded that SIS reporting could not be entirely trusted: "I never swallow all these things, and I am presented with a *selection*."[98] He probably did not, however, raise concerns about SIS reporting at the meeting. After all, he strongly agreed with Sinclair's advice; he, too, did not believe that a firm hand would deter Hitler, while it could lead to war. A warning would therefore be disastrous. Britain would either be weakened by her bluff or would have to go to war before she was ready. Cadogan made the argument succinctly. "As the evidence of German armed strength, Hitler's determination, French defeatism, and British weakness in arms" had accumulated, "the risks [of "a firm stand"] could be run only in the last resort."[99] Cadogan believed artful diplomacy could yet probe and test Hitler's ultimate aims.

Halifax and Chamberlain were inclined to agree with Cadogan, in part because they had a gambit in mind.[100] Before this meeting, Halifax had probably told Cadogan about Chamberlain's "Plan Z"—the prime minister's idea to fly to Germany to negotiate Czechoslovakia's fate directly with Hitler. Such a plan might gather diplomatic intelligence on Hitler's larger plans and willingness to achieve limited, "chemical" solutions to unviable borders. If so, they might still settle the Sudetenland problem short of war. As the meeting at 10 Downing

Street evolved into a discussion of Chamberlain's idea of negotiating directly with Hitler, Cadogan was almost certainly on board with it.

There remained, however, the issue of timing, and the not incompatible idea of issuing a warning of some kind. Kordt's intelligence suggested Hitler's attack might take place as early 19 or 20 September, creating a new sense of urgency.[101] Everyone in the room knew that Hitler was planning a major speech at Nuremberg on the eleventh, which could harden his position. Chamberlain was adamant that he would not embarrass Hitler by forcing him to back down in public, as he believed he had done during the Czech crisis in May. Should Chamberlain fly to Berlin for an urgent private meeting?

Perhaps, Halifax suggested, Vansittart should come and present a case as the devil's advocate. No one could have been pleased by this suggestion, least of all Cadogan. Halifax's support for Vansittart irritated everyone who found the latter's contrarian views on appeasement as irritating as a stuck record.[102] Yet the recent and passionate message from Kordt, one of Vansittart's and MI5 most secret sources, made it seem judicious to hear Vansittart one more time.

Sir Horace Wilson

As Chamberlain sent for Vansittart, Horace Wilson could not have been happy, despite being confident about how the meeting would come out. What could Vansittart add? Wilson knew how committed Chamberlain was to the idea of flying to Germany. He suspected the effort would help pry Mussolini further away from the Führer, and thus induce caution in Berlin.

Chamberlain's interest in dividing his enemies was an essential element of his strategy of appeasement, and Wilson knew it. After all, GC&CS had broken Italy's encrypted communications "all but completely," thanks to the heavy communications during the Ethiopian and Spanish Civil Wars. To preserve the insights gleaned and develop a broader relationship with Rome, Britain had eschewed decision-advantages at critical moments. For example, London had good insight into Rome's intentions toward Ethiopia from 1935 to 1936, but had remained quiet.[103]

Wilson suspected he had a jump on some of the others in the room because he was such a close adviser to Chamberlain that he knew some secrets they did not. He was, for example, the Downing Street contact for Chamberlain's éminence grise, Sir Joseph Ball.[104] Ball was in secret contact with the legal adviser at the Italian embassy, Adrian Dingli, who had previously worked for MI5. Dingli was the intermediary for the Italian ambassador, Dino Grandi. Communications through this channel to the Italian government, carried out behind the back of the Foreign Office and SIS, had been one of the reasons Halifax's predecessor,

Sir Anthony Eden, had resigned.[105] Chamberlain hoped to press Mussolini to get Hitler to compromise. Ball worked to make that happen almost from the beginning of Chamberlain's tenure in 1937.[106] Given that Hitler and Mussolini had thoroughly compromised the Italian embassy, this backchannel made some sense, provided it was managed with expertise and discipline.

Ball had long been an intelligence operative of one kind or another. Once head of MI5's Investigation Branch, he had become the first director of a research unit attached to the Conservative Party for the purpose of partisan intelligence gathering and dissemination. The party's chairman at the time (1930), J. C. C. Davidson, called the unit "a little intelligence service of our own," and allowed Ball to employ MI5 tactics against the Labour Party, including placing agents in the opposition's headquarters and scooping ad campaigns before they were printed.[107] Davidson hired Ball because he "had as much experience as anyone I know in the seamy side of life and the handling of crooks."[108] Ball and his intermediary, Wilson, had Chamberlain's trust and his ear.

The British Decision?

When Vansittart came into the room, he was prepared to make his case to a group he knew to be hostile. He likely repeated the arguments he had been making for some time: Hitler's objectives were domination of Europe; Britain would not be spared; the Nazi regime would, in fact, carry out the abhorrent plans outlined in *Mein Kampf*. The British government needed to join with France and Russia in taking a firm stand against any German territorial aggrandizement. In the meantime, London should create a solution to the Sudetenland issue within Czechoslovakia, confront Hitler with a fait accompli, and prepare as rapidly as possible for war. Vansittart likely reiterated his assessment that appeasement was feeding a beast with promise of pacification and an ever-stronger bite. He had long emphasized that this assessment was based less on estimative judgments than on Hitler's own words, his record of behavior, and reliable clandestine reporting. His warning was prescient:

> If we lend ourselves to the beginning of this process, the future is fairly obvious—in two stages. In the first Russia will be evicted and retire into sulky isolation. In the second she will be penetrated by Germany, and Bismarck's traditional policy of close Russo-German relations will follow. The consequences to Europe are too obvious to need enlargement here.[109]

In conclusion, Vansittart observed that Plan Z, as it had been described to him, amounted to Henry IV going to Canossa again. This was a reference to the French monarch during the Middle Ages who, having battled with Pope Gregory II to the point of excommunication, humbled himself by walking over the Alps and waiting for days to negotiate the pope's forgiveness, only to be excommunicated again later. Vansittart admitted that Czechoslovakia could not continue to exist in its present state, but he argued passionately for a solution through local engagement with stakeholders and strategic deterrence, including naval maneuvers.

Vansittart apparently changed no one's mind. As Cadogan wrote in his diary: "We argued with him [Vansittart] and I think demolished him."[110] Chancellor of the Exchequer Sir John Simon, who disliked Vansittart, summarized his position as a bluff that, if it failed, meant continental war:

> In the modern world there is no limit to the reactions of war. This very case of Czechoslovakia may be so critical for the future of Europe that it would be impossible to assume a limit to the disturbance that a conflict might involve, and everyone in every country who considers the consequences has to bear that in mind.[111]

Chamberlain, nonetheless, seemed troubled and uncertain. The meeting dissolved with no decision taken on either the warning or the trip. Vansittart was asked to participate in drafting option papers so that, over the next few days, Chamberlain could consider alternative courses of action. These included having the press endorse the latest Czech position in the Runciman talks (Vansittart); having Chamberlain issue a public or perhaps private warning that if France went to war, Britain would have to back her (Vansittart); sending a private letter to Hitler suggesting a meeting (Henderson, Halifax, and Cadogan); or surprising Hitler with an unannounced trip to see him (Chamberlain).

Chamberlain grappled with the options. Voluminous intelligence had confused as much as it enlightened him. On 2 September Hitler had apparently met with Henlein and told him he would act soon. Henlein reported to his French contacts, and thus to the British, that Germany's aims were limited and pacific, which was not true. Diplomats and intelligence officers reported that civilian officials in the Reich, such as Weizsäcker, were also saying Hitler's goals were limited. Officials in both London and Berlin received reports that high-level military officers were rebelling, insisting that Hitler was mad because he was intent on boundless expansion. French and British diplomatic channels were reporting well on both scores, with secret sources from overseas adding at the margins.

As the pace of discussion increased, however, Ambassador Henderson's views became weightier than anyone else's because any message to Hitler would have to go through him. Henderson opposed a press campaign or a warning, public or private, of the kind the Foreign Office had drafted. He instead supported Chamberlain's plan to propose a trip to Hitler via Ribbentrop. After many redrafts, this proposal was made to Hitler, he agreed, and Chamberlain flew to

Germany on 15 September. His departure prompted a ditty repeated in the halls of MI5: "If at first you don't succeed, Fly, fly, again."[112] MI5 and Vansittart had lost the argument. Chamberlain was not flying to Berlin to stand up to Hitler but to see if there was some new mix of concessions that might appease him. They knew they had failed to offer Chamberlain a credible alternative. Covert intrigues could not dull Hitler's appetite for land, and threatening war was difficult when most of the Cabinet believed that Britain was too weak to fight and win against Germany. Hitler might yet listen to reason, especially if Britain eschewed any move to "encircle." Vansittart had been able to make his case to Chamberlain, who knew what he did not know—well enough, in fact, to entertain the idea of gathering some diplomatic intelligence himself. Unfortunately, the prime minister failed to appreciate how much the terrain of uncertainty would shift against him once he directly engaged his adversary on foreign soil.

Decision Set 2: Chamberlain's Decision to Cede Sudetenland to Germany; Hitler's Decision to Swallow Czechoslovakia in Two Bites Rather Than One

Chamberlain's decision to fly to Germany would change the intelligence equation in Europe. Flying was a risky venture still, and this move by the British prime minister was meant to be a dramatic signal to Germany and Italy of Britain's engagement in the Eastern European question. It was also a way to gain critical intelligence firsthand. Chamberlain intended that this time, unlike WWI, there would be no misunderstanding or miscalculation. Britain was going to engage Germany directly and stick by France in the interest of European security.

In contrast, Hitler was confident he knew Chamberlain well enough to control the outcome of any "negotiation." He had established ties with the Sudeten Germans through Konrad Henlein's organization—the one that Vansittart had penetrated and clandestinely contacted through his star agent, Christie. While Henlein was "enlightening" Britain and France regarding the prospects of reaching a settlement with the government in Prague, his organization was also accepting subsidies from Berlin, probably without London's knowledge. In fact, the SS and Reinhard Heydrich's operators, known as the Sicherheitsdienst, or SD, were conducting sabotage and disruptions as a buildup to the Munich discussions.[113]

The Berchtesgaden Meeting of 15 September

On 15 September, Chamberlain arrived in Munich, traveling by train to Berchtesgaden, where he and Hitler conversed in private, with only a translator present. For reasons explained earlier, neither man knew his intelligence on relative military capabilities was either incomplete or wrong, leaving both fairly certain of German superiority.[114] But Hitler had the advantage in tactical intelligence because, operating on his own turf, he could monitor the British delegation and embassy both before and after the meeting.

Chamberlain nonetheless startled Hitler. First, he refused to listen to any ultimatums and declared his intent to go home if any were issued. Hitler reacted by flying into a rage over the situation of Germans in Czechoslovakia, pointing to outrages against the German Czechs without, of course, revealing that he had secretly sponsored them. After Chamberlain threatened to leave, Hitler declared his willingness to negotiate solutions to the problem provided Chamberlain accepted the principle of self-determination for the Sudetenland. He pledged that he had no other interests in territorial aggrandizement and that he was open-minded on the idea of a plebiscite. Chamberlain saw these demands as workable and left for home, convinced agreement would be possible if he could force the Czechs to yield. He also concluded that, while Hitler's will was supreme in the formulation of German policy, his aims could be limited.

Whereas Chamberlain's conclusions almost certainly got back to Hitler because he was eavesdropping on the British discussions, Hitler's net assessment did not get to London. Without communications intelligence comparable to Germany's, Chamberlain's relatively rosy reports became the primary intelligence for the British Cabinet. The Cabinet, along with the French government, pressed Czechoslovakia to accept Hitler's demands should the plebiscite prove the Sudetenland's population wanted what Hitler wanted.

In fact, Hitler planned to use Chamberlain's optimism (that ceding people to Germany could be done with safeguards, international supervision, and compensation) to create a form of diplomatic shock and awe. He knew that Chamberlain was working with the French to influence the Czechs, straining the Paris-Prague alliance. Indeed, while the Cabinet in London was deciding to force the Czech government to accept all Henlein's demands, Hitler secretly had been directing Henlein's right-hand man, Karl Hermann Frank, to instigate provocative incidents so negotiations would fail and he would have an excuse to intervene. In the next round of discussions, Hitler intended to use this unrest in Czechoslovakia to issue the ultimatum that Chamberlain had preemptively dismissed.

Hitler had his territorial requirements literally mapped out by 19 September. On that day, Hitler revealed to Goebbels a map of the territorial demands he planned to make on 22 September when he and Chamberlain were scheduled to meet in Bad Godesberg. He would demand the much more broadly defined "Sudetenland" territory be vacated immediately so that his army could occupy

INTELLIGENCE AND DECISION IN 1938   391

it within eight days. A plebiscite would be unnecessary but could be held, in the event of any dispute, by the end of December.

Bad Godesberg

On 22 September, Chamberlain flew to the next meeting with Hitler, this time in the Rhineland at Bad Godesberg. He had no warning of Hitler's next move. When he brought his carefully negotiated Czech concessions to the meeting and heard Hitler's new demands, it was his turn to be enraged and, then, diplomatically paralyzed.

Meeting on German soil with no source of intelligence other than embassies whose communications, security, and diplomatic sources were compromised, Chamberlain found himself in a fog as thick as General Hooker's at Chancellorsville or Philip II's admiral in the stormy English Channel in 1588. On enemy turf without means for navigating, he faced an adversary better prepared than he was for diplomatic next steps. Hitler pointed to the (largely manufactured) unrest swelling within the Czech territories, now including Polish and Hungarian interests, to argue that he needed a swifter solution than any plebiscite could deliver: he would move German troops into the newly delineated territory in nine days.

Chamberlain, calling Hitler's new demands an ultimatum, stayed put in his hotel the next morning. Hitler knew what he was thinking. According to the historian Ernest May, "The Forschungsamt worked quickly enough so that . . . at Godesberg, Hitler was able to read the British delegation's report on his first meeting with Chamberlain before he met with Chamberlain on the morning of the next day."[115] Although Chamberlain's report stirred Halifax to say, back in London, that Hitler's demands amounted to a crime, Chamberlain was committed to seeing what he could do about Hitler's new demands. When Hitler learned that Edvard Beneš, the Czech president, had mobilized his forces, he relented only insofar as he allowed 1 October to become the date of any Czech withdrawal. At Chamberlain's request, he put his position in writing.

Hitler had seemingly won round two. He would not win round three. Chamberlain went home ready to report Hitler's new demands with the prospect of war engulfing him. By all accounts, Chamberlain still hoped for peace. Yet his own reporting, which delivered new intelligence on Hitler's frame of mind, caused key advisors to shift to Vansittart's position. Cadogan was one of the first to be convinced that appeasement was not just a pointless strategy but now possibly a dangerous one:

> I was completely horrified—[the prime minister] was quite calmly for total surrender. More horrified still to find that Hitler has evidently hypnotised him to a point. Still more horrified to find P.M. has hypnotised H [Halifax] who capitulates totally. P.M. took nearly an hour to make his report, and there was practically no discussion. J.S. [John Simon]—seeing which way the cat was jumping—said that after all it was a question of "modalities," whether the Germans went in now or later! Ye Gods! . . . They don't yet understand and they haven't seen the map. (They're going round after dinner to have it explained to them by Horace [Wilson]!) Pray God there will be a revolt.[116]

Appeasement was slipping from a strategy to explore Hitler's objectives and limits while revising the balance of power in Europe, to accommodation to German dictates. Part of the explanation for the defeatist mood in London was "a shattering telegram" from Phipps, the ambassador in Paris, detailing why the French were in no position to fight. It also made clear that Chamberlain's negotiation had exposed Hitler's true aims.

> All that is best in France is against war, almost at any price (hence the really deep and pathetic gratitude shown to our Prime Minister). Unless we are sure of considerable initial successes we shall find all that is best in France, as well as all that is worst, turn against us and accuse us of egging French on to fight what must have seemed from the outset a losing battle.
>
> To embark upon what will presumably be the biggest conflict in history with our ally, who will fight, if fight she must, without eyes (Air Force) and without real heart must surely give us furiously to think.
>
> It may be asked why I have not reported sooner in the above sense. The answer is that up to the last hour the French had hypnotised themselves in to believing that peace depended upon Great Britain, and not upon Herr Hitler. They were convinced, that is to say, that if Britain spoke with sufficient firmness Herr Hitler would collapse. Only now do they realize that Herr Hitler may well be meaning to take on both our countries.[117]

Phipp's military assessment was wrong—misled by the pessimistic French intelligence—but he was right about what most saw as the implications of Hitler's position: "*that Herr Hitler may well be meaning to take on both our countries.*" And these implications had effects in both France and Britain. As Cadogan put it: "I know we and they are in no condition to fight, but I'd rather be beat than dishonoured. How can we look any foreigner in the face after this? How can we hold Egypt, India and the rest?"[118] Cadogan began to press for urgent rearmament and leaned hard on Halifax to see Hitler for what he was—not the man Chamberlain believed was "anxious to secure the friendship of Great Britain" and "willing to work with him"—but a totalitarian bent on war.[119] By the time of the crucial Cabinet meeting on next steps, Halifax had changed his mind and accepted Cadogan's view:

> Alec, I'm very angry with you. You gave me a sleepless night. I woke at 1 and never got to sleep again. But I came to the conclusion you were right, and at the Cabinet, when P.M. asked me to lead off, I plumped for refusal of Hitler's terms.

Chamberlain had told the Cabinet that he thought he had the measure of Hitler and could work with him, but the Cabinet had Hitler's written demands and backed Halifax's view.

Although Chamberlain was initially stunned, he accepted the Cabinet's decision and informed France that Britain would back her if Germany's invasion of Czechoslovakia triggered hostilities with France. He also informed Germany via Wilson that no more concessions would be forthcoming, but further negotiations would be preferable to violence. Britain's position was then announced publicly, and the Cabinet steeled itself for the results. Tensions rose to fever pitch—the small meeting of ministers "frightened out of their wits"—as incoming intelligence continued to suggest that war would bring defeat by a stronger foe. The Chiefs of Staff still held their pessimistic view:

> It is our opinion that no pressure that Great Britain and France can bring to bear, either by sea, on land, or in the air, could prevent Germany from overrunning Bohemia and from inflicting a decisive defeat on Czechoslovakia. The restoration of Czechoslovakia's lost integrity could only be achieved by the defeat of Germany and as the outcome of a prolonged struggle, which from the outset must assume the character of an unlimited war.[120]

The Chiefs added that the entry of Italy and Japan in any war in 1938 would lead to defeat, even if Russia and France were to come to Britain's aid. Even the prime minister's premises were adjusting to include the belief that Hitler's aims might not be limited—that the issue might not be defense of a "far away country" but rather "great issues," such as whether one power should be permitted to "dominate the world by fear of its force." When asked whether or not Britain should mobilize the fleet, Chamberlain nodded in the affirmative and held firm to his new stand, despite the insistent military position that the country was likely to martyr itself on the altar of principle.[121]

Hitler was not prepared for London's sudden stiffening. On the same day as the British Cabinet meeting, September 27, Sir Harry Wilson reported from Berlin that Hitler had received Chamberlain's message and had reiterated his intention to smash Czechoslovakia if the demands in his memorandum (the Godesberg ultimatum) were not accepted. He added that, given Britain's refusal to press Czechoslovakia to make additional concessions, if France attacked Germany he would assume Britain was obliged to attack as well. Hitler said that he had already taken full account of this possibility. "Not for nothing had he spent 4½ billion marks on fortifications in the West."[122]

Yet Hitler soon decided to retreat to his earlier, pre–Bad Godesberg position; in fact, he took the decision before he could have known about the mobilization of the British fleet. This decision was probably informed by widespread outrage registered in the foreign press and resistance at home. Berliners were evidently sour, and while Hitler was not fond of Berliners, Goebbels "made no secret of believing that the mood was not confined to Berlin."[123] Hitler thus learned that, unintentionally, he had unified Britain, if not France, in opposition to his purposes—a dangerous turn in developments.

Hitler, therefore, changed course. At 10:30 p.m. on the twenty-seventh, Chamberlain received a letter saying that German troops would only move into the territory the Czechs had already ceded, that the plebiscite would be carried out by free vote, and that Germany would join the guarantee of Czechoslovakia's borders. He thus retracted his new territorial demands and timetable. Chamberlain replied immediately, saying that he felt sure that agreement could be reached without war and offering to return to Berlin for discussions. Just to be sure, Chamberlain pressed Mussolini through backchannels to help bring this agreement about. At 2:30 p.m. on the twenty-eighth news arrived of Mussolini's success at delaying German mobilization; at 3:30 p.m. Henderson called from Berlin to say Hitler had agreed to the four-party conference. Chamberlain had won round three.[124]

Conclusion

The rest of the story of Munich is well known: the four powers met; agreement was struck along the lines of the deal anticipated at Berchtesgaden; then, in early 1939, Hitler invaded and occupied the rest of the Czechoslovakia. As Britain girded for war, Hitler's troops went on to attack Poland, where Britain had drawn a red line, launching WWII.

Winners and Losers

So, did either side gain intelligence advantage in 1938 and, if so, how was it won? At the time, Hitler regarded the Munich Agreement of September 1938 as a frustrating defeat. In a sense, he was right. Despite seemingly inferior forces and a divided public, Chamberlain had stared him down, colluded with Mussolini, delayed Hitler's march through Europe, and strengthened public opinion in Britain against him. Asked in October 1938 whether Hitler should be believed when saying he had no more territorial ambitions in Europe, 93 percent of British respondents said no. And while opinion remained divided on the policy of appeasement, 46 percent believed that the policy would at least prevent war until Britain had time to rearm.[125] (Indeed, by 1939, the British military had regained its confidence in Britain's capacity to win a war, especially one in the air, thanks to the development of radar and new fighter planes.)

Seen in this light, Chamberlain's diplomatic negotiations were "fact-finding" trips that provided the intelligence the Cabinet and the British population needed for sorting out who Hitler was and what he intended—an advantage that infuriated a man such as Hitler, who counted on a better capacity to read the public than wobbly politicians could in France and Great Britain. To Hitler's dismay, no doubt, the tempest from Bad Godesberg forced an awakening in France to the fact that the problem was not Britain's failure to stand up to Hitler, but Hitler himself.

Yet the results of Munich should not dim the clarity of the moments before: Chamberlain went into Munich relatively blind—that is, without the intelligence he needed to create the outcomes he wanted—and he knew it. His diplomatic intelligence was poor; his military intelligence unimaginative; his air force intelligence wrong; and his civilian intelligence service weak, underfunded, and widely compromised. The government's ability to put reporting from all sources together into comprehensive assessments had been undermined by bureaucratic feuding and personality conflicts. Chamberlain's ability to find workarounds, such as through Ball or the Czechs, could relieve these disadvantages, but he had no reason to expect they would as he flew to Munich. In fact, his emissary to Czechoslovakia was a dead diplomat walking. His mission had been penetrated and totally compromised by Hitler, who knew Chamberlain's bottom lines perhaps better than Chamberlain did.[126]

If, therefore, the outcome in 1938 seems to have had no clear overall winner, this is to a certain extent true: both sides gained and lost. But because of Hitler's poor understanding of diplomatic intelligence, decision advantage shifted in Britain's favor. Of the three key lessons from this case study of diplomacy in an era of total war, this lesson is probably the most important, so will be summarized first.

Intelligence, Negotiation, and Diplomatic Decision-Making

Diplomacy entails a bazaar-like process of probing an adversary's position, discerning common interests, and then probing some more. Such activity is not just negotiation or policymaking; it is information gathering. The process can lift veils, creating winners and losers through diplomatic tradecraft. It is, at least in part, an elicitation technique that is as much a form of intelligence as interrogation of defectors or spying. Before WWI, diplomatic intelligence gathering failed; in the midst of professional and military intelligence failures before WWII, the British revived it, gaining decision-advantage.

It follows that, although the legacy of "Munich" has been the seemingly sure lesson one should not bargain with bullies and dictators, such conclusions mistake diplomacy for war-fighting, during which objectives are zero-sum. Diplomacy is *about* the bazaar, including intelligence gathering; the alternative is war or isolation. If war must be avoided for reasons of weakness or excessive cost, it is up to diplomatic intelligence, conducted by savvy negotiators, to discern who needs to know what in order to get the necessary trades done, including finding options for reconciling or firming up interests.

Chamberlain may have flown to Germany relatively blind, knowing that Hitler was still an enigma, but he came home having gathered evidence that proved Hitler was not—though Chamberlain was one of the last to realize that fact. After Bad Godesberg, which threw the British and French press into a fury, almost no one in Britain or France believed Hitler's aims were limited. In this sense, Chamberlain's trip was the perfect overt intelligence operation. It exposed for men like Halifax and Cadogan, as well as the general public in Britain and France, that the problem was not British will or Germany's rights; the problem was Hitler.

The history of 1938 thus reveals lessons about how to navigate when intelligence is scarce and options seem few, including how intelligence institutions can sometimes make things worse, and traditional diplomatic methods can help states learn. But the lesson is not that one is better than the other. Chamberlain's decision to confront Hitler in person clarified matters, but not as much as it could have, had Chamberlain had a professional intelligence team supporting him on hostile territory. Instead, he had traditional diplomats in compromised embassies. The concept of intelligence support to diplomatic operations (SDO) had not yet been born, and British decision-making suffered as a result.[127]

Relative advantage is most often gained when diplomacy and intelligence work together to increase advantage and manage risks. Chamberlain, like his predecessors before WWI, was poorly served on both counts.

Diplomatic Advantage Requires Good, Useful, Military Intelligence

Another lesson is crisp in its clarity: British military intelligence before WWI was inadequately shared with statesmen. Before WWII it was shared but failed to get the military balance right, which convinced British statesmen that they were relatively weak, even in concert with France and Czechoslovakia, when, in fact, they were relatively strong, if not fully prepared for war. Technological change and the attending uncertainties of understanding air power explain part of this problem. Aerial surveillance was new and Germany a particularly hard target.[128] Yet what the British Chiefs of Staff claimed to know was also positively wrong. The sources for this bad intelligence were largely in France, where the armed forces produced apocalyptic assessments as a way to gain more resources from French politicians they did not trust. Their calculations, produced by military men jealous of civilian interference and seemingly speaking truth to power, infected the calculations not just of statesmen in Paris, but also of their liaison partners. The result was handicapped diplomacy and fears of bluff.

Making matters worse was the notion that civilians should have no say in how military intelligence might assist diplomacy. Vansittart, the antiappeaser, railed against flawed military intelligence, but had no standing to question it at a time when departments claimed rights to preeminence in their own areas. In this sense, Britain's power was lessened not just by bad intelligence, but by prejudices against methods for its legitimate collection and by management rivalries over who had rights to collect and present military data. That Hitler mistook this gap in British intelligence for weakness of will, command, or character reflected his own serious intelligence gaps. These gaps would be apparent briefly after Bad Godesberg, and more continuously during the coming war.

If war becomes likely in circumstances of apparent military imbalance, the role of diplomacy on either side is to ensure that its timing and location is as advantageous as possible—a process that requires that diplomatic intelligence be coordinated with military intelligence and overall strategy, which certainly was not the case before WWI. By Munich, civil-military planning, including intelligence coordination, was more advanced in London than in Berlin, where military uncertainties were increasing as Hitler's personal power grew. Although the store of political and military information was rich in Nazi Germany and interdepartmental intelligence-sharing surprisingly regular, the exchanges were common only at the lower levels of bureaucracies. Moving up the chain of command, intelligence became more of a currency to be hoarded and used to gain access and praise from the Führer. Hitler, in turn, cultivated the factionalism, including the intelligence it generated to good effect. But privatized intelligence, which is intelligence used for personal advancement, is a dangerous source no matter how distributed it might be among vendors.

Counterintelligence and Diplomacy

Another lesson from this case study has to do with the problem that attends influence operations through diplomatic channels. Because diplomatic interlocutors seek to influence as much or more than enlighten, diplomacy needs counterintelligence—that is, a capacity to know if sources are compromised and, if so, how to limit damage from them.

At one time, when all intrigue revolved around thrones, diplomats were masters of counterintelligence. But once *national* politics, *national* security, and *national* industries complicated matters, diplomats no longer had reliable access to all key decision-makers. After the industrial revolution, the more chaotic diplomatic bazaar raised the risks of offending counterparts through increasingly networked connections. Sensitive deals required counterintelligence; but they could be squashed if such operations went bad, causing a worse outcome. Therefore, diplomatic bargains were, by the 1930s, still being made based on relationships, past deals, and the dynamics of logrolling, favors, and trades without good counterintelligence input.

An appreciation of this aspect of peacetime diplomacy is crucial, or one risks misunderstanding how Chamberlain could detest Hitler and fear war yet eschew the risks of running operations against him. He needed validation for the intelligence he was receiving through diplomatic channels about Hitler's "reasonableness," but tended to go back to the sources he knew were compromised by penetration: his ambassadors in Rome and Berlin. The rebel, Vansittart, understood the problem but was too disliked and bereft of good alternative sources to make it stick.

The case of Weizsäcker, the source for much British diplomatic intelligence, is illustrative. Weizsäcker seems to have been a sincere believer in the kind of "chemical solutions" for European order that British leaders believed appeasement might deliver. He constantly reinforced the notion that Hitler was a reasonable man whose aims were achievable without force. If policy was to hang on his words, the British government needed to know if his basis for judging Hitler was sound. Was he a part of the inner circle or blowing smoke? Weizsäcker, the number two at the Foreign Ministry, claimed that his boss, Foreign Minister Ribbentrop, had a malevolent influence on Hitler, and his words carried inordinate weight in London. Although the British embassy in Berlin was known to have been compromised by the Germans (as was the one in Rome), London should have suspected that Weizsäcker was being tolerated for a purpose—that is, to mislead. It was the British ambassador to Germany, Neville Henderson, who intervened to persuade Chamberlain to travel to Munich—the same ambassador who found the idea of counterintelligence abhorrent because it got in the way of doing business.

Henderson was not, of course, the only policymaker affected by poorly integrated counterintelligence operations. Vansittart was too, and he knew it. He admitted to being manipulated by rebel generals in the German military; he knew they were using him to get Chamberlain to supply the threat that German generals needed to muster the courage to bring Hitler down. Yet, as the historian

Ernest May, has suggested, there "is not one shred of evidence," at least dating from 1936, that Hitler's generals would have stood more firmly against Hitler than they did;[129] that Vansittart did not know or acknowledge this fact was a counterintelligence failure on his part.

Vansittart excused himself by pointing to the fact that MI5 agreed with him about Hitler's imperial intentions. What he did not understand was that intel-ligence advantage is achieved decision by decision. Sources such as Kordt, who insisted on a "firm stand" in late August, were suggesting a timing perhaps right for those he represented, but not for Britain—a fact that Vansittart could not see, although he should have. With each successful territorial grab, Hitler's opposi-tion within military ranks shrank in numbers, if not in intensity of feeling. At the same time, his opposition among the French and British grew exponentially. The firm stand Chamberlain was able eventually to make came after Hitler's outra-geous demands at Bad Godesberg; Halifax and Cadogan were likely right that it would not have worked before.

The Importance of Intimacy in the Intelligence-Policy Relationship

Despite his counterintelligence blind spots, Vansittart was largely right on the facts of his case. He was among the first to understand Hitler's strategy as con-tinental domination through the stoking of mutual antipathy between Britain and the Soviet Union, and the legitimization of territorial claims through covert sponsorship of civil unrest. On issue after issue, from balance of air power to strategic objectives, Vansittart was more often right than not.

But being "right" was not enough. In the run-up to the Munich Crisis, Chamberlain did not trust that Vansittart had the true measure of Hitler. Trust is crucial if intelligence is to influence decision, especially in conditions of un-certainty. But Vansittart was annoying. He talked too much and too stridently. He had also catered to Churchill, Chamberlain's rival, and was obviously a Germanophobe—so biased that he seemed politicized to the point of advocacy. On this point, Vansittart would have heartily agreed with them; but he would have also insisted he was right on the facts. So what was the problem?

To deliver decision-advantage, an intelligence service needs both good col-lection and a trusted delivery system. SIS, bereft of platforms, spies, and any de-cent network of clandestine communications, failed at the first; Vansittart largely failed at the second. Few knew at the time, however, how crippled Vansittart and the SIS were. After all, under much older, nonprofessional intelligence sys-tems, kings only truly trusted appointed emissaries or men like Vansittart whose politics were clear. With the professionalization of intelligence in democracies, however, bias could no longer be reliably calibrated to changing sets of decision-makers. To prevent lost access, professional tradecraft eventually turned to scientific objectivity to foster trust.

Unfortunately for Vansittart and Chamberlain, neither the old nor the new system was in full effect in the 1930s. The gap-fillers were men such as Halifax, the British foreign secretary, who instinctively knew how to do both. At the key planning meeting before Chamberlain's decision to meet Hitler, he advised bringing Vansittart into the room to brief contrarian facts. He listened to Cadogan's arguments before and after Bad Godesberg, and then delivered his changed view that Vansittart, whom he disliked, was right after all. His openness, trustworthiness, and change of mind were the critical factors leading to Chamberlain's decision to stand firm.

But what then, of Germany, where Hitler trusted almost no one? If Britain won decision-advantage after Bad Godesberg, it was true, nonetheless, that from 1934 to 1939, Hitler won many more at the tactical and operational level. What accounts for these successes in an atmosphere of distrust at the highest level?

One answer is domestic counterintelligence, which can substitute for trust when other forms of oversight are lacking. Hitler made it a specialty. He tested people, eliminating some and leaning on others, such as Ribbentrop, whose loyalties were solid. In fact, for the Führer, intelligence was always more about offensive counterintelligence (security, propaganda, and influence peddling) than fact-finding. This attitude partly reflected his intention to gather his own facts, which he used to gauge public opinion and create his own reality. With the exception of Munich, where he underestimated public reaction to his bullying tactics, he was actually quite good at this. Indeed, by mid-1938 he had accomplished what experts had told him would be impossible without triggering war: remilitarizing the Rhineland, overturning prohibitions on rearmament, and swallowing Austria—all without a fight and, indeed, with applause in some quarters. To accomplish these ends, he knew he needed to keep secrets and conduct well-informed covert action. Yet this hardly meant he trusted his intelligence services to resolve his uncertainties. In fact, he threw out as irrelevant credible reports of military imbalances in his adversaries' favor.

The weakness in this kind of intelligence strategy is that the diminished interest in collecting on adversaries and increased interest in disloyalty at home become institutionalized. Intelligence providers become wary of delivering not just bad news, but any news at all, and so start looking for customers elsewhere, deepening the loyalty problem and the counterintelligence challenges. Hitler would not suffer the worst of these consequences until WWII was well underway. In the meantime, he gained intelligence advantages by spying on domestic enemies, knowing when opportunities for intervention were ripe, and gaining surgical control of his military in order to exploit them. He did not believe he needed diplomats or intelligence operatives to tell him how the masses at home or overseas would react.[130] On matters of diplomacy and war, he alone would decide and intelligence would serve him unflinchingly. His strategy required a unified state, including an intelligence apparatus that would jump to his command. This unity required, in turn, both public loyalty and unquestioned military obedience.

Hitler's overall purpose was, therefore underappreciated. Four sets of knowable facts could have revealed Hitler's intentions: his covert methods for pruning the German high command of those skeptical of Europe-wide aggression; his use of counterintelligence (embassy penetrations) and influence operations (Weizsäcker and Ribbentrop) for deception; his use of the Nazi Party for covert action to stimulate irredentism; and in particular, his striking inattention to the negotiating strategies of his opponents—the dog that did not bark.

Hitler was *disinterested* in British and French diplomatic strategy—the hallmark of a warrior or terrorist on the offensive—determined not to bargain at the bazaar but to shoot it up. A man with a robust intelligence service, but few informational requirements about his enemy's strategy, is a man disinterested in buying and selling at all.

Neither the British nor the French intelligence services in 1938 convincingly documented these facts for decision-makers, especially those who inherently distrusted them. It is true that a few men such as Vansittart put together Hitler's own expressed intent, secret intelligence from inside the Reich, and counterintelligence collection and analysis to estimate Hitler's next moves and overall strategic purpose. A few more had the same intelligence, but differed in their conclusions. In the mix, however, no one had enough evidence to win Chamberlain's confidence. In fact, British intelligence was so divided among competing services, special envoys, and diplomatic institutions that it exacerbated Chamberlain's uncertainties.

Absent reliable and trusted secret intelligence, Britain's policy of appeasement was, whether intended or not, a diplomatic strategy of telltale bargaining that teased out Hitler's intentions, split adversaries, and bought the time that the British Chiefs of Staff said they needed. Intelligence served this coping strategy, but only in the most minimalist sense. It did not, and perhaps could not have prevented the shootout that Hitler wanted. Arguably, no policy would have prevented war, but the inability of the intelligence systems in France and Britain consistently to offer up better options amounted to lost intelligence-advantage nonetheless.

Relating Intelligence Advantage to Diplomatic Opportunity

In diplomacy as in war, intelligence needs to help exploit opportunities, not just counter threats. Decision-makers often request this kind of support, but intelligence organizations struggle to provide it, lest they be accused of policy bias. Nevertheless, good ones do flag opportunities. Here Hitler had an advantage. With an offensive frame of mind, he looked less for how he might be hurt than how he might gain. With a defensive frame of mind, British leaders looked less for how to gain diplomatic advantage than how their actions might damage themselves by triggering war. The famous historian F. H. Hinsley unintentionally reflected that bias when summarizing the pre-WWII intelligence performance:

> Since the approach of the Munich crisis its over-riding concern had ceased to be the difficulty of discovering what Germany would do next, and had become the difficulty of deciding whether and in what way Great Britain should act to check her, and thus of calculating how Hitler and other governments would respond to whatever the British government might do. No more than any other source could agents, however well placed, assist with such calculations. Nor could they be believed if they professed to be able to do so: the other governments, not excluding Hitler's, did not know themselves what their response would be.

Unfortunately, Hinsley's wariness of support to the diplomatic bazaar would characterize intelligence establishments well into the twentieth century. Intelligence can't help unless it can gauge opportunities as well as threats, collect evidence of enemy contingency-planning, and lower the risk of surprise. It was possible to know Stalin's intentions, Mussolini's likely response to the British four-power initiative, and other, similar moves. Hinsley was right that guessing is usually dangerous and estimative judgments too often overrated; he was wrong to think that intelligence professionals, including diplomats, would have to engage in it to aid policy in this way. He underappreciated the worth of intelligence collection.

This "lesson" was as wrong to learn in diplomacy as it was in war. General Grant knew this when he marshaled intelligence for the steamrolling Union offensive that would win the Civil War. When a Confederate flank attack rolled back a Union line, a Union general rushed to Grant, delivering his estimate of the threat:

> "I know Lee's methods well by past experience; he will throw his whole army between us and the Rapidan, and cut us off completely from our communications." Grant sprang to his feet, snatched his cigar from his mouth, and chastised the panic-stricken officer. "Oh I am heartily tired of hearing about what Lee is going to do," he said with uncommon vehemence. "Some of you always seem to think he is suddenly going to turn a double somersault, and land in our rear and on both of our flanks at the same time. Go back to your command,

and try to think what we are going to do ourselves, instead of what Lee is going to do."

Grant was not deprecating intelligence-advantage, he was criticizing a defensive mindset among decision-makers and the intelligence orientation that went with it. Intelligence advantage can be gained not just by knowing in advance about an enemy's moves, but also by knowing what opportunities there might be for making those enemy moves irrelevant. Scouting terrain is not just to locate the enemy, but also to find the best road, the most accessible way to ford a river, and the highest ground so decision-makers have options before the enemy does.

In this regard, Vansittart was perhaps the best at generating alternatives to appeasement. Yet he could not generate options beyond what seemed risky bluff without a better relationship with his superiors and better net assessment from colleagues in military intelligence. It is possible that a better sense of Britain's relative power or a more opportunistic decision-maker in the mold of a Ulysses S. Grant might have made a difference; but they could only have made a difference together. As Vansittart himself later wrote:

> I conceded no superiority to politicians except that in a clash they must win....
> The task lay rather in correcting the adverse balance of evil, whether displayed
> in ferocity or apathy; and it proved hopeless. . . . Professionals must be good
> losers, but they might have more access to the Cabinet.[131]

Given that the public chooses its leaders, however, the problem from an intelligence policy standpoint was less with leadership than with intelligence on options that would permit opportunistic decisions. This would have had to begin with improving military intelligence for diplomatic purposes—using assessments of relative power to deter and compel when Hitler's hand inside Germany was still resisted by the army's top brass. Vansittart had repeatedly and vociferously complained about deficiencies in air force intelligence, but the Foreign Office, even supported by SIS and MI5, was in no position to second-guess the Chiefs of Staff.

Yet, if an offensive frame had been all there was to Hitler's intelligence strategy, it would have been ruinous because, in order to generate opportunities for himself, he needed to perpetuate both uncertainty and a defensive mindset on the other side. He therefore employed an offensive counterintelligence strategy involving agents of influence, deceptions, and domestic conspiracies designed to taint resisters within his military. Although this choice may have been more intuitive than deliberate, it worked because British intelligence was still (but not for long) naive on matters of deception. Hitler knew that France and Germany saw the German army as a stabilizing force—a perception that Hitler, by declaring the army a pillar of his regime, had reinforced. Hitler also knew this premise was one basis for the British notion that appeasement would work. So it was something of a trick to remake his army while projecting intent to not only leave it intact, but leave it a "pillar" of the state. If Hitler were ever to appear to be purging the army, as Stalin had done, he would be seen for the revolutionary he was.

It seems reasonable to conclude that decision-makers are crucial to the analysis of opportunity-oriented intelligence. Although Hitler was better at this than Chamberlain, neither was adept. This case study has not reviewed in depth how both systems generally functioned, but historians who have taken a close look have shown that Hitler was largely incurious about the thinking of foreign policymakers because he relied on his own intuitions and information gathering on such matters. As his intelligence apparatus conformed, agencies jockeyed for influence rather than advantage against adversaries. Goering correctly understood that Hitler wanted to exploit diplomatic opportunities, but did not want bad news about military preparations for them. Ribbentrop correctly divined that Hitler wanted news, but not analysis of its meaning in terms of either threats or opportunities. He therefore ensured that the Foreign Ministry complied, subordinating traditional diplomatic methods to an emphasis on foreign news reporting. No effort was made at senior levels to reconcile civilian departments' views on diplomatic opportunities with those of the armed services or Abwehr because Hitler did not want it done.[132]

As far as assessing Chamberlain's role, he gets a barely passing grade. His commitment to adjusting power relationships without war required knowing the enemy better than he did. But neither he nor the SIS spent enough time and resources mastering how the gap might be overcome. So, in a crisis, he threw himself into the breach with almost no capacity for tactical intelligence support. Such naivete showed up, too, in his belief, prior to Munich, that the German army *had to foresee* the probability of European devastation, including Germany's, in any great power war. He was shocked when he eventually realized in 1938 that Hitler's view had effectively become the army's view and that was all that really mattered. Mirror-imaging is a problem that originates in the minds of decision-makers who are bereft of good intelligence, and thus compelled to fill in the gaps with what they already know or firmly believe.[133] Seen in this larger perspective, those of Cadogan's persuasion, including MI6 (SIS), may have gotten it "right" in terms of what Germany *could and should* do given its interests, but wrong in terms of how far Hitler would go to accumulate power.

13

A Theory of Intelligence in International Politics

This book has gone back several centuries to reveal the essentials of successful intelligence, but could have gone much further. Humans have always been competitive animals served by their curiosity and learning. Neither excessive passivity nor blind groping has ever put food on the table, protected a family, guided a spear, or extended life. Besides brute strength, *knowing* when and how to fight, flee, rest, or cooperate with others has been key to longevity. Intelligence, which is the measurable capacity to learn despite being opposed by others, has always been the essential supplement to pure muscle—especially in international politics, where no overarching government enforces rules or arbitrates what is fair.

Useful lessons about how to win with wit as well as muscle should work for all competitions, whether they involve ancient warriors, Renaissance monarchs, army generals, or modern politicians. A good theory will not just *describe* how competitors engineer informational advantages, but also explain how this engineering affects war, peace, and international stability. In fact, a good theory of intelligence will do even more: It will explain why superior force does not necessarily predict outcomes in international politics.

Lessons from the Past: A General Theory of Intelligence

What, then, is such a theory? It seems sensible to begin by noting that intelligence has been shown to be a form of power—both a force multiplier and a disrupter. We need to know how this kind of power can be measured. The issue of measurement is riddled with problems, however, because absolute measures matter less than relative intelligence capabilities in diplomacy and war. Intelligence is both a way to read the distribution of power among competitors, and a component of that power itself.

This chapter argues that, tricky as intelligence power is, it can be measured, increased, and thus made an explicit part of grand strategy. If correct, this claim should change how we think about intelligence systems, international security, national security policy, and the general causes of war and peace. Given that

Decision Advantage. Jennifer E. Sims, Oxford University Press. © Oxford University Press 2022.
DOI: 10.1093/oso/9780197508046.003.0013

these latter implications rest on the claim that intelligence is power that can be measured, however, we should begin with those claims first.

Measuring Intelligence Capabilities

The introduction to this volume suggested four simple but fundamental requirements for achieving intelligence advantage:

1. Superior *capacities to collect* relevant information[1]
2. Sufficient *detachment* of collection from current policy and known threats to enable the discovery of the unexpected[2]
3. Superior *transmission of intelligence and strategy* among intelligence providers and decision-makers to create advantages over competitors[3]
4. Superior capacities for *selective secrecy*[4]

The case studies in this volume have substantiated these four requirements, but have not added to their basic number. They have also shown that the foundational capacity upon which all other capabilities depend is collection, without which the mind of man will tend to guess or rely on old mindsets. What the case studies have added, however, is that any one aspect of intelligence power may surpass the others in importance for gaining relative advantages, depending on the intelligence capabilities of the other side and the game in play. If these games or relative capabilities suddenly change, a state's intelligence power may collapse.

We can therefore propose the following:

- States build intelligence *readiness* for any new threat or opportunity by increasing capacity across all four ingredients of intelligence power listed above.[5]
- States can increase prospects for *intelligence advantage* by adjusting intelligence systems to the *terrain of uncertainty* they face.[6]
- States *sustain intelligence advantage* and *minimize the consequences of surprise* by achieving the former with as little damage to overall readiness as possible.[7]
- States *achieve decision-advantages* by developing and executing strategies that *use intelligence (and counterintelligence) to increase their options* as well as to identify and assess threats.[8]
- Competitors with intelligence advantages over others can use them to influence what others know (or think they know) through *counterintelligence* policies targeting opponents' intelligence readiness.[9]

- States lacking intelligence advantage but engaging in counterintelligence operations risk self-deception, confusion, and manipulation by their adversaries.[10]
- When all competitors are ignorant, a little knowledge can go a long way (General Lee during the Battle of Chancellorsville). Sound strategy takes account of that fact and will seek to fight contests on ground favorable to intelligence and operations.[11]

All these propositions reinforce the notion that mapping uncertainties must precede successful efforts to reduce them.

It follows, at least in theory, that if all states optimize their capacities to learn competitively, they will tend to gain an ever more efficient bartering of their interests, optimizing those as well. Thus, the international system will tend toward a dynamic stability as more transparency helps states adapt to the consequences of redistributed power. In particular, wars will not be started by those unlikely to win them and treaties will not be complacently maintained as others prepare to break them.

The reason intelligence persists is that it is powered by human nature: natural curiosity and self-interest. In judging when to fight, flee, bargain, or rest, the well-informed state can save its people, treasure, and other vital interests better than ignorant ones can. Moreover, a state able to know how powerful it is relative to others will tend to be more influential than those that are ignorant, especially if that knowledge can be shared. Such "win-wins" in the intelligence world can help break down what has been termed "the prisoner's dilemma": suboptimal decisions taken in the absence of knowledge about what others are deciding to do.

Preempting the Complaints

Intelligence power may exist, but it probably doesn't matter to policymaking or political theory if it cannot be measured and controlled. Before addressing these issues, however, other potential objections must be overcome. One might concern methodology. It would be unacceptable to posit the requirements for good intelligence and then, finding examples in historical cases, merrily assert that the requirements are proven. Political scientists call such theorizing tautological.

What this study has done, however, is something quite different. It has offered a definition of intelligence (information for competitive advantage), a method for finding when it might have mattered (winning and losing decisions), a way to track the knowing and confusion back to sources (finding connections between decision-makers and the collectors supporting them), and then determined whether and to what degree those connections were engineered rather than lucky. In following this methodology, it has, moreover, selected difficult but well-documented cases in which the side with notoriously "weaker" intelligence won (Lee at Chancellorsville) the role of intelligence has long been discounted (the Spanish Armada and First Manassas) or maligned (appeasement of Germany before WWII), or outcomes seemed unavoidable due to military factors (the July Crisis of 1914 and the circumstances of mobilization). In other words, this study identifies the informational roots of significant wins and losses using hard cases, historical tracing, and the conceptual tools of "platforms" and "sensors." It is this process and its revelations that have substantiated the four characteristics of success listed above, while adding nuance and some surprises.[12]

For example, although it might not seem surprising to suggest that the more collectors the more likely the win, we also found that collectors need not operate in great numbers or secretly if their opponents are relatively incurious due to mindsets and certainties. Consider, for example, the piratical intelligence about the vulnerabilities of the Spanish galleon. These weaknesses were actually widely known, but the Spanish discounted them because their naval doctrine judged them unimportant. The English, in contrast, used this knowledge to redesign their ships, change doctrine, and thus turn open facts into intelligence advantage.[13] The English success in 1588 involved relatively well-integrated collection systems (sea captains, ships, and crews) and a reliable, trusted way to share what they knew (through John Hawkins, the Navy Board, and the blueprints made by a mathematician, Peter Baker). Similarly, it is unsurprising that states with superior technology will tend to also have better platforms and sensors for collection. But we also found that technological superiority can degrade decision-making and trust. The elaborate system of balloons, spies, cavalry, and telegraph that served Hooker proved so poorly interconnected, managed, and trusted during battle that it failed relative to General Lee's simpler system built on his cavalry and mapmaker. Thus, this study's methods revealed *unexpected* synergies and surprises, including how militarily weaker parties can reliably and predictably win, and why intelligence-related capacities on all sides must be factored into strategies meant to defeat them.

All-Source Analysis?

Another critique might be the absence of all-source analysis on the list of core intelligence capabilities. This point might at first seem a very good one. After all, analysis is "thinking" in rigorous form, and is implicit whenever thoughtful decision-making is involved.[14] Good analysis has been important to successful intelligence in all cases covered in this volume—a fact that suggests rigorous thinking is an integral, cross-disciplinary requirement much like good people skills and facility with languages.

To make "analysis" a separate mission, however, would be to put it in a box, disconnecting it from its critical role in every piece of the puzzle-finding, puzzle-making, and puzzle-solving process. For example, collectors need analysts (codebreakers, target-finders, translators, reports officers) to access a target and assess the meaning of what they collect.[15] Counterintelligence (CI) operatives need analysts (forensic experts, surveillance experts, classifiers, and double agents) to block, deceive, or otherwise adjust the enemy's capacity to learn. They may be the best at knowing enemy strategy because they are learning what he is risking his lifeblood to find out. Decision-makers want analysts (synthesizers, policy "wonks," and trusted team members) to help them sift wheat from chaff and then imagine what to do next. In fact, decision-makers may sift the collection themselves, if not overwhelmed by their portfolios.

Given that analysis is integral to all stages of the hunt for decision advantage, the *separate* and *primary* function modern "all-source analysts" perform is *the orchestration of intelligence in light of the competitive moment.* This job is best thought of as *lubricating choice* and is as managerial as it is analytical. What makes it different from the other elements of performance is skill at binding intelligence producers to intelligence users *in an organized and relevant way.* Because the flow between decision and intelligence must be two-way, however, the term "transmission" works better than "orchestration." When driving a competitive intelligence system, the decision-maker has as much of a role to play as the professional intelligence officer with her hand on the gearshift. That said, if the engine falters, it is the skilled mechanic who will know when, where, and how to fix it. And that requires an expert in the intelligence system as a whole.

Indeed, it is the demand for this "transmission function"—smooth management of intelligence production and requirements using a complex mix of collection assets—that may explain the salience of what we call "all-source analysts" in most modern intelligence systems. Decision-makers, who traditionally orchestrated intelligence for themselves, increasingly look now to all-source analysts to manage intelligence production on their behalf, especially in the United States.

This relatively new transfer of authority to intelligence agencies has contributed to the now widespread (and erroneous) view that intelligence is one thing and command or policymaking something else, with all-source analysts guarding the gates between. In fact, the complexity of modern sensor and platform technologies means guards are less necessary than are trusted experts who can bridge the divide between policy and collection. Commanders just need help understanding collection systems, driving them, archiving data, and synchronizing intelligence products with decision-making. Collectors need help aligning their work with decision-makers' needs. General James Clapper, on becoming the US director of national intelligence in 2010, recognized the problem and created national mission managers to tighten connections between collectors, analysts, and decision-makers. National intelligence officers (NIOs) once thought such work was theirs to do but, consumed by the task of orchestrating topical estimates, they had evolved into high-level managers of analysis, not collection. As one US expert has written, "In reality, the collection and analytical communities do not operate as closely as some expect." The collection system is seen as a "black box" that most analysts cannot penetrate.[16]

There is, too, another reason for the preeminence of all-source analysts and, perhaps, confusion about their value added. As the behavioral revolution made a science out of politics, so the idea gained currency that sound and "objective" all-source analysis was beyond policymakers' abilities. At the same time, the rapid expansion of technical collection systems after WWII threatened to overwhelm policymakers increasingly alienated from the systems meant to serve them. All-source intelligence analysts, seeing the problem as an opening, planted a flag and then mined the gap.[17]

Such internal reform can be useful, but also misguided. What makes all-source analysts valuable to the policymaker is their help with managing as well as sense-making, both of which should serve to fit intelligence production to the policymaker's hand, not to substitute for it. All-source analysts' knowledge of the intelligence system should align intelligence collection to decision-making; decision-makers' knowledge should help all-source analysts report requirements back into the system. Whereas Hooker needed to create such a system, modern policymakers are given it, so often miss its true value. Having planted their bureaucratic flags, all-source analysts, in turn, tend to guard both their privileged access to policy and "red lines" meant to keep decision-makers at arm's length, purposefully deepening separations. Such walls are defended as means to avoid politicization, but they are also costly. It is noteworthy that the US military, better at intelligence orchestration and command, has more flexibility in these regards. Civilian decision-makers and their all-source analysts risk decision-advantage when they build walls and guard gates better than they bridge them. As late as the twenty-first century, some senior US policymakers still know little about how intelligence works. They prefer to read the contents of the classified pouch than to discuss policy dilemmas with their briefers.

In fact, it is not all-source analysis but rather the transmission function binding the policy and intelligence kingdoms that gives modern all-source analysts their potentially *unique* value added, whether they are called analysts, mission managers, or something else. To confirm all this is true, just imagine taking away all-source analysts from the halls of policy. Decision-makers would still analyze and decide, but they would despair of any means for synchronizing intelligence production to their requirements.

Counterintelligence and Covert Action?

Another objection to the list of core intelligence functions might be confusion over the treatment of counterintelligence and covert action. As explained in our opening chapter, counterintelligence shapes what an opponent learns through information denial and influence operations, including deception. Covert action employs intelligence to gain advantages against an adversary while keeping sponsorship secret. Neither of them is included in the core intelligence capacities listed above because they represent missions peculiarly *reliant* on core intelligence capabilities, but *are not such capabilities themselves.*

Covert action can be an important part of a strategy for winning—as the successful hunt for the mastermind of 9/11, Osama bin Laden, well demonstrated—but it is best understood as secretly sponsored policy, not intelligence. Covert action, like all policy, uses intelligence for decision-making, relying on selective secrecy while purposefully limiting or damaging the transmission function in the interest of plausible deniability. Covert action's potential for systemic damage is part of why it is so dangerous for those attempting it and why intelligence agencies are often asked to do it. Policymakers will suffer failures, however, if they do not understand that covert action can degrade their decision-making and put collection assets at risk to a far greater degree than any other kind of policy. As was clear in the case of King Philip II's intelligence against Queen Elizabeth I, covert actions exhaust sources and can damage overall intelligence readiness, blinding the user. For this reason, decision-makers who use covert action without sufficient oversight also risk losing control of outcomes.

The historical cases studied here also reveal that counterintelligence is policy too: the manipulation of what an enemy can and cannot learn. In theory, counterintelligence overlaps with policy much as covert action does, because it exploits intelligence to shape an adversary's ability to learn, thereby affecting what they know and how they act. Being policy, counterintelligence depends on the four core intelligence functions to succeed, but is not a core function itself. Absent policy rationale, counterintelligence is just another name for selective secrecy unmoored from the larger strategic enterprise. In fact, one of CI's primary tools, secrecy, is often hived off for purposes of the lesser goal of security. As stressed in the opening chapter, the two ought not be confused. Security protects assets, often through secrecy and analysis of threats, while counterintelligence requires selective secrecy in service to policy, which may include demarches, influence operations, and confidence-building through the *advantageous release* of intelligence.

This last point requires further discussion because it is so poorly understood, even among some intelligence professionals. Effective counterintelligence *analysis* considers not just threats, but also what and how targets are trying to learn—that is, what they think they do not know at any competitive moment. Counterintelligence *strategy*, which includes both offensive and defensive policies, shapes that knowledge. If CI policies are purposeful, they may be used to educate a target ill-served by corrupted or underperforming intelligence assets. Or they may be used to confuse, distract, deny, and misinform, thereby shaping what the target does next. If CI activities are not purposeful, these effects on the opponent's learning will still occur. It is therefore useful to think of CI as a form of information withholding and influence peddling, not unlike what diplomats do in a relatively more open and usually more truthful way.

Thinking of counterintelligence as policy might seem shocking. In the United States analysts are used to thinking of it as an attribute of law enforcement, which should not be about politics at all. In fact, the Federal Bureau of Investigation (FBI) secures US secrets and arrests those attempting to steal them, with limited regard for the policy or political consequences. In this sense, the FBI is a security organization that has been intentionally denied full counterintelligence authorities. Any other arrangement would risk politicizing those with authorities to arrest—a mix that Hitler wanted for the Gestapo, but that President Truman explicitly rejected for the United States when designing its intelligence services after WWII. Truman understood that counterintelligence targets the intelligence capacities of opponents and allies, thereby influencing what they know, how they think, and what they do, which is dangerous for politics in democracies.

These distinctions are, therefore, not just semantics or theoretical niceties. Policymakers who do not understand them risk putting their best-laid plans at risk. Our case study of the run-up to WWI shows that Austrian efforts to keep decision-making secret became policymaking in this larger sense, with unintended consequences. By shutting down diplomatic channels in July 1914, Austrian policymakers helped create the crisis in decision-making that they had hoped to avert. Political and military leaders who forget this lesson, or confuse security with counterintelligence, care less than they should about who runs counterintelligence and how what they are doing might be conflicting with overt policymaking. When sponsorship of an offensive counterintelligence operation is hidden, it can be almost indistinguishable from covert action that, as defined in the US legal system at least, is the secret sponsorship of political, economic, military, or law enforcement activity for policy purposes. And most policymakers know how significant and dangerous covert action can be.

Since counterintelligence may seem benign or esoteric, it is often delegated almost completely to intelligence professionals. In some states CI is assigned to a specialized set of decision-makers: those who have the power to lie, to incarcerate or kill, and to deny information to the public. Counterintelligence is, therefore, a dangerous mission that makes achieving effective decision-advantage particularly difficult for democracies, many of which have wisely established strict constraints while unwisely allowing its tools and tradecraft to atrophy. Thus, the paradox: to stay safe from lies and deceits, democracies tend to keep domestic counterintelligence a matter for law enforcement, limiting authorities to security and counterespionage, and thus increasing the likelihood that deception campaigns will go unrecognized. Such blindness is why Secretary Stanton's bold moves against John Wilkes Booth seem historically anomalous, why Britain was so disadvantaged in 1938, and why America was so vulnerable to terrorists in 2001 and to social media hacking—whether legal or not—in 2016. When it comes to counterintelligence, democracies tend to fumble in the dark, not knowing exactly what they are touching or what to do about it when they do.[18]

Measuring Intelligence Power

In the following sections, each of the four core functions or missions of intelligence will be discussed, along with what the previous case studies have suggested may be the best ways to measure their performance. The quality of US modern capabilities will also be covered briefly in order to demonstrate how theory can serve intelligence management and reform.

Unfortunately, of the four core functions, only collection is easily quantifiable. It is, therefore, the most useful measure for assessing the general distribution of intelligence power among large numbers of states. It is important to keep in mind that intelligence power is additive, which is to say that it supplements the traditional elements of state power such as population, material resources, and weapons, which are, for our purposes, understood to be constant. This generalization has its flaws because intelligence and diplomatic or military endeavors must often share platforms, sensors, or communications, forcing trade-offs. Any useful assessment of intelligence power must recognize this fact. In any event, when intelligence advantage cannot be certain because the opponent's capabilities are hidden or nonquantifiable, the surest way to gain advantage is to imagine, develop, retain, and manage a diverse range of robust and flexible collection systems appropriate to one's strategy.

Collection

Among our opening hypotheses was the idea that any collection system involves five pieces:

- Command, Control, and Communications (C3; a way to get decision-makers' requirements to the system)
- Platforms (vehicles to host sensors and access the target)
- Sensors (sniffers and listeners, etc.)
- Processing and Exploitation (P&E; translating, decoding or analyzing data obtained by the sensors)
- Data exfiltration (a way to get collected data "home")

The introduction illustrated these pieces with a dog-walking metaphor that now must be adjusted for national intelligence systems. After all, when training a dog, one assumes the dog and trainer both have working nervous systems that connect sensors (nose, eyes, and ears) to brain. This assumption does not hold when evaluating national intelligence systems. In fact, the integrity or connectedness of a state's nervous system for collecting information is essential to winning intelligence advantage, whatever an opponent's capabilities are. The historical case studies in this volume suggest that to gain superiority, a competitor is better off if he has *more* collection systems with *better integration of parts, greater range,* and *better management* than his adversaries have.

Integration

The parts of a collection system that must be integrated are the platform and its communications, sensors, and data processing. A platform that

- Ventures beyond the limits of its communications;
- Carries sensors unsuited to the environment in which the platform operates;
- Dumps data faster than its processors can handle; or
- Limits the relay (exfiltration) of critical data

is a platform unsuited to its task. Any such system would lack integrity, coherence, and suitability to the target. In this domain, Drake proved an exceptional platform manager: he could rely on his mercenary crews to sail almost anywhere, identify opponents from afar, and at his command, turn his ships away from treasure and toward intelligence targets. He commanded an integrated system that Philip II did not apparently even attempt to copy or penetrate. That Drake could sail his ships to all the Spanish empire's vulnerable points made him so valuable to his queen that she made him a British lord even as she railed against her limited ability to control him once his ships left English waters.

Compare Drake's collection system with Britain's before WWII and one sees the latter's problem: embassy "ships" full of leaks; ambassadors distrusting agents; collectors at war with one another; and no integration of findings for a prime minister desperately in need of them. That Britain pulled off some wins nonetheless proves the point that absolute capabilities matter less than relative ones: Hitler's diplomatic platforms were underused and leaky too, albeit to a lesser degree. Moreover, he forgot the elementary rule that political leaders, such as Chamberlain, can be collectors too. The prime minister may have acted instinctively, but he nonetheless gained close access, ferreting out Hitler's evil side and exposing it in a way the British public could appreciate. To ensure integrated operations, one needs each collection system to have a Drake—a captain familiar with all the parts and empowered to align and repair them as needed.

Range

The purpose of integrated management is to target and track other competitors while engineering useful, continuous access to them. Assuming good integration of a collector's components, its *ability to gain and retain this access*, will depend on the following:

- The manager's ability to know whom to target, on whose behalf, by what deadline (command and control)
- The mobility of the platform relative to the target
- The sensitivity and "tunability" (retargeting capacity) of the sensors
- The reach of its communications, including the separate missions of command and control and data exfiltration
- The capacity of the collection system to "go dark" or operate under cover

This last point is crucial because range may also depend on applicable laws, such as sovereign rights to control borders and treaties. Such rules raise the political risks of collection; they do not necessarily limit range if the stakes are high enough and policymakers are willing. Treaty regimes may inhibit or improve collection by either excluding zones from interstate competition, adding collection platforms for verification purposes, or mandating intelligence sharing. Arms control treaties that entail on-site inspections of an adversary's weapons facilities may fall into several of these categories.[19]

The legal terrain must therefore be part of any effort to map the terrain of uncertainty because it influences risk assessments and therefore the range of intelligence collection on all sides. This terrain can be particularly difficult to read. Treaty regimes that seem to enhance monitoring may, for example, provide cover for unsanctioned, clandestine, or covert operations. Liaison partners may unilaterally create laws to hobble themselves for political purposes, putting joint operations unexpectedly at risk. Most democracies sensibly limit intelligence collection within their own borders and against their citizens to preserve civil rights and to prohibit those in power from using the advantages of national office against domestic political competitors. Collectors operating within democracies do best when planning for these constraints by building open-source systems. Citizens and journalists in healthy democracies can provide the eyes and ears for a state under attack—a kind of neighborhood watch that formal intelligence services would have difficulty replicating. They can, however, only extend the range of collection episodically and of their own volition.

As suggested earlier, the range of a collection system generally depends on well-integrated components; it also depends on good management. A collection manager does not need to chase a target if he can get close to it one way or another, which in turn requires not just integrated components, but choreography: designing systems of platforms, sensors, and communications that can dance with the target most productively. Rose Greenhow, the Confederate spy, did not try to collect much outside her home because she was a social magnet; targets came to her door. She controlled everything that went on inside of it.[20]

In most cases, however, adequate range for a collection system cannot be predetermined because intelligence is always a competitive project and opponents are often on the move. Balloons extended the range of vision for Union generals, with the consequence that Confederate generals operated more in the woods and at night. Collectors had to adjust operations to pursue them. Booth's range of collection, which turned on wartime Confederate networks, collapsed around him as Stanton pressed forward with his cavalry and the South angled for favorable terms. And every time General Lee ventured above the Mason-Dixon Line, his collectors thinned relative to the Union's because his collectors, while robust in the South, had poor range outside of it. This fragility is why collection systems are often so highly secret: after so much investment, any exposure of capabilities (or lack of them) can lead to loss of range against multiple targets and deeply compromise overall intelligence readiness. Adversaries will inevitably seek workarounds, so the value in collection systems rests not just in what they collect, but in their forcing function; the ways their suspected or known presence limits the mobility of targets in profitable ways or patterns, making targeting easier for lesser-known collectors.

Management

For all these reasons, it is wrong to equate a collection system's range with integration, platform mobility, or even "Drake" styles of command. While these attributes are necessary, they may not be sufficient. Collectors may have to extend their range by acting as a system linked back to competitors. *If each collection manager adheres to a target by mixing, matching, and securing the components of collection that she controls, then central collection managers, working on behalf of the decision-maker, can orchestrate access through retargeting and handoff. In this way, individual collectors, even seemingly nonproductive ones, can boost each other's work over a larger territory.* For example, surface ships tracking an illicit shipment of weapons should be able to hand that mission to ground-, space-, or air-based platforms once the shipment comes to port and moves onto trucks or planes. Knowing when and how best to do so is a job for central collection management. To force an adversary to change course in helpful ways—that is, ways vulnerable to collection or interdiction, requires knowing, intimately, the capabilities of all collectors, using some to boost the work of others. Central managers can achieve this kind of agility through innovation and centralized orchestration.

Herein lies a crucial role for decision-makers working with intelligence systems: identifying for these central managers who is making decisions on both sides as competitions evolve. Without a lubricated process for keeping decision-makers in the loop, managers may design collection systems with insufficient range. Collectors may become untethered, missing their marks by gathering useless information to demonstrate productivity some other way or by delivering good intelligence to the wrong place. Identifying targets and recipients is not, therefore, a job only for all-source analysts but for policymakers and collection managers as well. This is the meaning in which "centralized" management is used here: "central" to the decision-maker served, whether the latter is the leader of a counterterrorist unit operating within a larger network or a prime minister or president. Indeed, decision-makers can and often have played this role themselves, as Queen Elizabeth I did in the sixteenth century.

Central management is also important for innovation. Decision-makers and established collectors will tend to favor proven ways of doing business with familiar platforms, sensors, processing, and communication systems. Recall the US Army's early resistance to balloon reconnaissance before the start of the Civil War and British diplomats' reluctance to accept intelligence professionals operating under diplomatic cover before WWII.[21] Such tension between innovators and defenders of proven methods is both valuable and dangerous. On the one hand, investing in innovation helps competitors gain and retain access to evasive targets using unexpected new sensors, platforms, and communications. The case studies in this book have shown that the distribution of technology, basic science, and industry shapes the terrain of uncertainty and, thus, opening advantages. States with strong scientific and industrial sectors, such as Britain had before WWII, are better positioned to develop innovative methods of collection than those without them. Collectors who resist innovation put their missions at risk from bold first-adopters.

On the other hand, however, skeptics are correct to point out that money, innovation, and industry do not always equate to extended range or collection capacity. Innovation introduced in the wrong ways can disrupt collection methods, prevent sharing among incompatible systems, threaten central managers' orchestration of collection efforts, and reduce confidence in security. The 1861–63 war among US telegraphers, each promoting a better technological system for wireless communications in battle, documents the point. And then, too, states with limited resources but savvy management can find other solutions, such as cannibalizing some collectors to augment others, reverting to "obsolete" but unexpected and better understood methods, or finding ways to skirt technological "eyes" as the terrorists did on 9/11.

Innovation is, however, essential for competitive advantage, because other competitors will otherwise learn how each other learns and penetrate, corrupt, or defeat it. Central management is the only way to balance old, reliable methods against new techniques. Sometimes innovation simply means remixing old components of collection in new ways; other times it means creating completely new platforms, sensors, or communications through cooperation with private industry. It took Britain decades to learn how to develop the connections between its private sector and intelligence agencies that helped it fight its "wizard's war" against Germany's industrial machine. The United States eventually learned these lessons too, exploring how to reduce the risks of incorporating commercial technologies, including those with components made by foreigners, into secure, classified collection systems. For better or worse, the answer was the development of an intelligence-industrial complex that rivaled the military-industrial one, with classified intelligence requirements feeding into innovative, new, and integrated platforms, sensors, and processing and communications systems. When the Soviet Union closed itself off during the Cold War, the United States was able to innovate, developing the capabilities to monitor Soviet capabilities first from high-flying U2 aircraft and then from space. The US CIA initially served as a central manager, developing a technical and scientific arm. Later, it worked in cooperation with the National Security Agency, National Reconnaissance Office, and military services to develop unmatched technical collection systems operating on land, in space, at sea, under water, and in the air. Success has been much more difficult in the area of encryption, where commercial advances have improved capacities for secrecy that have steadily eroded capacities for decryption and, thus, threatened collectors' capacities to process and exploit data on the move.

Although striking the balance between innovation and proven methods is both difficult and necessary, the best balance in any competition will have to be judged case by case by those responsible for collection management. In any event, the measure of *intelligence* value is not the cost of the collection system or the sophistication of its methods, but rather its ability to deliver advantages against an adversary. For example, a state initially incapable of launching imagery satellites might compensate to some degree by running large numbers of human spies off ground-based platforms or conducting aerial overflights. A central manager intimately connected to collection systems and knowledgeable of the targets can improve the viability and productivity of such trade-offs.

It follows that strong central managers and individual platform managers must have close connections because the work of each depends on the performance of the other. Frictions between central managers and individual collectors need not arise if both accept that their jobs are to improve each collector's productivity, efficiency, targeting flexibility, connectedness, usability, robustness, *and capacity to boost the performance of other collectors*. Collection management is, therefore, no place for bureaucratic loyalties or other restrictive mindsets.

Measurement Challenges and Collection Reform

The management factor, while crucial for the productivity of collection, is difficult to measure and assess. Indeed, when assessing the overall intelligence power of states, the most direct way would be to count their respective collection systems and just assume related platforms, sensors, communications, and P&E systems are well integrated. Central management and integration can be indirectly measured by the degree to which collection systems fill gaps when a collector is compromised or a new target is created. Technological innovation, including links between industry and the state, is also important, but perhaps less than the broader measures just mentioned. The number and quality of links between information-contractors and state agencies may serve as an indirect measure of capacity for innovation.

Measuring capabilities is, however, one thing; repairing deficiencies is quite another. Excellent central managers can do little about collection shortfalls if, for example, embassies are mismanaged or liaison partners balk. Sometimes bureaucratic or other interests get in the way, as they did for Quex Sinclair and Vansittart in the run-up to WWII. At other times competing interests do. Consider the example from the case of the Armada: Sir John Hawkins and Drake were devilishly successful collection managers at sea, but they had their own agendas that limited their trustworthiness and utility for further reforms. If the queen had not played a strong hand in managing them in 1588, she might have lost.[22] The failure of traditional diplomatic establishments before both WWI and WWII makes this same point in the negative: poorly designed, equipped, and integrated embassies failed repeatedly to deliver good intelligence in time. Senior officials knew the problem was serious, but few knew how to repair it. British embassies in Italy and Germany during the 1930s employed diplomats who performed more as sensors for Hitler than for Chamberlain: they were repeatedly compromised and bamboozled even as they retained their influence with political leaders. Once superior collection systems bound tightly to royal courts, many embassies had become, by the twentieth century, indifferently managed shells fighting to secure timely reporting.

This discussion reveals that, while collection may be the most quantifiable aspect of intelligence power, much of it still depends on the unquantifiable, such as management savvy, imagination, and capacity to reform. Imagination is essential for the crucial business of mixing and matching the components of collection. Over centuries of practice, platforms have included prisons, ships, churches, and embassies, but also horses, citizens' homes, and telegraph stations. Industrialization led to the use of planes, cars, and balloons, prompting innovators to adapt sensors and communications appropriate to them. In every case, platforms were only as good as the sensors that rode on them, the processors, the communications that they could accommodate, and the managers who made certain they were not overused and thus exposed.

In sum, then, a superior intelligence service will have highly integrated and managed collection systems that are numerous, flexible, and mobile enough to be orchestrated over the entire domain of competition without losing connectivity to decision-making. So how does one use this measure to assess a particular state's capabilities?

US Collection Issues

The current US intelligence community, which grew up rapidly after WWII, involves the largest, most diverse, and technologically sophisticated collection system in history, with collection platforms deployed in space, on land and sea, under water, and in cyberspace. As a democracy, the United States has set domestic limits on collection and delegated significant national security responsibilities to law enforcement. The wall between what law enforcement can legally know and pass on to national intelligence services has shifted over the years depending on shifts in public perceptions of threat.

Performance is also hurt, however, by barriers to integrated collection. For example, diplomatic platforms, communications, and reporting are poorly integrated with other forms of collection, despite chief-of-mission authorities to oversee all overseas US government activities outside of war zones. This mission makes ambassadors or chiefs of mission de facto central collection managers outside the intelligence community (IC) with responsibilities for managing a wide range of sensors. Yet, some intelligence operations work targets without ambassadors' knowledge, risking a mismatch of communications and security with high-risk operations. If operations go wrong, chiefs of mission are held accountable.

The problem here reflects the dual-use nature of diplomatic platforms. If ambassadors are political appointees with little overseas experience or understanding of intelligence, they may represent Washington well, but also have a steep learning curve as collection managers, putting sensitive operations at risk. If chiefs of mission are foreign service officers (FSOs), they may be better collection managers than they are channels to the president, provided they have not been burned by failed operations in the past. Yet even knowledgeable FSOs have been hamstrung by their lack of resources to, for example, adjust platform security to operational risks. For decades, State Department operating budgets and personnel have been in steady decline in comparison to other agencies. As nondiplomatic activities have expanded overseas, the demands on US platforms (embassies and consulates) have often outpaced the physical space and support services available, with no supplemental funds flowing to fill the gap. Thus, critical collection platforms and the security that goes with them, funded by one set of committees in Congress, are not shaped dynamically to fit the sensors, communications, and operational requirements developed by intelligence agencies and military programs funded by another set of committees.

As mentioned earlier in this volume, the Department of State identified this problem in the 1990s and created a program, Support to Diplomatic Operations, or SDO, to organize the requirements of platform management, coordination, and reconciliation of intelligence functions overseas. Efforts to integrate SDO into the central management of overseas operations ran, however, into serious difficulties. One had to do with the funding issue mentioned above: the US Code distinguishes intelligence (Title 50) from combat operations (Title 10), and both of these from foreign affairs (Title 22) and law enforcement (including counterespionage, Title 18) in ways that have made good collection management and planning difficult from a programmatic standpoint.[23]

Although the creation of the position of US director of national intelligence (DNI) after 9/11 was meant to solve the problems of coordinating multi-agency programs, it did not entirely succeed. The Department of Homeland Security has, for example, a new transmission function regarding domestic threats but few authorities to manage collection in support of it. The DNI also has limited ability to influence those agencies running platforms, sensors, and communications under their respective agency accounts. And because integrated management is important to the State, Defense, and Justice Departments for their own purposes, efforts to coordinate for intelligence purposes are difficult at best. These circumstances, which include split staffs in the Office of Management and Budget and multiple, competing oversight and appropriations committees in Congress, has meant that agility in the crucial collection function has long been compromised.[24] In particular, the managerial split between the FBI and the rest of the IC has led to miscommunication and operational trip-ups working against drug-, terrorist-, crime-, and gang-related targets that overseers have only gradually come to understand and repair.

If the United States has generally exceled at collection, the performance has not always translated to superiority because of the dynamics of the competitive context.

- US adversaries such as the USSR, and then Russia, China, Iran, and North Korea, have countered US collection capabilities with ramped-up secrecy, becoming exceptionally hard targets to penetrate. To block satellite surveillance, for example, countries have moved operations underground. To block diplomatic intelligence, they have heightened threats to them or limited diplomatic access—moves that congressional overseers have so far been unwilling to counter with increased funding.
- Adversaries know the range of US intelligence collectors is limited as far as domestic operations are concerned. By running bold collection operations inside the United States, they can tempt overreach and force increases in US security that set the public against government intelligence operations. Secrecy and other forms of security can be a black hole unless one calibrates "threats" according to the interests of the state.
- Although positive intelligence collection and counterintelligence work best when coordinated, the respective collection managers in the United States often come from two different cultures, so do not coordinate well. The advent of cyberwar has forced collection managers to repair this divide out of recognition that gaining access, exploiting it, defending against it, and attacking with it are all part of the same enterprise. This same coordination should be happening in all collection disciplines.[25]
- US adversaries can overwhelm dual-use platforms managed by military commands (ships and planes) and diplomatic services (embassies, consulates). Already somewhat insensitive to each other's needs and poorly coordinated, dual-use platforms under pressure can lose their ability to boost each other as part of an overall collection system. More than one

secretary of state has been stunned to find, in the midst of crisis, that intelligence on the target country has disappeared just when he or she has needed it most, because departmental managers have closed a threatened embassy or the military has re-oriented a satellite. That such calls weighing benefits and risks must be made is certain; that they should be made without interagency policy and intelligence input is foolhardy.

The problem of disaggregated collection management, particularly on the diplomatic side, has plagued US intelligence for years; it still needs to be fixed, ideally by someone who values and understands both diplomatic and military decision-making.

Anticipation

A superior intelligence system will be independent enough from the decision-making process to collect what decision-makers do not believe they need to know just in case they suddenly do. In this way, intelligence can lower the risks of strategic surprise and prepare to exploit the unexpected. By mapping the terrain of uncertainty, including how uncertainty is distributed across the international system, anticipatory intelligence lays the foundation for strategic planning should matters turn hot. It follows that if an adversary's strategy seems misaligned with his opening advantages, intelligence should suspect a hidden agenda, including surprise attack. Anticipatory intelligence is not the study of everything; rather, it maps the terrain and then collects against unexploited adversarial advantages, "black swans," and other gaps likely to matter, even if the current decision-makers are not alarmed by them.

This last point requires emphasis. Anticipatory intelligence goes beyond basic intelligence, strategic intelligence, and tactical warning. Whereas these latter three missions are all necessary, they serve decision-makers' express needs. Anticipatory intelligence goes further. Its purpose is to imagine and collect against what future decision-makers (on all sides) discount or choose to ignore, making it the only mission that is not driven by policymakers' expressed requirements.

The case studies in this volume include two instances of foresight and another striking lack of it. Queen Elizabeth I's decision to rebuild her navy along race-built lines was almost certainly based on the expectation that Spain would be a mortal enemy, and knowledge of how to beat her in the Channel. A similar clear-minded foresight was demonstrated by Lord Vansittart, who decided to take *Mein Kampf* seriously and so found (insufficient) evidence that Hitler meant what he said. The standout failure was Edward Grey's failure to foresee a coming crisis in the Balkans that Great Powers might not be able collectively to resolve.

From these handlings and mishandlings some lessons about foreknowledge become clear. It would seem that anticipatory capacity can be judged using a fourfold measure:

- The capacity to collect against adversaries (see above)
- The regularity and accuracy of strategic knowledge-mapping: that is, reporting on the terrain of uncertainty, not just "threat assessments"
- The degree to which intelligence policymakers have a budgetary reserve for independent collection priorities
- The strength of intelligence oversight

The first measure has already been discussed as a foundational requirement. The second measure recognizes that those who estimate (identify gaps in knowing) and those who command and control collection systems (fill in gaps in knowing) are variably linked; the better their connections, the more likely will be the ability to anticipate as well as warn. The third measure recognizes the importance of swift movement of resources into collection gaps, whether or not policymakers yet see the need to do so. The last measure hinges on the prior one, although that idea may seem paradoxical. Although one cannot have anticipatory intelligence without intelligence managers having a measure of independence in money and mission, one will be unlikely to gain the latter if policymakers cannot monitor and verify worth.

Oversight is therefore best thought of less as a check on intelligence than as an enabling function that keeps intelligence on the rails and fully fueled as it speeds forward toward competitive wins. In the case of anticipatory intelligence, it ensures that funding for "watchful waiting" and warning are sufficient and properly used. This kind of oversight requires a nonpartisan, sophisticated understanding of how intelligence works. With resources tight, policymakers almost always prefer to put money against targets they know that alarm them, rather than ones they do not know or find inconsequential. They want to pre-arrange intelligence deliveries to themselves and those they select, not to new, less trusted decision-makers on subjects they do not yet understand. For these reasons, some degree of independence for an intelligence service is both intolerable and essential. This paradox can only be resolved by sound oversight that, done well, makes the independence both tolerable and doable.

That Queen Elizabeth exercised strong oversight both personally and through her Naval Board has been thoroughly discussed and requires no further elaboration. That the miserly monarch was willing to spend so much on a naval redesign suggests something else: she had more than a hunch about how she might win at sea. She acquired that knowledge thanks to a group of men who financed their experimental designs *independently*, and then impressed her with the results. Such independent action was fueled by their own sense of fight—the anger with Spain over the treachery at San Juan de Ulúa—and the stash of money they had to test out their ideas. It was that independent funding combined with the Navy Board's watchful waiting that turned a hunch into anticipatory decision-advantage.

In the absence of strong policy oversight, independent collection can become more tolerable if subcontracted to someone else and overseen by intelligence managers. This arrangement was key to Vansittart's ability to anticipate Hitler's strategic plans. The author of that arrangement was Lord Halifax, the foreign minister, who found Vansittart intolerable, so removed him as permanent undersecretary, but also necessary, so kept him as an independent advisor free to conspire with the likes of Churchill, Léger, MI5, and his network of unauthorized spies.

Such an arrangement made anticipatory collection seem both cheap and deniable if things went wrong; it nonetheless infuriated those ruffled by devil's advocacy. Lacking his own resources, however, Vansittart had to lean on the French. Intelligence services lacking resources often barter with each other to fill gaps. Remember the dog on the leash in the first chapter? A liaison service's ongoing sniffing may serve to watch a partnering service's back at seemingly low cost for either party. Problems arise, however, when the dog seems excessively jumpy (as the French seemed to be) or turns to bite (as Stalin threatened to do). For this reason, relying on allied services *may be* safer (though not risk-free) than bartering with adversarial ones. Throughout the Cold War, the United States engaged in intelligence sharing with its allies—especially the "Five Eyes" of Britain, Canada, France, Australia, and New Zealand—to supplement US-based collection systems to get global coverage. The more attractive the cause seemed, the more US intelligence gained watchful volunteers.[26] The downside is that these services will likely have similar intelligence requirements, so be equally blind to the unexpected. Real gains can come from liaison with those holding a different point of view. Liaison with private-sector entities can be particularly fruitful, even if it sometimes includes less professional collaborators. WWII witnessed the race for nuclear weapons, sparked by initiatives coming from self-organizers and volunteers within the scientific community. In modern times, liaison with private firms managing social networks or cyber-related technologies have offered intelligence advantages—a subject to be discussed in the concluding chapter.

The role liaison and private networks play in anticipatory intelligence underscores the importance of counterintelligence as an aspect of proper oversight. Whether anticipatory intelligence is based on volunteers or liaison services, it needs to be managed as a peculiar mission for collection; seen as such, it introduces special problems of platform management, source validation, processing, exploitation, and data exfiltration. Even friendly services can have weaknesses or be penetrated by hostile powers eager to "share" and thus influence or deceive. Before the 2003 estimate on Iraqi weapons of mass destruction (WMD), for example, a trusted intelligence partner provided strategic warning of Iraq's growing capabilities, but refused access to sources for some of its most sensitive human intelligence. The result was dissemination of bad intelligence, with disastrous effects.[27] Intelligence services need to run counterintelligence operations against liaison partners, including "friendly" services whose weaknesses may be exploited by hostile powers seeking to spread disinformation under the guise of warning. The more hostile and weak the liaison service, the more costly will be the vetting and the stronger, necessary counterintelligence oversight. At some point, the gains in efficiency from liaison may be reduced to zero and overall costs may even go up.[28]

Another difficulty for anticipatory intelligence is that it often requires collection on what is *not* happening. Lord Grey saw little point in this, so was complacent about what was going on in the Balkans, and deployed few competent collectors there. After the archduke's assassination, a time when nothing seemed to be happening, the ambassador to Serbia went on holiday—a move that apparently did not strike Grey as inappropriate at the time, but denied him the foreknowledge he needed about what Vienna was planning. Architects of anticipatory intelligence think and behave quite differently: To prevent strategic surprise, they monitor and control terrain an adversary might believe is unknown or unwatched. Consider the importance of Secretary Stanton's knowing, after Lincoln's assassination, that the Confederacy was *not involved* and *would not try to capitalize* on the panic in Washington. With no good evidence that this was the case, and with Jefferson Davis still on the run, he had Lincoln's choice for Virginia's governor declare the state's pacific interests and intentions. In this way he pre-emptively adjusted the terrain of uncertainty in favor of Federal action on Virginia's soil. No latent Confederate network could assume an advantage even if, in fact, they had one. The deception may have worked—one cannot really know for sure—but Virginia's official declaration to Stanton probably lowered the risks of using the US cavalry to quit Washington and pursue Booth.

The Stanton case poses the question of how states can *anticipate security*— that is, the absence of threat. Knowing what an enemy will not do is perhaps the most difficult of all the kinds of foreknowledge. But it is possible with persistent surveillance, such as Hooker had of gaps in Confederate lines before Chancellorsville. Watchful waiting showed (and a bit of deception ensured) that this gap was not going to be filled, so Hooker could plan to march through it. In peacetime, such persistent surveillance of nothing is far more difficult to achieve. Again, this sentry-like role is the proper domain for diplomatic intelligence, which is supported by international law worldwide, but has lost so much of its footing in recent years. The United States even had this capacity within its borders, at least briefly, after 9/11. Consider how the FBI knew, after the terrorist attacks during the Boston Marathon, *that there were no co-conspirators* preparing follow-up bombings. This anticipatory awareness came from having collected unprocessed telephone metadata before the bombings took place. Once the bombers were caught, the FBI could exploit the metadata for the purpose of tracing the terrorists' prior activities with possible co-conspirators. *Finding nothing*, the FBI was able to reassure the public, let planes fly, and focus its work on prosecuting the two terrorists they had.

This capacity to know that nothing is brewing requires persistent surveillance of nonactivity until something happens; it also often requires trusted oversight to know that the right of surveillance is not being abused. Arms control treaties require this kind of monitoring of foreign compliance, which the parties jointly oversee. But in domestic cases, mass surveillance carries obvious risks to liberty that only strong oversight can assuage. US law enforcement only briefly had this capacity to anticipate after 9/11. As threats and public confidence in oversight institutions waned, the tether on intelligence tightened and ability to anticipate declined. This decline will not be felt until the next attack, when capacity to know what has not taken place will matter, leaving decision-makers unable to anticipate calm as well as heightened threat. Ironically, but perhaps justifiably, those critics most irritated by the tendency of intelligence officials to hype threats opposed the IC's use of its passive metadata tool, even though it carried extensive oversight provisions and allowed the rapid restoration of normal national activities, including air travel and normal urban life in Boston and other major cities. They were probably right to do so. With effective oversight on the wane in a politically riven Washington, this domestic tool was potentially wasteful and dangerous; that most of the overseers of this program claimed they did not understand it, just makes the point. The intelligence problem was, however, with the program's oversight, not its operations, which, like many intelligence operations, carried both risk and reward worth the cost and the leash.

Democracies are particularly prone to whipsawing intelligence institutions— blaming them for doing too little in the wake of crisis, and then too much after the crisis dissipates. This is why oversight is particularly critical to the warning or anticipation function. Anticipation is analogous to the baby-monitor concept for guardians: parents want to hear when their baby cries, but they also benefit from collecting "nothing" because it means their baby is sleeping soundly and lets them focus on other things. If an intruder enters—as unlikely as the parents may think this to be—the baby monitor will warn. The device contributes to decision advantage in three ways: alarms for the unexpected, alarms for warning of the expected, and silence for focus. Anticipatory intelligence (or counterintelligence) is like a baby monitor for distracted decision-makers; it is productive because it reveals no surprise is brewing; it serves to catch *what is not expected*; and it allows decision-makers to focus on what they are doing.

But herein lies the rub: anticipatory collection, like a stake-out, involves a lot of seemingly nonproductive waiting and expenditures. As fears diminish, the felt need for the collection diminishes, and managers are tempted to move collectors to more pressing concerns. Worse, baby monitors spy on the baby. When employed by a government, such systems seem to spy on citizens even when supposedly collecting nothing for current use. And babies eventually grow up. Much as parents might want to monitor their teens, it is not going to happen unless the arrangements are negotiated by both parties.[29] If oversight is poor or future leaders prove untrustworthy, anticipatory intelligence will break down; it cannot work to achieve decision-advantage without oversight and trust. The best and safest intelligence systems are, therefore, "semi-independent" in the sense that they operate according to the best judgment of the intelligence service in consultation with overseers charged with tightening and lengthening its leash as required and as publicly tolerated. Few democratic states have invested in true anticipatory intelligence because, in the absence of strong oversight, it hands tremendous power to intelligence services. This is as it should be, but it means democracies have a structural weakness in this dimension of intelligence power.

US Capabilities and Implications

The US intelligence system has a significant capacity for anticipatory intelligence thanks to its rich collection of technical intelligence collectors, its relatively sophisticated requirements system that leaves room for persistent collection or watchful waiting, and the Defense Department's experience as a collection manager. Five developments have, however, undermined US capabilities to warn and anticipate foreign threats:

- Hollowing out of diplomatic intelligence worldwide
- The post–Cold War deployment of military forces into hotspots requiring commitment of intelligence resources to their missions
- Heightened partisanship and the weakening of congressional oversight
- The advent of cyberwar, which has increased the requirement for technical knowledge
- Budget constraints that have limited the resources available for monitoring low-risk but high-impact events

When military forces deploy intelligence collectors devote resources to force protection, limiting what is available for other national missions, including anticipatory intelligence. For example, during the 1990s when national decision-makers wanted to monitor Saddam Hussein's WMD, there were competing needs for monitoring the no-fly zone over Iraq and related force protection. That collection trade-off was decided in the military's favor. As a result, however, analysts lost confidence in their assessments of Saddam Hussein's WMD and, in the run-up to the Iraq war of 2003, overestimated what he had. An inability to collect beyond the military's force protection requirements in the 1990s meant the IC was forced to estimate in 2003 using data from an interrupted stakeout. The IC got it wrong.

The United States has at least a partial, potential solution to the modern problem of anticipatory intelligence. Networks of embassies and consulates overseas could serve as better warning systems than they are now equipped to do. Sometimes maligned for their old-fashioned ways and presence in marginal countries, these ground-based platforms could help with collecting the "nothing" that, nonetheless, is the critical "something" on which strategic warning hangs. Recall that Ambassador Prudence Bushnell sounded the alarm about terrorist threats in Africa well before the embassy bombings there in 1998 that were the direct precursors of al-Qaeda's attacks in 2001. Embassies and consulates have long been the mailboxes for foreign governments and even foreign citizens to raise alarms. Unfortunately, as already mentioned, the US Department of State has long had insufficient resources to perform this monitoring function either flexibly or dynamically. FSOs have lost much of their reporting function and capabilities because of budget cuts. Many embassies are run by political appointees unfamiliar with what intelligence requires and pressed, as all ambassadors are with missions more challenging than their budgets seem to recognize, from diplomacy, reporting, communications, and management to diplomatic security.

To fix these gaps in anticipatory readiness, Congress would need to invest in its diplomatic platforms and Foreign Service reporting around the world, providing the secretary of state with funds for more FSOs and a financial reserve for surging diplomatic platforms and Foreign Service reporting in anticipation of crises, as well as in hotspots. The State Department's Bureau of Intelligence and Research might also be enlarged to help coordinate the collection management necessary for such surges. The US diplomatic network of platforms, sensors, reporting, and communications worldwide is ready-made for the job—a job it has done, in fact, with varying success for centuries. It would just need more savvy budgetary overseers, perhaps developing a stronger relationship with the intelligence oversight committees, for this aspect of its operations.

Transmission

The transmission function of intelligence is the crucial link, as already described, between the entire intelligence system and those whose policy decisions depend on it, whether diplomatic, military, law enforcement, or intelligence-related. Close, two-way connectivity is essential if intelligence is to be believed and collectors are to risk their lives providing it. General Hooker engineered near perfect connectivity with his intelligence service prior to the Battle of Chancellorsville, creating the conditions for successful surprise attack; the failure of the BMI to sustain that connectivity in battle created the conditions for Hooker's subsequent blindness and defeat. Like the transmission in a truck, the wheels will not turn if the gears are mishandled, no matter how powerful the engine.

There are five indicators of a good transmission function:

- Officials accountable for mapping and connecting collection to decision-making
- Comparable subject matter expertise among decision-makers and their primary intelligence contacts
- Capacity and willingness to share sensitive information—sources, methods, strategy, and tactics—across that intelligence-policy divide (two-way communications)
- Responsive collection, measured as upticks in the ratio of factual assessments to estimates in intelligence products
- A lack of substantive intelligence leaks to the public

Regarding the first measure, it should now be obvious that intelligence providers and users are best off when they know each other and have the means to work closely together. Intelligence officers within a military chain of command or a government bureaucracy have this kind of confidence and can know where intelligence needs to go by looking at a flow chart.[30] When they do not, as Winfield Scott failed to do before First Manassas, it is reasonable to charge incompetence.

Attentiveness across the intelligence-decision divide is difficult to assess. One way is highly subjective: the degree to which intelligence providers and users share *subject matter expertise*. Shared expertise gives decision-makers confidence that an intelligence provider knows at least as much as they do about the target. Their uncertainties are comparable and relatable. For this reason, subject matter analysts are often best at the job. Analysts will nonetheless fail at this task if they do not develop expertise in collection, stay in touch with collectors, and understand the strategy and tactics they are meant to support. Absent this knowledge, trust will evaporate. Recall that the all-source analysts with the BMI who helped Hooker plan his surprise attack at Chancellorsville became useless when uninformed about constraints on collectors, disconnected from the evolving battle, and ignorant of bottlenecks in the telegraph system.[31] The transmission function had broken down.

In circumstances such as this last example, subject matter expertise can actually cause problems for transmitting intelligence and requirements. Analysts may substitute what they think *should* suffice for what decision-makers need. This form of politicization is difficult for experts to recognize, even in themselves, but nonetheless undermines trust. Walsingham lost favor with Elizabeth I when he *insisted*, despite her objections, that the analytical thresholds for a war with Spain had been met; Burghley withstood similar disfavor when he *knew* the evidence against the Catholic Mary, Queen of Scots, was more than sufficient for a beheading when Queen Elizabeth did not. Looking back, it seems both men were substantively right but still wrong from an intelligence standpoint. Such analytical hubris begins with the notion that "analysis" is the primary product of the intelligence officer; this hubris ends when decision-makers insist that their perception of informed choice matters most. In the cases of Walsingham and Burghley, their presumptions were overruled by a forceful monarch who sent them scurrying to get more evidence. In democracies, decision-makers must insist on what they truly need—speaking decision-truths to intelligence power. Their interlocutors, who are often all-source analysts, should understand that their primary job is not just to know more and to convince, but to lubricate the machinery of choice, which may require better analysis, more evidence, more time, or something else.

In the modern US system, analysts tend to see themselves more as academics than as transmission specialists. This is a problem. US intelligence analysis has, since WWII and the postwar behavioral revolution in the social sciences, become a highly academic enterprise. The government's first national intelligence analysts came from the Library of Congress and Ivy League schools. Their academic expertise was admirable, but their practical expertise in stimulating collectors to close gaps or alerting leaders to critical unknowns proved lacking.[32] The ivory tower quality of the original Board of National Estimates was both laudable and dangerous, with the latter aspect most difficult to see and repair. The problem has become more challenging over time as collection systems have become more complex. One recent director of the National Intelligence Council has noted that most of the national intelligence officers he supervised saw managing resources, analytical training, and collection issues "more often as a burden distracting . . . from their central business of analysis."[33] Modern, civilian, all-source analysts, trained to internalize the "red line" between analysis and policy, still see their jobs as making "calls" based on available evidence. Most, recruited and promoted for their analytical skills and estimative tradecraft, are reticent to express doubt, draw attention to what they do not know, or offer insights on underlying collection issues. In fairness, they often lack the power to close collection gaps themselves. As a result, they often take refuge in their distance from decision-making while treating estimative tradecraft—an analytical way to deal with uncertainty—as the highest level of intelligence production. National intelligence estimates are important, but they should be used to clarify what is not known about high-priority targets so collectors can reduce those uncertainties through a redistribution of resources. Estimative judgments can then be briefed along with the new priorities, revealing known unknowns and how they will be overcome. In general, decision-makers prefer facts over guesswork, and solutions over probabilities and hypothetical scenarios.[34]

When estimates serve the collection mission, both decision-maker and collector benefit. Therefore, another good indicator of healthy transmission will be *upticks* in the ratio of factual assessments to estimates in intelligence products. Evidence of adversaries' capabilities and intentions will always be more persuasive than guesses. Estimates might be required if the problem has no present, factual answer (what will the stock market be in ten days?), or collection and exploitation of data have been insufficient (how often have threatening aerial phenomena remained unidentified over the past ten years?). But when analysts see their job as getting better at guessing intentions than clarifying gaps in collection, they are shirking their duty to gain evidence of an adversary's plans, and will lose decision-makers' trust. In healthy intelligence systems, estimating is, or should be, the first rung of the analytical ladder because the analytical objective is to *decrease* the proportion of guessing and *increase* the relevant facts with each successive cut at a problem.

This rule does not mean that there is no place for estimating in fact-based assessments, or that estimates are not important to analytical production.[35] Indeed, estimative work is highly desirable when mapping what we have called the "terrain of uncertainty." Insofar as such mapping entails creative thinking, identifies opening advantages or opportunities, and establishes the foundation for a competitor's strategy, it may be prescriptive and therefore sensitive. US intelligence estimates of global trends should never be unclassified—unless, of course, the insights offer no particular advantage. In the latter case, the reports may be generally informative, but they should come from a public service agency or university, not an intelligence agency with classified budget and the mission to gain advantage over opponents.

Perhaps the most powerful indicator of a sound transmission function may be *the sharing of sensitive information*—sources, methods, strategy, and tactics—across the intelligence-policy divide. When a classification system is biased against rapid sharing of such sensitive intelligence and instead becomes sticky, managers have chosen to sacrifice the transmission function (lubricated choice) for preservation of institutionalized mistrust. Decision-makers choose to withhold policy-planning from collectors, and collectors choose to protect of sources and methods from decision-makers. Each believes the other indiscreet and more self-serving than not. Modern intelligence institutions are supposed to overcome this problem with a system that vets people for access to classified material even when strangers are involved. Yet when this system gets too large, it can lose credibility. As membership grows, multiple classification levels, compartments, and "bigot lists" will signify increasing *internal mistrust* and a "need to withhold" as much as need to know.

In this light, it should not be surprising that after the capture of Aldrich Ames, a Soviet mole inside the CIA, investigators castigated the agency for too liberal sharing of intelligence among cleared insiders only to later castigate the agency after 9/11 for insufficient sharing against the terrorist target. In fact, the deficiency in both circumstances reflected an impoverished transmission function, which requires good balance in vetting personnel for trustworthiness *and* agility in intelligence handoffs among the vetted, whether provider or decision-maker. Failures in handoff are not always deliberate. Routine intelligence flows can lead to good connections with current decision-makers, but crippling resistance to new ones.[36] This dynamic suggests that a superior intelligence service will put in place sharing protocols that might be triggered in national emergencies.

Whenever the transmission function's two-way trust breaks down, internal frustration will go up and, with it, a tendency toward leaks. Leaks are therefore another indicator of a broken transmission function. When Vansittart briefed Churchill on the Nazi threat before WWII, he did so because he did not trust that Prime Minister Chamberlain was listening to him, which was true, but his actions made Chamberlain distrust him all the more. Leaks damage intelligence, not just because secrets are revealed, but also because intelligence relationships break down. Vansittart's successor, Cadogan, was appalled by his behavior, which drove the wedge between them ever deeper. The press and other media, which tend to view leakers as crucial to intelligence oversight in a democracy, often ignore this darker side. The leaker may be acting less against intelligence malpractice, as Vansittart claimed, than a system that has denied him access, which was true in this case. Leaks should thus serve as a red flag. Any system that cannot fix its transmission function by shedding bad actors, retraining the misguided, or re-evaluating the distrusted will suffer leaks. If the system simply blames the leaker without recognizing the underlying problem, the leak's damage will be far greater than it might initially appear.

US Capabilities

In many ways, the US intelligence system excels at the transmission function. For example, the US government wisely distributes intelligence analysts across the national security community in organizations such as the State Department's Bureau of Intelligence and Research (INR) and the Department of Defense's Defense Intelligence Agency and the CIA. This distribution ensures that departmental analysts become more than substantive experts; they also become trusted soldiers in bureaucratic wars. They use intelligence to help policymakers frame issues, get evidence their policymakers need, and counsel on the validity and sensitivity of sources and methods. Acting less as academics than as trusted intelligence-providers for decision-makers competing to influence national policymaking, they inevitably become associated with policy preferences. Sometimes these embedded shops appear to be redundant, or their analysts politicized; but such judgments miss their core function: less freestanding scholarship than transmission and less objectivity in the sense of neutrality than in the sense of honesty regarding the facts, including the validity of sources and methods.[37] The best analysts in INR often "get it right" on intelligence because collectors trust them with sources and methods, and decision-makers trust them to know what is important to know.

INR is a good example, however, of the challenges the transmission function holds for any intelligence endeavor. This bureau is responsible on behalf of the secretary of state for coordinating departmental approval of sensitive operations, including covert action programs. This work of INR *should* build two-way trust between intelligence collectors, embassy administrators, and diplomats when done well, but such has not always been the case. Other intelligence agencies have cut INR out of sensitive intelligence flows when it has unsuccessfully opposed risky collection programs on the department's behalf. When excluded, INR has lost access to policymaking and related intelligence requirements, even when the operations subsequently failed. At the same time, INR's mission will fail if it becomes so protective of departmental interests that it refuses to countenance operational risks of any kind, engenders distrust, and so fails to bridge policy and operations.[38] INR's coordination work, crucial to the transmission function, often goes unrecognized and unsupported by policymakers and other intelligence agencies; indeed, it is sometimes seen as an ancillary function even within the bureau itself.[39]

Finally, the United States would seem to need dynamic mapping of decision-making for domestic contingencies, including protocols for rapid handoff of intelligence from private collectors to national agencies. Before 9/11, national intelligence agencies had, at best, inflexible ways to coordinate intelligence flows with state governors, police, city mayors, and private institutions. Some of these restrictions were based on Watergate-era revelations of domestic intelligence operations against suspected Communists. Congress determined that infiltrating student protest groups, civil rights organizations, and radical political parties was antidemocratic and an infringement on civil liberties. But raising the threshold for legitimate domestic surveillance also had consequences. When the IC issued warnings in 2001 about al-Qaeda's threat to the United States, the director of central intelligence alerted national security officials in Washington, but was limited in what he could provide for mayors, governors, airlines, or local police who were in a position to actually stop or limit damage inside the United States. In the aftermath of 9/11, local authorities and national intelligence agencies struggled to develop sharing protocols for joint operations that subsequently had to be rolled back.[40] The 2020 pandemic of COVID-19 also demonstrated the need for ways to channel sensitive private data to government officials during emergencies. If the pandemic had been a biological attack by a foreign power, the inability to collect domestic data from hospitals would have been deemed an intelligence failure of alarming proportions.

Selective Secrecy

An intelligence service should be judged not by the number of secrets it steals or retains, but by *the facility with which the service hides and releases information for competitive purposes.* This ability depends on having optimized capabilities in the other three areas of intelligence performance: collection, anticipation, and transmission.

- Rich collection makes any loss of source or method less critical to the outcome of a contest.
- A capacity to anticipate helps a service identify and protect newly decisive information before the opponent knows to protect, steal, or otherwise acquire it.
- And a strong working relationship among decision-makers and intelligence providers helps a service to weigh risks against the gains of intelligence sharing, release, or secrecy in complex operations.

In fact, if an intelligence service just protects what it knows, it will be unable to influence others or act on opportunities. If an intelligence service simply aims to steal the secrets an adversary protects, then that service will be easily deceived. The adversary can win by keeping useless knowledge hidden or by "leaking" secrets for purposes of deception.

Agile secrecy is difficult, especially for democracies, for several reasons:

- Facility in keeping and releasing secrets requires, in the first instance, a capacity for secrecy, which limits the free exchange of ideas, and biases that exchange in favor of those holding the secrets.

- "Sources and methods" (the way intelligence is acquired) are enduring, while policy changes with every newly elected leader, so the trust necessary for keeping and releasing secrets suffers peaks and troughs that may not match the needs of either policy or intelligence communities.
- Because gaining advantage may be relevant to multiple competitions involving a variety of different government departments (Defense, State Department, Treasury, etc.), intelligence institutions seem best positioned to judge the costs of intelligence sharing across all domains, but have an inherent incentive to keep rather than release them.
- Ethical considerations: even after a competition is over, releasing information on sources may make them vulnerable to retribution.

Managing secrecy is, therefore, a fraught aspect of all national-security-related decision-making. Any attempt by a government to press another state to act—to stop developing bioweapons, for example—may require some sensitive proof. Thus, policymakers will want to use intelligence, and collectors will want to withhold it so they can continue to collect against this target and other adversaries in the future. The tension is, in fact, between intelligence advantage and decision advantage.

Whether and how to protect intelligence at any given moment is a difficult question of intelligence policy that demonstrates why decision-makers must see themselves as fully part of the process. During World War II, Winston Churchill was famously intent on keeping knowledge of sources and methods from decision-makers whose actions might inadvertently reveal them, but whose need to know was indisputable. The capacity at all moments to decide whether to use, classify, or release intelligence is essential to gaining and keeping intelligence advantages over an adversary and correctly timing the use of any decision-advantages that result. Sometimes, information will need to be hidden; sometimes it cannot be; and sometimes it needs to be exposed, divulged, or released at the just the right moment and to the right person(s) for the best effect. An intelligence service that focuses just on hiding what it views as secret is just showing its hand in a different way. And sticky intelligence can undermine policy or raise costs in subtle but destructive ways.

It follows that the best indicator for superior performance is not the number of secrets held or the capacity for retaining or releasing them considered separately, but rather the capacity to create, sort, retain, and release them at appropriate moments for optimum effect and ethical accountability. This capacity, which must be reliable, trustworthy, and routine, is enhanced in at least one way by the professional intelligence institutions of the modern administrative state. Political leaders may come and go, but intelligence institutions remember the sources owed for their service over time. Observing this indebtedness is not just ethical but serviceable for gaining intelligence advantages in the future. Consider, for example, how the US CIA assembled an offensive against al-Qaeda in Afghanistan so rapidly after 9/11; its operatives did so by re-engaging past sources and contacts that they had carefully maintained for years. But note the downside: by re-engaging their sources, these operatives put them at risk. They nonetheless did so. A death grip on sources and methods would have created advantages for the enemy by slowing decision-making, increasing costs, losing opportunities, and creating confusion on the ground. In the context of war, protecting intelligence advantages would have valued inputs (sources) more than outcomes (wins). Short of war, the balances had been struck differently because *anticipating* al-Qaeda's moves in Afghanistan did not seem worth the price. Decision-advantage in peace is, from an entirely rational intelligence standpoint, less worth the price than decision-advantage in war. Intelligence institutions will therefore tend to favor protecting secrets in case wars come, even as diplomats are seeking to prevent them through advantageous release and intelligence-sharing. This tendency makes intelligence power as potentially provocative as military power is when unchecked by civilian control. If not careful, intelligence institutions can, through ill-informed, inept, or constipated classification systems, bring an otherwise competitive state to its knees.

Intelligence officers and decision-makers gain advantages when they can jointly work to achieve selective secrecy. Decision-makers need to understand that they will, at times, need to forfeit decision advantage in the present to retain intelligence advantages for the future—a future in which decisions may be more consequential than they are today. Collectors need to understand that divulging secrets, such as President Kennedy did by showing allies classified satellite images during the Cuban Missile Crisis, can serve a greater good. If one side or the other fails in such understanding, the intelligence system can become so clogged with secrets that plans fail, as happened to the too tight-lipped Hooker at Chancellorsville and to the Austrian diplomats denied Conrad's military secrets in 1914. In both cases, excessive secrecy handicapped decision-making, leading to lost decision-advantage. The tactical wins, such as they were, proved to be precursors to strategic defeat.

The relationship of intelligence advantage to decision advantage lies at the heart of all intelligence operations, whether the purpose is risky collection, deception, or simply influencing another government to do the right thing based on sensitive sources. "Plausible deniability" is, in this sense, an artifice for limiting political blowback after the fact; it should not be a prescription for keeping policymakers out of policymaking. Intelligence operations of all kinds, including deception, require policymakers to weigh risks, including what truths to divulge to convince an enemy to trust a double agent or a false story. Policymakers need to take responsibility for the intelligence wins and losses that may result—if not publicly, then internally with respect to the intelligence system they adopt. This kind of responsibility would not be surprising or difficult to accept for a modern military general, but it would be for civilian leaders engaged in the less morally clear-cut business of diplomacy.

Optimizing intelligence against a target, collectors have to trust policymakers not to waste assets needed for future competitions, while the latter have to trust collectors to weed out deception, and not to hide or otherwise protect sources and methods at the expense of today's objective. Given that peacetime intelligence serves many diplomatic ends on any given day, no bureaucratic hierarchy will be able to broker the question of timely release, so decision-makers must be trained sufficiently in intelligence practice to help make these calls.

An intelligence system overburdened with expired secrets can become unwieldy, confusing, constipated, and expensive. Good classification policies are for secrets as laundering is for clothes: it refreshes them, helps sort the worn from the useful, matches pairs, sends the appropriate assets to the right drawers for use by the right people, and helps eliminate the no longer useful to make the whole process more efficient. Besides a smoothly functioning dissemination system, good indicators of a superior capacity for selective secrecy include the following:

- gains from well-timed surprise;
- agility in alliance building and secret diplomacy;
- successful double-agent programs;
- the absence of unauthorized leaks;
- civil service and military training on the decision-intelligence nexus;
- strong lessons-learned studies, including historical scholarship, based on carefully declassified documentary records;
- a well-regulated classification system; and
- rapid entry into and departure from the intelligence system for both intelligence officials and decision-makers.

Good indicators of weakness in this area are the following:

- unauthorized leaks;
- slow decision-making on national-security-related issues;
- lack of protocols for (current or contingent) of sharing national intelligence with senior civilian authorities at all levels of government and in the private sector;
- slow recruitment and discharge of intelligence-related personnel;
- repeated losses from diplomatic or military surprise;
- repeated counterintelligence failures; and
- sudden losses of collection assets.

In this volume's case studies, the Austro-Hungarian government stands out for bringing about the worst intelligence failure in this area. Beyond poor internal sharing between diplomats and military, the Austrians developed an ill-considered plan for a diplomatic blackout as it prepared its ultimatum, purposefully robbing itself of agility in managing secrecy in service to policy. The Austrians intended the blackout to create surprise, but overlooked the difficulties of simultaneously influencing other great powers to see the rationale for their position and their limited objectives in Serbia. Vienna failed, disastrously, at selective secrecy. The Austrian case serves as a good example of how intelligence policy can tie a state in knots that are both hard to see and consequential in their effects.

Selective Secrecy in the United States

The importance of the decision-collection nexus is currently underappreciated in the United States. There is less training among intelligence and policy professionals about the requirements for releasing intelligence than there is for keeping it. Both will vary depending on circumstances of battle or diplomatic campaign.

For example, I know of few if any intelligence-policy "campaign games" in the United States during which decision-makers are faced with the kinds of trades that were made during WWII, when the British Double Cross system maintained double agents for years. The agents' purpose then was deception, so they fed truly sensitive intelligence to Hitler on the bet that at some point their established credibility would allow them to deliver useful lies. In the meantime, the loss of good intelligence represented *purposeful* intelligence disadvantages to which both intelligence and military leaders had to agree. They and their political leaders had to understand and accept such "give-aways" in order to create an advantage for later. When the time came, they used the double agents to steer Hitler toward believing that the primary Allied landing in 1945 might be at Calais instead of Normandy. By triggering the delivery of a lie, intelligence chiefs had to accept that the double agents would likely be exposed, putting them at grave risk for their lives and forfeiting any hope of using them again.[41] This kind of intimate and interconnected understanding of the tools of diplomacy, war, and intelligence, and the trust engendered by repeated experience in making such calls, is currently lacking, especially on the civilian side. Instead, grievances are nurtured over recalled losses and gains of any particular moment. A highly regarded US station chief once divulged to this author that, in his experience, the State Department was more of an adversary than the professionals he operated against in foreign intelligence services. He called the former conflict "the real war."

Judgment calls regarding losses and gains, timing, and secrecy or release are integral to strategy and should engage policymakers, not just intelligence professionals. Although the modern US national security establishment suffers from these problems, specialists in the classification problem tend to see its dilemma as more the proliferation of secrets than the lost agility required for gaining information advantages. This attitude stems from President Harry Truman's decision to standardize what seemed to be the highly uneven handling of sensitive information across the national security community after WWII. He put in place a more sweeping, modern classification system in 1951. This decision improved the security of sensitive source's methods, but at the expense of requiring decision-makers to manage secrecy at all. Decision-makers finding safety in overclassification have abdicated their responsibilities for weighing in on the issue, even when obviously hobbling themselves in the process.

Democracies with relatively poor capacities for selective secrecy can nonetheless beat dictatorships if they are relatively good at securing the trust and loyalty of their populations and at innovating thanks to open and competitive markets. Dictatorships, less trusted by their populations, can beat democracies, nonetheless, if they undermine intelligence institutions by manipulating the public's distrust of secrecy, undermining the oversight of secret programs, or arranging leaks of legal programs for deceptive purposes.

It should be recalled, however, that, over time, advantage has tended to fall to the side with superior positive intelligence rather than counterintelligence capabilities. This is because superior denial and deception generally requires superior capacities to collect, transmit, and anticipate—the equivalent of drawing to an inside straight in poker. Thus, the historical arc of intelligence will tend to increase international transparency over time.

* * *

All these points reinforce the importance of mapping uncertainties and measuring relative intelligence power. A preliminary attempt at doing this for the twenty-first century follows in the next chapter. This exercise is not a mapping of threats. *It is a mapping of uncertainties.* These will be of a general nature and specific to known or brewing conflicts with other states or transnational powers. In certain circumstances, the ignorance of other states will be dangerous, so improving their intelligence capabilities will be crucial to decreasing the risks of war. International institutions can help with this process if they are treated more as liaison services instrumental to transparency, but also subject to manipulation by all state parties, than as allies or neutral actors.

14

The Twenty-First-Century Terrain
of Uncertainty

The future of politics or warfare is always a guess, but a safe one for the twenty-first century is that the competitive use of information will play a starring role in conflicts of all kinds: political, economic, and military. In particular, the cyber-threat posed by online conspiracy theories, radicalization, and networked action has left a marked trail since the turn of the century.

That trail is by now well known. In 2000, terrorists used online and open-source information to learn how to fly US airliners, which they then crashed into skyscrapers and the Pentagon. In 2010, news of the self-immolation of Mohamed Bouazizi in Tunisia spread rapidly through digital media, sparking protests throughout the Arab world and leading eventually to the downfall of Egypt's Hosni Mubarak. In response, conservative Middle Eastern regimes traced protestors through social media and cell phones, incarcerating or killing many of them.[1] In 2016 the Russian government demonstrated how a militarily and economically weaker state could attack a stronger one using private-sector allies and weaponized social media. From 2016 to 2021, an American president armed with conspiracy theories, the Internet, and extremist media profited from the fracturing and dissolution of American political culture, weakening the state from within. It was not just that Americans disagreed; it was that they disagreed about what was true, such as whether the slaughter of American children at Sandyhook Elementary School *ever really happened*. On January 6, 2021, a stampede of American citizens, radicalized over the Internet and by Internet-driven news cycles, stormed the US Capitol, forcing its evacuation and demanding nullification of a presidential election—a legally settled win they believed *had not happened*.

Cyberattacks, as opposed to cyber-espionage and defense, come in two principal forms: direct offensives and indirect subterfuge, such as the manipulation of public opinion. Although the United States experienced both in 2020, the former was, at least until January 2021, treated as the more obvious national security threat. In late 2020, General Paul M. Nakasone, the man responsible for the cybersecurity of the United States, reported that intelligence agencies had missed SolarWinds, a Russian cyber-penetration affecting over 250 federal agencies and major corporations. US intelligence agencies did not detect the

Decision Advantage. Jennifer E. Sims, Oxford University Press. © Oxford University Press 2022.
DOI: 10.1093/oso/9780197508046.003.0014

attack; instead, one of the victims did—a small private security company named FireEye. The supply chain attack was embedded in a software update to security software that permitted wide-ranging penetration of the host computers. As 2020 came to an end, intelligence agencies had identified Russia as the culprit, but no one knew whether Moscow's purpose was espionage, sabotage, or both. And no one knew how deeply critical national infrastructure had been damaged.

In a more slowly unfolding, indirect cyberattack, QAnon, an anonymous, conspiratorial network online, recorded impressive gains in its undermining of American democracy. An NPR-Ipsos polling report in early 2021 showed that 17 percent of Americans believed QAnon's foundational lie that "a group of Satan-worshipping elites who run a child sex ring are trying to control our politics and media," with another 37 percent apparently unable or unwilling to refute the lie.[2] This enemy is new—a metastasizing online "intelligence" network hawking crowd-sourced myths and falsehoods even within Congress.[3] QAnon's intelligence engine creates new conspiracies like a participatory novel generates alternative endings, roping people into its falsehoods and, at the same time, empowering them through the stories they help create. The narratives are propagated online where "researchers" add their rumors, amplifying personal grievance and collective outrage. It is the personal investment in such stories that engenders a cultist's loyalties and passions and leads to radicalization. Certain news services and politicians, including the American president, have been hungry to harness such loyalties for their own ends.

Not so long ago, few would have predicted the transformative effect information technology would have on national security. In his book *Dark Territory*, Fred Kaplan notes that the 1983 movie *War Games*, in which a kid hacks into the Pentagon and nearly starts WWIII, so shocked President Ronald Reagan that he ordered a much-needed upgrade to the Pentagon's computer network.[4] Although *War Games* might seem quaint in retrospect, the movie made it possible for the US president to see the digital "battlefield" as a terrain all its own—one in which a superpower could be dragged into war by a teenager. *War Games* made the dangers of network vulnerability both vivid and actionable in Reagan's time. Since then, however, the digital terrain has changed quickly, making matters more complicated. By 2016, experts were claiming that the Internet had become the world's nervous system.[5] Information, traveling the world at light speed, was creating an ocean of data to be used, stored, and supplemented by ever-more-connected appliances, such as refrigerators, heart monitors, and self-driving cars. Utilities, such as water reservoirs and electrical grids, were connecting to this nervous system and relying on it for their operations. Manufacturers were embedding computers in our watches, phones, "digital assistants," tollbooths, child monitors, and security cameras, offering to connect them all to the Internet for our convenience. For better or worse, teenagers can hack these things too, or affect world events from their laptops. If *War Games* had its fictional teen star, the COVID-19 era had a real one: Avi Schiffmann, a seventeen-year-old boy who, in 2019, used a web scraper to track the virus and predict a pandemic months before most governments did.[6]

So, on the edge of the twenty-first century, the United States seemingly stands as the most militarily and economically powerful state in the history of the world, but also the most deeply vulnerable to intelligence penetrations and misinformation. By nurturing digital innovation and promoting the Internet during the twentieth century, the United States seeded international politics with the tools of its own disruption. Ironic as this turn of events may seem, it should not be surprising; it is exactly what the theory of adaptive realism would have predicted. The challenge now is to map what forces will shape outcomes in this turbulent new era. Who will likely be the winners and losers, and how can we affect the odds in favor of those who champion democracy and cooperative international security?

Mapping the Twenty-First-Century Terrain of Uncertainty

Exploring the future of conflict and cooperation in the twenty-first century raises a serious methodological problem: how to identify the uncertainties that will likely matter most for *future* conflicts. When we thus move from well-documented history to future challenges, we need to proceed somewhat differently than we have done in the prior case studies. After all, the further ahead we look, the less we can know about the conflicts that might arise and, therefore, the uncertainties that will matter most. The possibility of a viral pandemic had long been anticipated, but its appearance in 2020 still came as a major surprise full of uncertainties about how states should cooperate (or not) to stop it.[7] Creeping systemic change involving the Internet has been the stuff of much speculation and study; it has nonetheless surprised us with spikes in viral worldwide conspiracy theories, jeopardizing the civil societies on which modern democracies are predicated.[8] Perhaps most dramatically, pure science has surprised us with quantum physics, which is radically overturning our understanding of time, space, and consciousness itself. Although the "four-valued logic" that emerges from the quantum world (true; false; both true and false; neither true nor false) is beyond the scope of this book, its implications are likely to alter systems for "knowing" in the twenty-first century, fundamentally altering interstate relations forever.[9]

As just one example, consider recent news from the Pentagon: On May 4, 2020, officials released three navy videos of what it termed "unidentified aerial phenomena," or UAPs, that appear to perform maneuvers that are impossible, according to the classical laws of physics. F-18 pilots flying off the aircraft carrier *Nimitz* have witnessed forty-foot-long objects descend instantaneously from eighty thousand feet to twenty thousand feet, then hover fifty feet above the ocean, before flying off at incredible speeds—all without wings or exhaust. Navy press releases have also confirmed earlier revelations published in December 2017 and during the summer of 2019 on the same topic.[10] In fact, the Department of Defense acknowledged that the *Nimitz* encounter lasted almost ten days and was not a one-time event. Since 2004, multiple pilots have encountered, near or inside restricted military airspace, high-velocity objects flying in ways no modern US fighter aircraft could replicate, and that the Pentagon could not explain. Although Congress has received classified briefings on the topic and legislated a mandatory report from the intelligence community on the subject, few news organizations have kept the issue alive for the general public. The hesitancy of editorial boards perhaps reflects the fact that unidentified flying objects (UFOs) are associated with extraterrestrials whose visits here are widely deemed to be impossible, regardless of evidence from F-18 pilots.[11]

This idea that what we have dismissed as impossible cannot be investigated is a modern manifestation of the certainty paradox that is as dangerous today as it has been throughout history. The quantum revolution's conception of time and distance would seem to make the objects' presence possible even if extraterrestrial in origin. Furthermore, the quantum-theoretical notions of "observer participancy" and "spooky action at a distance" suggest observing or measuring objects may shape them in ways that make our own ignorance dangerous, creating conflict where it might not need to be.[12] Here is the kind of strategic uncertainty that intelligence—or engineered transparency—is meant to reduce, lowering the risks of unnecessary conflict. Yet for years we seemed determined to participate in our own strategic surprise by shunning the terrain that science now seems to be unveiling before our eyes.[13] The US Navy, admitting that it does not know what these UAPs are, has at last forced the US government to publically acknowledge it needs to find out. This job was the intelligence community's; it left it to navy pilots to do.

The point is that what distinguishes imaginary monsters from true strategic surprise is the collection of facts that decision-makers can trust, despite their inclination not to. And what separates black swans from other forms of surprise is the socio-psychological mindset that makes decision-makers *certain* that the seemingly outlandish cannot be true and intelligence service's to ride in their wake.

It therefore makes sense to map the uncertainties attending *implausible* conflicts as well as likely ones, rank-ordering them according to the challenges they pose for decision-advantage, the pursuit of which carries its own uncertainties that are almost certainly being mapped by the other side. In chaotic times when conflicts cannot be reliably foretold, intelligence does best by reinforcing readiness, including learning what uncertainties put that readiness in jeopardy.

With these thoughts in mind, this chapter will not try to summarize the literature on all known or potential areas of international conflict, such as Chinese or US power projection, or the consequences for various geographic regions such as the Middle East and the South China Sea. Such an endeavor, while useful, has been done elsewhere. Instead, the discussion will consider uncertainties of two types: those related to traditional forms of power and those related to intelligence power (both institutionalized and not) that jeopardize its readiness for conflicts of all types. Even in these two areas, the discussion cannot be comprehensive. The full range of topics would be a book in itself. Left out, for example, are important uncertainties about the course of the new space race, the aforementioned discovery of quantum physics, and the future scarcity of critical resources, such as water and strategic minerals. Using selected examples, however, we can show how the distribution of ignorance creates opening military advantages and introduces gaps in intelligence readiness that opponents may be mapping at our expense. This type of terrain mapping goes beyond alternative scenario analysis to explore what we don't know and what we feel sure we do know, but may not.

It may seem odd to ask ourselves what we don't know, not just what we do know. But the point of this book is to suggest that that is exactly where intelligence must begin. We need to think about who will have natural decision-advantages across all potential competitive spaces and, if it is us, ask intelligence to build on it or, if it is not us, try to outsmart those who should know better but do not.

This chapter concludes with a return to the crucial issue of ethics in intelligence—a subject that triggers mindsets and so tends to confuse. The fact that intelligence can deliver victory in war does not preclude it from serving diplomacy, disarmament, or cooperation whenever better learning offers wins for all sides. It can be an instrument of peace, as well as of war, oppression, and subterfuge. Still, the special problems posed by ethics in intelligence deserve a closer look if only to remind us that truth-seeking is instrumental, not core, to the mission of intelligence. Sound intelligence is factually true as far as it goes, but it is also often incomplete and full of residual uncertainties. The ultimate purpose of intelligence is to gain decision-advantage—and win—*despite* uncertainty and the absence of ultimate truths. It follows that if good intelligence institutions fall into the wrong hands, there is no guarantee that democracy can be saved. Brokering winners among contending political aspirants is not the mission of intelligence, nor should it be; but that makes the future of US democracy among the most consequential uncertainties of the twenty-first century.

Military, Economic, Territorial, and
Demographic Uncertainties

Indeed, rarely have the stakes in international politics been higher or the possibilities of its restructuring so extreme as now, at the start of the twenty-first century. Considering just traditional military and economic power, the United States, Russia, and China far surpass all other states, with Russia on the eclipse and Europe, perhaps, on the rise. The primary causes of *traditional* power shifts seem to be wealth redistribution and demographics. Globalization and climate change are reshaping economies, moving people into jobs and spaces formerly occupied by others. As state borders experience the pressures of migration and rising seas, weakened states will tend to lose land, and stronger or more desperate ones will tend to seize it (as Russia has done with the Crimea and threatens to do with Ukraine, and China is doing with the South China Sea). Technology, at the same time, is generating new wealth while obliterating the old—a process that is reordering traditional power structures within states, changing their politics. Great powers are losing their traditional engines, such as manufacturing, while seeking more solid footing in the digital economy, reinforcing transnational dependencies. This process is generating political shocks as the old economy's labor force loses standing while the new one finds itself in short supply. The former becomes riotous while the latter becomes rich, like today's young computer whizzes earning six-figure salaries, sometimes straight out of high school.

It is not surprising, then, that states seem buffeted by forces beyond their control. This structural disruption is happening in almost every advanced industrial society, as well as many less developed ones, causing widespread social dislocation, a rise in populism, and an atavistic retrenchment. History tells us that when economic dislocation happens in one sector, say steel or fossil fuel production, a particular region or segment of the population will suffer. What the twenty-first century's information revolution presents, however, is akin to the industrial revolution of the late nineteenth century: change that is spreading *across sectors* from healthcare to energy, manufacturing, services, communications, and war. No sector is unaffected as citizens adjust to new ways of banking, shopping, healing, accounting, researching, building, manufacturing, communications, and even getting from one point to another. Buffeted by change, displaced or confused workers look for leaders who can ease their pain, simplify matters, and make things "right"—often by finding some other group or state to blame. Angry and displaced laborers tend to look for security through authoritarian leadership, anarchy, or vigilantism.

The political effects of economic dislocation go beyond the appeal for retrenchment and authoritarian or sectarian politics, however. History suggests that, in such unstable times, great powers become prone to radical action: arms races, territorial aggression to secure resources, trade restrictions, and blame-shifting. Britain has stumbled toward a renegotiated position in Europe, delivering a body blow to political order on the continent; the United States has sown confusion by reprimanding allies, softening opposition to long-standing adversaries under President Trump, and then reversing under President Biden, who nonetheless executed a precipitous military withdrawal from Afghanistan. Russia has made a land-grab in Crimea and Ukraine. Turkey, lurching toward dictatorship, is joining Hungary's march toward authoritarianism. China, already authoritarian, is increasingly expansionist, but seems to be investing more in itself than in a particular international order. The United States, once open and free-trading, has turned nativist, transactional, and border-conscious. In sum, no great power is on a predictable trajectory, which has spread uncertainty throughout the international system.

Modern great powers are not that different from past ones insofar as they are bound to each other through trade and finance, but at odds over their respective spheres of influence. What seems new is the volatility of legitimacy and trust in state institutions. Where authoritarians rule, uncertainty seems less. Before the pandemic, the course of China's power, for example, seemed steadier than most. With the current blame-shifting over the source of the virus, China's international standing may be at risk, but its authoritarian tendencies are only strengthening. Europe, on the other hand, is fragmenting and the United States stands apart as a Gulliver unbound—a seemingly confused giant whose episodic interventionism appears either unreliable (to allies) or purposefully provocative (to all others). American engagements and retreats in Afghanistan, Iraq, and Syria have been fitful; its commitments to climate management and arms control have been irresolute. The result has been a level of global uncertainty not unlike that generated by the British at the end of the nineteenth century.

Whither the United States?

Given the enormous size of the US economy, its deficits, and its weapons arsenals, the scope and intensity of twenty-first-century conflicts will likely turn on the decisions the United States makes about its interests and how best to defend them. Those decisions should be informed, in turn, by what the United States knows relatively well, shaping political outcomes from a position of natural advantage. Instead, uncertainty has taken a foothold. Take as just one example, nuclear power—a sector in which the United States used to be dominant. Not long ago, most analysts believed the United States and other nuclear weapons states would just sustain their nuclear stockpiles, observe agreed limits on them, and gradually disinvest from nuclear power—all trends that tracked with public attitudes.[14] Now, however, the US public seems to be discarding the idea of a nuclear weapons taboo and accepting the idea that the United States, China, and Russia will competitively add to their nuclear arsenals, disinvest from their arms control agreements, and go separate ways on nuclear power.[15]

Such new trends are introducing uncertainties in all aspects of great power competition. Unlike Russia and China, the United States is not building new nuclear reactors, and projections for the industry are dismal. Formerly profitable companies such as Westinghouse have gone out of business due to lengthy licensing processes and public resistence. After the earthquake and tsunami of 2011, and the resulting catastrophe at Japan's Fukushima nuclear power plant, the public's hostility toward nuclear power rose, not just in the United States and Japan, but seemingly worldwide. At the same time, however, projections of future energy production continued to include nuclear power because of its relatively inexpensive and "clean" contribution to base power loads. In fact, most experts remain uncertain how to achieve a clean energy future *without* nuclear power. Perhaps for these reasons, recent polling data in the United States suggest the public now has highly variable views about nuclear energy, depending on the availability of alternative fuels and fears of climate change—a result that seems likely to apply to public attitudes elsewhere.[16]

The Janus-faced aspect of US nuclear attitudes, together with rapid technological change, is contributing to a global climate of uncertainty about the proliferation of nuclear weapons states. Nuclear energy continues to serve as a logical route to economic development and global power for any state, including those wishing to experiment with illicit weapons acquisition *or* wishing to cut carbon emissions. Will currently non-nuclear weapons states turn to nuclear energy to protect the planet while reserving the option of "going nuclear" to deter competitors? New technologies are on the horizon for enriching uranium cheaply to weapons-grade and for cheap 3-D printing of precision-engineered materials for explosive devices. Their realization would make it even more difficult to find and trace nuclear weapons capabilities, given the small quantities necessary (think softball) for a bomb. Precision engineering and 3-D printing also contribute to improving cheap, safe, safeguarded nuclear power. Whether the nuclear nonproliferation regime gives non-nuclear weapons states good cover for such illicit ends, or forces an end to it in exchange for the distribution of safe power, remains a source of global uncertainty.

The United States, *because of what it knows and knows how to do,* could operate on this terrain better than most, bringing home self-serving, yet stabilizing wins. Yet, so far, the United States has ceded that ground to Russia, which is exporting International Atomic Energy Agency–compliant modern nuclear energy plants while locking in political advantages. Rosatom, the state-owned nuclear agency, operates thirty-five nuclear plants at home and has up to thirty-three projects in the works—mostly in emerging markets increasingly bound to Moscow through contracts with sixty-year-long maintenance and fuel-supply provisions.[17]

The nuclear domain is just one area in which US policies (or the lack of them) are introducing uncertainties in other states' strategic calculations, including the integrity of transnational arms control regimes that the United States once championed as a linchpin of international order.

Whither the Arctic?

With clean energy struggling to gain a foothold in the global energy future, the melting Arctic is emerging as another source of uncertainty for most observers of modern international politics. As Scott Borgerson noted in a 2013 piece in *Foreign Affairs*, "Although climate scientists have known for some time that global warming was shrinking the percentage of the Arctic Ocean that was frozen over, few predicted so fast a thaw. . . . It is turning what has traditionally been an impassable body of water ringed by remote wilderness into something dramatically different: an emerging epicenter of industry and trade akin to the Mediterranean Sea."[18]

That point deserves respectful attention. It has been a long time since whole new territorial zones have opened up for international exploitation. The last great land rushes involved the competitive colonization of the American continent and its offshore islands, Africa, the Near East, Asia and the Pacific Islands by empires intoxicated by the idea of vulnerable, resource-rich lands and their own hubris. The Arctic is offering up that and something new: a northwest passage for global trade and a treasure trove of minerals and energy resources *on the territories of wealthy states*, including the United States, Canada, Denmark (representing Greenland and the Faroe Islands), Russia, Sweden, and Finland.[19]

So far, territorial disputes have been cooperatively addressed, but some outstanding issues and uncertainties remain. Former US president Donald Trump launched the idea that Arctic access might be a real estate transaction, prompting others to recoil or poke fun. Both reactions, while understandable, reflected false certainties regarding international management of this new international gold rush. Here, the United States has some natural intelligence-related advantages, as do Russia and Canada. Collaboration may not easily be sustained as additional resources are discovered, including on contested seafloors, and shipping times from Europe to China, shortened by two weeks or more, deflect trade from traditional ports. Even if peaceful joint management is sustained, the returns will tend to benefit already powerful states, rendering them even more dominant in an international system trending toward resurgent nationalism, restrictions on trade, and less wealth creation among poorer trading partners.

Whither Populations?

The increasing disparity in wealth among states, combined with climate change and the spread of access to information over the Internet, has already affected global demographics. The combination of advances in bioengineering and global transportation, the distribution of water, and changes in human habitat, especially in coastal zones, are increasing uncertainties related to the spread of infectious diseases, agricultural production, and mass migration.

The COVID-19 pandemic highlighted the difficulties states confront in identifying such threats and ascribing causes for them. Most states know their borders, but far less about what generates challenges to them or how to discern threats from opportunities as they cope with waves of contraband, disease, immigrants, and asylum-seekers—an uncertainty that aggressors, such as Belarus, have already exploited by weaponizing migrant waves to threaten neighbors. Those states ill-equipped with modern means for securing their borders or fighting outbreaks of disease will need to know more sooner, whether the victims are crops or human populations. The neediest states will lack the resources necessary to address outbreaks, which could easily trigger international crises. Wealthy states, in contrast, will be better able to protect themselves from either intentional use of bioweapons or the surprise emergence of a pandemic, both because their health systems can respond more swiftly and thoroughly, and because their borders tend to be better monitored and protected. But the COVID-19 outbreak of 2020 demonstrated that even such advanced states will be disempowered in their response by a lack of intelligence on the provenance and past history of the contagion.

Of course, rapidly changing technology plays a role in all this political uncertainty, much as it has done for centuries, albeit now with broader impact. Whatever the locus of future great power conflict, it seems likely that cyberspace will be involved, whether in diplomacy, predation, or as a theater of war. This means that one technological development is deserving of particular attention: the evolution of transnational, information-processing empires. The rise of such firms is not new, but the extent of their transnational power and influence is. They are the great twenty-first-century disruptors—contenders for public allegiances as powerful as transnational religions have been in the past. Over the course of centuries covered in this volume, public loyalties have shifted from church, to monarch, to representative governments. Now many people, losing trust in these institutions, are choosing to trust digital platforms and the influencers they find there. The winners of twenty-first-century international politics will likely be states or other transnational actors that learn how to grapple with this new type of power and harness it to their interests.

Uncertainty in Cyberspace: New Players, New Platforms, and a New Domain for Competition

The economic and technological revolution of the twenty-first century has involved information processing, so it directly affects intelligence and, at the same time, touches almost everyone's life. The triggering technologies have included most elements of our new digital world: silicon chips, computers, fiber-optic communications, servers, routers, blockchains, and the like. We now collect and process information through cyberspace—essentially the digital domain created by interconnected computers—that is still growing exponentially and remains largely ungoverned and unmapped.

What does this new digital territory mean for understanding and influencing the distribution of power? It seems likely that the states most able to map and augment it by, for example, translating new technologies into smart weapons and adapting command structures to cyberspace will have cutting-edge militaries. The United States, already in the lead in conventional and nuclear weaponry, has surged to the front in the relatively hidden application of information technologies to command structures, weapons, and warfare. But before we leap to the assumption that the United States is set to solidify its place as an unbeatable twenty-first-century superpower, we must remember the oddity of intelligence as a form of power: done poorly, it subtracts from power; done well, it can defeat far superior conventional forces. Expensive weapons, if smart, can potentially be hacked. Cyberattacks can breech civil-miliary divides, skirting traditional forms of warfare to achieve victories in other ways. And the more a state relies on the Internet for civilian and military infrastructure, the more connected but also vulnerable it may be. The Clinton administration recognized this vulnerability in the 1990s, launching a protection plan for critical infrastructure. Since then, we have seen how US adversaries have sought to gain advantages anyway.

Whether one believes the Russians affected the outcome of the US 2016 elections or not, it is indisputable that malign influence-peddling had a heyday. As one senior US official has written: "In 2016, a foreign adversary launched a wide-ranging attack on our nation's robust political debate, advancing its agenda with weapons of discord and division. This sort of aggression must be repelled just as surely as if it were an invading army. The path is clear: . . . shore up our cyber-security defenses."[20] The United States tried, but lost again in 2020 with the aforementioned SolarWinds attack, perpetrated by Russia, that compromised even the National Security Agency, the seat of command for US cyber-defenses.[21]

We can almost certainly expect the international system to be in for more massive jolts. The rapid spread of intelligence capacities is reshuffling the distribution of power in ways still poorly understood. Today, anyone with a computer and an Internet connection has roaming rights for the gathering of intelligence from connected devices and storage areas on the Internet. And while wealthy actors, including states, still have certain privileges, such as the capacity to rent private rockets or satellites, to purchase imagery, or to geolocate targets from space, once obtained and archived on servers, the products will be accessible to (or corruptible by) anyone able to access those archives online.

Given that cyberspace is the constantly changing brainchild of its users, it cannot be definitively described or its "high ground" definitively possessed. What can be notionally described is the worldwide web that floats on this cyber-sea. The "surface web," made up of sites any searcher can easily find through engines, such as Google Search or links such as those on Wikipedia, makes up only 4 percent of the entire web. Here, every person who searches can be known and their location ascertained. The rest—an estimated 96 percent of the web—is "deep," meaning it is not indexable by web crawlers. Roughly 90 percent of this deep web is made up of private or privileged records, such as health information, legal documents, and the like. Users either need special permissions to search here, or they must hack into these sites to steal. In either case, they usually leave "fingerprints" in the process. Finally, perhaps 6 percent of the deep web is also "dark." This zone is the digital version of a failed state, which is essentially ungoverned space.[22] There are few standards or rules, making it a platform for all kinds of illicit activity, such as drug-trafficking, hacker forums, illegal pornography, terrorist communications, and deception campaigns. To gain access to the dark web, one must be anonymous and use special encryption software, such as Tor. Here, credit card bandits and hitmen market their services. Fingerprints on transactions are absent, thanks in part to new blockchain technologies that verify but anonymize them. From 2011 to 2013, a site called Silk Road operated as a sort of dark Amazon, selling everything from drugs to fake passports. In its few years, Silk Road moved over $1 billion in contraband, and it wasn't even the worst of its kind.[23]

The web is only one aspect of cyberspace, which infuses the international system in many ways, undermining and bolstering states. Indeed, with every passing year this cyber-terrain is quietly becoming more complex, integrated, and embedded in our daily lives, increasing the advantages flowing to its engineers and software developers. Interactive online devices, known collectively as the Internet of Things (IoT), increased 31 percent from 2016 to 2017, when they totaled about 8.4 billion items. These are the devices (including sensors embedded in ovens, cars, security systems, and the like) that collect, send, and receive data online. By the end of 2020, the IoT will likely include *thirty billion objects or more*, each a potential collection platform that can be controlled from afar by other connected devices—all without the necessity of human intervention. Mapping this digital terrain requires tracking all the "things" hooked to it, and the ever-changing pathways by which they connect and interact. Industry is constantly designing new attachments, each of which is a potential gateway to all others.

System engineers and computer jockeys are the modern pilots or piratical hackers on this cyber-sea of devices, websites, servers, and routers. If they want, they will be able to name their price to competitors seeking a political or military edge. To do so, however, they will need to live in cyberspace continuously, mapping it, navigating it, hacking it, and networking with others. Although conventional wisdom holds that this trend is a decentralizing one, it is uncertain whether this will be the case: perhaps the most power will flow to those who mine the web on behalf of rich organizations, such as governments and big corporations. Outside of China, at least for the time being, those responsible for the vertical and horizontal management of the IoT will be businesspeople, and they are already extraordinarily powerful, atop vertically integrated platforms that are increasingly interconnected.[24] In 2016, Amazon was Google's biggest customer.[25]

Although this argument cannot be pursued or resolved here, it is sufficient to note that there is no guarantee that these newly empowered cyber-navigators will abide by any rules or laws, which are in any case evolving rapidly.[26] Equipped with platforms ranging from watches, cell phones, and computer-equipped drones to popular applications and social media sites, modern computer-pirates can become privateers in an instant and switch loyalties just as fast.

So which states are naturally best positioned to achieve decision-advantage in this domain? First, it seems clear that wealthy, technologically advanced countries, such as the United States, will not *necessarily* have an advantage. Although early to connect its critical infrastructure to the Internet, the United States was also early in making its critical infrastructure (including communications, software, and hardware) both discoverable and vulnerable to the long reach of cyberwarriors. Although Washington woke to the counterintelligence implications of such connectivity in the 1990s and to the potential for asymmetric warfare after 2001, US law enforcement was still shocked by the use of it for political deception in 2016. Although some intelligence managers over these years saw the problem and treated it as an emergency, they had trouble moving government bureaucracies to address the implications.[27]

Still, it seems likely that the wealthiest organizations, whether states or multinational corporations, will have important advantages. New technologies, to advance rapidly, require both heavy investment and market pull. Although some advanced industrial states that once led in government-sponsored research and development are no longer doing so, other governments are taking their place. And wealth enables competitors to recruit and retain the best and brightest of the info-privateers whose loyalty is up for grabs.

Wealthy states are more able than others to lure the innovators of the next new "thing" with the unique incentives of citizenship, safe haven, and research dollars, gaining advantages from technological breakthroughs by paying for them in advance. Nonstate investors willing to take a leap of faith have to be rich enough to outbid what governments can offer. And as ever, innovators will be attracted to the highest bidder, sometimes regardless of the eventual applications their investors may envision. Backed by sufficient resources, natural curiosity fuels experimentation, regardless of the dangers—a truth that made the movie *Jurassic Park* plausible enough to be entertaining. Perhaps nowhere is that tendency in greater play than in the domain of artificial intelligence.

Artificial Intelligence: Command and Control or *Jurassic Park* Revisited?

Innovations (think CRISPR gene editing, autonomous robots, and 3-D printing) keep tumbling into the public domain despite their potential dangers. It would seem, then, that the future may feel like the fantastical world of *Jurassic Park* or the *Sorceror's Apprentice*, in which we seem perpetually terrified by overabundance and uncertain whether or even how to contain it.

Artificial intelligence triggers just such existential concerns. If the human purpose is not just to win, but to do so in service to greater interests, then the quest for competitive knowing should be tempered by varying commitments to other forms of knowing: pure science, as well as spiritual and creative endeavors, such as art, poetry, and faith. These pursuits are important in their own right because they fuel imagination, philosophy, and what some philosophers have called *useless knowledge*—the kind that machines cannot acquire.[28] This sort of knowledge helps us collaborate and pursue happiness as socially active humans: the life, cultural communities, and milieus that make life enjoyable. Part of the fight for state interests involves defining such things, which we want to preserve both nationally and transnationally. Knowing them involves what might be called nonintelligence intelligence or *competitively useless* smarts. Winners in competitive knowing or intelligence may lose these greater goods if they pursue decision-advantage without due regard for transcendent choice—that is, trading power for the human condition in an increasingly mechanized and digitalized international order.

It is this threat to our humanity that gives the problem of artificial intelligence its sharpness and clarity, makes its uncertainties so cloying, and renders the debate over its use for intelligence purposes so urgent. Whereas cyber and the Internet are widely acknowledged to have implications for national security, the subject of Artificial, Automated, Autonomous, and Anonymous intelligence (A4I) gets some of us, but not all of us, stuck on who we are—what sets us apart as human—and how far we will let technology go in service to our ambitions. Competitive learning is taking us down a dangerous path, into a terrain on which we cannot win with our current set of "intelligence" tools. It makes sense to explore this subject in somewhat greater depth than we otherwise might, because this is where we may have our most shocking, yet also most foreseeable, twenty-first-century surprises.

The Nature of A4I

To be clear, A4I includes a range of capabilities, from "smart" mechanical dishwashing (automation) to "smart" neural networks popularized in science fiction (deep learning). In between, A4I encompasses other capabilities associated with, but going beyond, simple machine learning through touch, vision, and audio inputs. One helpful way to think of A4I is to equate it with the function of intelligence, minus the competitive angle: it is technology that autonomously commands, controls, and executes the gathering of information, that processes and exploits that information, and then communicates the results, potentially anonymously, to a decision-maker. A4I is getting unnervingly smart, which makes humans uncertain that it can remain mastered, with humans in control.

Although the subject may seem daunting, A4I is understandable if terms are kept clear and used consistently. *Automation* is the process by which human activity is taken over by machines. The Mars rover is an automated platform hosting sensors that collect and send information to humans back on earth. *Artificial Intelligence* (AI) extends automation to data accumulation and analysis for the purpose of mechanized learning, judgment, and decision. IBM's Watson used narrow, rule-based learning to beat humans in games of Jeopardy and chess. Watson's type of AI is often called "narrow" because it is trained to the rules of a game that it plays many times to collect relevant information and develop superior expertise in that game. In contrast, "deep learning," employs "neural networks," and vast amounts of data to learn without relying on preset rules or prior play alone. In March 2016 a surprising demonstration of this latter capability sent China into an investment frenzy: over 280 million Chinese citizens watched Google's machine Alpha-Go beat a Korean master. There are 10 to the power of 170 possible board configurations in Go, so creativity and intuition, not just experience, were required to win. Then, in May 2017, the machine beat the reigning Chinese master of Go not just once, but repeatedly. The impact of those events has been called China's "Sputnik moment"; afterward, Chinese investment in AI surged, putting the country in contention for leadership in global A4I.[29]

China had suddenly appreciated, through a cultural and perhaps even an artistic lense, what had come at last. "General AI," as distinct from narrow AI, approaches human cognition: the ability to observe, orient, decide, and act when dropped in an unmapped, unruly environment.[30] Some experts argue that general AI approaches "the singularity" when human and machine become indistinguishable. In fact, some saw hints of this singularity in Alpha-Go because all masters of the game had long been revered for what seemed absolutely necessary to winning: a near-mystical, intuitive *feel for the game*. Others say the singularity will never happen, because human cognition has the capacity for transcendence, including self-abnegating choices that further spiritual, imaginative, or ethical ends for which machines cannot be, as it were, "aware."

The debate over prospects for the singularity still rages, especially in light of progress in making machines autonomous. Although the difference between narrow and general AI is enormous, capacities for autonomy exist in both. *Autonomy* refers to the unrestricted delegation of decision-making. Such decisions can vary from the simple, such as what to learn and when, to the complicated, such as what to do in the midst of complex contingencies involving multiple objectives and high stakes. *Anonymity* refers to the capacity for hidden sponsorship of any of these activities.

A4I and Mass Surveillance

A4I is the roll-up of all the foregoing tools in an integrated capability. One Chinese expert claims that deep learning will determine the superpowers of the twenty-first century and that China, with its early awakening, better capabilities for mass surveillance and better access to mass data, is well positioned to prevail.[31] For some analysts, the nightmare scenario entails weaponized, remotely controlled and anonymous drones as small as a particle or as large as jumbo jet, making kill decisions without human supervision. For others, the nightmare is a political or judicial system penetrated and remotely controlled by an unidentified puppeteer.

In general, engineers scoff at either scenario because they think it unlikely humans will allow matters to go that far. What the latter miss, however, is the competitive context that fuels the quest for decision-advantage. If A4I evolves as deep learning, is married to a weaponized platform of any kind, and is programed to have a competitive mission, it will observe an alien environment, orient to potential adversaries, and self-train to beat them, including opposing machines, *or potentially any human seeking to put them back on a leash*.

How could things get that far? Faced with an A4I-equipped adversary, governments could delegate more and more to their own A4I-enabled machines in the interests of gaining advantages in international politics and war. Machines can already process and think faster than humans do, particularly under stress. In a battle between two A4I systems, the more efficient and better-equipped system will win, which incentivizes designers to maximize the programmed battlefield while minimizing human control.

Of course, the problem is not confined to military institutions, doctrine, and traditional forms of warfare. Internet-enabled A4I spreads into the fabric of human society because it increases efficiency. The process seems innocuous: a dishwasher speeds kitchen clean-up (automation and robotics); then an improvement is made that allows the dishwasher to sense when meals are prepared and with what residue, helps it choose cycles to save soap and hot water; then the dishwasher connects to the Internet, allowing it to order more detergent or parts when supplies run low. But at that point the dishwasher has collected data that requires security: police would like to know if there are banned substances on the plates; insurance companies would like to know whether you eat healthful food so they can charge you higher premiums if you do not; thieves would like to know if you are home; others would like your DNA. Dishwasher manufacturers might introduce anonymity for your privacy, but others would insist on a trap door to ensure warrantees are met, or to prevent you from hiding your dishwasher's electrical burden from your utility company.

As a result, once your superconvenient appliances are online, your insurer, utility, local sheriff, or parts supplier can monitor, service, or press for legal access to them. Appliances would *begin* to do these things in the name of the owner's interests, which the owner would likely permit for convenience—much as most people agree to Facebook's or Apple's terms without reading the fine print. Unlike software services, however, such conveniences *may become* a long-term trap. It is one thing to throw out an Alexa personal electronic assistant for fear of being monitored, but it will be much harder to throw out a kitchen or garage full of machines. Whole houses are slowly becoming "smart" and, indeed, *intelligent.*

In sum, it seems likely that the states that will have a twenty-first-century edge will be autocracies or those democracies that recognize the dangers and develop protocols to manage the threats they pose. For democracies, A4I could eventually endanger individual freedoms and human rights by diminishing privacy and social trust in exchange for increased convenience and competitive learning, which will become potentially superhuman in scale and scope. This trade will tend to happen because the worst case, an Orwellian world, can also seem the best case: a superconvenient world where the smartest win. Whether we care about the social effects or not, efficiency still lures us to make the trade. Smart dishwashers of the kind described above would make life easier, plates cleaner, and diseases less rampant. Smart cars reduce energy consumption and save money. Biometrics on smart phones help track the spread of disease, contain the infectious, and manage the allocation of hospital equipment.

The transition to a hyperconnected AI economy is already happening worldwide. In China, an insurance company uses AI to analyze videos of prospective clients for indicators of deception, presumably without the clients' knowledge.[32] By sharply changing competitive learning practices and decreasing the role of trust in human interactions, A4I is making business smarter while also threatening to preempt and manipulate public discourse and private choice. The combination threatens the free market, investigative journalism, democratic elections, law enforcement, diplomacy, and war. Those financially able to equip themselves with massive data-processing capabilities will achieve elite levels of security. Everyone else will be on the defensive. Thus, the paradox: even as A4I is helping an elite few map reality and learn at increasing rates, uncertainty will rise for most of the rest of us, even as we feel so much smarter and more productive than we once were.

Returning to the Problem of Trust

The above discussion suggests a dystopia. Every "thing" linked to the Internet will collect, store, and share masses of data that autonomous machines may use to inform anonymous overseers. We know, however, that it is possible to hire gatekeepers in the form of security professionals or software. If every connected "thing" has a trusted gatekeeper empowered to monitor for intrusions and prevent malicious use, then bad actors may find intrusion too costly. *Trusted* gatekeepers can use A4I to keep a running list of suspicious probes, helping to anticipate hostile entry and to alert related platforms to brewing trouble. Networks of appliances, like neighborhood watches, could keep communities safer than ever from surprise attack.

The idea of having gatekeepers suggests at least someone or something will be trusted in cyberspace. But is that reasonable? The gatekeepers may themselves use A4I to wield extraordinary power. They will know with what "thing" it is safe or useful to link, thus telling their communities who or what can be trusted— that is, in addition to themselves.

Of course, the eruption of the Kaspersky Lab and Hauri scandals in 2017 exposed the extent to which gatekeepers can themselves become compromised.[33] In the former, Russia reportedly used Kaspersky's antivirus software to probe its clients' computers, including sensitive ones in the United States. In the latter, North Korea hacked into sensitive South Korean military files using Hauri's security software. Network security companies defended Kaspersky, which they said may not have been complicit in Russia's attacks. But note the shared interest at stake: security firms need the equivalent of cameras in every "room" of your computer. People *trust* security applications so allow these firms to put them there, even though that means allowing a stranger inside, because they have little choice. This makes firms such as Kaspersky or Hauri perfect, if perhaps unwitting, double agents, trusted by both sides but potentially working *against* the interests of one of them. And compromises may flow from profit motive alone. People trust their browsers to verify the authenticity of websites and keep their computers safe, but when security companies hide flaws they know exist just to keep clients they need, vulnerabilities will persist for hackers to later exploit.

In this competition for trust, the private sector is winning over government institutions. People trust system administrators at their place of work, their software providers to protect their data, and their phone company to protect their phone records. On a larger scale, they trust Facebook, Amazon, Pinterest, and Instagram as "gatekeepers" for their information. As Scott Galloway, author of *The Four: The Hidden DNA of Amazon, Apple, Facebook and Google*, writes, "We don't know how the Google algorithm works—but trust it to the point of betting our careers, even lives, on its answers."[34]

People tend to trust companies because, for one thing, they believe individuals are unlikely to be personally victimized by companies. Many users have not yet internalized Facebook's role in the 2016 Russian cyberattacks or its implications. The company did not intend to victimize anyone; *its platform simply enabled others to do so*. In any event, public trust has been shifting from slow-moving governments, whether elected or not, to private business, corporations and utilities.[35] There is no reason to suppose that, as interconnected "things" increasingly become gadgets, people will revert to trusting governing institutions over software. But even if they do, their world has already sorted into one where *they have to trust* corporate information aggregators or go off the grid, which will be an increasingly difficult thing to do and stay employed. The 2020 COVID-19 pandemic only accentuated some of these trends, as an increasing number of people began working from home and using web-based platforms for socializing.

Of course, corporations, especially social media platforms, recognize the trust required for selling gatekeeping services and are experimenting with ways to gain trust without having to work through governments' regulatory structures. These companies have advanced the development of blockchain software and its derivatives, such as Bitcoin. Blockchains offer a capacity for trusting the provenance of things, whether supply chains or financial transactions, using algorithms and distributed verification. They replace the friendly, local banker or professional handshake with an algorithm. In countries that permit its use, the technology is attractive because it offers accountability without any gatekeeper. One can anticipate that blockchain technologies, built to offer security in a decentralized way, will dramatically increase the efficiency of centrally managed corporations. And some might say, "Good for them." Yet here trouble brews. If good intelligence increases power and bad intelligence subtracts from it, the twenty-first century could operate much as the twelfth century did, with gated communities in which corporate lords protect only those weaker sorts who make them rich by tilling their soil.[36] In the modern case, the weaker or at least most trusting sorts will be offering up personal information that data aggregators can mine for a profit. Universities conducting sociological or political research using corporate metadata will have incentives to make deals with these corporations, recruiting students into their data-sharing communities for opportunities to publish new findings. Unlike elected political leaders, business leaders may worry less about such externalities as cultural impact, privacy, state power, or existential good than their competitive or scientific edge. It is only when Facebook, Twitter, or another platform bans scoundrels for their behavior, that individuals realize that these private companies will decide who can speak in what was thought to be their public squares. And soon these squares may be the most important ones in town.

In the twenty-first century, uncertainty will therefore likely grow over who is brokering digital norms on a cyber-terrain connecting polities around the world. This slide into seepening uncertainty will be hard to appreciate because technology is changing how norms are brokered. In the recent past, people looked to their governments to protect them from the downsides of a competitive market. Democratic governments in particular acted on their citizens' behalf by preserving liberties judiciously tempered with regulations, often after losses serious or repetitive enough to make regulation seem necessary for the greater good.[37] Laborers looked to government to protect them from dangerous workplaces. Consumers wanted protection from cribs that inadvertently but repetitively endangered babies, from airbags that killed passengers when they deployed, or cars that polluted communities to gain higher gas mileage. These were choices communities made through political processes. They resulted in manufacturing standards and car inspections.

But it is at least possible and perhaps likely that in the twenty-first century, A4I will take these choices from the public domain and put them in the private one by handing what were once regulatory decisions to companies seeking to shape what we think we know about their products. In an age of mass surveillance, governments may deserve a measure of mistrust; but imagine if business interests insinuate themselves into the world so efficiently that the social downsides of profit-making (false advertising, health insurance premiums indexed to genetic attributes, promotion of unsafe products for lower price points, or pyramid schemes) are only realized late in the game, after governments have been weakened by that mistrust. At that point, efforts to create and enforce norms could amount to whimpers in the rush to create designer babies and such. And if corporations are increasingly brokering norms and gating their communities, what happens to the "neighborhood watch" that has provided domestic intelligence against foreign interference for so long?

If we are well on our way to corporate brokered norms, it is because data aggregators, such as Google, Facebook, Amazon, Microsoft, and Apple, have actually become huge intelligence services working, seemingly, for each of us. Unsophisticated consumers, however, we cannot always tell when we are being manipulated. We appreciate evidence that confirms our point of view, admire success, and actually like wearing cool logos and interacting with "geniuses."

They increase our power in the most intimate kind of way, gradually rendering each of us dependent on them and yet, at the same time, enraptured and complicit. This is the stuff of intelligence power made manifest not at the level of the state or its institutions, *but inside our own homes*. Put a face on an AI-enabled computer and people have been known to bond, crying inconsolably when asked to give "her" up.

At the same time, Amazon, Google, Facebook, and Apple have become massive intelligence machines *for themselves*; they are executing the collection, transmission, and anticipation functions of intelligence for their customers while learning how they learn, influencing their decisions, reducing their capacity for selective secrecy, and trading their information for advertising dollars. This activity is neither good nor bad; it just is. The fault lies with the public—civil society—that has not yet conceptualized what is happening, and political leaders who find no advantage in educating them.

Shifting Loyalties and Offensive Intelligence in the Age of Cyberwar

Because users like the services these companies offer, they are slow to see that this kind of intelligence serves corporations' competitive interests with little regard for public interest (the integrity of the vote, for example) or the transcendent kind of knowing (what is right and wrong) that underpins societal norms. Because these businesses are profit-seeking, they have little interest in exposing deception or giving up decision-advantage unless they gain in other ways.

So, we return to the problem of gatekeepers and "influencers." According to the theory of decision-advantage, one need not fear an adversary's intelligence system if one can effectively influence, own, break, or outmaneuver it. Applying this logic to the private sector's growing intelligence architecture suggests that a regulatory structure that limits the power of data aggregators through direct regulations and controls may be one way to accomplish this end. China and Russia have taken this route. They are influencing others to follow their lead by advising on censorship and limitations on the movement, storage, and accessibility of data. Their strategies embrace sovereign Internets, government controls, firewalls, and the integration of the "information-space" (or traditional methods of "knowing") with government-controlled cyberspace.[38] In China, the e-commerce company Alibaba, which is also engaged in retail sales, Internet services, and technology development, *must* help the government keeps tabs on its citizens. Using Alibaba and other sources of big data, the Chinese government tracks and ranks citizens according to their trustworthiness.

State controls of this kind seek to manage risk, but they can prove disempowering over the long term if they slow innovation, alienate users, or prompt the best cyberwarriors to sabotage or flee. Government heavy-handedness can also hurt profits. Questions persist about whether a Chinese telecom giant, Huawei, would put Chinese interests ahead of the market if allowed to dominate the new 5G global infrastructure. The answer seems rather clear.

The United States has, in contrast, generally sought to keep the government's cyber-related intelligence institutions advancing in collaboration with private-sector data aggregators—that is to say with a light regulatory hand. This route has seemingly offered a more comfortable answer to the challenges posed by rapidly evolving and devolving intelligence power in the private sector. After all, protection of free speech, whose flip side is unleashed curiosity and innovation, is at the heart of the democratic-capitalist culture that most in the American government believe duty-bound to protect.[39]

Yet this approach is also risky. In the first place, using regulation as a soft route to public-private collaboration is something of an artifice. Corporations in this sector, like any other, will be self-interested, profit-oriented, and resistant to limits. Companies like Facebook and Twitter did little to prevent conspiracy theorizing and deception online before the January 6 attack on US Capitol because it was profitable; afterward, these firms suddenly banned right-wing extremists from their platforms. Whether public sentiment favored this move or not, corporations had unveiled their power: claiming their rights as platform-managers, they limited civic engagement by taking away social media in selected cases. They did so without reference to elected officials or political institutions, whose apparent powerlessness before the mob was rather obvious.

In the second place, managing cyber-intelligence systems requires expertise for which the government and private sector will increasingly compete, with the US government usually losing. This will make constructive regulation difficult. As employers such as the US intelligence community and Google compete for the best cyberwarriors, salaries and benefits will go up while the length of tenures on sensitive systems will head down, with abandoned employers left vulnerable to outside penetration unless loyalty can be won or enforced another way.[40] That contest will again likely favor the private sector, making effective regulation difficult, while at the same time increasing corporate distrust of government.

Such distrust is not particularly new, just newly important. Many of the best systems administrators launched their careers as self-taught computer jockeys. Their professional standards and ethics are often hacker-based (do anything we can), socially derived (do what peers are doing), and liberal (set information free for the greater good). Employers retain their employees not just by paying well, but by embodying their collective libertarian ethic, reinforcing employees' habits and loyalties, which tend to be in opposition to the state.

Third, and expanding on this last point, the basis for collaborative public-private regulation of information industries is limited. Part of the reason has to do with legal complexities. Europe has led in an effort to regulate by passing a privacy law, the General Data Protection Regulation, which took effect in May 2018.

The scheme makes collecting and managing personal information more difficult, lowering capacities to use data in beneficial ways. US companies such as
Google, Amazon, Facebook, and Apple come from a culture where free speech
is constitutionally protected, and privacy seems a rather more derivative and obscure right, mainly constraining government actions, not corporate ones. After
all, commercial data aggregators create products that get inside homes, such as
Amazon's Echo, or inside smartphones, such as Siri, whereas governments proposing to regulate how such penetrations are done and the derivative data managed are themselves suspect: the instruments of state monitoring are explicitly
prohibited from citizens' homes. These technical, cultural, and legal complexities
mean that governments need help from the industries they propose to regulate,
even as they make cases against these companies' core business practices on a
skeptical public's behalf.

Fourth, the popular support for a regulatory approach appears weak. As
already discussed, technology is deepening citizens' natural distrust of government, which is impersonal and taxes, while increasing their dependence
on transnational firms whose products they voluntarily purchase and interact with every day. Personal empowerment has led to the rise of networks,
as people use social media's platforms to search for any like-minded users
wherever they live, putting the coherence of the nation and the legitimacy of
the state at risk. As in prior centuries, the technological revolution has had
more than a leveling effect; it has created a revolutionary impulse with muscle.
Individuals (and objects) can access world affairs on the cheap, organizing in
swarms for a cause or hacking into information once protected by states using
walls, armies, distance, or secrecy. As national institutions lose their grip as
the primary socializing and acculturating mechanisms of the state, they lose
their grip on the public trust to regulate—especially when the public sees little
wrong and a lot right about the products they enjoy and the companies that
make them.

The concept of "the national security state" is thus under attack from within
and without, with declining prospects for managing the resulting chaos. In fact,
by the late 1990s, cyberspace had developed shrouded zones where terrorists,
black-hat hackers, and other criminals could plan, organize, strike, and then
swiftly disappear, threatening the state and triggering daily defenses unseen by
most citizens, law enforcement officers, or military officers. When attackers are
successful, victims blame government for failing to protect; when governments
are exposed for legally authorized but clumsy efforts to preempt, citizens blame
them, often rightly, for participating in mass surveillance or restricted freedoms.
Although the giants of the new digital industry dislike and resist the statist visions
of Russia and China, they have created a client-based, privacy-eroding culture
that is destabilizing those democratic governments on which they depend for

education, recruitment, profit, and infrastructure. Weak governments are not likely to construct useful public-private partnerships.

In sum, the cyber-revolution threatens to be individually empowering, piratical, and antidemocratic in its effects on governing institutions. It is not just that system managers, data aggregators, and gatekeepers are becoming a new, privileged elite, it is that they can appear heroic: making lots of money in industry while outwitting slow-moving, suspect government institutions. Big cyber-enabled companies like Facebook, Google, Wikileaks, and the like are increasingly housing the cyberwarriors, becoming political powerbrokers. By encouraging the sharing of information, they have become the facilitators and repositories of bulk data about people and places that they sell, mine, or fashion into tools for the public's convenience and their own profit. At the same time, the values they project make these corporations likable, and thus popular embodiments of a kind of antistate, individualist political ethic. Crowd-sourcing is not just a method for information collection, but has become a kind of antigovernment meme: Google Maps arbitrates discrepancies in a state's boundaries or road systems based more on user feedback than on governmental geographers, loosening the boundaries of sovereign controls.

Put another way, the new intelligence-related industries in cyberspace have become wealthy political rivals to states. They have their own foreign policy and "smart" weapons for influencing diplomacy and war. It should not be forgotten that while Russia may have used Facebook to skew the US elections in 2016, Facebook could have accomplished that task itself if it had wanted to. Intelligence is power, and these transnational companies have lots of it. What makes this technology-induced trend *populist as much as corporatist* is the loyalty *customers* (not just employees) show to these firms because they are "cool," approachable, and likable. What makes the trend antidemocratic is the appearance of purposeful public enlightenment but the actual effect of ignorance-peddling and thus, a degrading of expertise in public life in general. Such trends are encouraged by companies that put profit over public value in day-to-day operations.

The Question of Oversight

Whether transnational corporations will choose patriotism over profit at any particular point is thus one of the biggest uncertainties of our time. Whether elected politicians can exercise the kind of sensitive oversight that would be required to manage the risks and gains of any public-private collaboration in this area is an open question. Certainly, from the vantage point of 2021, Congress hardly seems up to the task.

One positive development for democracies has been the seeming growth in companies' interests in oversight themselves. In the wake of the 2016 elections, Facebook introduced new privacy controls, but also admitted that Russians were still trolling on its pages. In 2020, founder and chief executive officer Mark Zuckerberg was still refusing to fact-check content, intimating interest in the public's free speech, but at the same time doubling down on Facebook's right to manage that speech as a corporate "person." Zuckerberg's decisions reflect the tug of war between profit-seeking and market-building on the one hand, and patriotism on the other. Whereas duties to shareholders have tilted him toward the former, his actions after the January insurrection in Washington seemed to show that his firm—and Twitter and Amazon—know that a vibrant democracy is in their corporate interests, so requires self-policing to some degree.

Oversight of this new cyber-domain cannot be left to the private sector alone, however, particularly if public-private partnerships emerge. Data aggregators know that governments, especially law enforcement, will press for access to the data that the public willingly shares with corporations. In the United States, Ancestry.com and 23 and Me are collecting and storing people's DNA because people want to know themselves and their family trees. Law enforcement agencies have learned how to use these kinds of databanks for hunting criminals in ways that are simultaneously reassuring and vaguely Orwellian. The example of China shows that it is a short shift for these databanks to facilitate the identification and monitoring of individuals. And since the collector is a private entity with accountability only to its shareholders, how does the public get oversight of how the shared information is used?

The Upshot: Strategic Ambiguity and Authoritarianism on the Rise

The complexities, cultural clashes, competitive incentives, and legal sensitivies involved in the state management of cyberspace suggest that democracies will suffer greater uncertainties than autocracies. What remains uncertain is how long that advantage will last. Excessive state controls almost inevitably degrade capacities to collect, warn, and selectively release intelligence. Technology also tends to break down controls, first adopters work around them, and employees tend to take exception to government by corporation.[41]

What nonauthoritarian states will do about their vulnerability to privatized intelligence power, and how well their defenses will work are, therefore, among the big known unknowns for the twenty-first century. Most democratic governments resist liaising with (as opposed to regulating) private intelligence institutions because they view privatized intelligence as pathological for the state. As already discussed, companies seek advantage for private interests over collective ones. Yet, at the level of the individual, privatized intelligence seems righteous and enabling for that very reason—especially in capitalist democracies. It is difficult for individuals to see that their data-sharing enables third-party political agendas and profit-making at the original data-owner's expense. Unable to see the problem, individuals lose trust in governments trying to solve it, because it looks like overreach.[42]

If hostile regulation and state ownership are dangerous courses for democracies, the option of pursuing loose public-private partnerships may come to be seen as the safer course. Such cooperation can rest on shared interest in the construction of a secure and resilient cyber-infrastructure. After all, media moguls know that disinformation can hurt business (their advertisers). They too have uncertainties about how new technologies will be affected by older ones, such as metallurgy, genetic engineering, biological tracing, propulsion, miniaturization, or robotics. Companies need help measuring the trustworthiness of those business partners that could bring them down.

Good intelligence on the quality of components, and where bad ones originate, is already crucial for successful corporations as well as governments seeking to protect critical infrastructure. Many large corporations are dependent on complex systems with highly precise components. In just one illustrative case, Qantas airlines suffered an in-air explosion from an engine malfunction now attributed to a milling mistake of one ten-thousandth of an inch in one of the engine's tiniest pieces made by a small manufacturer in England.[43] Uncertainties embedded in supply chains offer common ground for public-private cooperation, not least because failure in this area could threaten people's willingness to trust an increasingly digitalized and transnational industrial infrastructure.

If shared interests suggest opportunities for public-private partnerships in the new information economy, cooperation may still not arise naturally, giving more authoritarian governments an advantage. This is because businesses may not see how markets may suffer from distorted facts—what manufacturing components are safe, which producer is untrustworthy, and where demand remains unmet—until it is too late for public-private partnerships to fix them. The twenty-first century has so far witnessed an unprecedented era of public deception, making private-sector liaisons with government seem unpalatable at the start, particularly in the information domain. And some businesses may expect, and like, that the information revolution will weaken democratic governments to their advantage. As already discussed, digital reporting from appliances could weaken the rationale for regulatory legislation and strengthen corporate foreknowledge, leading to stratified societies in which corporations rather than legislators are in the driver's seat.

The theory of decision-advantage predicts this problem and the forces that make it seem insoluble. When collecting and connecting outstrips capacity to assess information, intelligence tends to reinforce mindsets, not new learning. Absent extraordinary evidence, decision-makers will tend to trust their own estimates rather than someone else's. Similarly, people using the Internet have little capacity to assess the flood of information it offers, so they use it to bolster what they think they already know. Those wielding intelligence "power" will increasingly be able to process it and map others' ability to process it so well that they can send messages or deny information to particular audiences. Such conditions can either give rise to a new form of feudalism, where self-selected intelligence experts develop loyal political followers by defining, policing, and shaping their news, or a kind of syndicalism, where the information industry governs collaboratively with states. In either case, greater certainty will not necessarily prove "good" for international stability because it masks deepening public ignorance of the collective interest. As confidence goes up but education spirals down, decision-advantage can be attained at ever-more-impoverished levels of wisdom.

Threatening as these shifts may seem, the United States might still have a built-in advantage navigating these uncertainties both as a republic and as a world leader in advanced technologies. The point here is not to suggest that the more extreme dangers will be realized or exploited for new forms of diplomacy, warfare, or manhunts, but to point out that uncertainties about such matters are on the rise, and that states that exploit technologies, or partner with industry to overcome their uncertainties, will likely do better than those that do not.

The foregoing discussion suggests that information industries and authoritarian governments will have advantages on the new information terrain. They will compete for software engineers, web developers and systems administrators, who have quietly and relentlessly become the modern equivalents of the sixteenth century's privateers, peculiarly aware of how to navigate the cyberseas, bring ships to shore, and wreck hostile ones. Trained to network through hackathons and design sprints, the best of these tech-savvy entrepreneurs will lead information-based empires of extraordinary power. The most skilled of these teams will likely include A4I-enabled platforms ready to administer the IoT on behalf of the rest of us.

Such a projection might seem surprising. Just a few decades ago, the future looked massively democratic; it seemed people would decide their political fortunes through radical, unrestricted information-sharing, then organize in crowds or swarms for political purposes as they did during the Arab Spring. Individuals celebrated the advent of "free information" and the birth of Wikipedia, an online encyclopedia vetted by users. Hackers "liberated" information imprisoned on people's computers and released it into the public domain. Data aggregators loved the idea, because free information enables their business model.

But with time, organized authorities in democratic systems sensed trouble brewing. They agonized over users' rights *not to share*, including risks to proprietary information, copyright issues, and content control. Insurgents called such issues "old think." Julian Assange, founder of Wikileaks, best known for publishing content owned by others, seemed a hero of the antisecrecy counterculture. As the contest ripened, however, democratic governments understood they were paradoxically weakened by their citizens' newfound power to second-guess government themselves, rather than relying on government oversight institutions, and their vulnerability to outside manipulation through organized deception campaigns. Organized authority pushed back, warning of the dangers that "free" but nonfactual information posed for personal and national security. After the 2016 US election, those worrying that foreign hackers swayed the outcome lost some trust in both data aggregators and government institutions.[44] President Obama reportedly felt powerless to act against a threat to the US electoral system riding on the back of American industry. In the court of public opinion, the president was vilified more for his apparent confusion than the companies were for their complicity: Facebook's user base took an initial hit, but recovered and retained its top ranking.[45]

The problem for democracies is, however, larger still. Returning to the larger point raised at the beginning of this chapter: both material innovation and destruction are occurring across industrial sectors faster than popular politics can process, worsening trust in governmental institutions. No sooner have states come to grips with the challenge of cyberwar than A4I has made it possible for humans to delegate kill decisions to robots—a development that the private sector has enabled, professes to abhor, but has not attempted to slow. Capacities for gene-editing, which are making it possible to eradicate certain genetic diseases, can also create hybrid species or turn men into cyborgs, and are evolving faster than governments can monitor or regulate. Chemists, knowing that biodiversity amounts to a global library for curing disease or creating new materials, have been unable to convince politicians on the dangers of climate change, which is eradicating species, because those politicians reflect the popular angst of citizens fearful for their economic futures. For their part, political leaders have been slow to understand and convey the implications of this massive "book-burning," in part because citizens are losing traditional jobs brought about by their love affair with technology.[46] Industry, which has the most to gain from commoditization of flora and fauna, seems best positioned to shape the norms governing it.

So if the power both for organizing citizens, informing them, securing infrastructure, and setting norms is shifting to corporations with transnational interests, the question remains how this will affect international politics. Certainly, the United States would seem to be the technological leader in almost every domain. But will it lead in the taming of the technological future we do not want?

One of the most important implications of the theory of intelligence is that two of its critical components, the capability to anticipate and to learn, rest on trust. So long as humanity has some respect for transcendent truth, be it spiritual, artistic, or scientific, then public trust will require some agreement on morality and the expectation that delegated decision-making will embody ethical choice. These other, *noncompetitive* ways of knowing are beyond the domain of intelligence as defined here, but they, too, shape decision-advantage in a transcendent, collective sense that reflects what happens when a Mahatma Gandhi or a Martin Luther King Jr. steps into the arena.

There remains, therefore, the question of who or what will shape the morals of international politics when political parties choose winning over national good, slow-moving governments are no longer trusted, and leaders, trying to protect citizens from fast-moving threats, apply too heavy a hand.

Truth-Seeking: The Future of Faith, Art, and Science

Before closing this volume, it is worth revisiting the requirement for truth in intelligence. Honesty and accuracy are the forms of truth that are crucial to sound intelligence practices. Yet intelligence serves competitive advantage, so knowing everything must take second place to knowing enough for the competitive moment. Unregulated truth-seeking in intelligence work can increase risks and lead to failure, especially when it is pursued beyond what is needed for a decision, breaks laws, or confuses value judgments with facts. In intelligence, knowing everything is not as crucial as knowing enough, just in time, to get advantageous results for competitive wins.

If truth and power exist on both sides of the intelligence-policy divide, ethical choices in how to manage them rest, at least in democracies, with elected leaders of the state, not appointed ones in the intelligence profession. For example, the US government has determined that pursuing the truth about a terrorist's plans cannot legitimize torture, but it may legitimize spying on allies. The business of intelligence is to produce enough information to secure competitive wins, not to answer matters of right and wrong, or what a state should value most.

Searches for existential truths—the kind that bind societies and cultures together in service to political values such as freedom, liberty, or preservation of the planet—are properly the domain of science, art, and faith. Basic science precedes applied science, which springs upon us both glory and defeat. To the extent that advanced economies cut funding for pure science, they risk being unable to harvest applications in time.[47] To the extent that discerning good and evil is divorced from public purpose, societies can lose their way and descend into misery. In such matters, we are the makers of our own uncertainties.

The discipline of intelligence is, however, no natural corrective to foreseeable downward spirals to dystopia. It is a tool for sharpening the wits of leaders, not reordering their values. In fact, intelligence advocates positions on the ethics of strategy, the importance of human rights to foreign policy, or the morality of dealing with dictators at its (and society's) peril.

Successful intelligence must serve leaders of vastly different faiths, political preferences, and ideals. Intelligence is *applied knowledge* derived from *competitive, factual learning*, not an archive of invariable principles or a method for tapping into collective purpose. Values are what shape decision-makers' orientation toward war, attitudes about global efficiency, interest in the human condition, and commitment to building and securing their communities. Values serve purpose, not power. They are strengthened by art, science, and faith—the intertwined and distinctly human, truth-seeking obsessions. Scientists, artists, and theologians are also often at odds, each claiming superior methods. Yet the purists in all three camps agree about the human condition: we don't know it all yet.[48] Learning and teaching are so important, in fact, that their proponents agree that government should not interfere in the core, truth-seeking aspects of their business. Pure science, art, or faith requires autonomy from the power-hungry.

Of the three, science and faith have been most often at war with one another. Yet they have coexisted in the United States since the first industrial revolution because, at their best, their presumptive humility has leavened the entrepreneurial spirit and helped build community. Pure science enables applied science, which improves society, health, and well-being. Pure faith (whether in human spirit or a god) fuels ethical action in the midst of doubt. Technological change constantly reinforces the value of science while raising new ethical questions, thereby scouring our tarnished visions of truth and morality. In the United States, technological progress has been tamed by regulations, arms control, and social legislation in which both scientists and theologians have been deeply involved. Debates have involved lusty participation by religious leaders, scientists, and the state on questions of truth, such as whether the threat of "mutual assured destruction"—that is, threatening to wipe out an enemy's society—could be ethical if the purpose were to make war less likely. Even in the absence of answers, the debate itself keeps us human.

This debate between right and wrong is a ground on which state intelligence institutions cannot play if democratic institutions are to survive; but it is the ground that advanced technology in the twenty-first century now seems determined to obscure or chip away, forcing us to act. The normative debate has generally been presumed open and fair in advanced democracies, where the political process, although sloppy, has always held up. What is new is that modern technology is so manipulating the debate, that the ethical issues get lost and the truth-tellers cannot make their points. When climate change is raising sea levels or children and parents of asylum-seekers are separated at the southern US border, some Americans can be led to believe anything about how such situations came to be through conspiracy theorizing, misinformation, or propaganda. The debate about how one knows such things throws shadow over whether what is happening is wrong, and what the polity's interest is in righting it. In the United States, it is the job of leaders, the press, and political campaigns, not the state's intelligence institutions, to shine light on such questions so the electorate can answer them.

How polities manage the information revolution will redefine what it means to feel knowledgeable, to reason, and even to educate. It will determine whether we see reality for what it is, or instead, how someone else wants us to see it. And in these regards, liberal democracies have the most to lose, because faith, art, and science are, beyond sources of truth and joy, also the wellsprings of imagination and innovation that have long fueled competitive advantages in the more brutish world of power politics.

APPENDIX 1

Report by Nuño de Silva, Portuguese Pilot Captured by Francis Drake 19 January, 1578

What follows is reproduced from D. W. Waters, *The Art of Navigation in England in Elizabethan and Early Stuart Times* (New Haven: Yale University Press, 1958), 535–536. Waters added the notes in brackets, thus altering the document as he found it in H. R. Wagner, *Sir Francis Drake's Voyage around the World* (San Francisco, 1926), 338–349.

* * *

I am . . . a native of Lisbon . . . captain and pilot combined, of merchant ships . . . as I was entering the port of Santiago [Cape Verde Is.] for water and about to cast anchor February, 1578 . . . He captured my ship, took my men out of her. . . . He then put forty or fifty Englishmen aboard my ship . . . and took me along because he knew I was a pilot acquainted with the Brazilian coast. Drake took from me my astrolabe, my navigation chart which embraced, however, only the Atlantic Ocean as far as the Rio de la Plata on the west and the Cape of Good Hope on the east, and my book of instructions. He also took the charts of my master and boatswain and divided them among his officers. He caused a chart of the coast of Brazil to be translated into English from the Portuguese, and as we went along the coast he kept on verifying it down to 24° which is as far as the Portuguese charts reach. . . . March 10, we reached the coast of Brazil. . . . Continuing our voyage south from 13°, Drake kept making soundings until we reached 39°. . . .

In the port of Santiaga . . . captured the ship of Juan Griego . . . [in 1579] on the 8th . . . we departed, taking with us the ship, Juan Griego the pilot. . . . At Callao he left in her Juan Griego . . . on the 20th the Captain, with a pinnace took a ship bound for Lima. . . . Drake took out of her only the bread, some hens and a hog, and the pilot, an old man. Towards noon on the 1st of March we spied the ship laden with silver, called the *Cacafuego*. . . . On the 6th, at night Drake then let the ship go putting in her three pilots whom he had brought along. . . .

On the 20th a frigate passed close by, which they captured . . . on board two pilots. . . . Later Drake put the Spanish sailors in the pinnace and let them go, but took with him the ship and one of the pilots named Colchero with the letters, papers and maps which he had with him. Among the letters were those from the King of Spain to the Governor of China. These Drake prized highly, saying he would take them to his Queen. Among the maps were the sea cards by which the voyage was to be made. This pilot was acquainted with the China route and Drake consulted with him about matters concerning navigation. . . . [the 6th April] Drake turned her loose [another prize] leaving in her the China pilot and all the others who had been taken except one sailor whom we took along to show us where fresh water would be found . . . passing the port of Guatulco, on the 13th . . . Drake put me into the ship in the port whose Captain was Juan Gomez without previously having shown any intention of leaving me anywhere during the voyage. . . . While in Guatulco

Drake took out a map and pointed on it how he had to return by a strait which is in 66°
and that if he did not find it, then by way of China. He carries three books of navigation,
one in French [perhaps Nicolas de Nicolai's translation of Pedro de Medina's manual, *L'
Art de Naviguer*, Lyons, 1554], one in English [either, Eden's translation of Cortes's work,
The Arte of Navigation, London 1561 or, Bourne's *Regiment for the Sea*, London 1574], and
another, the account of Magellan's voyage, in a language I do not know [either Maximilian
of Transylvania's *De Moluccis Insulis*, Rome and Cologne 1523, or, Pigafetta's *Le Voyage
et Navigation faict par les Espanolz èc isles de Mollucques*, Paris, 1525, in a translation in
a language not known to Silva]. He carries a book in which he writes his log and paints
birds, trees and seals. He is diligent in painting and carries along a boy . . . who is a great
painter; shut up in his cabin they were always painting. He has a map of the world made in
Portugal but by whom I do not know, and some other maps which he said had been made
in England. The first thing he did when he had captured a vessel was to seize the charts,
astrolabes, and mariners' compasses which he broke and cast into the sea. . . . He is a very
skillful mariner.

Excerpt from Nuño de Silva's "Memory from Northern Costa Rica"

Account of the English privateer's trip given by the pilot Nuño de Silva before his Excellency the Viceroy of Mexico on 20 May of 79, and this he gave not piecemeal but rather as he was being questioned, he was responding.[1]

* * *

Nuño de Silva, native of Portugal living in Qaya, says that he left his house at the beginning of the year '77; that upon arriving near the port of the Cape Verde island of Santiago on 19 January of '78, six ships arrived that appeared to be English, and they spoke to him from the flagship [or tender] and took him and his people on a raft and put them in the flagship [or tender], leaving the crew of this witness useless, as some were youth [teenage boys or crew hands] and others sailors, and that from the stronghold they took four shots without causing the Englishman any harm whatsoever and from there they sailed that same day up to Brava Island, taking with them this Nuño de Silva's ship; and they took some barrels of water and from there, once at sea, they threw the crew of the ship in tow of this Nuño de Silva in a raft and took with them Nuño de Silva on his ship with the wines it was carrying, and Nuño de Silva says that the reason they took him was because they knew he was a pilot from Brazil and so that he would set sail and take them there[;] and that once they left Brava Island they made their trip toward Ara de Brazil; and that on the first of April they had her in sight at 30 degrees and that without dropping anchor or watering there they proceeded on their trip until the Plata River, where they watered. They went out in file [or on a current] that is at more or less 31 degrees, and from there they went up to 39 degrees and came to where some reefs emerged and left two of the six ships that he brought there and continued his trip with the four he had left and the one of this Nuño de Silva up to the bay that they say belongs to the islands that is at 49 degrees where they say Magellan wintered, and they went in on 20 June and came out so close to shore [at anchor] that they were within shooting range, and they saw that the shore was full of Indians covered in furs and with their bows and that their attire came down to their knees and half way down their arms, uncovered on their heads, they were bringing nothing whatsoever, and that they were well put-together and tall and that those that went out [while] at anchor [or in a file] were six men in search of fresh water, and that before they could pull anchor, four Indians arrived at the rowboat and the Englishmen gave them bread and wine; after having eaten, the Indians went up a hill and one of those Magellan Indians was saying this is my strip [or turf] and that six of the Englishmen followed and having gone up a bit the Indians recoiled and killed a Flemish and an Englishman and the rest went fleeing to the rowboat; and they stayed there until 17 August and went along the coast a league and a half from anchor more or less because everything is clean and 20 arm's-lengths deep; and that until arriving at the opening to sea it took them three or four days and that the wind was against them; it took them until 24 August and that the landing on the other side has a league of flat stretch and on the other side bare and that on the northern part they saw

Indians that were making great fires and that along the south side they saw nothing. And that around 24 August they started to sail along the strait with the wind to their northeast; and that he thinks this straight would be up to 110 leagues and that the latitude [width] was a league at the entrance and as far up as half the strait there are no rapids, and from there up about eight or ten leagues before the exit it has some rapids and one so great that it appears one current folds over another, and that from there to the exit it goes straight again although there are a some rapids but small, and exits to the west, and that eight or ten leagues before the exit it is half a league wide and the exit is widest of all where there is high stretch [water] at the end. After having gone eight leagues or so, it is flat stretch and that at the entrance of this strait they found currents toward the north sea that came from the part of the sea to the south and that later since they would sail with the northeast weather they ran to the inside part and not outside; and that the top strip was snowed over all on one part and another; and that the entire strait is clean and that they always were sailing one gunshot away from the strip [shore?] toward the northern part and the depth would be ten or eleven arm's-lengths and clean [clear] as it is high [deep?]; and that all along of it they could get out if they had to; and that on one side and the other the mountain ranges are full of trees up to the water; and that at other parts there is a plain here or there, and that there they saw no great rivers but rather some streams in the breaks [rocks or crags]; and at the part where there is the great swirl [as in rapids]. Toward the south they saw some fishermen Indians in canoes that are like the ones above that they say roam along the northern part; and that they saw no other people on the side of the southern part—and that having gone out of the strait that was on 6 of September of said year, they sailed three days to the north and on the third day they had northwest winds that forced them to sail west-southwest and they sailed ten or twelve days with little sail; because the wind took so much it took all the sails and they were en route at sea until the end of September and that by the 28th, the Englishman had lost his light boat and that would be 10 tons and from there taking sail because it was taking so long, they sailed northeast seven days, at the end of which they had sight of some islands to which it took more time they didn't have the opportunity, and from there came the wind to the northwest and he sailed with the southwest and that the next[?] day he lost another ship that would be 130 tons because the weather was too much such that the tender remained alone because the ship of this Nuño de Silva had been stuck [stranded] in the bay where they wintered and that from there it ran with the weather up to a height of 17 degrees where it made port on an island one shot opposite the strip [stretch of water] where it was 20 arm's-lengths deep and was there three or four days, and from there catching the wind from the south he sailed to the north for two days, at the end of which they took sight of a small, low island and took the sails and threw down the rowboat and there caught many birds and sea lions and the next day he took to the sail and sailing northwest and toward the north and up to another island, this one a firm strip [shoreline?] from the north side five or six leagues, and arriving there it emerged at a quarter league in 12 arm's-lengths; and that this island is small and low and very populated with Indians and that all of it was plowed; and that getting out of the rowboat, the Englishman went with eleven men, and with him there were twelve, and he went in search of water and supplies and that they took the Indians two Castilian rams and some corn for their rescue; and that being late he came back to his ship and the next morning another Englishman went out with the same eleven men who were riflemen and archers and sent two of them to shore with the barrels to get water and a band of Indians that was where they were supposed to water intercepted them and took these two and went to the ones in the rowboat, and stoning them and shooting arrows at them they wounded them all and the English captain took an arrow to his face and

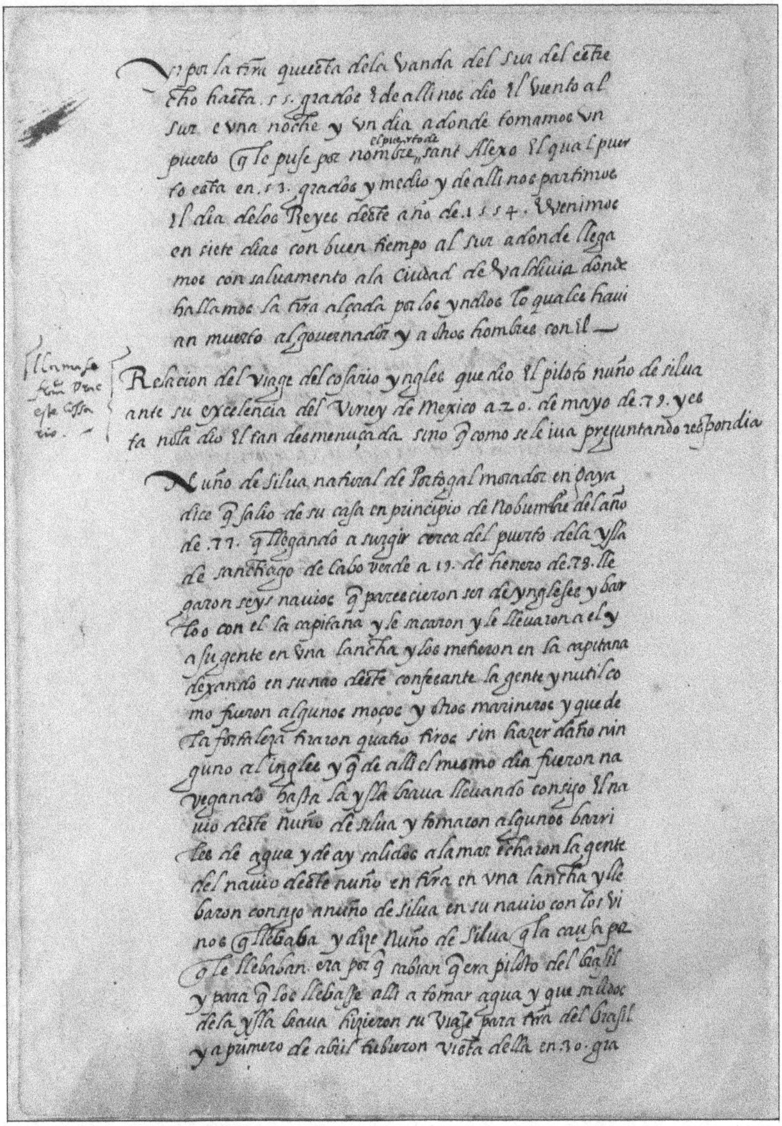
y por la tierra que esta dela vanda del sur del estre
cho hasta 55 grados e de alli nos dio el viento al
sur e vna noche y vn dia adonde tomamos vn
puerto q le puse por nombre el puerto de sant Alexo el qual puer
to esta en 53 grados y medio y de alli nos partimos
el dia delos Reyes deste año de 1554. Venimos
en siete dias con buen tiempo al sur adonde llega
mos con saluamento ala ciudad de Valdiuia donde
hallamos la tierra alçada por los yndios los quales haui
an muerto al gouernador y a otros hombres con el —

Relacion del viage del cosario yngles que dio el piloto nuño de silua
ante su excelencia del Virrey de Mexico a 20. de mayo de 79. y es
ta no la dio el tan desmenuçada sino q como se le iua preguntando respondia

Nuño de silua natural de Portogal morador en gaya
dice q salio de su casa en principio de Nobiembre del año
de 77. q llegando a surgir cerca del puerto dela ysla
de santiago de Cabo verde a 19. de henero de 78. lle
garon seys nauios q parecieron ser de yngleses y bar
los con el la capitana y le sacaron y le lleuaron a el y
a su gente en vna lancha y los metieron en la capitana
dexando en su nao deste confesante la gente y nutil co
mo fueron algunos moços y otros marineros y que de
la fortaleza tiraron quatro tiros sin hazer daño nin
guno al ingles y q de alli el mismo dia fueron na
vegando hasta la ysla braua lleuando consigo el na
uio deste nuño de silua y tomaron algunos barri
les de agua y de ay salidos ala mar echaron la gente
del nauio deste nuño en tierra en vna lancha y lle
baron consigo a nuño de silua en su nauio con los vi
nos q llebaba y dize Nuño de Silua q la causa por
q le llebaban era por q sabian q era piloto del brasil
y para q los llebasse alli a tomar agua y que salidos
dela ysla braua hizieron su viaje para tierra del brasil
y a primero de abril tubieron vista della en 30 gra

Figure A2.1 Page from Nuño de Silva's "Memoria de la Costa Rica del norte." The document contains six pages in total.

Source: The Kraus Collection of Sir Francis Drake. Courtesy of Library of Congress, Rare Book and Special Collections Division.

another to his head, and with that they turned and left without the Englishmen having wounded any of them even though the Indians had come up to the rowboat and taken four oars; and that after this they left the coast at hand and with the south wind they sailed and passed six more leagues ahead of the port they call Santiago and there they took port.

APPENDIX 3

Propositions about Intelligence Power

Additional propositions about intelligence power deserve special mention, including the outlines of a theory one might call "adaptive realism." The idea that intelligence is a measurable form of power, if true, has consequences. To recap earlier arguments: if all great and aspiring powers optimize their capacities to know their own ignorance and competitively learn, the international system will adapt to the inevitable rise and fall of great powers and sudden spikes in innovation, global pandemics, or climate change. In particular, wars will not be started by those unlikely to win them, and treaties will not be complacently maintained as others prepare to break them. If they do not, the probability of excessively costly or unnecessary wars increases.

Before moving to a more thorough discussion of adaptive realism, however, some additional points require clarification.

- First, achieving intelligence readiness—that is, the optimization of all four components of intelligence—is not straightforward, because of the contradictions among them.

For example, increasing collection can make the transmission function worse, by swamping decision-makers with too much information. Increasing the capacity to anticipate threats will draw resources away from current policy priorities, straining the transmission function. Balances must be achieved across all four capabilities in response to the requirements of the competitions at hand.

History has shown that an intelligence system can excel against one adversary and then lose disastrously against another unless the state monitors how the ramping-up of one capability may degrade others, and actively adjusts as new adversaries emerge. If walls between agencies, such as ministries of defense and foreign affairs, prevent their timely coordination, the chances of intelligence failure increase; yet if these walls are torn down in service to collection management, trusted relationships with decision-makers may cause failures of another kind. Given that superior performance in one competition may not require perfection across all four core competencies, the unused ones will tend to atrophy unless deliberately nurtured.

A few examples help to make this last point. After the end of the Cold War, the United States fought and won the Persian Gulf War, which was widely regarded as an intelligence success. That success owed much to the relevance of Cold War intelligence systems to the ground battle there. Those same intelligence systems failed, however, when attempting to deliver advantage against the 9/11 terrorists, who benefited from operating on American soil where US intelligence was weak. After the United States reorganized intelligence institutions to better fight the war on terror, cyber intrusions by Russia required connecting with decision-makers uncertain of their legal ground when seeking decision advantage against a state seeking to bias a presidential election. The intelligence community was relatively unprepared to sort "need to know" in the midst of US elections.

The transmission function is particularly sticky. There are many reasons, but an overarching one has to do with the reluctance of current stakeholders to identify and support new decision-makers likely to compete with them for intelligence resources or use those resources to trespass on their "turf." For example, some Civil War generals found President Lincoln's awareness of battlefield developments, thanks to the telegraph, an unwelcome intrusion of politics into war-fighting. When high-priority threats shift (say from surprise attack with strategic nuclear weapons to terrorists targeting civilian infrastructure), both providers and customers of intelligence have to agree to a redistribution of capabilities. During the Cold War, this kind of redistribution was rarely exercised because the foreign policy agenda was relatively constant. So the flexibility of the transmission function atrophied. After 9/11, national security officials noticed the rigidity and sought to do better against terrorists by, for example, creating teams of law enforcement and intelligence analysts in major cities and creating new offices at the top of the intelligence community, including a counterterrorism center. But such changes did not fix the core problem in other areas. The transmission function in general has atrophied. In some ways, creating whole new bureaucracies dedicated to counterterrorism made matters worse. Collaboration among intelligence components, law enforcement officers, and policymakers became locked into the counterterrorism fight, but at the expense of overall readiness in other areas. When, for example, the Russians interfered with the 2016 election and the COVID-19 pandemic hit, the transmission function was as rigid as ever. The overall point is that adversaries will always hunt for weaknesses and exploit them. Sometimes even viruses can reveal the flaws. Intelligence readiness requires superior nurturing of all the core competencies, even if at any given moment the target's vulnerabilities and the user's strengths make one or more of those capabilities seem irrelevant.

- Hostile counterintelligence strategies may aim to exacerbate the inherent contradictions among the core intelligence functions, even when those functions are operating well. Indeed, the better the core functions, the more likely such tensions will arise.

There is always more profit in manipulating a successful intelligence service than in damaging or manipulating a poor one. In other words, intelligence failure is not always an indicator that the core intelligence capabilities are flawed; it may instead be that counterintelligence—the *mission* to deny success to other intelligence services—has failed, often for reasons of *policy*. Consider, for example, the idea of running counterintelligence operations against a very important ally whose intelligence service is exploiting good relations to steal secrets from industry or run dangerous operations against third parties. A decision to not expose the ally's incompatible operations may lead to failure—not because his moves were unknown, but because the risks of taking them down would come at too high a political cost if discovered.

To optimize intelligence performance, managers, and policymakers must be aware that others are working to stoke the tensions that naturally arise in even a well-functioning intelligence system. Intelligence "wars" are familiar to intelligence professionals operating against each other in the field. They are the often-unseen fights for informational advantage that undergird all international politics. State power turns, in part, on a capacity to damage and defend the instruments of intelligence power and the dynamic balance among them.

This last observation underscores the importance of updating modern notions of international politics, particularly as political scientists understand it. "Political realism"— the idea that humankind is essentially selfish and security-obsessed—holds that human beings want to accumulate power to stay safe from predation. When people feel their lives are at risk, they want safety, even if it means denying the means of protection to others, especially strangers. The essential validity of political realism played out during the recent pandemic involving the coronavirus.

Yet that pandemic also demonstrated that our egotistical nature can be served (our power and survival enhanced) by collective transparency. During the 2020 pandemic, states learned that the better their competitors were able to protect themselves, the more protected they were, even though all states sought advantages in protecting their own populations. Preventing self-destruction required fact-finding and sharing about the disease (science-based testing), self-denial (isolation), and resource-sharing (e.g., personal protective equipment). In this way, self-serving intelligence, is not just additive to coercive power; if done well by everyone, it can lead to better odds for survival through informed, but self-interested joint action. Man's innate curiosity is, therefore, the wellspring for cooperative action—the tantalizing possibility that someone or something else might help one survive or improve one's lot in life. Intelligence power is the only kind of power that can help the self-interested escape the security dilemma, and so transcend the impulse to think "small."

Adaptive Realism: A General Theory of Intelligence in International Politics

The theory of intelligence presented so far diverges from most "realist" political thought insofar as it holds that intelligence is a measurable form of power and that uncertainty, while persistent, varies over time at all levels: individual, state, and international systems. Intelligence theory also delinks action from rationality by contemplating ways of "knowing" that are nonrational. In its normative form, however, the theory implies that rational decision-making is more likely, in general, to be winning behavior in competition. Chapter 13 in this volume offered ways to measure "intelligence power" for individual states, and assess its distribution across the international system. This appendix recaps these points as it discusses in greater detail the implications of intelligence theory on international political theory.

Underpinnings and Assumptions

At the level of the international system, uncertainty arises out of four persistent factors:

- The rate of innovation among states (curiosity on the loose)
- The grip of certainties among states (curiosity bottled-up)
- The wrenches nature throws, such as disease, earthquakes, and other natural disasters, in the workings of interstate relations
- The changing identity and number of great powers (as determined by wealth, military, and intelligence capabilities)

The first factor rests on the idea that humans are not simply self-interested and safety-conscious, but also naturally curious. Exploration is as endemic to human affairs as competition is. Being self-interested explorers, we innovate and apply what we learn in an effort to improve our condition. Thus, the more we discover, say, how to encode complex data or split an atom, the more we want to apply these discoveries and learn more.

This impulse to learn fuels technological and social changes that affect the power and interests of states. As humans build telegraphs, wireless devices, computers, and the internet or design a new bomb, uncertainties ebb and flow about the meaning of these developments for the safety and well-being of ourselves and others. We wonder how, for example, the internet will hurt or help our prospects for employment, or whether someone else will get a new ship, satellite, bomb, or source of energy before we do. This dynamic is at work today as we worry about how artificial intelligence and gene-editing, both of which we pursue with relentless vigor, threaten the technological, moral, and political future of mankind. Collective uncertainty thus feeds states' natural impulses to discover and innovate faster than others, which in turn keeps mankind in varying states of competitive darkness.

The second factor refers to the natural human inclination to lock-in "truths." We do this to build a framework of consensual knowledge and so organize society. Humans, threatened by uncertainty, create consensual paradigms and institutions because they make life more predictable and, thus, safer. We lock up found "truths" by teaching them and handing them on to others.[1] Yet this learning process implies investment in an existing paradigm; the curious may explore the boundaries of what is known, but do so by first defending the ground on which they stand. Thus, science seems tethered to "known" physical laws or paradigms; faith becomes rigidified as religious certainty and even zealotry; and social institutions such as "king," "state," and "family" seem immutable until revolutionaries say they are not. When knowledge is fenced like this, whether for divine, organizational, or some other purpose, some ideas are considered out of bounds, and learning is constrained. Uncertainty (and conflict) can thus spike at any moment because a foundational "truth" has been proven wrong, or a new source of power has been discovered.

The third factor, natural disruption, suggests that, despite all humans might do to prepare, nature will always threaten to upend plans, significantly altering the terrain of uncertainty with storms, viruses, meteors, and the like. Although science can help against nature's challenges, it will never eliminate the uncertainty that they inspire because it is often constrained not just by the paradigm within which it works, but by limits on funding and government intervention.

The fourth factor, the changing number of great powers, reflects the fact that, given the equal distribution of curiosity worldwide, the identity and number of the most powerful states will always be subject to change, increasing the uncertainty of relations among them. The ultimate source of that change is the innate curiosity of mankind that provides the wealth, population, and military and intelligence capabilities that increase the power of states.

Yet, it is also true that those societies that reward exploration, learning, and creativity will tend to increase their power relative to others that do not—albeit at the risk of instabilities and uncertainties. Herein lies, perhaps, both the vulnerability and potential power of capitalist systems. The impulse to create generates both changing power relationships and the uncertainties that make other states hostile. In any event, such entrepreneurship makes structural change endemic to the international system, creating the uncertainties that drive the search for intelligence power or decision advantage. In such a world, complete transparency may be mankind's unspoken goal, but it is utterly unreachable because of who we are—security seeking competitors.

Assuming curiosity is equally distributed among humans, the four factors cited above will cause variations in global levels of uncertainty at any moment, for any competition, and over time. We have called this unlevel playing field the "terrain of uncertainty." Varying uncertainty is hardwired into the international system, shaping the interaction of states. When all four of its contributing factors are changing rapidly, the international system will go very dark. In other words, the distribution of power will be almost indecipherable and, so, its effects on outcomes will be relatively low. At such times, competition will tend to be fierce, risk-taking will tend to be high, and weak states will be able to engineer intelligence advantages relatively easily, increasing their power relative to others. This is because great powers have too many competitors to watch to respond in time to all challenges posed. They will focus on near-peers, rather than longshots.

Dark periods are, therefore, the times when great powers are most at risk to upstarts. So it is hardly surprising that the era of total war followed so swiftly after the industrial revolution, and that modern intelligence institutions trace their origins to this period. Competitive learning (intelligence) is the means, after all, by which leaders and governments have long attempted to roll back darkness for particular purposes at particular times. States rich in intelligence power (curiosity harnessed to state interests) see the international system, its structure, and the distribution of threats and opportunities more clearly than more impoverished ones do.

It is important to note that, while relative capacity matters to outcomes, systemic capacity (the capacity of all states to learn on the terrain of uncertainty and map the distribution of power across it) matters too, because it has structural effects. At times of great systemic uncertainty, a little intelligence can seem to go a long way because advantages seem relatively (and often deceptively) easy to achieve. The reverse is true when the international system is relatively transparent to all: states will be able to read the distribution of power well, including who knows what and which states are lying about how strong they are. In such circumstances, uncertainties are relatively low, gaining advantage will seem difficult, and silly wars should be few. Yet, if transparency rests on the certainty of a shared underlying paradigm, any breakthrough to a new truth, such as quantum mechanics, can enlighten us while throwing a shroud over everything political.

It is important, therefore, to distinguish how intelligence advantage in any given competition is affected by the structure of power in the competitive moment and outside of it, including the distribution of "knowing" at the systemic level.[2] Theorists of the realist school speak of "poles" when describing the structure of (or number of great powers in) the international system—a simplification that both limits and clarifies what we can learn about structural effects. During the Cold War between the United States and the USSR, for example, we would describe the international system as "bipolar."

From an intelligence standpoint, however, we have shown that things can look different, and consequentially so, inside as opposed to outside such polar relationships determined only by calculations of traditional forms of power (military, demographic, and economic). *Inside* bipolar competitions *transparency will tend to peak* for the two competitors because they will dedicate most of their resources to the contest. The resulting mimicry tends to lead to balanced capabilities. Negotiated restraint may be coupled with intelligence to verify the arrangements, including on-site inspections, advantageous release of secret data (such as telemetry during the Cold War's arms race), and the like. Stability results inside that competition as transparency dampens down the chance of war.

Bipolar systems contain, however, the seeds of their own destruction. The reasons are several, but two of the most important deserve mention here. First, instability arises from the phenomenon of mirroring. As each party stares ever more intently at the other, it will invest ever more heavily in reducing uncertainties within that relationship, while learning from and even mimicking the other. In this process, each party will tend to disinvest intelligence resources from wider-ranging exploration, including the capacity to collect elsewhere or probe for the unexpected, thus lowering the capacity to anticipate surprise, as well as the readiness of the intelligence system as a whole. Put simply, the two great powers in a bipolar system will tend to invest most heavily in what has already made them rich and in monitoring and mirroring near peers, not in what might upend them from the margins. Indeed, *inside* the bipolar contest, allied partners may build intelligence power by piggybacking on the capabilities of their superpower, wittingly or unwittingly serving as collection platforms for penetration by anyone in liaison relationships with them. *Outside* the bipolar contest, curiosity and natural threats will gather in the relative darkness, as non-peer competitors seek intelligence advantages, study the best moment for surprise and nature does its own work, cooking up new pandemics, climate change, alien visitation, or the occasional asteroid.[3]

Second, bipolar competitions tend to be exhausting, hollowing out economies as military capacities spiral. As domestic resources are diverted to defense requirements, disloyalty to the state among publics and alliance partners will tend to increase, increasing the competitors' uncertainties relative to others and offering opportunities for deception, penetration, and espionage.

In sum, the intelligence performance of each party in a bipolar competition will tend to be defined and institutionalized in terms of its success against the other. The resulting transparency *inside* the bipolar contest will augment the intelligence powers of each party relevant to that contest, and so tend to reduce the likelihood of war between them (even if one side collapses, as happened at the end of the Cold War). At the same time, however, bipolar transparency will tend to undermine the adversaries' intelligence power with respect to rising peer competitors, giving rise to opportunities for lesser states that, operating in the great powers' blind spots, go on building their capabilities.

Understood in systemic context, intelligence is the means by which states bootstrap themselves to a higher ranking in the international system in general, and a bipolar system in particular. Adaptive Realism therefore holds that bipolar systems will therefore tend to be stable (structurally unchanged) in the short run but unstable (structurally changing) in the longrun as the engines of uncertainty grind on. The process is, in fact, inevitable.

To stave off upstarts, great powers may have incentives to cooperate, establishing international institutions, beholden to each of them, to improve (and control) what other states know while keeping themselves apprised of emerging threats. But any increasing systemic transparency and stability will inevitably create blind spots that other states' intelligence systems will exploit. In fact, any such cooperative institutions will be vulnerable to manipulation by state-parties and their aptitudes for selective secrecy and deception. War is more likely to arise from instability when the structure of the international system is dark, which it almost always is at its boundaries or in multi-polar contests. When it is bright, as it is in bipolar ones, such as at the end of the Cold War, rapid, extreme change can occur peacefully. Consider the collapse of the Soviet Union, when the international system adjusted to the implosion of a superpower that released new, weak states into the international system. Unlike the case of Austro-Hungarian empire before WWI, the USSR disappeared without major war.

It follows that, when the structure of power is unipolar, the international system will tend to be unstable (changing) and prone to war. A single "all-seeing" imperial power has no focus; it must regard every actor on its periphery as a potential or actual threat, and either divide its intelligence resources among them or choose to focus on the greatest among them while ignoring the rest. Upstart powers can focus on finding vulnerabilities acting either alone, or in liaison with others. Whereas the single superpower must be "intelligence ready" across the entire list of potential adversaries, lesser powers can focus on just one top dog, bartering intelligence to gain power. To envision this dynamic, consider the trouble that afflicted Philip II in the 16th century as Drake popped up to from nowhere to "singe his beard."

It is, therefore, the loss of decision advantage relative to rising powers that drives structural change in the international system. Multipolar systems tend toward darkness because the number of competitions in play tends to stretch intelligence capabilities thin in each great power and makes readiness harder to sustain. Bipolar systems tend toward transparency between the two competing powers, and thus great power stability, but suffer from the atrophy of attention to the intelligence threats emerging among their own allies and the noncommitted. Of course, complete transparency in the international system is unattainable because the causes of uncertainty are so persistent: curiosity, innovation, natural monkey-wrenches, and mindsets. And, as we have seen, man's natural curiosity makes for constant changes in the distribution of it. Still, the natural trajectory of the international system is perpetually in the direction of transparency because *engineered darkness* (counterintelligence) depends on superior positive intelligence to win over the long haul.

Two of the causes of competitive uncertainty—curiosity and innovation—also enlighten mankind in absolute terms, lifting the deepest darks, if not eliminating them entirely. Man's curiosity keeps improving his capabilities to sense, communicate, and, therefore, "know" in absolute terms, even if not relative to other competitors at any particular point. Thus, intelligence power is the mechanism by which the international system, composed of curious, tinkering, and competitive states, transforms itself, creating structural effects but also moving us ever closer to transparency. And the closer we get to transparency, the more the possibilities for a dynamically stable peace.

This last point deserves more emphasis because it is so consequential. The business of intelligence is never easy, but its unethical manifestations have made it seem undesirable as well. This mindset needs to change. Wars persist and peace is hard won, not just because governments wrestle with particular adversaries over particular interests, but also because the international system is naturally but variably dark, constantly veiling and revealing the distribution of power. As states compete to learn, they will tend to imitate each other's best practices, increasing the baseline transparency of international politics—an ethically good thing, despite the unethical reputation of certain competitive learning practices we call "intelligence." Transparency is ethically good because it increases the chance that solutions to global threats will be shared, and that bartering will secure states' vital interests without the need war.

Intelligence, understood as competitive learning, is, however, a malleable tool. There are many ways it can get off track or fail. It can lead to corruption if autocrats privatize these institutions for self-aggrandizement or persecution. It can disempower states that stick with winning competitive practices that are unsuitable for a new day and age. When this happens, however, intelligence power will tend to decline as the state's corrupted collection system becomes ever more tied to old ways or an autocrat's personal battles and agenda, reducing agility and the capacity to counter surprise. Such states will, in general, lose over the long haul.

The Power of Adaptation

How then do we measure the power to adapt—that is, intelligence power? After all, even when all four measures of intelligence readiness are optimized, a state's intelligence capability is not assured in any particular conflict. Some battlefields require emphasizing one capability over others, creating a tension between the power to know in any given competition and the power to adapt to the next one.

In fact, the only sound measure must be intelligence readiness. Readiness—measured by adding the absolute capacities of all four attributes of intelligence power—reduces the drama, time, and damage involved in sustaining intelligence power over time while minimizing the chance of grand failure. It is, therefore, a better measure of a state's capacity to adapt to a changing international system than is its momentary power to gain decision-advantage in a particular competition.

Readiness is difficult to sustain. Intelligence systems built for one kind of world can become irrelevant if innovation suddenly disempowers collectors or a pandemic suddenly changes priorities. Then too, some leaders do not understand their critical role in the intelligence process at all. The situation is not unlike military capability as a component of power. If military tools are not well used by commanders for the purpose of gaining battlefield advantage, all the "readiness" in the world will not help with the outcomes.

The same is true of intelligence power. If particular decision-makers fail to develop readiness or fail to use intelligence advantages as a component of strategy, then a "strong" intelligence service will lose to a relatively "weak" one that lures the former onto unfamiliar, disadvantageous terrain where it cannot quickly adapt. It is when the intelligence function is in motion over time that we can best evaluate its strength and weaknesses.

Notes

Preface

1. Michael Howard, "The Lessons of History," *History Teacher* 15, no. 4 (1982): 494, quoted in Katherine C. Epstein, "Scholarship and the Ship of State: Rethinking the Anglo-American Strategic Decline Analogy," *International Affairs* 91, no. 2 (2015): 319–331.
2. I will not directly address the argument that international politics need not be competitive, because this volume takes competition as a premise. For more discussion the reader is invited to explore the vast literature in political science on this subject. I would note here, however, that the competitive basis of the world does not preclude agreement, cooperative endeavors, and acceptance of the rule of law. It simply means that when matters of survival remain unsettled, such as who gets what in the divvying up of limited global resources, competition will be endemic.

Acknowledgments

1. Walter M. Miller Jr., *A Canticle for Leibowitz* (New York: J.B. Lippincott, 1959), 22.
2. Epstein, "Scholarship," 319.
3. Kenneth N. Waltz, *Man, the State, and War*, 2nd ed. (New York: Columbia University Press, 2001). In this classic work, foundational to realist theory on the causes of war, Waltz explores the ideas of the major philosophers of Western civilization since the ancient Greeks.

Chapter 1

1. Even if you are outgunned in a fight, good intelligence can make your defeat as inexpensive as possible. Also note that the term "intelligence" can sometimes be used to refer to what certain government institutions do in some countries, such as political repression, or assassination. The term as we will use it here refers only to the deliberate gain or loss of winning information.
2. In terms of the frequency and duration of war and the percentage of years of the total involving armed conflict (95 percent), the years from 1500 to 1700 were Europe's most ferocious. Feudal states in China engaged in unusually intense warfare from 770 to 221 BC.

3. David Kahn, "The Rise of Intelligence," *Foreign Affairs*, September–October 2006, 125–134.

4. John Keegan, *Intelligence in War: Knowledge of the Enemy from Napoleon to Al-Qaeda* (New York: Alfred A. Knopf, 2003), 6.

5. John Mearsheimer, a leading neorealist theorist, has said intelligence is irrelevant to theories of international politics because intentions of states cannot be foretold, and efforts to do so are too hit-or-miss to be related in theoretical terms to state power (panel discussion, Forty-Eighth Annual Convention of the International Studies Association, Chicago, February 28–March 3, 2007). Exceptions to this position exist, however. Robert Jervis considers intelligence in the context of discussions of the causes of war in his "Arms Control, Stability and the Causes of War," *Political Science Quarterly* 108 (Summer 1993): 167–181 and with respect to decision theory, for example, in his *Perception and Misperception in World Politics* (Princeton, NJ: Princeton University Press, 2017). These works put Jervis in the forefront, along with Richard Betts, *Enemies of Intelligence: Knowledge and Power in American National Security* (New York: Columbia University Press, 2007), of those modern political scientists working on the practical and theoretical relationship of intelligence to power and statecraft. Thomas Schelling, Robert Powell, James D. Fearon, and others have looked at intelligence more obliquely in their work on bargaining, communications, and conflict resolution.

6. A deep dive into political science, including its contending theories of structural realism, game theory, liberal institutionalism, and constructivism is beyond the scope of this book. That said, the case can be made that structural realism and related tools for exploring its implications through game-theoretic models offer the richest returns for considering intelligence in international politics, but only if intelligence power as developed in this volume is explicitly factored into structural precepts of "the system" or "the game." Theorists avoid the problem of agency—that is, how changes in the international *system* affect *state* behavior (foreign policy)—by insisting that levels of analysis be kept distinct so that theory does not become too descriptive. That insistence will, however, prevent any hope of achieving a grand theory of politics, which, it seems to me, would be nice to have and a good theory of intelligence might serve. For the levels-of-analysis problem see G. John Ikenberry, ed., *American Foreign Policy: Theoretical Essays*, 4th ed. (Addison-Wesley Educational Publishers, 2002), especially 1–12.

7. See Richard Betts, *Enemies of Intelligence: Knowledge and Power in American National Security* (New York: Columbia University Press, 2007); Mark Lowenthal, *Intelligence: From Secrets to Policy*, 4th ed. (Washington, DC: CQ Press, 2009); and Abram N. Shulsky and Gary J. Schmitt, *Silent Warfare: Understanding the World of Intelligence*, 3rd ed. (Washington, DC: Brassey's, 2002). This observation is not unreasonable, but it leads too easily to the assumption that intelligence success is tied to the limited prospects for perfecting the tradecraft of estimative analysis. It assumes that decision advantage cannot be obtained by reducing the requirements for the latter, or by increasing intimacy with what decision-makers know and need. It therefore reflects the limitations of the Cold War paradigm.

8. The intelligence cycle has been featured in the Central Intelligence Agency's publication *A Consumer's Handbook to Intelligence* (Langley, VA: Central Intelligence Agency, 1993). Its deficiencies have been noted by Mark M. Lowenthal, *Intelligence: From Secrets to Policy*, 5th ed. (Washington, DC: CQ Press, 2012), 68. One adaptation of the conventional notion of the intelligence cycle is the idea of the "OODA loop," or the "observe, orient, decide, and act" maxim developed by a US Air Force colonel James Boyd. By connecting intelligence gathering to decision-making and by timing one's own OODA loop to the adversary's decision-intelligence cycle, Boyd took an important step in taking the cyclical model toward a more dynamic and interactive theory. The OODA loop was, however, meant to offer less a generalized theory of intelligence than an explanation of the connection between cognitive agility and decision advantage. It explains how to improve the relative efficiency of tactical decision-making over time, not how intelligence systems fail or succeed more generally.

9. See, for example, Abram Shulsky, "What Is Intelligence? Secrets and Competition among States," in Roy Godson, Ernest R. May, and Gary Schmitt, eds., *US Intelligence at the Crossroads: Agendas for Reform* (London: Brassey's, 1995), 17–27. Shulsky's argument about competitive context is crucial; his argument about secrecy is not.

10. Steve Strasser, ed., *The 9/11 Investigations* (New York: Public Affairs, 2004), 398. The perpetrators rented properties, got driver's licenses, and took flying lessons in their own names. The terrorists also used aliases on occasion, especially when traveling abroad. See 398–401.

11. The literature on reform includes many interesting ideas with theoretical underpinnings, if not claims to a general theory. William E. Odom, former director of the National Security Agency, the US signals intelligence provider, has found the cause of intelligence failures in organizational issues and reform, much like re-engineering a ship to float higher, to steer more accurately, and to accommodate a larger crew. See *Fixing Intelligence for a More Secure America* (New Haven: Yale University Press, 2003), especially 1–7.

12. Lowenthal, *Intelligence, Fourth Edition*, 7. Lowenthal, who eschews truth as a goal, goes on to distinguish truth from honesty and "proximate reality," which are more reasonable ones (6–7).

13. There is a substantial literature on the problems of intelligence reform. For a modern sampling, see Odom, *Fixing Intelligence*; Paul R. Pillar's *Intelligence and U.S. Foreign Policy* (New York: Columbia University Press, 2011); Gregory F. Treverton, *Reorganizing US Domestic Intelligence: Assessing the Options* (Santa Monica, CA: Rand Corporation, 2008); Richard Betts, *Enemies of Intelligence* (New York: Columbia University Press, 2009); Jennifer E. Sims and Burton Gerber, eds., *Transforming US Intelligence* (Washington, DC: Georgetown University Press, 2005); and Jennifer E. Sims and Burton Gerber, eds., *Vaults, Mirrors and Masks: Rediscovering U.S. Counterintelligence* (Washington, DC: Georgetown University Press, 2008).

14. See Betts, *Enemies of Intelligence*, for a critique of reform efforts along these lines.

15. This premise reveals the realist foundations of this book. For more on the intellectual development of these ideas, see Jennifer E. Sims, "A Theory of Intelligence in International Politics," in Gregory F. Treverton and Wilhelm Agrell, eds., *National*

Intelligence Systems: Current Research and Future Projects (New York: Cambridge University Press, 2009), 58–92.

16. For example, good intelligence policy turns on understanding that secrecy, which usually protects *intelligence advantage*, can encumber decision-making, slowing it down, and costing *decision advantage*—a common intelligence pitfall discussed in this volume.

17. Geoffrey Parker, *The Military Revolution: Military Innovation and the Rise of the West, 1500–1800* (New York: Cambridge University Press, 1996), 8–12.

18. Parker, *Military Revolution*. The innovation of the angled bastion became known as the *trace italienne*.

19. Parker, *Military Revolution*, 26. For example, Henry VIII, believing English tradesmen to be superior, rejected ideas on fortress evolution, such as the *trace italienne*, as late as the early sixteenth century and built many deficient ones along England's coast.

20. This terrain, of course, would tilt in your favor in the city, where urban smells might overwhelm the dog's senses, almost no dogs are off-leash, and you know better than she does where the off-leash ones are likely to be.

21. Note that we have so far mentioned two types of strategic surprise. We might call them Type A and Type B. Type A concerns a game-changing move from an expected competitor. The December 7, 1941, attack by Japan on Pearl Harbor would be an example. Type B concerns a strategic move by an unexpected competitor in a completely new game. Type B surprises are sometimes referred to as "black swans," in reference to Nassim Nicholas Taleb's conceptualization of surprise in *The Black Swan: The Impact of the Highly Improbable* (London: Penguin Books, 2008).

22. The following section borrows substantially from the author's chapter "The Future of Intelligence: The 21st Century Challenge," in Isabelle Duyvesteyn, Joop van Reijn, and Ben de Jong, eds., *The Future of Intelligence: Challenges in the 21st Century* (London: Routledge, 2014), 58–79.

23. Each of these types of operations, in turn, can be sorted into active and passive techniques. A fence is passive defense; camouflage would be passive offense. Catching foreign agents is active defense; distracting the dog with a treat when she sees another dog approach would be active offense.

24. To understand how all this works, consider a common analogy used by CI experts: a homeowner grappling with a band of thieves. If the owner is interested only in securing his possessions, he will immediately repair a broken lock. If, however, he is interested in clearing all the thieves out of the neighborhood, he might leave a window ajar or a lock broken, allowing repeated thefts until everyone involved in the criminal effort is identified and arrested. If the homeowner has better televisions stored in his garage than he has in his house, he may actually leave weak locks on the front door to encourage the thieves to steal the old stuff. In such a case, security and CI, while different missions, work together to support overall policy. Understanding the importance of selectively using lures and locks during times of rapid scientific or technological change, strategists might *encourage* information flows among scientists rather than enforce secrecy—if they believe that their own side will gain more from such exchanges. Much depends on how quickly and intensely a competition

is crystallizing and how technologically capable an opponent is judged to be—all assessments in which intelligence and counterintelligence officials must collaborate if they wish to strike a wise balance between defense and offense.

25. To understand the measurement problem, it may be helpful to consider two views of the somewhat analogous mission of a librarian. In its most limited sense, the job of a librarian is to keep track of books in order to keep them safe and available for users. Libraries, therefore, might measure their staff's success by assessing whether all of the library's holdings are in proper order on the shelves. In a larger sense, however, a librarian's mission is to serve a community of learners. Understood in this way, the number of books accounted for but *not on the shelves* would be positively correlated with success. Overdue books, in fact, might be less of a worry than books that are safe but never checked out. Counterintelligence officers ought to differ from security officers in a similar way: the former should measure success in terms of the strategic purpose of those they serve, not the security of information per se. Security most certainly matters, because secrets or advantages lost cannot usually be regained; but, if security rules, then the strategists may lose opportunities to go on the offensive or the flexibility they need to shape their opponent's perceptions.

26. A striking example comes from WWII, when cable and radio censorship included, among other things, "the civil, military, industrial, financial, or economic plans of the United States, or other countries opposing the Axis powers, or the personal or official plans of any official thereof," "weather conditions (past, present, or forecast)," and "criticism of equipment, appearance, physical condition or morale of the collective or individual armed forces of the United States or other nations" opposing the Axis powers. US Cable and Radio Censorship Regulations,1801-18(d), (g), (k), 7 Fed. Reg. 1499, 1500 (1942), cited in Harold Edgar and Benno Schmidt, "The Espionage Statutes and the Publication of Defense Information," *Columbia Law Review* 73 (1973): 934. Press dispatches were excluded from this particular rule and were covered in another regulation

27. David Holloway, *Stalin and the Bomb: The Soviet Union and Atomic Energy, 1939–1956* (New Haven: Yale University Press, 1994), 78–79.

28. The presumption here is that these shifts do not confuse the decision-makers' own intelligence providers; otherwise, everyone would be worse off.

29. The vignette used earlier may be helpful to fully understand this point. Recall that the focus on controlling your dog gives you both *intelligence* and *decision advantages* over her. Suppose training goes on for a while. One day, you pick up signals of an approaching dog and whip around as fast as usual, but your dog now knows what your action implies and so rips the leash from your hand. Racing down the road, she attacks the other dog before you can catch her. Neither of you had better intelligence *capabilities* than you had previously, but your dog *has learned* that she needs to speed up her decision-making in response to yours. Neither her senses nor her athletic capabilities have changed, just her timing, which secures decision-advantage for her.

30. A superior intelligence service seeks robust decision advantage by penetrating the decision-making apparatus of the adversary so that changes in decision-making are known immediately. An inferior or untrustworthy intelligence service will

undermine decision advantage, causing decision-makers to disengage from it. Such disengagement can be smart intelligence strategy for decision-makers if it leaves opponents busily collecting secrets from agencies that do not themselves have a clue where policy is headed. But it cannot work for long.

31. As we shall see, Confederate general Robert E. Lee did choose to fight most of his battles on familiar ground, but the question is whether he did so more by instinct or because of deliberate intelligence assessments.

32. Note that in the vignette, both dog and human start with inherent advantages and disadvantages in relative knowledge and capacity to learn. Because the competition defines the terrain of uncertainty, the dog-walking case does not include the human's relative knowledge about how to write a PhD dissertation or drive a truck, both of which are irrelevant to dog training,

33. Leslie H. Gelb, "Letter of Transmittal of the Study," in *The Pentagon Papers: The Defense Department History of the United States Decisionmaking on Vietnam*, vol. 1, Gravel ed., (Boston: Beacon Press, 1971), xvi.

34. Marc Trachtenberg, *History and Strategy* (Princeton, NJ: Princeton University Press, 1991), 263.

35. This is another reason why it would be unwise to reform intelligence on the basis of a single spectacular success or failure. One would be allowing the adversaries' capabilities to dictate one's own.

36. In other words, a general prediction that terrorists will use airplanes to strike the United States tomorrow would be unlikely to help the secretary of state conduct diplomacy, but it might help the FBI increase vigilance and the secretary for homeland security increase Transportation Security Administration operations.

Chapter 2

1. Quoted in Geoffrey Parker, *The Grand Strategy of Philip II* (New Haven: Yale University Press, 1998), xix. The free Dutch were in alliance with England against the Spanish during the great battle at sea.

2. Asymmetric wars are contests between two powers or blocs that are seriously mismatched in power, including resources, military methods, and population.

3. "Philip mobilized sufficient resources . . . only to be thwarted by something that he had failed to foresee, and for which his plans left no place." Parker later attributes Philip's loss to his deficient character (*Grand Strategy*, xx) and specifically discounts the role of intelligence. See his chapter "The Worst-Kept Secret in Europe? The European Intelligence Community and the Spanish Armada of 1588," in Keith Neilson and B. J. C. McKercher, eds., *Go Spy the Land: Military Intelligence in History* (Westport, CT: Praeger, 1992), 49–72.

4. See Stephen Budiansky, *Her Majesty's Spymaster* (London: Penguin Books, 2005).

5. For a review of the classic argument on intelligence during the Armada, see Parker, "Worst-Kept Secret."

6. The best work on this topic is Parker, *Grand Strategy*.
7. For a sympathetic treatment of English commanders, as well as English incompetency during the battle, see John Sugden, *Sir Francis Drake* (New York: Henry Holt, 1990), especially 235–252.
8. Perhaps the best historical treatment of intelligence issues related to the sailing of the Armada itself is Colin Martin and Geoffrey Parker, *The Spanish Armada*, revised ed. (Manchester: Manchester University Press, 1999).
9. See Chapter 1 of this volume for more on this concept, which describes competitive learning in detail, and the conclusion, which discusses its implications.
10. Some have credited the successful explorer, privateer, and pirate Sir Francis Drake with using a "secret crystal" that allowed him to see distant objects during these years. For more on English development of sixteenth-century "perspective glasses," see D. W. Waters, *The Art of Navigation in England in Elizabethan and Early Stuart Times* (New Haven: Yale University Press, 1958), 298–299.
11. As the value of telescopes spread among seamen in the seventeenth century, the advantages afforded by having one became less certain, and the playing field became more level once again. Most history books cite the early seventeenth century as the origin of this innovation in this regard, although perspective glasses existed in the sixteenth.
12. The focus of this analysis will remain on England, the Netherlands, and Spain. It will extend to other allies, such as the pope or the Turks, insofar as liaison with them gained or confused the intelligence acquired by the battle's principal parties.
13. See Paul Kennedy, *The Rise and Fall of the Great Powers: Economic Change and Military Conflict from 1500 to 2000* (New York: Vintage Books, 1989), 31–72. Also, Parker, *Grand Strategy*, 85. The king won French recognition of his position in the Low Countries and Italy in the Peace of Cateau-Cambrésis in 1559. After this, France was wracked by civil war, though still capable of harassing Spanish interests.
14. King Philip II partly accomplished his goal with victory against the Turks in the Battle of Lepanto. This was the last great battle dominated by galleys, which were great ships powered by oarsmen.
15. The conflict went back further than these dates suggest. As early as 1559, when Elizabeth changed her religious affiliation from Catholic to Protestant, the Catholic king wrote of "the evil" gathering there. Meanwhile, Catholic underlings began plotting the queen's demise. See Parker, *Grand Strategy*, 148–149.
16. Quoted in Parker, *Grand Strategy*, xix.
17. See Sugden, *Sir Francis Drake*, especially 200–201, for more on this point.
18. Parker, *Grand Strategy*, 113.
19. There were at least seven assassination attempts against Philip II, so his security was not assured. The queen, however, was the target of larger and more persistent conspiracies. See Parker, *Grand Strategy*, 14. The Venetian ambassador attested to Philip's legitimacy by saying that the Spanish monarchy "is held together by the authority and wisdom of the king, and if he were to die everything would fall in confusion and danger." Parker, *Grand Strategy*, 13.

20. Both the Protestants of the Reformation and the Anglicans will be referred to as "Protestants" in this volume—a term widely used to refer to non-Catholic Christians during this era.

21. A good example of this problem is the Duke of Norfolk, who engaged in the Northern Rising but escaped punishment by pledging to remain loyal to the queen. He was then dragged reluctantly into the Ridolfi plot, caught, and executed. The uncertain loyalties of nobles created incentives for the queen's government to use stings and domestic covert action to eliminate threats preemptively.

22. Anne Somerset, *Elizabeth I* (New York: Anchor Books, 2003), 405. An Englishman wanted to know if it would be a sin to assassinate Elizabeth, so he asked the Vatican. The papal secretary of state, Cardinal Como, consulted with the pope and said, "Since that guilty woman of England rules over·two such noble kingdoms of Christendom and is the cause of so much injury . . . there is no doubt that whosoever sends her out of the world with the pious intention of doing service, not only does not sin but gains merit." Somerset, *Elizabeth I*, 405–406.

23. Parker, *Grand Strategy*, 14.

24. Parker, *Grand Strategy*, 15.

25. The Councils of War and of State both dealt with military affairs, with the latter responsible for all matters, including the imperial army, in Europe.

26. Pedro Fernandez Navarrete, *La Conservación de Monarquías* (Madrid, 1626), quoted in Geoffrey Parker, *The Army of Flanders and the Spanish Road: 1567–1659* (Cambridge: Cambridge University Press, 2004), 110.

27. This intelligence challenge was exacerbated when the king moved his base of operations from Brussels back to Madrid, which he did soon after Elizabeth's ascension.

28. Some fortifications were partial, but others were complete and built in the modern Italian style. The military problem they posed was more Spain's than England's in 1588. See Geoffrey Parker, *The Military Revolution: Military Innovation and the Rise of the West, 1500–1800* (Cambridge: Cambridge University Press, 1996) and Parker's *Army of Flanders* for the definitive discussion of these military developments.

29. Owen Feltham, an English travel writer, quoted in Parker, *Grand Strategy*, 115.

30. Geoffrey Parker, *The Dutch Revolt* (London: Penguin Books, 1985), 14.

31. Parker, *The Dutch Revolt*, 14. Parker's is the best account.

32. Discerning *the meaning* of Spanish policies and deployments required understanding the motives of the king, who could, according to his contemporaries, be both secretive and dissimulating: "I can certainly say—because his own ministers say it—that he knows how to pretend and conceal his intentions better than any king . . . up to the time and the hour at which it suits him to let them be known." Comment by Ambassador Fourquevaux; cited in Parker, *Grand Strategy*, 33.

33. Drake had successfully recruited *cimarrones* to his crew and his anti-Spanish cause while conducting reconnaissance missions along Spain's land-based treasure routes. He aspired to recruiting five thousand of these in the isthmus by 1586 as part of his campaign to capture Havana. Sugden, *Sir Francis Drake*, 177.

34. Entrepreneurs contributed ships and provided returns on investment through the capture of treasure vessels. The queen resisted taxing them for this reason, even when

war with Spain threatened. Merchants selling wares to new outposts along treasure routes and entrepreneurial nobles purchasing shares in voyages of discovery gradually became less beholden to their monarchs than to their wallets.

35. Chapter 4 reveals that there were opportunities for grand strategic compromise. In return for the king's commitment not to unseat her, the queen could have removed support for Protestant insurgents in the Netherlands and squelched her privateers. Both parties missed this deal for several reasons, but mostly because it required understanding each other's shared interests at the strategic level. It also required a better capacity for monitoring a strategic agreement than either side could generate. As we shall see, neither side's intelligence capabilities were good enough to overcome mutual uncertainties and build confidence in the resolution of competing interests at that level.

36. The Portuguese taught the Spanish their navigational techniques. See Waters, *Art of Navigation*, 62–63. Writing of the circumnavigation of the globe in the fourteenth century, Sir John Mandeville wrote: "For that it asketh so long tyme and also there are so many perils to passé . . . few men assay to go so, and yet . . . it might be done." Quoted in Waters, 41. It was common knowledge by this time that the earth was round.

37. See John Guy, *Tudor England* (New York: Oxford University Press, 1992), for the role of sea power versus land power at the time.

38. See Parker, *Army of Flanders*, for the definitive book on imperial Spain's logistical challenges in the Netherlands.

39. Neil Hanson, *The Confident Hope of a Miracle: The True History of the Spanish Armada* (New York: Vintage Books, 2006), 81. Ironically, Sir Francis Drake made this former symbol of international collaboration at sea one of his targets for attack in 1586.

40. Waters, *Art of Navigation*, 80–82.

41. The knowledge gap was to narrow somewhat in the years immediately prior to the Armada, with the first publication of an English book on navigating the Channel, which every sea captain in the Royal Navy had on board as the Spanish sailed north in 1588.

42. See Martin and Parker, *The Spanish Armada*, 60–61.

43. See E. G. R. Taylor, *The Haven-Finding Art: A History of Navigation from Odysseus to Captain Cook* (London: Hollis and Carter, 1956); also, Waters, *Art of Navigation* for an extensive, if somewhat dated, discussion of the evolution of navigational technology.

44. Waters, *Art of Navigation*, 10–11.

45. Waters, *Art of Navigation*, 10–11.

46. Taylor, *Haven-Finding Art*, 131.

47. Waters, *Art of Navigation*, 15. Waters quotes from William Bourne's "Preface to the Reader" in the *Regiment for the Sea*, probably first published in 1574, but this preface dates from the 1577 unauthorized edition.

48. "Thus, as Cortes explained, whereas two ships 100 leagues apart on the equator which sailed due north to latitude 60 degrees N finished up only 50 leagues apart, on the plane chart they appeared to be still 100 leagues apart and "one errour bryngeth in an other; and so an other . . . whereof to speak any more here . . . shall . . . be an endlesse

confusion," adding somewhat bitterly that to do so was in any case but "to certen Pilottes . . . to paynt a house for blynd men." Quoted in Waters, *Art of Navigation*, 66.

49. Sugden, *Sir Francis Drake*, 91.

50. See Fernand Braudel, *The Mediterranean and the Mediterranean World in the Age of Philip II*, vol. 1 (New York: Harper and Row, 1972), 103–104. Braudel's rich discussion of the pace, character, and complexities of European life in the sixteenth century is an important backdrop to any consideration of intelligence and decision-making during this period.

51. Waters, *Art of Navigation*, 101. Waters quotes from Cal. S. P., Venetian ambassador in France, April 8, 1588.

52. This was especially true of pirates, whose survival among a crew of bandits and knowledgeable prisoners required persuasion and cajoling as much as fighting.

53. See Sugden, *Sir Francis Drake*, 120–121.

54. Among the most difficult trade-offs had to be gun emplacement. Master forgers worked to increase range, stability, and the integrity of gun barrels as wrought-iron cannon gave way to cast iron and bronze. The number of guns on a ship and the quality of materials used meant little if the evolving size of the guns or their characteristics of firing and recoil were unappreciated by the shipwright, who had to ensure seaworthiness despite the extra weight distributed on decks. That merchant vessels could be refitted for war does not mean that they ended up well designed for it, especially as the technology and doctrine for naval engagements evolved. Warships and merchant ships were built to very different specifications in the sixteenth century, even though merchantmen could be armed. See Kennedy, *Rise and Fall*, 46, for another view.

55. Galleys, which relied on oars for propulsion, were highly maneuverable even on windless days. They were ideal ships for the Mediterranean but often unseaworthy in the North Atlantic. Galleasses were galleys with sails—a hybrid that gained speed in high winds but had similar problems to galleys when on the open ocean. Round-bellied, square-rigged cogs had plenty of room for storage of large cargoes, but they were slow and hard to steer. Spanish galleons, which sported guns and high castles fore and aft, were optimized for carrying soldiers who fought by grappling and boarding adversaries' ships.

56. Given the costs of hiring shipwrights, maintaining ships, and victualing crews, monarchs had trouble sustaining large standing navies. Therefore, they often supplemented their fleets by embargoing and refitting merchant ships. Accomplishing refits quickly and expertly was, in some ways, as demanding a task as building ships from the ground up.

57. The distinction between pirate and privateer in Elizabethan times had more to do with manner than motivation. Both robbed ships for prizes, but privateers, who had letters of marque from their sponsoring monarchs, had to consider political factors. Drake, who often (but not always) depended on the queen for his financing, mastered the tactics of piracy, but considered his strategic interests and usually operated to optimize them. While most historians might, therefore, categorize Drake a privateer, it is not clear he ever carried the queen's formal authorization for his activities. This is,

in part, because Lord Burghley regarded him as a pirate, and King Philip certainly called him one. So the queen adopted a policy of plausible deniability.

58. Budiansky, *Her Majesty's Spymaster*, 22–23.
59. For an extensive discussion of the time lags and uncertainties in sixteenth-century European communications, see Braudel, *Mediterranean*, 355–374.
60. See one of the best works on this subject: Parker, *Army of Flanders*, especially 70–90. Efficient use of such roads by the military meant little for subsequent civilian use. As Parker writes: "The Spanish Road, like all other routes, consisted of several parallel or semi-parallel strings of fixed points . . . and the tracks between them." Without an army, which provided security and built and destroyed bridges for water-crossings, delays and brigandage still plagued travelers (72).
61. Parker, *Grand Strategy*, 48.
62. Such problems made bonfire warning systems hardly instantaneous or reliable. In England, for example, ponderous procedures were in place to ensure that false alarms would not occur, making the utility of beacons for early warning questionable.
63. Parker, *Grand Strategy*, 52. Much of the subsequent discussion of Spain's particular problems in these regards rests on Parker's work, and especially 47–75.
64. The advantages France gained from its position as a European crossroad for communications set it on a course to develop an intelligence capability heavily weighted toward domestic counterintelligence—a characteristic that was highlighted and strengthened before and after the French Revolution.
65. Indeed, it was just such a connection that confirmed, and thus foiled, the Ridolfi plot on the queen's life. A merchant had informed Lord Burghley, then the queen's secretary, that the Duke of Norfolk wanted a shipment of gold, and enciphered letters shipped up the coast.
66. Parker, *Grand Strategy*, 48.
67. It is important to remember here that English pirates or privateers were hardly the only ones—or the most ruthless—operating against Spain. However, by the sixteenth century, the English had a long history of piratical practice in the Mediterranean. Braudel, *Mediterranean*, 619.
68. Braudel, *Mediterranean*, 619.
69. Budiansky, *Her Majesty's Spymaster*, 123.
70. Somerset, *Elizabeth I*, 323.
71. See Somerset, *Elizabeth I*, 451–452. Some have attributed the prophecy to the fifteenth-century mathematician Johan Muller, otherwise known as Regiomontanus; it was based on numerology of the Revelation of Saint John. In any case, the effects were insidious.
72. Hanson, *Confident Hope*, 195–197. See also Somerset, *Elizabeth I*, 451–452.
73. See Geoffrey Parker, *The Imprudent King* (New Haven: Yale University Press, 2014), 61–79, 213–227, and 305–323 for more on the king's work habits and errant decision-making.
74. Parker, *Grand Strategy*, 13.
75. Martin and Parker, *The Spanish Armada*, 85.
76. Martin and Parker, *The Spanish Armada*, 25.

77. Martin and Parker, *The Spanish Armada*, 63–64.
78. Parker, *Grand Strategy*, 60–61. His archive of seafaring knowledge had increased significantly with the conquering of Portugal in 1580. This archive, which extended beyond Europe, was kept relatively up to date. Philip's Escorial atlas of the European continent contained maps, based on surveys and mathematical calculations, that were the best of those days.
79. Scottish and Scandinavian coasts and ports were slowly making their way onto the maps of Europe that were circulating among merchants by mid-century.
80. John Hawkins developed, for example, a technique for protecting English ships from the burrowing worm that infested Caribbean waters and turned ships into Swiss cheese. A paste made from the combination of tar and hair protected most English ships by the time the Armada sailed in 1588.
81. That David's legendary victory may actually have been a triumph of intelligence over raw power is an intriguing argument in Malcolm Gladwell's *David and Goliath: Underdogs, Misfits, and the Art of Battling Giants* (New York: Little, Brown, 2013).

Chapter 3

1. The decisions that ultimately and directly led to the Armada's defeat involved Philip, his principal advisors, and his military commanders and admirals on the one hand, and the queen, her Privy Council and Naval Board, and her commanders at sea on the other.
2. Most historians agree that she made a choice for open war as early as 1586, and perhaps even 1585, when she unleashed her privateer, Sir Francis Drake, to attack Spanish interests in reprisal for the impounding of English ships.
3. We must bear in mind that decisions for war may not have seemed as grave in centuries past as they do now to us. In particular, we should not presume that our modern views about war and, particularly our preoccupation with its causes, were shared by leaders centuries ago. See Michael Howard, *The Causes of Wars*, 2nd ed. (Cambridge, MA: Harvard University Press, 1983), 7–9.
4. Other decisions probably mattered too, such as the Turks' decision to stay out of the brawl, or the pope's decision to support Irish resistance to English rule, but their relevance to the eventual battle in 1588 became indirect. The Turks, Scottish pretenders, Protestant loyalists, and recalcitrant Catholic nobility played important roles, but ones examined here are only as they related directly to the contest between England and Spain. To weigh the value of Elizabethan and Spanish intelligence in this particular competition requires highlighting the militarily relevant choices that, properly informed or not, led to the destruction of the Armada and its larger mission.
5. Colin Martin and Geoffrey Parker, *The Spanish Armada*, revised ed. (Manchester: Manchester University Press, 1999), 62.

6. The plot apparently evolved over time. One idea was to spirit Mary to shore, where she would be transported to Spain with the help of John Hawkins. There she would marry Philip's brother, Don Juan of Austria, and Mary's son, James, would marry Philip's daughter, Isabella. Later, the king endorsed a plan favored by the king's court advisor on English affairs, the Duke of Feria: Spain would ally with the English insurgents for a more violent purpose: dethroning Elizabeth and marrying off Mary to the Duke of Norfolk. See Parker and Martin, *The Spanish Armada*, 64–65. Also, Stephen Budiansky, *Her Majesty's Spymaster* (London: Penguin Books, 2005).

7. See Geoffrey Parker, "The Place of Tudor England in the Messianic Vision of Philip II of Spain," Prothero Lecture, 2001, appendix (provided to the author by Parker).

8. Martin and Parker, *The Spanish Armada*, 65.

9. After the uprising, the Privy Council strengthened homeland defense by engineering the passage of a new Treason Act, which protected Elizabeth's title to the throne, and an Act against Bulls from the See of Rome, which made it illegal to possess papal bulls.

10. If so, his tradecraft was sloppy. Sometimes, he wrote to Mary without cipher or code at all. His lack of operational security, whether purposeful or not, allowed Burghley, who had access to Mary's mail, to stay informed on the plot. For a discussion of the evidence of Ridolfi's double-dealing, see Parker, *The Spanish Armada*, 70 and n. 5, but especially the appendix to Parker's "Place of Tudor England."

11. When Ridolfi was turned into a double is not as clear. Burghley's investigation of the plot probably was designed to protect his role in it. Ridolfi, in any event, not only returned to Rome, but was made a senator by the pope, living until eighty at home in Florence. See Budiansky, *Her Majesty's Spymaster*, 80.

12. Hawkins, though an English privateer and trader, did business with Spain because of his need for licenses from Madrid to trade between Africa and the Americas. At the same time, he bore a grudge toward Spain over its surprise attack at San Juan de Ulúa, which had cost him ships, men, and the confidence of the queen. See Parker and Martin, *The Spanish Armada*, 60. See Chapter 2 for the rules of trade, including the Treaty of Tordesillas, that shaped Hawkins's decision-making.

13. See Parker, *The Spanish Armada*, 61–65.

14. "This fundamental policy difference between Brussels and Madrid was perhaps Elizabeth's greatest asset during the series of crises that lay ahead." Parker, *The Grand Strategy*, 157.

15. John Guy, *Tudor England* (New York: Oxford University Press, 1992), 281–282.

16. Walsingham initially shared the position Burghley had vacated with Sir Thomas Smith, but he acted as primary and eventually served in the position alone until his death in 1590. Budiansky, *Her Majesty's Spymaster*, 76.

17. It is likely that Walsingham also played a role in the covert publication of pamphlets advertising Mary's treasonous behavior and in "lurid and exacting detail" charges against her. Budiansky, *Her Majesty's Spymaster*, 81.

18. John Guy reports that Walsingham was the primary chief of espionage, especially after Burghley became Lord Treasurer (July 1572). See his *Tudor England*, 280–281.

19. Geoffrey Parker, *The Grand Strategy of Philip II* (New Haven: Yale University Press, 1998), 168–169. The French, engaged in a civil war, were nonetheless making trouble

for Philip at the time. The Duke of Alençon (Anjou), who was courting Elizabeth I, had been named sovereign ruler by the rebel Dutch in 1581; the strategic enclave of Cambrai had been transferred from Spanish hands to French control by rebel Dutch; and Henry III, king of France, had helped Dom António defend the Azores against Spanish efforts to conquer it. Parker, *Grand Strategy*, 170.

20. The king of France, Henry III, had been ignorant of the plans.

21. Anne Somerset, *Elizabeth I* (New York: Anchor Books, 2003), 403.

22. Receiving news of plans by the Duke of Guise to murder Elizabeth in 1583, Philip wrote in the margin: "It was thus I believe that we understood it here; and if they had done it, it would have been no harm." Somerset, *Elizabeth I*, 406.

23. For reasons too complex to discuss in this case study, the historical record suggests that Sir Edward Stafford was almost certainly a double agent. It appears that Stafford did not, however, contribute significant advantages to either side's decision-making, so the particulars on this matter are beyond the scope of this book. For the most in-depth treatment of the subject, see Geoffrey Parker, *Success Is Never Final: Empire, War, and Faith in Early Modern Europe* (New York: Basic Books, 2002), 67–96.

24. Robert Poley was the second of these double agents. Having ingratiated himself with Catholics in France, he used their help to insinuate himself into the household of Walsingham's daughter, much to the delight of his controllers in Paris. Actually, he was under Walsingham's thumb throughout. See Budiansky, *Her Majesty's Spymaster*, 123–171. Walsingham never completely trusted Gifford. In fact, the beer merchant had been bribed twice: once by Gifford to permit the hidden messaging, and another time by Paulet because Walsingham insisted that he also read the messages himself.

25. Somerset, *Elizabeth I*, 406.

26. For an explanation of the line and its significance, see Chapter 2.

27. For a firsthand account of Drake's commitment to intelligence gathering and his methods, see the report of a Portuguese sea captain included as Appendix 1.

28. Parker, *Grand Strategy*, 155.

29. Parker, *Grand Strategy*, 153.

30. John Sugden, *Sir Francis Drake* (New York: Henry Holt, 1990), 149. The total amount is not known, but exceeded that officially recorded to ensure Drake received a share that could not be impounded or returned to the Spanish via negotiations.

31. Sugden, *Sir Francis Drake*, 150.

32. Sugden, *Sir Francis Drake*, 164.

33. Sugden, *Sir Francis Drake*, 41. The Spanish were engaged in an expensive war in the Mediterranean until 1577, which made financing a war against England particularly difficult. Distracted and hobbled, the king chose, reluctantly, to back covert planning. The king's financial vulnerability was an opportunity the queen understood, partic-ularly after 1568; it made her English privateers a useful instrument to deter Spanish invasion, as we shall see subsequently.

34. After the queen offered safe harbor to one of the king's ships in 1568, and then claimed the loan it carried as her own, Philip had made the English ambassador to his court, the Protestant Dr. John Man, pointedly unwelcome. Elizabeth recalled Man but

did not replace him. That said, as part of her negotiation—or ploy—in 1571, she had begged to be allowed to replace Man for the purpose of opening negotiations.

35. The States General of the Low Countries renounced their allegiance to the Spanish king on July 22, 1581, and gave it to a Frenchman of royal blood, the Duke of Alençon, who sought Queen Elizabeth's hand in marriage, and commanded the combined forces fighting the Spanish in Flanders. The queen decided to support these Protestant rebels and their French Huguenot allies less out of religious sympathy than out of fear that their loss would strengthen Spain's aggressive intentions toward her, and make invasion more likely. Philip II, for his part, decided to sponsor rebels working against Alençon's brother and backer, Henry III, the king of France. Philip's military commander, now the Duke of Parma, won battle after battle, reclaiming important coastal cities and culminating in a bold siege of Antwerp.

36. Henry de Guise was attempting to win the French throne, vacated by the death of Henry III, for the cardinal of Bourbon.

37. The list is of her intelligence requirements. It is lengthy. We do not have a record of the answers the Privy Council provided. See Conyers Read, *Mr. Secretary Walsingham and the Policy of Queen Elizabeth I*, reprint ed., vol. 3 (Harwich Port, MA: Clock and Rose Press, 2003), 73–75.

38. For background on Walsingham's channels, as well as others, see Read, *Mr. Secretary Walsingham*, 125–128.

39. Even if Walsingham had taken these backchannel discussions seriously, erratic communications (messages to and from Madrid sometimes took months), doomed a policy that depended on good timing for its success. Walsingham used an intermediary for the later contact—a Portuguese physician in London who corresponded with Castillo. The king's reply, which inquired about terms, was not received until March 1586. See Read, *Mr. Secretary Walsingham*.

40. Sir John Crofts, a Spanish sympathizer, as well as a member of the queen's Privy Council, explored opportunities for peace through his relative William Bodenham, who was close to the Duke of Parma. As this effort got underway in 1585, a perhaps related channel opened through Carlo Lanfranchi, an Italian merchant living in Antwerp and friendly with Parma's governor there. He wrote to a Flemish merchant living in London, Andrea de Loo, urging him to use his contacts to open a channel for negotiations with the Privy Council. None of these additional channels appears to have involved high-level intelligence exchanges for confidence-building, even though Lord Burghley seems to have been incidentally involved in the last. Accordingly, they fizzled.

41. The Anglo-Spanish contacts had a downside risk for England: they could convince the Dutch that the English were unreliable allies, leading the Dutch to suspect betrayal and act accordingly should war ensue. In fact, leaks of the peace feelers helped Parma deceive Dutch forces in Flanders that the Armada might sail against them, not the English. This potential split was one of England's most serious intelligence vulnerabilities, because Dutch sea dogs could have helped Spain. A few did.

42. Martin and Parker, *The Spanish Armada*, 76.

43. Parker, *Grand Strategy*, 174. Parker writes: "The Spanish government never seems to have paused to consider how the inclusion of English and Hanseatic along with Dutch vessels might be interpreted in London." That the English were willing to sell out the Dutch was evident to them, and should have been evident to the Spanish, but was not. The king's diplomatic victory in isolating the Dutch from potential continental allies only nailed them to the English cause, whether they liked it or not, when the Armada sailed (Parker, 200). The Dutch learned the details of Anglo-Spanish negotiations in 1587 from a captured Spanish envoy, forcing the queen to reveal her apparent double-dealing.

44. For a discussion of the points made in this paragraph, see Geoffrey Parker, *The Imprudent King* (New Haven: Yale University Press, 2014), 305–307.

45. Parker, *Grand Strategy*, 180.

46. It is interesting that there is no evidence that the king, a sponsor of many complicated covert actions against the queen, ever contemplated one against Drake.

47. Philip's ambassador in London, de Espés, misjudged Hawkins's affinity with the Spanish cause, in part because he wanted to orchestrate Elizabeth's fall. Santa Cruz tended to underestimate the English navy and the viability of an amphibious invasion after his success in the Azores. Although Santa Cruz may have had an intelligence network in England as Alba and Parma almost certainly did, they were all likely compromised by the king's covert operations. Philip encouraged his emissaries to share information with each other and his councils, but required the best be sent "eyes only" to him.

48. Geoffrey Parker, "The Worst-Kept Secret in Europe? The European Intelligence Community and the Spanish Armada of 1588," in Keith Neilson and B. J. C. McKercher, eds., *Go Spy the Land: Military Intelligence in History* (Westport, CT: Praeger, 1992), 61.

49. Guy, *Tudor England*, 339–340.

50. His innovation was not just in building his fleet, but in equipping it with superior artillery. James and Mary Tudor maintained his fleet and, in fact, improved it.

51. See Chapter 2 for a discussion of the uncertainties surrounding naval construction during this period.

52. "The construction of sailing ships in general, and in particular of the carracks with their lofty 'forestages' . . . seemed to make it difficult if not impossible to mount heavy guns firing foreward." Nicholas A. M. Rodger, *The Safeguard of the Sea: A Naval History of Britain, 660–1649* (New York: W.W. Norton, 1997), 109. Rodger is widely considered the preeminent authority on English ships and naval warfare during this period.

53. This process of observation and adaptation cannot be considered intelligence, because Spain and England were at peace, and the sharing of knowledge flowed naturally from Philip's and Mary's joint governance.

54. Race-built galleons had sleek lines, reduced castles fore and aft used in the past for housing noble soldiers and their staff, and longer gun decks. The ships carried fewer soldiers and more sailors. See Martin and Parker, *The Spanish Armada*, 34. Maneuverability and superior artillery allowed the English ships to avoid Spanish

efforts to board them, which would have been fatal. For the Spanish underpinnings of the race-built galleon, see Angus Konstam, *Tudor Warships (2): Elizabeth I's Navy* (Oxford: Osprey Publishing, 2008).

55. Out of the thirty-four ships England had in her fleet in 1588, eleven had been built since 1584, and twelve of the others had been rebuilt along race-built lines. Martin and Parker, *The Spanish Armada*, 33. See Chapter 2 for additional information on the English race-built galleon and the development of doctrine for its use.

56. Neil Hanson, *The Confident Hope of a Miracle: The True History of the Spanish Armada* (New York: Vintage Books, 2006), 252.

57. For an extensive discussion of English and Spanish gunnery during this period, see Angus Konstam, *Sovereigns of the Sea: The Quest to Build the Perfect Renaissance Battleship* (Hoboken, NJ: John Wiley and Sons, 2008), 183–205.

58. Konstam, *Sovereigns of the Sea*, 204. The Spanish had access to Hawkins's flagship, the *Jesus of Lubeck*, after the battle in Mexico in 1568, so they would have known of the use of trucks for managing cannon fire. Awareness of the technical advance did not, however, change their approach to naval operations, which is testimony to the cognitive biases that operated then, as now, when trying to make sense of technological change.

59. Hawkins had commanded a small fleet that engaged in the slave trade between England, Africa, and the Spanish Main. While Hawkins was forever tainted by his treatment of slaves, Drake by all accounts found the work so morally objectionable that he refused later participation in it, and became renowned for the diversity of his crews and his willingness to ally and even defend native populations against their Spanish persecutors. By one account, Drake retaliated for the killing of an African boy he employed as a messenger by hanging two Spanish priests. He also burned part of the town where the incident took place in order to force the handover of the perpetrator, who was peremptorily killed by the Spanish.

60. Hawkins and his ship captains, including Francis Drake, had sought shelter to supposedly refit after a storm. A Spanish *flota* arrived and agreed to share the port peaceably. Suddenly the Spanish attacked the English ships. Only Drake's *Judith* and the *Minion*, now captained by Hawkins, got away. Hawkins's flagship, the *Jesus of Lubeck*, was destroyed, and most of his crewmen were killed or captured. Hawkins realized that Don Martín Enriquez, viceroy of New Spain, and Don Francisco de Luxán, commander of the Spanish *flota*, had conspired on the attack. The viceroy saw the English presence as an illegal infringement of Spanish rights west of "the line" and its laws regarding the licensing of trade in Spanish domains. The ambiguity of the situation made the incident provocative for both sides—a circumstance that was enflamed by the king's treatment of his English prisoners and Hawkins's attempts to get Spanish compensation for his losses.

61. According to one of Drake's biographers, "For the rest of his life Francis Drake pictured himself an avenger, bent upon rewarding the treachery of Don Martin Enriquez." Sugden, *Sir Francis Drake*, 38.

62. Arthur Nelson, *The Tudor Navy: The Ships, Men and Organization* (Annapolis, MD: Naval Institute Press, 2001), 1485–1603.

63. Konstam, *Tudor Warships (2)*, 13.

64. Konstam, *Tudor Warships (2)*, 13.

65. The *Foresight* was built, according to Konstam and Nelson, in 1570. Other authors claim it was later. Although resolving this discrepancy would seem to be essential to determining whether Hawkins originated the race-built design, his role in the English naval revolution more generally seems beyond doubt. See Nelson, *Tudor Navy*, 102.

66. Neil Hanson and a few other historians credit Mathew Baker with the primary redesign of the English ships. See Hanson's *Confident Hope*, 177–179.

67. Konstam, *Tudor Warships (2)*, 15. Konstam and Nelson (*Tudor Navy*) credit Hawkins with the design innovations. Other historians argue there is no proof the original designs were his, as opposed to the independent work of shipwrights Peter Pett and Matthew Baker. It would seem, however, that Baker got his expertise in how to correct sailing deficiencies from Hawkins. See Hanson, *Confident Hope*, 177.

68. Although Hawkins's employment in the queen's service could be explained by his familial connections to the treasurer of the navy and the queen's desire to keep him land-bound during a period of sensitive relations with Spain, two other factors suggest his continuing role reflected his deeper influence on decision-makers in the Privy Council and Royal Navy. The other key decision-maker on the Navy Board, in addition to Godson, was William Wynter, its surveyor and master of ordnance. Both Godson and Wynter had sensed the tension with Spain could develop into war and began looking for ways to improve the English navy's performance against the Spanish fleet. Tellingly, their campaign had involved the building of three new galleons in the "old way," based on Queen Mary's earlier program aping the Spanish ships. These new galleons of old design were the *Elizabeth Jonas* (1559), the *Triumph* (1561), and the *White Bear* (1563). The last of these was slightly beamier than the others, suggesting a merger of the Iberian emphasis on narrower length-to-beam ratios and the English emphasis on a stable gun platform. Thus it was that when Hawkins returned from his voyage in 1569, the Navy Board was not only prepared to listen to his ideas about how to redesign ships, but had begun a program themselves to do so, specifically to address the Spanish threat. Konstam, *Tudor Warships (2)*, 10–12. In making his pitch for the position of treasurer, however, Hawkins criticized the Wynter brothers for their keeping of the books and, in consultation with Baker and Pitt, assured the Board that the costs of the new navy could be lowered. See Harry Kelsey, *Sir John Hawkins: Queen Elizabeth's Slave Trader* (New Haven: Yale University Press, 2003), 153.

69. Konstam, *Tudor Warships (2)*, 25. This view seems supported by the fact that Baker and Pett met with Hawkins and helped him prepare his report to Cecil on the Navy Board's management of the books prior to his employment by the Crown. See Kelsey, *Sir John Hawkins*, 151.

70. John Sugden writes, "The changes have been attributed to John Hawkins . . . but they had an older history and were evident from the first years of Elizabeth's reign. If credit must be attached to particular individuals, it would more justifiably rest with William Winter [*sic*], who had been surveyor of the navy from 1549, and with the shipwrights, Richard Bull, Peter Pett and Matthew Baker." *Sir Francis Drake*, 231. This argument

follows Parker, but begs the question of why the changes were made at such expense and under the controversial guidance of Hawkins. The building of the *Foresight* in 1570 underpins Konstam's argument in favor of Hawkins and Chapman because the queen's shipwrights had not made significant changes in their designs at this point. Parker, however, records the *Foresight* as built in 1581. Parker, *Grand Strategy*, 254. Somerset also concludes that Hawkins was primarily responsible for the innovations. *Elizabeth I*, 453–454.

71. Konstam, *Sovereigns of the Sea*, 236.
72. Among other things, Hawkins revealed to a Spanish agent that his revolutionary ship, the *Foresight*, needed to be tested against the Spanish galleons. Kelsey, *Sir John Hawkins*, 113.
73. Martin and Parker, *The Spanish Armada*, 35, fig. 9.
74. Wynter was deeply enmeshed in the private-public partnership that underlay England's naval defenses. As a trusted admiral and naval official, William Wynter had helped support privateering in the Channel by fitting out small ships to attack and plunder Spanish ships ferrying goods to the Spanish Netherlands. Sugden, *Sir Francis Drake*, 45.
75. Hanson, *Confident Hope*, 179.
76. Martin and Parker, *The Spanish Armada*, 201.
77. It is important to note that the battle of Smerwick mostly involved firing against troops already ashore at the Golden Fort in County Kerry, not crippling a fleet bent on an amphibious assault.
78. Konstam, *Sovereigns of the Sea*, 136–160.
79. Most of the Spanish fleet sailed with plenty of guns, but many were old-fashioned wrought-iron, breech-loading types with heavy wooden carriages. The bronze guns they did have were often mounted on cumbersome two-wheeled carriages. The recoil on any of these weapons was destabilizing and prevented rapid reloading. This configuration contrasted sharply with the English "trucks," which allowed guns to be fired repeatedly and relatively easily during battles. Konstam, *Sovereigns of the Sea*, 202–203.
80. Konstam, *Sovereigns of the Sea*, 203.
81. Hanson, *Confident Hope*, 30.
82. Parker, *Grand Strategy*, 263.
83. Martin and Parker, *The Spanish Armada*, 124.
84. Martin and Parker, *The Spanish Armada*, 125.
85. Parker, *Imprudent King*, 309.
86. Hanson, *Confident Hope*, 182.
87. Parker, *Imprudent King*, 307.
88. Given Drake's modus operandi discussed below, penetration by Spanish agents would certainly have been possible. Yet there is no evidence that it was ever successful, let alone seriously attempted.
89. Interestingly, some of Drake's prisoners reported on the pirate and his ships once they were released and returned home. But most of them did little to deflate Drake's reputation, and largely confirmed what was already known about him and his ships.

90. Philip entertained many more than three strategies, as suggested earlier, but these were the most important ones.
91. See Chapter 2 on the problems of untimely communications in the mid-sixteenth century.
92. Given his concern for speed and secrecy, it seems strange that Parma chose to send his proposal to the king by the most circuitous and lengthy route possible, though this may have been done to ensure security.
93. Quoted from Martin and Parker, *The Spanish Armada*, 115.
94. Other members included Don Juan de Idiáquez, Basque secretary of state and member of Council of War; Don Cristobal de Moura, advisor on Portuguese affairs; and the Count of Chinchón.
95. Hanson, *Confident Hope*, 102.
96. Lord Howard was not only admiral of England but a Privy Councilor. His brother-in-law was Edward Stafford, who was England's ambassador to France and probably a double agent.
97. For discussion of the controversy concerning Stafford's role, see Parker, *Success Is Never Final*, 67–95. The author believes Stafford was a double agent, for reasons too lengthy to explain here. Stafford's role did not deliver a significant intelligence-advantage to the English or Spanish.
98. Nelson, *Tudor Navy*, 125.
99. Although tangential to the story of the Armada, it is worth noting that this prize also included much of the paperwork on the Portuguese trading operation out of India. This was a prize of a different kind, and Drake recognized it, bringing home the papers, providing them to the queen, and thus helping to launch the East India Company. See Nelson, *Tudor Navy*, 129.
100. She erred in this judgment, however, as Drake and the other captains knew that recruiting loyal crews was their key to success. They treated their men well, while enforcing strict discipline aboard ship. Lord Howard wrote to the queen to protest her treatment of veterans, noting that recruiting good seamen would be difficult if the Navy Royal could reliably offer neither pirate-prizes nor pay.
101. Nelson, *Tudor Navy*, 133. "Under sail alone" refers to the fact that soldiers would not be boarding and fighting each other for the win.
102. This was hardly surprising since Elizabeth had indicated the primacy of her own interests in this alliance. In mid-1587, she engaged with Parma in negotiations over a peace settlement that would have significantly compromised Dutch interests. Parma used the opportunity to press the siege of Sluys, which played into his plans for a combined operation to deceive the Dutch and wiggle his ships out of Flanders to ferry troops to Kent, in conformity with Philip's plan. The queen was, for her part, probably just buying time herself. She had sent Drake to harass Philip that same year, so she knew that negotiations were likely to break down in any case. See the excellent detail provided in Read, *Mr. Secretary Walsingham*, 262–263.
103. Burghley's man in the Netherlands was Andrea de Loo.
104. Not to be confused with Drake's *Golden Hind* of the same name.

105. Roughly half of these twelve hundred administered her various estates. This number compared with forty thousand officials serving the king of France, for example. See Budiansky, *Her Majesty's Spymaster*, 49.

106. Philip regarded himself as an expert on England long after his tenure on the English throne ended. He also continued to rely for years on men such as Count (later Duke) Feria for expertise—a man who had married one of Mary Tudor's aides and had been ambassador to England from 1557 to 1559.

107. Placed in power by the Privy Council and often members of it, JPs and provincial governors had a regularized system of communications with the court that reinforced both loyalty to London and regulations for the movement of resources from one province to another as national security might require.

Chapter 4

1. Colin Martin and Geoffrey Parker, *The Spanish Armada*, revised ed. (Manchester: Manchester University Press, 1999), 258.

2. This is exactly how this book is helping sharpen our understanding of intelligence.

3. Neil Hanson, *The Confident Hope of a Miracle: The True History of the Spanish Armada* (New York: Vintage Books, 2006), 111.

4. Hanson, *Confident Hope*, 116 (emphasis added).

5. Hanson, *Confident Hope*, 108.

6. Hanson, *Confident Hope*, 108.

7. Nassim Nicholas Taleb, *The Black Swan: The Impact of the Highly Improbable*, 2nd ed. (New York: Random House, 2010).

8. Hanson, *Confident Hope*, 199. All ships required that their hulls be scraped of barnacles, tarred to prevent rot, and treated against worms that could infest the wood. Pirates relied on speed more than most, so they careened their ships often. The process required beaching the craft, rolling it on its side, and literally scraping off debris. It was a time-consuming process that left crews vulnerable even as it allowed them to rest ashore.

9. "The wages being so small, cause the best men to run away, to bribe and make means to be cleared from the service and insufficient, unable and unskillful persons supply the place." Hanson, *Confident Hope*, 187.

10. "Proper" refers here to nonpiratical. The Spanish had known that pirates, privateers, and guerrilla naval operations were part of sixteenth-century naval warfare since at least the spring of 1523, when French corsairs began attacking Spanish treasure ships. Sea battles using warships were assumed to be different. Angus Konstam (author) and Angus McBride (illustrator), *The Elizabethan Sea Dogs, 1560–1605* (Oxford: Osprey Military, 2000), 24–26.

11. Hanson, *Confident Hope*, 203.

12. "Most of the Armada commanders had only the most limited charts." Hanson, *Confident Hope*, 110. Spain seems to have employed only two English pilots and one Flemish one. Hanson, 203.

13. The fate of the English Armada, also known as the Drake-Norris Expedition, which tried to attack Spain after the Armada's defeat, demonstrated the difficulties for the English in operations farther from their shores. In contrast, the Spanish needed covert or even open-source collection against tactical requirements when fighting in the Channel. As we know, however, Philip discounted the possibility that his admirals would have questions he had not foreseen.

14. See the author's "Foreign Intelligence Liaison: Devils, Deals, and Details." *International Journal of Intelligence and Counterintelligence* 19, no. 2 (Summer 2006): 195–217.

15. More than one counterintelligence expert has reminded us that there are no friends in intelligence. For one of the best books on this subject, see James M. Olson, *To Catch a Spy: The Art of Counterintelligence* (Washington, DC: Georgetown University Press, 2019). Olson is former chief of CIA counterintelligence.

16. Hanson, *Confident Hope*, 204.

17. In retrospect, the king's choices may seem silly, but modern decision-makers have failed in much the same way. Within the Warsaw Pact, Romania played both sides during the Cold War; Israel has run active spying operations against its allies; and the United States has spied on third parties within the borders of its NATO allies without their permission. Perhaps the most famous US case of "friends on friends" spying was the capture of Jonathan Pollard, an Israeli asset. Despite Israel's repeated requests for him to be released, the damage he caused to US intelligence was so grave that the United States refused to do so until 2020, when Pollard was permitted to leave for Israel. See Olson, *To Catch a Spy,* 164–170.

18. See the works of John MacGaffin, a US expert on all matters related to human intelligence, for more on this crucial subject. See, in particular, his "Clandestine Human Intelligence: Spies, Counterspies and Covert Action," in Jennifer E. Sims and Burton Gerber, eds., *Transforming US Intelligence* (Washington, DC: Georgetown University Press, 2005), 79–95.

19. MacGaffin, "Clandestine Human Intelligence."

20. Credit for this breakdown of the levels of counterintelligence belongs to MacGaffin, "Clandestine Human Intelligence," 82–83.

21. The US debate over how to handle industrial espionage in the 1990s was a case in point. The FBI wanted to liaise with private firms to protect them from the theft of their proprietary information, while CEOs worried about losing their right to overlook their own proprietary losses for business gains, and policymakers worried that selective protection would amount to back-door industrial policies.

22. See note 28 and Geoffrey Parker, *Success Is Never Final: Empire, War, and Faith in Early Modern Europe* (New York: Basic Books, 2002), 67–95, for a discussion of the Stafford case. My view differs from Parker's. There are indications Stafford was a "dangle"—bait for the gullible Spanish ambassador in Paris, Mendoza.

23. Some leaders want agents they can trust, so they look for those who agree with them politically. This is sometimes a smart choice, such as when engaging in civil war when sides to a dispute remain unclear and political screening becomes essential to counterintelligence. But political motives can also lead agents to lure their sponsors into their own favorite policies, including covert action.

24. Her desire to perpetuate this norm may have contributed to her uncertain handling of Dom Antonio's pretensions to the Portuguese throne after 1580, which enraged Philip, or order the death of her rival, Mary, Queen of Scots.

25. Hawkins likely did this more as a compartmented liaison operation with the Privy Council than under their direct control; for example, he almost certainly did not know that Ridolfi was working for the queen.

26. That he was working for Burghley in an effort to provide a more balanced picture to the queen seems validated by his generous treatment after the Armada and his service in Paris was over.

27. It is difficult to prove a historical figure acted as a double agent, but there are clues in this case. Stafford sent letters concerning his actual mission and loyalties to a trusted backup (in this case, a relative in England), which is a common double-agent practice to avoid retribution should his sponsors die or disavow him. He also had a plausible mission: the queen, pursuing deterrence as late as 1587, used Stafford to convince Philip that Anglo-French peace negotiations might succeed despite both countries' religious differences. Also, it is worth noting that she rewarded Stafford after the Armada was defeated. See note 253.

28. "Sir James Croft was semi-Catholic—he owed his appointment to Elizabeth's habit of balancing points of view." John Guy, *Tudor England* (New York: Oxford University Press, 1992), 279. Neil Hanson opines that Elizabeth I's "need for favorites and sycophants" explains why "she retained traitors such as the Staffords, Sir James Croft and Lord Henry Howard . . . and entrusted Sir Edward Stafford and Croft with two of the most crucial posts in the Armada years, when she must have known that all were at least sympathetic to Spanish aims and at worst—as was in fact the case—in Spanish pay." See *The Confidant Hope*, 48. Hanson is one of a group of historians who have argued, based on her decision-making style, that Elizabeth I was incapable of strategic thought. This case study argues just the opposite, supported by substantial evidence.

29. Geoffrey Parker, "Treason and Plot in Elizabethan Diplomacy: The 'Fame of Sir Edward Stafford' Reconsidered," in his *Success Is Never Final*, 67–95. His analysis of the Stafford affair is the best available. Although he discounts the possibility Stafford was a double agent, he provides evidence this was the case. Apparently, Stafford sent all copies of his dispatches to Lord Burghley, of whom he asked the following: "I beseech your Lordship [to] seal up this in another paper and to deliver ytt to my mother, sealed, as all coppyes that hereafter I shall send you." Parker notes that this request "marked an intrusion of bedchamber influence into foreign affairs not always communicated to the Privy Council" and increased the influence of Stafford's mother with the queen. It seems likely, however, that this was Stafford's effort to ensure that

evidence of his true loyalties had a second channel to the queen through a trusted route. This is common practice for double agents.

30. For an excellent discussion of the larger factors in play, see James M. McPherson, *Battle Cry of Freedom: The Civil War Era* (Oxford: Oxford University Press, 1988), especially 646–649 for factors prior to Gettysburg.

Chapter 5

1. These, however, were rather different traditions. Jackson championed the ideal of the citizen-soldier; Scott advocated more formalized, professional training for a regular army. This chapter relies on classics of American military history, especially Russell F. Weigley's *History of the United States Army*, enlarged ed. (Bloomington: Indiana University Press, 1984). Obviously, Jackson did not serve in the Civil War. He simply influenced its fighting methods.

2. "Most Civil War officers learned about the intelligence 'business' on the job." William B. Feis, *Grant's Secret Service: The Intelligence War from Belmont to Appomattox* (Lincoln: University of Nebraska Press, 2002), 3.

3. Edwin C. Fishel, *The Secret War for the Union: The Untold Story of Military Intelligence in the Civil War* (New York: Houghton Mifflin, 1996), 1.

4. See Russell F. Weigley, *The American Way of War: A History of United States Military Strategy and Policy* (Bloomington: Indiana University Press, 1973), especially 90–91, on the effects of rifles on battlefield engagements. This is a contentious issue discussed later in this chapter. The fact remains, however, that the *potential* killing radius of a soldier had increased even if these effects were not always realized in battle, and it is this uncertainty that concerns us here.

5. Fishel, *Secret War*, 1. For an insightful study of the role of civilian leaders in war, see Eliot A. Cohen, *Supreme Command: Soldiers, Statesmen and Leadership in Wartime* (Sioux City, IA: Anchor, 2003), especially 15–51.

6. For more on the impact of technological change on the mid-century battlefield and commanders' inexperience with it, see Mark Grimsley, "Surviving Military Revolution: The American Civil War," in McGregor Knox and Williamson Murray, eds., *The Dynamics of Military Revolution, 1300–2050* (New York: Cambridge University Press, 2001), 74–91. Also, Martin van Creveld, *Technology and War: From 2000 BC to the Present*, revised ed. (New York: Free Press, 1991), and Charles Ross, *Trial by Fire: Science, Technology and the Civil War* (Shippensburg, PA: White Maine Books, 2000).

7. Quoted from Thomas B. Buell, *The Warrior Generals: Combat Leadership in the American Civil War* (New York: Three Rivers Press, 1997), 199.

8. Strategic intelligence was important for the war overall. Lincoln and his secretary of state worked hard to uncover British intentions by cultivating espionage and open source networks in England. See, for example, David Hepburn Milton, *Lincoln's Spymaster: Thomas Haines Dudley and the Liverpool Network* (Mechanicsburg,

PA: Stackpole Books, 2003). For our purposes here, however, we will examine only the intelligence requirements of winning on the battlefield.

9. Earl B. McElfresh, *Maps and Mapmakers of the Civil War* (New York: Harry N. Abrams, 1999), 10.

10. Neil Kagan and Stephen J. Hyslop, eds., *Atlas of the Civil War* (Washington, DC: National Geographic, 2009), 9.

11. The flow of rivers from south to north in the Shenandoah Valley explains references to going "up" the Valley (south) and "down" the Valley (north) in accounts of the movements of troops at the time. This convention will be used here, as well.

12. The "Railroad and Township Map" series, published by Joseph H. Colton's New York firm, in particular, became valuable to Federal commanders during the course of the war. Kagan and Hyslop, *Atlas*, 9.

13. Jack Coggins, *Arms and Equipment of the Civil War* (Mineola, NY: Dover Publications, 1990), 99.

14. McElfresh, *Maps and Mapmakers*, 22.

15. McElfresh, *Maps and Mapmakers*, 22.

16. Kagan and Hyslop, *Atlas*, 9.

17. McElfresh, *Maps and Mapmakers*, 21.

18. William J. Miller, *Great Maps of the Civil War: Pivotal Battles and Campaigns Featuring 32 Removable Maps* (Nashville: Thomas Nelson, 2004), 14–15.

19. "Minutes on Council of War," July 9, 1861 *The War of the Rebellion: A Compilation of the Official Records of the Union and Confederate Armies*, Series I, vol. 2 (Washington, DC: US Government Publishing Office, n.d.) Author: US War Department, John Sheldon Moody, Calvin Duvall Cowles, Frederick Caryton Ainsworth, Robert N. Scott, Henry Martyn Lazelle, George Breckenridge Davis, Leslie J. Perry, Joseph William Kirkley. Located online at http://collections.library.cornell.edu/moa_new/waro.html; hereafter *OR*. Citations of official documents in this case study have been located at this site unless indicated otherwise.

20. *OR*. Emphasis has been added.

21. See Hotchkiss's first map in Miller, *Great Maps*, 6. Also see the excellent reproductions in McElfresh, *Maps and Mapmakers*.

22. Jedediah Hotchkiss, *Make Me a Map of the Valley* (Dallas: Southern Methodist University Press, 1973), 10.

23. Hotchkiss, *Make Me a Map*, 11. Hotchkiss went on to work under Confederate generals A. P. Hill, Ewell, and Early.

24. McElfresh, *Maps and Mapmakers*, 26–27.

25. The author was able to compare Hotchkiss's maps with Federal ones at an exhibition at the Shenandoah Valley Museum, held in cooperation with the National Archives, in 2008. It is important to keep in mind, however, the varying purposes for which maps were made when making such comparisons. Maps were not only created to inform tactics and operations, which required sensitivity to decision-makers' requirements, but to record the detailed, and often complex, outcomes of battle.

26. Hotchkiss also produced highly detailed, all-purpose maps and after-action maps designed to record major movements during a battle for the purposes of documenting

history. The point is that he understood the connection between what he was producing and what a commander needed at a particular moment.

27. See Robert Knox Sneden, *Eye of the Storm*, ed. Charles F. Bryan and Nelson D. Lankford (New York: Free Press, 2000). Also, Charles F. Bryan Jr., James C. Kelly, and Nelson D. Lankford, eds., *Images from the Storm: Robert Knox Sneden* (New York: Free Press, 2001).

28. Kagan and Hyslop, *Atlas*, 15.

29. Technologies other than those listed in the title of this section mattered to the outcome of the Civil War more generally, such as innovations in ship design, but we focus here on the sources of uncertainty in land battles.

30. Grimsley, "Surviving Military Revolution, 74–75."

31. See Cohen, *Supreme Command*, especially 15–51, for a study of civilian command, including the impact of telegraphy and the role of Lincoln in the Civil War.

32. Important innovations such as submarine and ironclad technologies, used along the coast and in inland waterways, will not be discussed here because they were not directly related to the battles in this case study.

33. Edwin B. Coddington, *The Gettysburg Campaign: A Study in Command* (New York: Simon and Schuster / Touchstone, 1997), 245.

34. Coddington, *Gettysburg Campaign*, 242.

35. Coddington, *Gettysburg Campaign*, 247.

36. Coddington, *Gettysburg Campaign*, 245–246. Coddington's descriptions of these issues are compelling. Earl J. Hess's work is, however, probably the best on the impact of weaponry, training, and doctrine on troop effectiveness during the American Civil War. See *The Rifle Musket in Civil War Combat: Reality and Myth* (Lawrence: University Press of Kansas, 2008) and *Civil War Infantry Tactics: Training, Combat, and Small-Unit Effectiveness* (Baton Rouge: Louisiana State University Press, 2015). Grimsley takes his analysis to another level by considering the larger sociopolitical dynamics.

37. Rifle-muskets were muzzle-loading single-shot weapons manufactured with rifling for extended range and accuracy. Rifled muskets were smoothbore muzzle-loading, single-shot weapons that were modified with rifling after their initial manufacture. Most of the discussion in this section relies on the important work of Earl J. Hess and Mark Grimsley, updating the standard history found in such classic works as Weigley's *American Way of War* and Coddington's *Gettysburg Campaign*.

38. See for example, Weigley, *American Way of War*, 90–91.

39. Hess, *Rifle Musket*, 38.

40. Hess, *Rifle Musket*, 39.

41. Hess, *Rifle Musket*, 42.

42. Coddington, *Gettysburg Campaign*, 256.

43. Edward Porter Alexander, *Fighting for the Confederacy: The Personal Recollections of General Edward Porter Alexander*, ed. Gary W. Gallagher (Chapel Hill: University of North Carolina Press, 1989), 121–122.

44. Weigley, *American Way of War*, 90. Notice the difference here with Alexander's estimate at the time, cited above.

45. Hess, *Rifle Musket*, 27. Worries about the cost, ammunition requirements, and reliability of breech-loading rifles meant that the US Army was not equipped with these relatively rapid-firing weapons as standard issue during the war, though they were available as early as the 1850s. Hess, 26.

46. Hess, *Rifle Musket*, 27. Thanks to historian Earl J. Hess and others, we now know the new technologies probably only had a marginal impact on killing zones in actual firefights. For a different view, see the debate referenced in notes 51 and 52 below.

47. Hess, *Civil War Infantry Tactics*, 33.

48. John Hennessy, *The First Battle of Manassas: An End to Innocence, July 18–21, 1861,* 2nd ed. (Lynchburg: H.E. Howard, 1989), 72.

49. Hardee's book, *Rifle and Light Infantry Tactics,* was adopted in 1855. Both sides in the US Civil War used this manual or other versions of it. Hess, *Civil War Infantry Tactics*, 30–31.

50. Hess, *Civil War Infantry Tactics*, 31. The statistics Hess has uncovered make his case strong and one many Civil War scholars find convincing. (Personal correspondence with Professor Mark Grimsley, December 2017–March 2018.)

51. Other factors also played starring roles in these disasters. Grant was forced to delay his attack at Cold Harbor, for example, allowing Lee to erect fortifications. Burnside also had trouble synchronizing his forces. He ignored seemingly good intelligence on the Confederate defenses the day of the attack on Maryes Heights. See Fishel, *Secret War,* 268–270. Yet, in commenting on the results of the Peninsula Campaign of 1862, the US Army historian Russell F. Weigley, has written: "The war was beginning to reveal that rifled weapons extracted horrendous losses from the makers of such (Napoleonic) attacks." *American Way of War,* 106.

52. See Coddington, *Gettysburg Campaign,* 242–259, and Earl J. Hess's excellent works *Civil War Infantry Tactics* and *Rifle Musket* for good discussions of the problem of ordnance and tactics. See Cohen, *Supreme Command,* 23–25 and note 51 above for a different view.

53. Union general George McClellan's letters reveal that he either appreciated the uncertainties weaponry had introduced, or he was unwilling to pay the price of war with the lives of men. As he wrote to Colonel E. D. Townsend on July 5, 1861, "Assure the General [Winfield Scott] that no prospect of a brilliant victory shall induce me to depart from my intention of gaining success by maneuvering rather than by fighting; I will not throw these men of mine into the teeth of artillery and entrenchments, if it is possible to avoid it." Stephen W. Sears, ed., *The Civil War Papers of George B. McClellan: Selected Correspondence, 1860–1865* (Boston: Da Capo Press, 1992), 45.

54. Sears, *Civil War Papers,* 363. The ballistic trajectory of rifle-muskets had a higher parabola than that of smoothbores, so aiming at closer targets required a lower elevation of the barrel.

55. John Emmet O'Brien, *Telegraphing in Battle: Reminisces of the Civil War* (Scranton: Forgotten Books, 2012, originally published 1910), 27. Emphasis added.

56. Southern states each had responsibility for equipping their own militias, and the discretion on how to do so was broad. At the same time, Richmond required all states to turn over stockpiles of arms to the Confederacy, with varying results. "Procurement

and issue of arms at the general government and state levels continued on a com-
petitive basis in the South as it did in the North, but usually with far less harmony."
Frederick P. Todd, *American Military Equipage, 1851–1872*, vol. 2 (Providence,
RI: Company of Military Historians, 1977), 445.

57. Todd, *American Military Equipage*, 445.
58. Eliot A. Cohen has documented the president's pressure, especially early in the war,
for the distribution of breechloaders. He also holds to the traditional view that rifles
mattered to tactical outcomes in the war. See his *Supreme Command*, 24–25. As Jack
Coggins has written, "It is hard to understand why the Federal government never
made a determined effort to arm the troops with breechloaders. There was no question as to their effectiveness, and the men were so anxious to have them that in many
cases companies would save their small pay and purchase the arms themselves." See
Coggins, *Arms and Equipment*, 28.
59. "It is plain that a less conservative approach to the problem of the ideal weapon might
have shortened the war and saved tens of thousands of lives. It was a great tragedy
for the North that, despite the wealth of ideas, technical ability, and manufacturing
facilities at its disposal, the head of the Bureau of Ordnance should have hindered
the adoption of the very weapons which might have brought speedy victory to the
Union." Coggins, *Arms and Equipment*, 28.
60. Fred B. Wrixon, *Codes, Ciphers, Secrets and Cryptic Communication: Making and
Breaking Secret Messages from the Hieroglyphs to the Internet* (New York: Black Dog
and Leventhal, 1998), 53–55.
61. William R. Plum, *The Military Telegraph during the Civil War in the United States,
with an Exposition of Ancient and Modern Means of Communication, and of the
Federal and Confederate Cipher Systems*, 2 vols. (Forgotten Books, 2012; http://
www.forgottenbooks.org), vol. 1, 62, originally published (Chicago: Jansen,
McClurg & Co., 1888).
62. Henry worked independently of the English scientist Michael Faraday, who was first
to publish the discovery.
63. Telegraphy is the long-distance signaling of messages using code. The electrical telegraph and flag signaling were the principal forms of telegraphy during the US Civil
War. For the remainder of this volume, "telegraphy" will refer to the electrical form,
unless otherwise specified.
64. Cohen, *Supreme Command*, 27.
65. There were three major telegraph companies in 1861. The first was the American
Telegraph Company, which extended lines east of the Hudson River through New
England and west as far as Ohio, then also along the Atlantic seaboard and the Gulf to
New Orleans. The Western Union Telegraph Company joined up with the American's
northern lines and extended them westward as far as San Francisco (by 1862). The
Southwestern Telegraph Company, whose headquarters were in Louisville, Kentucky,
linked with American's seaboards lines in the South and extended them inland, and
as far west as Texas.
66. Fishel, *Secret War*, 12.
67. Fishel, *Secret War*, 11–12.

68. The first Union censor was a Mr. A. Watson from the War Department, who inspected every incoming and outgoing message, once communications were restored. When Southern colleagues asked why their communications remained unanswered (on the nineteenth and twentieth) operators were told to reply, "It's none of your business." Plum, *Military Telegraph*, vol. 1, 64.

69. The railroads relied on telegraphers to run their trains, so railroad companies had a number of skilled operators well trained in Morse code for that purpose. Later, they adopted a transposition cipher for military communications.

70. Plum, *Military Telegraph*, vol. 1, 68.

71. Fishel, *Secret War*, 18. The line from Alexandria to Richmond remained open until the capture of the former on the twenty-fourth. According to Plum, little could have been done to repair communications without private-sector cooperation and financing. "Colonel Scott invested David Strouse with powers to erect and maintain such Federal telegraphs as should be required by the military authorities at Washington and in the Department of the Potomac, but left him dependent upon the American Telegraph Company for nearly every dollar necessarily expended in building, operating and maintaining such lines." See Plum, *Military Telegraph*, vol. 1, 68.

72. O'Brien, *Telegraphing in Battle*, 21.

73. O'Brien, *Telegraphing in Battle*, 32. The Stager transposition cipher was named after Anson Stager, once superintendent of Western Union Telegraph Company, then reporting to the governor of Ohio for military purposes, then on May 27 becoming superintendent for all military purposes of all the telegraphic lines within the Department of Ohio (West Virginia, Ohio, Indiana, and Illinois). For the cipher see Wrixon, *Codes, Ciphers, Secrets*.

74. Wrixon, *Codes, Ciphers, Secrets*, 62.

75. Unschooled in Morse telegraphy, Myer helped develop a competing system for encoded communications on wires that was easier to operate but underpowered and vulnerable to disruption. Initially championed by the Signal Corps, this competing system was abandoned after Chancellorsville—a clue to part of what went wrong for the Union during that battle.

76. See Wrixon, *Codes, Ciphers, Secrets*, 56–57.

77. The railroad-trained professionals contended that the accessibility of their rival's easier to use but underpowered system was not worth the loss in efficiency per mile offered by the tried-and-true railroad equipment. Field disputes complicated decision-making for commanders in the field.

78. For example, a telegrapher angered cavalry officers by reporting gaps in pickets before Chancellorsville—gaps that Colonel John Mosby's Confederate raiders eventually exploited in capturing General Stoughton on raids near Fairfax Station. Fishel, *Secret War*, 326.

79. See Eric Wittenberg and David Petruzzi, *Plenty of Blame to Go Around: Jeb Stuart's Controversial Ride to Gettysburg* (New York: Savas Beatie, 2011), 264–265. These authors relieve Stuart of much responsibility for the failure, however, and place most of it at Robertson's feet.

80. See Plum, *Military Telegraph* for excellent accounts of Civil War telegraphy.

81. Sherman, in fact, spared a journalist from execution after he discovered and reported an intercepted and deciphered Southern telegram, prompting the Confederacy to change their codes. That newsman's near execution by firing squad prompted others to exercise more caution. See Buell, *Warrior Generals*, 360.

82. Stephen Z. Starr, *The Union Cavalry in the Civil War: From Fort Sumter to Gettysburg, 1861–1863*, vol. 1 (Baton Rouge: Louisiana State University Press, 1979), 60. This volume discusses the history of the prewar cavalry and the sources of Confederate advantages in 1861 at some length (especially 47–61).

83. Phil Livingston and Ed Roberts, *War Horse: Mounting the Cavalry with America's Finest Horses* (Albany, TX: Bright Sky Press, 2003), 44–45. Apart from a limited number of dragoons (mounted infantrymen), the US had not invested much in cavalry before 1832, when it organized a battalion of self-supplied mounted rangers for controlling the state's rapidly expanding territories. The following year, that effort was disbanded in favor of a regiment of dragoons to fight the Indian tribes of the western Plains. Eventually, Congress realized the need to organize a cavalry, and created the first and second Cavalry Regiments.

84. James M. McPherson, *The Battle Cry of Freedom: The Civil War Era* (New York: Oxford University Press, 1988), 40.

85. McPherson, *Battle Cry of Freedom*, 40.

86. Apart from a limited number of dragoons, the United States did not invest much in cavalry before 1832, when it organized a battalion of self-supplied mounted rangers for controlling the state's rapidly expanding territories. The following year, that effort was disbanded in favor of a regiment of dragoons to fight the Indian tribes of the western Plains. Eventually Congress realized the need to organize a cavalry, and created the First and Second Cavalry Regiments.

87. For more on how crucial horsemanship was to cavalry operations—including such seemingly inconsequential but critical issues as recognizing correctly sized horseshoes—see Wittenberg and Petruzzi, *Plenty of Blame*, 276–278.

88. Lynne Raff, *My Heart Is Too Full to Say More: The Horse in the Civil War* (Beaumont, TX: Art Horse Press, 2010), 117–118.

89. Prior to the war, the US Army had only limited cavalry operations. Wars with the British had not involved cavalry in any significant degree. Growing confrontations with Native Americans had begun, however, to expose the imbalance between cavalry and infantry, and in 1832 Congress authorized the first dragoons and, eventually, cavalry. They were limited in their training and in the supply of good horses. See Livingston and Roberts, *War Horse*, 43–51. Some officers had cavalry experience, of course. Men like Captain George A. Custer and General Alfred Pleasanton were excellent, experienced horsemen; their reputations were burnished by their mastery of their horses.

90. Raff, *My Heart*, 26. These comparisons are broad generalizations. Obviously, there were fine horsemen in both Union and Confederate armies even at the start of the war. But the overall superiority of the Confederate horse and rider was commonly known, even at the time.

91. The Union cavalry's lack of horses meant that "for the first few months the men simply performed their cavalry drills and training on foot." Raff, *My Heart*, 25–26.

92. Livingston and Roberts, *War Horse*, 44–45. "On July 28, 1863, the Union Army set up the Cavalry Bureau within the Office of the Quartermaster General. By then, Union forces were requiring up to 500 remounts per week." Livingston and Roberts, 45.

93. Wars with the British had not involved cavalry in any significant degree. Growing confrontations with Native Americans had begun, however, to expose the imbalance between cavalry and infantry and, in 1832 Congress authorized the first dragoons and, eventually, cavalry. They were limited in their training and in the supply of good horses. See Livingston and Roberts, *War Horse*, 43–51.

94. Raff, *My Heart*, 26.

95. Quoted in Raff, *My Heart*, 26.

96. E. D. Townsend, assistant adjutant-general, to Patterson, July 7, 1861.

97. Buell, *Warrior Generals*, 209.

98. Stephen W. Sears, *Chancellorsville* (Boston: Houghton Mifflin, 1996), 91.

99. See Raff, *My Heart*, 117–118.

100. "The cavalry of the South, who brought to their job their tradition of horsemanship and the proper care of horses, hit the ground running well in advance of the Union Cavalry." Raff, *My Heart*, 17. Also see Coddington, *Gettysburg Campaign*, 259: "Stuart could well boast of the verve, the dash and the skill of his riders, for as expert cavalrymen they had no peers. Their disadvantage lay in mediocre equipment and inadequate arms."

101. See Christopher Andrew, *For the President's Eyes Only: Secret Intelligence and the American Presidency from Washington to Bush* (New York: Harper Perennial, 1996), 20. Andrew does not take a position on the utility of balloons, but notes that Lincoln did: he supported the creation of the first balloon corps.

102. Gary W. Gallagher, ed., *Fighting for the Confederacy* (Chapel Hill: University of North Carolina Press, 1989), 115.

103. Gallagher, *Fighting for the Confederacy*, 115.

104. Fishel, *Secret War*, 5. Artillerists tried to shoot down balloons but were never successful. Signal stations were also repeatedly targeted with a good rate of success.

105. See Charles M. Evans, *War of the Aeronauts: A History of Ballooning in the Civil War* (Mechanicsburg, PA: Stackpole Books, 2002), for an interesting history of ballooning.

106. Evans, *War of the Aeronauts*, 50–52. Lowe's monster balloon initially failed because the maximum rate of inflation in New York was insufficient to compensate for the loss of gas through the woven silk envelope. The ship, renamed the *Great Western*, successfully ascended for Lowe's later experimental flight out of Philadelphia. Evans, 56–57.

107. Evans, *War of the Aeronauts*, 56. Lowe lifted off from Philadelphia, traveled to Atlantic City, New Jersey, and then returned within eighteen miles of his launching point.

108. See Stephen Poleskie, *The Balloonist: The Story of T.S.C. Lowe—Inventor, Scientist, Magician and Father of the U.S. Air Force* (Savannah, GA: Frederick C. Beil, 2007), 70–84 for the entire story of this escapade.

109. See Evans, *War of the Aeronauts*, 60–62 and 84–87 for more on the military's resistance to balloons, especially during the Mexican war. The location proposed for aerial bombardment by balloon was San Juan de Ulúa, of all places—the same place that, in 1571, Sir Francis Drake had his revelation about how to redesign galleons for effective bombardment from the sea. Evans, 61.

110. See Evans, *War of the Aeronauts*, 117–121, for a discussion of the logistics of transporting and inflating Lowe's Civil War balloons.

111. Evans, *War of the Aeronauts*, 92–93. The head of the Smithsonian at the time validated the potential of the new airborne platform and argued repeatedly for patience with the technology despite early failures. In a letter to Simon Cameron, secretary of war, Joseph Henry (of telegraph fame) provided assurances that the balloon prepared by Lowe, inflated with ordinary street gas, would retain its charge for several days; be easily towed in an inflated condition for twenty or more miles, given normal conditions; permit observation for twenty miles or more, depending on the weather, light, and length of tether; permit telegrams to be "sent with ease and certainty between the balloon and the quarters of the commanding officer"; and probably could conduct round-trips by exploiting wind currents at varying altitudes. Henry went on to convey his judgment that, by using Lowe's balloons, "information may be obtained in regard to the topography of the country and to the position and movements of an enemy" and that "Mr. Lowe is well qualified to render service in this way." He also pointed out, however, that "the balloon which Mr. Lowe now has in Washington can only be inflated in a city where street gas is to be obtained." Long-distance reconnaissance would be more difficult and costly to execute.

112. The aeronauts' superiors in the Signal Corps were often skeptical of the utility of balloons and complained of difficulties finding sufficient men to support operations.

113. Thomas B. Allen and Roger McBride Allen, *Mr. Lincoln's High-Tech War: How the North Used the Telegraph, Railroads, Surveillance, Balloons, Ironclads, High-Tech Weapons and More to Win the Civil War* (Washington, DC: National Geographic Books, 2009), 42.

114. Alexander, *Fighting for the Confederacy*, 115.

115. See Mark Grimsley, *The Hard Hand of War: Union Military Policy toward Southern Civilians, 1861–1865* (Cambridge: Cambridge University Press, 1995), for more on this important and misunderstood issue.

116. Sears, *Civil War Papers*, 45.

117. Gallagher, *Fighting for the Confederacy*, 124.

118. Fishel, *Secret War*, 14.

119. Federal officials seized all telegraphic messages from Richmond on May 20, 1861, that had accumulated over the previous twelve months, including the time during which Union use of the lines had been suspended in order to uncover potential traitors. The effort was hampered, however, when the American Telegraph Company

took the unilateral decision to sever the line from Washington to Richmond only two days later.

120. Virginia was not entirely loyal to Richmond, either. Thomas B. Buell has noted, for example, that Virginia residents living in the western Allegheny Mountains opposed secession. See his book *Warrior Generals*, 45.

121. See Ann Blackman, *Wild Rose* (New York: Random House, 2005), for an example of a well-researched study but an incomplete analysis in these regards.

122. The secret power of covert action is the capacity to fuse *intelligence gathering* and decisive *action* together. The modern definition of covert action, however, implies secret sponsorship by a foreign state of open activity, such as riots or sabotage by a lone entity. Lone-wolf saboteurs do not fit that definition, though they may be designated criminals, assassins, or terrorists. While covert action requires intelligence to succeed, and is often therefore, executed by intelligence agencies, it requires more than intelligence alone; it involves the execution of policy, whether political, military, or economic in nature.

123. Fishel, *Secret War*, 257.

124. Proper use of terminology is important here: "Covert" activity, whether "action" or "espionage," signifies *open activity* (whether by agitation or passive observation) that is *clandestinely sponsored*. "Clandestine" activity is hidden both in its sponsorship and in its execution.

125. Fishel, *Secret War*, 11. Fishel notes that Scott's conversation with Lee lasted three hours, before Lee made his decision to serve the South.

126. See Grimsley, *Hard Hand of War*, for an extensive and excellent review of Union military views toward Southern civilians during the conflict.

127. See Sears, *Civil War Papers*, McClellan to Townsend, July 5, 1861, 45.

128. Feis, *Grant's Secret Service*, 197. Grenville Dodge, Grant's secret service chief during and subsequent to his Vicksburg Campaign, achieved successes similar to the BMI's.

129. The distinction is explained in Chapter 1 of this volume.

130. After Pinkerton went to battle with McClellan, Lafayette C. Baker, chief of the War Department's National Detective Bureau, further developed the Union's counterintelligence capabilities in Washington. Besides searching for spies, he focused on investigating fraud and corruption while earning a reputation for being corrupt himself—a reputation only partially assuaged by his successful tracking of John Wilkes Booth after Lincoln's assassination. William B. Feis, "That Essential of Success," in Aaron Sheehan-Dean, ed., *Struggle for a Vast Future: The American Civil War* (Oxford: Osprey Publishing, 2006), 156–157.

131. If an enemy's intelligence efforts are known to be misleading them, counterintelligence officials might find gain in letting them continue, while security officials would not, and could not, do so, since their mission involves defending against theft at all costs.

132. CIA, Office of Public Affairs (Thomas Allen), *Intelligence in the Civil War* (Washington, DC: Central Intelligence Agency, Office of Public Affairs, 2012).

133. Fishel, *Secret War*, 120. The report may not have been accurate, however.

134. Elizabeth Van Lew ran more than twelve agents, passing messages in hollowed-out eggs, baked goods, and sewing patterns. Her reports included the location of new artillery batteries, the reasons for diminishing cavalry (Lee's shortage of horses), and the conditions and movements of prisoners of war. See CIA's *Intelligence in the Civil War*, 20.

135. Fishel, *Secret War*, 552.

136. Feis, "Great Essential of Success," 165.

137. Feis, "Great Essential of Success," 155.

138. Adam Goodheart, *1861: The Civil War Awakening* (New York: Alfred A. Knopf, 2011), 159.

139. Goodheart, *1861*, 160. This number was, according to Goodheart, "several thousand fewer than the rebel forces at Charlestown alone."

140. Sears, *Chancellorsville*, 43–44.

141. J. H. Stine, *History of the Army of the Potomac* (Washington, DC: Gibson Bros., 1893), 314–315.

142. It is also important to recall that this study only examines intelligence in support of battlefield decision-making. Intelligence operations in support of covert action to alter political outcomes, such as the November 1864 presidential elections in the North, are not covered here. See Feis, "Great Essential of Success," 154–157, for more on this.

143. A note on terminology: An "agent" is a hired source. A "double agent" is a source two services have hired, but who is actually only working for one—usually against the other. (There is really no such thing as a "triple agent" in modern professional terminology. An agent is either doubled or not.) A "dangle" is an agent one side uses as bait in hopes of creating a double agent, while a "turned" agent is a source once working for one side but since "doubled" by the other. Technically, a "mole" is similar to a "double agent" in that he or she is embedded in one intelligence service but actually works for another. The difference is that a "mole" is not necessarily a source or agent for the other side (e.g., he or she could be an analyst). An "operative" is an intelligence official executing intelligence or political policies in the field.

Chapter 6

1. William B. Feis, "That Great Essential of Success: Espionage, Covert Action and Military Intelligence," in Aaron Sheehan-Dean, ed., *Struggle for a Vast Future* (Oxford: Osprey Publishing, 2006), 153.

2. Notable exceptions include Edwin C. Fishel, *The Secret War for the Union: The Untold Story of Military Intelligence in the Civil War* (New York: Houghton Mifflin, 1996), and Stephen W. Sears, *Chancellorsville* (Boston: Houghton Mifflin, 1996). Historians have blamed General George McClellan's failed Peninsula Campaign on his faulty intelligence, including overestimation of the enemy.

3. Stephen W. Sears, *Gettysburg* (Boston: Houghton Mifflin, 2003), 106.

4. The Confederates termed the battle "First Manassas," while the Federals referred to it as "First Bull Run." This volume will adhere to the Confederate name since the South won this battle.

5. Virginia's electorate endorsed secession on 23 May. Russell H. Beatie, *Army of the Potomac*, vol. 1, *Birth of Command, November 1860–September 1861* (Cambridge, MA: Da Capo Press, 2002), 153.

6. Although the president had rejected Scott's plan, it served as the underpainting of Federal strategy and decision-making until the close of the war. See Donald Stoker, *The Grand Design: Strategy and the US Civil War* (Oxford: Oxford University Press, 2010), 411.

7. "It had been given out by prominent men and officials that it would be a short war; Secretary Seward placed its duration at sixty days, therefore the first volunteers were called for ninety days only." J. H. Stine, *A History of the Army of the Potomac* (Washington, DC: Gibson Bros., 1893), 1.

8. He did so on 4 July in an address to the joint houses of Congress. Stoker, *Grand Design*, 40.

9. Fishel, *Secret War*, 31. A preliminary meeting had been held on 25 June, but McDowell had been unable to attend. Attendees on the twenty-fifth included the president, Mansfield, Winfield Scott, General Montgomery Meigs, and Lincoln's cabinet.

10. McDowell was named to this position on 28 May 1861. The problem of rank confused and delayed early decision-making in Washington. In early 1861, governors still had the power to appoint general officers, so a state was able to endow an individual with a rank that other states' troops and officers had to acknowledge when mustering for a Federal force. Sandford was a major general in New York who, to follow his troops to Washington, had to waive rank so that he would not be reporting to a Federal officer (Mansfield) of lesser rank. A general order would soon curtail governors' authorities in these matters.

11. Beatie, *Army of the Potomac*, 205.

12. Stine, *Army of the Potomac*, 1–4. Matters of policy and command that had divided Lincoln's advisors since March seemed settled by the Confederacy's growing strength and belligerency, and with the selection of the Union's new major generals: Frémont, Halleck, and McClellan.

13. Bradley M. Gottfried, *The Maps of First Bull Run: An Atlas of the First Bull Run (Manassas) Campaign, including the Battle of Ball's Bluff, June–October 1861* (New York: Savas Beatie, 2009), 2.

14. Beatie, *Army of the Potomac*, 206. Scott thought the prospect unlikely.

15. Beatie, *Army of the Potomac*, 87. In fact, this statement was broadly untrue if horsemanship, skills with firearms, and knowledge of terrain were taken into account. See the previous chapter.

16. For a good recounting of these problems, see Eliot A. Cohen, *Supreme Command: Soldiers, Statesmen and Leadership in Wartime* (Sioux City, IA: Anchor, 2003), 15–51.

17. Scott earned fame for his victory at Veracruz during the Mexican-American War.

18. Doris Kearns Goodwin, *Team of Rivals: The Political Genius of Abraham Lincoln* (New York: Simon and Schuster Paperbacks, 2006), 338–340. Lincoln dispatched a long-time friend, Stephen Hurlbut, to Charleston to ascertain whether or not there might be hope, as Seward was suggesting, that public sentiment would grow Unionist over time if Lincoln abandoned Sumter without a fight. Hurlbut reported the contrary: "Unionist sentiment in the city and state was dead," and "Separate nationality was a fixed fact." The report helped consolidate Lincoln's determination to resupply the fort. Goodwin, 348.

19. Goodwin, *Team of Rivals*, 369.

20. John Hennessy, *First Battle of Manassas: An End to Innocence, July 18–21, 1861*, 2nd ed. (Lynchburg: H.E. Howard, 1989), 5.

21. Stine, *Army of the Potomac*, 2–3. Goodwin, *Team of Rivals*, 365.

22. Goodwin, *Team of Rivals*, 366.

23. Similar problems would show up on the brink of battle as two balloonists with competing orders fought for access to equipment for inflating their envelopes.

24. See the previous chapter for more background on this conflict.

25. The fort's brewing problems managing its telegraphers were probably just reaching the War Department as the council met; relatively slow steamers were still the principal means of communication with coastal places as distant as Newport News. No military telegraph line could be extended that far in early 1861. Howe's ascents at Falls Church established the Confederate presence at Fairfax.

26. Charles M. Evans, *War of the Aeronauts: A History of Ballooning in the Civil War* (Mechanicsburg, PA: Stackpole Books, 2002), 75.

27. Evans, *War of the Aeronauts*, 75.

28. Evans, *War of the Aeronauts*, 6. The question of whom Scott supported is not resolved by the historical record. Fishel, for example, seems to believe Scott preferred Mansfield (*Secret War*, 35).

29. The agents reported to Parsons, the head of the espionage unit under Mansfield. After the battle, Parsons said his men were ill-used, and that had they been properly heard, the battle would likely have ended differently. See Fishel, *Secret War*, 34–35.

30. Likely by the name of William Johnston; see Fishel, *Secret War*, 34–35.

31. Colonel Stone, who had been working his way up along the Potomac to secure lines to Harpers Ferry, supported Patterson's views. He, too, was relentless in his requests for help in securing Harpers Ferry, the upper Potomac, and its canals, which were necessary for Patterson's resupply. Federals had already lost control of the lower Potomac when, in response to Lincoln's announced embargo of Southern ports in April, the Confederates had built artillery batteries at Aquia Creek (Stafford County) and Cockpit Point (Prince William County), effectively blocking shipping. John S. Salmon, *The Official Virginia Civil War Battlefield Guide* (Mechanicsburg, PA: Stackpole Books, 2001), 5–6.

32. The maps were apparently devoid of engineering notes regarding the fordability of streams, the strength of bridges, and the like.

33. William R. Plum, *The Military Telegraph during the Civil War in the United States, with an Exposition of Ancient and Modern Means of Communication, and of the Federal*

and Confederate Cipher Systems, vol. 1 (Forgotten Books, 2012; http://www.forgott enbooks.org), 73.

34. Bradley M. Gottfried has suggested that modern scholarship is concluding that Patterson should not have been essential to McDowell's strategy, since the latter expected to fight reinforcements from the South that never showed; Johnston's forces were just substitutes coming from a different direction. This argument is flawed for reasons made clear in the prior chapter. McDowell explicitly stated that any support to Beauregard from Johnston's *demonstrably effective forces*, which included Jackson and the troops that had captured Harpers Ferry, would make his plan too risky. In this, he was right. *Maps of First Bull Run*, map 2, note 4, 113.

35. Evans, *War of the Aeronauts*, 80. See also 74–75.

36. Fishel, *Secret War*, 36. This spy's first report in May covered the number, positions, and ranges of enemy batteries along the Potomac near Harpers Ferry; the disruption to railways on the Maryland side of the river; the number of cavalry; the extent of Confederate pickets around Harpers Ferry; and the fortifications, cannon, and troops along the Maryland Heights opposite the ferry. In fact, Beauregard actually had about fifteen thousand troops by that time, and McDowell's were growing.

37. *OR*, Col. Stone to Lt. Col. E. D. Townsend, Assistant Adjutant-General, Poolesville, June 15 and 16, 1861; Chapter 9, 108–109.

38. Fishel considers Mason's recollection an error and that Mason actually learned of the fallback to Winchester on his *third* trip.

39. What the maps did not show was how little was known about the terrain around Bull Run, ignorance of which proved to be another obstacle to McDowell's plan.

40. General Butler and Fort Monroe was the locus of both fights. Butler, suffering from the effects of a failed operation at Big Bethel, had called for help from John La Mountain, a civilian balloonist eager for a role. Mountain's move to Fort Monroe contributed to the dust-up already underway between Howe and John Wise, who underbid Howe at the last minute, getting the formal nod for support to military operations prior to the battle. The confusion debilitated the operations of both aeronauts throughout July. See Evans, *War of the Aeronauts*, 74–85.

41. *OR*, Col. Stone to Lt. Col. E. D. Townsend, June 17, 1861; Chapter 9, 110–111.

42. *OR*, Col. Stone to Lt. Col. Townsend; Chapter 9, 109.

43. See Plum, *The Military Telegraph*, 74. Plum writes: "It is sufficient to say that Generals Scott and Patterson seem not to have properly understood one another, owing in a large part to a lack of telegraphic services" (74).

44. Beatie, *Army of the Potomac*, 205.

45. John Emmet O'Brien, *Telegraphing in Battle: Reminisces of the Civil War* (Scranton, PA: Forgotten Books, 2012), 21.

46. Plum, *The Military Telegraph*, 74.

47. Plum, *The Military Telegraph*, 74.

48. See J. H. Stine's *Army of the Potomac*, 10. In Stine's version of the events, Scott is intensely critical of McDowell's plan. He is recorded as saying that if McDowell's strategy depended on Patterson holding Johnston in check, then "his plan was not

worth the paper it was drawn on." Although Stine's version does not comport with the record, it may have reflected Scott's later doubts.

49. Baker's memoir is, according to most historians, an exaggerated account of his exploits. Fishel, a more trustworthy source on Baker, writes: "A week before the army marched for Bull Run, Baker was sent South, not by Brigadier General Irvin McDowell, who was to command the field army, but by General Scott." *Secret War*, 25.

50. If Beauregard were to spearhead the counterattack, he would need Davis's backing to get the higher-ranking Johnston to support him with a flanking maneuver that would bring Johnston across Patterson's front. In this event, Patterson was well positioned. Alternatively, if Johnston were to command some combination of Confederate forces between Winchester and Manassas, then Patterson's hope of catching him was slim, given Patterson's logistical constraints (lack of adequate supply train and regulars). It seemed possible that Beauregard's activity in Manassas might be a feint masking a dash to Johnston in the Valley, and a march on Washington from there.

51. Although Patterson's source, if any, remains unknown, his impression of his circumstances had all the earmarks of deception—whether self-induced or created by the enemy. See *OR*, 2, 159. R. Patterson to Col. E. D. Townsend, July 5, 1861.

52. *OR*, Chapter 9, 164. To Maj Gen. Patterson, Martinsburg, VA, from W. Scott, Washington, July 11, 1861. In communicating this intelligence to Patterson, Scott wrote that "the author of the following is known, and he believes it authentic."

53. Scott sent the intelligence forward, with its bona fides, to Patterson at a moment of the latter's most acutely felt vulnerability. Why Scott would have done so if he did not believe the report had merit is hard to imagine, and may be further testimony to his incompetence.

54. See Fishel, *Secret War*, 24–28. Historians, including Fishel, generally discount Baker's assertions about the significance of his role and believe his memoir overinflates events. He nonetheless may have played a crucial, if debilitating, role at First Manassas. Fisher notes, for example, that Baker's cover as a "photographer" was weak because he carried an empty camera box. Yet if his purpose was to get behind enemy lines (to determine enemy dispositions and plans), then his "cover" more than served its purpose. Fisher writes: "Baker did make a trip to Manassas and Richmond about the time he claims. The record that supports his claim is sketchy but authoritative. It consists of his bill for $105 in expenses, naming Manassas and Richmond as the points visited, citing General Scott's orders as authority for the mission and bearing endorsements by Secretary of State Seward and a disbursing officer of the War Department. These were the officials who customarily passed on expenditures for 'secret service' at this period, and . . . they were cautious about paying even the most obviously legitimate claims." Fishel, 26.

55. For more on these Confederate opening advantages, see Chapter 5.

56. Scott's orders to Patterson were, at best, unclear. We know, for example, that he ordered Patterson to both keep Johnston busy in the Valley and, if possible, make his way to Alexandria, VA.

57. Fishel, *Secret War*, 604 n. 3.

58. Contemporary participants in this debate have included historian Edwin Fishel, who argues her role was important but has been exaggerated (*Secret War*, 58–68) and Greenhow's biographer, Ann Blackman, who suggests it was crucial but does not establish exactly why, perhaps because her purpose was more autobiographical than analytical in a strategic policy sense. Ann Blackman, *Wild Rose* (New York: Random House, 2005), 40–46.

59. Quoted in Fishel, *Secret War*, 37.

60. Recall that the spies focused on numbers of troops rather than terrain and mapping. They were run by William C. Parsons, a lawyer employed by Colonel Mansfield, the officer in command of the Department of Washington. Fishel, *Secret War*, 21. Parsons did infiltrate a spy behind Beauregard's lines in late June and provided good information on Confederate numbers, weapons (a hodge-podge), quality of horseflesh, troop morale, food, and disease. Fishel, *Secret War*, 35–36.

61. *OR*, Patterson to Townsend, July 10, 1861.

62. And the insights available from balloon reconnaissance could not have helped McDowell appreciate the steep banks, weak bridges, and narrow lanes that slowed his advance.

63. Fishel, *Secret War*, 382.

64. See Peter G. Tsouras, *Major General George H. Sharpe and the Creation of American Military Intelligence in the Civil War* (Haverton, PA: Casemate, 2018), for a thorough history of Sharpe and his work creating the BMI.

65. Edwin Fischel, *Secret War*, 283–285. This led to repeated run-ins between himself and Lafayette Baker, who collected intelligence on army field operations on behalf of the War Department, for which he served. Baker's men may have gotten away with it by collecting intelligence on the commanding generals' gambling and womanizing and threatening retaliation.

66. Fischel, *Secret War*, 287.

67. Babcock was a "walking encyclopedia" of the Confederate order of battle. Fischel, *Secret War*, 300.

68. United States Mine Ford above Fredericksburg had employed Union men now out of work and willing to cooperate. For more on the analysis of the fords, see Fishel, *Secret War*, 344–345.

69. Fishel, *Secret War*, 291–294. Spying may have been considered lowly work for officers, but the policy of using them for overseeing espionage had the benefit of ensuring that operations were managed from above.

70. Other US generals had attempted an intelligence effort, but these prior attempts were not all-source analytical enterprises, and did not manage all collection on the battlefield situation.

71. Thomas B. Buell, *The Warrior Generals: Combat Leadership in the Civil War* (New York: Three Rivers Press, 1997), 211.

72. Buell, *Warrior Generals*, 211.

73. Buell, *Warrior Generals*, 212–213. During this time, Lee employed Hotchkiss to make maps of past engagements. Asked to prepare maps late, Hotchkiss produced uncharacteristically inaccurate ones, according to Buell.

74. Buell, *Warrior Generals*, 212.
75. Fishel, *Secret War*, 360–362.
76. Fishel, *Secret War*, 360–369.
77. Quaker guns were nonfunctional, wooden cannon erected to deceive the enemy. Fishel, *Secret War*, 366.
78. Fishel, *Secret War*, 352.
79. Technically, scouts became spies when they crossed into enemy territory, but the terms were used loosely. See Fishel, *Secret War*, 331.
80. Since the commander of these Federal troops was assigned on rotation every forty-eight hours, oversight was minimal; the men felt safe consorting in this way.
81. Fishel, *Secret War*, 332.
82. Fishel, *Secret War*, 332. Emphasis added. See Fishel's note 66 on Freeman's similar judgment.
83. Fishel, *Secret War*, 370.
84. Edward Porter Alexander, *Fighting for the Confederacy: The Personal Recollections of General Edward Porter Alexander*, ed. Gary W. Gallagher (Chapel Hill: University of North Carolina Press, 1989), 200.
85. Fishel says Hooker's injury was partly to blame for the defeat (*Secret War*, 404), while pointing out many other causes related to intelligence. Stephen Z. Starr (*The Union Cavalry in the Civil War: From Fort Sumter to Gettysburg, 1861–1863*, vol. 1 [Baton Rouge: Louisiana State University Press, 1979], 361) blames it on Hooker's "loss of nerve and loss of grip on the battle." Stephen W. Sears emphasizes the injury when writing about the critical loss of Federal advantages on 3 May (*Chancellorsville*, 337–341).
86. Plum, *The Military Telegraph*, 363–364.
87. Plum, *The Military Telegraph*, 365. "Even the yard and out-buildings were filled with the wounded. The office itself was also invaded and the operators, when possible, eased the sufferers. At night the ground wire was broken, and [one operator], in feeling around in the dark for the trouble, found the dead body of a poor soldier lying upon it."
88. Recall that Stonewall Jackson had found a path to the Federal right, marched there with the aid of a cavalry screen and the impenetrable Wilderness, and then, using several of J. E. B. Stuart's men, had located the exact point where the Federal right ended.
89. Stoneman had also proceeded slowly and ineffectively, without timely communications back to Hooker.
90. In fact, Hooker's placement of his chief engineer, Captain Cyrus Comstock, in charge of the balloon corps hurt morale and increased bureaucratic red tape. Just before the battle, Comstock cut Lowe's pay and required all reports go through him. See Evans, *War of the Aeronauts*, 263–270.
91. Fishel, *Secret War*, 396–397.
92. These pathologies should be distinguished from others with which they are often confused: "Politicization" is the skewing of intelligence to get preferred policy prescription; "privatization" is the skewing of intelligence to advance a career or other

personal, non-policy-related interest. Both pathologies are endemic to conflicts and must be managed as a matter of intelligence policy.

93. An important exception to this broad judgment was the night of 1 May, when the BMI interrogated prisoners and defectors, coming up with a fairly accurate picture.

94. Sears, *Chancellorsville*, 56.

95. Fishel, *Secret War*, 367.

Chapter 7

1. The quotation is from General Sheridan. See the opening of the previous chapter. William B. Feis, "That Great Essential of Success: Espionage, Covert Action and Military Intelligence," in Aaron Sheehan-Dean, ed., *Struggle for a Vast Future* (Oxford: Osprey Publishing, 2006), 153.

2. William R. Plum, *The Military Telegraph during the Civil War in the United States, with an Exposition of Ancient and Modern Means of Communication, and of the Federal and Confederate Cipher Systems*, 2 vols. (Forgotten Books, 2012; http://www.forgottenbo oks.org), vol. 1, 97. Recall that the Signal Corps had set up the wire linking Falmouth with the US Ford using weak wires and the "Beardslee" telegraph system of the Signal Corps rather than the competing "Morse" system of the USMT. Once Union forces had advanced to Chancellorsville, Morse men operated the line from Falmouth west to the Union station at US Ford (east of Kelly's Ford). The other telegraph company (the Signal Corps) operated the line from US Ford across the Rappahannock toward Chancellorsville.

3. See Plum, *The Military Telegraph*, vol. 2, 106–153, for an excellent discussion of the relationship between telegraphers and the military chain of command in both the Union and Confederate armies.

4. In fact, these assets were employed more tactically than strategically, though between engagements mapmakers' responsibilities often extended into damage assessment and illustrations of engagements for the purposes of maintaining records.

5. Fred D. Seth Jr., "'Gittin Stuff': Equipping Confederate Armies at the Onset of the Civil War (1861–1862)," *Property Professional* 16, no. 3 (2004): 16–27. Accessed online at http://cdn.ymaws.com.

6. The problems of tapping and monitoring private expertise were, of course, not new. During the sixteenth century, England's Naval Board had found privateers such surly operators that some counseled against employing them. Spain's Philip II knew England's Naval Board was working with privateers to build new ships, but remained complacent about the consequences for Spanish naval doctrine. This attitude persisted even as English sailors tested the new ships and doctrine in several engagements before the Armada sailed.

7. For a more nuanced view, see Peter B. Tsouras, *Major General George H. Sharpe and the Creation of American Military Intelligence in the Civil War* (Havertown,

PA: Casemate Publishers, 2018); especially 70–73. Tsouras offers a sympathetic, detailed account of Sharpe's role throughout the war.

8. Tsouras, *Major General George H. Sharpe*, 72.

9. It is instructive to consider the positions of historians who are expert in the Civil War. They all have access to the same facts but nonetheless argue over the meaning of them to this day. Such is true of contemporary experts on any intelligence issue: all may be experts but none may claim exclusive hold on "the truth" or the one correct vision of current events, let alone estimative judgments about the future. To suggest that policymakers demanding more from them are necessarily politicizing intelligence is to suggest that all-source analysis is more oracle-like than deliberative, and that analysts are more priestly than scholarly. Politicization can be a real problem, but claims of it may also be erroneous, causing oversight to become corrupted and intelligence to become ungovernable in a democracy.

10. Edwin C. Fishel, *The Secret War for the Union: The Untold Story of Military Intelligence in the Civil War* (New York: Houghton Mifflin, 1996), 298–299.

11. Hooker himself had to learn. Fishel, *Secret War*, 300.

12. Fishel, *Secret War*, 495. Meade, however, later advised Grant to disband the BMI. Grant did not.

13. William B. Feis, *Grant's Secret Service: The Intelligence War from Belmont to Appomattox* (Lincoln: University of Nebraska Press, 2002), 268.

14. For reasons of brevity we are not revisiting here Hooker's disastrous decisions to deploy his cavalry, so essential for intelligence dissemination, on missions far south of the battlefield.

15. Before 9/11, intelligence chiefs, inclined to gather leads from watching targets, waited too long to interdict known terrorists plotting inside the United States. Law enforcement officers, inclined to gather evidence for arrest and prosecution, not serve policy, had lost opportunities to turn tables on foreign governments in years past. For these and other reasons, the FBI and US intelligence agencies often had experienced difficulties cooperating with each other.

16. Fishel, *Secret War*, 400–402. Sears instead suggests the charges against Devens in this case amounted to 20/20 hindsight. Stephen W. Sears, *Chancellorsville* (Boston: Houghton Mifflin, 1996), 265. In any event, the widely reported Federal inertia contrasts sharply with the quick reactions of Confederate officers during First Manassas, when they reacted to picket reports of a surprising Federal flanking maneuver by reorienting their troops. Their fast action saved the battle. Interestingly, Devens's previous encounter with intelligence failure had happened during the disastrous battle of Balls' Bluff, when he too quickly accepted an erroneous report of an enemy encampment and, acting on it, fell into a Confederate ambush. Likely remembering this mistake, he made the opposite one at Chancellorsville.

17. This was General Jackson's brilliance: he married secrecy to an unerring sense of when and to whom to release it. As a general, he also had the authority to decide.

18. Committee on Armed Services, House of Representatives, *Intelligence Successes and Failures in Operations Desert Shield/Storm: Report of the Oversight and Investigations*

Subcommittee, 103rd Congress, First session, no. 5 (Washington, DC: US Government Printing Office, 1993), 13–18.

19. Covert action is an openly observable activity that is clandestinely (secretly) sponsored.

20. Technically, "clandestine" refers exclusively to secret activity and "covert" refers only to secret sponsorship or reporting of overt activity. The words have separate meanings and are not interchangeable.

21. See Christopher Andrew, *Her Majesty's Secret Service: The Making of the British Intelligence Community* (New York: Viking-Penguin, 1986), 446. This issue is an enduring one. For example, despite repeated British intelligence failures in 1940, its Expeditionary Force escaped back to Britain thanks largely to luck and Nazi error. Defenders captured top-secret documents in a German staff vehicle venturing too close to British lines in Belgium. Those documents revealed German knowledge of a gap that allied forces had discounted or overlooked, and British worked to fill it. Had they not filled it in time, that gap could well have prevented their successful escape across the Channel. The point is, the Allies should have recognized the vulnerabilities the enemy saw without having the need for secret documents.

22. The Federal cavalry had become better at reconnaissance, espionage, couriering, and security, but still lacked confidence in their ability to outride Stuart's men. The Battle of Brandy Station, which took place on 9 June, right after Chancellorsville, demonstrated the improved horsemanship and daring of the Federals, and increased their confidence. Then, in a series of battles near Aldie, Middleburg, and Upperville, Virginia from 17 June to 21 June, the Federal cavalry skirmished with Jeb Stuart's cavalry. Stuart was working to screen Lee's movements in the valley, but in a skirmish at Upperville, Pleasanton's men beat Stuart for the first time in open engagement, driving his men back over Ashby's Gap (the same gap Joe Johnston had used to get from the Valley to Beauregard during the Battle of First Manassas).

23. As we have seen, Rose Greenhow found out not just when McDowell would attack, but how and with what objective, eliminating Beauregard's and Johnston's need to guard against feints by either him or Patterson. Papers left by Confederate troops at Centerville showed how much they knew of McDowell's plans in advance. This intelligence haul led to the arrest of Greenhow and the roll-up of her Washington network of spies.

24. See the previous chapter for a discussion of opportunities lost in this regard.

25. Patterson noted in early July that he was in Martinsburg but that his "post office" would remain in Hagerstown, about twenty-two miles away. A confidential message sent to him from Washington on 1 July did not get to him until 4 July.

26. Recall that balloons could not have helped with the assessment of fords across the Run, but they could have helped Scott see Johnston's vanguard cross Ashby's Gap on the nineteenth, or the massing of Johnston's forces at Delaplane (Piedmont) as they waited to board trains on the twentieth. The War Department, however, would have had to invest quickly and generously in the technology to do so. It did not, despite the president's enthusiastic support for balloons and at least two experienced aeronauts who were ready to serve the Union. Historians have too quickly dismissed the role of

balloons without analyzing why they failed to deliver the advantages commanders said they needed.

Chapter 8

1. A number of authors have provided insights into more modern cases. See for example, Peter L. Bergen, *Manhunt: The Ten-Year Search for Bin Laden from 9/11 to Abbottabad* (New York: Crown Publishers, 2012); Robert L. Grenier, *88 Days to Kandahar: A CIA Diary* (New York: Simon and Schuster, 2015); and Henry A. Crumpton, *The Art of Intelligence* (New York: Penguin Books, 2012).

2. The vulnerability of a state does not necessarily turn on the size of an attack against it. The Oklahoma City domestic terrorist attack of April 19, 1995, killed over 168 people and injured more than 680, prompting a large-scale rescue and law enforcement investigation. Although some in the press immediately and erroneously blamed foreign terrorism, President Clinton was hesitant to frame the attack in terms of national security or foreign culpability, and normal criminal procedures were followed. In contrast, when the terrorist bombings in Paris, France, and its suburb, Saint-Denis, on 13 November 2015, killed 131 people and injured 413, the French president regarded the attack as an act of war and launched a national security manhunt that covered territory from France to the rest of Europe and on to Syria. Intelligence empowered each president to make the correct call.

3. Ron Chernow, *Grant* (London: Penguin Press, 2017), 527.

4. The lone actor on stage was Harry Hawk, playing a folksy American rebuking an elegant Englishwoman who had just walked offstage. The rebuke would elicit a laugh that Booth hoped might muffle his shot. See Terry Alford, *Fortune's Fool: The Life of John Wilkes Booth* (New York: Oxford University Press, 2015), 265.

5. For the best background on the conspirators see Alford, *Fortune's Fool*, 221–223.

6. James L. Swanson, *Manhunt: The Twelve-Day Chase for Lincoln's Killer* (New York: Harper Perennial, 2007), 17.

7. Stanton had also ordered military guards for all cabinet members, including the vice president (Swanson, *Manhunt*, 101 and 111–112). He had decided this immediately after confirming the attack on Seward. Stanton's notion that the whole cabinet might be targeted was an estimative judgment based mostly on the circumstances of the attack on the secretary of state. It was an easy (low cost, high return) decision that required little intelligence.

8. Swanson, *Manhunt*, 111–112.

9. The secretary of the navy, Gideon Welles, shared this belief. Swanson, *Manhunt*, 101.

10. William Marvel, *Lincoln's Autocrat: The Life of Edwin Stanton* (Chapel Hill: University of North Carolina Press, 2015), 327–329.

11. Marvel, *Lincoln's Autocrat*, 369.

12. Marvel, *Lincoln's Autocrat*, 369. Emphasis added.

13. Marvel, *Lincoln's Autocrat*, 348.

14. Marvel, *Lincoln's Autocrat*, 331.
15. This mindset is reminiscent of President George W. Bush's decision to increase domestic surveillance in the immediate aftermath of 9/11, regardless of the legal requirements for prior court approval.
16. The evidence was in the form of a letter to Booth from someone named "Sam" whose words hinted at a preplanned conspiracy that required input from Richmond. See Marvel, *Lincoln's Autocrat*, 369; also, Swanson, *Manhunt*, 119.
17. Swanson, *Manhunt*, 122 and Marvel, *Lincoln's Autocrat*, 368.
18. Swanson, *Manhunt*, 116, 122, 147.
19. Alford, *Fortune's Fool*, 281.
20. As discussed later, some have judged Stanton harshly for his decision to prosecute the conspirators in military tribunals, not civil courts. This decision did eventually divide the country, but Stanton judged the risks of this choice to be less than the risk of prolonged court procedures that might have allowed the assassins to gain some public sympathy.
21. Swanson, *Manhunt*, 135.
22. At one point, General Grant ordered the arrest of all paroled Confederate officers and surgeons in Richmond. He rescinded the order only when subordinates protested that this might reignite the war—particularly if General Lee were included. Swanson, *Manhunt*, 118.
23. Swanson, *Manhunt*, 119.
24. Atzerodt had left incriminating evidence at his hotel. He also spoke too freely about the assassination. Atzerodt was located and arrested at 4:00 a.m. 20 April as he slept at his cousin's house in Maryland. Swanson, *Manhunt*, 219–221.
25. For this characterization of Atzerodt, see Alford, *Fortune's Fool*, 211–212. Swanson recounts that Booth saw Herold as his guide, but if so his trust was misplaced given Herold's later incompetence. Atzerodt certainly had greater familiarity with the river. Swanson, *Manhunt*, 86–87.
26. Southern Maryland was full of Confederate sympathizers in a state that had become increasingly allied with the Union cause over four years of war. The state had emancipated slaves, infuriating slaveholders in this rural peninsula close to Washington. Confederate agents came and went through the area, transporting contraband and rebel communications to Richmond. See Alford, *Fortune's Fool*, 190.
27. Swanson, *Manhunt*, 125–127.
28. Booth and Herold likely kept their recent business secret from Mudd. When Booth showed up, Mudd probably did not yet know that the president had been shot. But Mudd knew Booth and had been involved in prior plotting against the president. That there was no conversation between them about the circumstances of Booth's flight or his broken leg seems unlikely, at best.
29. Swanson, *Manhunt*, 147. This message was of particular importance because Booth's shout on the stage of Ford's Theater, "Sic semper tyrannis" ("Thus always to tyrants") was Virginia's state motto at the time, seemingly implicating its citizens in the act.

Pierpont, however, was a Lincoln loyalist. He was from one of Virginia's northern counties that had split from secessionist Virginia to become West Virginia. He was not recognized officially as the governor of Virginia until 9 May 1865.

30. Alford, *Fortune's Fool*, 282.

31. There is some controversy on this point, as well as the subsequent actions of Dr. Mudd. For example, the memoirs of John Turner, who helped Booth and Herold cross the Potomac, suggest Mudd traveled separately to Bryantown and informed authorities via his brother of the presence of two strangers on his property. Turner's narrative probably reflects, however, the tainted testimony of Mudd, who was on trial for his life when he gave it. Mudd was later pardoned.

32. For an extensive discussion of the controversy over Mudd's role in the assassination plot, see John Paul Jones, ed., "Dr. Mudd and the Lincoln Assassination: The Case Reopened," published by the Richmond School of Law, University of Richmond UR Scholarship Repository (Law Faculty Publication, 1993) at https:// scholarship.richmond.edu.

33. Some historians (Alford, *Fortune's Fool*) have used this spelling; others have used "Swann" (Swanson, *Manhunt*). The spelling used here has the added benefit of helping distinguish Oswell's family from that of Cox's housekeeper, whose name was Swann, and was unrelated.

34. Swan's name has varied in historical accounts between "Swan" (Alford, *Fortune's Fool*, 278) and "Swann" (Swanson, *Manhunt*, 163) and sometimes appears as Ausy, Oswald, Oscar, and the like. Swan was a poor tobacco farmer, married, with eight children.

35. If Booth truly had experienced a poor reception at Rich Hill, he likely understood that he was unwelcome even among Confederate sympathizers in Maryland. It seems more likely, however, that the act was some theater for Swan's benefit.

36. Jones may have been playing a double game, committed to the rebel cause but unwilling to risk his life and his Confederate network underground to secure Booth's life. He did not speak of his role or knowledge about Booth's escape for years. See Swanson, *Manhunt*, 242–244.

37. Alford, *Fortune's Fool*, 279.

38. See Booth's entry into his diary in Swanson, *Manhunt*, 206.

39. Alford, *Fortune's Fool*, 282.

40. Swanson, *Manhunt*, 174.

41. Swanson, *Manhunt*, 246.

42. Alford, *Fortune's Fool*, 286.

43. Jones and Cox were imprisoned for only one month after Booth's death. Lacking sufficient evidence against them, the authorities let them go.

44. Among the hundreds arrested in the roll-up of suspicious characters up to this point were Samuel Arnold, linked to Booth through the letter found in Booth's hotel room; Michael O'Laughlen, a Confederate veteran associated with Booth's prior plots; and Edman Spangler, who had held Booth's horse behind Ford's Theater. Alford, *Fortune's Fool*, 284.

45. Swanson, *Manhunt*, 297.

46. Swanson, *Manhunt*, 297. These words come from an account by Captain William Cross Hazelton of the Eighth Illinois Cavalry in a letter to his mother. Swan was, therefore, a "walk-in" who should have received the monetary reward. He never did.
47. Swanson, *Manhunt*, 253.
48. Swanson, *Manhunt*, 254.
49. Swanson, *Manhunt*, 315.
50. According to Swanson, Rollins, the ferryman, agreed to be a guide only if he was placed under mock arrest to shield him and his family from retribution. Swanson, *Manhunt*, 302.
51. It may be that Booth intended Stanton to be killed along with Seward, Johnson, and Lincoln. If so, he hinged too much of his overall plan on the outcome of this one part of his assassination plot. His journal reveals that he had little confidence in the team he had rapidly put together on 14 April.
52. For an excellent discussion of the problem of interdiction and the successes the nonproliferation community have recently achieved, see Zachary S. Davis, "Bombs Away: Interdicting Proliferation," *American Interest*, January–February 2009, 33–38.
53. See Mark Bowden, "The Ploy," *The Atlantic* 299, no. 4 (May 2007): 54–68. Bowden's article on the interrogation process used in the hunt for Abu Musab al-Zarqawi, which proved successful on 7 June 2006, is an excellent explanation of how hostile interrogation is done (as opposed to friendly interviews and cooperative elicitation).
54. The United States would use similar teams of hunters in the pursuit of terrorists before and after 9/11. Los Angeles, Chicago, and New York City developed joint operations and concepts such as "intelligence-led policing" to tackle the threat of foreign agent penetration of urban centers.
55. As one of the city's officials wrote to his king: "In search of the corsair, this city has sent out three expeditions on which were expended more than 4,000 pesos; and he has always had the luck to escape. Once the fleet is gone, when the town and port are deserted, it is plain we are going to suffer from this corsair and others." John Sugden, *Sir Francis Drake* (New York: Henry Holt, 1990), 51. Quotation is from Gonzalo Nuñez de la Cerda in a letter to Philip II, May 24, 1571.
56. Sugden, *Sir Francis Drake*, 51. Officials in the Spanish town of Nombre de Dios, a critical junction of land and sea treasure routes, sent three expeditions in 1571 to interdict the raiding Englishman. All of them failed.
57. See Isaiah Berlin, *The Hedgehog and the Fox* (London: Weidenfeld and Nicolson, 1953); Jim Collins, *Good to Great: Why Some Companies Make the Leap and Others Don't* (New York: Harper Business, 2001).

Chapter 9

1. Diplomacy and diplomatic operations are generally, but not always, performed by foreign ministries and other agencies involved in "foreign affairs," including ministries of defense. The term "diplomacy" will be used in this larger, all-inclusive sense,

534   NOTES

although the two functions of foreign policymaking and representation were not always joined.

2. "Diplomacy" will be understood in this chapter to include the framing of state interests in terms of foreign policy, the representation of state interests between governments, the conduct of negotiations regarding those interests, and the collection of intelligence in support of foreign policy. "Diplomatic operations" include the logistical and management functions involved in the execution or practice of diplomacy and diplomatic intelligence.

3. Henry Kissinger, *Diplomacy* (New York: Simon and Schuster, 1994), 508.

4. George Kennan, *Memoirs, 1925–1950* (Boston: Atlantic Monthly Press / Little, Brown, 1967), 233.

5. Kennan, *Memoirs*, 354–367. The ideas in Kennan's "long telegram" (22 February 1946) led to Kennan's anonymous (July 1947) *Foreign Affairs* ("Mr. X") article, "The Sources of Soviet Conduct," which arguably became the intellectual basis for the US Cold War military policy of containment rather than a more political approach, much to Kennan's later chagrin.

6. Andrew Kydd, "Facing Impediments: Information and Communication," in I. William Zartman, ed., *How Negotiations End: Negotiating Behavior in the End Game* (New York: Cambridge University Press, 2019), 211.

7. In a remarkable case of obduracy, the British ambassador in Rome persisted in defending an Italian butler that wandered unsupervised for years, stealing sensitive documents and jewelry for his government. See Christopher Andrew, *Her Majesty's Secret Service: The Making of the British Intelligence Community* (New York: Viking-Penguin, 1986), 402–404.

8. Vansittart was here discussing Prime Minister Baldwin's capacity to process foreign policy paperwork, but the point remains: modern diplomacy requires reading and processing under pressure. Lord Vansittart, *Mist Procession* (London: Hutchinson of London, 1958), 352.

9. Correlli Barnett, *The Collapse of British Power* (Atlantic Highlands, NJ: Humanities Press International, 1986), 239.

10. For more on this historical period and what has been termed the "Gehlen Affair," see Richard Helms, *A Look over My Shoulder: A Life in the Central Intelligence Agency* (New York: Random House, 2003), 82–91.

11. See Robert E. Osgood, "The Expansion of Force," in Robert J. Art and Kenneth N. Waltz, eds., *The Use of Force: International Politics and Foreign Policy* (Boston: Little, Brown, 1971), 29–55. Also, Martin Van Creveld, *Technology and War: From 2000 BC to the Present* (New York: Free Press, 1991).

12. Christopher Andrew, "The Nature of Military Intelligence," in Keith Nelson and B. J. C. McKercher, *Go Spy the Land: Military Intelligence in History* (Westport, CT: Praeger, 1992), 3.

13. See John Ferris, "Lord Salisbury, Secret Intelligence, and British Policy toward Russia and Central Asia, 1874–1978," in Nelson and McKercher, *Go Spy the Land*, 115–152.

14. Strobe Talbott, *The Master of the Game: Paul Nitze and the Nuclear Peace* (New York: Vintage Books, 1988), 54.

15. Robert Blackwell and Jack Davis, "A Policymaker's Perspective on Intelligence Analysis," in Loch K. Johnson and James J. Wirtz, *Intelligence and National Security: The Secret World of Spies*, 2nd ed. (New York: Oxford University Press, 2008), 153–159.

16. Christopher Clark, *The Sleepwalkers: How Europe Went to War in 1914* (New York: Harper Perennial, 2014), 528–529.

17. Eventually, of course, the US military did experiment with embedding journalists and even designed strategies, such as "shock and awe" to take account of public effects.

18. Clark, *Sleepwalkers*, 45.

19. Ferris, "Lord Salisbury," 129.

Chapter 10

1. This was true despite the scale of bloodletting during the American Civil War and Japan's sanguinary victory over Russia in 1905. See Raymond Aron, *The Century of Total War* (Boston: Beacon Press, 1954), 18–20. Also see James Joll and Gordon Martel, *The Origins of the First World War*, 3rd ed. (London: Pearson Longman, 2007), for a comprehensive discussion of the origins of WWI and the sources of uncertainty.

2. Aron, *Century of Total War*, 13. Aron's full argument is not nearly so spare, but this excerpt conveys Aron's bottom line. Observing that it was not the same Germany that launched the two world wars, nor the same technology that turned them "hyperbolic," Aron maintains that the *underlying causes* of these confrontations were not the same, but *diplomacy's inadequacy* in dealing with them proved a constant. His entire analysis, more fully summarized on 164, is as suggested in the quotation above: "It is man, or rather it is men, who by their action or inaction, produced this history which they did not want." Aron's discussion is worth reading in full. See especially 9–98.

3. "Versailles Revisited," *The Economist*, July 6, 2019, 16.

4. Ernest May, *Strange Victory: Hitler's Conquest of France* (New York: Hill and Wang, 2000), 5.

5. Luigi Albertini, *The Origins of the War of 1914*, translated by Isabella M. Massey, vol. 2 (New York: Enigma Books, 2005), 641–642.

6. See Christopher Clark, *The Sleepwalkers: How Europe Went to War in 1914* (New York: HarperCollins, 2013). At times, the ignorance seemed almost willful. Just before the outbreak of war the French prime minister, Raymond Poincaré, arranged for a neophyte to take charge at the Foreign Ministry because Poincaré wanted to run foreign policy himself. And though he apparently tried to teach Minister Viviani something about alliance politics as they sailed to St. Petersburg on the eve of WWI, he ultimately despaired of it. Viviani was not only ignorant of foreign affairs, but alarmingly disinterested. As storm clouds gathered, he persevered on the fate of the famous wife of a political leader, Madame Caillaux, who was on trial for murdering a newspaper editor in Paris. See Clark, 406, 441–442.

7. Clark, *Sleepwalkers*, 581.

8. The increase in dispatches was part of a trend that accelerated for other reasons, including the advent of the telegraph. In Britain, Foreign Office dispatches increased steadily from 1829 (6,000) to 1905 (111,000). See Zara Steiner, *The Foreign Office and Foreign Policy, 1898–1914* (Cambridge: Cambridge University Press, 1969), 4.

9. Joll and Martel, *Origins*, 131. In fact, there is little evidence that Grey, Europe's longest-serving foreign minister (foreign secretary in his case) as of July 1914, understood the British military's (or admiralty's) strategy for a European war, including premises about how it might start or end. Among European statesmen, he was hardly alone. Most in the German Foreign Office, though aware of Berlin's strategic challenges, anticipated a quick victory because they hoped and expected Britain to remain neutral. The German general staff, reasoning otherwise, did not disabuse them of this happy prediction.

10. The year 1903 was when the Wright brothers flew for twelve seconds and up to 120 feet in altitude.

11. See Katherine C. Epstein, "Scholarship and the Ship of State: Rethinking the Anglo-American Strategic Decline Analogy," *International Affairs* 91, no. 2 (2015): 319–331. This is an article on perception and power in international politics before WWI. The author's suggestion that commercial and financial instruments become "WMD" equivalents when used seems a stretch. Nevertheless, her points reinforce those made in this volume: globalization increases the uncertainties of international politics. Her larger argument, that the old paradigm of British decline (in relative power) before WWI reflects faulty scholarship, is not supported by the good case she makes that British naval strategy did not accept or reflect that decline, but rather reimagined strategic necessities.

12. Col. Terrence J. Finnegan, *Shooting the Front: Allied Aerial Reconnaissance and Photographic Interpretation on the Western Front—WWI* (Washington, DC: National Defense Intelligence College Press, 2006), 9.

13. Aron, *Century of Total War*, 18.

14. Nicholas Lambert has written a well-regarded revisionist history on the effects of uncertainty on British naval decision-making before WWI. Advances in chemical explosives brought uncertainties for surface ships, prompting Britain to excel in developing subsurface mines, expend significant resources on purchasing them, but then sending them to storage because of uncertainty about what to do with them. Advances in mine-related technologies arguably reduced Britain's relative power and triggered the need for 360-degree surveillance at sea. *Planning Armageddon* (Cambridge, MA: Harvard University Press, 2012).

15. It would not be until the mid-twentieth century that diplomats, military officers, economists, and business leaders joined in pursuit of a theory of deterrence intended to manage the uncertainties weapons of mass destruction had introduced through increased transparency and shared vulnerability. "Mutual assured destruction," or MAD, was a force-sizing concept originating in the 1950s that captures the idea of deterrence through fear of inevitable, catastrophic retaliation against nuclear attack. The idea was that, when "mutual," both sides would refrain from starting a war they could not win. The catch was that each side had to be willing to leave itself vulnerable,

believe that all opponents were doing likewise, and believe that all involved were rational.

16. This naval competition has generated a substantial literature, including strong revisionist works that make the argument that British naval strategists, cognizant of the sociopolitical impact of the first wave of globalization, planned to use British supremacy in communications, credit, and oceangoing merchant shipping to attack enemies while insulating Britain itself from any fallout. That this strategy triggered hostile reactions from neutral powers, such as the United States, and so ultimately failed is testimony to the uncertainties that the industrial revolution introduced. See Epstein, "Scholarship"; and Nicholas A. Lambert, *Sir John Fisher's Naval Revolution* (Columbia: University of South Carolina Press, 1999), and his *Planning Armageddon*. I am grateful to Lambert for his helpful communications on this topic, September–December 2017.

17. The kaiser's decision also increased uncertainties for Britain, however. The British navy not only expanded its own intelligence operations to monitor the threat, but also sponsored the development of MI-6, Britain's civilian foreign intelligence service, to help spy on Germany's program. Thus, one silent consequence of the kaiser's obsession was the launching of intelligence cooperation between civilians and naval offices in the British government.

18. See Chapter 6 in this volume on the rise of the telegraph. Alexander Graham Bell invented the telephone in 1876.

19. Perhaps the most important study of the impact on cable and wireless communications during this period is Jonathan Reed Winkler's *Nexus: Strategic Communications and American Security in World War I* (Cambridge, MA: Harvard University Press, 2008).

20. Winkler, *Nexus*, 9.

21. These were the Anglo-American Telegraph Company, the Direct United States Cable Company, the Companie Francaise du Telegraphe de Paris a New York, the Western Union Telegraph Company, and the Commercial Cable Company. See Winkler, *Nexus*, 9, and "The Submarine Cables of the World—1892," in *Manufacturer and Builder* 24, no. 5 (May 1892) (Western and Co.). Found at http//atlantic-cable.com.

22. Christopher Andrew, *Her Majesty's Secret Service: The Making of the British Intelligence Community* (New York: Viking-Penguin, 1986), 108.

23. Among the best books on the US effort to secure its own global communications is Winkler, *Nexus*.

24. Solutions became increasingly complex as communications began to "hop" from wire to wireless and back, creating vulnerabilities at each juncture.

25. Logistical coordination also contributed to her sinking Britain's *Prince of Wales* and the *Repulse*, her taking of Guam, Wake, Hong Kong, Singapore and Malaya, the Dutch East Indies and the Solomons, the Philippines, and Siam.

26. Much later, terrorists would exploit the expanded potential of the Internet and social media to achieve networked "wolf packs" in the twenty-first century. The idea is the same in all such cases: exploit instantaneous communications to send intelligence for joint decision-making over surprising distances.

27. Winkler, *Nexus*, 62. Anyone interested in this subject can do no better than to read this superb book on the evolution of electronic communications prior to WWI.
28. Winkler, *Nexus*, 61–62.
29. Traffic analysis maps flows of communications even if content is encrypted. It contributed both to the rolling up of Allied spy networks on the Continent during WWII, and to the defeat of the German submarine "wolf packs," which preyed on Allied convoys during WWII's battle for the Atlantic.
30. John Chapman, "Japanese Intelligence 1918–1945," in Christopher Andrew and Jeremy Noakes, eds., *Intelligence and International Relations, 1900–1945* (Exeter: Exeter University, 1987), 140. William Friedman broke JN25b after only twenty months of work. Japan knew it needed to change its code, but had to do so over such a broad expanse that persistent administrative problems made the change difficult (146). Yamamoto was planning to grab Midway Island and, thus, gain control of the central Pacific while, at the same time, destroying the remainder of the US fleet. But US cryptanalysts could read many of his orders and discern his plan. On 1 June, the Japanese changed their code, but too late. Admiral Chester Nimitz had brought his aircraft carriers from the SW Pacific to wait off the flank of the Japanese and attack the fleet when it was most vulnerable.
31. By WWII, when Japanese ships used the main fleet code of 1940 (US designated JN25b) for about half of its messages, the US Navy was able to read the key communications that enabled a decisive and war-changing victory at Midway.
32. By the twenty-first century, communications forensics on the Internet would turn traffic analysis into a software application, allowing governments to track terrorists by skimming metadata off digital communications and individual civilians to map their Internet traffic in potentially fine detail. The authorities for tracking "wolf packs" in peacetime would be, however, more problematic for democracies than dictatorships, opening opportunities for the latter to gain advantages.
33. Reginald V. Jones, *The Wizard War: British Scientific Intelligence, 1939–1945* (New York: Coward, McCann and Geoghegan, 1978). The role of Carl's brother Robert, founder of the Bosch precision machines and electrical equipment company, in the anti-Nazi resistance is mentioned in Andrew, *Her Majesty's Secret Service*, 382.
34. The 1941 report by the MAUD Committee, "Use of Uranium for a Bomb," influenced decisions in Britain, the United States, and the Soviet Union, which got the report from its British agent, Donald MacLean. The scientists who wrote it suggested a bomb was feasible, albeit only with a very large commitment of funds.
35. Private communication with Burton Gerber, Washington, DC.
36. In 1945, Eugene Rabinowitch, a biophysicist, joined with colleagues in launching the *Bulletin of the Atomic Scientists* with the specific intent of educating civilians about the dangers of atomic weapons for international politics.
37. Kodak Corporation was founded in 1888; Convair Corporation in 1943.
38. For a history of cryptology during WWII, see R. A. Ratcliff, *Delusions of Intelligence: Enigma, Ultra and the End of Secure Cyphers* (Cambridge: Cambridge University Press, 2006). For a more general history of codes and ciphers, see David

Kahn, *The Codebreakers: The Comprehensive History of Secret Communication from Ancient Times to the Internet* (New York: Scribner, 1996).

39. Kahn, *Codebreakers*, 230–235.
40. Kahn, *Codebreakers*, 233.
41. For an early description of WWI cryptology, see Nicolai Batyushin, "Cryptography during WWI: A Tsarist Russian's View," *CIA Studies in Intelligence* 1, no. 2 (Summer 1977). Declassified 2005.
42. For an enlightening discussion of the role of intelligence in war, including the Battle of Tannenberg, see David R. Stone, *The Russian Army in the Great War: The Eastern Front, 1914–1917* (Lawrence: University Press of Kansas, 2015), especially 69–76.
43. For example, on 25 August 1914, at 8:00 a.m. at Mantovo, General Ludendorff reported the following intercepted orders from the enemy: "VI [Russian] Corps, on the flank guarding the Narev [Second] Army would advance through Ortelsburg to Bischofsburg; the Russian XXIII Corps would advance from Neidenburg at Allenstein; its forward units would be positioned along the Gimmendorf-Kurken line. The Russian XXIII Corps itself would be positioned along the Nadrau-Paulsgut line, etc." These details are quoted from Batyushin, "Cryptology during WWI," 29.
44. The best work on this topic is probably Ratcliff, *Delusions of Intelligence*.
45. For more on this history and the other characters playing important roles in it, see Kahn, *Codebreakers*, 415–434.
46. The quite different Japanese type-step device known as "Purple" was broken by a brilliant effort at reverse-engineering it, thanks to the US mathematician and "bright genius of a dark science," William Friedman. A description of Friedman's contributions is found in the definitive work on the history of ciphers and codes in Kahn, *Codebreakers*, 384–393.
47. Ratcliff, *Delusions of Intelligence*, 1.
48. "In 1914 only two manufacturers in the world made the heavy crown barium glass necessary for building high-speed, high-power lenses. Germany's Carl Zeiss firm and France's Parra-Mantois factory were the world's leading manufacturers of high-quality optics. Parra-Mantois became the de facto sole supply source of heavy crown barium glass for the Allies." Quoted from Finnigan, *Shooting the Front*, 354. This work is an important contribution to intelligence studies and provides many illustrations of how the Allies engineered aerial platforms, cameras, processing, and exfiltration technologies into effective and balanced collection systems before and during WWI.
49. The French edged ahead before WWI, however, because they focused on marrying cameras to airplanes while the Germans bet on dirigibles. The former proved better for long-range reconnaissance in war due to their speed, maneuverability, and relative invulnerability. The Germans pursued "lighter than air" alternatives out of an interest in long-dwell surveillance and air-to-ground attack. These craft had certain advantages for monitoring static forces, including trench warfare. Unfortunately for the Germans, these "dreadnoughts of the sky" proved logistically complicated to deploy and vulnerable in war, much as balloons had been during the US Civil War. Their inflation before battle led to the phrase, "When the balloon goes up . . . "

50. Much has been written about Redl and his impact on Austro-Hungarian defenses before WWI. For an interpretative biography, see Robert Asprey, *The Panther's Feast* (New York: G.P. Putnam's Sons, 1959).
51. For the state of the art by WWI, see Finnegan, *Shooting the Front*, 395–413.
52. John S. Gregory, "New Things in War," in Walter Hynes Page and Arthur Wilson Page, *The World's Work*, vol. 28 (1914), 97–102. Developed to be a luxurious airliner before the war, the huge aircraft was reportedly fitted out with wicker chairs, a bedroom, a saloon, and even a bathroom. The maximum crew size was twelve. Sikorsky, born in Kiev, emigrated to the United States in 1925, establishing Sikorsky Aircraft Company. He built the first workable helicopter in 1942.
53. It is important to note here that some collection systems are valuable because they can scoop up and store vast quantities of *noise* so the signals of interest can be discerned, compared, refined, or studied. MASINT systems, such as sonar, fall into this kind of *data-forward* collection. *Signal-forward* collection systems, on the other hand, refine sensors to signals and only collect what is of interest at the time of collection. *Elicitation* collection systems are designed for the absence of either noise or signal. They purposely excite a target so sensors can work. These methods are not necessarily mutually exclusive, but they can be. What makes human intelligence so valuable is that it can perform all types of collection (vacuuming, sensing, and eliciting) with minimal re-engineering, but it does so by putting human lives at risk.
54. Some, most notably Winston Churchill, learned more quickly because they had experience using new surveillance capabilities in more limited or controlled circumstances, such as domestic law enforcement matters. Churchill, as home secretary, used intelligence for lawful manhunts long before he used it in war. See Christopher Andrew, *Defend the Realm: The Authorized History of MI-5* (New York: Alfred A. Knopf, 2009), 29–31.
55. Paul Kennedy, *The Rise and Fall of the Great Powers: Economic Change and Military Conflict from 1500 to 2000* (New York: Random House, Vintage Books, 1989), 202.
56. Kennedy, *Rise and Fall*, 194, 200. Indexed to Great Britain in 1900 at 100, Britain stood at 157 in 1938, while the United States, Germany, and France stood at 167, 144, and 73 respectively.
57. Russia also experienced significant growth from 1905 to 1914, including in agricultural and industrial production. Russia was not, however, blessed with invulnerable borders, so it did not benefit as the United States did from a natural sense of security. See Kennedy, *Rise and Fall*, 198–202 and 232–241.
58. Kennedy, *Rise and Fall*, 194. The European powers did not upgrade the rank of their representatives in Washington until 1892, when the posting became ambassadorial.
59. Kennedy, *Rise and Fall*, 194.
60. For more on this point, see Nicholas Lambert's two volumes *Sir John Fisher's Naval Revolution* and *Planning Armageddon*.
61. The effect was to set private economic interests at odds with public policy, creating confusion.
62. "In 1906 a Foreign Office official characterized the British Empire as being like 'some gouty giant' with fingers and toes spread across the world, which could not

be approached 'without eliciting a scream.'" Keith Jeffery, *The Secret History of MI-6: 1909–1949* (New York: Penguin Press, 2010), 4. One of the most adventurous of the British soldiers and agents of empire was Sir Richard Burton. See Edward Rice, *Captain Sir Richard Francis Burton: The Secret Agent Who Made the Pilgrimage to Mecca, Discovered the Kama Sutra, and Brought the Arabian Nights to the West* (Cambridge, MA: Da Capo Press, 1990).

63. Rice, *Captain Sir Richard Francis Burton*, 5.

64. Steven Wade, *Victoria's Spymasters: Empire and Espionage* (Gloucestershire: History Press, 2009), 14.

65. There were, of course, important differences between the conundrums faced by the Habsburg king and Edwardian England that directly affected the intelligence demands of statecraft. The most important of these has already been addressed: the communication revolution that shifted decision-making to capitals and situational awareness toward land empires. This development contrasted sharply with the sixteenth century, when, as we have already seen, Sir Francis Drake could challenge mighty Spain by sailing faster into ports than news could travel between those ports on land, thus achieving surprise.

66. From a meager six million pounds in 1815, British investment overseas had climbed to seventy-five million annually by 1870. This performance was complemented by territorial acquisitions—about one hundred thousand square miles annually between 1815 and 1865 that inspired competitive claims by other Great Powers.

67. Germany's chancellor, Count Otto von Bismarck, was the mastermind behind this growth of German power, the reordering of Europe and the distraction of Britain and France. Jealous and erratic, Germany's new leader, Kaiser Wilhelm II, not only fired him, but also quickly undid his work. Convinced by his leading admiral that all Great Powers had to go to sea, Wilhelm launched a naval challenge to Britain by building dreadnoughts and top-of-the-line battleships.

68. See Kennedy, *Rise and Fall*, 198–249.

69. Sir Edward Grey, Viscount of Fallodon, *Twenty-Five Years, 1892–1916* (New York: Frederick A. Stokes, 1925), 11.

70. Germany used her support for Britain's position in Egypt, which was threatened by the French, as leverage for British concessions to German interests in Turkey (e.g., railway contracts) and elsewhere.

71. Britain's vulnerabilities were masked by the popularity and influence of Alfred Thayer Mahan's book, *The Influence of Sea Power upon History*, published in 1890. Admiral Sir John Fisher understood, however, that advantages in naval power, nonetheless, required a revolution in naval strategy to secure, among other assets, Britain's increasingly important merchant marine. See Lambert, *Sir John Fisher's Naval Revolution*.

72. The phrase is Seeley's; see John Robert Seeley, *The Expansion of England*, 1883. Quoted in Charles Emmerson, *1913: In Search of the World before the Great War* (New York: Public Affairs, 2013), 22.

73. Grey, *Twenty-Five Years*, 6–7.

74. Emmerson, *1913*, 22.

75. For a theoretical discussion of ambiguity in international politics, see Jaqueline Best, "Ambiguity, Uncertainty, and Risk: Rethinking Indeterminancy," *International Political Sociology* 2, no. 4 (December 2008): 355–374. The literature on indeterminacy and risk is broad, but Best offers an introduction to it.

76. France sought territory claimed by Siam, a trading partner of Britain that hosted British assets. A crisis developed as Britain sent ships to protect her assets, and France pressed for concessions, instituting a naval blockade the British refused to recognize. Several naval incidents raised the prospect of war, which was avoided when the Siamese backed down and the French removed the blockade. For more on Grey's views on this event, see his memoir, *Twenty-Five Years*, 15–17.

77. Grey, *Twenty-Five Years*, 15.

78. Grey, *Twenty-Five Years*, 15.

79. Russia's per capita GNP and national product declined relative to those of other European powers from 1830 to 1890. By 1850, Russia had about five miles of railroad; the United States had eighty-five hundred miles of it. See Kennedy, *Rise and Fall*, 170–172. Russia's efforts to close this gap with France's help made Russia's power seem salient and more threatening than it probably should have been, given her internal weaknesses, which were not well appreciated in 1914.

80. See Solomon Wank, "Desperate Council in Vienna in July 1914: Berthold Molden's Unpublished Memorandum," *Central European History*, March 26, 1993, 281–310. Cited in Annika Mombauer, ed. and trans., *The Origins of the First World War: Diplomatic and Military Documents* (Manchester: Manchester University Press, 2013), 198–202. Emphasis added.

81. John C. G. Röhl, *Wilhelm II: Into the Abyss of War and Exile, 1900–1941* (Cambridge: Cambridge University Press, 2014), 1075.

82. Most famous at the time was the kaiser's rant against England, occasioned by his interview with the American journalist, Dr. William Bayard Hale, in 1908, in which the kaiser stated his expectation that Germany would soon go to war with Britain—and "the sooner the better!" For more on this astonishing interview, see Röhl, *Wilhelm II*, 622–628. Britain, after several unsuccessful attempts to persuade the kaiser of its lack of hostile intent, seems to have accepted the kaiser's temper as part of his nature.

83. Recall that, to counter France, Bismarck created the Three Emperors' League with Russia and Austria-Hungary. After Kaiser Wilhelm II came to power in 1890, however, German moves seemed irrational. First, the kaiser fired his chancellor; then he canceled the arrangement with Russia, leaving Europe's central powers, Germany and Austria-Hungary, in a potential Franco-Russian vice.

84. In the 1890s, Britain had suggested, fleetingly, a preference for the land-based solution, which would have countenanced German domination of Central and Eastern Europe. Britain's entente with France had then seemed to preclude it. When Germany launched her naval building program, the British tightened their entente with the French and began naval discussions with the Russians, all the while proclaiming their options open. British policy on the German question was thus unsettled right up to WWI and, arguably, through WWII—an uncertainty that made Stalin suspicious that Britain was interested in Hitler's eastward expansion at his expense.

85. "Had Anglo-American cooperation been effective in the Far East, British policymakers might have been able so to manage their complicated affairs that the threats could be prevented from materializing simultaneously. In the absence of such co-operation, the British found themselves unable to concentrate sufficient force in the right place and at the right moment." David Dilks, ed., *The Diaries of Alexander Cadogan: 1938-1945* (New York: G.P. Putnam's Sons, 1972), 29–30.

86. The superpowers would "solve" the German problem by dividing her—a temporary deal that left uncertainties for the future of Europe should Germany eventually be reunited. While few civilian decision-makers understood the political, military, and intelligence disconnects, many military leaders did, but avoided the implications. In such a context, Britain's ostensible role as both balancer and entente partner in Europe was both confusing and, because unsupported by strategic intelligence on relative power, largely untenable.

87. Such uncertainties had relatively little effect on Britain's response to the Catholic uprising in Ireland, or to the rising tide of anticolonialism in India. The policing infrastructure in these areas, combined with her worldwide communications system, usually generated timely intelligence.

88. A news department was not established in the Foreign Office until WWI; prior to this, influencing the press was not a familiar or institutionalized diplomatic tool. "Almost everything in the way of press relations depended on personal contacts and individual friendships." Steiner, *Foreign Office*, 192.

89. Christopher Clark uses this phrase to describe the ad hoc decision-making of Russia's ambassador in Serbia, Nicolai Hartwig, while alluding to the wider phenomenon among others representing St. Petersburg at the time. *Sleepwalkers*, 260.

90. Clark, *Sleepwalkers*, 184.

91. France had become a republic through radical and violent revolution, whereas Britain had stripped its monarchy of its military authority, while leaving some of its political purpose intact. In any event, by 1940, the only monarch to retain significant legal powers in Europe was King Leopold III of Belgium, who was commander in chief of the Belgian army and president of the cabinet. See Lynne Olson, *Last Hope Island* (New York: Random House, 2017), for more on the role of monarchs at the outset of WWII.

92. Clark, *Sleepwalkers*, 174. Zara Steiner argues, in contrast, that the king's role has been overinflated, and that Edward VII was more gadfly than strategic visionary. The truth would seem to lie somewhere in between. *Foreign Office*, 202–207.

93. Clark, *Sleepwalkers*, 528. The British king supposedly said, "We shall try all we can to keep out of this and shall remain neutral" to the kaiser's brother, Prince Henry of Prussia, on 28 July.

94. For more on the role of monarchs and leaders of occupied Europe in WWII, see Olson, *Last Hope Island*.

95. Clark, *Sleepwalkers*, 175.

96. Clark, *Sleepwalkers*, 176–177.

97. As the tsar heard about the threat to timber industries along the Yalu River, for example, he felt emboldened to declare red lines, stating that "under no circumstances

can I allow Japan to become firmly established [in Korea]. That would be a *casus belli.*" Clark, *Sleepwalkers*, 176.

98. Aleksandr Mikhailovich Bezobrazov, a former member of the Chevalier Guards, used his connections with the tsar to promote his commercial interests in Korea. According to the historian Christopher Clark, the tsar had "no personal secretariat and no personal secretary, so outsiders could use direct, personal connections to influence the Tsar's decisions" (*Sleepwalkers*, 175).

99. Clark, *Sleepwalkers*, 177. Although the tsar's private policymaking frustrated and confused his own government officials, particularly his experts in the Russian Foreign Ministry, note that his outside contacts were performing an intelligence function at which the government insiders were failing.

100. Clark, *Sleepwalkers*, 177. The chairmen of the council, Sergei Witte (until 1906), P. A. Stolypin (1906–11, when he was assassinated), and Vladimir Kokovtsov (1911–February 1914), all fell victim to the tsar's machinations. Clark, 178.

101. Clark, *Sleepwalkers*, 178.

102. Not a few diplomats speculated that the emperor was more relieved than aggrieved by his heir's assassination. Albertini, *War of 1914*, Vol. 2, 3.

103. Graydon A. Turnstall Jr., "Austria-Hungary," in Richard F. Hamilton and Holger H. Herwig, eds., *The Origins of World War I* (Cambridge: Cambridge University Press, 2003), 116.

104. Laurence Lafore, *The Long Fuse*, 2nd ed. (New York: J.B. Lippincott, 1971), 152.

105. "Like Nicholas II, Wilhelm frequently—especially in the early years of his reign—bypassed his responsible ministers by consulting with 'favourites,' encouraged factional strife in order to undermine the unity of government, and expounded views that had not been cleared with the relevant ministers or were at odds with the prevailing policy." Clark, *Sleepwalkers*, 178.

106. Joll and Martell, *Origins*, 91.

107. Clark, *Sleepwalkers*, 183.

108. William C. Fuller Jr., "The Russian Empire," in Ernest May, ed., *Knowing One's Enemies* (Princeton, NJ: Princeton University Press, 1984), 101–102.

109. Clark, *Sleepwalkers*, 186.

110. Fuller, "The Russian Empire," 100.

111. Clark, *Sleepwalkers*, 202.

112. Clark, *Sleepwalkers*, 202.

113. Steiner, *Foreign Office*, 83.

114. Steiner, *Foreign Office*, 84–85.

115. These disagreements chiefly concerned the fate of the union with Ireland, and the challenge posed by Germany.

116. Henry Bienen and Nicolas van de Walle, *Of Time and Power: Leadership Duration in the Modern World* (Redwood City, CA: Stanford University Press, 1991), 170–171.

117. Clark, *Sleepwalkers*, 193–195.

118. Clark, *Sleepwalkers*, 196.

119. Daladier, an experienced war minister, cemented relations with his Foreign Ministry through liaison with the ministry's popular and brilliant secretary general,

Alexis Léger. Léger received the Nobel Prize for Literature in 1960. May, *Strange Victory*, 741.

120. Fuller, "The Russian Empire," 125. Civil-military tensions were especially high in Russia after the ascension of Alexander III. Soldiers rarely advised diplomats in Russia between 1907 and 1913.

121. See Steven E. Rowe, "Labor," in *International Encyclopedia of the First World War: 1914–1918* (online at encyclopedia.1914-1918-online.net, version 1.0, last updated October 8, 2014).

122. Correlli Barnett, *The Collapse of British Power* (Atlantic Highlands, NJ: Humanities Press International, 1986), xi.

123. See Richard Popplewell, "The Surveillance of Indian 'Seditionists' in North America," in Christopher Andrew and Jeremy Noakes, eds., *Intelligence and International Relations, 1900–1945* (Exeter: Exeter University, 1987), 49–76.

124. Barbara W. Tuchman, *The Guns of August* (New York: Random House, 1962), 1.

125. Keith Jeffrey, *The Secret History of MI-6: 1909–1949* (New York: Penguin Press, 2010), 284–285.

126. Mombauer, *Origins*, "1 May 1914, Grey to Bertie (83)," 129.

127. These were the ingredients of fascism. Corporatism is the binding of labor to management using threats, punishments, and rewards enforced from the top for the purpose of collective power against all challengers.

128. Statesmen were, however, only beginning to appreciate the value of counterintelligence as opposed to simple security; whereas the first interdicts foreign intelligence for the purpose of gaining advantages in intelligence and decision-making, the latter simply thwarts it, regardless of the political results. Jennifer E. Sims, "Twentieth Century Counterintelligence: The Theoretical Basis for Reform," in Jennifer E. Sims and Burton Gerber, eds., *Vaults, Mirrors and Masks: Rediscovering U.S. Counterintelligence* (Washington, DC: Georgetown University Press, 2009), 19–51.

129. Larry D. Hill, *Emissaries to a Revolution: Woodrow Wilson's Executive Agents in Mexico* (Baton Rouge: Louisiana State University Press, 1973), 20–21.

130. International eugenic conferences were held in 1912, 1921, and 1932. Eugenics was taught as a scientific discipline in many colleges and universities around the world, but lost credibility in the 1930s, particularly after it became part of the Nazi program.

131. For example, see Röhl, *Wilhelm II*, 1096.

132. Human intelligence organizations exploited such secret societies, but found them more useful for conducting secret policies, such as counterintelligence operations and covert action inside foreign territory, than for gathering useful information for diplomacy. For an amusing discussion of the pre-WWI fascination with amateur intelligence and secret societies, see Andrew, *Her Majesty's Secret Service*, 34–85. For a startling, but less credible, read on this subject, see Richard B. Spence, *Secret Agent 666: Aleister Crowley, British Intelligence and the Occult* (Port Townsend, WA: Feral House, 2008).

133. Jeffrey, *Secret History of MI-6*, 282–283.

134. Röhl, *Wilhelm II*, 1096.

135. Andrew, *Her Majesty's Secret Service*, 207.
136. Governors responded by shaping and championing public agendas, whether Clemenceau's vision of a flattened Germany post-WWI or Wilson's vision of self-determination encompassed by his 14 Points, or Roosevelt's championing of a "New Deal." This was the dawning of the age of "perception management."
137. John Fox Jr. and Michael Warner, "Counterintelligence: The American Experience," in Sims and Gerber, *Vaults, Mirrors and Masks*, 51–69.
138. The literature on fascism and its relationship to Nazism is voluminous. One starting place is Zeev Sternhell, with Mario Sznajder and Maia Asheri, *The Birth of Fascist Ideology: From Cultural Rebellion to Political Revolution*, trans. David Maisel (Princeton, NJ: Princeton University Press, 1994).
139. Russia proved an exception to this trajectory on intelligence sharing, but an exemplar of learned political mastery of intelligence. Bolshevik revolutionaries, once alienated from institutionalized intelligence, fused it to their covert political apparatus once in power. Then they used it to slaughter their political opposition by the hundreds of thousands, win control of the country, and destroy the Russian military. Stalin, a former intelligence chief, made the most of this Russian evolution.
140. There is some dispute on this matter between official historians of the war and others. For a contrary view, see Callum MacDonald, *The Lost Battle: Crete 1941* (London: Macmillan, 1993), especially 134.
141. See May, *Strange Victory* and Edmund L. Blandford, *S.S. Intelligence* (Shrewsbury, England: Airlife Publishing, 2000).
142. As F. H. Hinsley has written, the organizational problems in Britain before WWII "arose from the insularity and the rivalry that may bedevil relations whenever several bodies share responsibility in a single field." Moreover, the rise of professionalism among the services demanded coordination of input into the policy process—a development that "was either resisted or at best neglected by the departments most involved." (*British Intelligence in the Second World War*, abridged ed. (Cambridge: Cambridge University Press, 1993), 3.
143. In fact, Yardley's work was in decline already because, by the late 1920s, laws passed to restore the privacy of US communications in peacetime had led telegraph companies to turn off the "feed" for the government's cryptanalysts.
144. The SIS architecture for producer-consumer relationships developed during this time has been termed "the 1921 arrangement." See Philip H. J. Davies, *MI6 and the Machinery of Spying* (Portland, OR: Frank Cass, 2004), 56.
145. Christopher Andrew, "Secret Intelligence and British Foreign Policy 1900–1939," in Andrew and Noakes, *Intelligence and International Relations*, 20.
146. Andrew, "Secret Intelligence," 17–19.
147. Christopher Andrew, "Codebreakers and Foreign Offices: The French, British and American Experience" in Christopher Andrew and David Dilks, *The Missing Dimension: Governments and Intelligence Communities in the Twentieth Century* (London: Macmillan, 1984), 33–34.
148. For example, see the early mistakes of the SIS in Britain recounted in Andrew, "Secret Intelligence," especially 18.

149. Andrew, "Secret Intelligence," 12.
150. Andrew, *Her Majesty's Secret Service*, 45. Among the influential of these amateur spies was one William Le Queux, whose "immense clubability" and magnetic personality helped him network among the powerful. "His most important conquest was Lieutenant-Colonel James Edmonds who headed the counterintelligence and secret service attached to the War Office in 1907."
151. See Jeffery, *Secret History of MI-6*, 184–187. SIS and other national intelligence services used the diaspora and were deceived, repeatedly, by the Cheka's network of double agents. The latter provided false information and lured, among others, the gullible British agent Sidney Reilly to his death.
152. Having employed cryptanalysis against anarchists in the 1890s, the Sûreté gradually began intercepting diplomatic traffic after the turn of the century. In 1904 it got access to the Japanese diplomatic code and, within sixty days, had reconstructed most of its codebook—over sixteen hundred pages long. This singular feat bought trust in the Foreign Ministry. "For the remainder of the [Russo-Japanese] war all diplomatic telegrams exchanged between Tokyo and the Paris embassy were decrypted at the Sûreté and copies sent to the Quai." The Sûreté acquired a full-time cryptographic unit in 1907. Andrew, "Secret Intelligence," 35–36.
153. May, *Strange Victory*, 133.
154. May, *Strange Victory*, 132–137.
155. Such operations were hardly new, but the productivity was unprecedented given industry's new importance to war and the new capacities for secret, long-distance communications. The British ran WWI's covert White Lady Network, which used everyday citizens to observe the movement of German trains through Belgium and occupied France and then send the information to Britain using hidden radios. Port watchers did the same for US monitoring of naval assets in the Pacific during WWII. The growing capacity to collect useful intelligence through observation as opposed to theft proved a boost to classic espionage, as well. Agents could develop access to targets over long periods—living their cover more authentically—while still being secretly tasked by their sponsor.
156. That overt, open, or unclassified sources make the resulting intelligence necessarily unclassified and, thus, sharable with everyone is a common misconception. Intelligence does merit protection only to protect sources, but also to protect the methods used to sift, collate, and analyze it, and especially, to protect the advantages gained from it. Although the British learned the German order of battle from open observations, the fact they did so, and how, was necessarily secret.
157. See Andrew, *Defend the Realm*, 3–28. In Britain, talk of rampant German spying, and private efforts to thwart it, caused Prime Minister Herbert Asquith's government to ask the Committee of Imperial Defence in March 1909 to study "the nature and extent of foreign espionage that is at present taking place within this country and the danger to which it may expose us." The CID found an "extensive system" of German espionage, possibly for purposes of invasion, based in large part on "casual information" (17). Private citizens reported a wave of suspicious activities, and private citizens reacted. Spy novelists fueled much of the public alarm. The

notorious William Le Queux promoted himself as a spy and government insider, although his book, *The Invasion of 1910*, was a work of pure fiction. In the United States, some vigilantes during WWI were just in their teens, such as those involved in the Anti-Yellow Dog League. For more on the problem of vigilantism, the role of the American Protective League, and the early years of the Bureau of Investigation, see Fox and Warner, "Counterintelligence," 51–68, especially 53–54. The APL, while officially sanctioned, did not maintain full control of field operations carried out by private citizens against immigrants.

158. See Fox and Warner, "Counterintelligence," 51–68.

159. Direction-finding involves using multiple antennas on mobile vehicles to locate a radio emitter through triangulation.

160. The challenge of finding agents operating across borders led to the honing of skills in all-source intelligence, with human, signals, imagery, counterintelligence, and open-source collection all contributing to successful operations. See Nigel West, *MASK: MI5's Penetration of the Communist Party of Great Britain* (New York: Routledge, 2005).

161. Quoted from Emmerson, *1913*, 28.

162. Keith Neilson has pointed out, however, that Russia's economic situation was not as dire as some historians have suggested, with an annual growth rate of 3.5 percent and a national income that was 97.1 percent of Great Britain's. Russia's industrial production increased by almost 50 percent from 1908 to 1913, with defense industries in the lead. See Keith Neilson, "Russia," in Keith Wilson, ed., *Decisions for War* (Abingdon, Oxon: Routledge, 2003), 98 and 103.

163. Steiner, *Foreign Office*, 16.

164. Emmerson, *1913*, 88.

165. Emmerson, *1913*, 92–93. In fact, Austria had an efficient army; she just could not build internal power in response to external threat as fast as other states could. That her incapacity was, to some extent, her own doing masked her misery. In a bid for dynastic longevity in 1867, after Austria had been defeated by Prussia, the young emperor Franz Joseph proposed joint rule with the Hungarians to augment power against a consolidating German state. The subsequent arrangements so complicated the empire's governance that industrialization was effectively stalled and its benefits illiberally spread.

166. Andrew, "Introduction: Intelligence and International Relations 1900–1945," in Andrew and Noakes, *Intelligence and International Relations*, 6.

167. Much is made of the connected bloodlines among monarchs of this era. But the familial connections among diplomats was equally striking, especially before WWI. The brothers Cambon represented France in London and Berlin; Prince Lichnowsky, Germany's ambassador in London, was cousin to Britain's ambassador to Russia. Moreover, most European powers required that ambassadors have personal wealth, ensuring that most diplomatic representation came from the noble or bourgeois classes. And although Britain reformed its foreign service before WWI, most of those in senior positions came from one of the three most elite schools in Britain.

168. Davies, *MI6*, 27.

Chapter 11

1. From *Woodrow Wilson, 1913–1921*, published by the Center for the Study of Intelligence. Accessed on 2 February 2015, at https://www.cia.gov/static/14457f87b 514589917a4efc87ef83d49/Our-First-Line-of-Defense-Presidential-Reflections-on-US-Intelligence.pdf.

2. For a comprehensive review of this strategy and the argument for its coherence and deliberateness, see Luigi Albertini, *The Origins of the War of 1914*, 3 vols., trans. Isabella M. Massey (New York: Enigma Books, 2005). See also James Joll and Gordon Martel, *The Origins of the First World War*, 3rd ed. (New York: Pearson-Longman, 2007).

3. According to the constitution of the Dual Monarchy, the emperor should have chaired the council, but he had developed the habit, as explained in the previous chapter, of leaving this job to his foreign minister.

4. These details did not include, however, how a surprise attack, which required secrecy, and a strong diplomatic initiative, which required information sharing, could be compatible.

5. Although Hungary's Count Tisza had initial reservations about what to do in the wake of the assassination, he shared the mindset described, and was appeased by assurances that Austria-Hungary would not make territorial acquisition a war aim.

6. Apart from what Biliński knew (see below), intelligence was still scarce concerning Serbia's culpability in the assassination.

7. Albertini, *War of 1914*, vol. 2, 190.

8. Albertini, *War of 1914*, vol. 2, 25. As we will see below, the crime was actually perpetrated by a separate entity, the Black Hand, a terrorist organization opposed to the Belgrade regime and whose members were linked to the 1903 regicide in Serbia. If Viennese officials had correctly identified the perpetrators, their strategy for gaining the sympathy of the tsar might have had a better chance of success because the Russians backed Belgrade's efforts to defeat the Black Hand.

9. This matter is contested in the literature. Albertini (*War of 1914*, vol. 2, 101–105) claims that the Serbian minister made his remarks in a general way and on his own initiative. Christopher Clark notes the importance of the Serbian envoy's connections to both the Serbian government and pan-Serb nationalists, including the Black Hand, but seems to agree with Albertini (*The Sleepwalkers: How Europe Went to War in 1914* [New York: HarperCollins, 2013], 60–61). Sean McMeekin holds that Serbian PM was aware of the plot and that the envoy's warning, which may have gone to others, was explicit and purposeful. See his *July 1914: Countdown to War* (New York: Basic Books, 2019), 51.

10. Annika Mombauer, ed. and trans., *The Origins of the First World War: Diplomatic and Military Documents* (Manchester: Manchester University Press, 2013), 177. Potiorek seems to have told a French diplomat that Biliński was to blame for the outrage and would likely "soon be replaced." He was not. Biliński knew that the envoy had taken the information only to him because the man's relationship with Berchtold was bad,

but that the intelligence was deemed so important by his government that the failure to provide it would have been noticed.

11. See Albertini's discussion of the Biliński matter, *War of 1914*, vol. 2, 102–103.

12. Indeed, given the Russian influence in Belgrade and the Russian ambassador's dismay at learning of the success of the assassination, it is possible the Serb's effort to forewarn Vienna was prompted by Hartwig himself.

13. This leadership was uncharacteristic of him. According to the German historian Hermann Lutz, Berchtold was "by nature . . . soft, dependent, easily swayed," and so "irresolute" during the Balkan wars that he was subject to criticism. According to the Italian historian Albertini, Berchtold finally became convinced by the autumn of 1913 that war with Serbia was necessary. See Albertini, *War of 1914*, vol. 2, 125.

14. Graydon A. Tunstall Jr., "Austria-Hungary," in Richard F. Hamilton and Holger H. Herwig, *The Origins of World War I* (Cambridge: Cambridge University Press, 2003), 133.

15. Tunstall, "Austria-Hungary," 125.

16. For more on this group and their influence, see Fritz Fellner, "Austria-Hungary," in Keith Wilson, ed., *Decisions for War, 1914*, 10–12.

17. Fellner, "Austria-Hungary," 10–12. Fellner points out that Aehrenthal was, however, careful to avoid war by use of skillful diplomatic tactics that his followers could not, or in any case did not, emulate in the run-up to WWI.

18. According to Fritz Fellner ("Austria-Hungary," 12), Urbas called his group a "fronde of diplomatic cadets." The quotation is from Karl von Macchio, "Momentbilder aus der Julikrise 1914," *Berliner Monatshefte* 14 (1936): 763–788. Forgách was the strategic planner, Hoyos the agent of influence with the German government, and Musulin had a reputation for being among the most hawkish; he also had baggage, having been reprimanded for forging documents during court proceedings to implicate Serbia during the Freijung affair.

19. Tunstall, "Austria-Hungary," 127–128.

20. Albertini, *Origins of 1914*, vol. 1, 531. Czernin ended his report by comparing himself to "the leader of a reconnoitering patrol who sends back information of enemy concentrations to headquarters and finds all his reports and requests disregarded." Albertini, 532. That would soon change.

21. Albertini, *Origins of 1914*, vol. 1, 532.

22. Whether Berchtold knew the degree to which the Russian ambassador ran Russia's Balkan policies, including extensive espionage operations, is uncertain, but it seems likely he played a strong role. Hartwig was, in fact, worried about the assassination's effect on Serbia, fearing it would prompt an Austrian attack that Serbia could not defeat.

23. Gordon Martel, *The Month That Changed the World: July 1914* (Oxford: Oxford University Press, 2014), 103. Martel notes that the German ambassador to Austria-Hungary witnessed these demonstrations.

24. These views were reported by the German ambassador in a cable sent 30 June: "I frequently hear expressed here, even among serious people, the wish that at last a final and fundamental reckoning should be had with the Serbs" (Mombauer, *Origins*,

171). The Serbian ambassador reported similarly on the same day: "The tendency at Vienna to represent in the eyes of Europe the outrage . . . as an act of conspiracy engineered in Serbia is becoming more and more apparent." Mombauer, 170.

25. 27 June 1914: Bertie Memorandum, Document 102, in Mombauer, *Origins*, 151. See also n. 58. Grey complained of the leak to London's Paris ambassador, Sir Edmund Bertie, on 25 June, fearing it might hurt the good relations with Germany at the time.

26. See Document 87: 28 May 1914, Sazonov to Benckendorff, in Mombauer, *Origins*, 136.

27. Poincaré's "rise to high office took place against the background of a shift in the tone of French politics after Agadir that historians have called the 'Nationalist Revival.' " Paul Cambon saw Poincaré's "clarity" in his relations with Russia as stiffness and inexperience in diplomacy. See Clark, *Sleepwalkers*, 295.

28. For a copy of the Matscheko memorandum, see Mombauer, *Origins* (Document #117), 185–188.

29. This section, which accurately reflected the Hungarian premier Tisza's view, may have been drafted by him.

30. Mombauer, *Origins*, 188. Much of the memo was probably based on an earlier draft provided by the Royal Hungarian premier, Count Tisza, who was to become the sole skeptic of a policy of preventive war in the wake of the assassination.

31. Tisza had met with the emperor on 1 July to explain his concerns.

32. Neumann was a confidant of Wilhelm von Stumm, chief of the political department in the German Foreign Office. Neumann proved a good channel for Stumm to contact Count Hoyos, who was well known within German circles as an ardent, militant imperialist. Hoyos had become acquainted with Zimmermann, acting foreign secretary in the early days of the July Crisis, when Hoyos had been posted to China. Clark, *Sleepwalkers*, 402.

33. Clark, *Sleepwalkers*, 402. "Berchtold used the mission, in effect, to shut the Hungarian leader out of the decision-making process, and to ensure that Habsburg policy evolved in conformity with his own preference for a swift and decisive response to the outrage." See also Tisza's message to Franz Joseph of 1 July in which he counsels against war: Mombauer, *Origins* (#111), 1 July: Tisza to Franz Joseph, 174.

34. The German ambassador had told Berchtold on 3 July that "grandiose talk" of the kind Austrians loved could not replace a solid plan of action. See Clark, *Sleepwalkers*, 402.

35. The reporting from the bilateral ambassador (a member of Hoyos's hawkish circle at the FO), confirmed this view, although Hoyos later said (1933) that he had, in fact, drafted it, as well. The process of German decision-making, including the intelligence supporting the decision to offer a blank check, will be discussed further below.

36. See the reports from the Hoyos mission and the ambassador's meetings in Mombauer, *Origins*, 190–193.

37. Mombauer, *Origins*, 191.

38. Mombauer, *Origins*, 202.

39. McMeekin, *July 1914*, 108.

40. Mombauer, *Origins* (#119, 5 July: Hoyos's personal account), 190. The heading in Mombauer appears to be in error: Hoyos's mission was to Berlin, not London.

41. 6 July: Forgách to Tisza, Mombauer, *Origins*, 208.

42. Historians have noted that Berchtold's comments during the 7 July council meeting were strikingly similar to points made in the Molden memo, and that it is probable, if not certain, that he had read it beforehand. See Mombauer, *Origins*, 198 (Document #126 n. 35). Molden, a journalist and editor, was the Austro-Hungarian consul general in Warsaw. He was apparently in Vienna in July.

43. For Molden's memo, see Document #126 in Mombauer, *Origins*, 198–202; this quotation is from 201, emphasis added.

44. On 24 July, Sazonov told Buchanan that Russia would mobilize the moment Austria crossed the Serbian frontier, triggering a wider war. Grey understood this too, saying as much to Lichnowsky, the German ambassador, on the twenty-sixth. Sir Eyre Crowe's minute on Buchanan's message shows the foreign office was aware of the interlocking dynamics of the Great Powers' mobilization requirements, and thus, of Britain's vulnerability to being dragged into a war that was not, directly, in defense of her own interests. In this regard, he cites the precedence of Prussia in 1805. See Albertini, *Origins of 1914*, vol. 2, 408–410.

45. Albertini, *Origins of 1914*, vol. 2, 189–190. Recall that Otto Czernin was the younger brother of the ambassador to Romania at the time.

46. Count Metternich, who had been the German ambassador to Britain, had been one of those who helped shape a policy of Anglo-German détente that had come to fruition in 1913 and early 1914. He was replaced by Ambassador Lichnowsky, an Anglophile who enjoyed close relations with Sir Edward Grey, the British foreign minister, in 1914. Count Albert Viktor Julius Joseph Michael von Mensdorff-Pouilly-Dietrichstein (Mensdorff) was ambassador from Vienna to London, and was also very well connected both at the Foreign Office and at the court of George V, who was Mensdorff's distant cousin. Mensdorff had been promoted above his seniors at the request of George V's father, Edward VII. He worked with his Russian counterpart in 1913 to achieve a compromise on Albanian borders that Austrians believed entailed far too many concessions, and for which Berchtold received some of the blame. See Clark, *Sleepwalkers*, 284–285.

47. Most historians seem to agree that at least Berchtold had seen all the evidence and read the analyses described above. Tisza had certainly read the Matscheko analysis, and perhaps Molden's, as well. In any event, Berchtold used this intelligence to frame his remarks during the meeting. Most crucially, the intelligence from Germany was made available to all.

48. Mombauer, *Origins* (#134, 7 July: Minutes of the Joint Council of Ministers for Common Affairs), 211.

49. Mombauer, *Origins* (#134, 7 July: Minutes of the Joint Council of Ministers for Common Affairs), 211.

50. The quotation is a letter written by the Saxon military plenipotentiary in Berlin to the Saxon minister of war, Adolf von Carlowitz, on 3 July, reporting on impressions given him by the general staff in Berlin. See Mombauer, *Origins*, 178.

51. "Despite Conrad's attempts at modernization, the k.u.k. Army remained in poor shape to fight a major war. Its divisions generally consisted of two brigades each with two regiments of four battalions. The artillery complement of the division was about forty-two guns of varying calibres, and the total strength of the division came to about 15,000 men. Cavalry was organized into divisions of about 7,000, with twenty-four light field guns and a small number of machine guns. The only area in which the Austro-Hungarian forces might have been regarded as having an advantage was in mountain artillery, where they had pioneered the use of small, mobile guns that could easily be taken apart and reassembled. However, there were no significant mountainous areas where these might give Conrad's men an edge in a war against Russia." Prit Buttar, *Collision of Empires: The War on the Eastern Front in 1914* (Oxford: Osprey, 2014), 85.

52. The essential strategic dilemma had become worse over the past year. Colonel Redl's treason, discovered only in May 1913, had forced expensive and complicated changes in Austria's military structure, but had done nothing to change mobilization options, which were inflexible, potentially contradictory to the requirements of the alliance with Germany, and perhaps most importantly, also known to the Russians.

53. Germany had resisted Vienna's offensive moves in the Balkans during the recent wars because the kaiser was not ready for a continental war. Having pulled the reins, he came to regret these decisions by 1914. Austria-Hungary's and Italy's conflicting interests in the Balkans had long threatened to tear the Triple Alliance apart.

54. The question was not whether Austria was in a position to provide such deterrence herself, but whether she was in a position to force her ally's hand. When asked by Berchtold whether Austria would mobilize in Galicia at the start of war with Serbia, Conrad had said no. He had not explained why. Such a deterrent move, which was bound to trigger a Russian response, would have been suicidal. Austria did not have escalation dominance on that frontier, and Germany, which could have had it, had chosen not to.

55. Bethmann-Hollweg had told Hoyos that Germany would "cover (Austria's) back and fulfill her alliance obligations in every way." See Hoyos's personal account in Mombauer, *Origins*, 191.

56. See Hoyos's personal account of his mission to Berlin in Mombauer, *Origins*, 190–191.

57. For more on the Redl affair, see Clark, *Sleepwalkers*, 115–117.

58. Buttar, *Collision of Empires*, 84–85.

59. Conrad had decided to disembark troops further east to counter impressions likely held in Russia as a result of Redl's treachery.

60. Buttar, *Collision of Empires*, 85.

61. Buttar, *Collision of Empires*, 85.

62. Buttar, *Collision of Empires*, 85–86.

63. Albertini, *Origins of 1914*, vol. 2, 122. Emphasis added. The Austrian espionage network in Russia was significant before Redl's treachery exposed it, leading to the termination of many Austrian spies. In fact, Redl had blackmailed his Russian counterpart, who had blackmailed him, and they both agreed to secure their own positions by telling each other about penetration agents, permitting their capture, and thus

solidifying the counterintelligence chiefs' own reputations within their respective governments.

64. The quotations in this paragraph are based on Conrad's own notes of the meeting. See Mombauer, *Origins*, 189.

65. As explained above, the Hoyos mission would not reveal Austria's military conundrum. Indeed, Hoyos had received assurances of support. But the mission had been a diplomatic one and had received a diplomatic response. Conrad knew, and no evidence suggests he shared, that the German question was not just one of diplomatic intention, but of technical military capacities, and these were deficient to Austria's developing purpose.

66. "It is a measure of Conrad's limitations at the highest strategic level that he failed to grasp the impossibility of rapid mobilization given the state of the Dual Monarchy's railway system" (Buttar, *Collision of Empires*, 86).

67. Albertini, *Origins of 1914*, vol. 3, 529.

68. Conrad knew that Berchtold had some doubts about whether Germany would cover Austria-Hungary's rear. Conrad did not want to admit defeat before battle. When Berchtold later told him he was sending an emissary to learn whether Berlin would secure Romania's loyalty if Austria struck Serbia, Conrad replied that "Germany must first of all be asked whether she will cover our rear against Russia or not." At the moment of decision for war, Conrad's point should have served as a warning to the foreign minister. Albertini, *Origins of 1914*, vol. 2, 124–125.

69. Albertini, *Origins of 1914*, vol. 2, 127.

70. It was on this point that Conrad's intelligence was crucial. He could have countered Tisza by pointing out that Austria could not act independently to get Tisza's preferred outcome. That Conrad is not recorded as countering Tisza's view suggests that Conrad stayed mum in the hopes that Tisza would be persuaded by other arguments, as turned out to be the case.

71. It was not, of course. The faster Germany could defeat France, the faster it could swing east to engage Russia. This reply only underscored Berchtold's lack of appreciation for the two-front problem.

72. Where Berchtold had acquired his intelligence on this point is unclear; the last official Russian census had taken place in 1877, and the next was planned for 1915.

73. As we will see in the next section, this interpretation of the "intelligence" from Berlin was a stretch.

74. Redl, as counterintelligence chief, had used a list of spies provided by Russia to sustain his reputation as a spy-catcher. In turn, Redl provided his handler with not just the names of Austrian spies, who were fewer in number, but also reams of intelligence on allied war plans, fortifications, military hardware, logistics, and doctrine.

75. Albertini, *Origins of 1914*, vol. 2, 182–183.

76. For more on the impact of collegial thinking on intelligence analysis, see Ernest May, ed., *Knowing One's Enemies: Intelligence Assessment before the Two World Wars* (Princeton, NJ: Princeton University Press, 1984).

77. According to Joseph Redlich's diary entry of 3 November, 1916: "Yesterday evening alone at Alek Hoyos'. We talked very confidentially and companionably. He does not

regard peace as near! I was very touched when he told me openly that he has for a long time been depressed by the feeling really to have been the actual cause of the war because he had held and used decisive influence over Berchtold." Quoted in Mombauer, *Origins*, 184 n. 4.

78. See the prior chapter for a discussion of the role of the emperor and the chaotic decision-making structure in Vienna before WWI.

79. See Imanuel Geiss, ed., *July 1914: The Outbreak of the First World War—Selected Documents* (New York: Charles Scribner and Sons, 1967), 64–65. In the margins of the German ambassador's report conveying his efforts to soothe reactions in Vienna immediately after the assassination, the kaiser scribbled such phrases as "This is stupid!" and "It is none of his business as it is solely the affair of Austria, what she plans to do in this case."

80. See John C. G. Röhl, "Germany," in Wilson, *Decisions for War*.

81. Buttar, *Collision of Empires*, 102. The alliance in question was a defensive one involving Italy, whose leaders had not been informed of Austria-Hungary's plan when it was presented to Germany on 6 July or adopted on 7 July by the Council of Ministers in Vienna.

82. See the previous chapter in this volume for more background on this subject.

83. See Max Hastings, *Catastrophe 1914* (New York: Vintage, 2014), for a discussion of this problem.

84. On 18 May 1914, the quartermaster of the German general staff, Count von Waldersee, wrote a memo with a pessimistic analysis of Germany's military future (despite the Army Bill of 1913). He also wrote, however, that Germany's enemies were at present unlikely to start a war. France's army was in turmoil and had insufficient heavy artillery; Russia was reorganizing its army, and railways were still incomplete; Britain was distracted by domestic problems, particularly the Irish question, so had "absolutely no inclination to participate in a war." For these reasons, the balance of power was still in Germany's (and the Triple Alliance's) favor, and there was no reason to avoid war. Röhl, "Germany," 45.

85. This assumption was erroneous. See the previous chapter.

86. In June 1914, the British government was dominated by radical pacifists, who disliked notions of an "alliance" with France, and detested the idea of one with Russia. Liberal imperialists, such as Sir Edward Grey, Winston Churchill, and Prime Minister Asquith, believed in the need to support Entente partners against the rise of Germany. Although in powerful positions, the latter were a distinct minority.

87. This assumption was not incorrect, but it should have been understood as conditional. Britain had no equities in the Balkans, unless a war there triggered the defeat of France as a Great Power.

88. Even the kaiser believed he had vacillated in the past. In a comment to Krupp on July 6, he insisted he would not back down. See the previous chapter for more on the world view of the Germans in 1914.

89. Although 1913, the twenty-fifth year of the kaiser's rule, had been a year of celebration and of peace, 1914 portended the continuing rise of the political Left in the Reichstag, increasing tension between leftist and monarchist elements, and deepening divisions

between civilians and the Prussian military. See the previous chapter for further explanation of this context.

90. See Albertini, *Origins of 1914*, vol. 2, 182–183.

91. "This time I shall not topple over," he reportedly said to the German industrialist Gustav Krupp von Bohlen und Halbach. "The Kaiser's repeated emphasis on how nobody will be able to accuse him this time of indecision was almost comic." John C. G. Röhl, *Wilhelm II: Into the Abyss of War and Exile, 1900–1941*, trans. Sheila de Bellaigue and Roy Bridge (Cambridge: Cambridge University Press, 2014), 1029.

92. Mombauer, *Origins* (#122, July 5: Plessen Diary), 194.

93. See Hastings, *Catastrophe 1914*.

94. Mombauer, *Origins* (#135, 7 July : Riezler's Diary), 219.

95. Mombauer, *Origins* (#135, 7 July: Riezler's Diary), 219.

96. Mombauer, *Origins* (#135, 7 July: Riezler's Diary), 219.

97. The German military assumed a two-front war in any contingency involving Russia. On the twenty-fifth, in a letter to his wife, the head of the kaiser's military cabinet, Moritz Freiherr von Lyncker, wrote that it would "be hard to fight with 2 fronts, such as we have never before had on such a scale." So the German military believed the kaiser was risking a continental war well before the Russians mobilized, and the Serbs had even reacted to the ultimatum. See Wilson, *Decisions for War*, 38.

98. Mombauer, *Origins*, "5 July: Falkenhayn to Moltke," 195–196. The chancellor's aide, Kurt Riezler, recorded Bethmann-Hollweg's views on 7 July, two days after the meeting in Potsdam, but the sources of Bethmann-Hollweg's concerns predated that meeting. There are, however, some questions about the reliability of his diary. Mombauer, 20–21.

99. Mombauer, *Origins*, "5 July: Falkenhayn to Moltke," 195–196. Emphasis added.

100. Mombauer, *Origins* (#130, 6 July: Szögyény-Marich to Berchtold), 206. Emphasis added to indicate that Germany's assurances of full support seemed rooted in the notion that Austria was seeking approval of vigorous diplomacy to fundamentally change the character of the Triple Alliance. In the absence of a world war, this would have been a dramatic change in which Germany might have rightfully expected to take the lead.

101. Mombauer, *Origins* (#130, 6 July: Szögyény-Marich to Berchtold), 207.

102. Mombauer, *Origins* (#131, 6 July: Forgách to Tisza), 208.

103. Quoted in Albertini, *Origins of 1914*, vol. 2, 203.

104. See previous chapter.

105. Grey had learned from Lichnowsky that Chancellor von Bethmann-Hollweg wanted to convey Germany's hope that London and Berlin would continue to work closely together. Grey had conveyed at that time his strong endorsement of this approach, noting that, while Britain saw itself as part of the Entente grouping, she was committed to guarding against war. Britain would not fight on the side of an aggressor because "public opinion was against that." Grey understood Lichnowsky as he "regarded our intimacy with France and Russia without any misgiving." Grey, *Twenty-Five Years*, vol. 1, 304–305.

106. Grey, *Twenty-Five Years*, vol. 1, 302–303. Note Grey's self-perception as one "in the centre" of the troubles, when in fact, he knew little of developments on the ground. His reference is probably more to the "troubles" felt and conveyed by the governments of the Great Powers in view of Balkan insurgencies, terrorism, and war.

107. Albertini, quoting Grey's report of the meeting. *Origins of 1914*, vol. 2, 204.

108. Although Grey could not have known it at the time, the German chancellor had lost trust in Lichnowsky and had begun to plan to cut him out of plans for support to Austria.

109. Albertini, *Origins of 1914*, vol. 2, 204.

110. Albertini, *Origins of 1914*, vol. 2, 205.

111. Albertini, *Origins of 1914*, vol. 2, 206.

112. Albertini, *Origins of 1914*, vol. 2, 207.

113. Albertini, *Origins of 1914*, vol. 2, 207–208.

114. Albertini, *Origins of 1914*, vol. 2, 209–210.

115. Albertini, *Origins of 1914*, vol. 2, 215.

116. Albertini, *Origins of 1914*, vol. 2, 215.

117. The naval agreement led the French to move their naval forces from the northern coast of France to the Mediterranean and British ships to quit the Mediterranean to defend the Channel and France's northern coastline. Britain's military commitment to France entailed early deployment of an expeditionary force to defend a sector of Germany's expected invasion route through Belgium.

118. See Clark, *Sleepwalkers*, 88–90 for more on Forgách's past.

119. Recall from the earlier discussion of the 7 July Austro-Hungarian Council of Ministers meeting that Biliński had been warned by a Serbian envoy. Paschich knew the Serbian intelligence chief might be involved and tried, apparently, to warn Vienna.

120. There is evidence that the Russian military attaché in Belgrade actually knew of the assassination plot well before it occurred, and perhaps even offered Russian endorsement from higher-ups in St. Petersburg. Serbian and Russian military intelligence collaborated in supporting the Black Hand and the running of spies in Bosnia-Herzegovina, as well as Austria proper. See Albertini, *Origins of 1914*, vol. 2, 82–86. Such military collusion and prior knowledge in the field do not necessarily indicate, however, that Sazonov and other Russian decision-makers knew of them when deciding on the legitimacy of Austrian claims of Serbian complicity in the assassination plot.

121. Berchtold's strategy of deception and surprise required that his adversaries not compare notes or enflame each other's reactions to developments, which they might be inclined to do if the Austrian ultimatum to Serbia were made during this Franco-Russian summit.

122. Albertini, *Origins of 1914*, vol. 2, 184. Emphasis added.

123. It seems his source was Bunsen. See Albertini, *Origins of 1914*, vol. 2, 184–185.

124. Albertini, *Origins of 1914*, vol. 2, 185.

125. Joll and Martel, *Origins*, 20.

Chapter 12

1. For an introduction to the problem of illegals (intelligence officers operating clandestinely and without official cover) during this period and the later Cold War, see Nigel West, *The Illegals: The Double Lives of the Cold War's Most Secret Agents* (Reading, England: Hodder and Stoughton / Coronet Books, 1993). For more on Britain's interwar-period counterintelligence operations against the Communist International, see Nigel West, *MASK: MI5's Penetration of the Communist Party of Great Britain* (New York: Routledge, 2005).

2. Ernest May, *Strange Victory: Hitler's Conquest of France* (New York: Hill and Wang, 2000), 182.

3. See Geoffrey Wawro, *A Mad Catastrophe: The Outbreak of World War I and the Collapse of the Hapsburg Empire* (New York: Basic Books, 2015).

4. Czechoslovakia, a former part of the defunct Austro-Hungarian empire, contained German-speakers in a border area newly termed Sudetenland. The agreement was signed on 30 September 1938 in Munich, Germany by Germany, France, the United Kingdom, and Italy—all but one of the major powers of Europe. The Soviet Union was not invited to the conference, which had been called to discuss Hitler's demands to adjust the border to incorporate Sudeten Germans into Germany. Because the state of Czechoslovakia was also not invited to the conference, it considered itself to have been betrayed by the United Kingdom and France, with whom Czechoslovakia had a military alliance.

5. The Czech army was almost half the size of the German army at this point, and it has been argued by some that Britain's and France's strategic position was therefore better in 1938 than it was one year later, after the loss of Czechoslovakia.

6. Hitler was explicit: "The folkish State has to make up for what is today neglected in this field in all directions. It has to put the race into the center of life in general. It has to care for its preservation in purity. It has to make the child the most precious possession of a people. It has to take care that only the healthy beget children." Adolf Hitler, *Mein Kampf* (New York: Reynal and Hitchcock, 1950), 608. Also: "The National Socialist movement must endeavor to eliminate the discrepancy between our population and our area—the latter viewed not only as a source of nourishment, but also as a point of support for power politics. . . . It must, moreover, remain conscious that we are also obligated to a high duty as the guardians of the highest human race on this earth, and it will be all the more able to fulfill this duty, the more it contrives that the German people recovers its racial sense and, in addition to breeding dogs, horses, and cats, takes mercy on its *own* blood." Hitler, 940.

7. Although critics have been prominent, there is a historical debate on the wisdom of Chamberlain's policies. For less critical appraisals, see John Charmley, *Chamberlain and the Lost Peace* (Pan Macmillan, 1991) or David Dilks, "We Must Hope for the Best and Prepare for the Worst: The Prime Minister and the Cabinet and Hitler's Germany, 1937–1939," *Proceedings of the British Academy* 73 (1987): 309–352.

8. On the reaction of officials in MI5, see Christopher Andrew, *Defend the Realm: The Authorized History of MI-5* (New York: Alfred A. Knopf, 2009), 203. On Churchill's view, see May, *Strange Victory*, 191.

9. See Nick Baumann, "Neville Chamberlain Was Right," *Slate*, September 28, 2013, http://www.slate.com.

10. May, *Strange Victory*, 172.

11. For more on these uncertainties, see Chapter 10.

12. Andrew, *Defend the Realm*, 205.

13. Sir Robert Vansittart, *The Mist Procession: The Autobiography of Lord Vansittart* (London: Hutchinson, 1958), 429.

14. May, *Strange Victory*, 171.

15. May, *Strange Victory*, 170.

16. May, *Strange Victory*, 6.

17. Christopher Andrew, *Her Majesty's Secret Service: The Making of the British Intelligence Community* (New York: Viking-Penguin, 1986), 386.

18. For more on these uncertainties, see Chapter 9.

19. Notable exceptions included certain important British and French officials, and these men's sources will be discussed later in this section.

20. For example, in response to the army generals' expert opinion that the defenses against France (a fortified line known as the Westwall) could not hold in the event France attacked, Hitler visited the wall himself, declaring that it would hold not three weeks but "three years!"

21. May, *Strange Victory*, 188.

22. May, *Strange Victory*, 42.

23. For background on Hitler's assessment, see Chapter 10.

24. Despite the evidence of dissent, Hitler's presentation and the attendees' complicity were so clear that the memorandum of record, prepared by Hossbach, was later used at the Nuremberg war crimes trials as proof of conspiracy to commit aggression. Hossbach's memories of the meeting after the war emphasized the sharpness of the generals' dissent more than his notes at the time suggested. Quote and contextual information is from May, *Strange Victory*, 43–44.

25. Shortly after Munich, Hitler told his military officers that he needed '"officers who believe" with "blindly confident trust." See May, *Strange Victory*, 85.

26. Hitler thus determined early in 1938 that General Ludwig Beck, chief of the German general staff and a seemingly loyal devotee of Hitler himself, was nonetheless too independent of mind to be kept in his position. He was eased out too. May, *Strange Victory*, 73–77.

27. May, *Strange Victory*, 104. It seems that Hitler ordered Goering's wiretaps of senior officials mostly through their wives. Goering had created the agency in 1933, ran it as an independent entity, and served as its only link to Hitler. The Forschungsamt issued intercepts, known as "brown friends," to a carefully controlled group of recipients. According to May, it seems to have remained largely objective in its reporting.

28. May, *Strange Victory*, 38.

29. May, *Strange Victory*, 50. The full quotation from a foreign journalist witnessing Neurath's behavior: "so self-conscious, so servile, as he always is when Hitler is around, that you could almost see him wag his tail."

30. Edmund L. Blandford, *SS Intelligence: The Nazi Secret Service* (Shrewsbury, England: Airlife Publishing, 2000), 127–133.

31. This work complemented the military intelligence branches, whose operations remained under the control of the services. May, *Strange Victory*, 183. Most reporting from the military services—and indeed much from the Abwehr—concerned military weapons, deployments, and readiness, and so was of more interest to the services than to Hitler.

32. Hitler named SS chief Heinrich Himmler chief of the German police on June 17, 1936. All police powers were thus under Himmler's control, and dual membership in the Gestapo and SS became common. For more on the timeline and development of Hitler's internal control, see the website for the US Holocaust Memorial Museum at http://encyclopedia.ushmm.org. Accessed January 12, 2021.

33. For Hitler's views on propaganda and the management of public opinion, see *Mein Kampf*, vol. 2, chap. 11.

34. Plays for popular passion had, after all, almost derailed the Anschluss. Prompted by various Nazi patrons in Germany, factionalized Austrian Nazis had threatened to trigger a coup in late January 1938. A police raid ordered by the Austrian president, Kurt von Schuschnigg, revealed Nazi intention to assassinate key Austrian and German officials, which in turn, would have triggered German intervention. The Austrian president announced a plebiscite framed along nationalist lines. Hitler, enraged by the machinations of factionalized Austrian Nazis and Schuschnigg's unilateral decisions, took control by mobilizing his forces and leaning on Mussolini to not intervene should he need to use force. His tools of persuasion were propaganda (Goebbels) and military pressure, but the former took pride of place. To deal with Mussolini, Hitler sent a personal message carried by Prince Philip of Hesse. Mussolini sent his support in return. Thus, Hitler re-established control, but it was a near thing. See May, *Strange Victory*, 56–59.

35. Ian Kershaw, *Hitler: A Biography* (New York: W.W. Norton, 2008), 481.

36. Kershaw, *Hitler*, 100.

37. Kershaw, *Hitler*, 100.

38. May, *Strange Victory*, 183.

39. May, *Strange Victory*, 104–105.

40. Kershaw, *Hitler*, 433.

41. May, *Strange Victory*, 51.

42. An exception to the rule was Field Marshall Hermann Goering, who understood Nazi Party relationships that extended across borders to Austria and Czechoslovakia better than most of his military colleagues. See May, *Strange Victory*, 50–55.

43. May, *Strange Victory*, 53.

44. May, *Strange Victory*, 79–80.

45. May, *Strange Victory*, 81.

46. Weizsäcker lobbied visiting Hungarians, the deputy Führer, Rudolph Hess, and Ribbentrop throughout the summer of 1938. See May, *Strange Victory*, 81.

47. May, *Strange Victory*, 82.

48. Kershaw, *Hitler*, 433.

49. For a review of Britain's strategic situation and the uncertainties attending it, see the previous chapter.

50. See David Dilks, ed., *The Diaries of Sir Alexander Cadogan: 1938–1945* (New York: G.P. Putnam's Sons, 1972), 65. Both France and Britain had been worried about Japan's gravitation toward Germany since war had broken out between Japan and China in the summer of 1937. To defend interests there, both states had to contemplate sending warships, thus weakening their positions in Europe. See May, *Strange Victory*, 149.

51. The Chiefs of Staff had advised the Cabinet earlier in the year that the German air force could deliver a knockout blow against Britain. Statesmen were well informed on these assessments. Earlier that year, the chiefs of the military services had issued a gloomy report on the military balance. The lag in air capabilities was of particular concern. The Intelligence Branch of the Air Ministry had been handling a barrage of requirements for current assessments and future estimates of German air power, some of them originating at 10 Downing Street, the prime minister's offices.

52. Intelligence from French liaison sources and other sources from 1934–35 put the cap at fifteen hundred to two thousand planes—a goal that British analysts believed realistic, but which underestimated the "breakneck progress" Hitler and Goering were demanding (Wesley K. Wark, "British Military and Economic Intelligence," in Andrew and Dilks, *Missing Dimensions*, 80). After 1936, however, Air Staff estimates became much more pessimistic. Assessments of German capabilities were now overinflated, however, reflecting open sources, received propaganda, and intelligence feeds from the French services seeking to capture the attention of reticent policymakers in Paris. See Wark, "British Intelligence." This exaggeration of German capabilities may also have reflected the decision to dispense wholesale with "mirror-imaging" of British economic constraints on the German case.

53. In fact, those such as (former British permanent undersecretary at the Foreign Office) Vansittart, who were recommending a firm stand against Hitler had good intelligence that, at least as of 1938, the German air force was primarily meant to support battlefield operations, not strategic bombing. See Donald Cameron Watt, "British Intelligence and the Coming of the Second World War in Europe," in Ernest May, ed., *Knowing One's Enemies* (Princeton, NJ: Princeton University Press, 1984), 237–270.

54. Wark, "British Intelligence," 96.

55. Wark, "British Intelligence," 81.

56. Andrew, *Her Majesty's Secret Service*, 386.

57. Wark, "British Intelligence," 85.

58. Lloyd George, the architect of the Versailles agreement, was Chamberlain's nemesis, adding to the latter's distaste for the agreement and tendency to blame its terms for Europe's crisis.

59. As Chamberlain put it in 1937, "They want much the same things for the Sudetendeutsche as we did for the Uitlanders in the Transvaal"—that is, full political rights, including self-determination. May, *Strange Victory*, 176.

60. Chamberlain believed war was avoidable so long as the Nazi regime understood how to achieve its (limited) aims peacefully through "chemical solutions" to the nationality problem—that is, allowing nationalities to sort themselves among viable states through referendums, cross-border migration, plebiscites, and the like.

61. Before Munich, the British navy's principal concern had been Japan. See Watt, "British Intelligence," 260.

62. Wark, "British Intelligence," 86. In 1936, the War Department knew that Germany had breached its thirty-six-division army limit and that by August 1938 that army had surpassed the size the War Office had thought could not be reached until 1943. A net assessment of how those troops would do against Czechoslovakia, much less against France and Britain should they join in the latter's defense, was more assumed than rigorously analyzed—a gap that France shared. Although senior French officials were reticent to acknowledge Czech capabilities and relative French and German power, others pressed for better net assessments. (See Wark, 85–86, and Robert J. Young, "French Military Intelligence and Nazi Germany, 1938–1939," in May, *Knowing One's Enemies*, 306–308.) Whereas the British military attaché in Berlin thought Czech defenses pathetically inadequate, the attaché in Prague believed these views were influenced by the soft policies of Ambassador Neville Henderson, and strongly argued the opposite. The latter's assessments, in turn, were championed by Vansittart in his efforts to shape diplomatic policy.

63. The feeling was mutual. The Soviet ambassador in London, Ivan Maisky, saw Chamberlain as a committed anticommunist "bourgeois" who sought the destruction of the USSR. See John Erickson, "Threat Identification and Strategic Appraisal by the Soviet Union, 1930–1941," in May, *Knowing One's Enemy*, 406.

64. May, *Strange Victory*, 175. Indeed, Chamberlain would "die believing that war had resulted from Hitler's *miscalculation*."

65. May, *Strange Victory*, 175.

66. Cadogan, *Diaries*, 56.

67. May, *Strange Victory*, 82.

68. May, *Strange Victory*, 151.

69. May, *Strange Victory*, 151.

70. For reasons explained above, almost all of this intelligence was wrong, of course, reflecting a view shaped deliberately by Hitler and Ribbentrop.

71. May, *Strange Victory*, 177.

72. Christie's intelligence on Hitler's planned move on Czechoslovakia earlier that year was wrong, but that fact was not known in 1938. Andrew, *Her Majesty's Secret Service*, 391. Most of the information on Christie presented in this section relies on this volume.

73. After an interagency battle, the Air Ministry and the Foreign Office came to agreement on the matter of Luftwaffe production rates.

74. For background on Chamberlain's dislike of Vansittart, see Norman Rose, *Vansittart: Study of a Diplomat* (London: Heinemann, 1978), especially 206 and 207–208.

75. Andrew, *Defend the Realm*, 197.

76. Although not banned in 1938, the British government delivered intelligence on each individual to the police so that, when the decision was made to do so, the members could be rounded up—a step that was eventually taken when war was declared.

77. Andrew, *Defend the Realm*, 198.

78. Andrew, *Defend the Realm*, 195.

79. One source, Putlitz, later said that, when meeting with his handler, he saw himself as an agent of influence: "By this means I was able to lighten my conscience by the feeling that I was really helping to damage the Nazi cause for I knew [Ustinov] was in touch with Vansittart, who could use these facts to influence British policy." Andrew, *Defend the Realm*, 196. Vansittart later admitted to being used as an agent of influence, but more to stop Germany than to enable specific members of Hitler's domestic opposition.

80. Andrew, *Defend the Realm*, 195.

81. French and British negotiators had been pressing the Czech government to make concessions to Henlein that Vansittart believed might be unnecessary and demonstrated weakness; Vansittart did not know that Henlein had been stringing him along at Hitler's urging. Léger shared most of Vansittart's views. He was smart, hardworking, and powerful, having authority to order wiretaps by the Sûreté and to send the latest intelligence (including on domestic political adversaries) to the French PM, Daladier. Léger had shared with Vansittart his clandestine contacts with Henlein, the Sudeten German leader, whom Vansittart also knew via his source, Malcolm Christie. Henlein reported that the Czech crisis could be solved domestically, provided Britain lent a hand on the ground and stood firm. Vansittart's views thus reflected those of Henlein.

82. May, *Strange Victory*, 181.

83. Andrew, *Her Majesty's Secret Service*, 354–355. The Industrial Intelligence Center was created in 1931 after the Allied Control Commission, which tracked German armaments, ended (1928). In the interim, the Committee on Imperial Defense had set up the Foreign Countries Sub-committee (FCI). The FCI then recommended the creation of the IIC.

84. May, *Strange Victory*, 182.

85. Kershaw, *Hitler*, 433.

86. The parliamentary undersecretary, R. A. Butler, once commented that, "when faced with new proposals, Halifax would 'commune with himself, with his Maker, and with Alec [Cadogan].'" Andrew, *Her Majesty's Secret Service*, 387.

87. Cadogan, *Diaries*, 14.

88. Andrew, *Her Majesty's Secret Service*, 401.

89. This change also affected the service branches as well, which received and tasked SIS intelligence afterward.

90. This change, intended to correct disparities in military and diplomatic assessments, had sparked interagency battles. SIS, still largely a civilian organization within the FO, supported military and diplomatic decisions as part of a broad national security mandate.

91. According to Philip H. J. Davies, these consumer-oriented reforms were likely not simply the result of "lessons learned" in 1921, but likely stemmed from internal reforms flowing from the MacDonogh reforms of 1917. See his *MI-6 and the Machinery of Spying* (Portland, OR: Frank Cass, 2004), 58. In any event, the reporting chains followed a "consumer liaison" system that tied reporting to specific bureaucratic arrangements.

92. Cadogan, *Diaries*, 94.

93. Davies, *MI6*, 66.

94. Andrew, *Her Majesty's Secret Service*, 402–405.

95. For more on the ICC's role, see Wark, "British Intelligence," 93–98.

96. We now know, for example, that Thümmel's warning of Hitler's intent to attack Czechoslovakia in May, which included detailed reports of operational plans, was "more alarmist and less accurate" than usual—indeed, seems likely to have been false. British military attaches visited the border areas concerned and found no evidence of the massing of offensive forces on the border. See Andrew, *Her Majesty's Secret Service*, 392–393. When Britain overreacted and Hitler appeared to back down, A-4's apparent, but false, accuracy benefited Sinclair, bringing him close to the center of policymaking, even as MI6's reporting was weakening. Andrew, 394.

97. In fact, the decline of the PCO network had prompted the creation of a separate network "off the books." Called the "Z" or Dancey network, it was based in Holland and employed agents mostly within the business community. Unfortunately, in 1938 this network had scanty and unreliable reporting on Hitler's intentions, as well. Although its collection improved, it was later rolled up when penetrations of SIS stations implicated the Z network also.

98. Cadogan, *Diaries*, 94.

99. Cadogan, *Diaries*, 93.

100. Andrew, *Her Majesty's Secret Service*, 387.

101. Andrew, *Her Majesty's Secret Service*, 396.

102. Vansittart had called attention to German rearmament, had warned of the Anschluss with Austria, and was now warning that war in the west was not beyond Hitler's vision if the British and French governments seemed politically weak.

103. Andrew, *Her Majesty's Secret Service*, 401.

104. Andrew, *Her Majesty's Secret Service*, 386.

105. Andrew, *Her Majesty's Secret Service*, 386.

106. Andrew, *Her Majesty's Secret Service*, 386.

107. Andrew, *Her Majesty's Secret Service*, 339.

108. Andrew, *Her Majesty's Secret Service*, 340.

109. Cadogan *Diaries*, 93. This memo (or minute) was actually written on September 13, one day after Chamberlain flew to Germany. But these sentiments had likely been shared many times with the attendees at the meeting on September 8.

110. Cadogan, *Diaries*, 95.
111. Andrew, *Her Majesty's Secret Service*, 90.
112. Andrew, *Defend the Realm*, 202.
113. See Blandford, *SS Intelligence*, 144–145. As early as August 20, Helmuth Groscurth, a senior official with the Abwehr, saw the truth: "So, the Führer wants war."
114. For example, Goering, Hitler's head of the air force, was judged by at least one insider as largely ignorant about modern aircraft (May, *Strange Victory*, 109). Goering knew of the shortcomings of the Luftwaffe's planes, but deliberately pretended otherwise in his reports to Hitler. In fact, in 1938, he worried about "a big mess" (110).
115. May, *Strange Victory*, 105. May writes: "In peacetime the Forschungsamt supplied Hitler with information giving him tactical advantage in negotiations with foreign governments. Since Forschungsamt cryptanalysts broke most of the codes used by most embassies, including those of France and Britain, Hitler frequently knew what French and British ambassadors and attaches were reporting and what instructions they were receiving from home."
116. Cadogan, *Diaries*, 103.
117. Cadogan, *Diaries*, 104.
118. Cadogan, *Diaries*, 104.
119. Cadogan, *Diaries*, 104.
120. Cadogan, *Diaries*, 108.
121. Cadogan, *Diaries*, 107–109.
122. Cadogan, *Diaries*, 109.
123. May, *Strange Victory*, 83.
124. The US secretary of state, who had been conveying US preference for four-power talks, now advised that the US government would not try to supplant British trade should war break out. This first step in US support of a British Empire on the ropes during the crisis led the British ambassador to be "very much moved" and to express his deep satisfaction.
125. C. N. Trueman, "Public Opinion and Appeasement in 1938," *The History Learning Site*, 3 July 2015, https://www.historylearningsite.co.uk.
126. See Andrew, *Her Majesty's Secret Service*, 400, for more on the extent of Hitler's intelligence during and after Munich.
127. The concept of "intelligence support to diplomatic operations," or SDO, developed in the United States during the 1990s. It refers to intelligence for overseas diplomatic and Foreign Service operations, such as locating and building safe embassies, and monitoring threats to their operations, vetting visa applicants, conducting negotiations, protecting traveling diplomats, establishing and maintaining communications, and providing warning against peacetime threats in foreign countries. The Department of State advocated the concept as a counterpart to intelligence support to military operations (SMO). When SMO was first coined after the Persian Gulf War, it was designated the intelligence community's highest priority, even in peacetime. Tight post–Cold War budgets meant that this designation, together with the Defense Department's control of key collection agencies' budgets, threatened to undermine diplomatic intelligence in peacetime. The State Department responded

by pressing for SDO. The State Department gained support from key parts of the Defense Department and especially the CIA, which depends on diplomatic reporting and its platforms for collection worldwide. (The source for this information is the author, who developed and promoted the SDO concept while serving in the Department of State from 1994 to 2002. The work was rewarded by the director of central intelligence with the intelligence community's Distinguished Service Medal on 12 September 1998.)

128. F. H. Hinsley, *British Intelligence in the Second World War*, abridged ed. (Cambridge: Cambridge University Press, 1993), 3–12, esp. 10–11.

129. May, *Strange Victory*, 37.

130. Such a relationship of one-way intimacy could have made penetrations of his intelligence apparatus highly productive, had his counterintelligence capabilities not been as good as they were.

131. Vansittart, *Mist Procession*, 399. Vansittart regretted that "professionals" within government are treated as "servants" (400).

132. For an excellent review of Hitler's intelligence apparatus and Ribbentrop's role in it, see Michael Geyer, "National Socialist Germany: The Politics of Information," in May, *Knowing One's Enemies*, 310–346.

133. Seen in this larger perspective, MI6 (SIS) may have gotten it "right" in terms of what Germany *could and should* do given its interests, but wrong in terms of how far Hitler would go to accumulate power.

Chapter 13

1. Such capacities include numerous, wide-ranging, and centrally managed platforms with integrated sensors, processing, and communications.

2. Detachment is best measured by the degree of independence in executing the disposition of resources.

3. Transmission is measured by oversight and sharing across the decision-intelligence divide.

4. Selective secrecy enables the creation and retention of decision-advantage through offensive and defensive counterintelligence, and can be measured by fluidity and agility of classification systems.

5. Warranted by the case of Hooker before Chancellorsville.

6. Warranted by the case of Chamberlain's decision to go to Munich in 1938.

7. Demonstrated in the negative by Austria's trashing of diplomatic intelligence in the run-up to the July Crisis of 1914; see case study four in this volume.

8. Note the intelligence operations of the Confederates before First Manassas, especially as compared with the Federals; see case study two in this volume.

9. Notice how Stanton used propaganda to reduce Confederate support for Booth, his access to information, and his capacity to stay hidden; see the case study on Lincoln's assassination in this volume.

10. Consider King Philip II's operations against England from 1570 to 1588; see case study number one in this volume.

11. Consider Queen Elizabeth's limitations on Drake's ships discussed in the first case study in this volume.

12. Theorists of comparative politics understand that phenomena must first be delimited to their essential characteristics before they can be found in a world that might label them as something else. Once the phenomena are found, they can be compared, classified, and observed for variations or rules of behavior.

13. The idea here is that one side's mindset or certainty can eliminate the need for secrecy. Such mindsets may show up on one side as highly elongated "OODA loops"—the "observe-orient-decide-act" dynamic involved in most interactive competitions. John R. Boyd, "The Essence of Winning and Losing," 28 June 1995, at http://www.danford. net/boyd/essence.htm. When a competitor innovates, the wooden-headed competitor "observes" but fails to act on what he sees due to prejudice. In such circumstances, the knowledgeable innovator need not shroud his decisions in secrecy to achieve a competitive advantage.

14. See Mark Lowenthal, *Intelligence: From Secrets to Policy*, 4th ed. (Washington, DC: CQ Press, 2009).

15. Sometimes collectors may be the best briefers—as Drake was after disembarking from his floating worldwide collection platform—because their knowledge can convey an authenticity and specificity that leaders may want. At other times leaders may prefer independent assessments of a foreign power to lessen the influence of liaison relationships on analytical judgments. One reason the US government was surprised by the 1978-79 Iranian revolution that overthrew the Pahlavi dynasty was the reliance US intelligence had placed on the shah's intelligence services when gauging threats to the regime. CIA analysis underestimated the threat to the Shah's rule. See Milo L. Jones and Philippe Silberzahn, *Constructing Cassandra: Reframing Intelligence Failure at the CIA, 1947-2001* (Stanford: Stanford University Press, 2013), 80-101.

16. Lowenthal, *Intelligence*, 81.

17. This metaphor reminds one of the famous Louis Black joke about the colonial explorer who, landing in Africa, planted the imperial flag on African soil. When the inhabitants observed that the country was theirs, not his, the explorer scoffed: "Aha! But . . . do you have a flag?"

18. For a full discussion of these issues, see Jennifer E. Sims and Burton Gerber, eds., *Vaults, Mirrors and Masks: Rediscovering US Counterintelligence* (Washington, DC: Georgetown University Press, 2009).

19. Agreements to create such regimes do, however, raise the risks of collection on other matters that might, if exposed, put an end to the treaty regime.

20. Such fixed platforms may not always be the best way to learn about diplomatic targets. For centuries, states have used embassies and consulates for gathering foreign intelligence, often in cooperation with foreign governments interested in communicating and influencing, too. Unfortunately, for reasons of underfunding, lack of imagination, and prejudice, the range of diplomatic platforms, their tenability, and

their integration as intelligence platforms have suffered. At the same time, embassies struggle to gain access to diplomatic intelligence as power has seemingly shifted from capitals to business centers and the seats of populist unrest. In the Middle East and the Balkans, shuttle diplomacy required getting out of Sarajevo or Baghdad, where embassy platforms, communications, and diplomatic security could not safely go.

21. The best discussion of this problem may be Zara Steiner's *The Foreign Office and Foreign Policy, 1898–1914* (Cambridge: Cambridge University Press, 1969).

22. The key to Drake's intelligence success was sound collection management married to operations. Against the Spanish treasure fleet, Drake emphasized sensors over ships: he adapted whatever platforms floated, but made sure to recruit Iberian pilots and Central American natives who knew Spanish controlled ports and treasure routes the best. Against the Armada in 1588, he recruited English pilots who knew the Channel and were loyal to him. He used this loyalty for command and control: in the midst of battle he broke ranks to gather tactical intelligence off stranded Spanish ships, and then used what he learned for the fight, while never losing control of his platform to a mutinous crew. That Drake could make adjustments to each component of his seagoing operations reflected how tightly integrated all five of his collection components were: command, platform, sensors, exploitation, and data exfiltration. He could, and did, adjust his system as required, depending on his mission. In contrast, Philip II's ships were impoverished with respect to intelligence systems for operations. The soldiers on board knew little of sailing, the noblemen serving as captains were often deficient in experience, and the seamen rich in experience were treated as second-class. Whereas Drake and his like had learned to operationalize intelligence, the Spanish had bureaucratized it, leaving the navy to win through brute force rather than wit fueled by opportunistic learning.

23. For more on this point, see Fred Kaplan, *Dark Territory* (New York: Simon and Schuster, 2017), 110. During preparations for the invasion of Haiti in 1994, information warfare had to be coordinated with air operations, but the process was so convoluted that structural changes were made, leading to the creation of the first air squadron dedicated to information security and infowar: the 609th Air Information Squadron, which was created in 1995. But the practical gap between budgeting for military intelligence and operations remains.

24. The example of embassies often triggers dissonance because the history of US diplomatic intelligence has involved politically charged events such as the embassy bombings in Africa, where a highly competent ambassador (platform manager), working well with all agency components, received little help from headquarters bereft of funds when threats from terrorists spiked, or in uncoordinated platform operations in the Balkans that caused rifts and charges of betrayal from both the ambassador and the CIA. The point remains that, in the absence of integrated management of all components, any collection system can misfire or multiply in illogical and self-destructive ways. Consider the problems that attended having two telegraph companies and two (or more) competing balloonists running battlefield collection operations.

25. Michael Hayden, director of the National Security Agency in 1999, coined the acronym GEDA (gain, exploit, defend, attack) as a mantra for his agency precisely because he hoped to break down the cultural and bureaucratic walls separating information collection (exploitation) and information assurance (defense) within his agency, and raise awareness that both, online, could be weaponized.

26. Although the United States had this democratic advantage over autocracies and dictatorships, it was still vulnerable to opponents in creative liaison relationships themselves, such as Cuba was with the Soviet Union.

27. The CIA had demonstrated "serious lapses" in relying on a German intelligence source, code-named Curveball, who had falsely claimed that Saddam Hussein had mobile biological weapons labs. Michael Allen, *Blinking Red: Crisis and Compromise in American Intelligence after 9/11* (Washington, DC: Potomac Books, 2013), 29.

28. For more on the theory of counterintelligence and intelligence liaison, see Sims and Gerber, *Vaults, Mirrors, and Masks*, especially Jennifer E. Sims, "Twenty-First Century Counterintelligence: The Theoretical Basis for Reform," 19–50. Also: Jennifer E. Sims, "Intelligence Liaison: Devils, Deals and Details," *International Journal of Intelligence and Counterintelligence* 19, no. 2 (Summer 2006): 195–217.

29. Although good anticipatory intelligence has been historically difficult to sustain, the advent of the Internet has changed matters. The costs of waiting and watching online are low, and citizens in democracies worry about how easily powerful intelligence services can monitor, not only foreign communications and transactions, but also them. The necessity of preserving trust through strong intelligence oversight explains why Edward Snowden's full-throated attack on intelligence programs designed to anticipate terrorists, and his refusal to work through oversight mechanisms and the courts seemed so hostile. It was a master stroke for states eager to create fissures and lessened trust in American politics, whether the Russian government opportunistically supported Snowden or not.

30. This proximity to decision is, moreover, one reason why intelligence services want moles in another service's intelligence service, especially if the position is a trusted one with good, routinized access to decision-makers.

31. Similar problems arose in Europe in the run-up to WWI when diplomatic channels were blocked in order to blind others, but blinded the perpetrators too.

32. The disconnectedness of the Bureau of National Estimates from decision-makers during the Cuban Missile Crisis led to the system of national intelligence officers, and then national mission managers charged with improving the transmission function.

33. Christopher A. Kojm, "Intelligence Integration and Reform: 2009–2014," in Robert Hutchings and Gregory F. Treverton, eds., *Truth to Power* (New York: Oxford University Press, 2019), 161.

34. For an excellent discussion of the US "red line" between producers and consumers, policymakers' preferences, and intelligence practice in Israel, see Shay Hershkovitz and David Siman-Tov, "Collaboration between Intelligence and Decision-Makers: The Israeli Perspective," *International Journal of Intelligence and Counterintelligence* 31, no. 3 (Fall 2018): 568–592.

35. The highest estimative art may be the skill of interpretation: deriving meaning from facts when one looks at them through the enemy's eyes. What an enemy nonetheless thinks can be collected and documented, especially in this new information age.

36. In the case study of the Civil War battle at Chancellorsville, we saw that the Union's chain of command worked to simplify decisions about intelligence dissemination, but Hooker's decision to leave subordinates in the dark for purposes of surprise had the unattended effect of keeping them in the dark as the battle progressed.

37. On the downside, however, all-source analysts joined at the hip with policymakers risk losing touch with, and the trust of, nondepartmental collectors. To observe how often policymakers seek to work around the Bureau of Intelligence and Research (INR) in the Department of State, for example, is to recognize how isolated INR can become if its analysts are not *also* binding policymakers to other agencies' collection capabilities or worse, obstructing such connections and sowing distrust. INR's directorate for intelligence coordination works to overcome such tendencies, but, constantly short of funds due to misunderstandings concerning its role, only sometimes succeeds.

38. When INR has been *included* in a sensitive compartment but told by the secretary *not to brief* certain policymakers or ambassadors, perhaps because doing so would reveal policy developments they might oppose, INR has lost their confidence whenever the operations were later exposed or belatedly briefed. Although joint determinations of access to intelligence can represent trust and cooperation among some intelligence and policymaking officials, the creation of lists of insiders and outsiders within the national security community can breed suspicions. When the grounds for inclusion or exclusion are driven by policy disputes or bureaucratic warfare instead of need to know, the results may be more damaging than bureaucrats realize. Internal retribution may be part of any government, but using the classification system in this way drives wedges between intelligence analysts and decision-makers that are difficult to repair.

39. The IC similarly has "mission managers" to lubricate connectivity from collection through decision-making.

40. In some places, such as Los Angeles, sharing proved easier because the concept of "fusion centers" and intelligence-led policing was already accepted. But some cities, such as New York, pursued their own intelligence capabilities, including liaison relationships with foreign officials that exposed to overseas partners the extent of the disconnect with Washington.

41. The best book on deception and its use in WWII is Thaddeus Holt's *The Deceivers: Allied Military Deception in the Second World War* (New York: Scribner, 2004).

Chapter 14

1. Facebook and Twitter helped fuel the uprisings. Jeff John Roberts, "The Splinternet Is Growing," *Fortune*, May 29 2019. Accessed online at http://www.fortune.com.

2. Farhad Manjoo, "With One Presidential Phone Call, QAnon Shows Its Power," *New York Times*, January 6, 2021.

3. Manjoo, "One Presidential Phone Call." Marjorie Taylor Greene is a QAnon supporter from Georgia's Fourteenth District in the House of Representatives.

4. Fred Kaplan, *Dark Territory* (New York: Simon and Schuster, 2017).

5. Jason Silva, "IBM Event on Big Data and the Global Nervous System. BBC Speakers," *YouTube*, November 29, 2016.

6. "Extracurricular: Teen Tracker," *New Yorker*, March 30, 2020, 12.

7. Sylvia Mathews Burwell and Frances Fragos Townsend (Chairs) and Thomas J. Bollyky and Stewart M. Patrick (Project Directors), "Improving Pandemic Preparedness: Lessons from COVID-19," *Independent Task Force Report No. 78* (New York: Council on Foreign Relations, October 2020). See especially 89–100.

8. David Brooks, "America Is Having a Moral Convulsion," *The Atlantic*, October 5, 2020, http://www.theatlantic.com.

9. Paul Levy, *The Quantum Revelation* (New York: Select Books, 2018), especially 58 and 70. The most accessible but rigorous work on this subject, and especially its implications for political theory, is Alexander Wendt, *Quantum Mind and Social Science* (Cambridge: Cambridge University Press, 2015).

10. Helene Cooper, Leslie Kahn, and Ralph Blumenthal, "2 Navy Airmen and an Object That 'Accelerated Like Nothing I've Ever Seen,'" *New York Times*, December 16, 2017.

11. An interview (September 30, 2019) on background with former deputy assistant secretary of defense for intelligence, Christopher Mellon, established that these hearings, in fact, were held.

12. For more on these concepts, see Wendt, *Quantum Mind*, 54. "Spooky action at a distance" is the phenomenon of instantaneous causation between the states of two particles, regardless of the distance between them.

13. In 2009, NASA (National Aeronautics and Space Administration) launched the space probe *Kepler*, which revealed the existence of more than four thousand planets orbiting other stars. In fact, current models suggest that *most stars have planetary systems*, some of which may be habitable. Plans are afoot to look for bio-signatures of life on some of the closest of these planets, using tools such as the Extremely Large Telescope in Chile and the James Webb Space Telescope, due to be launched in 2021.

14. In 2002, a Chicago Council on Foreign Relations survey showed that 22 percent of Americans said the United States should never use nuclear weapons; 55 percent said only in response to a nuclear attack; 21 percent said possibly in other circumstances, as well. These numbers stayed essentially the same over the next decade. See Carl Brown, "Public Opinion about Using Nuclear Weapons," Roper: The Public Opinion Research Center, Cornell University, February 18, 2015. http://www.ropercenter.corn ell.edu.

15. On the decline of the nuclear taboo, see Scott D. Sagan and Benjamin A. Valentino, "Revisiting Hiroshima in Iran: What Americans Really Think about Using Nuclear Weapons and Killing Noncombatants," *International Security* 42, no. 1 (July 2017): 41–79.

16. Kuhika Gupta, "Tracking the 'Nuclear Mood' in the United States: Introducing a Long Term Measure of Public Opinion about Nuclear Energy Using Aggregate Survey Data," *Energy Policy* 133 (October 2019): 110888. https://doi.org/10.1016/j.enpol.2019.110 888. See also Ann S. Bisconti, "Public Opinion on Nuclear Energy: What Influences It," *Bulletin of the Atomic Scientists*, April 27, 2016. http://www.thebulletin.org.

17. Ben Aris, "Russia's Nuclear Power Exports are Booming," *The Moscow Times: Independent News from Russia,* May 9, 2019.

18. Scott Borgerson, "The Coming Arctic Boom," *Foreign Affairs* 92, no. 4 (July–August 2013): 76–78.

19. Thirteen additional states have observer status on the Arctic Council, including Switzerland, which joined in 2017.

20. Ellen L. Weintraub, Chair of the US Federal Election Commission, "Foreign Spending in Our Elections Isn't Trivial," op-ed, *Washington Post*, June 21, 2019, A23.

21. US Cyber-Command was created on May 21, 2010, and is one of eleven unified combatant commands. Its headquarters are at Fort Meade, in Maryland, where the National Security Agency is also headquartered.

22. For this breakdown of the web, see Neel Mehta, Adi Agashe, and Parth Detroja, *Bubble or Revolution? The Present and Future of Blockchain and Cryptocurrencies* (n.p.: Paravane Ventures, 2019), 54–55.

23. Mehta, Agashe, and Detroja, *Bubble or Revolution?*, 56.

24. China, which houses much of Bitcoin's infrastructure, ironically insists on remaining its citizens' gatekeeper for all online activity. China's contender for global internet reach is Alibaba, which China uses to collected data on its citizens and rank their loyalty to the state. For more on Bitcoin and other blockchain technologies, see Mehta, Agashe, and Detroja, *Bubble or Revolution.*

25. Galloway, *The Four*, 188.

26. For insight on this debate about the political and societal implications of the digital age and, in particular, individual empowerment versus corporate advantage, see Kevin Kelly, *The Inevitable: Understanding the 12 Technological Forces That Will Shape Our Future* (New York: Viking, 2016); Tim Wu, *The Master Switch: The Rise and Fall of Information Empires* (New York: Vintage, 2011); and Jared Lanier, *Who Owns the Future?* (New York: Simon and Schuster, 2013).

27. For a history of the effort to manage national security implications of cyber, see Joel Brenner, *America the Vulnerable: Inside the New Threat Matrix of Digital Espionage, Crime and Warfare* (New York: Penguin Press, 2011), and Fred Kaplan, *Dark Territory: The Secret History of Cyber War* (New York: Simon and Schuster Paperbacks, 2016). For the history and power of the information industry see, in addition to Tim Wu's *Master Switch*, Scott Galloway's *The Four: The Hidden DNA of Amazon, Apple, Facebook, and Google* (New York: Penguin, 2017).

28. See Abraham Flexner and Robbert Dijkgraaf, *The Usefulness of Useless Knowledge* (Princeton, NJ: Princeton University Press, 2017).

29. Kai-Fu Lee, *AI Superpowers: China, Silicon Valley and the New World Order* (Boston: Houghton Mifflin Harcourt, 2018), 1–18.

30. Military intelligence experts call this the "OODA loop" for "observe, orient, decide, and act."

31. Lee, *AI Superpowers*, 18.

32. Statistics cited are from "Non-tech Businesses Are Beginning to Use Artificial Intelligence at Scale," *The Economist*, March 28, 2018. Accessed online at http://www.economist.com.

33. Brian Barrett, "Kaspersky, Russia and the Antivirus Paradox," *Wired*, November 18, 2017. Accessed online at http://www.wired.com.

34. Galloway, *The Four*, 176.

35. Kathleen Dill and Kurt Wilberding, "More Trust in Business than in Government and Media, Survey Finds," *Wall Street Journal*, January 13, 2021.

36. As Galloway has put it: "America is on pace to become home to 3 million lords and 350 million serfs." *The Four*, 268.

37. Of course, regulation, which increases costs of production, can also make businesses less competitive and products more expensive. Whether the costs of regulation exceed the gains is always a question, but one that has so far been entrusted to government, not industry.

38. Laura Rosenberger, "Making Cyberspace Safe for Democracy: The New Landscape of Information Competition," *Foreign Affairs*, May–June 2020, 153.

39. For an excellent discussion of these issues see Laura Rosenberger, "Making Cyberspace Safe for Democracy: The New Landscape of Information Competition," *Foreign Affairs*, May–June 2020, 146–159.

40. As we have seen, Queen Elizabeth I knew that Sir Francis Drake's loyalty to her and the Church of England was unreliable; he had a nose for treasure and a personal gripe against Philip II that meant his interests did not exactly mirror hers. So she kept him loyal through generous rewards and restricted resources.

41. Jack Poulson, "I Used to Work for Google: I Am a Conscientious Objector," *New York Times*, Opinion, Privacy Project, April 23, 2019. https://www.nytimes.com/2019/04/23/opinion/google-privacy-china.html. Poulson sought to clarify his company's ethical choices concerning Project Dragonfly, Google's plan for meeting the Chinese Communist Party's requirements for censorship and surveillance: "When a prototype circulated internally of a system that would ostensibly allow the Chinese government to surveil Chinese users' queries by their phone numbers, Google executives argued that it was within existing norms. Governments, after all, make law enforcement demands of the company all the time. Where, they asked their employees, was the demonstrable harm?"

42. The concept of setting data "free" sounds good and right compared to the old ideas of copyright, privacy, or classification. But contributors of personal data to Google and Facebook are finding their data, freely given, now enabling billion-dollar industries. The kicker is that those databanks now archived by Google or Facebook are often more sharable, accessible, and sometimes hackable than the donors to them realize.

43. Simon Winchester, NPR broadcast interview, May 8, 2018.

44. Julian Assange, the editor and public face of Wikileaks, has been in hiding, investigated by the Unified Security Gateway for criminal activity, and implicated in Russian efforts to influence the US elections using timed release of stolen documents.

45. Facebook took a $42 billion hit in market value in March 2018 after revelations that Cambridge Analytica had "harvested private information from the Facebook profiles of more than 50 million users without their permission." *Daily Beast*, March 19, 2018. http://www.thedailybeast.com. Nevertheless, by April 2018, Facebook still had 2.2 billion monthly active users and sat at the top of all social networking leader-boards.

46. Nick Gallucci and Michael Shellenberger, "Will the West Let Russia Dominate the Nuclear Market? What the Westinghouse Bankruptcy Means for the Future," *Foreign Affairs*, August 3, 2017. https://www.foreignaffairs.com/articles/russian-federation/2017-08-03/will-west-let-russia-dominate-nuclear-market.

47. Flexner and Dijkgraaf, *The Usefulness of Useless Knowledge*. Yet the US federal research and development budget has dropped from 2.1 percent of the gross domestic product in 1964 to less than 0.08 percent at this writing. Funding for medical research by the National Institutes of Health has fallen 25 percent from 2007 to 2017.

48. For an exploration of the implications of crossing the science-intuition boundaries in the study of quantum consciousness and choice, see Wendt, *Quantum Mind*.

Appendix 2

1. "Memoria de la Costa Rica del norte," recorded as a debriefing to the viceroy for the king of Spain, in *Hans P. Kraus, Sir Francis Drake: A Pictorial Biography*, Library of Congress, Rare Book & Special Collections Division, transcribed and translated from the original Spanish by Rosa DeBerry King.

Appendix 3

1. Of course, true faith does not need human institutions to keep the faithful in line, or warriors to force religious belief on the conquered. The same is true of true science. While relying on rigorous testing to prove known theories, it also entertains the possibility that known theories are wrong, no matter how "true" they seem. It pursues truth by being creative, exploratory, and unshackled from existing laws or paradigms.

2. It will be noted here that the theory of adaptive realism departs from classical neorealism by insisting that the structural effects of power on state behavior cannot be analyzed at the structural level alone. Insistence on such purity may offer special insights for understanding the state system, but so does breaking through the levels of analysis to see how structure affects the sources of state power, including the curiosity that helps it innovate, and the loyalties that supposedly make demographics relevant to military might. This latter kind of analysis helps us understand structural change in international politics.

3. Surprised? If any of these possibilities is not on your list, a mindset that may be highly functional for your work and cultural setting nonetheless may be keeping you from being as curious as you could be about the challenges and opportunities on the edge of what we know; consciousness that may go "all the way down" (Alexander Wendt). The list is, of course, much shorter than it should be.

Bibliography

Albertini, Luigi. *The Origins of the War of 1914*. 3 vols. Translated by Isabella M. Massey. New York: Enigma Books, 2005.

Alexander, Edward Porter. *Fighting for the Confederacy: The Personal Recollections of General Edward Porter Alexander*. Edited by Gary W. Gallagher. Chapel Hill: University of North Carolina Press, 1989.

Alford, Terry. *Fortune's Fool: The Life of John Wilkes Booth*. Oxford: Oxford University Press, 2015.

Allen, Michael. *Blinking Red: Crisis and Compromise in American Intelligence after 9/11*. Washington, DC: Potomac Books, 2013.

Andrew, Christopher. *Defend the Realm: The Authorized History of MI-5*. New York: Alfred A. Knopf, 2009.

Andrew, Christopher. *For the President's Eyes Only: Secret Intelligence and the American Presidency from Washington to Bush*. New York: Harper Perennial, 1996.

Andrew, Christopher. *Her Majesty's Secret Service: The Making of the British Intelligence Community*. New York: Viking-Penguin, 1986.

Andrew, Christopher. "The Nature of Military Intelligence." In Keith Nelson and B. J. C. McKercher, eds., *Go Spy the Land: Military Intelligence in History*. Westport, CT: Praeger, 1992, 1-16.

Andrew, Christopher and Jeremy Noakes, eds. *Intelligence and International Relations, 1900-1945*. Exeter: Exeter University, 1987.

Aris, Ben. "Russia's Nuclear Power Exports Are Booming." *Moscow Times*, May 9, 2019.

Aron, Raymond. *The Century of Total War*. Boston: Beacon Press, 1954.

Art, Robert J. and Kenneth N. Waltz, eds. *The Use of Force: International Politics and Foreign Policy*. Boston: Little, Brown, 1971.

Asprey, Robert. *The Panther's Feast*. New York: G.P. Putnam and Sons, 1959.

Atkinson, Rick. *The Guns at Last Light: The War in Western Europe, 1944-1945*. Vol. 3 of *The Liberation Trilogy*. New York: Henry Holt, 2013.

Bain, David Haward. *Empire Express: Building the First Transcontinental Railroad*. New York: Penguin Group/Viking, 1999.

Barnett, Correlli. *The Audit of War: The Illusion and Reality of Britain as a Great Nation*. London: Macmillan, 1987.

Barnett, Correlli. *The Collapse of British Power*. Atlantic Highlands, NJ: Humanities Press International, 1986.

Barrett, Brian. "Kaspersky, Russia and the Antivirus Paradox." *Wired*, November 18, 2017. http://www.wired.com.

Batyushin, Nikolai. "Cryptography during WWI: A Tsarist Russian's View." *CIA Studies in Intelligence* 1, no. 2 (Summer 1977). Declassified 2005.

Bearss, Edwin. *First Manassas Battlefield Map Study*. 2nd ed. Lynchburg, VA: H.E. Howard, Inc., n.d.

Beatie, Russell H. *Army of the Potomac: Birth of Command, November 1860-September 1861*. Cambridge, MA: Da Capo Press, 2002.

Bergen, Peter. *Manhunt: The Ten-Year Search for Bin Laden from 9/11 to Abbottabad*. New York: Crown Publishers, 2012.

Berlin, Isaiah. *The Hedgehog and the Fox*. London: Weidenfeld and Nicolson, 1953.

Best, Jaqueline. "Ambiguity, Uncertainty, and Risk: Rethinking Indeterminacy." *International Political Sociology* 2, no. 4 (December 2008): 355–374.

Betts, Richard K. *Enemies of Intelligence: Knowledge and Power in American National Security*. New York: Columbia University Press, 2007.

Beymer, William Gilmore. *Scouts and Spies of the Civil War*. Lincoln: University of Nebraska Press, 2003.

Bienen, Henry and Nicolas van de Walle. *Of Time and Power: Leadership Duration in the Modern World*. Palo Alto, CA: Stanford University Press, 1991.

Bisconti, Ann S. "Public Opinion on Nuclear Energy: What Influences It." *Bulletin of the Atomic Scientists*, April 27, 2016. http://www.thebulletin.org.

Blackman, Ann. *Wild Rose: Rose O'Neale Greenhow, Civil War Spy*. New York: Random House, 2005.

Blackwell, Robert and Jack Davis. "A Policymaker's Perspective on Intelligence Analysis." In Loch K. Johnson and James J. Wirtz, eds., *Intelligence and National Security: The Secret World of Spies*. 2nd ed. New York: Oxford University Press, 2008.

Blandford, Edmund L. *SS Intelligence: The Nazi Secret Service*. Shrewsbury, England: Airlife Publishing, 2000.

Bloch, Marc. *Strange Defeat*. Important Books, 2013.

Borgerson, Scott. "The Coming Arctic Boom." *Foreign Affairs* 92, no. 4 (July–August 2013): 76–78.

Bowden, Mark. "The Ploy." *The Atlantic* 299, no. 4 (May 2007): 54–68.

Braudel, Fernand. *The Mediterranean and the Mediterranean World in the Age of Philip II*. 2 vols. New York: Harper and Row, 1972.

Brenner, Joel. *America the Vulnerable: Inside the New Threat Matrix of Digital Espionage, Crime and Warfare*. New York: Penguin Press, 2011.

Brooks, David. "America Is Having a Moral Convulsion." *The Atlantic*. October 5, 2020. http://www.theatlantic.com.

Brown, Carl. "Public Opinion about Using Nuclear Weapons." Roper: The Public Opinion Research Center, Cornell University, February 18, 2015. http://www.ropercenter.cornell.edu.

Budiansky, Stephen. *Her Majesty's Spymaster*. London: Penguin Books, 2005.

Buell, Thomas B. *The Warrior Generals: Combat Leadership in the Civil War*. New York: Three Rivers Press, 1997.

Burwell, Sylvia Mathews and Frances Fragos Townsend (Chairs) and Thomas J. Bollyky and Stewart M. Patrick (Project Directors). "Improving Pandemic Preparedness: Lessons from COVID-19." *Independent Task Force Report No. 78* (New York: Council on Foreign Relations, October 2020).

Buttar, Prit. *Collision of Empires: The War on the Eastern Front in 1914*. Oxford: Osprey, 2014.

Byman, Daniel. *Deadly Connections: States That Sponsor Terrorism*. Cambridge: Cambridge University Press, 2005.

Charmley, John. *Chamberlain and the Lost Peace*. Hampshire, England: Pan Macmillan, 1991.

Chernow, Ron. *Grant*. London: Penguin Press, 2017.

CIA, Office of Public Affairs (Thomas Allen). *Intelligence in the Civil War*. Washington, DC: Central Intelligence Agency, Office of Public Affairs, 2012.

Clark, Christopher. *The Sleepwalkers: How Europe Went to War in 1914*. New York: HarperCollins, 2013.

Coddington, Edwin. *The Gettysburg Campaign: A Study in Command*. New York: Simon and Schuster/Touchstone, 1997.

Coggins, Jack. *Arms and Equipment of the Civil War*. Mineola, NY: Dover Publications, 1990.

Cohen, Elliot A. *Supreme Command: Soldiers, Statesmen and Leadership in Wartime*. New York: Anchor, 2003.

Collins, Jim. *Good to Great: Why Some Companies Make the Leap and Others Don't*. New York: Harper Business, 2001.

Committee on Armed Services, House of Representatives. *Intelligence Successes and Failures in Operations Desert Shield/Storm: Report of the Oversight and Investigations Subcommittee*. 103rd Congress, First Session, no. 5. Washington, DC: US Printing Office, 1993.

Cooper, Helene, Leslie Kahn, and Ralph Blumenthal. "2 Navy Airmen and an Object That 'Accelerated Like Nothing I've Ever Seen.'" *New York Times*, December 16, 2017.

"The Cost of Succession." Video disc published and distributed by the Abraham Lincoln Presidential Library and Museum, 2010.

Cozzens, Peter. *Shenandoah 1862: Stonewall Jackson's Valley Campaign*. Chapel Hill: University of North Carolina Press, 2008.

Crumpton, Henry A. *The Art of Intelligence*. New York: Penguin Books, 2012.

Davies, Philip H. J. *MI6 and the Machinery of Spying*. Portland, OR: Frank Cass, 2004.

Davis, Zachary. "Bombs Away: Interdicting Proliferation." *American Interest*, 4, no. 3 (January–February 2009): 33–38.

Dexter, Byron. "Lord Grey and the Problem of an Alliance, Foreign Affairs, January 1952." http://www.foreignaffairs.com/articles/70945/byron-dexter/lord-grey-and-the-prob lem-of-an-alliance.

Dilks, David, ed. *The Diaries of Sir Alexander Cadogan: 1938–1945*. New York: G.P. Putnam's Sons, 1972.

Dilks, David, ed. *Retreat from Power: Studies in Britain's Foreign Policy of the Twentieth Century. Vol. 1, 1906–1939*. London: Macmillan, 1981.

Dilks, David. "We Must Hope for the Best and Prepare for the Worst: The Prime Minister and the Cabinet and Hitler's Germany, 1937–1939." *Proceedings of the British Academy* 73 (1987): 309–352.

Dover, Robert and Michael S. Goodman, eds. *Learning from the Secret Past: Cases in British Intelligence History*. Washington, DC: Georgetown University Press, 2011.

Duyvesteyn, Isabelle, Joop van Reijn, and Ben de Jong, eds. *The Future of Intelligence: Challenges in the 21st Century*. London: Routledge, 2014.

The Economist. "Versailles Revisited." July 6, 2019, 16.

Edgar, Harold and Benno Schmidt. "The Espionage Statutes and the Publication of Defense Information." *Columbia Law Review* 73 (1973): 930–1087.

Emmerson, Charles. *1913: In Search of the World before the Great War*. New York: Public Affairs, 2013.

Epstein, Katherine C. "Scholarship and the Ship of State: Rethinking the Anglo-American Strategic Decline Analogy." *International Affairs* 91, no. 2 (2015): 319–331.

Evans, Charles M. *War of the Aeronauts: A History of Ballooning in the Civil War*. Mechanicsburg, PA: Stackpole Books, 2002.

Fay, Sidney B. *The Origins of the World War*. 2nd ed. Vol. 1. New York: Free Press, 1966.

Feis, William B. *Grant's Secret Service: The Intelligence War from Belmont to Appomattox.* Lincoln: University of Nebraska Press, 2002.

Feis, William B. "That Great Essential of Success: Espionage, Covert Action and Military Intelligence." In Aaron Sheehan Dean, ed., *Struggle for a Vast Future.* Oxford: Osprey Publishing, 2006.

Fellner, Fritz. "Austria-Hungary." In Keith Wilson, ed., *Decisions for War, 1914.* Abingdon, Oxon: Routledge, 2003.

Ferris, John. "Lord Salisbury, Secret Intelligence, and British Policy toward Russia and Central Asia, 1874–1978." In Keith Nelson and B. J. C. McKercher, eds. *Go Spy the Land: Military Intelligence in History.* Westport, CT: Praeger, 1992.

Finnegan, Terrence J. *Shooting the Front: Allied Aerial Reconnaissance and Photographic Interpretation on the Western Front—WWI.* Washington, DC: National Defense Intelligence College Press, 2006.

Fishel, Edwin C. *The Secret War for the Union: The Untold Story of Military Intelligence in the Civil War.* Boston: Houghton Mifflin, 1996.

Flexner, Abraham and Robert Dijkgraaf. *The Usefulness of Useless Knowledge.* Princeton, NJ: Princeton University Press, 2017.

Fuller, William C. Jr. "The Russian Empire." In Ernest R. May, ed., *Knowing One's Enemies.* Princeton, NJ: Princeton University Press, 1984.

Gallagher, Gary W., ed. *Fighting for the Confederacy: The Personal Recollections of General Edward Porter Alexander.* Chapel Hill: University of North Carolina, 1989.

Gallagher, Gary W., ed. *The Richmond Campaign of 1862: The Peninsula & the Seven Days.* Chapel Hill: University of North Carolina Press, 2000.

Galloway, Scott. *The Four: The Hidden DNA of Amazon, Apple Facebook, and Google.* New York: Penguin, 2017.

Gallucci, Nick and Michael Shellenberger. "Will the West Let Russia Dominate the Nuclear Market? What the Westinghouse Bankruptcy Means for the Future." *Foreign Affairs,* August 3, 2017. https://www.foreignaffairs.com/articles/russian-federation/ 2017-08-03/will-west-let-russia-dominate-nuclear-market.

Geiss, Imanuel. *July 1914: The Outbreak of the First World War.* New York: Charles Scribner's Sons, 1967.

Gladwell, Malcolm. *David and Goliath: Underdogs, Misfits, and the Art of Battling Giants.* New York: Little, Brown, 2013.

Godson, Roy, Ernest R. May, and Gary Schmitt. *US Intelligence at the Crossroads: Agendas for Reform.* Washington, DC: Brassey's, 1995.

Goldsmith, Barbara. *Other Powers: The Age of Suffrage, Spiritualism, and the Scandalous Victoria Woodhull.* New York: Alfred A. Knopf, 1998.

Goodheart, Adam. *1861: The Civil War Awakening.* New York: Alfred A. Knopf, 2011.

Goodwin, Doris Kearns. *Team of Rivals: The Political Genius of Abraham Lincoln.* New York: Simon and Schuster Paperbacks, 2006.

Gottfried, Bradley M. *The Maps of First Bull Run: An Atlas of the First Bull Run (Manassas) Campaign, including the Battle of Ball's Bluff, June--October 1861.* New York: Savas Beatie, 2009.

Gregory, John S. "New Things in War." In Walter Hynes Page and Arthur Wilson Page, eds., *The World's Work* 28. New York: Doubleday, Page and Company, 1914.

Grenier, Robert L. *88 Days to Kandahar: A CIA Diary.* New York: Simon and Schuster, 2015.

Grey, Viscount of Fallodon. *Twenty-Five Years, 1892–1916.* New York: Frederick A. Stokes, 1925.

Grimsley, Mark. *The Hard Hand of War: Union Military Policy toward Southern Civilians, 1861-1865.* Cambridge: Cambridge University Press, 1995.

Grimsley, Mark. "Surviving Military Revolution: The American Civil War." In MacGregor Knox and Williamson Murray, eds., *The Dynamics of Military Revolution, 1300-2050.* Cambridge: Cambridge University Press, 2001, 74-91.

Gupta, Kuhika. "Tracking the 'Nuclear Mood' in the United States: Introducing a Long Term Measure of Public Opinion about Nuclear Energy Using Aggregate Survey Data." *Energy Policy* 133 (October 2019): 110888. https://doi.org/10.1016/j.enpol.2019.110888.

Guy, John. *Tudor England.* New York: Oxford University Press, 1992.

Gwynne, S. C. *Rebel Yell: The Violence, Passion and Redemption of Stonewall Jackson.* New York: Scribner, 2014.

Hamilton, Richard F. and Holger H. Herwig, eds. *The Origins of World War I.* New York: Cambridge University Press, 2003.

Hanson, Neil. *The Confident Hope of a Miracle: The True History of the Spanish Armada.* New York: Vintage Books, 2006.

Harari, Yuval Noah. *Special Operations in the Age of Chivalry.* Woodbridge: Boydell Press, 2007.

Hastings, Max. *Catastrophe 1914.* New York: Vintage Books, 2014.

Hazlewood, Nick. *The Queen's Slave Trader: John Hawkyns, Elizabeth I, and the Trafficking in Human Souls.* New York: Harper, 2005.

Helms, Richard. *A Look over My Shoulder: A Life in the Central Intelligence Agency.* New York: Random House, 2003.

Hennessy, John. *The First Battle of Manassas: An End to Innocence, July 18-21, 1861.* 2nd ed. Lynchburg, VA: H.E. Howard, 1989.

Hershkovitz, Shay and David Siman-Tov. "Collaboration between Intelligence and Decision-Makers: The Israeli Perspective." *International Journal of Intelligence and Counterintelligence* 31, no. 3 (Fall 2018): 568-592.

Hess, Earl J. *Civil War Infantry Tactics: Training, Combat, and Small-Unit Effectiveness.* Baton Rouge: Louisiana State University Press, 2015.

Hess, Earl J. *The Rifle Musket in Civil War Combat: Reality and Myth.* Lawrence: University Press of Kansas, 2008.

Hill, Larry. *Emissaries to a Revolution: Woodrow Wilson's Executive Agents in Mexico.* Baton Rouge: Louisiana State University Press, 1973.

Hinsley, F. H. *British Intelligence in the Second World War.* Abridged ed. Cambridge: Cambridge University Press, 1993.

Holloway, David. *Stalin and the Bomb: The Soviet Union and Atomic Energy, 1939-1956.* New Haven: Yale University Press, 1994.

Holt, Thaddeus. *The Deceivers: Allied Military Deception in the Second World War.* New York: Scribner, 2004.

Holzer, Harold. *Lincoln and the Power of the Press.* New York: Simon and Schuster Paperbacks, 2014.

Hopkirk, Peter. *The Great Game: The Struggle for Empire in Central Asia.* New York: Kodansha USA, 1994.

Hotchkiss, Jedediah. *Make Me a Map of the Valley: The Civil War Journal of Stonewall Jackson's Topographer.* Edited by Archie P. McDonald. Dallas: Southern Methodist University Press, 1973.

Howard, Michael. *The Causes of Wars.* 2nd ed. Cambridge, MA: Harvard University Press, 1983.

Hutchings, Robert and Gregory F. Treverton, eds. *Truth to Power*. New York: Oxford University Press, 2019.

Jackson, Peter and Jennifer Siegel, eds. *Intelligence and Statecraft: The Use and Limits of Intelligence in International Society*. Westport, CT: Praeger, 2005.

Jeffery, Keith. *The Secret History of MI-6: 1909–1949*. New York: Penguin Press, 2010.

Jervis, Robert. *Perception and Misperception in International Politics*. Princeton, NJ: Princeton University Press, 1976.

Johnson, Loch and James J. Wirtz. *Intelligence and National Security: The Secret World of Spies*. 2nd ed. New York: Oxford University Press, 2008.

Joll, James and Gordon Martel. *The Origins of the First World War*. 3rd ed. London: Pearson-Longman, 2007.

Jones, John Paul, ed. "Dr. Mudd and the Lincoln Assassination: The Case Reopened." Published by the Richmond School of Law. University of Richmond UR Scholarship Repository. Law Faculty Publication (1993). http://www.scholarship.richmond.edu.

Jones, Milo L. and Philippe Silberzahn. *Constructing Cassandra: Reframing Intelligence Failure at the CIA, 1947–2001*. Stanford: Stanford University Press, 2013.

Jones, Reginald V. *The Wizard War: British Scientific Intelligence, 1939–1945*. New York: Coward, McCann and Geoghegan, 1978.

Kagan, Neil and Stephen G. Hyslop, eds. *Atlas of the Civil War*. Washington, DC: National Geographic, 2009.

Kahn, David. *The Codebreakers: The Comprehensive History of Secret Communication from Ancient Times to the Internet*. New York: Scribner, 1996.

Kaplan, Fred. *Dark Territory: The Secret History of Cyber War*. New York: Simon and Schuster Paperbacks, 2016.

Kaplan, Fred. "The Rise of Intelligence." *Foreign Affairs* 85, no. 5 (September–October 2006): 125–134.

Keegan, John. *Intelligence in War: Knowledge of the Enemy from Napoleon to al-Qaeda*. New York: Alfred A. Knopf, 2003.

Kelly, Kevin. *The Inevitable: Understanding the 12 Technological Forces That Will Shape Our Future*. New York: Viking, 2016.

Kelsey, Harry. *Sir John Hawkins: Queen Elizabeth's Slave Trader*. New Haven: Yale University Press, 2003.

Kennan, George. *Memoirs, 1925–1950*. Boston: Atlantic Monthly Press / Little, Brown, 1967.

Kennedy, Paul. *The Rise and Fall of the Great Powers: Economic Change and Military Conflict from 1500 to 2000*. New York: Vintage Books, 1989.

Kershaw, Ian. *Hitler: A Biography*. New York: W.W. Norton, 2008.

Kertzer, David I. *The Pope and Mussolini: The Secret History of Pius XI and the Rise of Fascism in Europe*. New York: Random House, 2014.

Kissinger, Henry. *Diplomacy*. New York: Simon and Schuster, 1994.

Kojm, Christopher. "Intelligence Integration and Reform: 2009–2014." In Robert Hutchings and Gregory F. Treverton, eds., *Truth to Power*. New York: Oxford University Press, 2019.

Konstam, Angus. *Sovereigns of the Sea: The Quest to Build the Perfect Renaissance Battleship*. Hoboken, NJ: John Wiley and Sons, 2008.

Konstam, Angus. *Tudor Warships (1): Henry VIII's Navy*. Oxford: Osprey Publishing, 2008.

Konstam, Angus. *Tudor Warships (2): Elizabeth I's Navy*. Oxford: Osprey Publishing, 2008.

Konstam, Angus and Angus McBride. *Elizabethan Sea Dogs, 1560–1605*. Oxford: Osprey Press, 2000.

Kydd, Andrew. "Facing Impediments: Information and Communication." In I. William Zartman, ed., *How Negotiations End: Negotiating Behavior in the End Game*. Cambridge: Cambridge University Press: 2019.

Lafore, Laurence. *The Long Fuse*. 2nd ed. New York: J.B. Lippincott, 1971.

Lambert, Nicholas A. *Planning Armageddon: British Economic Warfare and the First World War*. Cambridge, MA: Harvard University Press, 2012.

Lambert, Nicholas A. *Sir John Fisher's Naval Revolution*. Columbia: University of North Carolina Press, 1999.

Lambert, Nicholas A. "Strategic Command and Control for Maneuver Warfare: Creation of the Royal Navy's 'War Room' System, 1905–1915." *Journal of Military History* 69 (April 2005): 361–410.

Lanier, Jared. *Who Owns the Future?* New York: Simon and Schuster, 2013.

Lee, Kai-Fu. *AI Superpowers: China, Silicon Valley and the New World Order*. Boston: Houghton Mifflin Harcourt, 2018.

Leimon, M. and G. Parker. "Treason and Plot in Elizabethan Diplomacy: The 'Fame of Sir Edward Stafford' Reconsidered." *English Historical Review* 111 (1996): 1134–1158.

Levy, Paul. *The Quantum Revelation*. New York: Select Books, 2018.

Lincoln, Abraham. *Speeches, Letters, Miscellaneous Writings, Presidential Messages and Proclamations, 1859–1865*. Selected by Don E. Fehrenbacher. New York: Library of America / Literary Classics of the United States, 1989.

Livingston, Phil and Ed Roberts. *War Horse: Mounting the Cavalry with America's Finest Horses*. Albany, TX: Bright Sky Press, 2003.

Lowenthal, Mark. *Intelligence: From Secrets to Policy*. 4th ed. Washington, DC: CQ Press, 2009.

Lowenthal, Mark. *Intelligence: From Secrets to Policy*. 5th ed. Washington, DC: CQ Press, 2012.

MacDonald, Callum. *The Lost Battle: Crete 1941*. London: Macmillan, 1993.

MacGaffin, John. "Clandestine Human Intelligence: Spies, Counterspies and Covert Action." In Jennifer E. Sims and Burton Gerber, eds., *Vaults, Mirrors and Masks* Washington, DC: Georgetown University Press, 2008.

MacMillan, Margaret. *The War That Ended Peace: The Road to 1914*. New York: Random House, 2013.

Malcolm, Noel. *Agents of Empire: Knights, Corsairs, Jesuits and Spies in the Sixteenth-Century Mediterranean World*. Oxford: Oxford University Press, 2015.

Manchester, William. *The Arms of Krupp, 1587–1968*. Boston: Bantam Books, 1973.

Manjoo, Farhad. "With One Presidential Phone Call, QAnon Shows Its Power." *The New York Times*, January 6, 2021.

Martel, Gordon. *The Month That Changed the World: July 1914*. Oxford: Oxford University Press, 2014.

Martin, Colin and Geoffrey Parker. *The Spanish Armada*. Revised ed. Manchester: Manchester University Press, 1999.

Marvel, William. *Lincoln's Autocrat: The Life of Edwin Stanton*. Chapel Hill: University of North Carolina Press, 2015.

May, Ernest, ed. *Knowing One's Enemies: Intelligence Assessment before the Two World Wars*. Princeton, NJ: Princeton University Press, 1984.

May, Ernest. *Strange Victory: Hitler's Conquest of France*. New York: Hill and Wang, 2000.

McDermott, James. *England and the Spanish Armada: The Necessary Quarrel*. New Haven: Yale University Press, 2005.

McElfresh, Earl B. *Maps and Mapmakers of the Civil War*. New York: Henry N. Abrams, 1999.

McMeekin, Sean. *July 1914: Countdown to War*. New York: Basic Books, 2019.

McPherson, James M. *The Battle Cry of Freedom: The Civil War Era*. New York: Ballantine Books, 1989.

Mehta, Neel, Adi Agashe, and Parth Detroja. *Bubble or Revolution? The Present and Future of Blockchain and Cryptocurrencies*. N.p.: Paravane Ventures, 2019.

Miller, William J. *Great Maps of the Civil War: Pivotal Battles and Campaigns Featuring 32 Removable Maps*. Nashville, TN: Thomas Nelson, 2004.

Milton, David Hepburn. *Lincoln's Spymaster: Thomas Haines Dudley and the Liverpool Network*. Mechanicsburg, PA: Stackpole Books, 2003.

Mombauer, Annika, ed. and trans. *The Origins of the First World War: Diplomatic and Military Documents*. Manchester: Manchester University Press, 2013.

Neilson, Keith. "Russia." In Keith Wilson, ed., *Decisions for War*. Abingdon, Oxon: Routledge, 2003.

Nelson, Arthur. *The Tudor Navy: The Ships, Men and Organization*. Annapolis, MD: Naval Institute Press, 2001.

Nelson, Keith and B. J. C. McKercher, eds. *Go Spy the Land: Military Intelligence in History*. Westport, CT: Praeger, 1992.

Neustadt, Richard E. and Ernest R. May. *Thinking in Time: The Uses of History for Decision Makers*. New York: Free Press / Macmillan, 1986.

O'Brien, John Emmet. *Telegraphing in Battle: Reminiscences of the Civil War*. Wilkes-Barre, PA: Raeder Press, 1910.

Odom, William E. *Fixing Intelligence for a More Secure America*. New Haven: Yale University Press, 2003.

Olson, James M. *To Catch a Spy: The Art of Counterintelligence*. Washington, DC: Georgetown University Press, 2019.

Olson, Lynn. *Last Hope Island*. New York: Random House, 2017.

Osgood, Robert E. "The Expansion of Force." In Robert J. Art and Kenneth N. Waltz, eds., *The Use of Force: International Politics and Foreign Policy*. Boston: Little, Brown, 1971.

Otte, T. G. *July Crisis: The World's Descent into War, Summer 1914*. Cambridge: Cambridge University Press, 2014.

Overy, Richard J. *The Origins of the Second World War*. 2nd ed. New York: Longman, 1998.

Parker, Geoffrey. *The Army of Flanders and the Spanish Road, 1567–1659*. 2nd ed. Cambridge: Cambridge University Press, 2004.

Parker, Geoffrey. "The Dreadnought Revolution of Tudor England." *The Mariner's Mirror*, August 1996. https://snr.org.uk/dreadnought-revolution-tudor-england/.

Parker, Geoffrey. *The Dutch Revolt*. London: Penguin Books, 1985.

Parker, Geoffrey. *Global Crisis: War, Climate Change and Catastrophe in the Seventeenth Century*. New Haven: Yale University Press, 2013.

Parker, Geoffrey. *The Grand Strategy of Philip II*. New Haven: Yale University Press, 1998.

Parker, Geoffrey. *The Imprudent King*. New Haven: Yale University Press, 2014.

Parker, Geoffrey. *The Military Revolution: Military Innovation and the Rise of the West, 1500–1800*. 2nd ed. Cambridge: Cambridge University Press, 2013.

Parker, Geoffrey. "The Place of Tudor England in the Messianic Vision of Philip II of Spain." Prothero Lecture, 2001. Provided by the author.

Parker, Geoffrey. "Queen Elizabeth's Instructions to Admiral Howard, 20 December 1587." *The Mariner's Mirror*, May 2008. https://snr.org.uk/queen-elizabeths-instruction-to-admiral-howard-20-december-1587/.

Parker, Geoffrey. *Success Is Never Final: Empire, War and Faith in Early Modern Europe.* New York: Basic Books, 2002.

Parker, Geoffrey. "The Worst-Kept Secret in Europe? The European Intelligence Community and the Spanish Armada of 1588." In Keith Neilson and B. J. C. McKercher, eds., *Go Spy the Land: Military Intelligence in History.* Westport, CT: Praeger, 1992.

Pillar, Paul R. *Intelligence and U.S. Foreign Policy.* New York: Columbia University Press, 2011.

Plum, William R. *The Military Telegraph during the Civil War in the United States, with an Exposition of Ancient and Modern Means of Communication, and of the Federal and Confederate Cipher Systems.* 2 vols. Chicago: Jansen, McClurg & Company, Publishers, 1882.

Plum, William R. *Running Account of War between the States.* 2 vols. Chicago: Jansen, McClurg, 1882.

Poleskie, Stephen. *The Balloonist: The Story of T.S.C. Lowe—Inventor, Scientist Magician, and Father of the US Air Force.* Savannah, GA: Frederick C. Beil, 2007.

Popplewell, Richard. "The Surveillance of Indian 'Seditionists' in North America." In Christopher Andrew and Jeremy Noakes, eds., *Intelligence and International Relations, 1900–1945.* Exeter: Exeter University Studies of History, 1987.

Porch, Douglas. *The French Secret Services: A History of French Intelligence from the Dreyfus Affair to the Gulf War.* New York: Farrar, Straus and Giroux, 1995.

Poulson, Jack. "I Used to Work for Google: I Am a Conscientious Objector." *New York Times.* Opinion, Privacy Project, April 23, 2019. https://www.nytimes.com/2019/04/23/opinion/google-privacy-china.html. Accessed online November 11, 2019.

Raff, Lynne. *My Heart Is Too Full to Say More: The Horse in the Civil War.* Beaumont, TX: Art Horse Press, 2010.

Ranft, Bryan, ed. *Technical Change and British Naval Policy. 1860–1939.* London: Hodder and Stoughton, 1977.

Read, Conyers. *Mr. Secretary Walsingham and the Policy of Queen Elizabeth I.* 3 vols. Reprint ed. Harwich Port, MA: Clock and Rose Press, 2003.

Reverton, Gregory F. *Reshaping US Intelligence for an Age of Information.* Cambridge: Cambridge University Press, 2003.

Rice, Edward. *Captain Sir Richard Francis Burton: The Secret Agent Who Made the Pilgrimage to Mecca, Discovered the Kama Sutra, and Brought the Arabian Nights to the West.* Cambridge, MA: Da Capo Press, 1990.

Richelson, Jeffrey T. *A Century of Spies: Intelligence in the Twentieth Century.* New York: Oxford University Press, 1995.

Roberts, Jeff John. "The Splinternet Is Growing." *Fortune*, May 29, 2019. http://www.fortune.com.

Rodger, Nicholas A. M. *The Safeguard of the Sea: A Naval History of Britain, 660–1649.* New York: W.W. Norton, 1997.

Röhl, John C. G. *Wilhelm II: Into the Abyss of War and Exile, 1900–1941.* Translated by Sheila de Bellaigue and Roy Bridge. Cambridge: Cambridge University Press, 2014.

Rose, Norman. *Vansittart: Study of a Diplomat.* London: Heinemann, 1978.

Rosenberger, Laura. "Making Cyberspace Safe for Democracy: The New Landscape of Information Competition." *Foreign Affairs* 99, no. 3 (May–June 2020): 146–159.

Ross, Charles. *Trial by Fire: Science, Technology and the Civil War.* Shippensburg, PA: White Maine Books, 2000.

Rowe, Steven E. "Labor." In *International Encyclopedia of the First World War: 1914–1918.* Online at http://encyclopedia.1914-1918-online.net, version 1.0. Last updated October 8, 2014.

Sagan, Scott D. and Benjamin A. Valentino. "Revisiting Hiroshima in Iran: What Americans Really Think about Using Nuclear Weapons and Killing Noncombatants." *International Security* 42, no. 1 (July 2017): 41–79.

Salmon, John S. *The Official Virginia Civil War Battlefield Guide.* Mechanicsburg, PA: Stackpole Books, 2001.

Sawyer, Ralph D. *The Tao of Spycraft: Intelligence Theory and Practice in Traditional China.* Boulder, CO: Westview Press, 2004.

Schecter, Jerrold and Leona Schecter. *Sacred Secrets: How Soviet Intelligence Operations Changed American History.* Washington, DC: Brassey's, 2002.

Sears, Stephen W. *Chancellorsville.* Boston: Houghton Mifflin, 1996.

Sears, Stephen W., ed. *The Civil War Papers of George B. McClellan: Selected Correspondence, 1860–1865.* Cambridge, MA: Da Capo Press, 1992.

Sears, Stephen W. *Gettysburg.* Boston: Houghton Mifflin, 2003.

Sears, Stephen W. *Landscape Turned Red: The Battle of Antietam.* Boston: Houghton Mifflin, 1983.

Seth, Fred D. Jr. "'Gittin Stuff': Equipping Confederate Armies at the Onset of the Civil War (1861–1862)." *Property Professional* 16, no. 3 (2004): 16–27. Accessed online at http://cdn.ymaws.com.

Sheehan-Dean, Aaron. *Struggle for a Vast Future: The American Civil War.* Oxford: Osprey Publishing, 2006.

Shulsky, Abram N. *Silent Warfare: Understanding the World of Intelligence.* 3rd ed. McLean, VA: Brassey's, 2002.

Shulsky, Abram N. and Gary J. Schmitt. "What Is Intelligence? Secrets and Competition among States." In Roy Godson, Ernest R. May, and Gary Schmitt, eds., *US Intelligence at the Crossroads: Agendas for Reform.* Washington, DC: Brassey's, 1995.

Silva, Jason. IBM Event on Big Data and the Global Nervous System: BBC Speakers.: *YouTube,* November 29, 2016.

Sims, Jennifer E. "The American Approach to Nuclear Arms Control: A Retrospective." *Daedalus* 120, no. 1 (Winter 1991): 251–272.

Sims, Jennifer E. "The Future of Intelligence: The 21st Century Challenge." In Isabelle Duyvesteyn, Joop van Reijn, and Ben de Jong, eds., *The Future of Intelligence: Challenges in the 21st Century.* London: Routledge, 2014, 58–79.

Sims, Jennifer E. *Icarus Restrained: An Intellectual History of American Arms Control, 1945–1960.* Boulder, CO: Westview Press, 1990.

Sims, Jennifer E. "Intelligence Liaison: Devils, Deals and Details." *International Journal of Intelligence and Counterintelligence* 19, no. 2 (Summer 2006): 195–217.

Sims, Jennifer E. "What Is Intelligence? Information for Decision Makers." In Roy Godson, Ernest R. May, and Gary Schmitt, eds., *US Intelligence at the Crossroads: Agendas for Reform.* Washington, DC: Brassey's, 1995.

Sims, Jennifer E. and Burton Gerber, eds. *Transforming US Intelligence.* Washington, DC: Georgetown University Press, 2005.

Sims, Jennifer E. and Burton Gerber, eds. *Vaults, Mirrors and Masks: Rediscovering US Counterintelligence.* Washington, DC: Georgetown University Press, 2009.

Smith, Huston. *The World's Religions*. New York: HarperCollins, 1991.

Sneden, Robert Knox. *Eye of the Storm*. New York: Free Press, 2000.

Sneden, Robert Knox. *Images from the Storm*. New York: Free Press, 2001.

Somerset, Anne. *Elizabeth I*. New York: Random House, 2003.

Spence, Richard B. *Secret Agent 666: Aleister Crowley, British Intelligence and the Occult*. Port Townsend, WA: Feral House, 2008.

Stackpole Books, eds. *Gettysburg: The Story of the Battle with Maps*. Mechanicsburg, PA, 2013.

Starr, Stephen Z. *The Union Cavalry in the Civil War: From Fort Sumter to Gettysburg, 1861–1863*. Vol. 1. Baton Rouge: Louisiana State University Press, 1979.

Steiner, Zara. *The Foreign Office and Foreign Policy, 1898–1914*. Cambridge: Cambridge University Press, 1969.

Sternhell, Zeev, with Mario Sznajder and Maia Asheri. *The Birth of Fascist Ideology*. Translated by David Maisel. Princeton, NJ: Princeton University Press, 1994.

Stevenson, David, ed., and Kenneth Bourne and D. Cameron Watt, general eds. *British Documents on Foreign Affairs: Reports and Papers from the Foreign Office Confidential Print, Part I from the Mid-Nineteenth Century to the First World War; Series F, Europe, 1848–1914*. Vol. 5 of *The Low Countries II: Belgium, 1893–1914*. Bethesda, MD: University Publications of America, 1987.

Stine, J. H. *History of the Army of the Potomac*. Washington, DC: Gibson Brothers, 1893.

Stoker, Donald. *The Grand Design: Strategy and the US Civil War*. Oxford: Oxford University Press, 2010.

Stone, David R. *The Russian Army in the Great War: The Eastern Front, 1914–1917*. Lawrence: University Press of Kansas, 2015.

Strasser, Steve, ed. *The 9/11 Investigations*. New York: Public Affairs, 2004.

Sugden, John. *Sir Francis Drake*. New York: Henry Holt, 1990.

Swanson, James L. *Manhunt: The Twelve-Day Chase for Lincoln's Killer*. New York: Harper Perennial, 2007.

Talbott, Strobe. *The Master of the Game: Paul Nitze and the Nuclear Peace*. New York: Vintage Books, 1988.

Taleb, Nassim Nicholas. *The Black Swan: The Impact of the Highly Improbable*. London: Penguin Books, 2008.

Tarrant, V. E. *The Red Orchestra: The Soviet Spy Network inside Nazi Europe*. New York: John Wiley and Sons, 1995.

Taylor, E. G. R. *The Haven-Finding Art: A History of Navigation from Odysseus to Captain Cook*. London: Hollis and Carter, 1956.

Todd, Frederick P. *American Military Equipage: 1851–1872*. 2 vols. Providence, RI: Company of Military Historians, 1974–1977.

Trachtenberg, Marc. *History and Strategy*. Princeton, NJ: Princeton University Press, 1991.

Trevelyan, George Macaulay. *Grey of Fallodon: Being the Life of Sir Edward Grey afterwards Viscount Grey of Fallodon*. London: Longmans, Green, 1937.

Treverton, Gregory F. *Reorganizing US Domestic Intelligence: Assessing the Options* Santa Monica, CA: Rand Corporation, 2008.

Treverton, Gregory F. and William Agrell, eds. *National Intelligence Systems: Current Research and Future Prospects*. Cambridge: Cambridge University Press, 2009.

Trueman, C. N. "Public Opinion and Appeasement in 1938." *History Learning Site*, July 3, 2015. https://www.historylearningsite.co.uk.

Tsouras, Peter G. *Major General George H. Sharpe and the Creation of American Military Intelligence in the Civil War*. Havertown, PA: Casemate Publishers, 2018.

Tuchman, Barbara W. *The Guns of August*. New York: Random House, 1962.

Tuchman, Barbara W. *The Proud Tower: A Portrait of the World before the War: 1880– 1914*. New York: Macmillan, 1966.

Tuchman, Barbara W. *The Zimmermann Telegram*. New York: Ballantine Books, 1994.

Tunstall, Graydon A. Jr. "Austria-Hungary." In Richard F. Hamilton and Holger H. Herwig, eds., *The Origins of World War I*. Cambridge: Cambridge University Press, 2003.

US Government. *The 9/11 Commission Report including Executive Summary: Final Report of the National Commission on Terrorist Attacks upon the United States*. Official Government Edition. Claitor's Publishing Division, 2004.

US Government. Official Records of the War Department. Extracts from the report of the Board of Police Commissioners, May 3, 1861. Available online at http://ebooks.library. cornell.edu.

US War Department. *The War of the Rebellion: A Compilation of the Official Records of the Union and Confederate Armies*. Series 1, vol. 2. John Sheldon Moody, Calvin Duvall Cowles, Frederick Caryton Ainsworth, Robert N. Scott, Henry Martyn Lazelle, George Breckenridge Davis, Leslie J. Perry, Joseph William Kirkley. Washington, DC: US Government Publishing Office, n.d.

Van Creveld, Martin. *Technology and War: From 2000 BC to the Present*. Revised ed. New York: Free Press, 1991.

Vansittart, Lord. *The Mist Procession: The Autobiography of Lord Vansittart*. London: Hutchinson, 1958.

Wade, Steven. *Victoria's Spymasters: Empire and Espionage*. Gloucestershire: History Press, 2009.

Walton, Timothy R. *The Spanish Treasure Fleets*. Sarasota, FL: Pineapple Press, 1994.

Wank, Solomon. "Desperate Council in Vienna in July 1914: Berthold Molden's Unpublished Memorandum." *Central European History* 26, no. 3 (1993): 281–310.

Waters, D. W. *The Art of Navigation in England in Elizabethan and Early Stuart Times*. New Haven: Yale University Press, 1958.

Wawro, Geoffrey. *A Mad Catastrophe: The Outbreak of World War I and the Collapse of the Hapsburg Empire*. New York: Basic Books, 2014.

Weigley, Russell F. *The American Way of War*. Bloomington: Indiana University Press, 1977.

Weigley, Russell F. *History of the United States Army*. Enlarged ed. Bloomington: Indiana University Press, 1984.

Weintraub, Ellen L. "Foreign Spending in Our Elections Isn't Trivial." Op-ed. *Washington Post*, June 21, 2019, A23.

Wendt, Alexander. *Quantum Mind and Social Science*. Cambridge: Cambridge University Press, 2015.

West, Nigel. *The Illegals: The Double Lives of the Cold War's Most Secret Agents*. Reading, England: Hodder and Stoughton / Coronet Books, 1993.

West, Nigel. *MASK: MI5's Penetration of the Communist Party of Great Britain*. New York: Routledge, 2005.

Williamson, James J. *Mosby's Rangers: A Record of the Operations of the 43rd Battalion Virginia Cavalry from Its Organization to the Surrender*. New York: Ralph B. Kenyon, 1896.

Wilson, Keith, ed. *Decisions for War, 1914*. Abingdon, Oxon: Routledge, 2003.

Winik, Jay. *April 1865: The Month That Saved America*. New York: Harper Perennial, 2001.

Winkler, Jonathan Reed. *Nexus: Strategic Communications and American Security in World War I*. Cambridge, MA: Harvard University Press, 2008.

Wittenberg, Eric J. *Like a Meteor Blazing Brightly: The Short but Controversial Life of Colonel Ulric Dahlgren*. Roseville, MN: Edinburgh Press, 2009.

Wittenberg, Eric J. and David Petruzzi. *Plenty of Blame to Go Around: Jeb Stuart's Controversial Ride to Gettysburg*. New York: Savas Beatie, 2011.

Wohlstetter, Roberta. *Pearl Harbor: Warning and Decision*. Stanford, CA: Stanford University Press, 1962.

Wrixon, Fred B. *Codes, Ciphers, Secrets and Cryptic Communication: Making and Breaking Secret Messages from the Hieroglyphs to the Internet*. New York: Black Dog and Leventhal, 1998.

Wu, Tim. *The Master Switch: The Rise and Fall of Information Empires*. New York: Vintage Books, 2011.

Young, Bennett H. *Confederate Wizards of the Saddle: Being Reminiscences and Observations of One Who Rode with Morgan*. Nashville: J.S. Sanders, 1914.

Zartman, William I., ed. *How Negotiations End: Negotiating in the End Game*. Cambridge: Cambridge University Press, 2019.

Index

For the benefit of digital users, indexed terms that span two pages (e.g., 52–53) may, on occasion, appear on only one of those pages.

Figures are indicated by *f* following the page number

Faraday, Michael 268, 514n.62
FBI (Federal Bureau of Investigation) 412,
    421–22, 426–27
FCI (Foreign Countries
    Sub-committee) 563n.83
Federal Bureau of Investigation. See FBI
Feis, William B. 510n.2, 519n.128, 519n.130,
    520n.1, 520n.136, 520n.137, 520n.142
Fellner, Fritz 486, 550n.16, 550n.17, 550n.18
Feltham, Owen 494n.29
Ferdinand, Franz 263
Fermi, Enrico 272
Fernandez Navarrete, Pedro 494n.26
Ferris, John 534n.13
Finnegan, Col. Terrence 536n.12
FireEye, Inc. 441–42
First Bull Run, Battle of 116–17
First Manassas, map of 161
First Manassas, Battle of 114–15, 117, 121, 132,
    135–36, 139, 143, 150–54, 156, 157, 160,
    163, 182–86, 195, 198, 200, 202–5, 207,
    210, 214, 218, 219, 298, 407–8, 430, 521n.4,
    524n.54, 528n.16, 529n.22, 566n.8
First Moroccan Crisis 297–98
Fishel, Edwin C. 115–16, 149–50, 184, 188,
    510n.3, 510n.5, 513n.51, 514n.66, 514n.67,
    515n.71, 515n.78, 517n.104, 518n.118,
    519n.123, 519n.125, 519n.133, 520n.2,
    520n.135, 521n.9, 522n.28, 522n.29,
    522n.30, 523n.36, 523n.38, 524n.49,
    524n.54, 524n.57, 525n.58, 525n.59,
    525n.60, 525n.63, 525n.68, 525n.69,
    526n.75, 526n.76, 526n.77, 526n.78,
    526n.79, 526n.81, 526n.82, 526n.83,
    526n.85, 526n.91, 527n.95
Fleming, Thomas 86–88
Flexner, Abraham 572n.28, 574n.47
Foch, Ferdinand 267
Ford's Theater 223, 224, 227–28, 531–32n.29,
    532n.44
Foreign Affairs 1, 488n.3
Foreign Countries Sub-Committee 563n.83.
    See FCI
Foresight 68, 504n.65, 504–5n.70, 505n.72
Forgách, János 324, 329–30, 350, 354, 356,
    550n.18, 552n.41, 556n.102, 557n.118
Forschungsamt 366, 368, 559n.27, 565n.115
Fort Perkins 166–67
Fort Sumter 133, 145, 163–64, 166–67, 170,
    522n.18
Fox, Jr., John 546n.137
Franckenstein, Georg von 324
François-Poncet, André 379

Frank, Karl Hermann 390, 564n.91
Franz Ferdinand 293–94
Franz Joseph 293–95, 548n.165
Franz-Ferdinand 301
Freeman, Douglas Southall 188
Frémont, John Charles 121–22, 164, 521n.12
Friedjung trial 356
Fritsch,Baron Werner von 366–67, 368–69
Frobisher, Martin 80–81, 88–89
Fukushima nuclear power plant 448
Fuller, William 295–96, 298–99
Fundamental Laws of April 1907 295–96

Gallagher, Gary W. 526n.84
Galloway, Scott 459, 572n.27, 573n.34
Gallucci, Nick 574n.46
Gamelin, Maurice 364
Gandhi, Mahatma 468
Garrett Farm 238–39, 242, 244, 245
Garrett, Richard 238–39, 244, 245
GC&CS (Government Code and Cryptologic
    Service) 383
GDPR (General Data Protection
    Regulation) 462–63
GEDA (gain, exploit, defend, attack) 569n.25
Gehlen affair 253, 534n.10
General Data Protection Regulation. See GDPR
George V 264, 292
George, Lloyd 561n.58
Gerber, Burton 489n.13
German Navy 267–68
Gestapo. See SS
Gettysburg 114, 115–16, 118, 124–25, 129–30,
    150, 188, 197, 201, 217,
Gettysburg, Battle of 22, 114–16, 127, 129–30,
    137–38, 142, 197–98, 201, 212, 217–19,
    512n.33, 512n.34, 512n.35, 512n.36,
    512n.37, 512n.42, 513n.52, 515n.79,
    516n.87, 517n.100
Geyer, Michael 566n.132
Gifford, Gilbert 58, 500n.24
Gladwell, Malcolm 498n.81
Godesberg ultimatum 393–94
Godson, Benjamin 68, 504n.68
Goebbels, Joseph 371–72, 390, 394, 560n.34
Goering, Nazi Reichsmarschall Hermann 362,
    366–67, 368, 369–70, 371–72, 404,
    559n.27, 560n.42, 561n.52, 565n.114
Golden Hind 86–88, 506n.104
Goodheart, Adam 520n.138
Google 452, 455, 459–61, 462–63, 464, 467,
    572n.27, 573n.41
Google Maps 464